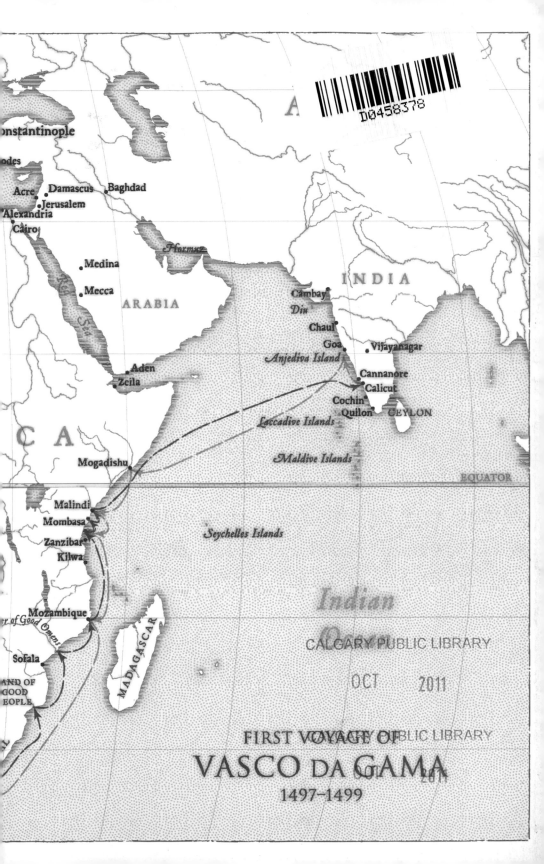

FIRST VOYAGE OF
VASCO DA GAMA
1497–1499

HOLY WAR

ALSO BY NIGEL CLIFF

The Shakespeare Riots:
Revenge, Drama, and Death
in Nineteenth-Century America

HOLY WAR

HOW VASCO DA GAMA'S EPIC VOYAGES
TURNED THE TIDE IN A CENTURIES-
OLD CLASH OF CIVILIZATIONS

NIGEL CLIFF

HARPER

An Imprint of HarperCollins*Publishers*
www.harpercollins.com

HarperCollins books may be purchased for educational, business, or sales promotional use. For information, please write: Special Markets Department, HarperCollins Publishers, 10 East 53rd Street, New York, NY 10022.

FIRST EDITION

Designed by William Ruoto

Library of Congress Cataloging-in-Publication Data

Cliff, Nigel.
  Holy war : how Vasco da Gama's epic voyages turned the tide in a centuries-old clash of civilizations / by Nigel Cliff.
      p.   cm.
  ISBN 978-0-06-173512-7
  1. Gama, Vasco da, 1469–1524. 2. Gama, Vasco da, 1469–1524—Influence. 3. Africa—Discovery and exploration—Portuguese. 4. India—Discovery and exploration—Portuguese. 5. Africa—Discovery and exploration—Religious aspects. 6. India—Discovery and exploration—Religious aspects. 7. East and West. 8. Christianity and other religions—Islam—History—16th century. 9. Islam—Relations—Christianity—History—16th century. I. Title.
  G401.G3C44   2011
  909'.4—dc23   2011021331

11 12 13 14 15   OV/RRD   10 9 8 7 6 5 4 3 2 1

For Viviana

CONTENTS

PART I: ORIGINS

PART II: EXPLORATION

PART III: CRUSADE

ILLUSTRATIONS

THIS STORY SPANS three continents and more centuries, and most of the people and places in it have been known by different names, at different times, and in different languages. Fittingly perhaps, Vasco da Gama has never been rechristened; I give his family name as Gama in the Portuguese manner, though some historians have preferred da Gama or Da Gama. In most cases—not least that of Gama's great rival, born Cristoforo Colombo, but called Cristóvão or Cristóbal Colón in his adopted Portugal and Spain—choices have had to be made. Where a well-established English name exists, it is given; where one does not, Western names are given according to prevailing usage in the language in question, while non-Western names are transcribed in their simplest and most recognizable form.

Other decisions have been made to remove thickets of qualifications from the reader's path. Broad-brush terms for epochs or regions—"the Middle Ages," or "the East"—are moving targets at best, but they are used, in context, as necessary signposts. Dates are rendered in the Western form, with reference to the Common Era. Quotations from non-English sources are variously given in translations old, recent, and brand-new, as period flavor or clarity dictates. Distances at sea are stated in the leagues used by the explorers; one Portuguese league is roughly equivalent to three modern miles. Finally, having whiled away many a day learning how to gammon the bowsprit, peek the mizzen, and cat the anchor, I have kept sailing terminology to a minimum. I hope specialists of all stripes will not be too offended.

THE LIGHT WAS fading when the three strange ships appeared off the coast of India, but the fishermen on the shore could still make out their shapes. The two biggest were fat-bellied as whales, with bulging sides that swept up to support sturdy wooden towers in the bows and stern. The wooden hulls were weathered a streaky gray, and long iron guns poked over the sides, like the barbels on a monstrous catfish. Huge square sails billowed toward the darkening sky, each vaster than the last and each surmounted by a bonnet-shaped topsail that made the whole rig resemble a family of ghostly giants. There was something at once thrillingly modern and hulkingly primeval about these alien arrivals, but for sure nothing like them had been seen before.

The alarm was raised on the beach, and groups of men dragged four long, narrow boats into the water. As they rowed closer they could see that great crimson crosses were emblazoned on every stretch of canvas.

"What nation are you from?" the Indians' leader shouted when they were under the side of the nearest ship.

"We are from Portugal," one of the sailors called back.

Both spoke in Arabic, the language of international trade. The visitors, though, had the advantage over their hosts. The Indians had never heard of Portugal, a sliver of a country on the far western fringe of Europe. The Portuguese certainly knew about India, and to reach it they had embarked on the longest and most dangerous voyage known to history.

The year was 1498. Ten months earlier, the little fleet had set sail from Lisbon, the Portuguese capital, on a mission to change the world. The 170 men on board carried instructions to open a sea route from Europe to Asia, to unlock the age-old secrets of the spice trade, and to locate a long-lost Christian king who ruled over a magical Eastern realm. Behind that catalog of improbability lay a truly apocalyptic agenda: to link up with the Eastern Christians, deal a crushing blow to the power of Islam, and prepare the way for the conquest of Jerusalem, the holiest city in the world. Even that was not the ultimate end—but if they succeeded it would be the beginning of the end, the clarion call for the Second Coming and the Last Judgment that would surely follow.

Time would tell whether this quest for the Promised Land would end at anything more than a castle in the air. For now, bare survival was uppermost in the crews' minds. The men who had signed up to sail off the edge of the known world were an odd assortment. Among them were hardened adventurers, chivalric knights, African slaves, bookish scribes, and convicts working off their sentences. Already they had rubbed uncomfortably close against each other for 317 days. As they swept in a great arc around the Atlantic, they had seen nothing but the bounding main for months on end. When they finally reached the southern tip of Africa they had been shot at, ambushed, and boarded in the dead of night. They had run out of food and water, and they had been ravaged by mystifying diseases. They had wrestled with heavy currents and storms that battered their ships and tattered their sails. They were assured they were doing God's work and that, in return, their sins would be wiped clean. Yet even the most seasoned mariner's skin crawled with morbid superstitions and forebodings of doom. Death, they knew, was just a swollen gum or an unseen reef away, and death was not the worst conceivable fate. As they slept under unknown stars and plunged into uncharted waters that mapmakers enlivened with toothy sea monsters, it was not their lives they feared to lose but their very souls.

To the watching Indians, the newcomers, with their long, filthy hair and their bronzed, unwashed faces, looked like the rougher species of sea dog. Their scruples were soon overcome when they found they could sell the strangers cucumbers and coconuts at handsome prices, and the next day the four boats returned to lead the fleet into port.

It was a moment to make the most stoic seaman stand and gape.

For Christians, the East was the wellspring of the world. The Bible was its history book, Jerusalem its capital of faith suspended between heaven and earth, and the Garden of Eden—which was firmly believed to be flowering somewhere in Asia—its fount of marvels. Its palaces were reportedly roofed with gold, while fireproof salamanders, self-immolating phoenixes, and solitary unicorns roamed its forests. Precious stones floated down its rivers, and rare spices that cured any ailment dropped from its trees. People with dog's heads ambled by, while others hopped past on their single leg or sat down and used their single giant foot as a sunshade. Diamonds littered its gorges, where they were guarded by snakes and could be retrieved only by vultures. Mortal dangers lurked everywhere, which put the glittering treasures all the more tantalizingly out of reach.

At least so they said: no one knew for sure. For centuries Islam had all but blocked Europe's access to the East; for centuries a heady mix of rumor and fable had swirled in place of sober fact. Many had died to discover the truth, and now the moment was suddenly at hand. The mighty port of Calicut, an international emporium bursting with oriental riches, the hub of the busiest trade network in the world, sprawled in front of the sailors' eyes.

There was no rush to be the first ashore. The anticipation—or the apprehension—was too much. In the end, the task was given to one of the men who had been taken on board to do the dangerous work.

The first European to sail all the way to India and step on its shores was a convicted criminal.

The men in the boats took him straight to the house of two Muslim merchants from North Africa, the westernmost place they knew. The merchants came from the ancient port city of Tunis, and to the visitor's surprise they were fluent in both Spanish and Italian.

"The devil take you! What brought you here?" one of the two exclaimed in Spanish.

The convict drew himself up.

"We have come," he grandly replied, "in search of Christians and spices."

On board his flagship Vasco da Gama waited impatiently for news. The Portuguese commander was of medium height, with a strong, stocky build and a florid, angular face that looked as if it were welded from plates of copper. By birth he was a gentleman of the court, though his beetling brow, beak nose, cruelly sensuous mouth, and bushy beard made him look more like a pirate leader. He was just twenty-eight when he was entrusted with his nation's hopes and dreams, and though he had been a surprise choice, his men had already learned to respect his boldness and mettle and to fear his flaring temper.

As he surveyed his floating realm, his large, sharp eyes missed nothing. Keen ambition matched by an iron will had brought him through dangers and across distances that no one had conquered before, but he was well aware that his great gamble had just begun.

THE QUESTION THAT motivated this book tugged at me several years before the story began to take shape. Like most of us I was bewildered by the eruption of religious war into our everyday lives, and as I found out more, I realized we were being drawn back into an ancient conflict about which we had developed collective amnesia. Reason, we believed, ruled the world in place of religion. War was about ideology and economics and ego, not about faith.

We were caught taking a nap from history. The march of progress is a tale victors tell themselves; the vanquished have a longer

memory. In the words of modern-day Islamists who see their struggle not as one to come to terms with the West but to defeat the
West, the rot set in half a millennium ago. That was when the
last Muslim emirate was expunged from western Europe, when
Christopher Columbus landed in the Americas—and when Vasco
da Gama arrived in the East. Those three events unfolded in one
dramatic decade, and their intimately entwined roots reach deep
into our common past.

Seven centuries before that pivotal decade, Muslim conquerors
had marched deep into Europe. In its far west, on the Iberian Peninsula, they had founded an advanced Islamic state, and that state
had played a vital role in lighting Europe out of the Dark Ages.
Yet as Christians and Muslims alike began to forget that the God
they worshipped in their different ways was one and the same deity,
the fires of holy war were lit in Iberia. They burned fiercely as the
Portuguese and Spanish carved their nations out of Islam's lands,
and they were still burning when the Portuguese embarked on a
century-long mission to pursue their former masters halfway around
the globe—a mission that launched Europe's Age of Discovery.

The timing was no coincidence. For hundreds of years history had marched from east to west, and on the eve of the Age
of Discovery its drumbeat was getting faster. In the middle years
of the fifteenth century Europe's greatest city had fallen to Islam,
and Muslim soldiers were once again preparing to advance into
the heart of the continent. At a time when no one suspected that
new continents lay waiting to be found, Christendom's hopes of
salvation were pinned on reaching the East; in Europeans' frustrated fantasies, Asia had become a magical realm where an alliance
against the enemy could be forged and the dream of a universal
church could finally be fulfilled.

Tiny Portugal had set itself a truly audacious task: to outflank
Islam by making itself the master of the oceans. As the collective
effort of generations built toward Vasco da Gama's first voyage, the
Spanish scrambled to join the race. Since they had a deal of ground

to make up, they decided to take a chance on an Italian maverick named Christopher Columbus. In 1498, as Vasco da Gama sailed east into the Indian Ocean, Columbus sailed west and finally reached the mainland of the Americas.

Both explorers were searching for the same prize—a sea route to Asia—yet Vasco da Gama's achievement has long been over-shadowed by Columbus's magnificent mistake. Now that we are returning to the world as it was in their time—a world where all roads lead east—we can finally reset the balance. Vasco da Gama's voyages were the breakthrough in a centuries-old Christian cam-paign to upend Islam's dominance of the world. They dramatically changed relations between East and West, and they drew a dividing line between the eras of Muslim and Christian ascendancy—what we in the West call the medieval and the modern ages. They were not, of course, the whole story, but they were a much bigger part of it than we choose to remember.

The Age of Discovery used to be glorified as a quixotic quest to push the boundaries of human knowledge. These days, it tends to be explained as a drive to reverse the global balance of trade. It was both; it transformed Europe's sense of its place in the world, and it set in motion a global shift of power that is still unraveling today. Yet it was not just a new departure; it was a deliberate attempt to settle an ancient score. Vasco da Gama and his men were born in a world polarized by faith, where fighting the Infidel was the high-est calling of a man of honor. As the bloodred crosses on their sails broadcast far and wide, they were embarked on a new holy war. They were told they were the direct successors to four centuries of Crusaders, knightly pilgrims who had swung their swords in the name of Christ. They were charged with launching a sweep-ing counteroffensive against Islam and inaugurating a new era—an era in which the faith and values of Europe would be exported far across the earth. That, above all, was why a few dozen men in a few wooden tubs sailed off the edge of the known world and into the modern age.

To understand the passions that drove Europeans into distant seas—and that shaped our world—we need to go back to the beginning. The story starts among the wind-carved sand dunes and scorched mountain ranges of Arabia, with the birth of a new religion that swept with breathtaking speed into the heart of Europe itself.

PART I

ORIGINS

CHAPTER I

EAST AND WEST

W HEN MUHAMMAD IBN Abdallah first heard the word of
God in or around the year 610, he had no intention of
founding a world empire.

He was not even sure he was sane.

"Wrap me up!" the forty-year-old merchant said, shivering miserably as he crawled up to his wife, who threw a cloak around him
and held him, stroking his hair as he wept. He had been meditating
in his usual cave outside Mecca—a luxury afforded him by marriage to a rich widow fifteen years his senior—when the angel Gabriel appeared, threw him into a painful, ecstatic trance, and spoke
to him the words of God. Muhammad was terrified that he was going mad and contemplated throwing himself off the mountain. But
the voice kept coming back, and three years later Muhammad began to preach in public. Gradually the message emerged: the faith of
Abraham and Jesus was the true faith, but it had become corrupted.
There was one God, and He demanded *islam*—complete surrender.

This was bad news for the rulers of Mecca, who had grown fat
on religious tourism to the city's 360 shrines. Mecca had sprung up
around a palmy oasis in the Hijaz, the baked barrier of mountains
that stretches along the Red Sea coast of the Arabian Peninsula. Its
authority radiated from the Kaaba, the square, squat sanctuary at
its center that housed the Arabs' chief idols. Every year hordes of
pilgrims emerged from the desert, descended on the holy precinct,
and circled the stone cube seven times, straining to kiss each corner
before the press of bodies pushed them back into the whirl. Over

time one tribe, the Quraysh, had orchestrated their guardianship of the Kaaba into a stranglehold on Mecca's commercial lifeblood, and at first Muhammad's revelations were aimed squarely at them. The greedy Quraysh, he accused, had severed the egalitarian threads of Arab society; they had exploited the weak, enslaved the poor, and neglected their duty to care for the needy and oppressed. God had taken note, and they would all go to hell.

What infuriated the Quraysh was not so much Muhammad's talk of the one merciful God, or even his claim to be God's mouth-piece. To the north a kingdom of Christian Arabs had existed for centuries, and in the Kaaba itself the figures of Jesus and Mary stood proud among the idols. Jewish migrants to Arabia had been influential for even longer; the Arabs considered themselves the Jews' fellow descendants of Abraham, through his firstborn son, Ishmael, and many identified their high god with the god of the Jews. In Muhammad's time poet-preachers perpetually roamed the deserts, exhorting their tribesmen to renounce idolatry and return to the pure monotheism of their forefathers. Nothing could be less controversial; what was uniquely intolerable was that Muhammad was an insider. His family clan, the Hashemites, was a minor branch of the Quraysh. He was a respected businessman and a small but solid pillar of the community, and he had turned on his own kind.

The Quraysh tried everything from bribes to boycotts to discredit the troublesome preacher, and finally they turned their hand to midnight assassination. Just in time Muhammad slipped out of his house, evaded the blade, and fled to a distant oasis settlement that would become known as Medina, the City of the Prophet. There, as his following grew, he implemented the radically new society he had only dreamed of in Mecca: an *ummah*, or community of equals, united not by birth but by allegiance, bound by laws that gave unprecedented rights to women and redistributed wealth to the neediest. As the revelations continued, he began to believe that God had chosen him not just to deliver a warning to his tribe but to be a Messenger to humanity.

For his message to spread, he first had to reckon with Mecca. Eight years of ferocious wars with the Quraysh bloodied the establishment of Islam. At the darkest hour, his face smashed up and smeared with blood, Muhammad was dragged from the battlefield by one of his warriors, and only the rumor that he was dead saved the remnants of his army. The ummah's morale was crushed, and it was about then that Muhammad made his fighters a promise that would echo through history. The slain in battle, it was revealed to him, would be swept up to the highest level of Paradise: "They shall be lodged in peace together, amid gardens and fountains, arrayed in rich silks and fine brocade. . . . We shall wed them to dark-eyed houris."

The Muslims—"those who submit"—clung on, and clinging on against the odds itself seemed a sign of divine favor. The decisive moment was not a battlefield victory but a spectacular public-relations coup. In the year 628 Muhammad unexpectedly appeared before Mecca with a thousand unarmed pilgrims and asserted his lawful right as an Arab to worship at the Kaaba. As he solemnly performed the rituals, while the Quraysh stood sullenly by, the rulers of Mecca suddenly looked more foolish than invincible, and opposition began to crumble. In 630 Muhammad returned with massed ranks of followers. He once again circled the sanctuary seven times, intoning "Allahu akbar!"—"God is great!"—then climbed inside, carried out the idols, and smashed them to pieces on the ground.

By the time he died, two years later, Muhammad had pulled off a feat that no other leader in history had even envisaged: he had founded a flourishing new faith and an expanding new state, the one inseparable from the other. In little more than a year the armies of Islam crushed the Arab tribes that held out against the new order, and for the first time in history the Arabian Peninsula was united under one ruler and one faith. Driven by religious zeal, a newfound common purpose, and the happy alternatives of vast spoils in life or eternal bliss in death, God's newly chosen people looked outward.

What they saw were two superpowers that had been doing their utmost to obliterate each other from the face of the earth.

For more than a millennium, East and West had faced off across the River Euphrates in Mesopotamia, the fertile land long known as the cradle of civilization and today home to Iraq. On the eastern side was the illustrious Persian Empire, the guardian of an ancient, refined culture and of the world's first revealed religion, the monotheistic faith of the visionary priest Zarathuster—a faith known after his Latinized name, Zoroaster, as Zoroastrianism—that told of creation, resurrection, salvation, apocalypse, heaven and hell, and a savior born to a young virgin centuries before the birth of Christ. Led by their great *shahanshahs*—"kings of kings"—the Persians had been the inveterate foes of the Greeks until Alexander the Great had smashed their armies. When Persia's power revived, it had simply transferred its hostility to the Greeks' successors, the Romans. The ancient struggle was the formative East-West clash, and in 610, just as Muhammad was receiving his first revelations, it had finally exploded into total war.

As waves of barbarians ran riot around western Europe, the emperor Constantine had built a new Rome on Europe's eastern brink. Glittering Constantinople looked out across the Bosporus, a strategic sliver of water that leads from the Black Sea toward the Mediterranean, at Asia. Ensconced behind the city's impregnable walls, Constantine's successors watched helplessly as the Persians swept across their rich eastern provinces and headed toward holy Jerusalem. Long ago the Romans had razed Jewish Jerusalem to the ground, and a new Christian city had risen over the sites identified with Jesus's passion; Constantine, the first Christian emperor, had himself built the Church of the Holy Sepulcher over the purported places of Jesus's crucifixion, burial, and resurrection. Now, to Christian anguish bordering on the apocalyptic, the Persians carted away the True Cross on which Jesus was believed to have died, along with the Holy Sponge and Lance and the city's patriarch, and left the Holy Sepulcher smoldering and hollowed out against a blackened sky.

On the brink of oblivion, the Romans struggled back and emerged triumphant, and Persia imploded into civil war. But the victors, too, were exhausted. Roman cities had been laid waste and were overwhelmed by refugees, agriculture had been blighted and trade had ground to a halt, and everyone was heartily sick of the crushing taxes that had paid for imperial deliverance. In a time of churning Christian controversy, most damaging of all was Constantinople's remorseless drive to enforce its orthodox version of Christianity across its lands. Having first fed Christians to the lions, the Romans had turned to persecuting anyone who refused to toe the official line, and across a large swath of the eastern Mediterranean, from Armenia in the north to Egypt in the south, Christian dissidents were far from unhappy at the prospect of a new regime.

With breathtaking bravado, the Arabs attacked both ancient empires at once.

In 636, eleven centuries of Persian might ended in a bellowing elephant charge near the future site of Baghdad. "Damn this world, damn this time, damn this fate," Iran's national epic would rue, "That uncivilized Arabs have come to make me Muslim." Islam's path opened north to Armenia, northeast to the Asian steppes bordering China, southeast to Afghanistan, and onward to India. That same year, an Arab army crushed a vastly larger Roman force at the Battle of Yarmuk and annexed Syria, where Saul of Tarsus had been converted on the road to Damascus and where, in Antioch, he had founded the first organized Christian church. The next year Jerusalem was starved into submission and opened its gates to the new set of conquerors, just eight years after the Romans had triumphantly restored the True Cross to its rightful place. The faith-torn city was holy to Islam as well as to Judaism and Christianity, and centuries of struggles between Romans and Jews over the sacred places gave way to centuries of clashes between Muslims and Christians.

Four years later, fertile, gilded Egypt, the richest of all Roman provinces, fell to the Arabs. While Constantinople stood impotently by, the truculent desert tribesmen it disparagingly labeled

Saracens—"the tent people"—had taken all the lands it had so recently reconquered, at such great cost. As kingdoms and empires were humbled and fell, even bishops began to wonder if Muhammad had been commanded from on high.

From Egypt, the armies of Islam marched west across the Mediterranean shores of Africa—and there, quite unexpectedly, their seemingly unstoppable onrush stalled.

The trouble was partly domestic. Muhammad had died without naming an heir, or even leaving clear instructions about how a successor should be chosen. Ancient rivalries soon resurfaced, sharpened by the booty of conquest that snaked in endless caravans across the deserts and invariably ended up in the pockets of the Quraysh, the very tribe whose monopolistic greed Muhammad had so roundly attacked. After some tribal jockeying, the first four caliphs—"successors" to the Prophet—were selected from among Muhammad's close companions and family, but even that high status failed to protect them. An irate Persian soldier thrust a dagger into the second caliph's belly, gutted him, and knifed him in the back while he was at prayer. A cabal of Muslim soldiers incensed at the third caliph's lavish lifestyle and blatant nepotism bludgeoned him to death, and the ummah erupted into civil war. Ali, the fourth caliph—the Prophet's cousin, son-in-law, and closest confidant—was stabbed with a poisoned sword on the steps of a mosque for being too willing to negotiate with his fellow Muslims. His followers, who had always maintained that Ali was Muhammad's divinely anointed successor, eventually came together as the Shiatu Ali—"the party of Ali"—or Shia for short, and split irrevocably from the pragmatist majority, who became known, after the term for the path shown by the Prophet, as Sunnis.

Out of the turmoil the first caliphal dynasty emerged in the form of the Umayyads, who moved the capital away from the snake pit of Arabia and ruled for nearly a century from ancient, cosmopolitan Damascus. Yet opposition continued to plague the young empire, this time from outside. In North Africa the Arab armies were bogged down for decades by ragged hordes of blue-eyed Berbers, the ancient indigenous peoples of the region. The Berbers had rampaged down from their mountain redoubts every time previous waves of conquerors had paid them a visit, and they were not inclined to adapt their behavior merely because they professed themselves converts to the new faith. At the head of the Berber charge was a fearsome Jewish warrior-queen known to the Arabs as Kahina, or "the Prophetess," who galloped into battle with her fiery red curls streaming out behind and drove the invaders far back east, until she was finally hunted down by a vast Arab army and died fighting, sword in hand.

As the eighth century dawned the Berbers' revolts petered out, and many swelled the ranks of their vanquishers. In little more than the span of a single lifetime, the armies unloosed by Muhammad had swept an unbroken crescent around the Mediterranean basin all the way to the shores of the Atlantic Ocean.

From there they gazed on Europe.

With staggering speed, the world had turned full circle. A religion that had erupted in the deserts of the East was about to burst into a stunned Europe from the west. But for the obstreperous Berbers, it might well have stormed straight across the continent before Europe's warring tribes had roused themselves to respond.

In time, it would turn again. When Western Christendom eventually recovered from the shock, a struggle of faiths would rage on the mainland of Europe—a struggle that would drive Vasco da Gama into the heart of the East.

SINCE THE AGE of legends, two stony peaks had marked the western end of the known world. The ancients called them the Pillars of Hercules, and they told how the mighty hero had fashioned them on his tenth impossible labor. Hercules was sent to the far shores of Europe to steal the cattle of the three-headed, six-legged monster Geryon, and to clear his path he smashed a mountain in two. Through the gap the waters of the one ocean that ringed the world rushed into the Mediterranean. Beyond was the realm of the writhing, shape-shifting Old Man of the Sea and the sunken civilization of Atlantis, fragments of old tales lost in the fog of time and the terrors of a millennium of mariners.

For more than two thousand years a port city called Ceuta has sat in the shadow of Hercules' southern pillar. Ceuta occupies a twist of land anchored to the northern shores of Africa by a jagged mountain range known as the Seven Peaks. The little isthmus drifts out into the Mediterranean until a large mound called Monte Hacho—Beacon Hill—brings it to an emphatic end. From its summit the limestone fist of the Rock of Gibraltar is easily visible on the Spanish coast. Gibraltar is Hercules' northern pillar, and it gives its name to the turbulent strait that opens into the Atlantic Ocean. Here Africa and Europe are separated by a mere nine miles of water, and here, time after time, history has made its crossing.

Today we think of Africa and Europe as two starkly different continents sundered by a chasm of civilization, but until quite recently that distinction would have made no sense. For many centuries goods and men moved more easily on water than on land, and trade and empire brought the peoples of the Mediterranean together. The path-finding Phoenicians mined silver in Spain and tin as far away as Britain. Where Sicily juts down toward Africa they built the fabled city of Carthage, and with the same feel for the strategic value of a bottleneck, they established Ceuta as their western outpost. Greek colonists followed, founding settlements from Spain to Sicily and installing the descendants of Alexander the Great's bodyguard as the Ptolemaic pharaohs of Egypt. Next came the Romans, who leveled Carthage and fortified Ceuta into the military camp at the end of the world. The term *Mediterranean* comes from the Latin for "the middle of the Earth," but political reality as much as imperial pride prompted the more common Roman name *Mare Nostrum*—"Our Sea." That sense of entitlement made it all the more intolerable when the barbarian Vandals swept through France and

Spain, poured across the Strait of Gibraltar, marched east across Rome's African provinces, and launched themselves into the Mediterranean, where they settled its larger islands, specialized in piracy, and finished up by sacking Rome itself.

No amount of sea traffic, though, could have prepared the northern shores of the Mediterranean for the events of 711. That year a Muslim army massed at Ceuta, sailed across the strait, and ushered in 781 years of Islamic rule in Western Europe. The leader of the expedition was a Berber convert called Tariq ibn Ziyad, and the rock beneath which he landed was named the Mountain of Tariq—in Arabic *Jebel al-Tariq*, or to us Gibraltar.

At the time, Spain—the name that medieval Europe applied to the whole Iberian Peninsula, including the future homeland of Portugal—was ruled by the barbarian Goths, who had seized it from the Vandals, who had taken it from Rome. In a little over three years the Goths were sent scurrying to the uplands of the north, where they had plenty of time to contemplate the ruin of their state as divine punishment for the sinful wickedness of their rulers. Having secured most of the peninsula, the Arab commanders and their Berber troops streamed northeast over the mountainous necklace of the Pyrenees into France.

At stake was nothing less than Christendom itself.

Twice, in Islam's first century, colossal Arab armies had besieged Constantinople and had failed to penetrate its monumental walls. Twice the city on the Bosporus had seen off enormous fleets of Arab warships amid seas slicked with a lethal new concoction called Greek fire. Constantinople was now the eastern bulwark of a diminished, fragile Christendom, but it showed no sign of caving in. In contrast, beleaguered western Europe was a disaster waiting to be conquered. The invasion of Spain had begun as a daring bit of opportunism, but it was soon directed from the heart of the Islamic empire. Its leaders planned to march straight across Europe, annex the lands abandoned by Rome, and attack Constantinople from its Balkan backyard. If they succeeded, the crescent that Islam had mapped around the Mediterranean would become a complete circle.

Tens of thousands of Arabs and Berbers burst into France, swept through Aquitaine, burned Bordeaux, and set off down the old Roman road that led from Poitiers to the holy city of Tours. A century to the year after the death of Muhammad, a Muslim army was on the march barely 150 miles from the gates of Paris.

In the fog of war that enveloped Dark Ages Europe, the momentous events that had gripped the far shores of the Mediterranean had come carried on the uncertain winds of rumor. The idea that those distant rolls of thunder presaged a lightning strike in the very heart of Christendom was so remote as to be incomprehensible. Yet here was a turbaned army, driven by a strange faith, riding under unknown pennants, heralded by the wail of unfamiliar horns and the jarring crash of cymbals, crying out chilling oaths in a foreign tongue, and picking up speed on the autumnal fields of France.

The tug of war between Islam and Christianity changed course that day in 732. On the road outside Poitiers the armies of Islam slammed into an immovable wall of shaggy but resolute Franks— West Germanic peoples who had long ago settled in Roman territory—led by Charles Martel, who was known to his men as the Hammer. The lines of infantry buckled as eddies of fleet Arab horsemen crashed into the front ranks, but they refused to break. The Arab tactics that had reaped such spectacular rewards for a century—cut up the front line, scatter while unloosing arrows, swarm back around the confused huddles, and pick them off one by one—failed for the first time, and Muslim bodies piled up in front of Frankish shields. Sporadic fighting continued into the night, but by morning the surviving invaders had melted away, headed back to Spain.

For decades huge Islamic armies would continue to march across the Pyrenees; they would briefly reach the Alps and send the Hammer racing back into the fray. When the invasions finally petered out, it was more thanks to rancorous power struggles among the tens of thousands of Arab and Berber immigrants who had begun to pour into Spain than to military prowess on the part of Western Christendom. Even then, Muslim bandits would control the Alpine passes—their greatest catch was the abbot of Cluny, the richest monastery in Europe, who brought them a king's ransom—and Muslim pirates would overrun the seas until Christians, gloated a caliph's chief of staff, could "not even put a plank on the water." Yet in the West, the Battle of Poitiers would be remembered as the turning point.

It was to describe Martel's men that a chronicler first coined the term *europenses*—"Europeans."

No such people had existed before. The geographical dividing lines between the continents were first drawn by the Greeks, who for their convenience named the land to their east Asia, that to the south Africa, and everything else Europe. As they explored farther, they puzzled over which northern river marked the boundary between Europe and Asia, or whether Africa started at the borders of Egypt or at the River Nile, and they questioned the sense of separating a single landmass into three parts. To everyone else the division was perfectly arbitrary. When northern Europe was still a hinterland of blue-faced savages and the Mediterranean was the lake of Western civilization, the Continent's peoples dreamed of no shared identity; nor were Rome's Asian and African provinces any less Roman because they were outside Europe. When the teachings of Jesus of Nazareth traveled in every direction out of Roman Judea, no one predicted that his followers' faith would be claimed as a European religion; Ethiopia was among the first nations to adopt Christianity, while St. Augustine, the church father who profoundly influenced the evolution of Christian thought, was a Berber from Algeria. It was Islam's armies and the empire they spread across three continents that reduced Christianity, with a few scattered exceptions, to a European faith.

Nor was there ever a single European Christianity. Most of the barbarians at first adopted Arianism, a popular creed that taught that Jesus was purely human; one Arian tribe, the Longbeards or Lombards, made it their mission to murder every Catholic clergyman who came their way. The popes, many the scions of old senatorial families, clung on amid the overgrown ruins of Rome until Clovis, a sixth-century king of the Franks, saw the light during a particularly tight battle with the Goths. The Franks made a pact with Rome that gave its kings legitimacy and the papacy military backing, and the deal was sealed on Christmas Day, 800, when Charles Martel's grandson Charlemagne climbed the steps of St. Peter's on his knees, prostrated himself before the holy father, and was crowned Augustus, Emperor of the Romans. The other emperor in Constantinople impotently fumed. The pope, the mere bishop of Rome, had effectively staged a coup, and the stage was set for schism with the Orthodox Church of Eastern Europe.

As Charlemagne's short-lived empire disintegrated and the Vikings launched waves of ravaging attacks from Scandinavia, as the barren countryside sprouted stone castles and its sparse population huddled under their walls, Europe became a backward peninsula precariously perched between the ocean and the green sea of Islam. In that, for want of much else, it found its identity. The modern concept of Europe was born not from geography alone, nor simply from a shared religion. It slowly emerged among a patchwork of fractious peoples that found common purpose in their struggle with Islam.

There was one conspicuous exception to that emerging identity: Iberia was still dominated by an imposing Islamic state. As the Christian counteroffensive began, it was there that the most zealously Catholic nations of all would be born. The reason was frighteningly simple. Christianity and Islam are sister religions, and in Iberia they long lived side by side. If you are about to hunt your sister out of your home, you need to work yourselves into a much more self-righteous frenzy than if you were expelling a stranger.

At the western end of the known world the forces of fundamentalism were about to be let loose among Christians and Muslims alike. The repercussions would be felt far and wide for centuries to come.

IT COULD ALL have been very different. In Arabic, Islamic Spain was called al-Andalus—the name would pass on to the Spanish region of Andalusia—and for three centuries al-Andalus was home to the most cosmopolitan society in the Western world.

From the first years of Islam, Muslims had classed Christians and Jews who submitted to Islamic rule as *dhimmi*, or "protected peoples." Pagans were fair game—they were given the stark alternatives of conversion or death—but Muhammad himself had forbidden his followers to interfere with the religious freedom of their fellow Peoples of the Book. The early Arab conquerors had gone even further: they had made it as difficult as possible for Jews and Christians to convert, not least because anyone who joined the Muslim elite was absolved of paying the *jizya*, the poll tax on unbelievers. As mass conversions became the norm, though, tolerance proved to have its limits. One ninth-century caliph with a flair for petty humiliations ordered Jews and Christians to hang wooden images of the devil from their houses, wear yellow, keep their graves level with the ground, and ride around only on mules and asses "with wooden saddles marked by two pomegranate-like balls on the cantle."

In al-Andalus, non-Muslims were not classed as equals—that would have gone against Islamic teaching—but they were rarely required to make more than token gestures of submission. Instead a radical concept was born: *convivencia*, or peoples of different faiths living and working together. Jews and even Christians began to take prominent roles in government as scribes, soldiers, diplomats, and councilors; one urbane, learned, and devout Jew became the Islamic state's unofficial but all-powerful foreign minister, while a bishop was one of his ambassadors. Jewish poets revived Hebrew as a living language after centuries of liturgical desiccation, and the Sephardi Jews—named after Sepharad, the

Hebrew term for al-Andalus—were released from a long era of barbarian persecutions into a Golden Age. Christians took just as happily to Arab culture; along with dressing, eating, and bathing like Arabs, they even read the Scriptures and recited the liturgy in Arabic. That earned them the nickname *Mozarabs*, or "wannabe Arabs," from a handful of refuseniks who made it their mission to insult Islam; one, an aristocratic monk named Eulogius, claimed among his many colorful insults that Muhammad had boasted he would deflower the Virgin Mary in heaven. Most met with the martyr's death they were after, and various bits of their corpses were spirited across the border to become favored attractions in far-flung Christian towns. Al-Andalus was never quite a multicultural melting pot, and yet as different traditions commingled and refreshed each other, as difference itself was celebrated in place of the conformity enforced by less confident societies, individuals with their own perceptions and desires emerged from the shadows of a rigidly hierarchical world.

This was a remarkable phenomenon in Dark Ages Europe, which had plunged into a continent-wide depression and was convinced the world was growing old and apocalyptic fires were flickering on the horizon. Spain, in contrast, was vibrant with exotic new crops transplanted from the East and heady with the fragrance of orange blossom wafting across the land. Córdoba, the Islamic capital on the banks of the Guadalquivir River, was transformed into the most magnificent metropolis west of Constantinople, its markets heaped with delicate silks and carpets, its paved and brightly lit streets hung with signs offering the services of lawyers and architects, surgeons and astronomers. The shelves of the main library—one of seventy in the city—groaned with four hundred thousand books, a thousand times the number boasted by the greatest collections of the Christian West. The Great Mosque—in Spanish the Mezquita—was a Gothic church transformed into an optical illusion, a shifting dream space of dainty marble columns supporting arches piled on arches in red and white candy stripes. With its population approaching half a million, Córdoba was for a while the largest city on earth; it was, wrote a Saxon nun, "the brilliant ornament of the world."

Al-Andalus reached the peak of its power in the tenth century, when its ruler discovered he had become too grand to stomach his status as a mere *emir*, or governor, and proclaimed himself the true caliph, the heir to the legitimate line of succession from Muhammad and the leader of all Muslims. To match his new magnificence Abd al-Rahman III built himself a sprawling palatine city outside Córdoba. Teeming with treasures, with doors carved from ivory and ebony that opened onto moated gardens complete with exotic menageries, gaudy sculptures fashioned from amber and pearls, and gargantuan fish ponds whose inhabitants were fed twelve thousand freshly baked loaves a day, it was a blazing statement of dynastic intent. The long line of ambassadors who tripped over themselves to offer fitting gifts to the new caliph were received in a hall of translucent marble, with at its center, beneath a giant pendant pearl, a pool filled with mercury that dazzled them when it was stirred at the operative moment.

Yet after three centuries, the Islamic powerhouse on mainland Europe crumbled to nothing in a historical flick of the fingers. Like every nation that succumbs to a superiority complex, it had grown too complacent to heed the danger signs. The fairy tale that climaxed with its haughty caliphs sequestered in their palace of marvels came to a fitting end at the hands of an evil courtier named Abu Amir al-Mansur—"the Victorious"—who was indeed so victorious that he won fifty-two out of his fifty-two battles. Most were fought with unprecedented fanaticism against the descendants of the Goths who had clung on in the northern fastnesses of Spain, and al-Mansur's notoriety earned him the Westernized name of Almanzor. Almanzor locked up the boy caliph who was on the throne, built himself a rival palatine city on the opposite side of Córdoba, turned al-Andalus into a police state, and outraged his urbane subjects by roping rough Berbers and even Christian mercenaries into his military campaigns. On his death in 1002, Muslim

Spain imploded into civil war; a few years later, resentful Berber troops tore down the showpiece home of the caliphs, just seventy years after it had risen to astonish the world.

Al-Andalus fragmented into a patchwork of competing city-states, and the Christian kings across the border finally saw their chance.

The Christian revival in Spain was a long, squabbling business, and the endless churn of its miniature kingdoms is a mind-numbing affair. By long-standing tribal tradition, its rulers left their territories to be divided among their children, and their children duly launched themselves into orgies of fratricide. As the ripples of war eddied back and forth, the rival monarchs made alliances of convenience with Muslim raiders as often as with their religious brethren. Yet gradually they moved south into the weakened city-states, and suddenly a spectacular upset of history was within their grasp.

Around the turn of the millennium, western Europe had finally begun to throw off its bloodstained blanket of darkness. The Vikings had started to settle down and convert to Christianity. France had begun to emerge from the western parts of Charlemagne's old empire, while the Holy Roman Empire, the forerunner of Germany, soldiered on in its eastern lands. The Roman Church had recovered from an ignominious low point, and once again it had begun to dream of increasing its flock. It saw its chance in Spain.

In 1064 the papacy gave its backing to war against the Muslims of al-Andalus—the first Christian war overtly fought against an enemy that was defined by its faith. From then on the Spanish marched—protected, if never exactly united—under the papal banner. They went into battle armed with an ironclad guarantee from Christ's representative on earth: mass indulgences for those who died, which absolved them of doing penance for their sins and guaranteed immediate admittance to heaven.

The struggle soon developed a name—the Reconquest—that swept aside the inconvenient fact that most of the peninsula had been Muslim territory for longer than it had been Christian. A haphazard flurry of battles fought for personal glory and territorial expansion was transformed into a war of religious liberation, and it boasted its own patron saint in the form of the Apostle James. St. James—*Santiago* in Spanish—had been beheaded in Jerusalem a few years after Jesus's death, but a hermit guided by a star had miraculously unearthed his bones in a Spanish field. In his unlikely new afterlife, Jesus's companion was transformed into *Santiago Matamoros*—"St. James the Moor-slayer"—with *Moro*, from the Roman name for the Berbers, being the catchall term that Iberia's Christians applied to Muslims, Berber and Arab alike. The Moor-slayer lent his name to the Order of Santiago, one of many military brotherhoods that sprang up to wage war on Islam, and the order adopted a stirring motto: "May the sword be red with Arab blood." From then on the Apostle regularly showed up in the heat of battle, dressed in shining armor and riding a white horse, urging on his followers to stick it to the Infidel.

Even now, not all of Spain's Christians were so sure where their loyalties lay. This was the time of El Cid, who earned a glowing reputation as a Spanish hero despite being a soldier for hire by Muslims and Christians alike. In 1085 El Cid's sometimes master, the wily and ambitious Alfonso the Brave of Castile and Leon, inveigled his way into control of the old fortress city of Toledo, and Christian Toledo took over from ruined Córdoba as Europe's capital of culture. Inside a synagogue designed by Muslim architects, its Christians, Muslims, and Jews celebrated their rites alongside each other. In its School of Translators, Muslims and Jews collaborated to translate medical, scientific, and philosophical texts from Arabic to Latin. Travelers crisscrossed the Pyrenees, introduced Islamic culture and learning to the rest of Europe, and transformed its intellectual life along with its decorative styles, recipes, fashions, and songs. In the twilight of convivencia, the Spanish had become the masters of modernity.

Toledo was one last bright flare of what could have been, one final, chaotic explosion of creativity. As Christian armies pushed on farther south, Iberia's remaining Muslim rulers began to fear their days were numbered. When Alfonso the Brave's enthusiasm carried him a step too far and he prematurely proclaimed himself emperor of all Spain, al-Andalus finally resorted to calling in help from abroad.

It was a fateful mistake.

The Almoravids were a ferocious Muslim sect from the Sahara Desert that had sprung up around a hard-line missionary who insisted on strict discipline and regular bouts of scourging. They had already expanded south to sub-Saharan Africa and north to Morocco, and they were only too ready to hop across the Strait of Gibraltar to Spain. As soon as they arrived, they decided their co-religionists were a bunch of addled sensualists and went home to arm themselves with a *fatwa*, or legal opinion, confirming their right to depose them. When they returned, the proud Arabs of al-Andalus took a deep breath and caved in. The new caliphate duly reunited the squabbling city-states and beat back the Christians until it, too, grew lax and was chased out of power by the Almohads, yet another all-conquering Berber dynasty that poured over from Ceuta.

The Almohads were even more fanatical fundamentalists than the Almoravids, and they set out to transform al-Andalus into a jihadist state.

Long ago, as Islam had expanded far beyond Arabia, its scholars had divided the world into the *dar al-Islam*, the House of Islam, and the *dar al-Harb*, or the House of War. According to that doctrine, the first was duty-bound to press on the second until it withered to nothing. Armed jihad—*jihad* itself merely means "struggle," and often refers to an inner striving for grace—was the divinely sanctioned instrument of expansion. As the House of Islam fractured and Muslims fought Muslims, the strong arm of holy war had itself withered away. Yet the Almohads tolerated no such frailty, and besides imposing severe strictures on their fellow Muslims, they declared an everlasting jihad against Spain's Christians and Jews. In the Almohads' uprooted and fiercely pruned faith, Christians were no better than pagans: as worshippers of a divine trinity rather than the one true God, they no longer deserved the status of protected people. The dhimmi who still lived in al-Andalus were given an ultimatum: die or convert. Rather than choose, many fled.

Western Christendom had undergone a similar transformation. Christianity had begun as a humble movement of Jewish sectaries, but when it was adopted as the official religion of the Roman Empire, it had soon made peace with war. Rome's legions had marched into battle under the cross, and so had successive waves of barbarians, many of whom had themselves been converted to Catholicism at the point of a sword. St. Augustine, the first Christian thinker to frame the concept of a just war, had condemned battles fought for power or wealth as no better than grand larceny, but he acknowledged that violence had to be met with violence in order to keep the peace. The journey from Augustine had wound through marauding barbarians and Vikings, through grand papal dreams and a Europe overshadowed by military camps, until fighting for Christianity was seen as a noble struggle against the Antichrist. To Catholic theologians, as they finally began to unravel the mysteries of Islam, any accommodation between the two faiths made no more doctrinal than practical sense: while Muslims at least acknowledged Christians, however misguided, as their precursors in faith, to Christians the newer religion, intolerably, told them they had got it all wrong.

For all their differences, it was their similarities that most divided the two faiths. Unlike any other major religion, both claimed exclusive possession of God's final revelation. Unlike most, both were missionary faiths that strove to take their message to nonbelievers, whom they labeled infidels. As universal religions and geographical neighbors, they were natural competitors. In the West, those rivalries had been held in check by a handful of enlightened rulers, by the unwieldy extent of the Islamic empire, and by Europe's bloody introspection. But the final glimmer of tolerance was fast fading, the Islamic world had begun to splinter into sharper shards, and Europe was finally on the move.

The pope called the warriors of Western Christendom to arms. Tens of thousands of Christian soldiers marched south across Spain, their shoulders squared with a vengeful zeal to drive Islam from Europe.

At the western edge of the world, holy war had been unleashed at the same time on both sides of an increasingly unbreachable divide. It was no coincidence that the descendants of Iberia's freedom fighters would race across the oceans to conquer far-flung lands in the name of Christ. Fighting Islam was in their blood: it was the very founding mission of their nations.

As the battle for the West neared its climax, an energized Europe turned its sights eastward. The counterstrike against Islam that had begun in Spain was headed to Jerusalem itself, and now it came with a name that would haunt the coming centuries: Crusade.

CHAPTER 2

THE HOLY LAND

IN THE SCORCHING summer heat of 1099, thousands of sunbaked Christian soldiers marched across Europe, crossed into Asia, and converged on Jerusalem. Weeping with joy, singing prayers, and seeing visions in the sky, they crouched beneath a firestorm of Muslim missiles and wheeled their wooden siege engines up to the holy city's towering white walls. When they overtopped the battlements, they sliced their way through the time-scarred streets until the stones themselves seemed to bleed. Fresh from the slaughter, staggering under the weight of their spoils, they flocked to the Church of the Holy Sepulcher and prayed at the tomb of Christ. Four hundred sixty-one years after it had become Muslim, Jerusalem was Christian again.

The outpouring of European zeal that launched the First Crusade had begun four years earlier, far away in the mountainous forests of central France. There, on a cold November day, 13 archbishops, 90 abbots, 225 bishops, and a clanking train of nobles and knights had gathered to listen to an important announcement by the pope. The church was too cramped for everyone to fit in, and the assembly moved to a nearby field to hear the ringing call to arms that was to unloose centuries of holy war on the East.

Pope Urban II, by birth Odo of Châtillon, was the scion of a knightly family from Champagne. His grand scheme was inspired by the Iberian Reconquest, but he had been spurred to action by an urgent request from Constantinople.

Six centuries after the fall of Rome, Constantinople still regarded western Europe as imperial land under temporary occupation by barbarians, and it bluntly refused to acknowledge the pope as the supreme leader of Christendom. Just four decades earlier, the pope's legates had stalked under the dizzying heaped domes of the Hagia Sophia, Constantinople's great cathedral, and had excommunicated the patriarch on the spot, a fit of pique that sundered the Eastern Orthodox and Roman Catholic churches for good. To ask Rome for help was a galling prospect, but Constantinople had little choice.

With its squares and streets lined with the sculptures of ancient Greece and Rome, its Hippodrome ringed with gilded equestrian statues and seats for a hundred thousand, its churches a golden blaze of mosaics and its workshops heaped with exquisite icons and silks, Constantinople had only one rival for the title of the most glamorous metropolis in the known world. That rival city had been built by the Abbasids, an Arab clan that had ousted the Umayyad caliphs from their throne in Damascus and had delivered the coup de grâce by inviting eighty of their deposed cousins to a banquet in which they featured as the main course. In the eighth century the Abbasids had deserted enemy Damascus for a site on the River Tigris, at its closest point to the River Euphrates and twenty miles from the towering ruins of the old Persian capital at Ctesiphon. The new capital was optimistically called Madinat al-Salam, or the "City of Peace," and was later renamed Baghdad.

As the heir to centuries of Persian cultural splendor and the crossing point of the currents of knowledge that swept across the vast Islamic empire, Baghdad had quickly become the intellectual powerhouse of the world. International scholars gathered at its House of Wisdom to translate the vast corpus of Greek, Persian, Syriac, and Indian writings on science, philosophy, and medicine into Arabic, and Islamic scholars tested the Quran against Aristotle. Mathematicians imported and improved the decimal positional number system from India and unlocked the secrets of algebra and algorithms. The secret of papermaking was extracted from Chinese prisoners, and lending libraries circulated the burgeoning body of knowledge. Engineers and agronomists perfected the waterwheel, improved irrigation, and bred new crops; geographers mapped the earth, and astronomers charted the sky. Baghdad's renaissance of learning sent shock waves around the world—and yet, even then, it was going rotten at its core.

The Abbasid caliphs had built Baghdad as a perfectly round city, and at its heart was their monumental palatine complex, the Golden Gate. As their lifestyle grew steadily more kingly, the Golden Gate became a pleasure dome of wine, women, song, and spectacular feasts; in the world captured in the *Arabian Nights*, courtiers kissed the ground as they approached the caliph, who was followed everywhere by an executioner and escaped from his public duties to a vast harem that echoed with the soft steps of an international selection of concubines and wily, witty singing girls. In 917 an embassy from Constantinople was welcomed by mounted troops seated on gold and silver saddles, elephants wearing brocade and satin, a hundred lions, two thousand black and white eunuchs, and waiters offering iced water and fruit juice. The palace was hung with thirty-eight thousand curtains made of gold brocade and carpeted with twenty-two thousand rugs, while four gold and silver boats floated in a tin-lined lake. Another pool sprouted an artificial tree topped with fruit-shaped jewels, with silver and gold birds perched on its silver and gold branches; on order, the tree would start swaying, the metal leaves would rustle, and the metal birds would tweet. It was a far cry from the egalitarian ummah of Medina, and as outrage mounted, the caliphs built themselves an insurance policy in the form of a personal army of mamluks, Turkish slaves seized from the savage tribes that roamed the Central Asian steppes. The solution proved short-lived. The Turks converted to Islam, adopted the local culture, and mounted a series of military coups: in nine years, at least four out of five caliphs were murdered. As the outraged Baghdadis erupted in rebellion, the Turks burned down whole quarters of the city.

The center of Baghdad would not hold, and neither would the center of the far-flung Islamic empire. To the west, a Shia sect wrested control of Tunisia and Egypt; its ruling dynasty, who called themselves the Fatimids, after their claimed descent from Muhammad's daughter and Ali's wife Fatima, expanded their dominions to Syria, Palestine, and much of Arabia itself, and for two centuries they ruled as a rival caliphate from their new capital at Cairo. To the east Persian power revived for a time until China's westward expansion pushed entire Turkish tribes into Iran, where they carved out independent kingdoms and barely paid lip service to the caliphs. In 1055 the Seljuks, a Turkish dynasty named after their first leader, finally seized Baghdad, installed their leader as sultan, or "holder of power," and relegated the caliphs to the honorary status of religious figureheads.

Throughout these upheavals Constantinople had looked on contentedly. It had retaken some of its long-lost lands, and its armies had almost reached the gates of Jerusalem. Yet the decline of Baghdad turned out to be anything but a triumph for its rival city. The Seljuks soon surged across Constantinople's eastern borders; within two decades they had smashed its armies and decimated its territories. Now they were massing in front of the capital itself, and the treasure house of the classical world finally seemed on the verge of annihilation.

SCANDALOUS RUMORS THAT the Turks made Christian boys urinate in fonts and sodomized clergymen, monks, and even bishops had gripped Europe for years, but for anyone who had missed them, Pope Urban left nothing to the imagination. The Turks, he luridly pontificated from his makeshift pulpit,

> have completely destroyed some of God's churches and they
> have converted others to the uses of their own cult. They ruin
> the altars with filth and defilement. They circumcise Christians
> and smear the blood from the circumcision over the altars or

throw it into the baptismal fonts. They are pleased to kill others by cutting open their bellies, extracting the end of their intestines, and tying it to a stake. Then, with flogging, they drive their victims around the stake until, when their viscera have spilled out, they fall dead on the ground. They tie others, again, to stakes and shoot arrows at them; they seize others, stretch out their necks, and try to see whether they can cut off their heads with a single blow of a naked sword. And what shall I say about the shocking rape of women?

That litany of horrors was enough to make Christian blood boil, but Urban had more. It was a tough sell to ask Catholic knights to march to the aid of Orthodox Constantinople and its notoriously scheming emperors, and the pope spun the Crusade in a new direction: toward Jerusalem.

In an age when men and women made arduous pilgrimages to bathe in the divine grace emanating from the relics of obscure saints, the city where Jesus preached, died, and was resurrected was the holy grail of penitents. For centuries Jerusalem's Muslim overlords had been happy to charge Christians to worship at the holy places, but the new powers of the Islamic world had torn up the old policy. In 1009, one Egyptian ruler had taken umbrage at the number of Christian pilgrims wandering around and had ordered the Church of the Holy Sepulcher pulled down to its foundations. It had been reconstructed, on payment of a heavy tribute, but soon afterward the Turks had arrived at the gates of the holy city and set about persecuting pilgrims with renewed relish. Like a captive virgin, Urban tugged at knightly heartstrings, Jerusalem was begging to be liberated "and does not cease to implore you to come to her aid."

The situation in the holy city was an unholy embarrassment, but in reality Urban was as desperate to get Europe's knights out of the West as into the East. As the Dark Ages had finally lifted, a large class of expensively armed and trained warriors was left with noth-

ing better to do than attack one other, terrorize defenseless popu-
lations, or, to Rome's indignation, raid Church property. "Hence
it is," Urban remonstrated with the assembled knights, "that you
murder one another, that you wage war, and that frequently you
perish by mutual wounds. Let therefore hatred depart from among
you, let your quarrels end, let wars cease, and let all dissensions and
controversies slumber. Enter upon the road to the Holy Sepulcher;
wrest that land from the wicked race, and subject it to yourselves . . . for the remission of your sins, with the assurance of the
imperishable glory of the Kingdom of Heaven." Christ himself, he
proclaimed, commanded them to exterminate the vile Turks from
his lands.

"Deus lo volt! It is the will of God!" the knights cried out.

For all Urban's firebrand rhetoric, the notion of fighting in the
name of Christ was hardly new. What was unprecedented was his
coupling of armed combat with the pilgrimage of a lifetime. The
prospect was so beguiling that thousands of poor men, women, and
children flocked to hellfire preachers like Peter the Hermit, who
was widely believed to possess a letter from heaven in which God
called on his people to attack the Turks. Armed with little but the
simple faith that Christ would scatter the unbelievers in its path, the
People's Crusade set out east before the warriors of Europe had even
begun to gather. Along the way, many of the pilgrims practiced
their slaughter on wealthy Jewish communities before they arrived
at Constantinople, where the horrified emperor hastily diverted
them to meet a grisly end at the hands of the Turks.

When the real Crusade set out the following year, the gruesome
hardships of the journey turned proud warriors into starving beasts
who carved off the rotting buttocks of slain Muslims and roasted
them on fires, tearing into the flesh while it was still half cooked.
Yet it was the assault on Jerusalem itself that guaranteed retribution. Memories would not die of that day of slaughter in the summer of 1099: not in the Muslim world, where writers howled that
a hundred thousand had perished, nor among Christians, who with

grim relish wrote home about the "marvelous works" performed in God's name. Piles of heads, hands, and feet, reported eyewitnesses, were scattered around the streets. Women were stabbed as they fled. Knights were seen "seizing infants by the soles of their feet from their mothers' laps or their cradles and dashing them against the walls and breaking their necks," or splitting open the bellies of the dead to retrieve the gold coins they had "gulped down their loathsome throats while alive." In the al-Aqsa Mosque, venerated by Muslims as the house of worship to which Muhammad had ridden at night on a winged steed before he climbed to heaven from a nearby rock, the slaughter was so great that witnesses vied over whether the Crusaders were up to their ankles, their knees, or their bridle reins in blood. The stench hung in the air for months, even after thousands of rotting bodies were stacked up against the walls "in mounds as big as houses"—by the forced labor of Muslim survivors—and burned in blackening, smoldering pyres from which more swallowed gold was recovered. The scale of the massacre only swelled the Crusaders' belief that a glorious benediction was shining on them from heaven; one rapturous monk declared that the conquest of Jerusalem was the greatest event in history since the Crucifixion, the precursor to the arrival of the Antichrist and the battles of the Last Days.

Jerusalem became the capital of a Christian kingdom, and a long series of French kings, mostly named Baldwin, were crowned in the Church of the Holy Sepulcher. To Jerusalem's north, three more Crusader states—Edessa, Antioch, and Tripoli—stretched along the eastern coast of the Mediterranean. A cordon of castles rose above the parched landscape of Syria and Palestine, each more monumental than the last and each no more than a day's ride from the next. The biggest of all were manned by the famously disciplined and fabulously rich military orders that had grown out of fraternities set up to care for sick pilgrims and guard them on their travels. The Knights Hospitaller and Knights Templar had become elite corps of holy warriors that answered only to the pope. The Templars rode on warhorses armed with iron spikes in the advance guard of the Crusades; on the battlefield, with their white mantles emblazoned with red crosses flying behind them, they couched their lances and galloped in silent, tight formation into the enemy's front lines.

The Templars and Hospitallers lived like monks and fought like devils, but they were often bitter rivals. The land Westerners called Outremer—"Beyond the Sea"—was a curious anomaly from the start. A miniature Europe transplanted to the East and dressed in exotic colors, it was bedeviled by the same lordly egos that set nobles at each other's throats back home, and it soon fell prey to the same endemic feuds. Crusaders constantly intrigued against each other, while others left the fold and went native. Bloodthirsty newcomers were outraged to find their predecessors wearing kaffiyehs, dousing themselves with deodorant, and sitting cross-legged on a tiled floor next to a plashing fountain while being entertained by dancing girls. They came up with a derogatory name for them— *poulins*, or "kids"—and the mounting estrangement was bound to end badly.

THE CRUSADER STATES had always relied for their survival on the even greater disunity of the Muslims who surrounded them on three sides. To the north, the Seljuk Turks had fallen into ferocious internecine fighting. To the east were the feuding city-states of Syria, and to the southwest was Egypt, whose long-ruling Shia dynasty, the Fatimids, had pitched into terminal pandemonium. Stalking silently among them all was a renegade sect of Shia fanatics who knifed their fellow Muslims in the back with even more ardor than they murdered the Christian interlopers. Their headquarters were hidden deep in the tortuous hinterland of the Syrian coast, in a fortress built on a rocky prominence from which their leader, a spectral figure known to the Westerners as the Old Man of the Mountains, reputedly ordered his disciples to jump to their death to impress a passing Crusader. To the rest of the Muslim world the sect was known as the *hashshashin*, or "hash eaters," a popular term of abuse from which the Crusaders adapted the name "Assassins." From there it was a short step to the fantasies of Western fabulists, in which cultists were given a glimpse of Paradise in the form of a hashish-hazed orgy before being sent off on a suicide mission that they were told would admit them to the promised land for good. Stoned or not, the Assassins did away with large numbers of prominent Muslims as well as plenty of Crusaders.

The Second Crusade did a much better job of uniting Muslims than the Muslims themselves had done. Led by the kings of France and Germany in person, it set out in 1147 to recover Edessa, the first Crusader state to be won and the first to be lost, and farcically ended by attacking wealthy Damascus, the only Muslim city that was actually friendly to the Christians. Having patched up their differences and thrashed the pilgrim knights, the Syrians invaded opulent, disintegrating Egypt, which in desperation called in the Crusaders, who first defended Egypt and then attacked it.

The Egyptians were forced to call in their enemy to chase out their allies, and this time the Syrians came to stay. Their commander's nephew and right-hand man, a young Kurd named Yusuf ibn Ayyub, took over as governor of Egypt, and in 1171 he evicted the last Fatimid ruler. Yusuf, who would become known to the West as Saladin, then engineered a reverse takeover of Syria. When, in 1176, the Seljuks buried the hatchet long enough to inflict another devastating defeat on Constantinople, Saladin forged alliances with both sides. In a decade he had united the Crusaders' neighbors, removed potential threats to his power, and snapped a trap shut on the Christian states.

Saladin was the opponent the Crusaders had most feared: a master tactician who was also a man of deep faith. He was as committed to reviving the faltering Islamic jihad as the most zealous Christian was to the Crusades. Like Urban II, he put Jerusalem at the heart of his campaign to build a new Islamic superpower, but his ambitions were even more outsize than the pope's. When the holy city was won, he declared, he would divide his territories, make his will, and pursue the Europeans to their far-off lands, "so as to free the earth of anyone who does not believe in God, or die in the attempt."

In 1187 Saladin made good on the first part of his promise. That summer, he marched west across the Jordan River at the head of thirty thousand warriors, nearly half of them fast, light cavalry. Twenty thousand Crusaders advanced to meet him, including twelve hundred knights in heavy armor.

The two sides drew up near Nazareth.

The name alone was enough to quicken Christian pulses with the certainty of victory. But God, or tactical sense, was not on their side. As the nobles quarreled about whether to trek across the desert in the blazing sun or let the Muslims come to them, Saladin drew them out into the parched plains to the west of the Sea of Galilee. As the Christians' water ran out and night fell, the Muslim advance guard howled taunts at them, unleashed torrents of arrows over their heads, emptied water skins on the ground within their sight, and torched the brush around their camp, choking them with smoke. The next morning, the weakening Christian foot soldiers ran pell-mell up the slopes of an extinct volcano known as the Horns of Hattin and refused to come down. The knights charged again and again, but the fresh Muslim troops crushed them in hours.

Three months later, Jerusalem capitulated to the Kurdish conqueror. The pope immediately called a Third Crusade, and the mighty triumvirate of Richard the Lionheart of England, Philip II of France, and the Holy Roman Emperor Frederick I answered the call. The elderly Frederick fell off his horse while crossing a river and died of a heart attack in Turkey; as was the custom in such cases, his flesh was boiled off and interred, while his bones, tied up in a bag, accompanied the remnants of his army that stayed on. Richard besieged the coastal city of Acre, promised to spare its citizens, then massacred nearly three thousand prisoners when it surrendered. Philip quarreled with the English king over the spoils and went home, and the Crusade petered out before it reached its goal.

New waves of armed pilgrims set out from Europe to recover the holy city, with equally unhappy results. Most egregious of all was the Fourth Crusade, which diverted to Constantinople at the behest of its Venetian paymasters without coming anywhere near Jerusalem. In 1204 the Crusaders breached Constantinople's mighty walls for the first time in nine impregnable centuries and wrecked the greatest Christian city in the world. In the majestic Hagia Sophia, drunken knights hacked at the dazzling altar and stamped on priceless icons, while a whore plied her trade in the patriarch's chair. Nuns were raped in their convents, and women and children were murdered in their homes. The Venetians shipped off the gilded horses from the ancient hippodrome to paw the air above the entrance to St. Mark's Basilica, and they commandeered the commercial life of the city. The occupiers anointed one of their number emperor, and for half a century there were three Roman Empires: the ousted rulers of Constantinople in exile, the Holy Roman Empire in Germany, and the so-called Latin Empire of the Crusaders. None, of course, had any power over the city of Rome itself.

The great movement of the West into the East that Urban II had unleashed had fatally wounded the very city that had called on his aid.

Once again it could all have been different. In 1229, the Holy Roman Emperor Frederick II arrived in Jerusalem and sat down with its Muslim rulers to negotiate a lease on the holy city. Frederick was a religious skeptic who had grown up in cosmopolitan Sicily, the only Christian state to match al-Andalus in favoring a fruitful interchange between the three Abrahamic religions, and he had already been excommunicated by the pope for failing to go Crusading. He feasted with the sultan, speaking the Arabic he knew well, and the next morning the muezzins, the men who called the faithful to prayer from the minarets of the city's mosques, kept mute out of respect. Returning the compliment, Frederick insisted that he had only stayed over to hear their mellifluous chants. The lease was signed and Jerusalem returned to Christian control for fifteen years, to the outrage of hard-liners on both sides.

Frederick, who was known to his peers, not always admiringly, as *Stupor mundi*—"the wonder of the world"—was a free-thinking anomaly. Once again a moment had arrived that seemed to shoot up the shadowy outline of a very different future, and once again it faded fast. In the end Frederick's intervention only roiled Europe the more, and the Crusades ground on to their inevitable end. For many, the final, shocking epiphany was the annihilation of the Seventh Crusade by famine, disease, and military defeat in Egypt, which Louis IX of France had confidently set out to conquer. "Rage and sorrow are seated in my heart," a Templar knight confided in an agony of faith, "so firmly that I scarce dare stay alive":

> It seems that God wishes to support the Turks to our loss . . . ah, lord God . . . alas, the realm of the East has lost so much that it will never be able to rise up again. They will make a mosque of holy Mary's convent, and since the theft pleases her Son, Who should weep at this, we are forced to comply as well. . . . Anyone who wishes to fight the Turks is mad, for Jesus Christ does not fight them any more. They have conquered, they will conquer. For every day they drive us down, knowing that God, who was awake, sleeps now, and Muhammad waxes powerful.

Though Louis was ransomed for an astronomical sum and was later canonized, some holy warriors lost all hope and defected to the Muslim side.

With the last Crusader strongholds set to topple and thousands of Christian refugees besieged on the shores of Palestine, it seemed as if only a miracle could prevent Islam from engulfing Europe itself.

It was at that point that a horde of ferocious warrior horsemen thundered across the East.

OF ALL THE nomadic invaders who surged west across Asia, the tribes united by Genghis Khan were the least heralded and the most devastating. In the early thirteenth century, the Mongol fighting machine swept across China, turned west, and burned a path through Iran and the Caucasus. The horsemen rode across Russia and into Poland and Hungary, where they wiped out a massed European army that numbered among its ranks large contingents of Templars and Hospitallers. In 1241 they marched on Vienna—and suddenly they vanished as quickly as they had come, called home by the death of their Great Khan.

Europe, which had been convinced the apocalypse was nigh, had been reprieved at the last possible moment. The Islamic world was not so lucky. There the Mongols stayed, and as they rolled inexorably on, countless great cities lay smoldering in their wake.

The caliphs were still ensconced in their Baghdad palaces when the new scourge from the steppes arrived at the gates. In 1258 the Mongols sacked the City of Peace and put a final end to five centuries of Abbasid rule. The victors had a taboo on spilling royal blood, so the last caliph was rolled up in a carpet and trampled to death by horses. Baghdad was burned, its people were massacred, and its palaces were pillaged and reduced to ruins. The irrigation system that had made Mesopotamia one of the most fertile regions in the world was broken for good, and the land that had cradled civilizations for more than five thousand years lay ravaged and desolate.

Islam's civilization would never fully recover from the loss. Many Muslims responded to the shock by withdrawing within themselves; this was the time of the whirling dervishes, mystics who redirected their sense of exile and estrangement into an interior battle, a means of stripping away the egotistical self to reveal the boundless divine. While some looked inward, others looked backward. With the loss of centuries of learning that followed the destruction of uncounted libraries, the ulama, Islam's body of religious scholars, retreated into a conservatism that sought stability in fundamental beliefs. Islam's early accommodation with Judaism and Christianity was finally forgotten as the ulama taught that all foreigners were suspect, and non-Muslims were banned from visiting Mecca and Medina.

By the mid-thirteenth century the Mongols had built with their battle-axes, scimitars, and bows the largest contiguous empire the world has seen. The beleaguered Crusaders who were clinging to the remnants of their former states began to see their enemies' enemies as potential allies, and for decades they entertained hopes of forging a world-spanning Mongol-Christian alliance against Islam. The Mongols themselves proposed a joint attack on Egypt, which was now ruled by the Mamluks, a dynasty of slave soldiers that had ousted Saladin's descendants. Yet the Crusaders insisted the Mongols had to be baptized before they would join them in battle, and another historic opportunity was lost to Western intransigence. Instead many of the Mongols converted to Islam, and they rebuilt the cities they had flattened on an even grander scale. Destroyers of civilizations, the Mongols also proved unexpectedly capable governors, and for a century a Pax Mongolica, or "Mongol peace," reigned across Asia.

Eventually the Mongols themselves grew sated and complacent, and their empire fell prey to internal quarrels. As it disintegrated into a patchwork of fiefdoms—one, the khanate of the Golden Horde, ruled Russia well into the fifteenth century—another cataclysm struck the Islamic world. In the middle years of the fourteenth century the bubonic plague arrived in Asia, carried in part by the fleet Mongol armies, and killed around a third of the population. Civilizations tumbled again, and the already weakened dynasties lost all authority. "Their situation approached the point of annihilation and dissolution," rued the Muslim historian Ibn Khaldun, who was born to a family of refugees from al-Andalus and lost his parents to the Black Death. "Cities and buildings were laid waste, roads and way signs were obliterated, settlements and mansions became empty, dynasties and tribes grew weak. The entire inhabited world changed."

The fourteenth century hurled Europe just as far backward. The Black Death wiped out as many lives as it did in the East, and once-burgeoning cities and commerce suddenly stilled. The dynastic bloodbath of the Hundred Years' War between France and England dragged interminably on. Superstition reigned again; this was a time when seventeen churches boasted that they housed Jesus's circumcised foreskin, and not one saw anything odd about the claim. The Church's moral suasion shattered; the papacy had already hobbled its own authority when, in 1309, it had moved to France under pressure from the French king. Catholicism toppled into its own Great Schism, the popes' legitimacy increasingly contested by the enemies of the French crown who backed rival contenders in Rome. A century after the move to France, the Council of Pisa declared both the French and Roman popes heretics and elected a third pope; the unholy mess was only solved eight years later at the Council of Constance, a three-year jamboree that was attended by 72,000 interested parties including 2 popes, 1 king, 32 princes, 47 archbishops, 361 lawyers, 1,400 merchants, 1,500 knights, 5,000 priests, and 700 prostitutes. When the first uncontested pope in generations returned to Rome, he found it so dilapidated that it was hardly recognizable as a city at all. The scaffolding went up, and the Eternal City turned into an eternal building site.

For more than a century, holy war had given way to a struggle for basic survival. Yet beneath the blasted surface, the deep-rooted rivalry between Islam and Christianity had not withered away. If anything, it had been fed all the more for being forced underground.

By the time the horrors passed, new Muslim rulers gazed out from the East. Their horizons enlarged by the Mongols' untrammeled ambition, they once again began to dream of a new world order born out of the end of the old. One family—the Ottomans—

consolidated their power across Turkey, marched into Europe across the Balkans, and trained their sights on Constantinople.

The Ottoman sultan Bayezid I—nicknamed "the Thunderbolt"—had called a new jihad. Three centuries after the first Crusaders had set out to rout them, the Turks were amassing again on the banks of the Bosporus.

As the front line between Christianity and Islam moved steadily west to the borders of Hungary, Europe finally began to respond. In 1394, the pope in Rome—there was still another in France—proclaimed a new Crusade against the fast encroaching Muslims. Its familiar vaulting goal was to expel the Turks from the Balkans, relieve Constantinople, and race across Turkey and Syria to liberate Jerusalem.

The outcome was predictable, too.

The Hundred Years' War had paused for one of its sporadic peaces, and Philip the Bold, the powerful duke of Burgundy and de facto ruler of France, saw in the papal call to arms a new way to parade his magnificent wealth. The question of how to defeat the Turks took up much less of his time, and Philip decided to send his eldest son, the twenty-four-year-old John the Fearless, in his place.

In April 1396, several thousand French Crusaders marched east to Budapest, breaking the journey with a string of lavish banquets, and joined forces with the embattled King Sigismund of Hungary. Also on the Western side was a large contingent of Knights Hospitaller, together with Germans, Poles, Spaniards, and a smattering of enthusiasts from across Europe. A Venetian fleet sailed up the River Danube to meet the land forces, and the combined army held a council of war to decide on the tactics for confronting the Turks.

Straightaway a bitter argument broke out. The first problem was that the Turks were nowhere to be seen. Scouts were sent out, but they came back none the wiser. The Hungarians argued that the Crusaders should sit tight and let the enemy do the marching, a lesson that should have been well learned from the Horns of Hattin. The glory-hungry French had already decided the Ottomans were cowards, and they overruled their allies. The army set out into Bulgaria and Muslim territory, where the French began pillaging and massacring with intent. Eventually, on September 12, the Crusaders marched up to the walls of Nicopolis, a fortress town built on a steep limestone cliff that commanded the lower Danube. Since they had no siege machines, they set up camp, partied on a grand scale, and waited for the defenders to give up. Most were still drunk when the news arrived that a massive Ottoman army was a mere six hours' march away.

The battle was so scarring that the medieval chroniclers later claimed as many as four hundred thousand combatants took part.

By now the French were bickering among themselves over who should have the honor of leading the charge. As usual, the rasher voices prevailed. While the Hungarians, the Knights Hospitaller, and the rest of their allies held back, the French knights galloped toward the hillside down which the Turks were advancing. They charged through the weak Turkish vanguard, only to impale their horses on rows of sharpened wooden stakes and expose themselves to a withering hail of arrows. Half of them were unhorsed, but they fought on bravely and managed to rout the main body of trained Turkish infantry. Again ignoring their elders' counsel, the younger knights clambered up the hill in their cumbersome armor, convinced it was all over. As they reached the top, kettledrums rattled, trumpets pealed, and to shouts of "Allahu akbar!" the Turkish cavalry thundered into sight.

Many of the French fled back down the slopes. The rest battled desperately on until John the Fearless's bodyguards, on the point of being trampled down, prostrated themselves to plead for their lord's life. As riderless horses stampeded across the plains, the rest of the Crusader ranks were surrounded and cut up. Many fled to the Danube, but in their frenzy to climb aboard the waiting boats, some were capsized, and the few men who managed to stay afloat fended off their fellow Crusaders. Only a small number made it to the far shore, where most were robbed, starved, and died.

Among the lucky few were King Sigismund of Hungary and the grand master of the Hospitallers, who got away in a fishing boat. "We lost the day," Sigismund later complained to his companion, "by the pride and vanity of these French." The French, though, paid a heavy price. Bayezid kept the youngest soldiers as slaves for his own army; many hundreds of the rest were stripped, bound, and decapitated or dismembered while the sultan and the French nobles, who were held for ransom, looked on. The bells tolled all day long in Paris when the horrifying news arrived.

Nicopolis was the very reverse of Poitiers: it had disastrously failed to halt Islam's advance deep into Europe. The shocking scale of the defeat marked the final death rattle of the medieval Crusades. Only a whirlwind Mongol revival under Timur the Lame, or Tamerlane, gave Constantinople and Eastern Europe one last reprieve; Timur, who claimed direct descent from Genghis Khan, exchanged a long series of insulting letters with Sultan Bayezid, the victor at Nicopolis, before seizing him in battle and leaving him to rot in prison, where he died in 1403.

No one in Europe now seriously proposed to send another army to the East. It would be a century before the crimson crosses were seen in Asia again—and then they would be blazoned on the sails of men who had come by sea.

Quite unexpectedly, those men would set out from the far western fringe of the known world.

The Crusades had begun among the knights of Iberia, but for a century and a half they had been too busy battling Islam at home to catapult themselves into the fight for the Holy Land. By the mid-thirteenth century the Christian conquest of al-Andalus was well advanced, but for another century and a half the knights were too busy fighting each other for territory to pay much attention to what was happening in the rest of the world. Yet the Crusading spirit they had kindled had never deserted them, and they carried none of the deadwood of failure in the East that had bowed down the rest of Europe.

When, in the fifteenth century, Iberia's new rulers began to dream larger dreams, they gazed across the Strait of Gibraltar at Africa and the lands of their former masters. They were not suddenly seized with a previously unsuspected craze for exploration; at first they were driven by the same malice against Islam and the same thirst for its wealth as were the holy warriors before them. Yet step by faltering step, led by a series of outsize personalities, they would launch a new Crusade that would lead them to the opposite side of the earth.

CHAPTER 3

A FAMILY WAR

K ING JOHN OF Portugal had been deeply pondering how to knight his three eldest sons in a manner befitting the heirs to an ambitious new dynasty.

Portugal was the westernmost of the five so-called Kingdoms of Spain, which had emerged in the wake of the Spanish Crusades. Three of the other four, Castile and León, Navarre, and Aragon, were Christian; only one, Granada, was Muslim. For more than a century bands of hardy, zealous warriors had battled to carve the new nation out of the old lands of al-Andalus, with a little help from Crusaders from northern Europe stopping off en route to the Holy Land, and its people were fiercely proud of their hard-won independence. The pope had recognized Portugal early on and had given it divine sanction to conquer land from the Moors, and its rulers continued to see themselves as closely allied to Rome. "God," a royal chronicler proclaimed, "ordered and wished to constitute Portugal as a kingdom for a great mystery of his service and for the exaltation of the Holy Faith."

Divinely ordained or not, at first the young country was Europe's wild west. King Peter I, who variously went by the sobriquets the Just, the Cruel, the Vengeful, and the Until-the-End-of-the-World-in-Love, was so crazed when his father's henchmen turned up at his trysting place and beheaded his beloved mistress, a beautiful Castilian girl named Inez de Castro, that the moment he assumed the throne in 1357 he tracked down the murderers and watched as their hearts were torn out, one from the front, the other from the

back. A few years later he had Inez's remains exhumed, draped in
royal robes, crowned, and propped up beside him on a throne. He
made his courtiers line up, and at his terrible cry of "The Queen
of Portugal!" they filed past and kissed her bony hand. Peter's heir,
Ferdinand the Handsome, was scarcely an improvement. Having
broken a promise to marry the heiress to the throne of Castile, Portugal's larger neighbor and constant foe, he instead took as his wife
the beautiful and very married Leonor Teles. Leonor began her
spectacular career of crime by ensnaring her brother-in-law into
murdering her sister by insinuating that she was unfaithful, only to
crow as soon as the deed was done that she had made it all up. She
then embarked on an adulterous affair of her own, and when Ferdinand's bastard brother John caught her in the act, she concocted
a letter that framed him for treason and had him arrested. When
her husband refused to execute his half brother, Leonor forged the
king's signature on the warrant, and John only escaped because his
jailers suspected foul play and refused to carry out the command.

On Ferdinand the Handsome's death Leonor assumed the re-
gency in the name of her eleven-year-old daughter, who was be-
trothed to the king of Castile. It was a toss-up whether the Portuguese hated their queen or the Castilians more; since both were
anyway openly in league, they erupted in rebellion and turned to
the only one of the royal brood who was not tainted with foreign
ties. As an illegitimate son, John had only a whisker-thin claim to
the crown, but with his powerful build and lantern jaw he looked
every inch a king. He emerged from hiding, broke into the queen's
palace, and murdered her lover with his own hands. The people's
assembly offered him the throne, and after consulting a holy hermit—he was pious as well as patriotic—he accepted. Castile took
his election as a declaration of war and invaded; that same summer
of 1385 John's army, though outnumbered seven to one, routed the
attackers and secured Portugal's survival as an independent nation.

A new dynasty needed a queen, and John looked to England.
The English and Portuguese had been allies before Portugal was

even a nation—many of the Crusaders who had piled into its wars were English—and they had recently signed a treaty of perpetual friendship and mutual defense. The bride John chose was Philippa, the eldest daughter of John of Gaunt, Duke of Lancaster. Gaunt was the uncle of the king of England and the richest and most unpopular man in the land, and growing up between the Lancasters' string of fortresses with their battalions of retainers and men-at-arms, his daughter had had a political education second to none.

Philippa arrived in Portugal with due pomp, but the marriage did not get off to a promising start. John failed to turn up for his wedding night; instead a courtier climbed into Philippa's bed to seal the deal, with the sword of chastity lying between them. The court was hostile; at twenty-seven, the new queen was extraordinarily old for a medieval bride. Philippa, though, was made of stern stuff, and she soon had the nobles speaking French and learning proper table manners. Whether out of love or awe, John was loath to do anything without consulting her, and the royal couple, so different in appearance—John bearded and burly, Philippa with pale skin, reddish gold hair, and "little blue Englishwoman's eyes"— were hardly ever apart. As for her primary duty—perpetuating the line—the superannuated queen bore eight children in quick succession, of whom five boys and a girl survived infancy. She took the lead in their education, passing on to them the love of poetry she had learned at the knee of Geoffrey Chaucer—she had also studied science, philosophy, and theology—and the chivalric code she had lived all her life. The mother of the family of princes that would become known as the Illustrious Generation was one of the most remarkable women of the medieval world.

After much thought, John settled on celebrating his sons' entry into the knighthood with a full year of feasts, complete with tourneys and jousts, dances and games, and lavish gifts for Europe's invited bluebloods.

The prospect of such a pampered entrée into the order of chivalry left a bad taste in the young princes' mouths. Playing games, they murmured to one another, was not worthy of their proud lineage. That summer of 1412, at their palace high in the cool hills outside Lisbon, Prince Edward, Prince Peter, and Prince Henry sat down and debated. Edward, the oldest, was twenty; Henry had just turned eighteen. They had decided to go to their father and ask him to come up with something more fitting—something that would involve "great exploits, courage, deadly perils, and the spilling of enemy blood"—when one of the king's ministers walked in. He was taken into their confidence, and he outlined a plan.

His servant had just come back from Ceuta, where he had been sent to extort a ransom for a band of Muslim prisoners who had been seized on the open sea. Portugal's nobles and even churchmen, like their peers elsewhere in Europe, were not above running a profitable sideline in piracy, and nor were their foes. Muslim corsairs had terrorized Europe for hundreds of years; their notoriety was so great that the Mediterranean shore of Africa would long be known, after its Berber pirates, as the Barbary Coast.

Seven centuries after an Islamic army first climbed the southern Pillar of Hercules and gazed covetously on Europe, Ceuta was still a name freighted with symbolism. Its recapture for Christendom would be an exquisite piece of revenge. Besides, the minister pointed out, it was fabulously rich. He had already suggested the idea himself, he added, though the king had treated it as a great joke.

By now Ceuta had grown into a major commercial port. Its famous granaries were piled high with wheat grown along Morocco's Atlantic coast. Camel caravans from the Sahara Desert terminated at its land gate, disgorging ivory, ebony, slaves, and gold. Jewish, Italian, and Spanish merchants regularly sailed there to trade; their factories, the buildings where they lived, stored their goods, and conducted business, lined the shore. Occasionally the religious temperature could rise and make life uncomfortable for foreigners, but Ceuta was hardly a hotbed of radicals. The Marinids, the dynasty that had ousted the Almohads from Morocco, had declared jihads against the Spanish and had occupied several coastal cities, including Gibraltar itself. But ever since 1358, when a sultan had been strangled to death by his own vizier, Morocco had been mired in a state of hopeless anarchy.

Niceties aside—as they usually were when glory and booty were in the offing—it was enough for the princes that Ceuta was an infidel city. The three went straight to their father, and once more the king fell about laughing. A few days later they tried again, this time armed with a list of justifications. An attack on Ceuta, they pointed out, would allow them to win their spurs in a real battle. It would also let the nation's nobles practice their knightly skills, which were in danger of becoming rusty since the expulsion of the Moors and peace with Castile had left them in the unwholesome position of having no alien enemies to fight. War, as the oldest brother put it, was an "excellent exercise of arms to be practiced, for lack of which many peoples and kingdoms have been lost, and to draw our subjects away from an idle life lacking in virtue." Besides, with a mainly rural population of around a million, Portugal was too small and too poor to keep a knightly class in the grand style, and a new Crusade meant new opportunities for plunder. Just as important to men raised on a diet of God-fearing chivalry, it would prove to the world that Portugal was at least as full-throated in its hatred of the Infidel as was any Christian nation.

John himself had been worrying that his battle-hardened knights would turn on one another if they had no other outlet for their energies. Even so, he cautiously sent for his confessors, scholars, and counselors. He wished to know, he told them, if this conquest of Ceuta would be a service rendered to God. Since the heyday of the Crusades, doubts had crept into the minds of Christian theologians and lawyers as to the pope's right, as the self-proclaimed sovereign of the world, to wield authority over non-Christians and approve wars of conquest against them. It was equally unclear whether Christian kings could legitimately wage war against infidels who posed them no direct threat; scripture, the antiwar camp pointed out, suggested they should be converted by evangelization, not arms. The papacy, which was still extricating itself from the fourteenth-century schisms, naturally took a different view. It was always keen to support rulers who were willing to put the papal prerogative into action, and several times it had granted bulls of Crusade to the Portuguese that licensed them to open a new front against Islam anytime they wished.

After pondering for some days, the royal advisers took the papal line that Christian princes had an unqualified license—an obligation, even—to attack any infidel or pagan simply because he was an infidel or pagan. The legal scruples dealt with, the princes persuaded their father out of his long list of practical objections—not least the crippling cost of the scheme—and the planning began.

The war council quickly realized that their best chance of success was to retain the element of surprise. Yet nobody in Portugal knew the first thing about Ceuta's defenses, anchorages, or sailing conditions. King John hatched a plot. The widowed queen of Sicily, which was then ruled by the crown of Aragon, had been angling to marry Prince Edward, the heir to the Portuguese throne. An embassy was prepared, but instead of Edward the ambassadors—a prior and a captain, both of whom had a well-earned reputation for cunning—were instructed to offer the hand of Prince Peter, the second-born royal son and the heir to nothing.

Two galleys were tricked out with banners, canopies, and awnings in the royal colors, with the sailors wearing matching livery. They headed into the Strait of Gibraltar, and dropped anchor near Ceuta. The prior made a show of relaxing on deck and committed the scene to memory, while the captain took a rowboat and, under cover of night, made a loop of the city. Their mission accomplished, they sailed on to Sicily, where the queen was predictably underwhelmed, and returned to Lisbon. When they were summoned to the palace, the prior asked for two sacks of sand, a roll of ribbon, a half bushel of beans, and a basin. He shut himself up in a chamber and built a giant sand castle that reproduced in miniature the hills, valleys, buildings, and fortifications of Ceuta.

Even in sand, it was a disconcerting sight. Monte Hacho was ringed with a web of perimeter walls, cross walls, and towers that rose from the beaches to the fort on the summit. More walls enclosed the main town, which occupied the peninsula that curled between the hill and the mainland. A moat stretched across the neck of the peninsula, separating the town from the suburbs on the shore, where a castle guarded the approach by land. Ships could anchor on both sides of the peninsula, but the winds often blew up and changed direction without warning, and the Portuguese would need to be ready to switch berths and tactics at a moment's notice. It was a daunting prospect for a small country that had never waged war by sea.

There was one more obstacle to overcome—the queen. Philippa was so well loved by her people, John solemnly explained to his sons, that nothing could be done without her consent. The princes were well aware of their mother's resolute nature, and they tried a little subterfuge of their own. They unfolded their plan to her and innocently asked her to approach the king on their behalf.

"Sire," Philippa addressed her husband: "I am going to make a request which is not such as a mother commonly makes in respect of her children, for in general the mother asks the father that he will keep their sons from following any dangerous courses, fearing always the harm that will come to them.

"As for me," she continued, "I ask you to keep them from sports and pastimes and to expose them to perils and fatigues." The princes, she explained, had come to see her that day. They had told her that the king was reluctant to take up their plan, and they had asked her to intercede.

"For myself, Sire," Philippa pressed, "considering the line from which they are descended, a line of very great and excellent emperors and kings and other princes, whose name and renown are broadcast all over the world, I would not by any means that they should lack opportunities of accomplishing, by their fatigues, their valor and their skill, the like high feats as were accomplished by their ancestors. I have therefore accepted the mission with which they have charged me, and their request gives me great joy."

John made a show of giving in, and the preparations went ahead. Only his immediate circle was in on the plan, and all manner of rumors started to fly: an assault on Aragonese Ibiza or Sicily, Muslim Granada, or even Castilian Seville. Eventually the full council was assembled, presented with a fait accompli, and sworn to secrecy. John's old comrades in arms had grown long in the tooth, but men as old as ninety reportedly leapt at the chance of one last fling on the battlefield. "On with you, greybeards!" one elderly councilor cried, and everyone burst out laughing. Gratifying though the prospect of the old soldiers squeezing themselves into their suits of armor undoubtedly was, as a precaution John quietly spread the word around Europe's knightly circles that a noble chivalric adventure was in the offing.

On the king's instructions a survey was made of the number and condition of the nation's ships. The reports were not encouraging, and orders went out to fell a sizable portion of the royal forests and hire every available carpenter, caulker, and cooper. Portugal's shipwrights were a privileged class; the nation's ports had become a vital way station between the Mediterranean and northern Europe, and many Italian merchants and sailors had settled there, bringing with them their expertise in nautical design and navigation. Yet it had nothing remotely like Venice's Arsenale, a state production line that cranked out huge galleys at a rate that astonished visitors. It quickly became clear that the only way to assemble a great fleet on short notice was to hire one, and John sent envoys to Spain, England, and Germany to charter as many tall ships as they could muster. To pay for them he commanded Portugal's salt producers to sell him their stocks at below-market rates, then sold them on at a large profit, and to defray more of the expenses he ordered anyone who held stockpiles of copper and silver to hand them over. The mint glowed and rang day and night, while the currency was stealthily devalued. To many of the nation's merchants, the enterprise seemed like a ruinous piece of chivalric nonsense.

Since a large war fleet could hardly be made ready out of sight, the king's men came up with another diversion. On the slender pretext that some Portuguese merchants had had their goods pilfered in Holland, an ambassador was dispatched to declare war on the Dutch. As soon as he arrived he arranged a clandestine meeting with the ruling count and took him into his confidence. The count was flattered to be let in on the secret, and he agreed to behave as if the threat were real. When the prearranged scene was acted out at court he played his part so convincingly that his counselors had to restrain him, and Holland made a show of preparing for battle.

Back in Portugal, Henry, the youngest and most zealous of the three princely plotters, was dispatched north to the ancient city of Porto to assemble one half of the fleet. His brother Peter was given the same task in Lisbon. The king busied himself with supervising the arms and artillery and left his oldest son, Edward, in charge of running the country, a responsibility that cost the delicate twenty-two-year-old prince months of sleepless nights and nearly brought on a nervous breakdown.

Across the land weapons were cleaned, tailors and weavers ran up racks of liveries, carpenters hammered away at ammunition chests, and ropemakers spun and twisted hemp. Sea biscuit, the hard, dry staple food of sailors, was baked in vast batches. Bullocks and cows were slaughtered in droves and their meat was flayed, salted, and packed in barrels. Along the docks gutted, salted fish lay drying in the sun like drifts of silver petals. The country buzzed with new opinions about the true purpose of the mysterious mission: a joint attack with England on France; a Crusade to the Holy Land to recover the Holy Sepulcher; even the unlikely war with Holland.

Portugal's neighbors were more worried than intrigued. Ferdinand of Aragon had been informed first that Portugal was going to attack his island of Ibiza, then his kingdom of Sicily, and finally

Castile itself, where he was locked in an uncomfortable co-regency with Philippa's sister, Catherine. Ferdinand dispatched a secret agent to Lisbon, wishing to know which, if any, of his possessions Portugal intended to assault. The Muslim rulers of Granada also decided to find out what was going on. Either out of a zealous refusal to kowtow to the Moors or a sense that this particular diversion had no downside, John utterly confused the envoys by first telling them he had no intention of attacking Granada and then refusing to give them any guarantees. Nonplussed by his prevaricating, they instead set off to see Philippa. The chief wife of the emir of Granada, they told the queen, begged her to intervene with her husband, since she knew well that the prayers of women had much power over their menfolk. As a thank-you, she would send Philippa the costliest outfits for her daughter's wedding.

"I do not know," Philippa haughtily replied, "what may be the manners of your kings with their wives. Among Christians it is not the custom for a queen or princess to meddle with the affairs of her husband." The first wife, she added at the end of a long diatribe, could do what she pleased with her gifts. The ambassadors finally tried to extract the assurances they were after from Edward, with the promise of more lavish bribes. "Those of my country who are in high places," the heir to the throne tartly replied, "have not the habit of selling their goodwill for a sum of money, for if they did so they would deserve to be called merchants and not lords or princes." If they offered him the whole realm of Granada, he added for good measure, he would not accept it—though, he added, their king really had nothing to fear.

IN EARLY JULY, young Henry's newly completed fleet raised anchor and sailed south along Portugal's wild Atlantic coast. After two hundred miles it rounded a rocky cape and filed through a narrow channel into the broad estuary of the Tagus River. In front was a calm expanse of water that had served as a spectacular deepwater harbor for two millennia, and on the north bank, behind the new shipyards and warehouses that were spreading along the waterfront, the Portuguese capital tumbled down a bowl of low hills. Across them a necklace of fortified ridges climbed up to the defensive crown of the citadel and its fortress, the former Alcáçova of the Muslims, which had been reborn as the Castle of St. George.

As the news spread, crowds poured down from the city to watch the seaborne pageant. Twenty-six goods vessels and numerous pinnaces led the way, followed by six twin-masted ships and finally, to the peal of trumpets, seven triple-masted war galleys. The prince's flagship was last of all. Every vessel flew a standard emblazoned with the eight-pointed cross of the Crusader, while smaller flags bore Henry's golden colors and insignia. Canopies embroidered with his new motto—"Power to Do Well"—shaded the decks of the seven galleys, and every sailor sported a silk outfit in his bold livery, a garland of holm oak overlaid with silver on a background of white, black, and blue. The prince and his captains wore simple woolen garments; Henry was pious, but he was also already a master of public relations.

Peter sailed up with eight royal galleys and dozens of smaller craft, these carrying the king's more discreet insignia. Fishing boats and river craft of every shape and size had been pressed into service to carry the troops, their horses, and the supplies for both men and beasts. With England about to march toward France and Agincourt, only a few foreign knights had shown up, mostly the usual suspects who would go anywhere for a good fight. Even so, the assembled army numbered more than 19,000: 5,400 knights, 1,900 mounted bowmen, 3,000 unmounted bowmen, and 9,000 footmen. It was a vast force for a tiny country that had struggled to maintain a standing army of 3,000 men-at-arms.

To more trumpet fanfares the combined fleet anchored a few miles from the Atlantic coast. For Henry it was a moment to savor, but all thoughts of celebration soon left his mind. One of the foreign ships had brought the plague to Portugal, and his squire hurried to tell him that his mother was dying. John had had his wife moved to a hilltop convent north of Lisbon, and Henry galloped there to join his family.

Before she fell ill Philippa had had three fine swords forged, their scabbards and guards gilded and studded with gems and pearls. She had intended to see her three sons knighted with them at their moment of departure. Now she knew she would not witness the proud scene, and she summoned her children to her side. Her desperate condition, it was said, could not stop her from presenting the swords from her sickbed, along with lucid instructions on how each of her grief-stricken sons should comport himself after her death.

On July 19, 1415, at the age of fifty-five, Philippa passed away. In another ominous omen, her death coincided with a lengthy eclipse of the sun. John's rattled counselors advised him to put off the departure for a month, until the funeral ceremonies could be observed and the plague had subsided. Instead the queen was buried with almost indecent haste at dead of night—because, it was explained, of the summer heat—and a brief funeral was held the next day, a huge crowd howling outside the church. Philippa's memorial would be the Crusade she had so robustly encouraged; there would be another time for mourning.

Henry, taking the lead as usual, invited his brothers to dine aboard his flagship. He hoisted the flags, raised the canopies, and ordered the trumpeters to climb the masts and strike up a merry tune. It was a Sunday, and the other captains were nonplussed. They rowed over, heard their departure was imminent, and rushed back to throw off their mourning clothes.

Three days later, on Friday, July 26—St. James's Day—the fleet weighed anchor and edged away from a subdued Lisbon. As crowds gathered on the hills and watched the sails recede toward the horizon, questions were being asked. How could the king have permitted such rejoicing while his wife's body was barely cold? Was it the influence of young Henry, whom the king had always held to be more of a man than his brothers? Hunting wild boar in the royal forests was one thing, but slaying armed warriors was quite another. Did the young princes think the looming battle would be yet another joust in which no one dared unhorse them? Perhaps, after all, it would come to a bad end.

The doubters' fears soon seemed to be confirmed, because the great mission quickly turned into a desperate fiasco.

Two days out of port, King John ordered the fleet to anchor and finally let the troops in on their destination. The king's confessor preached a stirring sermon and read out a new papal bull that reiterated Portugal's right to crusade against the Infidel and granted absolution to all who died in battle. Many among the ranks were so confused that they thought it was another trick.

The army had barely been exhorted to glorious savagery when the winds dropped. For a week the fleet bobbed around off Portugal's southern coast. Finally, on August 10, it headed into the Strait of Gibraltar, to the consternation of the Muslims who still controlled Ceuta's opposite pillar. Boats set out toward the king's ship bearing all manner of costly gifts. He accepted them, and flatly refused to promise peace.

The vast armada had equally astonished the Castilians who lived on the islet of Tarifa, just along the coast. According to one report they went to bed believing the ships were phantoms, woke up to a misty morning in which nothing could be seen at sea, and were only shaken out of their reveries when the sun suddenly illuminated the fleet as it drifted before their walls. When the Portuguese anchored outside the nearby Castilian port of Algeciras, the governor appeared on the shore with a sizable herd of cows and sheep and sent his son to offer them to the Portuguese king. John professed himself well pleased, but explained that his ships were well provisioned. Feeling the need to make a display of his own, the governor's son leapt on a horse and galloped along the beach stabbing the animals to death. John politely praised the effort and thanked him for his deed.

After that dramatic interlude, the king gathered his council and resolved to attack Ceuta the following Monday. They set sail just as a dense fog bank rolled in from the Atlantic. Worse was to come. Strong currents and high winds had always made the strait notoriously difficult to navigate, but the Portuguese sailors' dearth of experience made it all but impossible. The troopships commanded by Peter were swept off toward Malaga, the main port of Muslim Granada, while the royal galleys were blown straight to Ceuta, only to be forced by a sudden change of wind to weigh anchor and beat their way around to the opposite side of the peninsula. The city's banners streamed from the hilltop citadel, their two keys symbolizing Ceuta's control of the entrance to the Mediterranean and the exit to the Ocean Sea. Cannonballs hurtled from the walls, but the ships managed to stay out of range.

When the rest of the armada failed to appear, the king sent Henry off on their trail. He found half his brother's crews in the grip of the plague and the others groaning with seasickness. Between that, the fog, and the tricky currents, they appeared ready to give up. Henry gave out his father's orders, and eventually the troopships made it to Ceuta.

Immediately a storm blew up and drove the entire fleet back to Spain. The king and his commanders took to their boats, waded up a Castilian beach, and held a council of war on the sand. Many of John's advisers argued that he should heed the warning signs and head for home; others suggested launching a face-saving raid on nearby Gibraltar. He would rather choose certain death, the king stoutly replied, than abandon his Christian duty. In reality he had no choice: he had made such a big noise that to pull out at the last minute would have made him the laughingstock of Europe.

Finally the fleet made it back to the African coast.

From their observation posts, the bemused defenders had watched the first Portuguese ships approach and quickly vanish. The elderly governor had decided something at least was afoot, and as a precaution he had sent to the mainland for reinforcements. Plague and famine had been sweeping Morocco, and the city's defenses were badly undermanned. Yet since the Christians seemed incapable of steering in the right direction and had apparently retreated across the strait, he had sent many of the new troops home. For the Portuguese, the bad weather turned out to be a blessing in disguise.

That night the people of Ceuta set lamps in every window to make believe that the city was defended by a great multitude. Out at sea, the light of more torches and lanterns spilled across the water as the army made ready for the assault. At sunrise the Portuguese sprang into action, sharpening their swords, riveting their heavy plate armor, taking practice swings with their axes, confessing their sins to the priests, and breaking open barrels to tuck into the choicest food. The day had arrived for Europe's first colonial war since the time of the eastern Crusades.

The fleet's flounderings had revealed how little King John knew about navigation, but he had a lifetime's experience of fighting on land. His unintended sojourn outside Ceuta had given him ample time to form a plan. Its outline was simple. The objective was to take the fortress. Without it, the Portuguese would be exposed to attack, but with it, the town would be at their feet.

The king moved the main body of his war fleet in front of the city walls. It was a decoy: the attack would begin with an assault on Monte Hacho. A smaller group of ships sailed around the hill and anchored off the beach at its foot. Among them was Henry's royal galley. Long before the armada had set out, he had begged his father to let him lead the first action, and the king had given in to him as usual.

As they sweated in the hot sun and their enemies taunted them by waving their weapons on the shore, several hotheaded knights took to the boats without waiting for the order to attack. To his intense annoyance Henry was left watching from his galley as they waded to land and the fighting began. He leapt into a boat, commanded the trumpets to sound, and threw himself into the melee.

The Portuguese quickly pushed the defenders back to the wall that encircled the base of the hill and swarmed after them through a gate. Amid the confusion Henry suddenly saw his brother Edward fighting ahead of him. When he caught up, the two reportedly found time to exchange niceties. He thanked God, Henry beamed through his disappointment, for giving him so good a companion. "And to you, Lord," Edward replied, rubbing in his brother's late arrival: "I thank you a thousand times for your goodwill in coming thus to our aid."

One Muslim warrior, a head taller than anyone, was making mincemeat of the Christians; he was armed only with stones, but he threw them with the force of a catapult. A Portuguese chronicler noted, picturesquely, that he was naked and "black as a crow, and he had very long and white teeth, and his lips, which were fleshy, were turned back." Altogether he made a terrifying figure, but he fell, pierced by a lance, and his cornered comrades backed through a second gate that led into the city itself.

Five hundred Portuguese shouldered after them into the narrow alleys. Soon they were hopelessly lost, and to get their bearings Henry and his brother climbed what looked like a little hill and turned out to be the city dung heap. As the defenders closed in on them, they stood on their mountain of ordure, fending off attacks and waiting to be rescued. No one came. A large group of Henry's men had decided to cover themselves in glory by ignoring the open gates and attacking a firmly shut one. As they hacked away with their axes and tried to set fire to the planks, the defenders shied stones at their heads from the walls above and most were killed.

The two princes divided their troops into groups and finally fought their way off their dunghill. Edward headed for the steps that led up to the city walls, unbuckling and casting off his plate armor so he could climb faster in the mounting heat. Once again Henry was left behind, and he stripped down to his mail coat and ran after his brother.

King John was still on board his galley on the opposite side of the city, unaware that the battle was already joined, and impatiently waiting for some enemies to appear on the shore. Finally he sent Peter to the second fleet with the order to attack. When the prince returned and explained that there was no one left on the ships, the king sounded the signal for a full assault. John, it was diplomatically reported, "by no means betrayed his joy," but his knights made their feelings even clearer. They rushed at the walls, jealous that their comrades had seized the day and panicked at the prospect that the best booty had already been scooped up. Once inside, they fanned out and set about looting with intent. There was plenty to detain them; Ceuta's streets were lined with gorgeous mansions and palaces. "Our poor houses look like pigsties in comparison with these," one witness frankly reported. More soldiers smashed through the low, narrow doorways of smaller houses and came face-to-face with dozens of frightened families. Some were armed; many simply threw themselves at their attackers. Others dashed to drop bundles of their belongings into wells or bury them in a corner, hoping to retrieve them when the city was retaken. Gradually the attackers overwhelmed them, and many were killed.

The king was in no fit state to halt the mayhem, even if he had wanted to. He had been wounded in the leg as soon as he had reached the shore, and he sat down outside the city gate. To preserve his dignity, it was later reported that he had decided to reserve his royal person for the attack on the fortress, rather than join in the fray when the town was as good as taken.

With Edward and his troops busy fighting their way to the top of the city walls, Henry decided to regain the initiative by single-handedly storming the castle. As he made his way down the main street that led up to the citadel, he met several hundred Portuguese running away from an angry mob of Moroccans. Henry lowered his visor and thrust his arms through the straps of his buckler. He waited until his countrymen had passed him and flung himself at their pursuers. When the Portuguese recognized their prince they turned to follow him, and the Muslims fled down the street with the Christians in hot pursuit.

As the defenders reached the backs of the merchants' factories along the shore, they turned around and attacked again. Again the Portuguese soldiers fell back. Henry ran at the enemy in a rage, and they retreated through the nearby gate that led to the citadel.

The gate was set in a thick crenellated wall; behind it was a tower pierced with arrow slits protecting a second gate, followed by a passage ending in a third and final gate that led inside the castle. As fire rained down from the battlements, Henry pushed through the first gate with just seventeen men—so it was reported—at his side. Many of the rest had disappeared to plunder or find water, and others had simply become exhausted. Several had been killed, including the governor of Henry's household, who died while rescuing his rash young friend. Henry had tried to drag the wounded man away and had got into a gruesome tug-of-war over a corpse.

For two and a half hours, it was later said, the young prince battled his way forward in hand-to-hand combat. His seventeen companions were reduced to four, but somehow, perhaps because the defenders on the walls were wary of hitting their own people, they slipped inside the second gate. They stormed ahead, pushed through the third gate, and took the fortress. When King John finally arrived on the scene, he found it already abandoned. So claims the official account; far more likely is that the few remaining defenders saw the way the wind was blowing and decided to fight another day. Most of the civilians had already fled by the time the order was given for the garrison to withdraw; the rest, if they could, followed suit.

The next morning the city echoed with the cries of the wounded and the clanging of soldiers trying to unearth new treasure. In their frenzied search for gold, they managed to destroy tapestries, silks, oils, and spices of immense value. "This destruction caused much wailing among some of those of lowly origin," a chronicler reported, dutifully if unconvincingly adding that "respectable and noble persons did not trouble themselves about such things." Some Genoese traders who had been caught in the cross fire belatedly offered to help the conquerors, but the Portuguese, hopped up on victory, accused them of the invented crime of trading with the Infidel, and at least one was tortured to make him disclose the whereabouts of his valuables. Another band of soldiers broke into a huge underground cistern, and as they peered into the gloom, marveling at the walls covered with painted tiles and the vaults held up by three hundred columns, they made out huddles of Moroccans hiding in its depths. They destroyed the cistern with the townspeople inside.

That Sunday, King John ordered a mass to be held in the soaring space of Ceuta's main mosque. First it had to be scoured clean. The Moors, the chronicles explain, were in the habit of laying down new prayer mats over old worn-out ones, and they had to be dug up with spades and carted out in baskets. After the ritual scrubbing, the king, princes, and nobles assembled while the priests exorcised the ghosts of Islam with salt and water. Then, to trumpet blasts and Te Deums, they dedicated the building to Christ.

After mass, the three princes strapped on their armor and hung their mother's swords from their belts. They marched to the new church behind a file of trumpeters and drummers, knelt before their father, and were knighted. Soon afterward they sailed home to a victor's welcome, leaving three thousand troops behind to defend the city from the Moroccans who were already sniping at them from beyond the walls.

The conquest of a famous fortress city in a single day astonished the whole of Europe, even if it was overshadowed a month later by the news that King Henry V of England, like the Portuguese princes a grandson of John of Gaunt, had embarked on his long-awaited invasion of France. The three young princes had announced their nation's arrival as a crusading power in spectacular style, and at least one of the three had no intention of stopping there. The Portuguese had pursued their former masters across the same turbulent strait by which they had arrived, and stumblingly at first, then with gathering momentum, they would proceed to stalk Islam across the face of the earth.

It was only much later that the assault on Ceuta would be seen as a snapshot of Portugal's entire overseas odyssey. It had been fathered by the bitter struggle between Christians and Muslims in Iberia. It had been hatched in the zeal of youth. It had been nurtured by the collective effort, willing or otherwise, of an entire people. It had nearly met with a painfully premature end. Thanks in part to stout courage and in part to sheer luck, it had made a deep impression on the world. And it had left a legacy that would burden the ambitious young nation for centuries to come.

CHAPTER 4

THE OCEAN SEA

Henry, prince of Portugal, stands buffeted by the winds on a rocky promontory at the southwestern tip of Europe. A solitary figure dressed in a monk's garb, he gazes across at Africa, planning new missions to explore the unknown reaches of the world. At his back is the great school he has founded, where the most accomplished cosmologists, cartographers, and pilots of the age gather to advance the science of navigation. As his crews return from their daring missions, he debriefs them and adds the latest information to his incomparable collection of maps, charts, and travelers' tales. He is no longer Henry the Crusader: he is Henry the Navigator, discoverer of worlds.

So the carefully cultivated legend goes. The truth is rather different. Henry never set foot on an oceangoing ship. His school never existed as a formal institution, though he did take an interest in astronomy and he gave work to a number of leading mapmakers. He wore a hair shirt, was said to be a lifelong celibate, and was a dedicated student of theology, but he was equally fond of throwing wildly extravagant parties. He was the first man to mount a concerted campaign to explore the Ocean Sea, and yet his explorations started as little more than a sideline in piracy.

Henry's career as a corsair began soon after he earned his spurs at Ceuta. His vessels set out to buzz the coasts of Morocco and intercept Muslim shipping in the Mediterranean, though on occasion they were not above attacking Christian merchants as well, in one case drawing bitter complaints from the king of Castile. His first discovery of unknown lands came directly out of his raiding activities. In 1419 a storm drove two of his captains to an uninhabited archipelago in the middle of the Atlantic, and the following year an expedition was dispatched to claim the islands for the crown. Madeira, marveled one sailor, was "one large garden, and everyone reaps golden rewards," though Henry, as its lord for life, reaped more than most. It was quickly settled, and the first boy and girl born to the pioneers were named Adam and Eve.

Henry quickly developed a taste for discovery, but the proceeds of piracy were only going to take his ships so far. His prospects changed when, in 1420, King John petitioned the pope to install his favorite son as head of the Portuguese chapter of an infamous order of warrior monks.

Elsewhere in Europe, the Knights Templar had met with a downfall as swift as their spectacular rise. When the Templars had been turned out of the Holy Land, their aura of sanctity had quickly worn thin. Yet they retained a vast network of fortresses, estates, and entire towns that reached deep into European society. The Temple in London was the depository of much of England's wealth, including the valuables of the king, nobles, bishops, and many merchants and, for a time, the crown jewels. The Temple at Paris was a bristling fortress, ringed by a moat and enclosing a compound the size of a village, from which the order ran France's exchequer. Their power was prodigious, and Europe's biggest crowned heads had finally begun to resent the presence of so many mail-clad magnates in their midst, with their monastic discipline and their standing army, their fearsome treasuries and their direct line to the pope. In the early fourteenth century the French king Philip the Fair, who not coincidentally was massively in debt to the Templars, had had the knights arrested on the usual trumped-up charges of heresy, blasphemy, and sodomy, and had coerced the pope into dissolving the entire Templar edifice. Dozens were burned at the stake in Paris, including the grand master, an elderly man who confessed on the rack, recanted his statement afterward, and insisted on his innocence as he was consumed by the flames, his hands tied together in prayer.

Only in Iberia did faith in the warrior monks remain strong. Though their fame rested on their defense of the Holy Land, the Templars had been active in Europe's far west from their earliest days. They had ridden in the vanguard of the Reconquest, manned castles on the frontiers with Islam, and settled huge tracts of newly seized lands, and to the young Christian nations their zeal and deep pockets had been indispensable. In Portugal they never disappeared; as a sop to their newfound notoriety, they merely changed their name to the Order of Christ. Everything else, including their substantial wealth, stayed intact.

When the pope agreed to the king's request, Henry suddenly had the resources to match his ambitions, while the Templars, in their new incarnation, had an unexpected afterlife as the sponsors of the Age of Discovery. Even so, exploration was far from Henry's first concern. Instead he wasted enormous amounts of money and manpower on a vicious tussle over the Canary Islands with Castile, which laid claim to them, and the islands' Stone Age inhabitants, who covered Henry in military humiliation by beating back his armies three times in a row. With even greater ardor, he campaigned to follow up his heroics at Ceuta with another Moroccan Crusade.

Ceuta had turned out to be fool's gold for Portugal. The Muslim merchants had quickly diverted the caravan trade to nearby Tangier, and the shorefront warehouses at Ceuta stayed obstinately empty. The colony was permanently under siege; before long every house outside the land walls had to be torn down, since locals kept using them to launch attacks. The troops were badly fed and were forced to endure choruses of jeers from passing Spanish ships, and the posting became so unpopular that the garrison had to be reinforced with convicts working off their sentences. The permanent occupation of an isolated frontier post, supplied from overseas, was a terrible drain on Portugal's meager resources, and many Portuguese complained that hanging on to it was an act of folly.

Not Henry. To the glory-hungry prince, the debacle was an argument to do more, not less. The Islamic world no longer controlled the Pillars of Hercules, the stony guardians of the gateway to the great unknown. For the first time in seven centuries, Christendom had a foothold on the continent of Africa. The victory, he and his supporters insisted, was proof that God's benediction shone on their nation, and faith and honor demanded that they forge ahead. After all, North Africa had once been Christian territory; surely to recover it for Christ was merely to push ahead with the Reconquest?

For years Henry vainly pressed his father to launch an attack on Tangier. When John died, much mourned, in 1433 and was succeeded by the bookish Edward, Henry turned all his persuasive powers on his older brother. Edward caved in, and Henry took personal control of the new Crusade. He rushed ahead, overconfident as always, but without any of the subterfuge that had reaped such rewards at Ceuta. When the chartered transport ships failed to arrive on time he refused to delay, even though half the army had to be left in Portugal. Seven thousand men crammed into the available vessels and sailed to Africa, Henry rousing their wrath with increasingly bigoted diatribes against Islam. Yet as the Portuguese marched up to the gates of Tangier, waving a banner depicting Christ in a suit of armor and brandishing a portion of the True Cross sent by the pope, even Henry began to realize that faith alone would not carry the day. Tangier was much larger and much better defended than its neighboring port. The Portuguese artillery was too light to breach the sturdy walls, their ladders were too short to scale them, and the besiegers found themselves besieged in their stockaded camp near the beach. As more Muslim forces poured into the city and the usual sightings of crosses among the clouds failed to work their spell, hundreds of Henry's knights, including several members of his own household, took to the ships and abandoned him. His only remaining bargaining chip was Ceuta, and his envoys promised its surrender in return for safe passage for the remaining troops. Henry handed over his younger brother Ferdinand as a hostage, retreated to Ceuta, and crawled into bed, refusing to answer repeated summonses to go home and account for the calamity.

He never intended to honor the accord. Ferdinand languished in a Moroccan cell, and Ceuta moldered on in Portuguese hands. King Edward died the next year, aged forty-six, probably of the plague and not, as was widely believed, from a broken heart. After five years during which he had been increasingly maltreated and had beseeched his brothers in heartrending letters to negotiate his release, Ferdinand mercifully succumbed to a fatal illness. However tormented Henry may have been in private, in public he insisted that his younger brother—who was posthumously rewarded by being dubbed the Constant Prince—had been more than ready to die a martyr to the cause.

Henry, the younger son who would have been king, had exacted a terrible price for his unbridled ambition. Yet in an age of religious fanaticism, his relentless appetite for glory against the Infidel, however dark and devious the places it led him into, was seen by many as the mark of a true chivalric hero and worthy of nothing but praise.

HENRY TURNED BACK to the sea. Each year his raiding missions reached a little farther down the Atlantic coast of Morocco, and gradually he formed a bold new plan.

Like many educated Europeans, he was well aware of the insistent rumors that a fabulously rich gold mine was located somewhere in the depths of sub-Saharan Africa, a vast region that the Portuguese called, after its Berber name, Guinea. One widely influential map, the Catalan Atlas of 1375, pictured a Muslim trader on a camel approaching the fabled emperor Mansa Musa at his capital, Timbuktu. The heavily crowned Mansa Musa holds out a huge nugget of gold and squats on his throne over the heart of the continent. "So abundant is the gold which is found in his country," reads the legend on the map, "that he is the richest and most noble king in the land."

The fascination was understandable. Europe had almost exhausted its own gold mines, and it was desperately short of the bullion it needed to keep its economy liquid. Two-thirds of its gold imports arrived in bags slung over camels that had trekked across the Sahara Desert, yet Christians were almost entirely excluded from the African interior. Tapping the gold at the source, Henry envisioned, would bring a double boon: it would enrich his nation, and it would impoverish the Muslim merchants who benefited most from the trade.

The location of the mines, though, remained a closely guarded secret, and mounting frustration inevitably gave rise to a flurry of wild speculation.

From the fourteenth century, Europe's mapmakers began to draw an enormously long river that virtually bisected Africa from east to west. The river was named the Río del Oro, or the Gold River, and halfway across the continent, the maps showed it dividing around a large island that resembled the navel of Africa's torso. It was there that Henry was convinced the gold was to be found, and as his ships reached farther south, he began to dream of sailing up the Gold River and helping himself to the treasure.

There was one glaring obstacle. On nearly every world map the Atlantic was a small puddle of blue to the left, and beneath it the African landmass ran off the edge of the page. The last feature shown on the coast was usually a modest bulge, some five hundred miles south of Tangier, named Cape Bojador.

The very name struck fear into generations of sailors, and macabre legends wreathed around it. Boundless shallows made it impossible to approach the coast without getting marooned. Violent offshore currents swept ships into the unknown. Fiery streams ran into the sea and made the water boil. Sea serpents were waiting to devour intruders. Giants would rise up from the ocean and lift a ship in the span of their hand. White men would be turned black by the searing heat. No one, it was widely believed, could pass the cape and live to tell the tale.

Henry refused to be deterred. When, in 1433, his squire Gil Eanes sailed home and admitted his crew had been too afraid to approach the dreaded cape, the prince sent him back with strict orders not to return until the job was done.

Eanes's little ship crept up to the fearsome headland. The waves and currents were strong, the shallows reached a good way out from the coast, fogs and mists obscured the way, and the prevailing winds undoubtedly made it tricky to head for home. Yet past the sandy red dunes of the headland, the coast wore monotonously on. The perils were a myth, perhaps spread by Muslims to keep Europeans away from their caravan routes. Eanes returned in triumph and was knighted, and Henry loudly trumpeted his besting of generations of sages and sailors.

Nine years later, in 1443, Henry convinced his brother Peter, then regent of Portugal after Edward's death, to grant him a personal monopoly over all shipping to the south of Cape Bojador.

To claim the ocean as his personal possession was a bold move even for the enterprising prince, and it needed backing up with action. There were only so many Portuguese sailors with oceangoing experience and an enthusiasm for out-of-this-world experiences, and Henry was forced to look abroad for new recruits. Conveniently, his personal estates in the Algarve—the name came from the Arabic *al-Gharb*, or "the west"—were close to Sagres Point, a flat-topped promontory at Europe's extreme southwestern corner. In bad weather, ships heading from the Mediterranean to northern Europe took shelter behind its sheer cliffs, and Henry sent out his men to meet every vessel. They showed off samples of the wares his explorers had collected, they talked up the prince's discovery of new lands and the fortunes to be made there, and they coaxed the sailors into enlisting in his fleets.

In reality, Henry's ships had come home with little more than the pelts and oil from what had become a mass annual cull of seals, though in 1441 one captain had returned with "ten blacks, male and female . . . a little gold dust and a shield of ox-hide, and a number of ostrich eggs, so that one day there were served up at the Prince's table three dishes of the same, as fresh and good as though they had been the eggs of any other domestic fowls. And we may well presume," our informant added, "that there was no other Christian prince in this part of Christendom, who had dishes like these upon his table." Even so, plenty of daredevil sailors found Henry's blandishments impossible to resist. Alvise Cadamosto, a gentleman adventurer from Venice, was on his way to Flanders when his galley was blown onto the Algarve coast. He was immediately approached by Henry's recruiters and was regaled with the wonders of Africa. "They related so much in this strain," he recorded, "that I, with the others, marveled greatly. They thus aroused in me a growing desire to go thither. I asked if the said lord permitted any who wished to sail, and was told that he did." Like many others from as far away as Germany and Scandinavia, Cadamosto jumped ship and signed up on the spot.

Money, as much as manpower, was always in short supply in Portugal, and even with the key to the Templars' treasury, Henry could not fund the expensive business of exploration indefinitely. Wealthy Italian financiers set up shop in Lisbon, and Henry licensed Genoese, Florentine, and Venetian merchants to fit out ships and sponsor voyages, always reserving a share of the profits for himself. The new policy paid off: in 1445, fully twenty-six ships headed out for Africa flying the red Templar crosses of Henry's Order of Christ.

By now the prince's shipwrights and crews had hit on the ideal vessel for exploring the coasts and, equally important, making it back home. The caravel was a slim, shallow-draft craft that could skirt the shore and enter rivers. It was equipped with lateen, or triangular, sails—borrowed via the Arabs from the Indian Ocean— that responded to the lightest breeze and made it possible to sail closer to the wind than the traditional square rig allowed. With a solitary cabin in the stern it was also horribly uncomfortable, and progress was painfully slow. As the fleets picked their way down the Saharan coast, a constant watch had to be kept for breakers that warned of shoals and sandbanks ahead. The coastline had to be charted, and offshore islands had to be explored. The lead and line had to be dropped to sound the depths, and at night all work had to be suspended. Farther south, strong currents dragged the caravels toward the shore, and they were forced to sail out of sight of land. To return home, they had to head far out into the Atlantic, tacking—sailing in a zigzag pattern—against the northeasterly trade winds until they were far enough north to catch the westerlies that blew them back to Lisbon.

Yet there were many rewards. The ancient puzzle of where the birds went was solved: in the Saharan winter the sailors found swallows, storks, turtledoves, and thrushes, while in summer they saw the falcons, herons, and wood pigeons that wintered in Europe. Strange swordfish and suckerfish flapped in their nets, and the meat and eggs of showy pelicans and genteel flamingos made an exotic change of diet. As they put into shore, they marveled at the endless vistas of sand and rock and the variety of creatures that lived amid them. There were rats bigger than rabbits and snakes that could swallow a goat, desert oryx and ostriches, vast numbers of gazelles, hinds, hedgehogs, wild dogs, and jackals, and other beasts completely unknown. Swarms of red and yellow locusts filled the air for miles around, obscured the sun for days, and wherever they settled destroyed everything aboveground. Tornadoes made the barren land bloom in a single day, and sandstorms roared up like monstrous fires and hurtled turtles and birds around like leaves.

As they planted wooden crosses to announce that the land had been taken for Christ and set out to make contact with the local people, the explorers puzzled over the intricate African patchwork of kingdoms and tribes with their bewildering variety of languages. Since they introduced themselves by clambering onto beaches dressed in suits of armor, marching up to desert herders supping on camel milk or peaceable fishermen roasting fish and turtles over kelp fires, crying "Portugal and St. George!" and seizing a couple of prisoners to serve as informants and translators, the incomprehension was mutual.

When the Europeans grew bolder and struck inland, they came across remote mountains where the finest dates in the world were grown but the people were reportedly cannibals, and desert towns whose houses and mosques were built entirely of blocks of salt. Every so often, they encountered one of the famous camel caravans. The camels served both as transport and sustenance: the unluckier beasts were kept thirsty for months, then made to gorge on water so they could be killed on the march and tapped for a drink. The traders were brown-complexioned, wore turbans that partially covered their faces and white cloaks edged with a red stripe, and went barefoot. They were Muslims who traded silver and silks from Granada and Tunis for slaves and gold, and they were determined to keep the interlopers at bay.

Eventually the desert petered out, and the fleets sailed past the mouth of the Senegal River into the more densely populated tropics. Suddenly everything seemed larger and more vivid. "It appears to me a very marvelous thing," the Venetian adventurer Cadamosto expectantly wrote while still passing the Sahara, "that beyond the river all men are very black, tall, and big, their bodies well formed; and the whole country green, full of trees, and fertile: while on this side, the men are brownish, small, lean, ill-nourished, and small in stature: the country sterile and arid."

The Europeans' eyes had been opened to an unimagined new world. Here the men branded themselves with hot irons, and the women tattooed themselves with hot needles. Both sexes wore gold rings in their pierced ears, noses, and lips, and the females sported more gold rings dangling between their legs. The visitors marveled at the soaring trees, the sprawling mangrove forests, and the brightly colored talking birds. They bought apes and baboons to take home; they stared at hippopotami, witnessed elephant hunts, and sampled the huge animals' flesh, which turned out to be tough and tasteless. On their homecoming they presented exotic gifts to Prince Henry, including the foot, trunk, hair, and salted flesh of a baby elephant; Henry bestowed the tusk and foot of a fully grown specimen on his sister.

At first the Africans were equally fascinated by the newcomers. They rubbed spittle into their hands and limbs to see whether their whiteness was a dye. They seemed convinced that their bagpipes were some kind of musical animal. They paddled out to the caravels in dugouts, wondering, or so the Portuguese thought, whether they were great fish or birds, until they saw the sailors and fled.

To the Europeans' dismay it turned out that even here the people were Muslims. Even so, their faith was far from rigid, they were mostly poor, and at least some were happy to do business with Christians. On one sortie up the Senegal, Cadamosto was invited to a nearby royal capital, where, typically of his fellow pioneers, he fully expected to find a European-style monarchy and court. As he approached the throne he saw petitioners throw themselves on their knees, bow their heads to the ground, and scatter sand over their naked shoulders. Groveling in this way, they shuffled forward, stated their business, and were brusquely dismissed. Since it turned out that their wives and children were liable to be seized and sold as punishment for minor misdeeds, Cadamosto decided their trepidation was appropriate. The king and his lords, he approvingly noted, were obeyed much more readily than their counterparts in Europe—though, he added, they were still "great liars and cheats."

If many African customs seemed primitive, others made it hard to pass easy judgments. Cadamosto soon found himself debating the finer points of religion with the court's Muslim priests. As usual, the Europeans opened the discussion by informing the king that he had taken up a false faith. If the Christian God was a just lord, the ruler laughingly replied, he and his men had a much better chance of reaching Paradise than they did, since Europe had been so much more favored with riches and knowledge in this world. "In this," remarked Cadamosto, "he showed good powers of reasoning and deep understanding of men." The king showed a different type of understanding when he presented the Venetian sailor, as a mark of goodwill, with "a handsome young negress, twelve years of age, saying that he gave her to me for the service of my chamber. I accepted her," Cadamosto recorded, "and sent her to the ship."

Not every African ruler was so benevolent, and the explorers soon found themselves under relentless attack. Warriors emerged from the forests wielding circular shields covered with gazelle skins, spears with barbed iron tips poisoned with snake venom and sap, javelin-like lances, and Arab-style scimitars. Some launched into warlike dances and chants; others stealthily paddled out in canoes. All were fearless and much preferred to be killed than to flee. The caravels were equipped with small cannon that fired stone balls, but large numbers of knights, squires, soldiers, and sailors fell beneath the onslaughts, while the captives they tried to land as translators were invariably beaten to death on the beaches.

As more half-crewed caravels limped home, Henry began to grow alarmed at the escalating hostilities. He ordered his soldiers to fire only in self-defense, but by then their reputation for violence had already spread. When the next party of explorers arrived at the vast mouth of the Gambia River—more than fifteen hundred miles from Lisbon—they found they had been preceded by rumors that they were cannibals with a taste for black flesh. As they sailed upriver, massed ranks of Africans emerged from the cover of the forest, hurling lances and unleashing poisoned arrows. Fleets of war canoes paddled furiously at the intruders, the strongly built warriors dressed in white cotton shirts and white-feathered caps and, noted Cadamosto, "exceedingly black." In the parley that followed, the Europeans demanded to know why they, peaceful traders who had come bearing gifts, had been attacked. The Africans, reported Cadamosto, replied that they "did not want our friendship on any terms, but sought to slaughter us all, and to make a gift of our possessions to their lord." Even the shock of gunfire failed to make them back off for long, and once again the unwanted visitors beat a hasty retreat.

As the Portuguese trading network crept along the coast a few bags of gold dust began to make their way back to Lisbon; soon Portugal's first gold coinage in nearly a century, aptly named the *cruzado*, or "Crusader," would be proudly hammered out in Lisbon's mint. Yet the Gold River had turned out to be a mirage, and even less progress had been made with Henry's second great quest—the search for a powerful ally against Islam.

Somewhere far overseas, age-old stories told, was a lost Christian empire of fabulous wealth and power. Its ruler was known as Prester John.

THE WORD *Prester* comes from the Old French *prestre*, or priest, but John was no ordinary ecclesiastic. Europeans firmly believed him to be a mighty Christian king, and most likely a descendant of one of the three Magi who brought offerings of gold, frankincense, and myrrh to the infant Jesus. Centuries of speculation had endowed the Prester's kingdom with any number of marvels, including a fountain of youth that kept him alive through the centuries, a mirror in which the world was reflected, and an emerald table, illuminated by precious balsam burning in countless lamps, at which he entertained thirty thousand guests. In an age when Noah's life span was an accepted fact, Prester John's superannuated existence seemed perfectly plausible; or at least it validated Western Christendom's dreams of universality.

The story of Prester John was not just a popular fable. It had grown out of a string of rumors, frauds, and half-understood truths, but many powerful figures, including a succession of popes, took it at face value.

The known facts were these. In 1122 a man who announced himself as John, Bishop of India, had presented himself to the pope and had described his land as a wealthy Christian realm. Two decades later a German bishop reported the news that an Eastern

Christian king was at war with Iran; according to his informant, he added, the king was called Prester John and carried a scepter fashioned from solid emerald. Not much was made of either piece of information until 1165, when copies of a letter signed by the Prester began to appear across Europe. It was written in the supercilious tone befitting a man who claimed to rule over seventy-two kings and who styled himself "Emperor of the Three Indias." At his table, he informed his readers, he was served by "seven kings, each in his turn, by sixty-two dukes, and by three hundred and sixty-five counts. . . . In our hall there dine daily, on our right hand, twelve archbishops, on our left, twenty bishops." Count the stars of the sky and the sands of the sea, he helpfully proposed, and you might get a sense of the vastness of his realm and his powers.

Since medieval Europeans were sustained by a steady flow of marvels and miracles, these wild and wonderful claims made the letter all the more believable. The Prester further explained that his kingdom boasted "horned men, one-eyed ones, men with eyes back and front, centaurs, fauns, satyrs, pygmies, giants, cyclops, the phoenix and almost all sorts of animals which dwell on earth." Among those were bird-lions called griffins that could lift an ox to their nests, more birds called tigers that could seize and kill a knight and his horse, and a pair of royal birds with feathers the color of fire and wings as sharp as razors that ruled for sixty years over all the fowl in the world until they abdicated by plunging suicidally into the sea. A race of pygmies fought an annual and seemingly one-sided war against the birds, while a race of archers had the advantage of being horses from the waist down. Elsewhere, forty thousand men were kept busy stoking the fires that kept alive the worms that spun silk threads.

After mulling over this extraordinary communication for twelve years, the pope decided to send a reply. He entrusted it to his personal physician, who set out in search of the fabled king and was never heard from again. Nevertheless, the letter had gripped Europe's imagination; it was translated into numerous languages, and it was avidly read for centuries. Whenever Europe was under threat from overseas, Prester John was half expected to ride to the rescue and crush the infidels. During the Crusades he was rumored to be planning an attack on Jerusalem. As the Mongols invaded Europe he was relocated to Central Asia, where for a time he was believed to be Genghis Khan's estranged foster father. He was briefly killed off when reports arrived that he had enraged Genghis Khan by refusing him the hand of his daughter in marriage and had lost the war that broke out between them, but as Europe began to dream of converting the Mongols he was resurrected as a new Mongol ruler.

The Prester's population, it was said, was three times larger than that of the whole of Western Christendom. His standing army numbered a hundred thousand, and his warriors wielded solid gold weapons. If need be he could put a million men in the field; the rumor that many fought naked made them sound all the more fearsome. He was the most powerful man in the world, with unlimited supplies of precious metals and gems at his disposal. Allied with his invincible armies, Europe could surely wipe Islam off the face of the earth.

If only he could be found.

By the time Henry sent his crews to seek after Prester John, the great king had been relocated to East Africa. This was not such a leap from the old belief that he ruled over India, since Europeans had come to believe that India and Africa were joined together. East Africa was also known as Middle India, and to confuse matters further, Middle India had also been identified with the kingdom of Ethiopia.

Ethiopia was known to have been an ancient Christian land, but with Islam blocking the way Europe had long lost all contact with its people. Some said it was separated from Egypt by a desert that took fifty days to cross and was plagued by naked Arab robbers; others claimed that the Ethiopians were immune to disease and lived for two hundred years. In 1306, after centuries of silence,

Ethiopian ambassadors had suddenly turned up at the papal court in France, and no doubt from an eagerness to please on both sides, Prester John came out of the encounter invested as the patriarch of the Ethiopian Church. Since that was something of a letdown, he was soon elevated from patriarch to autocrat and was identified as the all-powerful emperor of the vast and mighty state of Ethiopia. By 1400 the supposition was sufficiently well established for King Henry IV of England to write to the Prester in his new capacity, on the back of rumors that the great ruler was once again planning to march on Jerusalem. The Europeans' insistence on calling their monarch Prester John caused no end of confusion to the occasional Ethiopian envoys who continued to reach Europe in the fifteenth century—in 1452 one caused a great stir by appearing in Lisbon—though no doubt they were flattered to be received as far more important personages than they had previously suspected.

Once again Europe's hopes soared that the priest-king would prove a decisive ally against Islam. Yet even if he had settled down, the problem was still how to reach him. The dilemma was seemingly solved when maps began to appear showing a colossal crescent-shaped gulf slicing into Africa from its west coast. Named the *Sinus Aethiopicus*, or Ethiopian Gulf, it seemed to lead straight to the heart of the Prester's realm.

For years, as Henry's ships sailed to the place where the gaping mouth of the gulf should have been, he instructed his crews to ask for news of the Indies and their priest-emperor Prester John. When, in 1454, the prince successfully petitioned the pope to confirm his Atlantic monopoly, he promised that his missions would soon reach "as far as the Indians who, it is said, worship the name of Christ, so that we can communicate with them and persuade them to come to the aid of the Christians against the Saracens." The Christian India for which the Portuguese would continue to search for decades was not India at all, but Ethiopia.

Henry never did find his Sinus Aethiopicus, his direct route to the Prester's lands. The search for the great king would go on, and

Western Christendom would continue to reach for miracles in its quest to dominate the globe.

GUINEA HAD TURNED out to be very different from the resplendent land of Europe's imagination. Its trading posts were scattered across vast wildernesses, and the seasonal caravans were almost impossible to track down. Apart from a little gold, the goods the explorers brought home—antelope skin, amber, civet musk and live civet cats, gum arabic, sweet resin, turtle fat, seal oil, dates, and ostrich eggs—were colorful but hardly world-changing. Even worse, the Africans were so dismissive of the bales of rough cloth the Portuguese offered to trade that Henry was forced to buy fine garments from Morocco for resale in Guinea. When his crews had run into concerted resistance and had been forced to adopt a more complaisant stance, he had explained that trade was just another way of advancing the struggle against Islam. Now even that claim was beginning to wear dangerously thin.

In Portugal, the rumblings of rebellion became impossible to ignore. Henry's colossal outlay of money and men seemed to be leading nowhere.

The dissent was stilled by the arrival of a commodity nearly as valuable as gold: human beings.

Henry's first full-fledged slaving mission sailed out in 1444 and brutally attacked the peaceful fishing villages of Arguin Island, just off the midpoint of Africa's western bulge. Setting out under cover of night in small boats, the soldiers sprang on the islanders at dawn with lusty cries of "Portugal, St. James, and St. George!" The chronicles recorded the ghastly spectacle:

> There you might see mothers abandoning their children and husbands abandoning their wives, each thinking only to flee as speedily as might be. And some drowned themselves in the sea, others sought refuge in their huts, others hid their children under the mud, thinking that thus they might conceal them

from the eyes of the enemy, and that they could come to seek them later. And at length Our Lord God, Who rewardeth all that is well done, ordained that in return for the work of this day done by our men in His service they should have the victory over their enemies and the reward of their fatigues and disbursements, in the taking of one hundred and sixty-five captives, men, women, and children, without reckoning those that died or that killed themselves.

The captors said their prayers and moved on to a nearby island. Finding one village deserted, they waylaid nine men and women who were tiptoeing away leading asses piled with turtles. One of the nine escaped and warned the next village, which had emptied by the time the Portuguese arrived. They soon spotted its inhabitants on a sandbank where they had fled by raft. Since the water was too shallow to reach them by boat, they went back to scour the village and dragged off eight cowering women. The next morning they returned for another dawn raid. The village was still deserted, and they rowed along the coast, landing men here and there to scout for new victims. Eventually they found a large party on the run and seized seventeen or eighteen women and children, "for these could not run so fast." Soon after, they saw many more islanders escaping on a score of rafts. Their joy quickly turned to grief, the chronicles rued, when they realized such a fine opportunity to win honor and profit would be lost because they could not fit them all in the boats. Nevertheless they rowed at them, "and moved by pity, albeit these rafts were filled with Infidels, they killed only a very few. However, it must be believed that many Moors who, seized with fear, abandoned the rafts, perished in the sea. And the Christians thus passing amidst the rafts chose above all the children, in order to carry off more of them in their boat; of them they took fourteen."

After giving thanks to God for their victory over the enemies of the faith, "and more than ever desirous of laboring well to serve God," the Portuguese set out the following day to renew the attack.

While they were still about their business a crowd ran at them and they fled. Far from making the aggressors look foolish, the chronicles claimed, the irate islanders had been sent by God to ward off the Christians before three hundred armed warriors arrived on the scene. Even so, before they had time to jump into their boats "the Moors were already upon them, and all were fighting in a great mellay." The Portuguese managed to get away and take more prisoners, including a young girl who had been left behind in her abandoned village. Altogether they carted off 240 men, women, and children to be bound and packed into the waiting ships, where the already crowded holds and decks, swarming with rats and cockroaches and stinking of bilgewater and rotting fish, now reeked with the filth of shivering and panicked slaves.

When the human cargo arrived in Portugal the news spread fast. Excited spectators crowded the docks, and Henry rode down to supervise the distribution of the spoils. Mounted on horseback and barking out orders, he turned the sordid spectacle into a crowd-pleasing stunt.

After the grueling journey the slaves were a sorry sight, and as they were paraded naked and made to show off their strength, even some of the Portuguese were horrified. "What heart could be so hard as not to be pierced with piteous feeling to see that company?" wrote Gomes Eanes de Zurara, an eyewitness who confessed he was moved to tears.

> For some kept their heads low and their faces bathed in tears, looking one upon another; others stood groaning very dolorously, looking up to the height of heaven, fixing their eyes upon it, crying out loudly, as if asking help of the Father of Nature; others struck their faces with the palms of their hands, throwing themselves at full length upon the ground; others made their lamentations in the manner of a dirge, after the custom of their country. And though we could not understand the words of their language, the sound of it right well accorded with the mea-

sure of their sadness. But to increase their sufferings still more, there now arrived those who had charge of the division of the captives, and who began to separate one from another . . . and then it was needful to part fathers from sons, husbands from wives, brothers from brothers. No respect was shewn either to friends or relations, but each fell where his lot took him . . . who could finish that partition without very great toil? for as often as they had placed them in one part the sons, seeing their fathers in another, rose with great energy and rushed over to them; the mothers clasped their other children in their arms, and threw themselves flat on the ground with them; receiving blows with little pity for their own flesh, if only they might not be torn from them.

Henry looked on contentedly. He had answered his critics: if he had not found fields of gold, he had earned Portugal a place among the major slave-trading powers of the world. When another bumper haul of slaves arrived in Lisbon the following year, the doubters were finally silenced. "Now," recorded Zurara as throngs of rubbernecks swarmed on board the ships, nearly capsizing them in the process, "there was no one around willing to admit to ever having been one of the critics. When they watched the prisoners bound with rope being marched through the streets, the tumult of the people was so great as they praised aloud the great virtues of the Prince that if anyone had dared to voice a contrary opinion to theirs he would very quickly have been obliged to withdraw it."

In their shackled servitude, the slaves had rescued Portugal's quest to explore the oceans.

Slavery was rife in the medieval world. Entire Muslim societies had been built on slavery; the numbers were so vast that in the ninth century half a million slaves had rebelled in Iraq. Many were sold by the mercantile republics of Italy; Genoa was particularly unfussy about where its human cargo came from, and large numbers of Orthodox Christians regularly appeared on its blocks. More were transported across the Caucasus and the Sahara, or were seized by the pirates of the Barbary Coast from Europe's shores; by one count the pirates carried away more than a million men, women, and children for sale in the markets of North Africa. Few nations were unblemished by the traffic, and few saw anything wrong with the trade. Most dismissed the victims as a lower form of humanity; many—including African warlords who sold their enemies for wheat, clothes, horses, and wine—thought anyone they captured was fair game. Tenderhearted Christians consoled themselves by imagining that the slaves had been rescued from an irreligious condition no better than that of beasts, and no one saw anything strange about taking away a man's liberty in order to save his soul. The tearful Zurara reminded himself that slavery originated with the curse Noah laid upon his son Ham after the Flood; the blacks, he explained, were descended from Ham and were subjected to all other races for all time. Any inconveniences they suffered, he reassured his readers, paled into insignificance next to the "wonderful new things that await them." Eternal salvation, as usual, was the payback for worldly suffering, and plenty more were to receive the same comfort. During Henry's lifetime, perhaps 20,000 Africans were captured or bought and transported to Portugal; by the turn of the century the number had risen to as many as 150,000.

Prince Henry's new identity as slave trader general never gave his admirers cause to question his Crusading convictions. Quite the reverse: they saw it as the clearest affirmation that the Atlantic explorations were an expansion of his lifelong Crusade. Since Henry was engaged in a permanent war against the Infidel, and since by most accounts a war against the Infidel was by definition a just war, anyone he captured was a legitimate prisoner of war and so, by the conventions of the age, liable to be enslaved. In contrast to the common run of slavers, Henry earned high praise for his incessant reminders that he had only got into the trade to bring the Gospel to unfortunate heathens. To his countrymen, his slaving raids were grand acts of knightly chivalry, no less worthy of praise than seizing captives on the field of battle. Henry himself undoubtedly believed that his new business was not just lucrative but eminently pleasing to God.

The Church not only agreed, it took pains to make its approval clear. In 1452, the pope issued a bull that authorized the Portuguese to attack, conquer, and subdue any "Saracens, pagans and any other unbelievers" they encountered, to seize their goods and lands, and to reduce them to hereditary slavery—even if they converted to Christianity. Rome had already granted full indulgences to any Christians who went Crusading under the cross of the Order of Christ, and in 1454 it subcontracted to Henry's order sole spiritual jurisdiction over all the newly discovered lands.

The astonishing notion that Africans who had somehow failed to find the true faith were "outside the law of Christ, and at the disposition, so far as their bodies were concerned, of any Christian nation" was the attitude that the first European colonialists carried with them around the world. They were not just traveling for the pleasures of discovery or the profits of trade: they were sailing to convert and conquer in the name of Christ. Religious passion joined to the opportunity for epic plunder was a lethally galvanizing combination, and it would draw the Portuguese inexorably on to India and beyond.

At the heavy cost of inaugurating the Atlantic slave trade, Henry had radically extended Europe's horizon. The endeavor he had begun still had a long way to go, but it took on a whole new urgency when devastating news arrived from the East.

CHAPTER 5

THE END OF THE WORLD

ON MAY 22, 1453, the sun set on a besieged Constantinople. An hour later a full moon rose in a crystal-clear sky, and suddenly it was eclipsed to a sickly sliver. All night long panicked crowds stumbled through the ancient streets, their way lit only by the flickering red glow from the enemy fires outside the walls. As the last Romans held aloft precious icons and chanted prayers to God, the Virgin, and the Saints, they knew that an ancient prophecy had finally been fulfilled. The heavens had blinked; the end was near.

For more than a thousand years Constantinople had stood firm against waves of barbarians and Persians, Arabs, and Turks. It had survived devastating plagues, blood-soaked dynastic mayhem, and marauding Crusaders. The golden city of the Caesars had gradually been reduced to a hollow honeycomb, its inhabitants, a tenth the number at its peak, scattered around fields strewn with the ruins of lost grandeur. Yet still it held on. Long ago it had lost its Latin language and had adopted the Greek of its majority population; western Europeans had long called its empire the Empire of the Greeks. Later historians would label it Byzantine, after the city over which Constantinople had risen. To its proud citizens it was always Roman, the last living, breathing survivor of the classical world.

For the twenty-one-year-old Ottoman sultan who had pitched his tent less than a quarter of a mile to the west, the glittering prospect in his sights was not so much the final end of the Roman Empire as its revival under his protection. Mehmet II, middling in height, stocky in build, with piercing eyes, an aquiline nose, a small mouth, and a loud voice, was fluent in six languages and a keen student of history. He was already master of nearly all the old Roman lands in the East, and history told him that the conqueror of the imperial city would inherit the mantle of the great emperors of long ago. He would be the rightful Caesar, and his vaulting ambition would restore the true ring of authority to that hallowed, hollowed-out name.

As the Turks closed in, the emperor behind Constantinople's walls had turned to the West one last time. In desperation he had visited the pope in person and had agreed to reunite the Orthodox and Catholic churches. His mission had fallen foul of centuries of bad blood between Greeks and Italians, and even in their last hour, the citizens of Constantinople had mounted a furious publicity campaign against reconciliation. Besides, while the papacy was as eager as ever to press its advantage, few in Europe had any appetite for more defeats at the hands of the Turks. This time there would be no papal coalition, no Crusading army, to defend the eastern bastion of Christendom.

Outside the land approach to the city the Turks had set up a monster cannon, its barrel twenty-six feet long and wide enough for a man to crawl inside, its weight so great that it took thirty yoke of oxen and four hundred men to heave it into place. For seven weeks its twelve-hundred-pound missiles had crashed into antiquity's ruins and had shaken the ground with the force of a meteor strike. Countless smaller cannon had pulverized the defenses, leaving soldiers, monks, and matrons scrambling to shore up the gaps. The monumental walls were badly battered, but they still held, and for one last time the few thousand remaining defenders took heart.

To the Orthodox, the capital of Eastern Christianity was not only the new Rome; it was the New Jerusalem, the cradle of Christendom itself. The entire city was a charnel house of holy relics that were credited with miraculous powers; reputedly among them were large parts of the True Cross and the Holy Nails, Christ's sandals, scarlet robe, crown of thorns, and shroud, the remnants of fish and bread from the feeding of the five thousand, the entire head of John the Baptist with hair and beard, and the sweet-smelling garments of the Virgin Mary, who was often sighted roaming the walls giving heart to the defenders. In Constantinople's glory days St. Andrew the Fool, a former slave turned ascetic whose patent insanity was taken by his followers to be a mark of his extreme holiness, had promised that the metropolis need never fear an enemy until the end of time: "No nation whatever shall entrap or capture her," he told his disciple Epiphanios, "for she has been given to the Mother of God and no one shall snatch her out of her hands. Many nations will attack her walls and break their horns, withdrawing in shame, though receiving from her gifts and much wealth." Only in the Last Days, he added, would God slice the earth from under her with a mighty sickle; then the waters that had borne the holy vessel for so long would cascade over her, and she would spin like a millstone on the crest of a wave before plunging into the bottomless abyss. To true believers, the end of the world and the end of Constantinople amounted to one and the same thing.

A week after the portentous eclipse, the end arrived.

Under cover of darkness, to the blare of horns and fifes, the rattle of kettledrums, and the thunder of cannon, a hundred thousand Turkish soldiers launched an all-out assault. As Christians and Muslims fought hand to hand on the hills of rubble that had once been the strongest defenses in the world, fate played one last, cruel trick on Constantinople. In the furor the defenders had left a gate open, and the Turks rushed straight through. As dawn broke in a cloud of dust, sulfur, and smoke, the last Romans collapsed back into the exhausted city and fell to their knees.

The Turks surged along the Mese, the main thoroughfare laid out by Constantine the Great more than a millennium before. Peeling off left and right, they burst into houses, claimed them as their own, and staggered off with the loot. They massacred the city's men and pressed themselves on its women, among them a goodly number of nuns. By the custom of battle, three days of plunder was the conquerors' right; Mehmet, with an eye on history, put a stop to the rapine at noon and insisted the survivors be taken as slaves. No one protested; even battle-hardened soldiers stopped to gaze in hushed wonder. Nearly eight centuries after an Islamic army had first besieged Constantinople, it was finally theirs.

Late in a golden May afternoon, Mehmet rode along the Mese and dismounted outside the Hagia Sophia. He bent down to scoop up a handful of earth, crumbled it on his turban, and walked through the heavy bronze doors, several of which were hanging off their hinges. As his eyes adjusted to the cavernous space with its rearing walls of glittering, dilapidated mosaics, he took his sword to a soldier who was levering a marble slab from the floor. The greatest church of Christendom would henceforth be a mosque.

IN EUROPE, THE news of the final end of classical antiquity was received as tragic but inevitable. The timeworn city had long seemed to belong to another world.

"But what is that terrible news recently reported about Constantinople?" the scholar Aeneas Silvius Piccolomini—later Pope Pius II—wrote to the then pope:

> Who can doubt that the Turks will vent their wrath upon the churches of God? I grieve that the world's most famous temple, Hagia Sophia, will be destroyed or defiled. I grieve that countless basilicas of the saints, marvels of architecture, will fall in ruins or be subjected to the defilements of Mohammed. What can I say about the books without number there which are not yet known in Italy? Alas, how many names of great men will now perish? This will be a second death to Homer and a second destruction of Plato.

As it turned out, the books—if not most of the churches—were safe. A steady stream of scholars had fled before the Turks, mostly to Italy, where they arrived with armfuls of volumes containing the literature of ancient Greece and spurred on the gathering Renaissance. Mehmet the Conqueror, as his people now knew him, guarded what was left in his prized library, and the cultivated autocrat soon turned his mind to rebuilding what he had destroyed. As ruler of the Renaissance world's only superpower, he had plenty of talent to call on. A new city, to be called Istanbul, would rise from the ashes of Constantinople, a capital illustrious enough to match the Conqueror's ambition. The Grand Bazaar, a fifteenth-century world trade center, would arch across the age-old streets, and the workshops would hum at a pace not heard for centuries. Christians and Jews would be invited back as artisans and administrators, the patriarch would resume his watch over his Orthodox flock, and the chief rabbi would take his seat in the divan, the council of state, beside the religious leaders of the Muslims.

Yet Mehmet had his life ahead of him, and he was not about to slumber on his jeweled throne. The self-declared Caesar was not satisfied with Constantinople, the new Rome of antiquity. For his claim to be complete, he would have to conquer the old Rome, too.

A few Europeans saw an opportunity in the looming disaster. George of Trebizond, a pugnacious Greek émigré who became a renowned Italian humanist and papal secretary, was convinced that Mehmet would fulfill the old prophecies by becoming sole ruler of the world. According to received wisdom, a long reign of terror would then hold sway until the last Christian emperor arrived to preside over an era of peace that would presage the End Times of the Earth. Seeing an opportunity to skip two centuries of hell on earth and go straight to the age of bliss, George wrote a series of long letters to the Ottoman sultan. Addressing him as the rightful Caesar, he suggested how to reconcile Islam and Christianity so that Mehmet could be baptized and himself become the last "king of all the earth and heavens." Though George's eschatological scheme was especially ambitious, he was not alone in attempting to convert the Conqueror: several more Greek scholars and even Pope Pius II wrote to Mehmet, proposing the same thing.

The rest of Western Christendom, unaware that salvation lurked in the Turkish onslaught and torn apart by its usual internal wars, could only look on aghast as Mehmet's armies marched deep into eastern Europe and set sail for Italy. The victorious sultan was on the verge of fulfilling the dream that had come to a halt, seven centuries before, on the fields of France.

Inevitably, Rome called a new Crusade. This time the genocidal papal plan was to reconquer Constantinople, invade the Ottoman heartlands, and exterminate the Turkish nation once and for all.

In February 1454, Philip the Good, the powerful duke of Burgundy—and the husband of Henry the Navigator's sister Isabel—threw the most spectacular of all fifteenth-century banquets to bang the drum for the mooted holy war. Hundreds of nobles converged on Lille for the Feast of the Pheasant and were entertained in a style befitting a man who was besotted with chivalric romances. Three tables were laid in the great hall, and each was decorated with a toymaker's fantasia of miniature automata. The top table alone boasted a castle whose moat was filled with orange punch trickling from its towers, a magpie perched on the rotating sail of a windmill that proved an elusive target for a file of archers, a tiger wrestling with a serpent, a jester mounted on a bear, an Arab riding a camel, a ship floating back and forth between two cities, two lovers eating the birds beaten out of a bush by a man with a stick, and a trick barrel that poured either sweet or sour wine—"Take some, if you dare!" read the label. For the pièce de résistance, a colossal pie was wheeled in and its crust was removed to reveal a twenty-eight-strong orchestra playing inside. While the masked guests worked their way through forty-eight courses, acrobats tumbled, actors performed interludes, a live lion roared next to the statue of a woman who poured spiced wine from her right breast, and two live falcons were released and killed a heron, which was presented to the duke. As the business of the evening approached, a giant dressed as a Muslim led in an elephant on a leash. A model castle was harnessed to the elephant's back, and on it sat a female impersonator dressed as a nun. The actor announced himself as Holy Church, and he proceeded to recite a "complaint and lamentation in a piteous and feminine voice" of the iniquities of the Turks. In line with long-standing knightly tradition, an officer solemnly carried a pheasant sporting a necklace of gold, pearls, and jewels to the high table. The duke made his crusading vow to God, the Virgin, the ladies, and the bird, and the assembled knights and squires followed suit. After such a show, it was hard to make a polite refusal.

For all Duke Philip's efforts the nobles turned out to be much keener on feasting than on fighting the Turks, and the papal call to arms was met with a great collective shrug. About the only nation that took the proposed Crusade seriously was Portugal. King Afonso V, King Edward's son and Prince Henry's nephew, had now come of age, and he was burning to eclipse the fame his forebears had won as holy warriors. The headstrong young king proposed himself as the commander in chief at the head of a twelve-thousand-strong Portuguese force, though when he sent an envoy to Italy to push his plan he was given a fast baptism in the muddy waters of Italian politics. Several Italian states had promised to join the Crusade, but the envoy reported that there was no chance whatsoever that they would keep their word. His skepticism was echoed by the Duke of Milan, who cattily wrote to Afonso in September 1456, admiring "the sublimity of spirit which led the Portuguese king, when barely out of his adolescence, to want to attack the infidel in a region so far away from the traditional Portuguese crusading arena in North Africa, and despite the fact that his plans might put Ceuta in danger." In a fit of pique, Afonso declared he would take on the Turks single-handed. Even his uncle thought he had lost his senses, and Henry hastily persuaded him to redirect his energies into a new Moroccan Crusade.

With its claim to overlordship of the earth looking shakier than ever, Rome increasingly turned to the stalwart Crusaders of Iberia to buttress its vast aspirations. In 1455, the pope rewarded young Afonso's ardor by bestowing on him the invented title of Lord of Guinea; so far as papal authority held sway, the Portuguese were now the rulers of vast swaths of Africa and the surrounding seas, discovered or still unknown. However far-fetched little Portugal's dreams might have seemed, Rome had nothing to lose, and potentially a world to gain, from backing them.

Afonso had the long papal bull read out in Lisbon's cathedral, a fortresslike structure that had been built on the site of the old Friday mosque, in front of an audience of international dignitaries. In glowing words, the pope praised Henry the Navigator as "our beloved son" and his discoveries and conquests as the work of a "true soldier of Christ." He also affirmed the new Lord of Guinea's right "to invade, search out, capture, vanquish, and subdue all Saracens and pagans whatsoever, and other enemies of Christ wheresoever placed, and the kingdoms, dukedoms, principalities, dominions, possessions, and all movable and immovable goods whatsoever held and possessed by them and to reduce their persons to perpetual slavery." It was the clearest possible sanction from the highest authority for any iron-fisted actions Europe might wish to indulge in overseas, and it would come to be known as the charter of Portuguese imperialism. Together with the bull granted to Henry in 1452, it would be trundled out time after time to justify centuries of European colonialism and the Atlantic slave trade.

Five years later, in 1460, Henry died. By then his ships had sailed two thousand miles south from Lisbon, and his lifetime's obsession had startlingly expanded Portugal's ambitions. Many of his countrymen revered him as a heroic visionary, the first man to launch a concerted exploration of the Ocean Sea and the father of an embryonic empire. Not all agreed: to some he was a rash opportunist, to others a reactionary medieval knight obsessed with Crusades and chivalry. He was all of those things, but his relentless pursuit of goals beyond the thoughts of more sober-minded men would

divert the course of history. He was the single flawed figure without whom Europe's knowledge of what lay beyond its shores might
have crept forward at a far slower rate, without whom Vasco da
Gama might never have sailed for India or Columbus for America.

Afonso had none of Henry's appetite for exploration. For nine
years the discoveries paused while he followed up his uncle's Crusade against Tangier, which was repeatedly won and lost until it
finally fell in 1471. Eventually he was persuaded to subcontract the
African enterprise to a rich Lisbon merchant named Fernão Gomes.
Without the royal distraction of Crusading, the voyages shot ahead.
Gomes's ships rounded the great continental bulge of west Africa
and followed the land due east. In Ghana—which the Portuguese
named the Mine Coast and the British would rename the Gold
Coast—Gomes's ships finally found the regular supplies of gold that
had eluded Henry, and in 1473, now heading south again, they
crossed the equator. In all, they had advanced another two thousand
miles.

Gomes had been too successful for his own good; the following year, his contract was terminated and the crown took back the
reins. Precious metal was not the only draw. When the Portuguese
suddenly found themselves in the Southern Hemisphere, an electrifying possibility finally began to spark the nation's collective imagination.

For centuries, Europeans had dreamed of finding a sure route to
the distant reaches of Asia. For centuries, the wall of faith built by
Islam had made the idea all but unthinkable. Yet if there was an end
to Africa, there might be a way to sail directly from Europe into
the East. The nation that pulled off that feat would transform both
itself and the world.

IN CLASSICAL MYTHOLOGY, Europe was born of an abduction
from the East. The legends told that a Phoenician princess named
Europa was dallying with her maids when Zeus, king of the Gods,
disguised himself as a fetching white bull, lured the object of his

desire to mount him, and swam off with her to Crete. Herodotus, the father of history, later explained that Europa was really seized by the Minoans of Crete in revenge for an earlier kidnapping by Phoenician traders, thereby inaugurating the enmity between Europe and Asia that climaxed in the Greco-Persian Wars. Either way, the mother of Europe evidently had no intention of quitting the attractions of Asia for foreign shores.

To medieval Europeans, the East was still a realm of marvels unmatched by anything to be found at home. Most were deduced from the Bible, as interpreted by the mystical medieval mind.

Cut off from firsthand knowledge of what lay beyond its borders, Europe had long ago retreated into a biblical literalism that had reshaped the world in its image. On its wheel-shaped *mappae mundi*, or schematic world maps, the three known continents were distributed around a T-shaped body of water. Asia was placed above the top bar of the T, which corresponded to the Nile and the Danube. Europe was to the left of the vertical bar, which represented the Mediterranean, and Africa was on the right. The Ocean Sea lapped around the edges of the circle, and at dead center was Jerusalem. In the European scheme of things, Jerusalem was quite literally the city at the center of the world. "Thus saith the Lord God; This is Jerusalem: I have set it in the midst of the nations and countries that are round about her," the Bible records the prophet Ezekiel as saying, and so it came to be drawn.

At the top of the map, or in the Far East, was the Garden of Eden, the spring of humanity itself. There was nothing symbolic about this piece of patristic geography. The vast encyclopedia compiled by St. Isidore of Seville—the most popular textbook of the Middle Ages and the early Renaissance—listed the earthly Paradise as an eastern province along with India, Persia, and Asia Minor. The entry on Paradise in the fourteenth-century *Polychronicon*, or "Universal History," further specified that it made up "a sizeable part of the earth's mass, being no smaller than India or Egypt, for the place had been intended for the whole of the human race, if man had not sinned."

The garden, of course, had been closed off after the Fall: it was shown on the maps guarded by a sword-wielding angel, a wall of flames, or a wilderness writhing with snakes, perched on a mountaintop so high that it touched the moon's orbit and thus stayed dry during the Flood, or immured on an island where the only entrance was a forbidding door marked GATES OF PARADISE. Inside were dense green forests, fragrant flowers, and gentle breezes, together with every conceivable form of beauty, happiness, and fortune. Paradise might be out of reach, but there was no question it existed.

Apart from the biblical authorities, for centuries Europe had little else to go on but the fragments of classical texts that had survived the barbarian onslaughts. In typical medieval style, it embellished them to its heart's content. The *Alexander Romance*, a medieval best seller recounting the adventures of Alexander the Great that ran to innumerable editions and became more far-fetched with each, told of an actual encounter with Paradise. In one version of the story, Alexander and his companions are sailing down the River Ganges when they find themselves alongside a towering city wall. After skirting its base for three days they finally see a small window and call up. The old guardian who answers tells them they have found the city of the blessed and are in mortal danger. Alexander leaves with a souvenir, a stone heavier than gold that, when it touches the earth, becomes lighter than a feather, a symbol of the end that awaits the most powerful of men. Classical lore buffed up by medieval ingenuity was also responsible for the belief that Alexander had encountered numerous "monstrous races" on his travels, including pygmies, cannibals, peoples with dogs' heads or faces in their chests, and others with heads but no mouths who fed on the scent of apples. Each species had an accepted name: the last were aptly called the apple smellers.

As well as showing Adam and Eve fleeing the garden, Christ rising from the tomb, and the dead departing to eternal bliss or damnation on Judgment Day, the mapmakers also had to find room for the vacant Tower of Babel, the indolent Happy Isles, the land of

the Dry Tree, the gold mines of Ophir, the Ten Lost Tribes of Israel, the kingdom of the Magi, and the barbaric nations of Gog and
Magog whose escape would unleash a battle for the End Times of
the Earth. The last two were placed in the far north of Asia, where
they were contained by an iron gate built by Alexander the Great
that also held back as many as twenty-two more evil races. The
maps depicted the fearsome tribes drinking blood and devouring
human flesh, including the tender flesh of children and miscarried
fetuses. Such dark imaginings were not limited to populist fear-
mongers; they were taken as gospel by the foremost minds of the
age. In the thirteenth century Roger Bacon, the medieval pioneer
of science, urged the study of geography so that Christendom could
plan against the coming invasion from the East.

As speculation piled on surmise and Europe came to believe that
fantastical places were real, so little was known about real places that
they became the stuff of fantasy in turn. Crucially, the far reaches of
the East were such a mystery that it was possible to imagine, at some
deep level at least, that they were Christian.

Of all the riddles, the whereabouts of India was the most perplexing. It was a source of untold frustration, because India was
known to be the main source of the most sought-after goods in the
world: spices.

NOTHING DELIGHTED THE medieval palate more than a fiery blast
of spice. In kitchens across Europe, spices were heaped into sauces,
steeped in wines, and crystallized as candies with the addition of
sugar, which was itself classed as a spice. Cinnamon, ginger, and
saffron were staples of any self-respecting cook's larder, and precious cloves, nutmeg, and mace were scarcely less ubiquitous. Even
countryfolk had a craving for black pepper, while wealthy gourmets
gobbled up the full range from anise to zedoary, a once-favored rel-
ative of ginger, at an astonishing rate. The fifteenth-century household of the first Duke of Buckingham worked its way through two
pounds of spices a day, including nearly a pound of pepper and half

a pound of ginger, and even that prodigious intake paled next to the sacks of spices that were emptied into cooking pots at the banquets of kings, nobles, and bishops. When Duke George "the Rich" of Bavaria married in 1476, the chefs sent out for a king's ransom of Eastern delights:

> Pepper, 386 lbs.
> Ginger, 286 lbs.
> Saffron, 207 lbs.
> Cinnamon, 205 lbs.
> Cloves, 105 lbs.
> Nutmeg, 85 lbs.

Spices did not just tickle the palate: by happy coincidence they were good for your health. Medieval medical students learned that the body was a microcosm of the universe, a concept that derived from classical Greek medicine and was transmitted to Europe by Muslim physicians. Four humors, or bodily fluids, were the internal equivalents of fire, earth, air, and water, and each conferred its own character trait. Blood, for instance, made you sanguine or irrepressibly optimistic, whereas black bile bred melancholy; and while no one was blessed with a perfect balance, an excessive imbalance brought on illness. Food was particularly important in maintaining the body's equilibrium, and like the humors it was classed according to its degree of heat and moisture. Cold, wet foods such as fish and many meats were thus rendered less dangerous with a healthy powdering of hot, dry spice. Even better, spices were believed to be highly efficient purgatives, a valued quality in an age that liked its remedies to be as violent as its diseases.

Individual spices had specific pharmaceutical uses. Under the sign of the mortar and pestle, apothecaries ground their desiccated treasure into cordials, pills, and resins and marketed the results as miracle drugs and health supplements. Black pepper, the most widely available spice, was used as an expectorant, to treat asthma, to heal sores, as an antidote to poison, and—when invigoratingly rubbed into the eyes—to improve vision; in a range of blends it was prescribed, among a great deal else, for epilepsy, gout, rheumatism, insanity, earache, and piles. Cinnamon had nearly as many applications, ranging from severe fever to bad breath. Nutmeg was invariably recommended for bloating and flatulence, while hot, moist ginger was the drug of choice for flagging male libidos. The author of one of many medieval sex manuals suggested that a man discommoded by "a small member,"

> who wants to make it grand or fortify it for the coitus, must rub it before copulation with tepid water, until it gets red and extended by the blood flowing into it, in consequence of the heat; he must then anoint it with a mixture of honey and ginger, rubbing it in sedulously. Then let him join the woman; he will procure for her such pleasure that she objects to him getting off her again.

Alongside the regular culinary spices, wholesale grocers and local merchants purveyed an exotic range of animal, vegetable, and mineral rarities from the far corners of the earth. These were also classed as spices, and many were meant to be inhaled.

Medieval men and women were not as universally unwashed as folklore holds, but life undoubtedly stank. The pungent aromas of tanneries and smelters wafted over residential areas. Sewage ran, or stagnated, in the streets, where it mixed with household garbage and dung from horses, rooting pigs, and cattle being driven to market. Floors were covered with rushes or straw and sprinkled with sweet herbs, but offending substances lingered underfoot. On a trip to England, the great Dutch humanist Erasmus noted that the rushes were renewed "so imperfectly that the bottom layer is left undisturbed, sometimes for twenty years, harboring expectoration, vomiting, the leakage of dogs and men, ale droppings, scraps of fish, and other abominations not fit to be mentioned. Whenever the weather changes a vapor is exhaled, which I consider very detrimental to health." The only way to combat powerful bad smells was with powerful good ones, and pungent spices were burned as incense, dabbed on as perfumes, and scattered around rooms to create a fragrant haven. For those who could afford them, expensive aromas were the most soothing of all; among the most prized aromatics were rare resins such as frankincense, myrrh, mastic, and balsam, and even rarer perfumed animal secretions such as castoreum from beavers, civet from wild tropical cats, and musk from small Himalayan deer.

Everyone knew a stench was a bad thing, even if they did little about it. What turned the craze for exotic aromatics into a full-blown addiction was the belief that foul odors were responsible for spreading epidemics, up to and including the Black Death itself. The supreme prophylactic against the plague was ambergris, a fatty secretion of the intestines of sperm whales that was coughed up or excreted, hardened in the water, and washed up on the beaches of East Africa as a crusty gray lump smelling of animals, earth, and sea. The medical faculty of the celebrated University of Paris prescribed a blend of ambergris and other aromatics—such as sandalwood and aloeswood, myrrh and mace—carried in pierced metal balls known as *pommes d'ambre*, or pomanders, though the king and queen of France, who were among the few who could afford it, inhaled pure ambergris.

In a world of mysteries and miracles, spices were among the deepest secrets of the earth. Ambergris was credited with magical powers precisely because it was so outlandish, and the same went for other equally strange substances. Also among the apothecaries' under-the-counter goods were "tutty," or crusty deposits picked out of the chimneys of the East, and "mummy," which was glossed in a leading drug handbook as "a kind of spice collected from the tombs of the dead"—a foul-smelling, pitchlike substance scraped from the heads and spines of embalmed corpses. One cherished commodity, solidified lynx urine, was believed to be a kind of amber or gemstone, while real gems and semiprecious stones were stocked alongside the rarer spices and were reputed to possess particularly strong curative powers. Lapis lazuli was prescribed for melancholia and malaria. Topaz soothed hemorrhoids. Jet, ground up and sprinkled around the house, induced menstruation and had the added benefit of warding off evil incantations. Crushed pearls were taken to stanch hemorrhages, to increase the flow of a nursing mother's milk, and for the truly self-indulgent, to treat diarrhea. Lavish concoctions of gems and spices were the last resort if all else failed: the pampered elite could combat the winter blues by downing powdered pearls blended with cloves, cinnamon, galangal, aloes, nutmeg, ginger, ivory, and camphor, and ward off old age with an exquisite blend of pearl, sapphire, ruby, and coral fragments mixed with ambergris and musk—a mixture barely easier to digest than the cheaper alternative of viper's flesh, cloves, nutmeg, and mace.

Gems, naturally, were for the rich, and a few doctors quietly expressed doubts that the exotic goods from the East were any more effective than common, or garden, herbs. But for those who could buy the best, the very fact that spices were borne across distant lands and seas from jungles and deserts unknown—and the sky-high prices they commanded—gave them a reassuring cachet of exclusivity. In an age that glorified conspicuous consumption, basking in a cloud of Eastern ambrosia was an essential ingredient of high living. Spices were the luxury goods par excellence of the medieval world.

The profits at stake were immense, and unscrupulous merchants, their sales patter heavy with the exotic Orient, were not above adulterating their goods by soaking them in water to add weight, hiding stale spices under fresh ones, or even adding shavings of silver, which was worth less than its weight in cloves. Their customers' fury knew no bounds: in 1444 one adulterator of saffron was burned to death in Nuremberg, though more often it was the spices that were incinerated. The increasingly vociferous anti-spice lobby, though, had larger concerns than a little local larceny; what really outraged it was the scandalous waste of money. Moralists fulminated that spices—even "that damned pepper"—merely inflamed the senses, generated gluttony and lust, and were gone in a flash. The habit, they fumed, was turning doughty Europeans into effeminate wastrels. Most egregiously of all, the taste for Eastern luxuries was draining Europe's treasuries of gold and funneling it into the grasping hands of the Infidel.

It was not that spices were seen as unholy; quite the reverse. The aromas of the East, the naysayers sternly warned, properly belonged to heaven and the saints and not to greedy mortals. Resins and spices had been used in religious rituals as incense, balms, and unguents at least since the time of ancient Egypt, and though the first Christians shunned perfumes as the whiff of the bathhouse, brothel, and pagan altar, the idea that fragrances summoned up the supernatural proved hard to dispel. Medieval Christendom believed that the bittersweet smell of spices was a breath of heaven on earth, a waft of the fragrant hereafter. The scent, it was said, clung to visiting angels and verified their presence, while devils could be detected by their telltale stink. Saints were also believed to smell miraculously spicy, and those who had endured a particularly gruesome death were held to enjoy a correspondingly fragrant afterlife. In the fifteenth century the corpse of St. Lydwine of Schiedam, who broke a rib while ice-skating as a teenager and was fated to live for another thirty-eight years while chunks of her body fell off and blood poured from her mouth, ears, and nose, was reported to exude an appetizing savor of cinnamon and ginger.

LONG AGO, EUROPEANS had traveled the spice routes. The Greeks had shown the way, and the Romans, after ousting Cleopatra from her throne, had established a regular trade between the east coast of Egypt and the west coast of India. As many as 120 huge freighters had sailed back and forth each year to satisfy the Roman penchant for piquant flavors and exotic perfumes, though even then purists were complaining about the vast trove of gold and silver that was being forked out for Eastern fripperies, a theme the satirist Persius took up in the first century CE:

> *The greedy merchants, led by lucre, run*
> *To the parch'd Indies and the rising sun;*
> *From thence hot Pepper and rich Drugs they bear,*
> *Bart'ring for Spices their Italian ware.*

By the third century the Arabs had taken over the sea routes, and the later rise of Islam had consolidated their control of the Eastern trade. As Europe's fortunes revived, the merchants of Venice and Genoa had haggled in the bustling spice markets of Constantinople, built by imperial edict beside the palace gate so the aromas wafted upstairs, and during the Crusades the Christian ports of Syria and Palestine had done a roaring trade in spices and jewels, oriental carpets and silks. Yet Europe's spice merchants were the last link in a long supply chain, and they were utterly in the dark about where their precious goods originated or how they were produced.

As usual, ignorance bred a heady swirl of speculation. Since spices clearly came from a blessed place, the reasoning went, the obvious location was the earthly Paradise. From a handful of classical authorities it was clear that spices were most abundant in India, so it followed that India must border Paradise. Even so, it was known that some spices came from other far-flung places, and the answer to that puzzle was found in the Bible. The book of Genesis revealed that the Garden of Eden watered four rivers, which had become identified as the Tigris, the Euphrates, the Ganges, and the Nile. It had long been believed that all four gushed forth from a single giant spring at the center of the Garden, but even Europeans had come to balk at that mangling of geography, so it was decided that the rivers ran underground until they surfaced at their apparent source. Of the four, the Nile was the most venerated, and since it could hardly flow through the sea, it had become accepted that the African hinterland from which it issued must be connected to India. This neatly

explained why spices were widely available in Egypt. A Frenchman who went there with the Seventh Crusade revealed that every
night, the people who lived along the banks of the Upper Nile cast
nets into the stream: "When morning comes, they find in their nets
such things as are sold by weight and imported into Egypt, as for
instance ginger, rhubarb, aloes, and cinnamon. It is said that these
things come from the earthly Paradise, for in that heavenly place
the wind blows down trees just as it does the dry wood in the forests
of our own land, and the dry wood from the trees in Paradise that
thus falls into the river is sold to us by merchants in this country."

As to the means of harvesting the spices, Europe's experts had
plenty to say. It was well known that pepper grew on trees patrolled
by poisonous snakes. "The pepper forests are guarded by serpents,
but the natives burn the trees when the pepper is ripe and the fire
drives away the snakes," Isidore of Seville expounded in his encyclopedia. "It is the flame that blackens the pepper, for pepper is
naturally white." Some authorities declared that the whole grove
had to be replanted after the blaze, which explained the high cost of
the crop. Collecting cinnamon was equally labor intensive:

> The Arabians say that the dry sticks . . . are brought to Arabia
> by large birds, which carry them to their nests, made of mud,
> on mountain precipices which no man can climb. The method
> invented to get the cinnamon sticks is this. People cut up the
> bodies of dead oxen into very large joints and leave them on the
> ground near the nests. They then scatter, and the birds fly down
> and carry off the meat to their nests, which are too weak to bear
> the weight and fall to the ground. The men come and pick up
> the cinnamon.

The more cynical suspected Arab merchants of spreading tall
tales to justify their prices, but the accounts were widely believed.
So were the old reports that precious stones were only found in
treacherous Indian gorges; since no man could climb down, the

only way to retrieve the gems was to fling chunks of raw meat at them and send trained birds to fetch the glittering morsels. This particular thesis also convinced the Islamic world—it turns up in the tales of Sinbad, the sailor from Basra—and traveled as far as China. Over the centuries snakes were added to the ravines, some of which could kill with a mere glance. Alexander the Great, of course, had the answer: he lowered mirrors in which the snakes stared themselves to death, though he still fell back on the meat-and-birds strategy to retrieve the stones.

The first real information about the origin of spices reached Europe during the long Mongol peace. The Mongols, who were not particularly hung up on faith, guaranteed security of travel to all comers across their empire, and to adventurous Europeans the prospect of penetrating Asia's hidden places was irresistible. Missionaries led the way, and merchants soon followed. The Italians, as usual, were in the vanguard, and among them was a young Venetian named Marco Polo. In 1271 the seventeen-year-old Marco set out for Beijing, where he became the trusted envoy of the Mongol emperor Kublai Khan. He set out to survey the Great Khan's lands, and after twenty-four years he returned to Venice laden with rich jewels and richer tales. Almost immediately he was imprisoned by the Genoese, who were then at war with Venice, and he whiled away the time by dictating his *Travels* to a fellow inmate.

Marco Polo's Asia was remarkably free of monstrous races, he poured cold water on the fireproof salamander, and he reshaped the unicorn into the less graceful rhinoceros. He—or his amanuensis—was not immune to all the old stories; diamonds, the *Travels* explained, were eaten by white eagles enticed into snake-infested Indian crevasses by lumps of raw meat, then fished out of the birds' excrement. Yet on the whole his was a practical businessman's report—and that was what made it startling reading. The China he described was a peaceful and prosperous nation of vast wealth and extent, a realm of countless cities built on a colossal scale, each with thousands of marble bridges and harbors teeming with junks.

Fifteen hundred miles off its coast—an overestimate that would greatly encourage a Genoese sailor named Christopher Columbus—was Japan, whose palaces were roofed with gold. Polo was the first European to report the existence of Japan and Indochina; he was also the first known to have reached India, and the first to pass on the information that many of its spices came from islands far to the east, the number of which he put at precisely 7,448.

The Mongols had never conquered India, and only a tiny trickle of Westerners made it to the subcontinent after Marco Polo. In 1291, shortly before he returned to an astonished Venice, two missionary friars visited India on their way to China, and they were soon followed by a third, an intrepid Dominican named Jordan of Sévérac, who spent much of his life single-handedly supporting the tiny Christian communities established by his predecessors. Both Jordan and his Franciscan counterpart Odoric of Pordenone wrote accounts of the marvels of India that were heavily embroidered to entice new recruits, but they also contained some fresh information. Odoric finally explained that pepper grew on vines and was dried by the sun; crocodiles stalked the groves, he added, but they were timid and ran away from a modest fire. Another Franciscan, named John of Marignola, who set out in 1338 as a papal envoy to China and wandered around much of Asia for fifteen years, described how pepper was harvested, and demystified the people with parasol feet by introducing the West to the umbrella.

Of all the new revelations, the most provocative was Friar Odoric's report that pepper was as abundant in India as grain was in Europe; the crop, he surmised, grew only on the Malabar Coast, the monsoon-soaked shoreline of southwest India, but it took a man eighteen days to travel from one end of the plantation to the other. This was news to feed Europe's mounting anger at the ruinous cost of its condiments. The more India became a real place to the West, the more the old awe at the inordinate rarity of spices was scoffed away in favor of new stories of their absurd abundance. Spices, polemicists began to claim, grew everywhere in the East and cost nothing; it was Christendom's enemies who spread wild stories and manipulated the supply and price.

It was all too much for many people. Vast stretches of the lands Marco Polo described were completely unknown to the ancients and the Christian geographers alike, and his claims were not widely credited. His was only one of many competing voices, and other travel writers continued to peddle and embellish the old stories, in some cases without ever leaving home. The highly imaginative *Travels of Sir John Mandeville*, likely written in the mid-fourteenth century by a French physician from Liège, came complete with dog-men, apple smellers, and one-eyed giants and was far more popular with the reading public than was Polo's sober report. "Mandeville" took in a large sweep of the Middle East, China, and India, with a detour to the mountain of Paradise with its gushing spring and its wall of flaming swords. The plausible guide insisted that the pepper plantations were, after all, infested with snakes, though they could easily be driven away with lemon juice and snails. Prester John, he added, was fabulously rich from his extensive pepper forests and from the emeralds and sapphires that sparkled in his rivers. His land was watered by a spring of marvelous flavors that cured any disease and preserved everyone at thirty-two years old, the exact age at which Jesus was crucified.

With the downfall of the Mongols the overland routes became unsafe and eventually impassable, and virtually all travel between the two continents ceased. Europe's tantalizing glimpse of the East was soon a dim memory, and it became harder than ever to tell fact from the fantasies supported by centuries of tradition. It was painfully clear, though, that with the Turks entrenched in Constantinople, any hopes Europe had of infiltrating the spice trade had receded further than ever. This was no epicurean's lament; the predicament posed a dire threat to Europe's economy, its political structures, and even its faith. As prices rose sky-high and demand barely wavered, the obsession with keeping up appearances left the privileged classes—including several royal courts—facing the real possibility of severe financial embarrassment. Even worse, the prospect of an ever richer Islamic world pushing on an impoverished Europe's doors seemed to spell Christendom's doom.

The European powers that appeared to have most to lose from the new order of things were Venice and Genoa. For centuries the two maritime republics had vied for control of trade with the East. One late-fifteenth-century visitor to Venice was astonished to discover that the whole world seemed to be doing business there: "Who could count the many shops," he marveled, "so well furnished that they almost seem warehouses, with so many cloths of every make—tapestry, brocades, and hangings of every design, carpets of every sort, camlets of every color and texture, silks of every kind; and so many warehouses full of spices, groceries, and drugs, and so much beautiful wax! These things stupefy the beholder." The wealth of both cities depended on a regular supply of Asian luxuries, and the supply had dried up.

Yet as Venice's councilors met inside the newly completed Doge's Palace, its architecture inspired by the mosques, bazaars, and palaces of the East, they scented an opportunity, not a disaster. The city's merchants still had deep contacts within the Islamic world, and since Muslim control of the trade routes was all but complete, the rest of Europe had even less chance of competing with them than before. Half afloat on its lagoon, Venice had always been tenuously anchored to Europe; to its neighbors its power had a cold, hard sheen, and its religious scruples came a distant second to trade. "*Siamo Veneziani, poi Cristiani,*" its people were fond of saying; "First Venetians, then Christians." Within months of the conquest of Constantinople the republics were back, buying their luxuries from the Ottomans and passing on the inflated tariffs to their customers. The entente did not last—Mehmet's conquering gaze soon turned on Venice's overseas colonies, and despite itself the republic was plunged into its own Crusade—but for all the Ottomans' triumphs they were not the only game in town. Mehmet was marching toward war with the Mamluk sultans of Egypt, and the Egyptians dispatched a series of dazzling embassies to Italy in a deliberate attempt to cut their fellow Muslims out of the market. One deputation arrived in Florence bearing balsam, musk, benzoin, aloeswood, ginger, muslin, Chinese porcelain, purebred Arabian horses, and a giraffe. Another reached Venice, and the republic soon switched much of its trade to the ancient Egyptian port of Alexandria.

To the rest of Europe, the situation was a scandal. Italy's merchants were conniving with Muslims to corner the spice trade, and their fellow Christians were paying the price. As so often, necessity was the mother of invention; with Islamic states once again lined up along Europe's land borders, the notion of reaching the East by sea no longer seemed quite so ridiculous.

It was still such a radical idea that few gave it a passing thought, but it was not entirely new. Back in 1291, as the last Crusader stronghold in the Holy Land had fallen to the Egyptians, two Genoese brothers had put into action a heroically suicidal plan. Ugolino and Vadino Vivaldi had equipped two oared galleys for a ten-year voyage and had set out with the intention of reaching India by sailing around Africa. They rowed across the Mediterranean and out through the Pillars of Hercules and were never heard from again, though persistent legends held that they circumnavigated Africa before being taken prisoner by an unexpectedly hostile Prester John. No one would attempt the same feat until Vasco da Gama set sail two centuries later, but the notion that the seaborne trade of the East was the key to undermining Islam gradually became an article of faith, and it kept resurfacing in the reams of propaganda that flew from the pens of Crusading revivalists.

In 1317 a Dominican missionary named William Adam wrote a lengthy memo to a cardinal-nephew of the pope titled *De modo Sarracenos extirpandi*—"How to eradicate the Muslims." Adam had spent nine months exploring the Indian Ocean, and he recommended enlisting the help of the Mongols of Iran to mount a naval blockade of Egypt using Genoese galleys. "Everything that is sold in Egypt," he explained, "like pepper, ginger and other spices, gold and precious stones, silks and those rich textiles dyed with Indian colors, and all the other valuables, to buy which the merchants from these countries go to Alexandria and expose themselves to the snare of excommunication, all these are brought to Egypt from India." According to Adam, two Genoese galleys had already been built on Mongol territory and had rowed down the Euphrates toward the Indian Ocean, but rival factions of sailors had quickly set upon each other and they were all dead before they had got very far. Seven years later Jordan of Sévérac, the Dominican friar who had taken it upon himself to establish the Catholic Church in India, wrote to his order echoing Adam's call for ships to be sent into the Indian Ocean to launch a new Crusade against Egypt. "If our lord the pope would but establish a couple of galleys on this sea," he urged, "what a gain it would be! And what damage and destruction to the Sultan of Alexandria!" He briefly journeyed back to Europe to press his case, and in 1329 the pope sent him back to India as a bishop, but soon after his return he was rumored to have been stoned to death.

Around the same time, a Venetian statesman named Marino Sanudo Torsello penned an elaborate manual for reviving the Crusades. It came complete with detailed if inaccurate maps, and it also made the case for a naval blockade. The papacy had responded to the loss of the last Christian port in Palestine by prohibiting all trade with the Islamic world, but Rome had soon started granting let-outs to Europe's merchants, in return for a hefty consideration. Sanudo forcefully argued that Christian merchants were funding Islam's wars against Christian armies by handing over Europe's wealth in return for spices. It was abundantly clear, he pointed out, that armed expeditions alone were not going to dislodge the Muslims from the Holy Land. What was needed was a total trade embargo backed by the threat of excommunication and enforced by patrolling galleys; the blockade would fatally weaken the Egyptian sultan, since his wealth flowed from his grip over the spice trade. A Crusader navy could then sail up the River Nile and finish off the job. From their new base in Egypt, the knights could forge an alliance with the Mongols, attack Palestine, and retake Jerusalem. Finally, a fleet would be established in the Indian Ocean to police its peoples and trade. Sanudo pressed his plan on two successive popes and the king of France, but since it required concerted action from Europe's fractious rulers, it came to nothing.

While the exhausted great powers shrugged off each successive proposal as yet another foolish flight of fancy, tiny Portugal had been busy preparing the way.

THE OLD MAPPAE mundi had no place for the Southern Hemisphere. Contrary to popular belief, the mapmakers did not think the earth was flat, but they did assume that no one lived in the Antipodes, the lands below the equator. The equator itself was widely believed to be a scorching ring of fire, and since Noah's Ark had come to rest on Mount Ararat in the north, it was hard to see how people could have made their way south. Besides, they would have been unreachable by the Gospel, which the Bible declared had gone forth over all the earth.

As that world picture wavered and collapsed, mapmaking underwent a revolution. For decades the new world maps were a curious blend of the medieval and the modern: half based on the remarkably accurate portolan charts, or coastal maps, of sailors, half filled with black giants who ate foreign white men, or with fish-women called Sirens. When cutting-edge cartographers began to search for more reliable information about the far-flung regions of the globe, like so much that was new in the Renaissance they harked back to the classical age.

In 1406, Ptolemy's *Geography* had reappeared in the West in the baggage of a scholar fleeing dying Constantinople. Ptolemy, a Roman citizen who lived in Egypt during the second century CE, was the first geographer to give detailed instructions on how to represent the globe on a flat plan, and the first to provide a comprehensive gazetteer of every known place on earth. The *Geography* was quickly translated into Latin, and it was soon a fixture in the library of any self-respecting prince, cleric, or merchant. It was a mark of Europe's long isolation that going back more than a millennium in time meant leaping forward in knowledge. Christian geographers had believed that six-sevenths of the earth was land and had imagined a single supercontinent fringed by a single Ocean Sea. Ptolemy spread his continents across a background of clear blue, and his maps gave a startlingly watery image of a world where the oceans led everywhere.

Everywhere, that is, except around the southern tip of Africa. Ptolemy's Africa had no end: its east and west coasts abruptly turned at right angles and stretched across the bottom of the page, like the tail of a humpback whale. The eastern extension curled around to join a long south-tending finger of Asia, leaving the Indian Ocean as an enormous landlocked lake.

The rediscovery of Ptolemy radically altered Europe's conception of the globe, but one daring mapmaker caught the spirit of the time and decided to go further. In 1459, King Afonso of Portugal commissioned a new world map from the renowned Fra Mauro of Venice. Mauro, a monk who ran a cartography workshop out of a monastery on the island of Murano, synthesized Ptolemy with Marco Polo and added in the intelligence gleaned from an even more intrepid Venetian traveler, an inveterate adventurer named Niccolò de' Conti, who left home in 1419, learned Arabic and Persian, disguised himself as a Muslim merchant, and toured the East for twenty-five years. On Fra Mauro's map, Africa stopped short of the bottom of the page, and a narrow channel linked the Atlantic to the Indian Ocean. It was the audacious monk who raised the tantalizing prospect of sailing around Africa, and yet his trailblazing scoop was almost certainly based on a misunderstanding.

In India, Niccolò de' Conti had learned of the great Chinese junks that sometimes visited its ports. The giant multistoried ships had five masts and a colossal rudder suspended from an overhanging bridge at the stern. The hulls were triple-planked to withstand storms and were divided into compartments, so that if one was holed the ship was still seaworthy. Inside were rows of cabins with lockable doors and latrines; herbs and spices were cultivated in gardens on the decks. The junks were vastly larger than any European vessel, and they were far from the biggest Chinese ships afloat.

The Central Kingdom, as China contentedly called itself, had traded with India and East Africa for centuries, but between 1405 and 1433 the Ming emperors had staged a spectacular piece of seaborne theater. Seven floating embassies had arrived in the Indian Ocean, under the command of Admiral Zheng He, a burly Muslim eunuch who was the great-grandson of a Mongol warlord. The first fleet alone comprised 317 ships manned by 27,870 sailors, soldiers, merchants, physicians, astrologers, and artisans. At its head were 62 nine-masted treasure ships, and yet in a display of munificence that would have utterly baffled Europeans, the ships were designed not to receive treasure but to dispense it. As they sailed into the harbors of Southeast Asia, India, Arabia, and East Africa, they disgorged huge quantities of silks, porcelain, gold and silver wares, and other marvels of Chinese manufacturing. Such terrifying munificence invariably had the intended effect: in the space of a few years the envoys of thirty-seven nations rushed to pay homage to the emperor at Beijing. Yet not even China could afford to dispense such largesse indefinitely, and in 1435, the Central Kingdom voluntarily abandoned its commanding presence in the Indian Ocean. Within decades its navies and merchant fleets dwindled away to nothing—a development without which Portugal's route to the East might have been well and truly blocked.

On Fra Mauro's map a caption carried the remarkable news that, around the year 1420, a junk had rounded Africa and had continued on a southwesterly bearing for two thousand miles, a course that would have taken it deep into the icy South Atlantic. Mauro credited the information to a "trustworthy source" that was likely his fellow Venetian Niccolò de' Conti. Yet Conti had set out on his travels only the year before the junk had supposedly made its voyage, and if he got wind of the story, it must have been from hearsay. Fra Mauro had more: his informant, he added, was himself driven two thousand miles to the west-southwest of Africa by a great storm. Yet Conti's own account of his travels merely mentions that he was blown off course while crossing to Africa in an Indian or Arab ship. Since Fra Mauro's depiction of the southern tip of Africa bears a strong resemblance to features of the east African coast much farther to the north, the most likely explanation is that the mapmaker read into the new information he had at hand the facts to support his own hypothesis—and, perhaps, to please his Portuguese paymaster.

On such slender threads rested the growing belief that the Indian Ocean was, after all, connected to the Atlantic. It was not a new idea, but its time had come.

CHAPTER 6

THE RIVALS

I N 1475 THE forty-three-year-old King Afonso of Portugal married his thirteen-year-old niece, Joan of Castile. It was not a match kindled by true love.

Joan's mother—Afonso's sister—was married to King Henry IV of Castile. Henry was also known as the Impotent, and Joan's real father was widely believed to be a nobleman named Beltrán de la Cueva, a scandal that saddled her for the rest of her life with the nickname La Beltraneja. A large part of the Castilian nobility revolted at the notion of the Beltraneja becoming their queen and threw their support behind Henry's stepsister Isabella. Isabella had eloped at age seventeen with her cousin Ferdinand, heir to the crown of Aragon, but at least her blood was pure blue. When Henry died in 1474, rival factions proclaimed both Joan and Isabella queen. Joan's backers hastily arranged her marriage with her uncle, and Afonso proclaimed himself the lawful king of Castile.

War broke out between the neighboring nations and quickly spread to the Atlantic. The Castilians sent their fleets to pillage the African coast, an activity they had anyway been surreptitiously engaged in for some years. Portugal's warships made short shrift of them, but Afonso's military maneuvers on land petered out amid an unusually cold Spanish winter, while Joan's coalition fell apart when the pope, who had initially supported her claim, switched sides and annulled her marriage. Joan took herself to a nunnery; Afonso fell into a deep depression, wrote to his son John abdicating the throne to him, and began to plan a pilgrimage to the Holy

Land. John had been king for less than a week when his father, who had changed his mind, returned home, and his official ascension to the throne was postponed until Afonso died in 1481.

If Afonso had embodied one side of his uncle Henry's character—his Crusading zeal and his love of chivalric tradition—King John II was the apotheosis of Henry's other side. He was the very picture of a modern Machiavellian ruler: driven by grand ambitions beyond ordinary men's ken, and not overly fussy about how to fulfill them. As intelligent as he was ruthless, he would become known as the Perfect Prince, though his victims termed him the Tyrant. Many of those victims were prominent aristocrats who had accrued broad powers at the crown's expense. When the twenty-six-year-old king found his coffers virtually empty, he lost no time in hacking away at their privileges. The outraged nobles plotted to overthrow him, and one by one their heads rolled.

The year before hostilities had erupted with Castile, the crown had taken back control of the discoveries after its brief flirtation with free enterprise. The African trade now promised real profits, and the new king acted quickly to shore up his watery empire. Lisbon rang with the hammer blows of African slaves working forges to make anchors, arms, and ammunition. John ordered his engineers to improve the aim and firepower of the rudimentary cannon that were carried aboard ships, and larger, newfangled models were imported at great expense from Flanders and Germany. The king also set about solving a problem that had bedeviled the fleets since they had neared the equator: the disappearance of the Pole Star, the reference point by which Portugal's navigators had learned to determine their latitude when out at sea. John immersed himself in the science of cosmography and gathered together a committee of experts. At its head were Joseph Vizinho and Abraham Zacuto, two Jewish mathematician-astronomers who set about redesigning the ships' simple navigational instruments and preparing tables that allowed sailors to read their latitude from the sun.

Regular fleets set out from Lisbon for Africa, carrying the materials and laborers to build forts along the coast—the first links in the backbone of an empire. Other ships pressed on south. In 1483 a sailor named Diogo Cão reached the delta of the Congo River and set up the first of the *padrões*—stone pillars topped with a cross bearing the arms of Portugal, the date, and the names of the king and the captain—that from now on would mark the boundaries of the Portuguese discoveries. "In the year 6681 from the Creation of the world and 1482 from the birth of Our Lord Jesus Christ," read the inscription on the second pillar he erected, "the most high, most excellent and powerful prince King John, second of Portugal, ordered this land to be discovered and these pillars to be put up by Diogo Cão, squire of his household." Cão was ennobled on his return and he set out again. In 1486 he reached rocky Cape Cross in Namibia, desolate except for its vast breeding colony of Cape Fur seals, and perhaps Whale Bay, a deep harbor protected by a sand spit that would prove an important staging post on the journey farther south. Whale Bay was just five hundred miles from the southern tip of Africa, but Cão's was not to be the name that history would remember: he died on his way home while trying to explore the Congo.

John II was as keen as his forebears to graft Christianity onto Guinea, not least because baptism made for more reliable allies. Gradually a trickle of Africans volunteered for conversion—or were brought back as hostages, instructed in the faith, and sent home as ambassadors—and they were treated as celebrities for both domestic and international consumption. One deposed Senegalese prince named Bemoi made a great stir by arriving in Lisbon to redeem the king's promise that he would help restore him to his rightful position if he converted. Bemoi was forty years old, tall, strong, and handsome, with a patriarchal beard and a majestic manner of speaking, and the king and court received him with full honors. He and twenty-four of his companions were baptized amid prolonged festivities that included, on the Portuguese side, tournaments, bull-fights, farces, and evening fetes, and on the visitors' side, spectacular horse-riding stunts. Twenty warships and a large contingent of soldiers, builders, and priests escorted them home, but to John's fury the commander of the fleet became paranoid that the African was planning treason and stabbed him to death en route.

Even without such rash acts, the pace of proselytization was painfully slow. Then, as Portuguese agents pressed farther into the interior of Guinea, an electrifying piece of intelligence suddenly emerged from deepest Africa.

News had arrived of Prester John.

In 1486 an envoy returned to Lisbon accompanied by an ambassador from the king of Benin. Twenty moons' march from the coast, he declared, there lived a monarch named Ogané who was revered by his subjects much as the pope was by Catholics. Many African kings visited him to be crowned with a brass helmet, a staff, and a cross, but all anyone had seen of him was his foot, which he graciously proffered to be kissed from behind a silk curtain.

The royal experts pored over their maps and decided it took exactly twenty moons to march from Benin to Ethiopia. The legend beckoned, and the discoveries leaped forward.

John decided on a two-pronged approach to locate Prester John and join forces with him to reach India. He would push ahead with the sea voyages, and at the same time he would step up his search for reliable information by land.

The only way to sort fact from hearsay was to send his own secret agents into the heart of the East.

KING JOHN'S FIRST attempt to send spies in search of Prester John was not encouraging. The two men got as far as Jerusalem, where they were warned they would not last long without speaking Arabic, and turned back for home.

The king sought advice and summoned a more promising pair. Pêro da Covilhã, who was about forty and was the senior of the two, had grown up among the granite crags and ravines of the Serra da Estrela in central Portugal. As a streetwise kid he had bluffed his way into the service of a Castilian nobleman—not least by naming himself, in the patrician manner, after his birthplace—and he had proved a useful swordsman in the endless cloak-and-dagger brawls between Spanish cavaliers. On his return from Castile he had insinuated himself into the service of King Afonso, first as a valet and later as a squire. King John had taken him on after his father's death and had sent him to spy on the Portuguese nobles who had fled his executioners to Castile; his information cost at least two lordly rebels their necks. John had subsequently reposted Pêro to Morocco and Algeria to negotiate peace treaties with the Berber kings of Fez and Tlemcen, and the dependable envoy had soon learned Arabic and familiarized himself with Muslim customs. Quick-witted and courageous, possessed of a phenomenal memory, and adept at appearing what he was not, he was an inspired choice for the treacherous mission. The companion chosen for him was Afonso de Paiva, the son of a respectable family from the same hardy mountain stock as Pêro. Afonso was a squire of the royal household, he had proved his loyalty in the Spanish wars, and he also spoke some Arabic.

Amid the utmost secrecy, the two men met in the Lisbon house of John's clerk of works. Also present were three of the king's closest advisers: his personal chaplain, who doubled as the bishop of Tangier and was a keen cosmographer; his physician Rodrigo, who was also an astronomer; and the Jewish mathematician Joseph Vizinho. The three men began analyzing maps and plotting the spies' route.

With the preparations complete, on May 7, 1487, the two men rode out to the palace at Santarém, forty-five miles outside the capital and safely away from the prying eyes of the spies who infested every European court.

Like most grand designs formed in ignorance of the practicalities, John's orders were simple to state and fiendishly difficult to carry out. The two men were to reach India and learn about the spice trade. They were to find Prester John and forge an alliance with him. They were to discover whether it was really possible to sail around Africa and into the Indian Ocean, and how to navigate once there. Only then were they to come home and make a full report.

The sheer audacity of the task briefly overwhelmed the irrepressible Covilhã, who expressed regret that "his capacity was not greater, so great was his desire to serve His Highness." He should be more confident, the king told him: fortune had shone on him, and he had proved himself a good and faithful servant.

John's future heir was also present at the meeting. Manuel was a moon-faced, delicate-looking young man with chestnut hair, greenish eyes, and fleshy arms "which were so long that the fingers of the hands reached below his knees." The young duke, a few weeks shy of his eighteenth birthday, handed the two spies the final map drawn up by the three wise men. The king gave them a bag filled with four hundred gold cruzados, purloined from a chest meant for the expenses of the crown estates, and a letter of credentials "for all the countries and provinces in the world." Before they left they knelt and received the royal blessing.

Carrying around so much money was an invitation to be robbed, or worse. The two men pocketed a handful of coins for their expenses and hastily returned to Lisbon, where they swapped their sack of gold for a letter of credit issued by a powerful Florentine banker.

That done, the two secret agents mounted their horses and rode across Portugal. They crossed the Spanish border and made their way to Valencia, where they cashed in their letter at a branch of the Florentine's bank, sold their horses, and took a boat along the coast to Barcelona. The bustling port had regular departures to North Africa, France, Italy, and the eastern Mediterranean, and after exchanging their gold for another credit note the pair booked a passage to Naples. After an easy ten-day voyage, they arrived in the sweeping bay at the foot of Mount Vesuvius. There were no banks that would welcome their business where they were headed, and they cashed in their check for the last time. Keeping their heavy pouches well hidden, they sailed down the Amalfi Coast, through the Strait of Messina, and across the Aegean Sea to the island of Rhodes, just off the coast of Turkey.

Rhodes was the home of the Knights Hospitaller and the last redoubt of long-spent Outremer. A forbidding constellation of crenellated walls and jutting towers loomed over the harbor. After they were ousted from the Holy Land, the Hospitallers had found new purpose in plundering Muslim shipping; seven years earlier, Mehmet the Conqueror had tried and failed to dislodge these final stubborn Crusaders from their island fortress.

The spies found lodgings in a monastery and set out to seek the advice of two Portuguese Hospitallers. The knights suggested they use their gold to buy a hundred barrels of honey and a new set of clothes. They were headed for Islamic lands, and from now on they were to pose as lowly merchants—though the disguise was not so much aimed at Muslims, who were unlikely to distinguish them from other Europeans, as at Italian merchants who jealously guarded their interests against interlopers.

From Rhodes, the two spies sailed south to Egypt and the ancient port of Alexandria, where their real mission began. From here on, their findings would be of the utmost importance to Vasco da Gama and his fellow seafaring pioneers.

Alexandria had once been the classical world's greatest metropolis, the hub of trade between Europe, Arabia, and India, and the model for imperial Rome itself. Its Arab conquerors had gasped at the gleaming marble streets lined with four thousand palaces and bathhouses and four hundred theaters, and repelled by such pagan splendor, they had relocated their capital to Cairo. Soon Alexandria had dwindled to a small town built on the hollow foundations of empire. The Great Library was long lost, along with the vast palace of the Ptolemies. Earthquakes had leveled the legendary Pharos, the towering lighthouse whose beam shone thirty-five miles into the Mediterranean, and just seven years earlier the last of its mammoth stone blocks had been recycled to build a harbor fort. "At this time [Alexandria] looks very glorious without," reported Martin Baumgarten, a wealthy German knight who was overwhelmed with grief at the untimely death of his wife and three children and embarked in 1507, at the age of thirty-two, on a pilgrimage to Jerusalem; "the walls as they are of a large compass, so they are well built, firm and high, and the turrets upon them are numerous; but within, instead of a city, there's nothing to be seen but a prodigious heap of stones."

The ship nosed between the submerged rocks of the harbor, its sails lowered in the usual sign of deference to the sultan, and as soon as it moored officials came on board to search the passengers and crew. Merchants regularly tried to evade taxes by hiding their goods in the strangest places; one group of Christians, a traveler boasted, "sav'd a great part of what we did bring, by hiding it in pork, which they abominate above all things."

Even as it crumbled Alexandria had carried on a trade in spices, silks, and slaves, and with the fall of Constantinople it had begun to regain its position as a world-class emporium. It was a messy, multilingual port city. On one side of the massive stone mole that once led to the Pharos, Italian warehouses were stacked with Eastern goods awaiting shipment to Europe; on the other side was a separate harbor reserved for Muslims. The two groups sometimes clashed violently, but the mutual search for profits usually sustained an uneasy standoff.

The spies plowed into the noisy streets and found suitably obscure lodgings. Their disguise held up, but they discovered that diseases as well as goods were exchanged in Alexandria's fetid climate. As they tossed and sweated with Nile fever, the sultan's deputy gave them up for dead and requisitioned their honey, which was much in demand in North Africa. By the time they recovered he had already sold it, and they retrieved what money they could and quickly left town.

The countryside was low-lying and bare but for the occasional clump of date trees. Fishermen popped up out of fens to extort protection money, and at night the two men slept fitfully on the ground, hugging their remaining belongings. Before dawn they started again, the winds shifting hillocks of sand and obscuring the road ahead. Eventually the minarets of Rosetta rose before them at the head of the Nile, and they hired a felucca, a narrow, lateen-rigged sailboat, to take them upriver. They whiled away the time spotting the crocodiles that lurked in the canes and the mysterious monuments that littered the banks, or watching as Egyptian men and women stripped off their long blue shirts, tied them on their heads, and swam across the river at astonishing speed. At dusk the crew lighted pyramids of lanterns, tied tinkling bells to the sails, and entertained themselves by shooting fiery arrows into the night sky.

As they approached Cairo, the real pyramids reared from the desert like mountains carved by giants. Even then no traveler could leave without paying them a visit. In the sixteenth century an Englishman named John Sanderson went mummy hunting in Egypt; along with several complete corpses he brought home six hundred pounds of broken mummy to sell to London's apothecaries and "one little hand" for his brother the Archdeacon of Rochester. Accompanied by two German friends, he crawled up to the King's Chamber in the Pyramid of Cheops, climbed into the lidless sarcophagus, and lay inside "in sport." Soon afterward an Italian traveler named Pietro della Valle clambered to the top of the pyramid and carved his name and the name of his lover in the stone. Like every foreigner, he was thoroughly taken in by the guides who claimed to be able to decipher the hieroglyphics, a tradition that dated back to classical times.

Cairo—in Arabic *al-Qahira*, "the Victorious"—astounded Europeans even more than its ancient precursors. The city was vast. "They do positively aver," recorded Martin Baumgarten, "whether true or false I know not, that there are about twenty-four thousand mosques in it." Many of the mosques boasted libraries, schools, and hospitals where treatment was free and musicians played to soothe the sick; all were built of white stone, some of it plundered from the pyramids, that dazzled the eyes in the intense light and almost bleached out the intricate vegetal carvings and calligraphic inscriptions that covered every surface. At nightfall, the minarets from which the muezzin, reported Baumgarten, "night and day, at certain hours, make a strange, loud and barbarous noise," were illuminated with burning torches and lamps. The German's informant also explained that the city boasted ten thousand cooks, most of whom seemed to ply their trade in the labyrinths of rush-covered alleys, carrying their pots on their heads and dressing their dishes as they went. He added another outsize if less impressive statistic: there were more homeless on the streets of Cairo than there were inhabitants in Venice.

Cairo had grown into the busiest and most advanced city in the Islamic world. Turks, Arabs, Africans, and Indians gathered there. Italian merchants had their own colony, as did Greeks, Ethiopians, and Nubians. Copts, the native Christians of Egypt, worshipped in ancient churches, and thousands of Jews gathered in synagogues. Muslim potentates grazed on banquets spread on rich carpets, while their numerous wives waited upstairs in rooms dripping with silk, fragrant ointments, and perfumes, peeping out through latticework screens at the street life below. The historian Ibn Khaldun lavished accolades on his beloved city: Cairo, he wrote, was the "metropolis of the world, garden of the universe, meeting-place of nations, anthill of peoples, high place of Islam, seat of power." What we see in dreams, he rhapsodized, "surpasses reality, but all that one could dream of Cairo would not come close to the truth."

The spies approached on donkeys—only high officials could enter on horseback—and passed under the minaret-topped towers of Bab Zuweila, the soaring main gate. Important visitors were announced with a tattoo beaten by drummers who sat in the loggia above, but the Portuguese pair were given the more common welcome: a shower of dirt, brickbats, and moldy lemons from the boys of Cairo.

The two men followed the jostling crowds down Muizz Street, the congested central artery of the city. Halfway along, amid ornate tomb-mosques built by rich eternity seekers, were the sources of much of Cairo's wealth: the teeming state spice and perfume markets. The perfume emporia were lined with flasks in which lumps of resin and rock were distilled into deep yellow-brown colognes and balms. The spice shops were heaped with sacks and barrels that stretched back to dark recesses where merchants weighed out the precious substances on finely calibrated scales; in the heat the smell of aromatic leaves, seeds, and roots was almost suffocating.

The visitors struck out into the dusty side streets, dodging the droves of donkeys standing around grazing or being driven to and from the souks. They found modest lodgings—no doubt with the help of the ubiquitous touts—and set out to plan the next leg of their journey. Before long they fell in with a group of merchants from Fez and Tlemcen, the very North African cities where Covilhã had been posted. The merchants were headed to Arabia and India itself, and the wily spy coaxed them in their own dialect into taking him and his companion along for the ride.

It was now the spring of 1488, and almost a year had passed since the pair had left Portugal. The camels were saddled and loaded and the long caravan set out, after a pelting from the boys at the gate, for the Red Sea port of Tor. Tossed and shaken by their noisy, smelly mounts, the Portuguese crossed the flat, stony Sinai Desert, then a range of barren granite mountains that shone in the sun as if they were oiled, and next a coastal path so narrow that in places they had to ride in the sea. For food they had tough twice-baked bread, dry cheese, and salted ox tongue, and they were forced to pay handsomely for water that wriggled with red worms. Robbers ambushed them in date plantations, stole their provisions, and had to be paid off with silver. The mule and camel drivers kept raising their prices, and if anyone complained, they drove off their animals with the baggage still on their backs. The two men barely slept; by the end of the trek they were sliding off their mounts from exhaustion and hallucinating that hands were grabbing at their last few crumbs of food.

It was becoming clear why spices cost so much in Europe, and the journey had only just begun.

As the caravan finally reached the Red Sea, the guides spun another favorite yarn. It was here, they explained, that the waters had parted for Moses and the children of Israel and had crashed over the pharaoh's pursuing host. Martin Baumgarten dutifully reported that the tracks of the pharaoh's chariots and the prints of his horses' hooves were clearly visible, "and tho' one should deface them this minute, they shall plainly appear the next."

THE 1,400-MILE-LONG RED SEA, which European travelers were surprised to find was not red at all, is shaped like an elongated slug crawling north toward the Mediterranean. Two feelers protrude from the slug's head: on the left is the Gulf of Suez, which separates Egypt from the Sinai Peninsula, and on the right is the Gulf of Aqaba, which divides Sinai from the Arabian Peninsula. At its southern end the slug's tail swishes into the Gulf of Aden and the Arabian Sea, the part of the Indian Ocean that lies between Africa and India. There, where the two bodies of water meet, the coast of Africa curves east in a sharp hook, cradling the southwestern corner of Arabia.

The tight channel between the two continents is known as the Strait of Bab-el-Mandeb; the name means "Gate of Tears." Strong currents and scattered islands make the passage precarious, and for much of its length the Red Sea itself is strewn with treacherous islets and sunken reefs. Gusting winds and choppy waves regularly drove heavily laden sailing vessels onto the rocks, and while a few oceangoing ships braved the strait and continued halfway up the east coast of the sea to Jeddah, the port of Mecca, small vessels skippered by experienced navigators mostly had the traffic to themselves. The two dhows—traditional Arab sailing ships—that the Portuguese spies boarded in the little port of Tor were typical of the craft that had plied the route for centuries. The hulls were made of planks sewn together with coconut fiber, and the sails were mats of woven coconut fronds. Lightly built for maneuverability—and because timber was in short supply—they were also leaky and unstable even in light swells. The pilots could only navigate by day, and since pirates infested the coasts, they had to stay well out to sea at night. By the time the merchants' party sailed through the Gate of Tears and headed for the southern Arabian coast, two excruciating months had passed since they had left Cairo.

The spies were about to discover the fabulously rich triangle at the heart of the spice trade. The first of its three points was the port they had just arrived at, and it was a forbidding sight.

The famed harbor of Aden lay in the crater of an extinct volcano that stood proud of the mainland of Yemen. The city nestled on the crater floor, and jagged black crags surmounted by a cordon of castles almost encircled it down to the sea. Behind the shore, strong fortifications completed the defensive bowl, which the Arab geographer al-Muqaddasi thought looked uncannily like a giant sheep pen. With its fine anchorage, natural defenses, and position commanding the entrance to the Red Sea, Aden had been a commercial center of the first order since ancient times, and as the main terminus for oceangoing vessels laden with Eastern spices and silks, precious stones, and porcelain, it was among the richest trading cities of the medieval world.

When the party from Cairo arrived, the monsoon winds that drove Arab ships southeast to India were already gusting fiercely. Crossing the Arabian Sea in high summer meant one of two things: death, or a quick journey of as little as eighteen days. Delaying too long would mean waiting another year, and the two men decided to split up. Afonso was to sail the short distance from Aden to Ethiopia, where he was to seek out Prester John, while Pêro was to continue to India. They arranged to meet back in Cairo at the end of their adventures.

The dhow that Covilhã boarded for India was much larger than the Red Sea boats, but it had the same single mast, raked forward and crossed by a long yard to which was bent the head of a lateen sail, and it was made of the same sewn planks. There was no deck; the cargo was covered with thick cane mats, and the passengers had to squeeze themselves in wherever they could. It was almost impossible to find shade from the burning sun, the only barriers to waves washing over the side were strips of matting or cloth smeared with pitch, and for food there was nothing but half-cooked dried rice sprinkled with sugar and chopped dates. The dhows were fast runners and their Arab captains were skilled navigators, but the few weeks it took to reach India passed slowly.

As the year neared its end, Covilhã headed along the Indian coast to a city whose marvels he had heard a great deal about on his journey. Calicut was the second point of the trade triangle, the gathering place of the spices and jewels of the East, and the spy stayed on for several months to investigate the sources and prices of the mysterious goods that sold in Europe for staggering sums. His report would have far-reaching consequences for his hosts: within a few years, Vasco da Gama would sail for India with orders to head straight for Calicut.

In February Covilhã made his way back up the coast, stopping to record the location and trade of more ports along the way. By now the Arab fleets were heading back home, and he secured passage on a ship bound for Hormuz, the third point of the fabled triangle.

The ship sailed into the Persian Gulf, the Red Sea's twin inlet on the eastern side of Arabia, and headed for a small island that commanded a narrow strait. As it approached, Covilhã made out a sizable city through the thicket of masts that filled the port. When he landed, he found it packed with merchants from every corner of Asia. Situated at the point where the Arabian Peninsula juts sharply out and seems to make a dent in the coast of Iran, Hormuz had no greenery and no fresh water, which had to be brought in flagons from the mainland, but it sat astride the junction of the sea routes from India and the Far East with the land routes that led through Iraq to Syria, Turkey, and Istanbul. Its markets were heaped with pearls, silks, jewels, tapestries, spices, perfumes, and drugs, and for sheer luxury it had few equals. Carpets covered the streets for the comfort of shoppers, and linen awnings draped between the rooftops kept off the scorching sun. Merchants' tables boasted fine wines and expensive porcelain, and gifted musicians played while they ate. A later Portuguese visitor reported that the food was better than in France, while an English adventurer marveled at the beauty of the women, though he found them "very strangely attyred, wearing on their noses, eares, neckes, armes and legges many rings set with jewels, and lockes of silver and golde in their eares, and a long bar of golde upon the side of their noses. Their eares with the weight of their jewels be worne so wide," he added, "that a man may thrust three of his fingers into them." Cultural chasms aside, there was no gainsaying the importance of the island city. If all the world were a golden ring, went an Arab adage, Hormuz would be the jewel on it.

Covilhã now had a vivid picture of the dazzlingly rich trade of the Arabian Sea—and of the dangers and exorbitant dues that dogged its merchants at every step. The sea route from Europe might take longer, but the oceans were gloriously untroubled by robbers and customs officials, and there was undoubtedly a killing to be made. One thing remained: to find out whether ships really could sail directly from Europe into the Indian Ocean.

The Portuguese spy left Hormuz on a ship bound for Africa and disembarked at Zeila, a busy Muslim port that exported gold, ivory, and slaves from Ethiopia. The great Moroccan traveler Ibn Battuta had found Zeila "the dirtiest, most disagreeable, and most stinking town in the world," and though the sea was rough, the reek of fish and camels slaughtered in the streets was so revolting that he spent the night aboard his ship. Covilhã did not stay much longer. He set out to see how far down the coast he could sail, and he soon had his answer. The Arabs had settled the shores of East Africa for centuries, but their dhows could not withstand the heavy seas to the south. Besides, even if they had had the technology, they saw no need for such a voyage and had probably never attempted it. Their caravans had long funneled the goods of the African interior north and east to the Mediterranean and the Indian Ocean, and it made no sense to switch that trade to the west and the apparently empty Atlantic. They had certainly not tried to sail all the way around Africa to reach wild Western Europe: why bother when they already controlled half the Mediterranean, including many of its leading ports, and the goods of Europe, along with much of its gold, came to them?

The riddle of Africa would take a while longer to solve. Covilhã returned north, and by early 1491 he reached Cairo. It had been an exhausting if exhilarating journey, and he had been away from home for nearly four years. He must have been looking forward to meeting up with his fellow spy and going back to his wife, his family, and his richly deserved rewards.

He never found his companion. While he was waiting in Cairo, Afonso had fallen ill and had died.

The indefatigable Pêro prepared to make the return trip alone, and he was about to leave when two Portuguese Jews turned up on his doorstep. King John had sent them, they explained, and they had tracked him down, with some difficulty, in the cosmopolitan confusion of Cairo.

One of the two was a shoemaker from northern Portugal named Joseph; the other was a rabbi named Abraham from the south. A few years earlier Joseph had traveled overland to Baghdad, perhaps to investigate the market for shoes, and there he had heard fabulous things about Hormuz. On his return he had sought out the king, who was always accessible to messengers from faraway lands. The rabbi had also been east, perhaps to Cairo. When the two spies had failed to reappear, John had decided to send the two Jews to search for them.

The newcomers had with them a letter from the king, which Pêro lost no time in reading.

Its contents could hardly have been welcome. If their mission was complete, John wrote, the two men should return to Portugal, where they would receive great honors. If not, they should send word of their progress by the shoemaker Joseph and not rest until they had fulfilled their quest. In particular, they were not to come home unless they had personally established the whereabouts of Prester John. Before they did anything, though, they were to conduct the rabbi to Hormuz. The king no doubt thought a rabbi was a more reliable informant than a shoemaker, and Abraham had sworn that he would not turn back without seeing Hormuz with his own eyes.

King John had no way of knowing that his spy had already been to Hormuz himself and was ready to give a full report of its operations. Pêro had his royal orders, and as usual he was determined to carry them out to the full. He wrote a long dispatch to the king, handed it to Joseph, and set off with his new companion. The shoemaker made for home, the bearer of news that would be of vital importance to Vasco da Gama's impending mission.

Once again Covilhã crossed the desert to Tor; once again he made the slow, perilous journey down the Red Sea. By now the spy was an habitué of the Arabian ports, and in Aden the pair easily found passage to Hormuz. When Abraham was satisfied that he had seen all he needed, the two men went their separate ways: the rabbi back to Portugal, probably via a caravan headed to Syria, and Pêro back to the Red Sea.

From there Covilhã made for Jeddah, the port of Mecca. He was about to deviate utterly from his instructions. By now he had developed a taste for the hard glamour of adventure—and the inveterate explorer's hunger to spice up life with a dose of danger.

Jeddah was rich, busy, and completely forbidden to Christians and Jews. Pêro, though, was bronzed from long voyages in uncovered ships and bearded from the usual sailor's distaste for shaving. Besides, he had spent the past four years living and traveling with Muslims. He had adopted their dress, he was fluent in their language, and he was utterly conversant with their customs. He went undetected in Jeddah, and he decided to go farther—to Mecca

itself. At the least sign that he was a Christian, he knew he would
have been executed on the spot.

Perhaps, with his head shaved and uncovered and his body
wrapped in the two white cloths of the pilgrim, the Portuguese
spy entered the sacred precinct of the Kaaba and circled the stone
cube seven times, tracing the path worn in the granite slabs by
millions of worshippers' feet. Perhaps, if he had arrived at the time
of the hajj, he followed the press of pilgrims to Mount Arafat,
where Muhammad was said to have preached his last sermon, then
threw pebbles at the devil at Mina and watched the mass slaughter
of animals that commemorated Abraham's sacrifice of a ram in
place of his son. Having seen his fill, he journeyed on to Medina
and visited the great mosque that was rising, after a lightning
strike had destroyed much of the previous building, over Muhammad's burial place.

His initiation complete, Covilhã left Medina for the Sinai Desert and dropped in on the ancient monastery of St. Catherine. The
skeletal Greek monks bundled him off, as they did all pilgrims,
to attend a service and to marvel at the Burning Bush that Moses
himself had seen, or at least that the emperor Constantine's mother
Helena had miraculously unearthed on a relic-hunting trip to the
Holy Land. Having squared everything with his faith, Covilhã continued to Tor and took for the fifth time to the Red Sea. It was now
1493. More than a year had passed since he had left Cairo with the
rabbi, and Prester John still needed to be found.

The spy landed in East Africa near the mountains of High Ethiopia, a formidable bulwark that for centuries had protected the interior from attack. After a perilous journey across deserts, plateaus,
and plains, he reached the court of Alexander, Lion of the Tribe
of Judah and King of Kings, the descendant, so he and his dynasty
claimed, of King Solomon and the Queen of Sheba. Ethiopia had
once been a great power, and in its remote fastness it had preserved
its ancient traditions. The king, who presided over a vast and intricate hierarchy of nobles, had numerous wives and dozens of daugh-

ters, some of whom virtually ran the country. Yet he was Christian, and so were his people.

Alexander warmly received the visitor, and Covilhã presented him with an address written in Arabic and a brass medal engraved in multiple languages that he had kept for this moment since leaving Portugal. Both were addressed to Prester John, but by now the Ethiopians were accustomed to the Europeans' baffling but harmless habit of calling all their kings John.

The monarch received the communication, Covilhã later reported, "with much pleasure and joy, and said that he would send him to his country with much honor." He never did. A few months later Alexander marched off to put down a rebellion, and unrecognized at night, he was cut down by arrow fire. His infant son succeeded him until he succumbed to a childhood disease, and after much confusion Alexander's brother Naod replaced him on the throne. Covilhã immediately petitioned the new king to fulfill his brother's pledge and was politely turned down. Covilhã outlasted Naod, too, but Naod's son and successor David was no more inclined to let the traveler go. Since his forebears had not given him permission to leave, he explained, "he was not in a position to grant it, and so the matter stood."

After years away from Portugal, no doubt long mourned by his family, Covilhã had become a dyed-in-the-wool expatriate. With his vast experience of the world and his fluency in several languages, he was a valued adviser to the court. He was rewarded with titles and estates, and eventually he was made governor of a district. After demurring as long as he could, he caved in to the king's wishes and took a wife. He was clearly able to choose well, because there, in the middle of Ethiopia, thirty-three years after the former spy had left home, a Portuguese embassy arrived and found him fat, rich, happy, and surrounded by his children.

While King John was waiting for his spies to return, he had forged ahead with the second prong of his master plan. To head up the next expedition by sea he chose Bartolomeu Dias, a cavalier of the royal household and an experienced captain. His mission was to answer once and for all the burning question of whether ships could sail around Africa, and if possible to press on to the lands of Prester John.

Dias quietly left Lisbon in August 1487, three months after Pêro da Covilhã and Afonso de Paiva had set out. The fleet consisted of two caravels together with a supply vessel captained by Dias's brother Pêro, an innovation that was designed to prevent the increasingly long voyages from coming to a premature end for lack of food, water, and spares. Though the ships were unnervingly small for such a venture, the preparations had been unusually thorough, and the crews were highly experienced. Also on board were two African men and four African women who had been seized on earlier voyages and who were to be set ashore to ask after India and Prester John. The royal planners thought the inclusion of the women was a masterstroke on the grounds that they were less likely than men to be attacked, though as it turned out, one of the women died en route to Africa while the other five envoys disappeared inland and were never heard from again.

The fleet sailed past the wide mouth of the Congo River, stopped in Whale Bay, and struggled south against a heavy coastal current. To make better progress Dias put out to sea, only to be swept up in a storm. For thirteen days the caravels were driven west and south before the gusting wind, with their sails at half-mast to prevent the prows from plunging into the rough seas. The temperature had dropped markedly by the time Dias was able to steer back east, and when the coast failed to appear after several days he instead turned north.

Soon mountains came into view on the horizon, and as the ships drew closer the men made out a sandy beach curving from east to west, backed by sloping green fields where herders were tending their cattle. The herdsmen took one look at the mystifying ships and drove their flocks inland. With no one in sight, several sailors set out to search for fresh water and found themselves the target of a shower of stones from the hills above. Dias shot one of the assailants with a crossbow, and the fleet hurriedly resumed its journey.

By now the frightened and exhausted crews had had enough. There was hardly any food left, they protested in chorus. The storeship had been left far behind, and if they went any farther they would die of starvation. They had discovered fourteen hundred miles of coastline that had never been seen by Europeans; surely that was plenty for one voyage?

Dias eventually gave in, though not before landing onshore with his officers and extracting a signed statement that they were determined to turn back. It was only as they headed home that he finally sighted the unmistakable rocky point of a great cape, backed by a dramatic series of high peaks that framed a mountain with a top as flat as a table. He ruefully named it the Cape of Storms, though on his return the king decided on the more optimistic Cape of Good Hope.

The voyage had lasted more than sixteen months. The ships were in tatters, and the survivors' health was broken. They had weathered a tempest, they had seen the southern tip of Africa, and they had come home with precise charts that proved the great Ptolemy wrong. An ancient mystery had been solved, and as the news leaked out, Europe's maps were hastily redrawn. Yet on the very verge of sailing into the East, Dias had had to admit defeat. When he made his report to the king, he apologized for failing to find either Prester John or the Indies. Those were his orders, and by that high benchmark he had failed. His were not the rewards, and his was not the name that would go down in history.

By now the Portuguese had mapped the entire western coast of Africa. It was a remarkable testament to the doughty determination of an entire people, and many had paid a high price. Yet on the brink of triumph, the possibility suddenly arose that it might all have been in vain.

Among the figures who gathered that December in 1488 to hear Dias's report was a Genoese sailor named Christopher Columbus.

ON MARCH 4, 1493, a lone caravel limped into Lisbon's harbor and anchored alongside Portugal's most powerful warship. The *Niña* had been battered by violent storms that had stripped off its sails, and its captain had been forced to seek the only shelter within reach.

It was not the homecoming that Christopher Columbus would have chosen. For years he had attempted to persuade the Portuguese king to sponsor his audacious venture to reach the East by sailing west. Yet John had decided the Italian was full of big boasts and hot air, and his council of experts had poured scorn on his proposals and rejected them out of hand.

Columbus, the son of a Genoese weaver, had been drawn to the sea as a boy. He had first arrived in Portugal in 1476, as an ordinary seaman on a merchant ship carrying a cargo of mastic to England. The convoy had come under heavy attack off the Algarve coast, close to Henry the Navigator's old center of operations, and when his ship began to founder the young sailor had dived overboard, grabbed an oar, and half swum, half floated the six miles to the shore. After that dramatic entrance he had found his way to Lisbon, married a nobleman's daughter, and launched himself into Portugal's naval affairs.

Columbus was not the first man to propose sailing west to the East. The notion dated back at least to Roman times, and it had recently been revived. In 1474, a prominent Florentine intellectual named Paolo dal Pozzo Toscanelli had written to one of his many correspondents, a canon at Lisbon Cathedral named Fernão Martins, to propose a scheme to sail westward to the Indies as "a shorter way to the places of spice than that which you take by Guinea." The priest had presented the letter at court, where the plan received short shrift but reached the ears of the Genoese newcomer. Columbus was struck by a grand vision of adventure and riches, and he wrote to Toscanelli for a copy of his letter. It duly arrived, along with a map showing the route the Florentine recommended, and Columbus threw himself into a crash course of research.

From his reading, he drew several conclusions that seemed to put a western passage tantalizingly within reach.

The first was that the circumference of the earth was much smaller than it really was. Here Columbus had a powerful authority on his side: the great Ptolemy himself had lopped several thousand miles off the remarkably accurate calculations of his Greek predecessor Eratosthenes. Ptolemy's own estimate had been superseded by a larger figure given by the ninth-century Persian astronomer Alfraganus in his *Elements of Astronomy*, a revised summary of Ptolemy that was still the most popular textbook on astronomy in both East and West. Columbus, though, assumed that Italian miles were identical to Alfraganus's Arabic miles, whereas they were in fact substantially shorter, and so he decided that the globe was even more compact than Ptolemy had envisaged.

Having shrunk the globe, Columbus stretched Asia. Estimates of the distance going east from Portugal to the Chinese coast ranged as low as 116 degrees of longitude, a figure that left anyone contemplating going in the other direction a gaping 244 degrees of open sea to sail. Ptolemy was more helpful—he had calculated the distance at 177 degrees—but that still left the impossible task of sailing more than halfway around the globe. Instead, Columbus turned to Ptolemy's contemporary Marinus of Tyre, who had come up with a figure of 225 degrees, leaving just 135 degrees to cross.

Even taking the lowest estimate of the circumference of the earth and the highest of the breadth of Asia, no crew could have survived such a voyage without regular stops for fresh food and water. What Columbus needed was evidence of land en route, and for that he turned to Marco Polo. Polo had reported that Japan lay fully fifteen hundred miles off the coast of China, and in Columbus's mind Asia leapt even closer. He was convinced that Japan was little more than two thousand miles west of the Canary Islands, with China, the Spice Islands, and India itself just beyond. With a fair wind, he would be there in a couple of weeks. Better still, there was a potential stepping-stone to Japan: the island of Antillia, which Christians fleeing the Arab invasions of Spain were rumored to have settled in the eighth century and which legend placed far out in the Ocean Sea.

Columbus was brazenly running against the consensus of his age. Having been rebuffed in Portugal, he had no more luck pressing his case in Genoa and Venice. His brother Bartholomew set off to sound out the kings of England and France, while Christopher abandoned Portugal for its old enemy, Spain. There he obtained an audience with Ferdinand and Isabella, who were now ruling Castile and Aragon from Córdoba, and presented his plan. The two monarchs kept the would-be explorer on a well-padded leash while their advisers deliberated, but the matter dragged on so long that Columbus slipped away to Portugal to try his luck again.

It was at that point that Bartolomeu Dias docked in Lisbon on his return from the Cape of Good Hope. Dias's discovery was a disaster for Columbus: it finished off any Portuguese interest in far-fetched western routes to Asia. Columbus slunk back to Castile, only to hear that Ferdinand and Isabella's experts had judged that his "promises and offers were impossible and vain and worthy of rejection."

Two years later everything changed.

On January 2, 1492, after a bitter ten-year campaign, Ferdinand and Isabella conquered the Islamic kingdom of Granada. It was said that the last sultan turned back as he left the city, looked one final time on the sunset-red towers of the Alhambra Palace gently glowing above the rooftops, and burst into tears. "You weep like a woman for what you could not defend as a man," his mother scolded him, and they went on their way. The Alhambra's new owners processed up the hill to its gate dressed in gorgeously colored silks: a final reminder of the glorious heritage of al-Andalus.

The last vestige of Muslim rule in Western Europe had been wiped out, and the royal couple immediately sent word to the pope.

"It pleased our Lord," they piously boasted, "to give us a complete victory over the king and the Moors of Granada, enemies of our holy Catholic faith. . . . After so much labor, expense, death, and shedding of blood, this kingdom of Granada which was occupied for over seven hundred and eighty years by the infidel . . . [has been conquered]." Unmentioned in the letter was the awkward fact that for much of the previous quarter millennium, Granada had been a vassal of Castile and had supplied it not just with desirable Muslim goods but with troops.

The Reconquest was complete, the foundations had been laid for the unification of Spain, and the Catholic Monarchs—the title the appreciative pope bestowed on Ferdinand and Isabella—set about purifying their realm. They were confident that the Muslims and Jews who remained in Spain would soon convert, but the public mood quickly turned vengeful. Horror stories of Jews crucifying Christian children and eating their still-warm hearts sent shudders running down Spanish spines, and though no one could point to any child who actually went missing, several scapegoats were arrested and burned alive. The date of August 2, 1492, was fixed as the deadline for all Jews to embrace the Christian faith or face execution, and just seven months after the fall of Granada, the Atlantic port of Cadiz was choked with tens of thousands of Jews fleeing Spain. The rush to leave was so great that captains extorted huge sums for standing space in their holds, then dumped their passengers overboard or sold them to pirates. Others escaped to North Africa, only to be banned from its cities and left to die in the fields. Sepharad had long been a fairy tale, not a real place. Now it was a nightmare.

Muslims fared no better. A treaty that had promised freedom of worship in Granada, including the protection of mosques, minarets, and muezzin, was quickly torn up. Spain's Muslims were soon converted by force, then marched to the torture chamber to find out how genuinely they held the faith that had been thrust upon them. The Inquisition was Spain's proof of its ideological purity, its claim

to be the most righteous Christian nation, and yet another consequence of the long battle between Islam and Christianity in Iberia.
It was also economically ruinous. That same year the Ottoman sultan Bayezid II, Mehmet the Conqueror's son and successor, sent his
navy to Spain to rescue its Muslims and Jews alike. He welcomed
the refugees to Istanbul as full citizens, threatened with death any
Turk who mistreated a Jew, and ridiculed the shortsightedness of
Ferdinand and Isabella in expelling so many valuable subjects. "You
call Ferdinand a wise ruler," he scoffed to his courtiers, "when he
impoverishes his own country to enrich mine!" The fires of religious war that had been stoked in Iberia had blown back home, and
they would blacken Spain for centuries to come.

Having scoured the foreign matter from their kingdom, the
royal couple turned their attention abroad.

A few weeks after the conquest of Granada, Isabella summoned
Christopher Columbus and rejected his appeal against her experts'
verdict. The would-be explorer was trotting off disconsolately on
a mule when, back at the court, Ferdinand's finance minister spoke
up. Columbus, he pointed out, had already secured half his capital
from Italian investors. The enterprise would cost no more than one
of the weeklong fiestas thrown for foreign ambassadors, and surely
the royal treasury could shift some funds around and find the cash?
Perhaps Columbus's wealthy rescuer even then suspected that he
would be forced to put up most of the money himself; perhaps, as
a baptized Jew, he had his reasons for insisting that the reward of
converting Asia to the Holy Faith was well worth the risk.

Isabella sent a messenger haring after Columbus and caught him
preparing to board a ship to France. Columbus's terms were outrageous: he would receive 10 percent in perpetuity of all revenues
from any lands he discovered, he would be their governor and viceroy, and he would control every colonial appointment. Not least,
as soon as he reached land he would be appointed Admiral of the
Ocean Sea. Most of his conditions were accepted, but then, no one
really expected him to succeed.

Half an hour before sunrise on August 3, 1492, as the ships crammed with Jews edged east out of Cadiz, Columbus set sail west for Asia. As soon as his small fleet was safely under way, he sat down in the cramped cabin of his flagship, the *Santa María*, and wrote the first lines of his journal.

"IN THE NAME OF OUR LORD JESUS CHRIST," he began.

Columbus intended to present the book to Ferdinand and Isabella on his return, and it was addressed to them. He celebrated the Catholic Monarchs' great victory over the Moors of Granada and their righteous expulsion of the Jews, and he reminded them that he was embarked on an equally holy mission:

> Your Highnesses, as Catholic Christians and Princes devoted to the Holy Christian Faith and the propagators thereof, and enemies of the sect of Mahomet and of all idolatries and heresies, resolved to send me, Christopher Columbus, to the said regions of India, to see the said princes and peoples and lands and [to observe] the disposition of them and of all, and the manner in which may be undertaken their conversion to our Holy Faith, and ordained that I should not go by land (the usual way) to the Orient, but by the route of the Occident, by which no one to this day knows for sure that anyone has gone.

Soon, he added, he would return with such wealth "that within three years the Sovereigns will prepare for and undertake the conquest of the Holy Land. I have already petitioned Your Highnesses to see that all the profits of this, my enterprise, should be spent on the conquest of Jerusalem."

Columbus's innate seafaring instincts had been well honed during his years in Portugal, and five weeks after he left the Canaries he sighted land. He was a less natural leader of men; even in that short span his crew more than once threatened mutiny. The land turned out to be a small island, but the friendly natives signaled that there was a much larger island nearby. Columbus sailed off, convinced he was headed to Japan, even though the locals called the place Colba, and explored a length of the shore. By the time the *Santa María* ran aground on Christmas morning he had visited a third island, and he set his course for Spain.

The three islands would later be revealed as one of the Bahamas, Cuba, and Hispaniola, but Columbus was convinced he had reached Asia. True, the East was not everything he had expected. He had found a bush that smelled somewhat like cinnamon and nuts that, though small and inedible, with a little imagination did seem like coconuts. The mastic trees were evidently not producing that year, and the gold he took away turned out to be iron pyrite—fool's gold. The islanders in their thatched huts were clearly among the poorer subjects of the Great Khan, but undoubtedly, he told his journal, the emperor's palace lay nearby.

When the battered *Niña* was blown off course and had to put into Lisbon, the new Admiral of the Ocean Sea sent a note to King John. In it he asked permission to enter the royal harbor, where he would be safely out of reach of treasure seekers, and stressed that he had arrived from the Indies, not from Portuguese Guinea. When Bartolomeu Dias rowed over from his warship, alongside which Columbus had anchored, the admiral could not resist showing off the captive "Indians" he had brought back as proof of his staggering discovery.

Four days after his unintended arrival, Columbus set out to meet the Portuguese king. With him he took the strongest of his captives and a few trinkets he had picked up on the islands. Spices, gems, and gold were conspicuously missing.

The king was not in the best of moods. Two years earlier, his only son, Afonso, had fallen off his horse while riding along the banks of the Tagus and had died in agony in a fisherman's shack. The seventeen-year-old Afonso had been married to Isabella of Aragon, the oldest daughter of Ferdinand and Isabella. The Catholic Monarchs' only son was dangerously ill, and since Afonso had looked increasingly likely to become the heir to both Spain and Portugal, many suspected foul play. Ferdinand and Isabella had tried every diplomatic maneuver to declare the marriage void, but the young couple, having been married for purely political reasons, had inconveniently fallen in love. More to the point, Afonso was an excellent rider, and his Castilian valet disappeared after the accident and was never heard from again. The possibility that Ferdinand and Isabella had stolen John's thunder by discovering the sea route to India was a bitter pill to swallow.

Columbus made matters worse by insisting the king address him by his string of new titles and pointedly reminding him that he had turned down the dazzling opportunity he, the Admiral of the Ocean Sea, had given him. Some of John's advisers offered to kill the impudent sailor, but the king heard him out. It was far from clear just what Columbus had discovered, but he had clearly discovered something. When the admiral was done, John pointed out that he had found no spices. Columbus explained that he had only got as far as the outlying islands of Japan, and the king tried another tack. He was pleased the voyage had gone so well, he said insincerely, but under the terms of the papal bulls and the treaties between Castile and Portugal, the discoveries no doubt lay within Portugal's orbit. Columbus replied that he had obeyed his monarchs' orders and had not gone anywhere near Africa; besides, no treaty had anything to say about new lands to the west, since no one had suspected there were any.

John smiled noncommittally, retired in a fit of anger that he had let such a chance slip, and dashed off a letter to Spain in which he threatened to send warships to ascertain the truth and if necessary claim the new lands for Portugal. It was not a bluff: he had a fleet readied to follow Columbus if he set out again, and an alarmed Ferdinand dispatched an ambassador to beg John to delay its departure until the matter had been discussed.

On May 4, 1493, shortly after Columbus finally reached Spain, the pope weighed into the fray by dividing the world in two.

Pope Alexander VI was not a neutral referee. He had been born in Spain, and his family name—Borgia—would become a byword for blatant nepotism. He had four children by his favorite mistress, and he parceled out to them large chunks of papal land. Spanish cutthroats, whores, fortune hunters, and spies were running riot in Rome, and the papal palaces were reportedly great writhing heaps of bodies. Rodrigo Borgia was even rumored to have bribed his way into the chair of St. Peter, but his candidacy had certainly been helped by the intervention of his friend Ferdinand of Spain. The Catholic Monarchs had ample reason to believe that Rome was on their side.

On the pope's orders, a line was drawn from the top to the bottom of the map a hundred leagues west of the Azores and Cape Verde Islands, two archipelagos discovered in Henry the Navigator's time that were still Portugal's westernmost possessions. Everything to the west of the line henceforth belonged to Spain. The long bull that laid out the new world order pointedly failed to mention Portugal at all, and soon Lisbon's predicament took an even more dramatic turn for the worse. That September, another bull revoked every previous license given to the Portuguese to colonize new lands. Since it might happen, the pope explained, that the Spanish, while sailing west or south, might "discover islands and mainlands that belong or belonged to India," they were to be granted any lands whatsoever, "found and to be found, discovered and to be discovered, that are or may be or may seem to be in the route of navigation or travel towards the west or south, whether they be in western parts, or in the regions of the south and east of India." Given the confusion over the extent of India, that was sufficiently ambiguous to cover almost anywhere, including much of Africa.

The long decades of Portuguese discoveries were suddenly at risk of leading nowhere.

In a piece of timing that reeked of papal collusion, the Spanish sent Columbus back west two days before the second bull was formally issued. This time the Admiral of the Ocean Sea commanded a fleet of seventeen ships and an army of twelve hundred men. He explored the Bahamas and the Antilles, discovered new islands, landed at Puerto Rico, and returned to Cuba. The stakes were high, and Columbus urgently needed tangible proof that he could bring home the riches of the East. His men went around sniffing trees and convinced themselves they bore spices, though they were no more in fruit than before. Columbus ordered his new subjects to hand over a quarterly tribute in gold; if they refused, he threatened, they would have their hands cut off. Since they had no way of reaching their quota, many were mutilated and were left to bleed to death, while thousands poisoned themselves to end the ordeal. Hundreds more were rounded up, mothers dropping their babies on the ground as they fled, to be shipped back to Spain and sold; many died on the journey. The Spanish set about pillaging and slaughtering with savage abandon, and the stark shapes of countless gallows rose up across the New World.

With Columbus still away, King John sent his envoys to negotiate directly with Spain. He had the stronger navy, and he was well aware that Ferdinand and Isabella were deeply in debt and were busy building their new nation. Besides, his informants on the Spanish royal council had told him that the Catholic Monarchs were willing to treat the pope's outrageous edict as a negotiating position.

The two sides met at the little Spanish town of Tordesillas, just across the border from Portugal. With a papal envoy acting as mediator, the negotiators hammered out a compromise. The Spanish agreed to move the boundary line 270 leagues farther west, roughly to the midpoint between the Cape Verde Islands and Columbus's West Indies. The Portuguese recognized Spain's sovereignty over any lands her sailors found to the west, and the Spanish conceded to Portugal the rights to all lands to the east, Indian or otherwise. The new treaty was signed on June 7, 1494, and in Portugal it was hailed as a triumph. More accurately, it was the most outrageous cartel of all time, but in the end it raised as many problems at it solved. It was

left to a future joint voyage to establish just where among the straggling islands the measurement of 370 leagues began, but the voyage never took place. In any case, there was no way for men at sea
to determine their longitude with any precision, and so no way to
know whether they had crossed the line. Nor did anyone think to
ponder whether the line merely bisected the Western Hemisphere
or stretched all the way around the globe.

Spain and Portugal were locked in a furious race to spread their
faith and dominion far across the earth. Soon nations whose names
were barely known to Europe would discover that they had been
parceled out between two European powers they had never even
heard of.

PART II

EXPLORATION

CHAPTER 7

THE COMMANDER

THERE WAS NOTHING obviously remarkable about the two ships that were taking shape under a wooden scaffold on the waterfront dockyards of Lisbon. As the carpenters completed the stout framework of ribs and nailed the planking into place, the hulls began to take on the same tubby form, the same bluff bows and high, square stern, as the dozens of cargo ships that were riding at anchor in the busy port. They were clearly being strongly built—the timber had been specially felled in the royal forests—but they were definitely on the small side, perhaps eighty or ninety feet overall in length. Only a few insiders knew that they were destined for an astonishingly long voyage through uncharted seas.

The shipwrights signed off on the hulls, and tall masts were raised toward the sky and secured to the keels. The decks were laid around them. A high forecastle and an even taller sterncastle, robust enough to serve as a last redoubt if the ships were boarded, took shape above the main deck. Rudders were mounted on long posts and were fitted to the sterns, and heavy wooden tillers were joined to the tops of the posts. Bowsprits were fixed to the bows, where they poked jauntily upward like unicorns' horns to serve as extra masts. The carved figureheads of the ships' patron saints were installed in pride of place on the prows, and the fitting out began.

Relays of dockhands wheeled cartloads of stones up the steep gangplanks and tipped them into the holds to serve as ballast. Ropemakers rolled over large wooden drums wound with hawsers and riggings fashioned from twisted flax, and sailmakers carried great wings of canvas. Iron anchors were fitted to the bows, and spares were stowed in the holds. The topsides of the hulls were painted with a black tarry mixture to protect the wood against rot. Below the waterline, oakum—hemp fibers picked from old tarry ropes— was rammed into the seams between the planks, and hot pitch was poured on top to make a water-resistant seal. Then the bottoms were daubed with a foul-smelling mixture of pitch and tallow to ward off the clinging barnacles that acted as a drag on ships' hulls, as well as the tropical worms that turned them into sieves. Meanwhile teams of laborers hauled over trolleys bearing great guns, their barrels made from wrought-iron bars hammered together in the furnace and reinforced with iron hoops. Twenty were installed on each ship, some heavy bombards lashed to wooden beds, others lighter falconets mounted on simple forked bases or iron swivels, though even the smallest weighed hundreds of pounds. Cannon had been carried on Portugal's Africa-bound caravels since mid-century, and strengthened ships had been especially designed to support large bombards, but a keen observer might have paused to think that these two were more heavily armed than most.

A figure cloaked in black watched every step of the progress. Bartolomeu Dias had been ordered by King John to begin construction of the two vessels. He had abandoned the caravels, which he knew from bitter experience were too small for comfort on voyages that were now measured in years rather than months, as well as dangerously light and low in the water to weather fierce South Atlantic storms. Instead he had based his designs on the versatile merchant vessels that had evolved from the combined shipbuilding traditions of northern Europe and the Mediterranean. The new ships were square-rigged on the mainmast and foremast, with a single lateen sail on the mizzenmast. They were heavier, slower, and less capable of tacking against the wind than the caravels, but they were also roomier, steadier, and safer. Dias deliberately kept them compact—100 or 120 tons burthen, about twice the size of the caravels—to allow them to sail in shallow coastal waters and enter deep rivers. Even so, there was no disguising the fact that a hugely dangerous voyage was about to be undertaken in ships meant for lugging bulk goods around European shores.

From the start John had intended the two vessels to sail for India, but he would not even see them leave Lisbon.

On October 25, 1495, the king finally succumbed to a long illness that some ascribed to grief at the death of his son Afonso and others to regular doses of poison. Kissing a figure of Christ on the cross, penitent for his ferocious temper, and refusing to be addressed by his royal titles, "for I am only a sack of earth and worms," he died, aged forty, in great pain. His cousin and brother-in-law Manuel took the throne.

King Manuel I had come of age in a court whose air bred conspiracy. John had murdered Manuel's older brother and brother-in-law during his wars with the aristocracy. He had brusquely dismissed Manuel himself as a spineless incompetent, and he had only named Manuel as his heir after he had failed to legitimize his bastard son Jorge. The new king was a vain and capricious man—he was so fond of new clothes that half the court was dressed in his castoffs—and he was sufficiently fearful of rivals that the national assembly met just three times during his long reign. Like more than a few vain men, he was also a pious puritan who drank only water and recoiled at food cooked or dressed in oil. He was quickly nicknamed the Fortunate, both because of his unlikely route to the throne and because he came to power at the critical moment in the great enterprise fostered by his forebears. Yet just as those kings and princes, in their different ways, had each given the discoveries new impetus, so for good and ill the profoundly religious Manuel would leave a deep mark on history. John's brief blast of modernity had relapsed into a royal worldview that was still substantially medieval, and faith, not reasoned calculation, would drive Portuguese ships directly into the heart of the Islamic world.

The twenty-six-year-old king had no queen, and soon after his accession Ferdinand and Isabella offered up their daughter for the task. The new bride was the same Isabella of Aragon who had married John II's son—and Manuel's nephew—Afonso. Isabella had been grief-stricken at Afonso's death and had gone home to Castile and self-imposed widowhood. Being thrust into the arms of her beloved's uncle was a ghoulish prospect, and she attached conditions to her compliance. The marriage, Manuel was told, could only proceed if he followed her parents' lead and expelled from his kingdom every Jew who refused to convert to Christianity. King Manuel harbored dynastic designs on his neighbors' lands, and his feelings for his bride dramatically heated up when the Catholic Monarchs' only son died, at the age of nineteen, on the way to his sister's wedding. Manuel suddenly found himself the heir to Castile, and thus potentially the overlord of the entire Iberian Peninsula.

Tens of thousands of Jews had fled from Spain to Portugal in 1492. Now they were on the run again.

Officially, Portugal's Jewish population had long been confined to quarters known as *judiarias*. They were among the better ghettoes in Europe: the oldest, in Lisbon, occupied prime real estate between the business district and the harbor, to the annoyance of Christians who were allowed in during daytime but had to traipse around it at night. In practice, though, prominent Jews had always been able to live where they pleased. They were a vital part of Portugal's economy, and they had played an equally important role in the discoveries. Henry the Navigator had employed Jewish experts in navigation, cartography, and mathematics; Jews had acted as trusted royal advisers and, like the shoemaker Joseph and Abraham the rabbi, as envoys and explorers. Yet on December 4, 1496, every Jew in Portugal was ordered to leave the country within ten months on penalty of death. By the following Easter the synagogues had been boarded up, Hebrew books had been confiscated, and children had been torn from their families to be brought up in Christian households.

In private, Manuel was less enamored of the new policy than he publicly professed. He was well aware of the brain drain that

would accompany a mass exodus, and he had no intention of letting most of his Jewish subjects leave. Those who chose exile were
only allowed to book passage on ships specified by the king; when
they arrived at the port, clerics and soldiers met them and coerced
or cajoled as many as possible into being baptized. In September
1497 most of the rest were rounded up, brought to Lisbon, and
baptized by force; perhaps only forty held out. Manuel announced
that all converted Jews and their descendants would henceforth be
called "New Christians," and he decreed a long grace period during
which no inquiries into their faith would be allowed. He had fulfilled the letter of his in-laws' wishes while completely disregarding
their spirit, but it was a subterfuge born of pragmatism, not religious tolerance. To those who protested that forced conversion was
far worse than exile—worse even than death—he replied that it was
a matter for exultation, since it had saved thousands of souls from
eternal damnation and brought them to the True Faith. Manuel had
lit a long fuse, and the fires of religious purification would burn in
Portugal, too.

Without any prompting from the Catholic Monarchs, at the same
time Manuel expelled every Muslim from his lands. Reminders of
Portugal's Islamic past were still everywhere, including directly beneath the ramparts of Lisbon's royal Castle of St. George. A maze
of streets wound down the hill, linked by cobbled stairways and
crisscrossing at tiny squares adorned with tinkling fountains, with
every so often a chink in the whitewashed walls giving a glimpse
of courtyards planted with fragrant orange trees. Yet only a few
Muslims remained, and they were confined to a few backstreets,
where they were taxed, banned from commerce, and made to wear
a half-moon symbol on their turbans. Economically they were no
loss, and unlike the Jews, they were allowed to leave. Several years
before the Spanish had completed their rites of purification, Manuel
unraveled the final strands of convivencia and declared Portugal a
purely Christian nation.

The king's advisers had few issues with the new domestic policy;

they were far more alarmed by his increasingly grandiose talk about changing the world. Many took advantage of John the Tyrant's death to voice long-held fears about the foolishness of trying to reach India. The hope was doubtful, they pointed out, while the perils were great and certain. Even if a miracle saw them across hazardous seas to that vast and mysterious place, who knew what dangers awaited? How could they hope to conquer India, when they had found it hard just to hold on to Ceuta? Even worse, surely an attack on the East would make enemies of far richer powers, not least Egypt and Venice, and threaten the homeland itself?

The advice fell on deaf ears. Manuel had inherited a sacred obligation, and he was determined to reap the glory. God, he replied to his critics after failing to persuade them with rational arguments, would look after his kingdom, and he put the affair in His hands.

The young king's belief that a divine hand impelled the Portuguese explorations was shared by many of his people. It came from the conviction that Portugal, as a nation born of the Crusades, was obliged to carry the fight against Islam to the ends of the earth. But Manuel went much further. The year 1500 was fast approaching, and in the wake of the fall of Constantinople all manner of apocalyptic figures were hovering on the horizon. Encouraged by his pious wife, Manuel had developed a startling messianic streak. He had come to believe that the Holy Spirit had directly inspired him to usher in a new global age of Christianity. The armada he was about to send to the East was to prepare the way for the overriding objective of Manuel's new foreign policy: a Last Crusade to recapture Jerusalem, the great event from which, Scripture foretold, the Last Days of the world would follow as light follows dark.

As THE SHIPS neared completion, Manuel ordered his factor to equip them with all due haste. The dockhands installed two rowboats, a longboat and a lighter yawl, on each deck and stowed long oars for rowing the ships in an emergency. The holds filled up with chests of iron and stone cannonballs and shot, spare sails and tackle, compasses and sounding leads, Venetian hourglasses and assorted trading goods. An armory of crossbows and pole-axes, lances and boarding pikes, spears and swords was stashed safely away. Porters shouldered aboard cases of wine, oil, and vinegar and barrels of sea biscuit, salted meat and fish, and dried fruit. The plans assumed that the crews would be away from home for three years, but no one really knew how long the voyage might take.

Two more vessels completed the fleet. The *Berrio*, a swift caravel of fifty tons, was purchased from a pilot named Berrios. Finally, a storeship of two hundred tons was bought on the king's orders from a Lisbon shipowner.

With the armada almost ready, its commander took control of filling the final positions in his crew.

The man in charge was not Bartolomeu Dias. It was not just that he had caved in to his mutinous men on the brink of sailing into the East. Dias was a professional mariner, and his task had been to explore and chart. The leader of the new mission needed to know the ways of the sea, but he also had to be a diplomat and, if necessary, a war leader. His task was not just to reach India; once there, he was to negotiate alliances that would oust Islam and entrench Portugal as an Eastern power—and all before the Spanish arrived. He would need to inspire, cajole, and threaten, and if argument failed, he would have to persuade at the point of a gun. In short, what was required was a captain who could command sailors, an envoy who could converse with kings, and a Crusader fit to carry the standard of Christ.

It was a tall order, and there was not a huge pool of talent to draw on. Portugal was still a rough place dominated by the Church and the military nobility. Its clergy was heavily procreative, and standards at the new university of Lisbon were so low that successive popes forbade it to teach theology. A Polish visitor who arrived in 1484 was deeply unimpressed with what he found. Portuguese men of every class, he reported, were "coarse, poor, lacking in good manners and ignorant, in spite of their pretense of wisdom. They remind one of the English, who do not admit any society equal to theirs . . . they are ugly, dark, and black, almost like negroes. As for their women, few are beautiful; almost all look like men, though in general they have lovely black eyes." At least, he added, they were less cruel and insensate, more loyal, and more sober than the English.

Eventually Manuel's gaze settled on a young courtier, a *fidalgo*—a gentleman of the king's household—who was eager to make his fortune and who seemed to promise the right balance of skills.

Vasco da Gama was such an unexpected choice that not even the Portuguese chroniclers could agree on the reason for his appointment. One explains that his father was given command of the mission, and that Vasco inherited it on his death. Another asserts that Vasco's older brother Paulo was offered his father's command and declined on account of poor health, though he was apparently fit enough to offer to serve as captain of one of the ships. A third simply declares that the king caught sight of Vasco walking through the palace and took a shine to him. The most likely explanation is that men of quality were not exactly lining up to lead a voyage that would mean living for three years amid appalling conditions and would in all likelihood end in death. Vasco da Gama was the best man Manuel could find.

Gama's lineage did not mark him out for more than a modest position in life, and even the place and date of his birth are uncertain. He was most likely born in 1469 in Sines, a small Atlantic seaport a hundred miles south of Lisbon. Tradition holds his birthplace to be a simple stone house under the gray battlements of the small castle where his father Estêvão was the local *alcaide-mor*, the chief magistrate and military governor. It was a respectable situation for a respectable family. Gamas had fought against the Moors in the Algarve and had carried the royal banner into battle against Castile, while Vasco's mother, Isabel, was the granddaughter of an English knight named Frederick Sudley, who had arrived in Portugal to fight the Castilians and had never left.

Vasco da Gama was probably the third of five legitimate sons; he also had at least one sister and a bastard half brother who was also called Vasco da Gama. By the time he was born his father had secured a sinecure as a knight in the service of the exceptionally well connected Ferdinand, Duke of Viseu. Ferdinand was the nephew, adopted son, and heir of Henry the Navigator, the brother of Afonso V, the father of Manuel I, and the master of both the Order of Christ and the Order of Santiago. He was a patron worth having, and Estêvão rose to a middling position in the order of the Moor-slayers. In 1481 young Vasco was invited to one of its council meetings and was presented with its monkish habit, a white robe embroidered with a red cross, the lower arm of which was shaped like a plunging sword. From an early age, the novice Crusader was schooled in the warrior monks' ancient malice toward Muslims.

From the castle the little town straggled down the hillside to a tiny harbor formed by a small cape and a rocky spit, where fishermen landed their catch and mended their nets. No doubt Vasco and his brothers first learned the ways of the sea from them. As the son of a minor nobleman, he may have been sent to school in the venerable and scholarly town of Évora, and in his late teens he may have fought alongside his peers in Morocco. Certainly, from an early age he was headstrong and proud. One night in 1492, he was out walking with a squire of the royal household when a magistrate challenged the two stop-outs. Gama stubbornly refused to identify himself, and the magistrate tried to rip off his cloak. The two young men fended him off, and he had to be rescued from the brawl by several of his fellow officials.

Despite his quarrelsome nature, by 1492 Gama had made the leap from the provinces to the royal court. That year a French privateer—a privately owned ship licensed by a state to attack and plunder enemy shipping—captured a Portuguese vessel that was returning from Africa with a large cargo of gold. In retaliation King John had all the French ships in Portuguese waters seized, and he sent the twenty-three-year-old Vasco to carry out his orders in the ports south of Lisbon. According to the chronicles, the young man had already served in Portuguese "armadas and naval affairs" and had earned the king's trust. Three years later Gama was a fidalgo of King Manuel's household, a professed knight of the Order of Santiago, and the recipient of revenues from two estates. He was unpolished and somewhat brusque in manner, but intelligent, ambitious, and willing to risk his life to make his fortune. Perhaps there was a question mark over his quick temper, but if it was hardly a desirable trait for a diplomat, at least it seemed likely to keep his crew in check. Either way, the king clearly saw in him the self-confidence and strong will that marked out a born leader. That, more or less, is all we know about the inconspicuous man who carried the future of Portugal—some thought of Christendom itself—on his young shoulders.

VASCO DA GAMA'S first choice for his crew was his brother Paulo. The two were deeply attached, and though Paulo had no discernible experience of navigation, loyalty was the most prized quality of all when a fleet was out at sea.

The two newly built ships were named after the two saints carved on their figureheads. Vasco da Gama took the slightly larger *São Gabriel* for his flagship and appointed Paulo captain of its sister ship, the *São Rafael*. He put Nicolau Coelho, a close family friend, in command of the *Berrio*, and Gonçalo Nunes, one of his own retainers, in charge of the storeship. With his authority firmly established, he selected the rest of the officers from among Portugal's most experienced mariners.

On the *São Gabriel*:

Pêro de Alenquer, chief pilot. Responsible for navigating the whole fleet, he had sailed with Bartolomeu Dias to the Cape of Good Hope and had since returned to the Congo.

Gonçalo Álvares, sailing master. Skipper of the flagship, he had served on Diogo Cão's second voyage.

Diogo Dias, clerk. Brother of Bartolomeu Dias. The clerks, also known as scribes or scriveners, were among the few truly literate men on board and were in charge of keeping all records.

On the *São Rafael*:

João de Coimbra, pilot.

João de Sá, clerk.

On the *Berrio*:

Pêro Escobar, pilot. He had served in Fernão Gomes's fleets and had also sailed with Diogo Cão to the Congo.

Álvaro de Braga, clerk.

On the storeship:

Afonso Gonçalves, pilot.

Petty officers—including boatswains, who supervised the deck crew, and stewards, who had charge of the stores and provisions—completed the roster.

As important as the officers to the mission's success was a small group of interpreters. Among them was Martim Affonso, who had lived in the Congo and had learned several African dialects, and Fernão Martins, who had mastered Arabic during a spell in a Moroccan prison.

Less well regarded, but hardly less valuable, were the ten or twelve men known as *degredados*—"exiles"—who had been recruited in Lisbon's prisons. They were convicts whose sentences had been commuted by the king to service on the ships. At Gama's will, they were to go ashore in dangerous places to act as scouts or messengers, or to gather information until a later fleet picked them up.

The able and ordinary seamen were selected from veterans of the earlier voyages to Africa, and where possible from those who had sailed with Dias. Some were skilled in the various crafts that were vital at sea: among them were carpenters, caulkers, coopers, and ropemakers. Gunners, soldiers, trumpeters, page boys, servants, and slaves completed the full company, which altogether numbered between 148 and 170 men. In sharp contrast to many of the preceding voyages, the mission's importance meant there was no place for foreigners. Naturally, women were not allowed on board.

Crucially, one of the sailors was given the responsibility, or took it upon himself, to keep a journal of the voyage. His is the only eyewitness account that has survived, and though there have been repeated attempts to identify him with one or another of the crew, we do not know his name. In our story, we will respect his anonymity and call him the Chronicler.

KING MANUEL HAD overseen the preparations from the old Moorish castle overlooking Lisbon, but as the warm weather returned and the heaps of rubbish in the streets began to raise their usual stink, he had decamped to a more salubrious spot. For their farewell audience Vasco da Gama and his captains rode east out of the city, passing through lush orchards and vineyards and waving fields of wheat and barley, then struck out across the rolling plains of the Alentejo to Montemor-o-Novo.

There they rode up through the village to another forbidding Moorish fortress. Behind its long crenellated walls the court was gathered in ceremonial dress. The king launched into a lengthy, high-flown address that laid out the glorious deeds of his ancestors and his determination to bring them to a still more glorious conclusion.

"Praised be God, by the power of the sword we have driven the Moors from these parts of Europe and Africa," Manuel recalled, before reminding his audience why the impeding voyage was a natural continuation of that long campaign:

I have decided that nothing is more fitting for my kingdom—as I have often debated with you—than to search for India and the lands of the East. In those places, though they are far from the Church of Rome, I hope with God's mercy that not only may the faith of Our Lord Jesus Christ His son be proclaimed and adopted through our efforts, and that we may win fame and praise among men as our reward, but also that we will wrest new kingdoms, states, and great wealth by force of arms from the hands of the Infidels.

Since Portugal had won titles and riches by exploring Africa, he added, how much more could be expected by pursuing the quest to Asia and acquiring "those Eastern riches so celebrated by the ancient authors, some of which have, through their business dealings, aggrandized such mighty states as Venice, Genoa, Florence, and the other great powers of Italy!" He was not about to reject an opportunity offered by God, he pointedly declared, and nor would he insult his ancestors by abandoning their long Crusade and the great expectations of which it held out hope.

When he had finished lecturing the numerous court skeptics who were less than ecstatic at the royal obsession with fantastical quests, Manuel introduced the man he had selected to lead the mission. Vasco da Gama, he told the assembly, had given a good account of himself in everything he had been asked to do, and he had chosen him "as a loyal knight, worthy of such an honorable enterprise." The king conferred on the young commander a title that coupled together his responsibilities as both navigator and military leader. From now on, he was to be known as the captain-major of his fleet.

Manuel enjoined the other captains to obey their leader, and he urged them to pull together to overcome the dangers they were bound to face. Then every man filed past the king, knelt, and kissed his hand. When Vasco da Gama's turn came, Manuel presented him with a white silk banner embroidered with the cross of the Order of Christ, and the captain-major knelt to speak his oath of allegiance:

"I, Vasco da Gama, having been commanded by you, most noble and mighty king, my liege lord, to discover the seas and the lands of India and the East, do swear on the sign of this cross, on which I lay my hands, that I shall hold it high in your service and that of God, and not surrender it to any Moor, pagan, or other race of people I may meet, and in the face of all perils, whether water, fire, or sword, always to defend it and protect it, even unto death."

The king dismissed the visitors, and Gama returned to Lisbon. With him he carried his sailing orders and a packet of letters addressed to some of the great figures he was expected to meet on his travels—among them, of course, Prester John of the Indies.

On the eve of the great voyage, with excitement and trepidation contending in its leaders' minds, perhaps none paused to weigh their king's words very exactly. If they had, Manuel's yoking together of religion, politics, and economics would scarcely have made them doubt their cause. Even men who did not concern themselves with such matters knew that a healthy, wealthy nation was a sign of God's favor and a signal to carry on His work. To seek riches from cornering the spice trade was to strengthen the states that defended Christendom and to weaken Islam in turn. If the Italian mercantile republics suffered in the process, so be it; they had always seemed closer to the East than to the West.

Each man had his own motives for signing up; each man knew he was part of a larger pattern. Perhaps it was just as well, though, that they did not know just how large that pattern was. Vasco da Gama's mission was not merely to reach India; it was to win allies and wealth there that would enable the Portuguese to invade the Arab heartlands and push on to Jerusalem itself. It was an astonishing thing, to be sure, that Europeans would sail halfway around the known world to end up near the eastern shores of the Mediterranean, but such was the belief in Prester John, the marvelous East, and the value of spices. It was extraordinary, too, that more than seven hundred years of history had been placed in the hands of at most 170 men, but true believers had an answer to that, too. If the means seemed hopelessly inadequate to the end, God would surely intervene to make up the shortfall.

PORTUGAL'S QUEST TO explore the oceans had begun with Henry the Navigator, but it had been advanced by the collective endeavors of a nation. Before he set sail, Vasco da Gama was entrusted with the intelligence gathered by four generations of Portuguese princes, captains, and sailors. The bishop of Tangier—the same ardent cosmographer who had prepared Pêro da Covilhã for his mission—

furnished him with maps, charts, and reports, perhaps including the letters sent back by the intrepid spy himself.

The last provisions—fresh water, fruit, and bread, live chickens, goats, and sheep—had been loaded. The ships had left the docks and had anchored four miles downstream from the city. Nearby, behind a fine sandy beach, was the little village of Belém—the Portuguese name for Bethlehem. From the same spot a great armada had once sailed for Ceuta, and Henry the Navigator had built a little chapel to mark the spot. It had become a ritual for departing crews to pray there for success and a safe return, and on the evening of July 7, 1497, Gama rode out with his brother and his fellow officers and kept vigil until daybreak.

As the sun rose above the silvery waters of the Tagus, the sailors and soldiers rowed over to join them. The officers were clad in steel armor, their men in leather jerkins and breastplates. The seamen wore loose shirts, knee breeches, long hooded capes, and dark caps. With their families, lovers, and friends crowding the entrance, they squeezed into the somber chapel and celebrated a final mass. Then the bells rang and the cowled monks and robed priests led the worshippers to the shore, each man carrying a lighted taper and intoning a litany. By now huge crowds had gathered, and they surged toward the beach, murmuring the responses and "weeping and deploring the fate of those who now embarked, as devoted to certain death in the attempt of so dangerous a voyage." All knelt as a priest received a general confession and absolved the departing Crusaders of penance for their sins, and the full company rowed out to the ships.

The trumpets pealed, the drums beat out a tattoo, and the royal standard was hoisted to the peak of the captain-major's mainmast. The banner of the Order of Christ fluttered from the crow's nest, and the same Crusader cross flew from the mastheads of the three other ships. The anchors were heaved to the rhythmic chant of a sea chantey, the deck crews hauled on the halyards, and the sails slowly spread to reveal their own great crosses—the same crosses beneath which the Knights Templar had ridden into battle for the Holy Land.

A brisk breeze filled the sails and the fleet edged forward, imperceptibly at first, then with gathering pace. Even the youngest boy on board could hardly have failed to feel an electrifying jolt. In that moment a new life seemed to begin, a life that would be shared with unfamiliar companions and that would unfold in unknown places. As their homeland retreated into the distance a vast horizon opened ahead, bright with the anticipation of adventure but tinged with the fear of danger and death. Over the coming years the picture would be filled in; for now, it was enough to watch, and wait.

On board Paulo da Gama's ship the Chronicler made his first entry. He noted the date—Saturday, July 8, 1497—and the place of departure. Then he added a brief, heartfelt prayer: "May God our Lord permit us to accomplish this voyage in his service. Amen!"

CHAPTER 8

LEARNING THE ROPES

A T FIRST EVERYTHING went smoothly. On Saturday, July 15, a week after leaving Lisbon, the four ships came in sight of the Canaries. They stopped at dawn the next day for a couple of hours' fishing, and by dusk they had reached the broad inlet the earlier explorers, seemingly a long time ago now, had named the Gold River.

That night came the first taste of the dangers ahead. As darkness fell, a dense fog rolled in, and Paulo da Gama lost sight of the lanterns hung out on his brother's ship. The next day the fog lifted, but an eerie silence remained; there was no sign of the *São Gabriel* or the rest of the fleet.

The Portuguese had long experience of such mishaps, and the *São Rafael* made for the Cape Verde Islands, the first appointed rendezvous. At daybreak the next Saturday, after nearly a week of empty horizons, the lookouts sighted the first of the islands. An hour later the storeship and the *Berrio* appeared, heading toward the same point. The *São Gabriel*, though, was still nowhere to be seen, and as the vessels regrouped the sailors shouted anxiously across to one another. They continued on the planned route, but almost immediately the wind died away and the sails sagged. For four days they drifted in a calm until finally, on the morning of July 26, the watch made out the *São Gabriel* five leagues ahead. By evening they had caught up, and the brothers brought their ships close enough to confer. It had been a bad omen, and to general joy the trumpets pealed and the gunners fired off round after round from their bombards.

The next day the reunited fleet arrived at Santiago, the largest of the Cape Verde Islands, and anchored off sheltered Santa Maria Beach. Already the yards and rigging needed repairs, and the ships stayed for a week, taking on board fresh supplies of meat, water, and wood. On August 3 they headed back out to sea, first sailing in an easterly direction toward the African coast and then changing course to the south. They were now in the dreaded doldrums, the region near the equator where dead calms trapped ships and threatened crews with slow death by thirst and starvation, then gave way to changeful gusts and sudden storms. As the vessels pitched and rolled, even veteran sailors were racked with seasickness, and the novices clutched their stomachs and threw up overboard for days on end. During one squall the main yard on the *São Gabriel* cracked in two and the great square mainsail hung flapping like a broken wing; for two days the fleet lay to while a new spar was fixed into place.

When they resumed, the ships steered to the southwest—a heading that took them into the very center of the Atlantic.

On every previous known voyage, every captain—up to and including Bartolomeu Dias—had kept his ships close to land as they labored down the African coast. Not this time. Perhaps the Portuguese had set out on secret missions—so secret that no trace of them survived—to unravel the wind patterns of the South Atlantic. Perhaps they had realized that square-riggers were much less well equipped than caravels to sail against the southeast trade winds and the north-going current. Or perhaps it was a mix of happenstance and intuition that led Vasco da Gama to head for the open ocean in search of the great wind wheel that would whirl him in a counterclockwise arc to the southern tip of Africa. If so, it was an astonishingly risky move. If he sheered off at the right moment, he would catch the westerlies that would speed him to his destination. If he got it wrong, he would be buffeted back up the coast of Africa—or even worse, he could be blown off the known face of the earth.

Gama's men had no choice but to trust their commander. Their only companions were the great flocks of herons that kept pace with the fleet until they flapped off at night toward the faraway coast. One day a whale caused great excitement by surfacing nearby; perhaps, as on another voyage, the sailors made a racket with drums, pans, and kettles in case it decided to turn playful and capsize the ships. Otherwise they went about their tasks, and gradually they adjusted to the daily routine of life at sea.

Half hour after half hour, day and night, the sand ran in the hourglasses. Each time the ship's boy turned the glass the ship's bell rang; after eight bells, the watch changed. The departing seaman of the watch handed over to the new team by chanting an ancient ditty:

"The watch is changed, the glass is running! We shall have a good voyage if God is willing."

Each day on board began with prayers and hymns. Every morning, on the boatswain's orders, the deckhands pumped out the water that had seeped into the bilges, swabbed down the salty decks, and scraped the woodwork. The sailors adjusted the rigging, repaired tears in the sails, and made new lines from frayed ropes, while the gun crews cleaned their cannon and tested them with some target practice. To prepare to fire, they first loaded a stone ball into the long barrel, then rammed a powder charge into a cylindrical metal chamber. They wedged the open tip of the chamber into the breech end of the barrel, and put a smoldering stub of rope to a touchhole. It was best to keep one's distance when firing, as King James II of Scotland discovered in 1460:

And while this Prince, more curious than became him, or the majesty of a King, did stand near hand the gunners when the artillery was discharged, his thigh bone was dug in two with a piece of a mis-framed gun that brake in shooting, by the which he was stricken to the ground and died hastily.

With no mishaps and enough precharged chambers ready to be wedged in place, a slow but steady rate of fire could be maintained.

While the guns boomed, the servants and cabin boys polished the officers' steel armor and washed and mended their clothes. Belowdecks, the storekeeper kept a daily check on the equipment and provisions. The galley boy cooked the single daily hot meal over a sand-filled firebox on the deck, and the men ate the results off wooden trenchers with their fingers or pocketknives. Every crew member, from the captains down, received the same basic daily rations: a pound and a half of biscuit, two and a half pints of water, and small measures of vinegar and olive oil, together with a pound of salt beef or half a pound of pork, or rice and cod or cheese instead of the meat on fasting days. Delicacies like dried fruit were reserved for the top brass and would prove vital in preserving their health.

The officers passed on orders from the quarterdeck, the part of the main deck abaft the mainmast, or climbed the ladder to the poop deck that formed the roof of the sterncastle to get a better view. Meanwhile the pilots calculated their position and corrected their course. With the simple instruments at their disposal, it was a laborious business. As the ships sailed south, the angle of the Pole Star above the horizon declined, and by a fairly simple calculation their latitude could be established. To calculate the angle the pilots used a smaller, simplified version of an instrument that had evolved over the centuries for celestial observation. The mariner's astrolabe consisted of a brass circle suspended from a ring at the top to ensure it stayed as vertical as possible on the swaying deck. The alidade, a sight bar that pivoted from the center of the circle, was aligned with the star—assuming it was not obscured by clouds—and the altitude was read off a degree scale marked around the circumference. It was a recent invention, and since it was made of light sheet brass it tended to swing in a strong wind, which made accurate readings exasperatingly tricky to take.

Each night the Pole Star rode lower in the sky until finally, about nine degrees above the equator, it touched the sea and disappeared over the horizon. To the novices who were spending their first nights under southern skies, it seemed as if the world had sud-

denly flipped over. Even veterans paused to wonder before read-
justing themselves to the unsettling new shape of the heavens. The
Portuguese were the first Europeans to confront the problem of
navigating south of the equator, and without the Pole Star as their
guide they had learned to calculate their latitude by measuring the
altitude of the sun at noon. Squinting directly at the sun—again,
assuming clouds were not in the way—was not a pleasant task, and
since no timepiece had been developed that was accurate at sea,
numerous readings had to be taken to hit the meridian, the point
when it was at the top of its arc. Besides, the sun was a much less
reliable partner than the Pole Star. Since its ecliptic does not follow the celestial equator—in other words, since its path through
the sky does not line up with the earth's equator projected out into
space—its meridian angle from the equator varies on each day of
the year. A navigator who wanted to know his latitude by reference
to the sun therefore needed to compensate for that variable. Again,
the Portuguese had a head start. Gama's ships carried with them the
Rule of the Sun, a series of lengthy tables and detailed instructions
that King John II's committee of mathematicians had drawn up in
1484. The tables gave a figure for the declination of the sun—its
angle from the equator at noon—on any given day, and the instructions told a navigator how to apply the figure to his reading. Faced
with such a laborious series of tasks, many preferred to forgo celestial navigation and trust their gut instincts, but Vasco da Gama was
a stickler for the rules.

So much for latitude; no useful way whatsoever had been found
to determine longitude. The navigators relied on dead reckoning,
which amounted to an informed guess about the speed of travel
constantly adjusted by the direction shown on the compass. That
all-important instrument was carried in a recess under the sterncastle, near to the spot where the tiller poked through the stern.
The magnetized needle was attached to a card marked with the
compass rose and set on a pivot in a round bowl; the apparatus was
lit by a tiny oil lamp and was encased in a hooded wooden box.

Spare needles and cards and lumps of adamant to remagnetize the needles were carefully stashed away. As the officer of the watch shouted instructions to change course and the helmsman heaved on the heavy tiller to turn the rudder, he kept a close eye on the compass at his side. With his vision obstructed by sails and forecastle, sailors and deck equipment, it was often the only way he knew where he was headed.

Between carrying out their duties a few men read books, and more gambled with dice and cards. Some fished with hooks, nets, and harpoons, and cleaned, filleted, and salted any of the catch that was left over. Others struck up a tune or sang a sea song; a few kept dogs or cats, which hunted down the population of rats and mice that gnawed their way through the ship's stores. Many merely ate and drank, lounged about, talked, argued, and occasionally brawled, lubricated by the wine ration of as much as two liters per man per day. All prayed. Cast on the unknown deep, with death always figuring on the horizon, the need for a beneficent god to guide their path was always in their minds. They prayed alone, while they worked, or in groups, sometimes led by the captain. They worshipped before the shipboard shrines, read prayer books and rubbed amulets, and observed holy days with lengthy devotions and festivities.

Each day ended with a religious service, and when it was over the night watches were set and the lanterns were hauled up the masts. The captain repaired to his cabin in the sterncastle, the officers to their bunks in the cabin below and in the forecastle. The rest of the men slept where they could—beneath the raised gang boards that ran between the castles, in the recess under the sterncastle, or on close tropical nights when the compartments smelled foul, in the open air; the top of the hatch, the only flat spot, was always in demand. On the much smaller caravel, where there was only one cabin and even less privacy, the men shifted even closer against one another.

August wore on, and the crews grew sick from the burning

heat. What food was left quickly went corrupt. The water began to reek, and the men held their noses while they drank. Strong odors were everywhere. Men hauling sails and anchors in the burning sun worked and slept in the same clothes for months on end. At sea their hair was never cut and seldom washed—seawater was too briny, and fresh water too precious—and their scalps teemed with lice. They squatted between the cables and gear on the forecastle and used an open box as a toilet, but their aim was at the mercy of the waves, storms made it impossible to maintain even that minimum of decorum, and the results invariably ended up being washed belowdecks. A passenger on a later Portuguese voyage to the East drew a painful picture of the worst moments:

> Amongst us was the greatest Disorder and Confusion imaginable, because of the Peoples Vomiting up and down, and making Dung upon one another: There was nothing to be heard but Lamentations and Groans of those who were straightened with Thirst, Hunger, and Sickness, and other Incommodities, and Cursing the time of their Embarkment, their Fathers and Mothers, and themselves, who were the cause thereof; so that one would have thought they had been out of their Wits, and like Mad-men.

When the scorching heat and the storms and calms near the equator were behind him, a new scourge struck the hapless sailor. Hot rain fell in sheets along the African coast and, he complained,

> afterwards turned to Worms, if that which was wet was not perfectly dried. It was a wonderful trouble to me, to see my Quilt wet, and Worms crawling all over. These rains are so stinking that they rot and spoil, not only the Body, but also all Cloths, Chests, Utensils, and other Things. And not having any more Cloths to shift my self withal, I was forced to dry upon me that which I wore, with my Quilt, by lying thereupon; but I was

well fitted for that; for the Fever, with a great pain in the Reins, took me in such a manner, that I had a fit of Sickness, almost, the whole Voyage.

September passed, then October, with few distractions except for a school of whales and huge herds of seals that floated like smooth boulders on the waves. By now, though, the fleet had reached the southwesternmost point in its great loop around the Atlantic, and the westerly winds were driving it at full speed back to Africa. Finally, on Wednesday, November 1, clumps of gulfweed began to float past: a telltale sign that land was near.

That Saturday, two hours before daybreak, the night watch lowered the lead and line and sounded the depths. They measured 110 fathoms, or a mere few hundred feet of water. From the latitude, they reckoned they were a mere thirty leagues north of the Cape of Good Hope.

At nine o'clock in the morning the watchkeepers sighted land. The ships drew close together, and every man put on his best clothes. The mightily relieved crews ran up the flags and standards, and the gunners blasted off the bombards.

It had been a grueling journey. The men had not seen land for ninety-three restless days, and it was a desperately long time since they had had fresh water or food. Yet the unprecedented sweep of the ocean had paid off handsomely: by avoiding the contrary coastal winds and currents they had shaved precious weeks off the voyage. In the infancy of his command, Vasco da Gama had discovered the fastest and surest sailing route from Europe to the Cape of Good Hope.

It was the first bold move of a man who was determined to push himself and his crews to the limits to attain his otherworldly goal.

THE SHIPS TACKED close to the coast, but the shoreline bore no resemblance to the charts and sailing instructions drawn up by Bartolomeu Dias. They stood out to sea again to catch the wind, and three days later they tacked back to land.

This time they found themselves in front of a wide bay backed by low-lying plains. Dias's veterans had not seen it before, and the explorers named it St. Helena Bay.

On Vasco da Gama's orders, the chief pilot set out in a boat to take soundings and find a safe anchorage. The bay turned out to be sheltered and crystal clear, and the next day, November 8, the fleet dropped anchor a short distance from the shore.

Four months at sea had already wreaked havoc with the ships. One by one they were run up into the shallows, and the arduous process called careening began. The stores were piled up against one side of the hold, and with some concerted tugging on cables the vessels were heeled over. The sailors climbed up ladders onto the exposed hull and scraped it clean of the barnacles that encrusted the wood like thousands of tiny volcanoes. They scrubbed off worms, snails, and weeds, and drove fresh oakum into the seams with a caulking iron. A fire was lit on the beach, and boiling pitch was poured along the seams. The same operation was carried out on the other side, then the ship was hauled back onto an even keel and towed out to sea. By now the ballast was sodden with foul bilgewater, reeking from the rubbish and ordure that had been washed belowdecks and crawling with rats, cockroaches, fleas, and lice. The noxious slurry was shoveled out and new ballast was tipped in. The decks were scrubbed and scraped, the sails were repaired, and the damaged spars and worn ropes were replaced with spares.

As the work got under way a landing party set out to reconnoiter the shore, find fresh water, and gather wood. A few miles to the southeast they came across a river that meandered through a grassy plain, and nearby they ran into a group of locals.

"The inhabitants of this country are tawny-colored," noted the Chronicler. "Their food is confined to the flesh of seals, whales and gazelles, and the roots of herbs. They are dressed in skins, and wear sheaths over their virile members." They carried spears of olive wood tipped with a sliver of fire-hardened horn, and packs of dogs accompanied them wherever they went. The Portuguese were surprised to find that the dogs barked just like the ones back home, and the birds, too—cormorants, gulls, turtledoves, crested larks, and many others—were equally familiar.

The day after the fleet arrived, Vasco da Gama went ashore in his ship's boat with several of his crew. While he was setting up a large wooden astrolabe to take a more accurate reading of the latitude than was possible at sea, his men spotted a party of Africans gathering honey. The bees made their hives on the drifts of sand that piled up around bushes near the shoreline, and the locals were busy smoking them out. The sailors crept up on them, grabbed one man who was conveniently small in stature, and dragged him off to the *São Gabriel*. Since he was clearly terrified, the captain-major sat him at his table and ordered two ship's boys—one of them a black slave—to sit beside him and tuck into a good meal. Gradually the visitor began to help himself to the food, and by the time Gama returned he was almost gregarious. He stayed on board overnight, and the next day Gama dressed him in handsome clothes, gave him a few trinkets—some bells, crystal beads, and a cap—and set him free.

Soon he reappeared on the shore, as Gama had hoped, with more than a dozen companions. The captain-major had his men row him to the beach, and once there he laid out before the Africans small samples of cinnamon, cloves, seed pearls, and gold. In gestures he asked if they had anything similar to sell. When it became clear that they had never seen anything of the sort, he handed out some more bells and tin rings and returned to his ship.

The next day another group appeared, and the day after, a Sunday, forty or fifty locals gathered on the shore. After dinner the Portuguese landed and exchanged some small coins for conch shells, which the Africans wore as earrings, and fans made from foxtails. The Chronicler, in search of a souvenir, bartered one copper coin for "one of the sheaths which they wore over their members, and this seemed to show that they valued copper very highly."

When the commerce was over, a loudmouthed sailor named Fernão Velloso asked Gama if he could accompany the natives to their village to see how they lived. The amateur anthropologist would not be dissuaded, and at his brother's urging Gama gave in. While most of the party returned to the ships, Velloso went off with the Africans to feast on freshly roasted seal served with roasted roots. Paulo da Gama and Nicolau Coelho, meanwhile, had stayed behind with some men to collect driftwood and lobsters from the shore. When they looked up they saw a pod of young whales gliding between the ships in pursuit of shoals of small fry in the shallows. Paulo and his crewmen jumped into their boat and set off in hot pursuit, brandishing harpoons that were attached to the bow by ropes. The sailors took aim, and a barbed head pierced one whale's back. As the pain hit, it thrashed and dived, pulling the line taut in seconds. The little boat flipped up and lurched into the bloody foam; only the shallow coastal water, which made the whale run against the bottom and cool down, stopped the men from being dragged out to sea.

A little later, as the sportsmen and foragers were returning to the ships, Fernão Velloso came pelting down a hill with his dining companions in hot pursuit. When he had eaten his fill, the Africans had gestured in no uncertain terms that it was time for him to go back to his people. He had run off in a panic, and he began hollering to the fleet.

Gama had been watching for his return. He signaled the boats to turn back and rescue the would-be ethnographer, and in case of more trouble he ordered his men to row him to the shore.

As Velloso pounded down the sands toward the boats, the Africans stayed back in the cover of the bush. The sailors, though, were in no hurry to rescue their cocky comrade. After four months they had already had enough of his boasting, and they decided to make him sweat it out. They were still enjoying the joke when two armed Africans ran purposefully onto the beach. The mood abruptly changed, but before the rescuers could climb ashore, the rest of the Africans emerged and unloosed a fierce volley of stones, arrows, and spears at the boats. Several men were wounded—including

Vasco da Gama himself, who had no sooner appeared on the scene than he was shot in the leg with an arrow—and the landing party retreated pell-mell to the fleet. Gama salved his wound with a paste of urine, olive oil, and theriac, and he salved his pride by ordering his crossbowmen to fire at will toward the shore.

The captain-major decided he had been taught a salutary lesson, and it would stay with him for the rest of his time at sea.

"All this happened," recorded the Chronicler, "because we looked upon these people as men of little spirit, quite incapable of violence, and had therefore landed without first arming ourselves."

NOTHING MORE WAS seen of the locals, and the Portuguese stayed for four more days to finish their repairs. On November 16, at first light, they left the bay and stood out to the south-southwest. Two days later they caught their first unmistakable glimpse of the Cape of Good Hope. Its stage set of mountains glowed in the setting sun, a milestone as monumental as the decades-long journey it marked.

Once seen, the Cape proved tricky to pass. The winds howled along the coast from the south, and for four days the ships battled out to sea and were blown back to land. Finally, at midday on November 22, with the wind now astern, they doubled the Cape. Only one fleet had sailed these waters before, and Bartolomeu Dias had only seen the legendary landmark on his way home.

The trumpeters blasted a fanfare, and the crews thanked God for guiding them to safety.

For three days the ships hugged the coast, passing lush woods and the mouths of numerous streams and rivers, until they reached an enormous bay, six leagues deep and six leagues wide at its mouth. This was the place where Dias had had an unfortunate encounter with some herdsmen, and Gama was forewarned.

The explorers sailed into the bay, past a little island whose shores were solid with seals, and anchored off the beach. It was to be a long stay. The supplies on the three main ships had already run low, and the contents of the storeship needed to be transferred to them.

A week passed with no sign of any inhabitants; only a mysteriously large number of fat cattle roamed the shores. Then, on December 1, ninety or so men emerged from the hills, and some came down for a walk along the beach. At the time most of the company were on the *São Gabriel*, and as soon as the Africans appeared they armed and launched the ship's boats. As they neared the shore, Gama threw handfuls of little bells onto the sand, and the curious locals picked them up. After a moment they came right up to the boats and took some more bells from the captain's hand. The veterans of Dias's voyage were perplexed; perhaps, the sailors surmised, before their recent skirmish the news had traveled that the visitors meant no harm and gave away gifts.

Gama, who was still recovering from his injury, was less sanguine. He told his men to row away from the overgrown spot where the Africans were gathered and make for the open beach, where there was less chance of a surprise attack. At his gesture the locals followed.

The captain-major landed with his captains, soldiers, and crossbowmen, and he signaled the Africans to approach in ones or twos. In return for his bells and a few red nightcaps, he was presented with some fine ivory bracelets. Clearly elephants were plentiful; great piles of their dung were all around.

The next day two hundred locals appeared on the beach, leading a dozen fat oxen and cows and four or five sheep. The fattest ox was ridden by a man sitting on a litter of twigs supported by a reed packsaddle; the other beasts had sticks through their nostrils, which turned out be signs that they were for sale. After months of chewing on dried and salted meat, an ox roast was a mouthwatering prospect. The Portuguese made straight for the shore, while their hosts produced some flutelike instruments, struck up a tune, and began to dance. Gama was now in high spirits, and he ordered the trumpeters to play. The Portuguese stood up in the boats and danced along, and the captain-major joined in.

The explorers bought a black ox for the bargain price of three bracelets and feasted off it for Sunday lunch the next day. "We found him very fat, and his meat as toothsome as the beef of Portugal," noted the Chronicler.

Both sides began to relax in the festive atmosphere. More curious locals began to appear, this time bringing their women and little boys as well as herds of oxen and cows. The women stayed back on a low hill just behind the shore, while the men gathered in groups on the beach, dancing and playing more tunes. As the Portuguese arrived the older men approached them, fanning themselves with more foxtails, and the two sides managed to communicate in signs. It all seemed thoroughly cheery until the sailors noticed the young men of the tribe crouching in the bush, weapons in hand.

Gama drew aside his African translator Martim Affonso and told him to try to buy another ox with some more bracelets. The Africans took the bracelets, drove their cattle into the bush, and pulled Affonso to a nearby watering hole where the Portuguese had been filling their barrels. Why, they angrily asked, did the strangers take away their precious water?

The captain-major was starting to get a bad feeling about the whole situation. He drew his men into a huddle and shouted to Affonso to get away and join them. The Portuguese retreated to the boats and rowed along the shore to the open space where they had first landed. The locals followed, and Gama commanded the soldiers to strap on their breastplates, string their crossbows, grasp their lances and spears, and line up on the beach. The show of strength seemed to work, and the Africans backed away.

Gama ordered the soldiers to the boats, and they rowed off a short distance. The captain-major was anxious, the Chronicler recorded, to avoid killing anyone by mistake, "but to prove that we were able, although unwilling to hurt them, he ordered two bombards to be fired from the poop of the longboat." The Africans were now sitting quietly, just off the beach in front of the bush. When the guns went off and the balls went whistling overhead they jumped up and fled, dropping their animal skins and weapons in their panic.

Two men ran out a minute later to gather up the scattered possessions, and they all disappeared over the brow of the hill, driving their cattle before them. No more was seen of them for days.

As the work of cannibalizing the storeship for spare parts and wood came to an end, Gama had a fire set in the stripped hull. For several days the burning hulk smoldered and smoked like a somber warning signal. The sailors, though, had quickly forgotten about the troubles onshore—that was the captain-major's problem—and were more interested in a bit of recreation. One party rowed to the island in the middle of the bay to take a closer look at the colony of seals. The animals were so tightly packed that from a distance the island itself seemed a mass of smooth, shifting stones. Some were as big as bears, roared like lions, and attacked men without fear; spears thrown by the burliest sailors glanced off their skin. Others were much smaller and cried like goats. The Chronicler and his party of sightseers counted three thousand before they gave up, and to amuse themselves they fired their bombards at them. There were strange birds, too, that brayed like asses and were "as big as ducks, but they cannot fly, because they have no feathers on their wings." They were Cape penguins, and the explorers massacred them, too, until they grew bored.

By their twelfth day in the bay the three remaining ships were almost ready to leave, and the sailors set out once again to fill the water casks. On one sortie they took with them one of the padrões, the stone pillars bearing the royal coat of arms, that they had carried from Portugal. Gama had had a large cross made out of the mizzenmast of the storeship, and after the pillar was set up, it was fitted to the top.

The next day, as the little fleet set sail, the Africans finally emerged from the bush. They had been keeping a watch on the uncouth strangers all along, and they seized their chance for revenge. A dozen men ran out and smashed the cross and the pillar to pieces in full view of the departing ships.

It was now December 7, and there was a palpable mood of

nervous excitement on board. Bartolomeu Dias had turned back home just a little farther ahead, and Vasco da Gama's men were about to trespass on nature's secret places. Many were convinced they were sailing toward an uncrossable threshold, and their worst fears soon seemed to be confirmed.

No sooner had the fleet left the bay than the wind dropped, the sails sagged, and the ships lay all day at anchor. The next morning—the day of the Immaculate Conception, the Chronicler piously recorded—they moved off, only to sail into a terrifying storm.

The waves reared into watery cliffs. The vessels heaved toward the inky clouds and dropped into the abyss. A piercing cold wind battered at the stern, and everything went pitch dark. With the ships under full canvas the prows plunged under the waves, and the captains hastily ordered the foresails struck.

Freezing seawater crashed on the decks and soaked the sailors' woolen cloaks. Belowdecks all hands were on the pumps, but water seeped and washed in faster than they could expel it, and the holds flooded. The howling heavens drowned out the pilots' commands, but even with several men hanging on to the tiller, the ships were almost impossible to control. As the tempest reached its worst Nicolau Coelho's caravel disappeared from sight, and the most seasoned sailors thought they had seen their last day. They wept and confessed to each other, and struggling to form a file behind a cross, they prayed God to show mercy and preserve them from disaster.

Finally the skies lightened, and at sunset the lookouts spotted the *Berrio* on the horizon, fully five leagues away. The two ships hung out their signal lights and lay to. Around midnight, at the end of the first watch, Coelho finally caught up, but only by chance. He had not seen the other ships until he was almost upon them; he had sailed in their direction because the spent wind gave him no choice.

The fleet had been blown far out to sea, and once more it made for land. Three days later the watchkeepers spotted a chain of low islands. Pêro de Alenquer recognized them at once: five leagues farther, on a headland that jutted out from the coast, was the last pillar erected by Bartolomeu Dias.

The next day, December 16, the three ships passed the mouth of the river where Dias's mutinous crew had forced him to turn around. They were now sailing where no European—almost certainly no man—had ever sailed before. That night they lay to, and specters of the dangers ahead filled every half-sleeping mind.

The next day they sailed briskly on with a following westerly wind, but in the evening the wind sprang around to the east. The ships were forced to stand out to sea again, and for two days they tacked as best they could. When the wind finally switched round to the west they headed back to land to find out where they were. They soon saw a familiar sight: an island where Dias had erected a cross, sixty leagues back from where they had reckoned they should be. A strong offshore current had dragged them halfway toward the bay they had left nearly two weeks before.

Many of the sailors were sure they had hit an invisible wall that divided East from West. Vasco da Gama, whose steely determination was daily becoming more evident to his men, was having none of it. The fleet resumed its course.

This time a stiff stern wind blew for three or four days, and the ships inched forward against the current.

"Henceforth," noted the Chronicler, who was as relieved as the rest, "it pleased God in His mercy to allow us to make headway! We were not again driven back. May it please Him that it be thus always!"

They were now sailing past lush woodland, and the farther they went, the higher the trees reached toward the heavens. It seemed like a sign, and sure enough, the coast was now clearly trending to the northeast.

After decades of questing and centuries of dreaming, the first Europeans had sailed into the Indian Ocean.

CHAPTER 9

THE SWAHILI COAST

CHRISTMAS DAY, 1497, passed in prayers before the shipboard shrines. In honor of the date the explorers named the land they were passing Natal, but there was no time to rest. The charts had run out; from now on, blank sheets had to be filled in. Everything needed to be observed and recorded, and there were the usual trials—a cracked mast, a snapped anchor cable, an adverse wind—to slow things down still more. Worst of all, the drinking water was nearly finished and the cooks were reduced to boiling salted meat in salty seawater, with nauseating results. The need to put into land was becoming urgent.

The new year was eleven days old when the watchkeepers sighted the mouth of a small river. The captain-major gave the order to anchor near the coast, and the following day a landing party set out in the boats. As they approached they saw a large crowd of men and women watching them. All were remarkably tall—much taller than the Portuguese.

Gama, who was leading from the front as usual, ordered Martim Affonso to land with a companion. The Africans gave them a quietly courteous welcome. Among them was one who appeared to be the chief, and as far as Affonso could make out, he seemed to be saying that the travelers were welcome to take anything they needed from his country.

In return Gama sent the chief a red jacket, a pair of red pantaloons, a red Moorish cap, and a copper bracelet. As night fell and the boats returned to the ships, Affonso and his companion set off with the Africans to their village. Along the way the chief shrugged on his new clothes. "Look what I have been given!" he announced, either in surprise or pleasure, to anyone who came up. They arrived in the village to general applause, and the chief paraded around the thatched houses. When he retired for the night the visitors were shown to a guesthouse and were fed with millet porridge and chicken. They slept lightly, not least because whenever they opened their eyes they found groups of villagers peering down at them.

The next morning the chief appeared with two men who were to lead the sailors back to the ships. He gave them some chickens for their commander, and he added that he would show their gifts to a great chief, whom the Portuguese took to be the king of the land. By the time Affonso, his companion, and their two guides had made their way to the landing place, they had attracted a two-hundred-strong following.

The Portuguese named the country the Land of Good People. It seemed to be densely populated, with many chiefs but twice as many women as men. The warriors, whose constant battles with neighboring tribes no doubt had much to do with that imbalance, went armed with long bows and arrows, spears with iron heads, and daggers with pewter hilts and ivory sheaths. Both men and women wore copper ornaments on their legs and arms and in their braided hair. Near the villages were pools in which seawater was carried in dried, hollowed-out gourds and was evaporated to obtain salt. The travelers eagerly deduced that they were on the verge of more developed lands. Even so, they stayed for five days, their ships riding at anchor on the waves, trading linen shirts for large quantities of copper and replenishing their water supplies. This time the Africans helped them carry the casks to the ships, but before they were finished a favorable wind blew along the coast and beckoned the explorers on.

After nine days' sailing the thick woods parted to reveal the mouth of a much larger river, guarded by sandy islets covered with mangrove thickets. Gama decided to risk a little reconnaissance, and on his orders the *Berrio* entered the waterway. A day later the two larger ships followed.

On either side were flat, marshy plains dotted with clumps of tall trees that produced strange but edible fruits. The people were dark, strong, and naked except for short cotton loincloths. The Portuguese quickly noticed that the young women were remarkably good-looking, even though their pierced lips were hung with a daunting array of twisted tin ornaments. The Africans, the Chronicler noted, took equal delight in the strange newcomers. Groups rowed up in dugouts to proffer the local produce and climbed on board without hesitation, as if the Europeans were old friends. They left with bells and other trinkets and led the sailors to their village, and they readily offered them as much fresh water as they could take.

A few days later two men wearing caps of green satin and embroidered silk rowed up to the fleet. They were clearly the local nobility, and they looked over the ships with a connoisseur's eye. One of their young men, they explained, had traveled from a distant country, and he had seen vessels that were just as big as these.

"These tokens," the Chronicler wrote, "gladdened our hearts, for it appeared as if we were really approaching the bourne of our desires." The Portuguese were less happy when the two men turned up their noses at the gifts they were offered—an alarming snub when they were still far from India. Still, the haughty gentlemen had huts built for them on the riverbank, and for seven days they sent servants to barter reddish dyed cloths for the strangers' trinkets until they grew bored and paddled back upstream.

The Portuguese stayed on the river for thirty-two days. Gama had decided his men deserved a rest after their trials, and they evidently enjoyed the company of the attractive and obliging women. At the same time they repaired the mast of the *São Rafael* and once again careened all three ships.

So far East Africa had turned out to be some kind of paradise, but danger lurked in the warm, moist air. Many of the crew fell seriously ill. Their feet and hands ballooned, and their legs broke out in hundreds of tiny spots. Their gums puffed up so far over their teeth that they were unable to eat, and their breath stank unbearably. Their eyes bled, and their eyeballs began to protrude from their shrunken faces. Seven months from home, the dreaded scurvy had struck.

Paulo da Gama, a kindly and solicitous man, visited the sick night and day, consoling them and dispensing remedies from his own stores. There was no doctor among the crew, though since ship's surgeons—who also acted as barbers—tended to be like the sort encountered by the Italian traveler Pietro della Valle, "a man of such unprepossessing appearance, that even in perfect health I would have sickened if he had felt my pulse," their effectiveness was anyway limited. The worst afflicted developed suppurating wounds that left them paralyzed, and their teeth dropped out. Perhaps thirty men died while the survivors stood by, baffled and helpless to act.

Eventually Vasco da Gama gave the order to move on. Before leaving he erected the second of his pillars and made a note of the name his men had given to their anchorage: the River of Good Omens. The signals, though, were decidedly mixed. The fleet had hardly passed the bar of the river when the flagship ran aground on a sandbank. Everyone was about to give it up for lost when the rising tide refloated it just in time.

THE LITTLE ARMADA regained the open sea on Saturday, February 24. At night the pilots set a course to the northeast to keep clear of the coast, and for the next week they followed the same heading, stopping at night to avoid missing anything but seeing little of note except for a few scattered islands.

On March 1 a larger group of islands heaved into view, this time close to the shore. It was growing late, and the ships stood out again and lay to, waiting until the morning to survey the scene.

The dawn light revealed a large flat lozenge of coral, fringed with white sand and spiked with green vegetation, embraced by a broad sweep of the mainland. Two smaller islands guarded the approach from the sea. Gama decided to send in the caravel first, and Nicolau Coelho set his sails and edged forward into the bay. It was soon clear that he had misjudged his approach, and the *Berrio* headed straight for a sandbank. As he was attempting to put about and dislodge himself, he saw a little flotilla of boats set out from the main island.

By now the other two ships had come up behind, and the island-ers excitedly tried to flag them down. The Gama brothers sailed on regardless to the sheltered roadstead between the mainland and the island, and with the welcoming committee in hot pursuit they cast anchor. Seven or eight of the boats came up to the ships, and a small orchestra struck up a tune. The Portuguese recognized their long, straight trumpets as the same instruments played by the Moors of North Africa.

The rest of the men in the boats warmly beckoned the new-comers to follow them into the island's port. Gama invited some of them on board, and they ate and drank their fill with the crew.

The Portuguese quickly realized the islanders spoke Arabic. This was both promising and puzzling. They were clearly Muslims, but they were much friendlier than any Muslims the explorers had met before.

Vasco da Gama decided he needed to find out more about where he was and what kind of people were there. Once again he ordered Nicolau Coelho to go ahead into the harbor and take soundings to see if the larger ships could follow. Coelho tried to steer around the island and struck a rocky point that broke his rudder. He managed to extricate himself, and the caravel limped into the deep, clear water of the port.

The *Berrio* had barely come to a standstill when the local sultan drew alongside and climbed on board with a large retinue. He cut a distinguished figure in a long linen shirt, a full velvet gown, a multicolored silk cap trimmed with gold, and a pair of silk shoes. His men were dressed in fine linens and cottons, elaborately worked and dyed in vibrant stripes. On their heads they wore caps with silk bands embroidered with gold thread, and Arab swords and daggers were thrust in their belts.

Coelho received the dignitaries with due deference, though he was only able to present the sultan with a single red hood. In return the sultan gave the captain the black rosary he fingered while praying, signaling that he was to hold it as a pledge of goodwill, and invited some of the sailors to come ashore with him.

They landed on a rocky belt of shoreline where small ships could dock at high tide. Warehouses lined the waterfront. Several substantial boats were being built nearby, their hull timbers sewn together with coconut fiber and their sails woven from more of the same versatile material. Behind was a sizable town, with small mosques, ornate graveyards, and stuccoed houses built of coral rag and blocks. Everywhere coconuts, melons, and cucumbers were piled up for sale, and in the streets women sold small fried fish and meal cakes baked over coals.

The sultan beckoned the men to his house. He fed them and sent them back with "a jar of bruised dates made into a preserve with cloves and cumin, as a present for Nicolau Coelho."

By now the two ships had followed the *Berrio* into the port. The sultan dispatched more delicacies to them, and Gama hastily prepared himself for a visit. After their arduous voyage, his men were hardly a presentable lot: the best were ragged and unkempt, while the worst were on their last legs. The captain-major ordered the sick and infirm belowdecks and summoned the strongest men from the other ships. They shrugged leather jerkins over their loose shirts, stepped into their boots, and concealed weapons under their clothes. The flags were run up, the canopies were put out, and the show was ready in the nick of time.

It was just as well. The sultan arrived in full ceremonial splendor, with attendants dressed in rich silks and musicians who played nonstop on ivory trumpets. Gama welcomed him on board, seated him under an awning, offered him his best meats and wines, and presented him with more hats, together with some tunics, coral beads, and other baubles from his chests. The sultan cast his eyes over the proffered gifts, dismissed them contemptuously, and asked if the foreigners had any scarlet cloth. Gama, through his Arabic translator Fernão Martins, was forced to reply that they did not. The visitors soon left, though the sultan was intrigued enough to come back several times, and the Portuguese carried on giving him what they had.

By now the explorers had learned that they were in a country called Mozambique. The well-dressed men were wealthy merchants who traded with Arabs—or white Moors, as the Portuguese insisted on calling them—from the north. Four Arab ships were in port, and they turned out to be heavily laden with "gold, silver, cloves, pepper, ginger, and silver rings, as also with quantities of pearls, jewels, and rubies, all of which articles are used by the people of this country." All apart from the gold, explained the Europeans' new friends, came from rich cities where precious stones, pearls, and spices were so common "that there was no need to purchase them as they could be collected in baskets."

The visitors' pulses quickened. Here was the first evidence of the fabled riches of the East they had come so far to seek. It was disturbing, of course, to discover that Muslims controlled the entire coast—the Swahili Coast, from the Arabic for coast dwellers, as they would learn to call it—but there was good news there, too. Nearby, the merchants told them, was a hugely wealthy island whose half-Christian, half-Muslim population was constantly at war. Half encouraged, the Portuguese inquired after the whereabouts of Prester John. He also lived nearby, they learned, and ruled over numerous coastal cities, whose inhabitants were "great merchants and owned big ships." The Prester's court, it transpired, was far in the interior and could only be reached by camel, but that deep disappointment was tempered by the revelation that the Arabs had two Christians from India itself on board their ships. Another dose of reality was delivered by the news that the Christians were the Arabs' captives, but the two were soon brought out to the *São Gabriel*. The instant they saw the saint's figurehead on the prow, they fell to their knees in prayer. Prisoners or not, this was surely the long-awaited proof that there were, after all, Christians throughout the East.

"This information," rejoiced the Chronicler, "and many other things which we heard, rendered us so happy that we cried with joy, and prayed God to grant us health, so that we might behold what we so much desired." The hopes and dreams of centuries were almost within their grasp: a Christian king of the East and his fabulously wealthy subjects, and cities overflowing with jewels and spices that could simply be scooped up.

Just as the travelers were becoming flushed with excitement, things started to go badly wrong.

On one of his visits the sultan asked the foreigners where they came from. Were they Turks, he wanted to know, or another distant Muslim people with whom he was unfamiliar? The Turks, he was aware, were a fair people like them. If they were Turks, he added, he would be very interested to see the famous bows of their country and to take a look at their copies of the Quran.

They were not from Turkey, Gama replied, wearing his best poker face, but from a kingdom in that neighborhood. He would willingly show him their weapons, but they did not have the religious books at sea. The soldiers brought out their crossbows, drew them, and shot them off, and the sultan seemed astonished and delighted. Over a spread of figs and sugared fruits and spices, Gama ventured to explain that he had been sent by a great and mighty king to discover a way to the Indies. He asked if he could hire two pilots who knew the Indian Ocean, and the sultan readily agreed. Two men duly reported for duty, and Gama gave them each a purse of gold and a tunic. His sole condition, he told them through Fernão Martins, was that from now on, one of them must stay on board at all times.

It was not long before the presence of the pilots caused trouble. The behavior of the pale visitors with their strange language and stranger ships had already raised suspicion. They seemed to know nothing about the coast or its produce; they asked too many questions and refused to give clear answers. It finally dawned on the two men that they had been recruited not by some exotic race of Muslims but by Christians, and one of the pair made his excuses and left. When he failed to reappear, the Portuguese set off for one of the small outlying islands, a league across the bay, where they had found out he lived. The ships anchored close by, and Gama and Coelho headed for the shore in two armed boats, taking the other pilot with them. Immediately half a dozen small dhows started out from the island to intercept them. They were packed with Muslim fighters armed with bows, long arrows, and round shields who gesticulated to the Portuguese to return to the town.

Gama had the pilot secured, and he ordered his gunners to fire their bombards at the boats.

Cannonballs roared out of the barrels and rumbled through the air.

The moment that Christians and Muslims had knowingly come face-to-face in the Indian Ocean, relations had skidded from jovial to hostile. The old bitter rivalry had been exported into new waters. The first shots had been fired, and the report would echo across centuries.

Paulo da Gama had stayed with the fleet in case he needed to send help, and at the sound of gunfire he sprang to action. As the *Berrio* bore down on the Arabs' boats they fled to the main island, where they disappeared into the town before Paulo could catch up with them.

The Portuguese returned to their anchorage. Relations with the sultan were clearly beyond repair. When he had taken them for Turks, the Chronicler noted, he had been markedly friendly. "But when they learned that we were Christians, they arranged to seize and kill us by treachery. The pilot, whom we took with us, subsequently revealed to us all they intended to do, if they were able." Making the best of it, the Portuguese decided the pilot had been moved by the Almighty to reveal the plot.

The next day was a Sunday, and the crews set out to the small island to celebrate mass. They found an isolated spot, and under the shade of a tall tree they set up an altar and took communion. Immediately afterward they set sail in search of more hospitable waters.

The elements had other plans. Two days later, as the ships sailed past a cape backed by high mountains, the wind dropped away and they ground to a halt. The following evening a breeze carried them out to sea, but the men woke up the next morning to discover that a powerful offshore current had dragged them all the way back past Mozambique Island. By evening they had made it to the island where they had celebrated mass, but by then the wind was against them again. They anchored, and waited. It was the last place they wanted to be.

When reports reached the sultan that the Christians had returned, he sent one of his men to the fleet with a message of friendship. The envoy was an Arab from the north who swore he was a sharif, a descendant of the Prophet. He was also blind drunk. His master, he told the Portuguese, wanted to make peace after their unfortunate misunderstanding. So did he, replied Gama, but first he required the return of the pilot whom he had hired. The sharif left and never came back.

Soon another Arab arrived with his little son and asked permission to come on board. He was the pilot of a ship from a port near Mecca, he explained, and he was looking for a passage back north. This seemed odd when there were so many Arab ships plying the coast, but Gama agreed to take him as a passenger, not so much out of hospitality as to ply him for information. The newcomer gave one piece of advice unprompted: the sultan, he declared, hated Christians, and they had better keep their wits about them.

After holding off for nearly a week, Gama ordered the fleet back into the harbor. He had little choice: the weather showed no sign of improving, and the drinking water was running dangerously low.

There was no freshwater source on the island: digging down

brought up brackish, salty puddles that gave anyone who drank from them a bad dose of dysentery. All the water came from the mainland, and there, the explorers were told, warring tribes of naked tattooed men with sharpened teeth dined off the flesh of the elephants they hunted and the humans they took prisoner.

Despite that alarming news, at nightfall the sailors quietly lowered the boats and loaded them with empty casks. Around midnight, Vasco da Gama and Nicolau Coelho took some men and rowed softly to the mainland. The pilot whom Gama had hired from the sultan had offered to show them to the watering place, and he came with them. Soon they were hopelessly lost amid mangrove swamps, and they began to suspect that the pilot was merely looking for a chance to escape. After rowing about all night they returned tired and angry to the ships.

The next evening, without waiting for nightfall, they tried again. This time the pilot quickly pointed out the place, but when the boats drew near, the Portuguese saw twenty men on the beach, brandishing spears at them and gesturing them to go away.

Gama was reaching the end of his tether, and he ordered his men to open fire. As the shot exploded out of the barrels, the Africans fled into the bush. The sailors landed and took all the water they wanted, though their satisfaction was spoiled when they realized that an African slave who belonged to João de Coimbra, the pilot of the *São Rafael*, had slipped away unnoticed. The Portuguese soon heard to their indignation that he had gone over to Islam, even though he had been baptized a Christian.

The next morning another Arab approached the fleet and delivered a threatening message. If the strangers wanted water, he said with a sneer, they could go and search for it, but they might meet something that would make them turn back.

The captain-major finally snapped. His gifts had been laughed off, one of his pilots had escaped, and now one visitor after another was toying with him. He was being made to look a fool, and he was determined to teach the Muslims a lesson before he lost any more face. He sent a message to the sultan demanding the return of the slave and the pilot, and the answer soon came back. The sultan was outraged. The men at the watering hole were only being high-spirited, and the Christians had killed them. As for the pilots, they were foreigners and he knew nothing of them. The visitors had ap-peared to be trustworthy people; now it seemed they were nothing more than low vagabonds who went around plundering ports.

Gama held a quick conference with his captains. All the boats were armed with bombards, and they bore down on the town.

The islanders were prepared for a fight. Hundreds of men were drawn up on the beach, armed with spears, daggers, bows, and slings with which they hurled stones at the approaching boats. The cannon fired back, and the islanders retreated behind a palisade they had built by lashing together rows of wooden planks. They were hidden but they could no longer easily attack, and for three hours the Portuguese bombarded the shore.

"When we were weary with this work," recorded the Chroni-cler with the feigned insouciance of the provoked, "we retired to our ships to dine."

The islanders began to flee, taking their belongings with them and paddling in dugouts to the mainland.

After dinner the Portuguese set out to finish off their work. The captain-major's plan was to take prisoners to swap for the slave and the two "Indian Christians" held by the Arabs. His brother overtook a canoe paddled by four Africans and hauled them off to the ships. Another group of sailors pursued a boat that belonged to the self-declared sharif. It was crammed with his personal property, but the rowers abandoned it as soon as they reached the mainland. The Portuguese found another aban-doned canoe and carted away "fine cotton-stuffs, baskets made of palm-fronds, a glazed jar containing some butter, glass phials with scented water, books of the Law, a box containing skeins of cotton, a cotton net, and many small baskets filled with mil-let"—the household possessions of a well-to-do merchant. Gama handed out everything to the sailors, except for the Quran, which he put away to show to his king.

The next day, a Sunday, the coast was deserted. The Portuguese topped up their water casks, this time unopposed. On Monday they rearmed the boats and set out again for the town. The remaining islanders stayed in their houses. A few shouted oaths at the brutal strangers. Gama did not want to risk a landing, and since there seemed no hope of recovering the missing men, he satisfied honor by ordering the gunners to discharge their bombards.

Having made their point, the Portuguese left the roadstead and returned to the small island. They had to wait another three days before the wind finally picked up.

ALARMING LEGENDS CIRCULATED about the coast the explorers were about to follow. In one place, a traveler reported, "the Blacks Fish for *Pisce Mulier*, which is to say Women Fish":

> This Fish resembles a Woman, having the Privy Parts after the same manner, and carrieth her young under her Fins, which are on each side, serving for Arms, and goes often on Land, and is there disburthened of her young: The Blacks who Fish, are to swear not to have to do with these She-Fishes: Their teeth are of great Virtue, (as I have experienced) against Hemorhoids, Bloody Flux, and hot Fevers, in rubbing them against a Marble, and agitating it with Water, and so to be Drunk.

Forbidden or not, he added, the Africans "are extream fond of these Fishes, and refresh themselves by having Communication with them," though far from being ravishing mermaids, the fish-women had "a hideous Face, like the Snout of a Hog." The purely human inhabitants of the coast were even more awful. Farther inland, it was reported, there ruled a great king whose subjects, "when they kill any of their Enemies, cut off their Privy-Members, and having dried them, give them their Wives to wear about their

Neck, of which they are not a little Proud: For they who have the most are the most esteemed, in regard that Evidences the Husband to be the more hardy and valiant." Possession of a "Chaine of mens members," another traveler helpfully explained, was equivalent to being knighted in Europe; for the warriors of East Africa it was as great an honor "as it is with us to weare the golden Fleece, or the Garter of England."

The Portuguese stoutly persevered, and on March 29 a light wind finally blew them north. Slowly they made headway against the current, the heavy work of continually casting and weighing anchor leaving a catalog of blisters on the seamen's hands.

On April 1 they sailed up to a large archipelago of tropical islands edged with mangrove forests and ringed by vibrant coral reefs. Boats plied between the islands and the mainland, and there were sizable trading posts near the shore. The night before, while the Portuguese were still too far away to make out the terrain, the Arab pilot had insisted that the islands were part of the mainland. By now Gama was convinced that everyone was conspiring against him, and he had the pilot soundly flogged. To commemorate the event, the Portuguese named the first of the islands the "Island of the Flogged One."

Gama decided to carry on, and three days later they came across another archipelago. This time both of the Muslim pilots recognized it. Three leagues back, they declared, the fleet had sailed straight past an island inhabited by Christians.

The captain-major was convinced the pilots had made him overshoot a friendly port on purpose. All day the ships maneuvered to reach it, but a strong wind was against them. It turned out to be a blessing in disguise, or, as it was later interpreted, a miracle sent by God, because the island of Kilwa was home to the most powerful ruler on the coast, and he was no Christian. Far from trying to lead the Portuguese away, the disappointed pilots had been trying to draw them into a trap.

When it became clear that there was no going back, the pilots tried a new tack. A big city called Mombasa lay four days' sailing ahead, they said, and powerful Christians also lived there. It was already late, but the wind was high and the fleet bore away to the north. As night fell the lookouts made out a large island ahead— another place, claimed the Mozambique pilot, with both Christian and Muslim towns. Gama pressed on regardless, and with the favorable wind the ships made good progress until the *São Rafael* suddenly hit a shoal and ran aground.

It was two hours before daybreak, and the fleet was several miles from land. The crew shouted at the top of their voices to the other ships, which were following behind and could easily have rammed them in the dark. The *São Gabriel* and the *Berrio* came to a stop just in time and lowered their boats.

By dawn the tide had fallen and the *São Rafael* was revealed sitting high and dry on its shoal. In the background, on the coast, was a magnificent range of lofty mountains with a settlement at its feet. Seeing a business opportunity, the locals paddled out to the stricken ship and did a brisk trade in oranges, which the sailors thought were much better than the fruit back home. Gama rewarded them with the usual trinkets, and two stayed on board.

By now the *São Rafael* had lowered all its anchors. The men in the boats laboriously heaved each anchor forward of the bow and away from the shoal before shouting out to their comrades on board to pay out the cable. When the tide rose later in the day, the ropes tensed and the ship floated off amid much relief and cheering.

Finally the fleet arrived off Mombasa.

It was April 7, a Saturday. Ahead was a lushly wooded island clasped by the protective arms of the mainland. A large walled city rose on a rocky height facing the ocean. A beacon marked the shoals in front, and a fort almost level with the water guarded the bar. The harbor was just in sight around the north side of the island, and the Portuguese could see a large number of ships moored there, dressed in flags as if for a celebration. They were clearly in a wealthy and important port, and not wanting to be outdone, they ran up their own flags. They put on a good show, but in reality the fleet was in poor shape. With many sailors dead from scurvy and many still painfully ill, the ships had been undermanned for weeks. The one thing that cheered up the survivors was the prospect of landing the next day to hear Sunday mass. The pilots had told them that the Christians had their own quarter of the city, ruled by its own judges and lords; they would receive the newcomers with great honor, they assured them, and would invite them to their fine houses.

The night watch took over and the rest of the men bedded down in their usual nooks, eager for morning to come.

About midnight the watch cried out. A dhow was approaching from the city carrying perhaps a hundred men, all armed with cutlasses and bucklers. It bore down on the flagship, and the armed men tried to clamber on board. Gama barked out orders and his soldiers lined up around the decks, blocking the way. He eventually allowed four of the leaders aboard, but only after they had laid down their weapons.

Gama slid from soldier to diplomat. He begged his visitors to excuse his precautions and not take offense; he was a stranger, he added as he offered them food, and he didn't know how things worked in their city. His guests, all smiles, explained that they had merely come to look at the fleet because it was such a striking sight; carrying arms, they added, was their custom in peace or war. The sultan had been eagerly expecting the foreigners' arrival; he would have come himself if it weren't so late.

The delicate parley continued for two hours. When the four men left, the Portuguese were still convinced they had come to see if they could capture one of the ships. They were, after all, Muslims, though they, too, had confirmed that there were indeed many Christians on the island.

Sunday morning arrived, and with it a present from the sultan of Mombasa: a sheep, together with crates of oranges, lemons, and sugarcane. Clearly the Europeans had already become minor celebrities along the coast, because they received a stream of callers all day. Among them were two envoys who presented Gama with the sultan's ring as a pledge of the visitors' security and promised that they would be supplied with everything they needed if they entered the port. The envoys were pale-skinned and said they were Christians; they were very plausible, and the Portuguese believed them. Gama sent them back with a string of coral beads for the sultan—an unremarkable gift on a coast brimming with coral reefs—and the message that he intended to head into the harbor the following day. At the same time, he sent two of the degredados to repeat his friendly greetings to the sultan in person and to reconnoiter the scene.

As soon as the two men landed, a crowd gathered around them and followed them through the narrow streets to the palace. A series of four doorways, each manned by a doorkeeper holding a drawn cutlass, led to the audience chamber. The sultan received the foreigners hospitably, and he ordered his men to show them around the city.

The group wound through handsome streets lined with three-story buildings. Fine plaster ceilings could be seen through the windows. The women were draped in silk and glittered with gold and precious stones, while coffles of slaves shuffled by in irons.

The tour halted at the house of two merchants who were introduced as Christians. They showed the visitors an image they worshipped, which seemed to be the Holy Ghost painted as a white dove. There were many other Christians in the city, the guides explained, and when their ships came into the harbor they would meet them all. The itinerary ended back at the palace, where the sultan reappeared and handed the two men samples of cloves, pepper, and sorghum. They were for sale in great quantities, he said, and he would permit the visitors to load their ships with them. He also had warehouses full of silver, gold, amber, wax, ivory, and other riches, and he promised to undercut the competition.

Gama received the messages and the reports of the city with much satisfaction. The three captains consulted. As an insurance policy in case anything went wrong in India, they decided to put into the port and stock up with spices.

The fleet weighed anchor, but the *São Gabriel* refused to turn and it drifted onto a shoal. The next ship ran straight into it, and all three anchored again to sort themselves out.

The shoal turned out to be another instance of divine providence at work. There were still several Africans and Arabs on the ships, and now they decided the Christians were never going to go nearer the shore. They signaled to each other, ran for the stern, and jumped into a dhow that was tied alongside. Seconds later the two pilots jumped overboard and swam to the boat.

Vasco da Gama began to suspect that a deep plot was in hand. That night, he set about interrogating two men from Mozambique who had not managed to escape. Since it was commonly believed that reliable answers were only given under torture, he had some oil heated to boiling point and dripped on their skin.

Between their shouts of pain they gasped out the gist of the plot. News of the Christians' arrival and their attacks on Mozambique had preceded them up the coast, and plans had been laid to capture them as soon as they entered the port.

Gama ordered more boiling oil applied to more smoking skin. One of the interrogees squirmed out of his tormentors' grasp and threw himself into the sea, his hands still tied together. The other suicidally followed suit a few hours later. The Portuguese thanked God for once again saving them from the Infidel's evil grasp.

Around midnight, two canoes paddled silently toward the fleet and halted just out of sight. Dozens of men dived noiselessly off the edge and swam up to the ships. Several surfaced at the side of the *Berrio*, took out their knives, and cut through the anchor cables. Their skin and weapons glinted in the moonlight, but the night watch took them for a school of tuna. As the caravel began to drift, the sailors finally caught on and raised the alarm. More swimmers had already climbed on board the *São Rafael* and were swarming around the rigging of the mizzenmast, about to sever the ropes. When they were spotted they slipped silently into the water and swam away.

"These and other wicked tricks were practiced upon us by these dogs," recorded the Chronicler, "but our Lord did not allow them to succeed, because they were unbelievers."

The Portuguese were still convinced that half the population of Mombasa was Christian, but they were troubled that there was no sign of them coming to their aid. They eventually concluded that there was a war going on between the Christians and Muslims; clearly the slaves they had seen were captured Christian soldiers. In any case the Christian merchants, they persuaded themselves, were only temporary residents and so were unable to do anything without the sultan's permission.

By now the crews had finally recovered their strength. Perhaps the ample supply of citrus fruit had helped; more likely, the Portuguese believed, it was another miracle. The captain-major waited two more days for Christians to arrive who might furnish him with a replacement pilot. Then, on April 13, he ordered the fleet to set sail, still none the wiser about how to cross the Indian Ocean.

AT DAWN THE next day the watchkeepers spotted two boats in the open sea, and the ships immediately set off in hot pursuit. If there were no pilots for hire, Gama had decided, one would have to be captured.

One of the boats escaped to the mainland, but by late afternoon the fleet caught up with the other. Inside were seventeen Muslims, some gold and silver, and a great deal of maize. One elderly man had a distinguished look about him, and clinging to his side was his young wife. As the ships closed in the sailors and passengers threw themselves overboard, but the Portuguese jumped in their boats and fished them out of the sea.

To Gama's annoyance, none of the new captives was a pilot, and the fleet was forced to continue up the coast.

Thirty leagues north of Mombasa the Portuguese found themselves near another sizable town. At sunset they anchored for the night, keeping a close watch for any signs of nefarious activity along the shore.

The next day was April 15, Easter Sunday, but only the usual morning prayers were said. The explorers looked warily around them, waiting to see who would make the first move.

Ahead the coastline curved majestically between two distant rocky points to form a broad, undulating bay. At low tide the surf crashed onto coral reefs that stretched well out from the sandy beach, exposing glinting pools and low rocks spread with tattered green blankets of algae in the shallows. The town spread along the shore amid extensive palm groves flanked by farms and orchards. Well-kept villas roofed with palm thatch stood tall and white against the limpid blue sky; unlike most blank-walled Arab houses, they had many windows and roof terraces that looked out to sea. The scene reminded the Portuguese of Alcochete, a favorite resort of Portuguese royalty—and the birthplace of Manuel I—on the Tagus estuary above Lisbon.

The men who had been seized from the boat told their captors that they were in front of the city of Malindi. They had just come from there themselves, they added, and they had seen four ships belonging to Christians from India in the port. If the strangers would let them go, they would provide them with Christian pilots, together with water, wood, and any other provisions they cared to name.

Gama was badly in need of some help, and he listened to their advice. He moved the fleet toward the city and anchored half a league away. The inhabitants kept their distance: perhaps they had already been warned that the foreigners went around capturing ships and kidnapping their passengers and crews.

The next morning, Gama had his men row the elderly Muslim to a sandbank in front of the city. They left him there, and he stood quietly until a canoe approached from the shore and picked him up. The foreigners were still holding his young wife hostage, and he went straight to the palace and passed on the captain-major's message. The newcomers, he related, were the subjects of a great and powerful king whom the sultan would rejoice to have as an ally;

they were headed for India, and would be glad of pilots. For once the diplomatic patter found a receptive ear; the sultan was at war with neighboring Mombasa and was eager for new allies, especially belligerent ones with fearsome-looking ships.

After dinner the old man reappeared with one of the sultan's men-at-arms, a sharif, and three sheep. The human callers relayed the ruler's eagerness to enter into friendly relations with the strangers and his readiness to give them pilots or anything else in his power. Gama sent them back with a surtout, two strings of coral, three hand basins, a hat, some small bells, two striped cotton scarves, and word that he would enter the port the next day.

The fleet edged nearer to the shore, and a boat arrived from the sultan with six more sheep and a gift of cloves, cumin, ginger, nutmeg, and pepper. Once again the expensive waft of spices quickened the sailors' pulses.

With the gifts came a new message: If the strangers' leader wished to talk with the sultan, he would come out in his dhow and meet him halfway. Gama agreed, and after dinner the next day the royal dhow pushed off from the shore. At the sultan's side was a band of trumpeters, two of whom played huge horns made from intricately carved ivory tusks, as tall as a man and blown through a hole in the side. Together the deep blasts and sweet peals made a harmonious, hypnotic sound.

The sultan wore a robe of crimson damask trimmed with green satin and a lavish turban. He was seated on a double chair made of bronze and piled with silk cushions. Over his head was a crimson satin parasol, and by his side stood an old retainer holding a sword in a silver sheath. His men were naked above the waist, but below they were wrapped in silk or fine cotton. On their heads they wore cloths embroidered with silk and gold, and they carried fancy daggers and swords decorated with silk tassels in a rainbow of colors. The Europeans were much taken with the pageantry and the dignified comportment of the royal party.

Gama was dressed in his best knightly gear and was accompanied by twelve of his principal officers. His boat had been decked out with flags and streamers, and as the sultan drew near, his sailors rowed him out. The two boats stopped side by side. In signs and through the translators, the two men exchanged cordial greetings, and Gama was flattered to find himself addressed with the deference due a king.

The sultan invited the captain-major to visit the city and stay in his palace, where he could refresh himself after the fatigues of his long voyage. Afterward, he suggested, he would pay a recip-rocal visit to the ships. Despite the soft comforts on offer, Gama demurred. He had come to the fixed conclusion that it was too dangerous to set foot in what were clearly strongly armed Muslim cities, however friendly the people seemed. He was forbidden from complying, he replied, by the orders of his king; if he disobeyed them, a bad report would be made of him.

What would his people say of *him*, the sultan responded, if he were to visit the ships without a sign of goodwill from the strang-ers? At the least, he would like to know the name of their king.

The Portuguese translator wrote down the name Manuel.

If the strangers called on him on their way back from India, the sultan declared, he would send letters to this Manuel, or even an ambassador in person.

Gama thanked him for his politeness, promised to return, and answered a string of questions about the mission. The sultan ex-pounded at length on spices, the Red Sea, and other matters of vital interest to the explorers, and he promised to provide them with a pilot.

The meeting went so well that Gama sent for his prisoners and handed them all over. The sultan vowed that he could not have been happier if he had been presented with a city. In great good humor he made a lap of honor around the fleet, admiring each ship in turn and doubtless estimating the damage it could inflict on his neighbors. The captain-major, who had followed in his own boat, ordered the bombards to fire off a salute. The alarmed Muslims lunged for their oars, and Gama quickly signaled for the guns to cease. The sultan, when he had recomposed himself, proclaimed that he had never been so pleased with any men and would be very glad to have some of them to help him in his wars. He had seen nothing yet, Gama intimated; if God permitted them to discover India and return home, his king would surely send a whole fleet of warships to his new ally's aid.

After a visit of three hours the sultan headed home, leaving his son and a sharif on board the fleet as a surety. He was still keen to show off his palace, and he took two sailors with him. Since the captain-major would not go ashore, he said as he left, he would return the following day to the beach.

The next morning Vasco da Gama and Nicolau Coelho took charge of two armed boats and rowed along the town front. Crowds had gathered on the shore, where two cavalrymen were acting out a duel. Behind were handsome streets and plashing fountains. The explorers learned that only Arabs—perhaps four thousand in number—lived inside the city walls, while the Africans, many of them slaves who worked the plantations, lived outside in mud-and-wattle huts. As all along the coast, after centuries of intermarriage there was little to tell physically between the two groups, but whatever their ethnicity the Muslim elite called themselves Arabs and labeled the non-Islamic population *kaffirs*, the Arabic word for infidels.

The sultan emerged from his seafront palace. He climbed into his palanquin—a covered litter mounted on poles—and was carried down a flight of stone steps to the water's edge. Gama's boat bobbed alongside, but it was hard to have a proper conversation, and again the sultan begged the captain-major to step ashore. He asked it as a personal favor, he added; his elderly, infirm father was keen to meet the man who had come so far and survived such dangers for his king. If need be, both he and his sons would wait as hostages on the ships. Even that was not enough to lower Gama's guard, and he stayed firmly seated in his boat to watch the entertainments that his hosts had laid on.

Of all the Indian Ocean cities ruled by Arabs, the Portuguese had hit upon the one most likely to give them help. The information about the four ships from India turned out to be accurate, too, and soon a party of Indians rowed up to the *São Rafael* and asked to come aboard. Vasco was there talking to his brother, and he told the crew to show the Indians an altarpiece that represented "Our Lady at the foot of the cross, with Jesus Christ in her arms and the apostles around her." Since these were the first Indians they had seen, the sailors examined them with unabashed curiosity and decided they looked nothing like any Christians they knew. They wore white cotton shifts, full beards, and their hair long and plaited up under turbans; on top of that, they explained that they were vegetarians, which sounded deeply suspicious to men who were ravenous for fresh meat. But the moment they saw the altar they prostrated themselves on the deck, and throughout the fleet's stay in the harbor they came daily to say their prayers before the shrine, bringing little offerings of cloves or pepper.

This was final confirmation, surely, that India was teeming with Christians. The Portuguese were even more stirred when the captain-major rowed past the Indians' ships and they fired off a salvo in his honor.

"Christ! Christ!" they shouted joyfully, raising their hands above their head; at least, so their chant sounded to European ears.

That night the Indians applied to the sultan for permission to throw a party in the strangers' honor. As darkness fell the sky blazed with rockets. The Indians fired round after round from their small bombards, and they sang strange hymns at the top of their voices.

After a week of fetes, sham fights, and musical interludes Gama was growing impatient. On April 22 the royal dhow arrived bringing one of the sultan's counselors, the first caller in two days. Gama had him seized, and he sent a message to the palace demanding the promised pilot. The sultan had hoped to keep the Portuguese diverted until they could join his war, but he immediately sent a man and Gama released his hostage.

To the Europeans' great joy, the pilot appeared to be another Christian from India. He unrolled a detailed map of the Indian coast, talked the officers through its features, and explained the winds and currents of the ocean. He was clearly an experienced navigator, and he was equally knowledgeable about the science of sailing. The ships' instruments failed to impress him in the slightest; the pilots of the Red Sea, he remarked, had long used similar contraptions to take the altitude of the sun and the stars, though he and his fellow Indians preferred another device. He showed it to them, and Gama's pilots decided to let him take the lead.

On Tuesday, April 24 the trumpets sounded, the sails were set, and the fleet left Malindi with all flags flying. According to one report, the sultan was heartbroken to see his new friends go and assured them that the name of the Portuguese "would never leave his heart where he preserved it, except when he died."

The weather was fair, and they made good progress. Directly north, their pilot told them, was a huge bay that ended in a strait: the Gulf of Aden and the Bab el Mandeb, the gate to the Red Sea and the Kaaba of Mecca. Nearby, he added, were many large cities, both Christian and Muslim, and six hundred islands, counting only those that were known. The Europeans still had a great deal to learn.

After two days the African coast disappeared from view. Three nights later the North Star reappeared on the horizon. The explorers had once again crossed the equator, but this time they were sailing in an ocean where no European ship had ever been. They held their course to the northeast, and India.

Behind them they had left more enemies than friends. Their picture of Africa was muddled at best, and they still had only the shadiest notion of where they were headed.

CHAPTER 10

RIDING THE MONSOON

FOR MORE THAN two millennia, the passage across the Indian Ocean depended on the simple fact that land heats and cools more quickly than water.

Every September, as the earth's tilt inclines the Northern Hemisphere away from the sun, the vast Tibetan Plateau loses heat fast. The air above the landmass cools in its turn and sinks, creating a huge pool of high pressure. The Indian Ocean retains its heat much longer, and since warm air rises and leaves a void, the colder air pours down over the plains of North India and across the water. By the end of the year, sailing ships departing from India are blown southwest to Arabia and Africa by a regular, dependable northeast wind.

As summer approaches and the sun climbs in the sky, the deserts, plains, and plateaus of north and central India quickly reach scorching temperatures. The heat forms a low-pressure area that sucks in the cooler, moisture-rich ocean air. The southwesterly winds pick up by May and race across the subcontinent in June, dragging with them banked storm clouds that glower low in the sky. As the air mass roars into the high wall of the Western Ghats in southern India and then the towering Himalayas to the northeast, the clouds are forced upward, the moisture condenses, and the rainfall turns parched sand and soil into fields of fertile coffee-colored foam. After three months the winds reverse direction and the pattern begins all over again.

The winter monsoon—the word comes from the Arabic

mawsim, or "season"—dictated the trading calendar of much of the world, from the markets of Alexandria to the annual fairs of northern Europe. Getting to India in the first place, though, required a finer calculation. An Egyptian or Arabian merchant who wanted to bring his goods to market in the shortest possible time would sail with the tail end of the southwest monsoon and return three or four months later. Yet the late-summer monsoon could be a deadly ally. In the 1440s, a Persian ambassador named Abd al-Razzaq was held up at Hormuz until the monsoon was more than halfway through and was paralyzed by the thought of the tempests that tore apart Arab ships and made them easy pickings for pirates:

> As soon as I caught the smell of the vessel, and all the terrors of the sea presented themselves before me, I fell into so deep a swoon, that for three days respiration alone indicated that life remained within me. When I came a little to myself, the merchants, who were my intimate friends, cried with one voice that the time for navigation had passed, and that everyone who put to sea at this season was alone responsible for his death, since he voluntarily placed himself in peril. . . . In consequence of the severity of pitiless weather and the adverse manifestations of a treacherous fate, my heart was crushed like glass and my soul became weary of life.

Less troublesome than fainting in a timely manner was to set sail earlier, even if that meant waiting out the torrential summer rains that shut down the ports of southwest India. By sheer luck—or, the Portuguese would later claim, with divine assistance—Vasco da Gama had left Africa at an opportune moment.

For twenty-three days the crews saw nothing but cerulean blue water passing at a regular clip, and on May 18 the lookouts sighted land.

Vasco da Gama stood on his poop deck and gazed at India.

The pilot had guided the ships straight to Mount Eli, a prominent, massy hill traditionally used as a marker by Indian Ocean
navigators. A decade earlier Pêro da Covilhã had arrived in exactly
the same spot, and like the resourceful spy, Gama was headed for
the spice emporium of Calicut.

At night the fleet put out to sea again, steering south-southwest
to skirt the coast. The next day they headed back to land, but a
heavy thunderstorm made it impossible to see where they were.
The day after, a lofty mountain range emerged from its inky wrap-
ping, and the pilot announced that the Portuguese were just five
leagues from the object of their quest.

Gama paid him his reward on the spot and summoned the company to prayers, "saying the *salve*, and giving hearty thanks to God,
who had safely conducted them to the long wished-for place." The
prayers soon gave way to celebrations. If there was a time to break
out the rum, this was it.

That evening, just before sunset, the little fleet anchored a league
and a half offshore, well clear of some treacherous-looking rocks.
The crews lined the bulwarks and climbed the rigging to take a
good look. In front, glowing in the sun's last rays, was a half-mile-
long crescent of fine golden sand backed by coconut palms and fir
trees. The bay was protected at each end by a rocky promontory,
and an old temple perched on a crag to the north. It was a paradise
beach, and after nearly a year at sea it looked every bit the Promised
Land conjured up in so many travelers' tales.

Soon four boats approached and the sailors, nut brown and naked except for small cloths around their waists, hailed the strangers
and asked where they were from. Some were fishermen, and they
climbed on board to proffer their catch. Gama told his men to buy
everything they were offered at the price they were asked, and the
fishermen doubtfully bit the silver coins to see if they were real. The
captain-major was rewarded with the information that the fleet was
anchored near a town called Kappad, which the pilot had mistaken
for Calicut.

The next day the Indians returned, and Gama sent the degredado who spoke Arabic with them to Calicut.

While the convict was being introduced to two astonished merchants from Tunis, no doubt on the grounds that they came from far to the west as well, the fleet moved in front of the city itself. Gama took in the scene. A broad sweep of beach was backed by tall coconut palms bent inland like reeds by the monsoon winds. Behind, backed by a range of tall hills, Calicut sprawled for miles amid lush palm groves.

The emissary soon returned, and with him came one of the merchants. The explorers soon took to calling him Monçaide, a Portuguese corruption of his Arabic name.

Monçaide was still in shock at the appearance of Europeans in India—and far from the most likely Europeans at that.

"Why," he and his colleague had asked their unexpected caller, "does the King of Castile, the King of France, or the Signoria of Venice not send men here?"

"The king of Portugal," he had dutifully replied, "would not allow them."

"He does the right thing," the two men had replied with wonder.

The merchants had taken the convict to their lodgings for a snack of bread and honey, and Monçaide had set out to see the ships with his own eyes.

"A lucky venture," he exclaimed in Spanish as soon as he stepped on board, "a lucky venture! Plenty of rubies, plenty of emeralds! You owe great thanks to God, for having brought you to a country holding such riches!"

The entire crew stood gape-mouthed.

"We were greatly astonished to hear this talk," recorded the Chronicler, "for we never expected to hear our language spoken so far away from Portugal." Several of the sailors wept for joy. "They all then joined in humble and hearty thanks to the Almighty, by whose favor and assistance alone this great happiness and good fortune had been accorded to them."

Gama embraced the man from Tunis and made him sit down beside him. Rather hopefully, he asked if he was a Christian.

The answer momentarily took the shine off things. Monçaide frankly explained that he was from the Barbary Coast and had come to Calicut via Cairo and the Red Sea. He had met Portuguese merchants and sailors, he explained, in his former home, and he had always liked them. He would do anything he could to help.

The captain-major, who was too invigorated to be too discouraged, thanked him and promised to reward him handsomely. He was very happy to meet him, he added; God must have sent him to advance the great mission.

The conversation passed on to Calicut and its ruler, the Samutiri, whom the Portuguese soon started calling the Zamorin. He was a good and honorable man, said the Tunisian, and he would gladly receive an ambassador from a foreign king, especially if he had valuable merchandise for sale. The Zamorin was very rich, he added, and all his revenue came from the customs he levied on trade.

MONÇAIDE WAS NOT exaggerating. Calicut was the busiest port in India, and for more than two centuries it had been the keystone of the international spice trade. A great bazaar stretched inland for a mile, its open-fronted shops busy late into the night and heaped, as the Portuguese soon discovered, with "all the spices, drugs, nutmegs, and other things that can be desired, all kinds of precious stones, pearls and seed-pearls, musk, sanders, aguila, fine dishes of earthen ware, lacker, gilded coffers, and all the fine things of China, gold, amber, wax, ivory, fine and coarse cotton goods, both white and dyed of many colors, much raw and twisted silk, stuffs of silk and gold, cloth of gold, cloth of tissue, grain, scarlets, silk carpets, copper, quicksilver, vermilion, alum, coral, rose-water, and all kinds of conserves." Pepper, ginger, and cinnamon were grown in the hinterland and were sold in vast quantities; the other spices and exotic goods were brought in convoys from points to the southeast. Platoons of porters plodded up and down the streets between overflowing warehouses, bent double under the weight of the sacks on their backs, stopping every so often to rest their loads on long, hooked staffs.

At this time of year the harbor was virtually empty, but soon it would fill up with the fleets from Aden, Hormuz, and Jeddah that carried the produce of India to Arabia and Iran, Egypt and Europe. The Chinese, too, had been regular visitors until the Central Kingdom had retreated into splendid isolation. The visiting merchants were not attracted by Calicut's port facilities—the Portuguese had already discovered that the stony seafloor gave little purchase to their anchors, there was no protection against the monsoon winds, and closer to land, the water was too shallow for all but the smallest boats—but by its carefully cultivated reputation for probity. The Iranian ambassador Abd al-Razzaq, when he finally made it to India, reported that merchants from far-flung ports were so confident in the security and justice of Calicut that they sent their valuable cargoes for sale without even bothering to keep an account: "The officers of the custom-house," he explained, "take upon themselves the charge of looking after the merchandise, over which they keep watch day and night. When a sale is effected, they levy a duty on the goods of one-fortieth part; if they are not sold, they make no charge on them whatsoever."

Locals told the story of a rich Arab merchant who was passing by when his ship began to sink under the weight of the gold he had brought from Mecca. He moored in the harbor, built a granite cellar in the Zamorin's basement, and filled it with his treasure. When he returned to the city, he broke open the cellar and found everything intact. He offered half to the ruler, who declined any reward. From then on the merchant refused to trade anywhere else, and the bazaar was born. Another legend held that an Arab merchant arrived one day with a challenge in the form of a pickle box, which he entrusted to the ruler's safekeeping. Every other king whom he had tested in the same way had opened the box and had stolen the gold he found inside, but the Zamorin came after him. "You mistook one thing for another," he pointed out. "This is not pickles but gold." That merchant, too, reputedly settled in Calicut.

Gama sent Fernão Martins and another messenger to the virtuous Zamorin, with the helpful Monçaide as their guide. Meanwhile, the Portuguese took the opportunity to find out more about his people.

Their first discovery seemed to confirm everything they had dreamed of for decades.

"The city of Calicut is inhabited by Christians," recorded the Chronicler.

True, they were unorthodox Christians. "They are of a tawny complexion," he observed. "Some of them have big beards and long hair, whilst others clip their hair short or shave the head, merely allowing a tuft to remain on the crown as a sign that they are Christians. They also wear moustaches. They pierce the ears and wear much gold in them. They go naked down to the waist, covering their lower extremities with very fine cotton stuffs. But it is only the most respectable who do this, for the others manage as best they are able."

"The women of this country," he ungallantly added, "as a rule, are ugly and of small stature. They wear many jewels of gold round the neck, numerous bracelets on their arms, and rings set with precious stones on their toes. All these people are well-disposed and apparently of mild temper. At first sight they seem covetous and ignorant."

To the newcomers' dismay there were, though, plenty of Muslims in Calicut. They were dressed in fine long coats and silk turbans embroidered with gold, they carried knives with silver hafts and sheaths, and they worshipped in elegant, pagoda-like mosques. One traveler observed that, unlike the majority of the Indians, who were "commonly very hayrie, and rough upon the breast, and on their bodies," the Muslims of Calicut were "verie smoth both of haire and skin, which commonly they annoint with Oyle to make it shine." They were also, he added, "verie arrogant and proud."

Martins and his companions soon discovered that the Zamorin was staying in a palace some way down the coast. The three men set off through vast deciduous and evergreen forests, marveling at the strange birds and fruits and watching warily for tigers, leopards, and pythons. When they reached the royal residence they announced, as Gama had instructed them, that an ambassador had arrived with letters from the great king of Portugal. If the Zamorin wished it, they added, he would come to him in person.

The Zamorin, who in the way of kings was not much inclined to betray surprise, undoubtedly had no notion of what or where Portugal was. In reply to his questions Martins explained that they were Christians from far away who had endured many dangers to reach his city. The answer seemed satisfactory, and the three men returned to Calicut with a large quantity of fine cotton and silk and a message for the ambassador. He was most welcome, the Zamorin said, and he need not trouble himself to make a long journey, because the royal party was about to set out for Calicut.

Gama was struck by the friendly tone of the message, and he was even more pleased when a pilot arrived with orders from the Zamorin to conduct the fleet to a safer anchorage. The harbor of Pantalayini, the pilot civilly explained, was four leagues north of Calicut, but it was usual for large ships to anchor there; the water was deeper, and a mudbank offered some shelter from the monsoon-whipped sea.

The Portuguese had been watching the worsening weather with alarm. In the evenings the ocean was an angry gray-green under banked storm clouds. Suddenly the wind whipped the shore, the rain splattered the land, and without warning men and women were lashed and blown along the unprotected coast. The ships had barely held their position, and the captain-major immediately gave the order to set sail—though for all the signs of favor, he still exercised caution. "We did not," noted the Chronicler, "anchor as near the shore as the king's pilot desired."

The fleet had no sooner reached its new berth than a messenger arrived and announced that the Zamorin had already returned to the city. Straightaway a party of dignitaries turned up to escort the visitors to the palace. At its head was the *wali*, or governor, of Calicut, who was also the chief of police and came attended by two hundred guards. The tall, slender soldiers were an arresting sight to the Europeans. They went barefoot and naked from the waist up; below the waist they wore a dhoti, a white cloth passed between the legs and tied at the back. Their long hair was knotted in a bunch on their heads, and they were never seen without their weapon of choice: sword and buckler, bow and arrows, or pike.

Despite the large turnout, Gama decided it was too late in the day to set off. He had another reason to delay. That night, he called a council of his principal officers to discuss whether he should break his own rule and go ashore in person.

His cautious older brother strongly objected. Though the natives were Christians, Paulo argued, there were many Muslims among them who were Vasco's mortal enemies. They would use every means to destroy him, and however friendly the Zamorin seemed to be, he could not bring him back from the dead. Besides, the Muslims were inhabitants of the place; his brother was a complete stranger. The Zamorin might even be in league with them to kill or capture him; the voyage would then be ruined, their toil would have been in vain, and they would all be destroyed.

All the officers took Paulo's side, but Gama had already made up his mind. It was his job to seal a treaty with the Zamorin, he insisted, and to procure the spices that would prove their discovery of the true Indies. The Zamorin might take it as an insult if someone went in his stead. He could not possibly explain to anyone else what to say and do in every situation that might arise. He was going to a Christian city, and he did not intend to be gone long. He would rather die, he vowed, than neglect his duty—or see someone else claim the credit.

The young commander had the hand of history at his back. His brother made no more objections.

The next day, May 28, Gama buckled his gilded belt around his waist and ran his sword into its scabbard. He fastened his gilt spurs onto his buskins, and placed his stiff, square cap, like the birettas worn by priests, on his head. When his ceremonial dress was complete, he emerged from his cabin ready to represent his king. Paulo was left in charge of the ships; Nicolau Coelho was to wait every day in a well-armed boat, as near the shore as was safe, until the delegation returned.

Gama had chosen thirteen men to accompany him. Among them were Diogo Dias and João de Sá, the scribes of the *Gabriel* and *Rafael*, and the interpreter Fernão Martins. The Chronicler was also one of the party. They were dressed in their finest clothes, the boats were decked out with flags, and the trumpeters blew a fanfare as the sailors rowed to the shore.

The wali stepped forward to greet the captain-major. A throng of onlookers had gathered, and they pressed in to catch a glimpse of the strangers. "This reception was friendly," noted the Chronicler, "as if the people were pleased to see us, though at first appearances it looked threatening, for they carried naked swords in their hands."

The reception committee had provided a palanquin for Gama's use, and he sat on the padded seat. Six strong Indians hoisted the bamboo poles onto their shoulders, the wali climbed into his own palanquin, and the convoy set off along the dirt road to Calicut.

When they reached the small town of Kappad, off which the fleet had first anchored, the porters set down the chairs in front of a handsome house. A local notable was waiting for them, and he gestured them to come inside and eat. Gama stoutly refused the proffered delicacies; his less scrupulous entourage tucked into a meal of well-buttered boiled fish and strange fruits. No doubt the Portuguese wondered at the cow dung that was spread over the floor, partly to fend off the columns of ants that marched everywhere. "They can keep nothing free from being destroyed by these little Animals, to prevent which they have also Cupboards born upon Piles, set in Vessels full of Water, where the Ants drown themselves by thinking to mount up," observed one European traveler.

After breakfast the party resumed its journey. Still some way from the town they came to a broad river that flowed parallel to the coast before turning toward the sea. The Indians helped the visitors into two lashed-together canoes, then climbed into dozens more craft that bobbed around them. More curious locals watched from the thickly wooded banks. As the boats pushed off into the middle of the river, the Portuguese caught sight of the silvery skein of backwaters that stretched far inland and the large ships that were drawn up high and dry on their banks.

The company disembarked about a league upriver, and Gama returned to his palanquin. Everywhere the land was divided into large walled gardens, with large houses just visible through the tall trees. Women cradling children in their arms came out to watch and joined the burgeoning procession.

After several hours the visitors finally arrived on the outskirts of Calicut itself. To their deep satisfaction, the first building they saw was a church.

It was a strange church, to be sure.

The complex was old and huge, the size of a monastery. It was built of rust-colored laterite blocks topped with slanting tiled roofs and a pagoda-style porch. In front was a slender bronze pillar as tall as a mast, with the figure of a bird, apparently a rooster, on top, and a stouter second pillar the height of a man. Seven small bells hung from the walls in the entrance.

Gama and his men stepped inside. The passage led to a large hall, which was lit by hundreds of lamps and smelled strongly of incense and smoke. In the center was a square chapel made of stone, with stone steps leading up to a bronze door.

The party was received by a procession of priests who were naked from the waist up, except for three threads slung across their chests like a deacon's stole. Four went inside the sanctuary and pointed toward a statue hidden in a dark recess.

"Maria, Maria," they seemed to the Portuguese to chant.

The Indians prostrated themselves on the floor, and the visitors knelt, too, in adoration of the Virgin Mary.

The priests doused the guests with holy water and offered them a white earthlike substance that, the Chronicler noted, "the Christians of this country are in the habit of putting on their foreheads, breasts, around the neck, and on the forearms." Gama submitted to the dousing, but he handed one of his men his portion of white earth, which would turn out to be partly composed of sacrificial ashes, and gestured that he would put it on later.

Having said their prayers, the explorers looked around them. The walls were covered with colorful portraits of figures they assumed to be saints—though since they boasted "teeth protruding an inch from the mouth, and four or five arms" and looked as ugly as devils, they were clearly an exotic species of saint.

With the ceremony over, the party emerged blinking into the light. Sunk into the ground outside was a huge brick tank filled to the brim with water, lotus flowers floating on the surface, not unlike many others the visitors had seen along the road. They paused to wonder at its purpose, then followed their hosts through a gate into the heart of the city.

The journey halted for a tour of another ancient church paired with another rectangular reservoir. By the time Gama and his men came out, crowds jammed the arrow-straight streets as far as they could see, and the beleaguered foreigners were hustled into a house to await rescue by the wali's brother. He eventually arrived, attended by soldiers firing muskets and a marching band playing drums, trumpets, and bagpipes. The explorers' entourage, the Chronicler noted, now included two thousand armed men; by one account, there were five thousand people trying to accompany them through the streets. India was turning out to be an unexpectedly frantic place.

The procession set off again, with more locals joining in and others lining the roofs and windows of the houses. As they finally drew near the Zamorin's palace, the sea of heads stretched so far that it was impossible to guess at their number. Despite the tumult, though, the Portuguese were struck by the great delicacy and respect shown the captain-major—"more than is shown in Spain to a king," remarked the Chronicler.

It was already an hour before sunset. In the square outside the entrance to the sprawling complex, royal servants were handing out coconuts and pouring fresh water from gilded pitchers set on tables under shady trees. A fresh committee of distinguished-looking figures came out to meet the visitors and joined the ranked dignitaries surrounding the captain-major. Everyone struggled on through the great gate, where ten doorkeepers bearing silver-mounted sticks were stationed.

"They little think in Portugal how honorably we are received here," Gama said to his men, a touch of wonder escaping beneath his usual imperturbability.

Inside was a vast leafy courtyard, with offices and lodgings dotted around amid flower beds, orchards, fish ponds, and fountains. A series of four doorways led to the audience court, and here the crush was so bad that courtesy bowed to necessity. The Portuguese had to force their way through, "giving many blows to the people," while more porters lay about them with sticks.

A small, wizened figure who turned out to be the Zamorin's chief priest emerged from the last door. He embraced the captain-major and ushered him into the royal presence. There was room for two or three thousand people in the court, but the excitement to get inside was so great that the Portuguese had to shove and batter even harder, while the Indians brandished knives and slashed several men. When the main party was through, the porters shouldered the door shut, fastened it with an iron bar, and mounted guard.

In the evening light, Vasco da Gama finally came face-to-face with the man he had come twelve thousand miles to meet.

The Samutiri Tirumulpad, King of the Hills and the Waves, was arranged like a Roman emperor on a mound of crisp white cotton cushions. The cushions were piled on a fine white cotton sheet, the sheet was draped over a well-padded mattress, and the mattress rested on a couch covered in green velvet. The floor was carpeted with the same velvet, the walls were hung with more precious drapes in a rainbow of colors, and above the couch was a canopy, "very white, delicate and sumptuous." The Zamorin was dressed in a long cotton *sherwani*, a coatlike garment worn open at the front, with his chest uncovered and a sarong-like *lunghi* knotted around his waist. The effect was of expensive simplicity, offset by the heavy jewels set in his ears and on his belt, bracelets, and rings. To his right was a gold stand supporting a cauldron-sized gold basin heaped with the royal drug of choice—paan, made from sliced areca nuts mixed with spices and lime made from oyster shells and wrapped in bitter betel leaves. A dedicated paan attendant stood by preparing the stimulating mixture, and the Zamorin chewed it nonstop. By his left hand was a huge gold spittoon into which he ejected the remains, and another attendant stood ready to moisten his palate with liquid refreshment from an array of silver jugs. Perhaps the visitors paused to think that much of Europe's bullion ended up here, where it was hoarded as treasure and worked into elaborate ornaments and until now had never been seen again.

Gama approached the Zamorin. He bowed his head, raised his hands high and touched his palms together, then made two fists in the air. He had been practicing the local etiquette, and he repeated the greeting twice more as he had seen the Indians do.

His men followed suit.

The Zamorin beckoned the captain-major closer. Gama, though, had been told that only the paan page was allowed to approach the royal person. He was determined not to cause offense, and he stayed put.

Instead the Zamorin cast his eyes over the rest of the Portuguese contingent and gave orders for them to be seated where he could see them. The thirteen men sat down on a raised stone pavement that ran around the court. Servants brought water for washing their hands and peeled small bananas and huge jackfruit for them. The visitors had never encountered either before, and they stared at them like confused children. The Zamorin watched them with languid amusement and made some wry comments to his paan attendant, revealing teeth and gums stained a deep orangey-red from too much chewing. For the foreigners' next trial, the servants handed them a golden ewer and signaled that they were to drink without touching the vessel to their lips. Some of the men poured the contents straight down their throats and started choking, while the rest tipped it over their faces and clothes. The Zamorin chortled even more.

Vasco da Gama had been given a seat facing the royal couch, and the Zamorin turned back to him and invited him to address his remarks to the assembled court. Later on, he indicated, his courtiers would inform him what had been said.

Gama demurred. He was the ambassador of the great king of Portugal, he declared, covering his mouth with his hand—the correct method of address, he had been told, to stop his breath from sullying the royal air. His message was for the Zamorin's ears only.

The Zamorin seemed to approve. A retainer ushered Gama and Fernão Martins, the Arabic-speaking interpreter, into a private chamber. The Zamorin followed with his chief factor, his head priest, and his paan supplier, who he explained were his trusted confidants. The factor, the Zamorin's commercial agent, was instantly recognizable from his clothing as a Muslim, but whatever the visitors' misgivings, his presence was essential: the addresses of the king and the ambassador—one speaking the local Malayalam language, the other Portuguese—had to be translated via Arabic.

The rest of the Portuguese delegation stayed outside, where they watched an old man struggle to remove the royal couch and tried to catch a glimpse of the princesses who peeked down from an upstairs gallery.

Inside the chamber the Zamorin arrayed himself on another couch, this one covered with gold-embroidered cloths, and asked the captain-major what he wanted.

Vasco da Gama gave his big speech, and the Chronicler later set it down.

He was the ambassador of the king of Portugal, Gama explained, who was the lord of many countries and was far richer than any Indian ruler. For sixty years his king's ancestors had sent ships to discover the sea route to India, as they knew that there they would find Christian princes like themselves, of whom the Zamorin was the chief. This alone was the reason they had ordered India to be discovered, and not because they sought gold or silver, which they already had in such plenty that they had no need of any more. Successive captains had voyaged for a year, even two, until their provisions had run out and they had been forced to return home without finding what they sought. A king named Manuel was now on the throne, and he had commanded himself, Vasco da Gama, to take three ships and not return until he had met the ruler of India's Christians, on pain of having his head cut off. His king had also entrusted him with two letters for the Zamorin, but as it was now past sunset he would present them the following day. In return, King Manuel requested that the Zamorin send ambassadors to Portugal; it was the custom among Christian princes, Gama added, and he did not dare show himself before his lord and master unless he had with him some men from Calicut. Finally, he finished, he was instructed to inform the Zamorin personally that the Portuguese king desired to be his friend and brother.

The captain-major was welcome to Calicut, the Zamorin more succinctly replied. On his part he held him as a friend and brother, and he would gladly send envoys to his king.

It was getting late, and the Zamorin asked—so the Portuguese understood—whether the visitors wished to stay the night with Christians or Muslims.

If the Zamorin was still puzzled about the newcomers' origins, Gama was still mindful of his narrow escape in Africa. "With neither," he warily replied, and he begged the favor of lodgings of his own. It was clearly an unusual request, but the Zamorin ordered his factor to provide the strangers with everything they needed. With that Gama took his leave, highly satisfied with the commencement of his business.

By now it was ten o'clock. During the interview the monsoon had crashed with full force on the city, and the rain was coming down in sheets. Gama found his men sheltering on a terrace lit by the flickering flames of a giant iron lamp. There was no time to wait out the storm, and with the factor in the lead they set off for their lodgings.

Shuddering rolls and claps of thunder filled the air, low flashes of lightning tore the sky, and sudden cloudbursts turned the streets into muddy rivers. Even so, large crowds were still milling around outside the palace gates, and once again they attached themselves to the procession.

The captain-major was ushered to his palanquin, and the six porters hoisted him onto their shoulders. The rest of the visitors trudged through the mud. As the storm bore down and the crowds pressed in, they found themselves lost at night in a foreign land, without even a room to call their own.

The city was large and scattered, and the lodgings Gama had asked for were a long way off. He was exhausted after the day's excitement, and as the journey wound interminably on, he crossly asked the factor if they were going to be out all night.

The factor obligingly ordered a change of direction and took the visitors to his own house.

The Portuguese were shown into a large courtyard enclosed by a broad verandah with an overhanging tiled roof. Carpets were spread everywhere, and more huge lamps illuminated every corner. To sailors used to shipboard living it was a sumptuous and somewhat disconcerting sight.

When the storm died down the factor sent for a horse to take the captain-major the rest of the way to his quarters. It turned out that the Indians rode bareback and there was no saddle. Ambassadorial dignity did not allow for sliding off into the mud, and Gama refused to mount. A day of ceremony was fast turning into a night of farce.

Eventually the Portuguese reached their lodgings and found some of their men already there. Among the items they had carried from the ships was the captain-major's much-needed bed.

The sailors had also brought with them the gifts earmarked for the ruler of Calicut. In the morning Gama had them laid out, and the Chronicler made an inventory:

> Striped cloth, 12 pieces
> Scarlet hoods, 4
> Hats, 6
> Coral, 4 strings
> Brass hand basins, 6 in a case
> Sugar, 1 case
> Oil, 2 barrels
> Honey, 2 casks.

Nothing could be presented to the Zamorin without first passing it by the wali and the factor, and Gama dispatched a messenger to notify them of his intention. The two men came to examine the goods and burst out in incredulous laughter.

These were not things to offer a great and rich king, they lectured the stony-faced captain-major. The poorest merchants from Mecca or anywhere in India gave better gifts. Gold was the only thing that would do; these trifles, the king would never accept.

The two men continued to scoff, and Gama's face fell. He hastily improvised to cover his embarrassment. He had brought no gold, he said; he was an ambassador, not a merchant. His king had not known whether he would reach India, and so he had not given him suitably regal gifts. What he had offered was his own, and it was all he had to give. If King Manuel ordered him to return to India, he would certainly entrust him with a splendid tribute of gold, silver, and much more. Meanwhile, if the Zamorin would not take what he offered, he would send it back to the ships.

The officials were unmoved. It was the custom, they maintained, for every stranger who was favored with a royal audience to make an appropriate donation.

Gama tried again. It was very proper, he agreed, that their custom should be observed, and he therefore desired to send these gifts, which were more valuable than they seemed for the reasons he had said. Again the two men bluntly refused to forward the insulting items.

In that case, replied the captain-major, he would go and speak with the Zamorin and then return to his ship. He meant, he added icily, to tell him exactly how things stood.

The wali and the factor at least acquiesced in this. If Gama waited a short while, they said, they would conduct him to the palace themselves. Since he was a stranger, the Zamorin would be angry if he went about alone; besides, there were large numbers of Muslims in the city and he needed an escort. With that, they left him to cool his heels.

It was a humiliating moment, and it exposed a flaw in Portugal's entire plan to infiltrate the East—a flaw so glaring, it seems incredible it was not foreseen.

CHAPTER II

KIDNAP

B Y THE TIME the explorers arrived, India's civilization was already four millennia old. Age had endowed the subcontinent with three major religions, a complex caste system, countless architectural marvels, and an intellectual culture that had transformed the world. Even the most jaded travelers were apt to gush.

In the 1440s, the Persian ambassador Abd al-Razzaq struck out from Calicut for Vijayanagar, the city that gave its name to the dominant empire of southern India. Along the way he came across an eye-boggling temple cast entirely from solid bronze but for a giant humanoid figure sitting above the entrance, which was made from gold with two prodigious rubies for eyes. It was just a foretaste of what was to come. Vijayanagar was set at the foot of a steep mountain range and was enclosed by triple walls that reached for sixty miles around. Inside the great gates, avenues lined with richly embellished mansions stretched toward the imposing backdrop; Abd al-Razzaq was particularly taken by an enormously long prostitutes' bazaar that was decorated with outsize animal sculptures and featured a seemingly endless selection of bewitching girls posing outside their chambers on thrones. The simplest artisans sparkled with pearls and precious stones, while the chief eunuch went around accompanied by parasol bearers, trumpeters, and professional panegyrists whose job was to fill their employer's ears with ever more artful praise. The king, reported the Venetian traveler Niccolò de' Conti, who reached Vijayanagar at about the same time, "is by far more distinguished than all the others: he takes as many as twelve thousand wives, of whom four thousand follow him on foot wherever he may go and are employed solely in the service of the kitchen. A like number, more handsomely equipped, ride on horseback. The remainder are carried in litters, of whom two or three thousand are selected as his wives on condition that they will voluntarily burn themselves with him."

The Vijayanagar Empire had been founded a century earlier, when a Hindu monk had inspired the fractious rulers of southern India to band together against the Islamic powers that were encroaching from the north. It was still the ruling power when the Portuguese arrived. For all its resplendence, though, it was a land empire, and its authority was patchy at best along the coasts. Many of its three hundred ports were independent city-states in all but name, and Muslim merchants were the key to their wealth.

Islam had arrived in India in 712, but mass invasions had begun at the end of the tenth century. Rampaging Turkish and Afghan armies, drawn like the Persians and Greeks before them by the subcontinent's fabled riches, had smashed Hindu power and had gradually folded their culture into India's rich skein of civilization. Only southern India had stayed out of reach of the Islamic empires, but even there, Muslim traders had flourished from the early years of Islam. Merchants arriving from Mecca, Cairo, Hormuz, and Aden had settled on the Malabar Coast and had married local women; their children, known as Mappilas, crewed the Arab fleets. Calicut, in particular, had been home to a rich and powerful Muslim community for so long that its beginnings were lost in legend. One Arab story held that it all started when a Hindu ruler named Cheruma Perumal—or Shermanoo Permaloo—converted to Islam and set off on the hajj to Mecca. Before leaving he divided his lands among his relatives, but he left the patch of land from which he embarked to a simple cow herder. The land grew into Calicut and the cowherd became the Zamorin, the first among the coastal kings. More likely it was the city's open-market tradition that had made it popular with Arab merchants, but either way, they had taken control of the kingdom's foreign trade, were ruled by their own emir and judge, and had forged a close alliance with the Zamorins.

The Zamorins had prospered accordingly. By one count they had a hundred thousand armed men—an entire caste of noble warriors called Nairs—at their command, and their lives had become a perpetual round of ceremonies, feasts, and festivals that started at their investiture and continued long after they had been cremated on a fragrant pyre of sandalwood and aloeswood. As a mark of respect for a dead Zamorin, every man in the kingdom shaved his body from head to foot, leaving only his eyebrows and eyelashes unpruned; for a fortnight all public business ceased, and anyone who chewed paan risked having his lips cut off. Since the women of the Zamorin's caste enjoyed an unusual degree of sexual freedom—and since by custom the Zamorin paid a Brahmin, a priest or scholar from the highest caste, to deflower his wife—inheritance passed through the sister's line, and the new Zamorin was usually a nephew of the deceased. His induction began with a sprinkling of milk and water and a ceremonial bath. The ancestral ankle bracelet—a heavy gold cylinder encrusted with jewels—was clasped into place, and he was blindfolded and massaged with meadow grasses. His attendants filled nine silver censers representing the nine planets that determined human destiny with sap and water, heated them over a fire into which they threw ghee and rice, and emptied them over his head. As a mantra was whispered into his ear, he proceeded to his private temple to worship his guardian goddess and the golden dynastic sword. He moved on to his private gymnasium, where he bowed before each of the twenty-seven tutelary deities and was presented with his own sword of state by the hereditary instructor-at-arms. After prostrating himself before the high priest and receiving the royal benediction three times—"Protecting cows and Brahmins, reign as king of the hills and the waves"—he returned to his dressing room to put on the rest of the ornaments of state. Finally he sat on a white rug spread on a black carpet, and in the twinkling light of hundreds of gold lamps, the Brahmins threw rice and flowers over his head. For a year he mourned his predecessor, letting his nails and hair grow wild, never changing his clothes and eating only once a day, until at last he came into his own.

Each day of his reign began with a prayer to the sun and an hourlong massage with perfumed oils. He bathed in the palace pool while his nobles buffed him from the side, and when he emerged, his attendants dried him off and massaged him with more precious oils. His valet daubed him with a paste of sandalwood and aloeswood pounded with saffron and rosewater, sprinkled him with leaves and flowers, and smeared the moistened ashes of his ancestors on his forehead and chest. While the grooming rituals were going on, a dozen of the comeliest teenage girls of the realm mixed fresh cow dung with water in large gold basins and handed them to an army of women cleaners, who disinfected every inch of the palace by rubbing in the diluted dung with their hands. Following a visit to his temple the Zamorin retired to his dining pavilion for three hours, and after briefly seeing to the affairs of state, he installed himself in his audience chamber. If no one came he passed his time with his lords, buffoons, and mountebanks, playing a game of chance with dice, watching his soldiers spar, or simply chewing paan.

Very occasionally he went out in a silk-lined palanquin slung on a bamboo pole studded with jewels; whenever he had to walk, baize was laid beneath his feet. A brass band headed up the procession, followed by archers, spear carriers, and swordsmen staging bravura displays of fencing. Four attendants walked in front of the royal litter holding parasols made of fine cotton and embroidered silk, pairs of servants fanned the royal person on either side, and the paan page was always ready with his golden cup and spittoon. More page boys followed, bearing the golden sword of state, a selection of gold and silver ewers, and piles of towels. "And when the king wishes to put his hand to his nose or eyes or mouth," one astonished Portuguese onlooker noted, "they pour some water from the ewer on his fingers, and the other hands him the towel, which he carries, to wipe himself." Bringing up the rear were the royal nephews, governors,

and officers, while all around acrobats tumbled and jesters jested.
If the procession took place at night, great iron lamps and wooden
torches lit the way.

It was into this ancient, intricate, and rich civilization that
the Portuguese had blundered. They had never heard of Hindus,
never mind Buddhists or Jains. In Mombasa, Gama's emissaries had
mistaken a picture of a Hindu pigeon god for the Holy Spirit. In
Malindi, his crews had misheard chants of "Krishna!" for cries of
"Christ!" In Calicut, the landing party had assumed that Hindu
temples were Christian churches, they had misconstrued the Brahmins' invocation of a local deity as veneration of the Virgin Mary,
and they had decided the Hindu figures on the temple walls were
outlandish Christian saints. The temples were also crammed with
animal gods and sacred phalluses, and the Indians' devotion to cows
was deeply puzzling, but the Portuguese merely looked askance at
anything that failed to fit their preconceptions. Since it was well
known that Muslims abhorred the worship of the human form, it
was clear to them that most of the Indians they met could not be
Muslims; and since Europe's with-us-or-against-us world picture
allowed for only two religions, Christians they had to be. As far
as the Indians were concerned, it was a mark of respect to invite
visitors to their temples, and if the visitors felt a kinship with their
religion, they were not going to protest. To be called Christians was
strange, to be sure, but perhaps the language barrier was to blame.
In any case, it was not something to pursue because in Calicut the
discussion of religion was frowned on from high. "It is strictly forbidden," one European visitor reported, "to talk, dispute, or quarrel
on that subject; so there never arises any contention on that score,
every one living in great liberty of conscience under the favor and
authority of the king, who holds that to be a cardinal maxim of
government, with a view to making his kingdom very rich and of
great intercourse."

Ignorance leavened with wishful thinking had driven Europeans halfway around the globe, and the success of the entire Portu-

guese scheme rested on two deeply Western-centric assumptions. The first was that India was peopled with Christians who would be so overjoyed to be reunited with their Western brothers that they would send their Muslim allies packing. The second was that, for all their inestimable riches, the Indians were simple people who would hand over their valuable goods for a song.

Only a handful of Europeans had made it to the Malabar Coast before, and to the people of Calicut the foreigners, with their pale skin and cumbersome clothes, were a curiosity worth witnessing. Despite their uncouth and dirty appearance they had been welcomed with due ceremony, and in return they had made an offering that would have been perfectly acceptable if it had come from a common grocer. In short, they had made themselves look ridiculous, and even worse, compared to the city's rich Muslim merchants they had made themselves look poor.

Vasco da Gama was way out of his depth, and he had no idea where to turn.

AFTER HIS GIFTS had been snubbed, Gama waited all day for the two officials to reappear. They never did, but news of his gaffe had clearly traveled fast. A steady trickle of Muslim merchants showed up at his lodgings and made a great show of ridiculing the rejected goods.

By now the captain-major was glowering at all around him. The Indians, he complained, had turned out to be an apathetic and unreliable people. He got ready to go to the palace, then at the last moment decided to bide his time. As usual, his men were less burdened with the need to maintain their dignity. "As to us others," the Chronicler recorded, "we diverted ourselves, singing and dancing to the sound of trumpets, and enjoyed ourselves much."

The next morning the officials finally showed up and led the Portuguese party to the palace.

The courtyard was lined with armed guards, and Gama was kept waiting for four hours. By midday it was ferociously hot, and tem-

peratures were rising all around by the time the ushers emerged and
told the captain-major he could only take two of his men inside.

"I expected you yesterday," the Zamorin rebuked his visitor as
soon as he was within earshot.

Not wishing to lose face, Gama mildly replied that the long
journey had tired him.

The captain-major, the Zamorin sharply rejoined, had said that
he came on a mission of friendship from a very rich kingdom. Yet
he had brought nothing to prove it. Just what sort of friendship
did he have in mind? He had also promised to deliver a letter, and
he had not produced even that.

"I have brought nothing," replied Gama, robustly ignoring his
frosty reception, "because the object of my voyage was merely to
make discoveries." It had been uncertain, he added, whether he
would reach Calicut by a way never before attempted. When other
ships followed, the Zamorin would see how rich his country was.
As to the letter, it was true that he had brought one, and he would
deliver it forthwith.

The Zamorin refused to be swayed. What was it, he asked, that
the captain-major had come to discover? Was it stones, or men? If he
had come in search of men, why had he not brought gifts with him?
Perhaps he had, but he did not want to deliver them. Aboard one of
the ships, he had been informed, was a golden statue of a St. Mary.

The statue, Gama indignantly replied, was not made of gold but
of gilt wood. Even if it were gold he would not part with it. The
Holy Virgin had guided him safely across the ocean, and she would
lead him back to his own country.

The Zamorin backed off and instead asked to see the letter.

First, Gama begged, he should send for a Christian who spoke
Arabic; since the Muslims wished to do him harm, they would no
doubt misrepresent its contents.

The Zamorin assented, and everyone waited until a young
translator appeared.

He had two letters, Gama explained when they resumed: one

written in his own language and the other in Arabic. He was able to read the first, and he knew there was nothing in it that might cause offense; as to the other, he could not read it, and while it might be perfectly good, it might contain misleading errors. Presumably he expected the "Christian" to confer in Arabic with Fernão Martins, whom he had brought with him into the court, in order to check the contents of the letter before rendering it into Malayalam. His careful plan was thwarted when it turned out that the young translator, though he spoke Arabic, was completely unable to read it, and in the end Gama was forced to hand his letter to four Muslims. They looked it over among themselves and translated it aloud into the king's tongue.

The letter was full of royal flattery. King Manuel, it said, had learned that the Zamorin was not only one of the mightiest kings of all the Indies but also a Christian. He had immediately sent his men to establish a treaty of friendship and trade with him. If the Zamorin would give them a license to buy spices, he would send him many things that were not to be had in India, and if the samples his captain-major had brought with him were not satisfactory, he was willing to send gold and silver instead.

The Zamorin unbent a little at the prospect of boosting his revenues with a new influx of taxable goods.

"What kind of merchandise," he asked Gama, " is to be found in your country?"

"Much corn," replied the captain-major, "cloth, iron, bronze, and many other things."

"Do you have any of this merchandise with you?" asked the Zamorin.

"A little of each sort," replied Gama, "as samples." If he was permitted to return to his ships, he added, he would order the goods to be landed; four or five men would stay at their lodgings as a guarantee.

To Gama's indignation, the Zamorin refused. The captain-major could take all his people with him right now, he said; he could bring his ships properly into the harbor like a regular merchant, land his cargo, and sell it for the best price he could get.

Gama had no intention of doing anything of the sort. He knew perfectly well that his trade goods were worth next to nothing; he had come to make a treaty directly with the Zamorin, not to barter baubles with Muslim merchants. He bowed out of the court, picked up his men, and returned to his lodgings. It was already late at night, so he made no attempt to leave.

The next morning the Zamorin's representatives arrived with another saddleless horse for his use. Whether or not they were being mischievous, Gama declined to embarrass himself further and demanded a palanquin. After a detour to borrow one from a wealthy merchant, the party set off on the long trek back to the ships, accompanied by another large detachment of soldiers and more curious crowds.

The rest of the Portuguese went on foot, and they soon fell behind. They were trudging through the mud as best they could when the wali overtook them in his own palanquin, but before long both he and the main group were out of sight. The men lost their way and wandered far inland, and they would have wandered farther if the wali had not sent back a guide to rescue them. Eventually, as the light faded, they regained the path and reached Pantalayini.

The sun had already set when they found Gama in one of the many rest houses that lined the road to the harbor to shelter travelers from the rain. He gave his men a black look and sharply pointed out that he would have been back on board his ship if they had kept up.

The wali was with him, along with a large group of his men, and Gama immediately demanded a boat. The Indians suggested he wait until morning. It was late, they explained, and he might lose his way in the dark.

Gama was in no mood to listen. Unless the wali provided him with a boat at once, he insisted, he would go back to the city and inform the Zamorin that his officials had refused to escort the visitors to their ships. They were clearly trying to detain him, he added; it was a very bad way to behave to a fellow Christian.

"When they saw the dark looks of the captain," reported the Chronicler, "they said he was at liberty to depart at once, and that they would give him thirty boats if he needed them."

In the gloom the Indians led the Portuguese to the beach. The boats that were usually pulled up there seemed to have vanished along with their owners, and the wali dispatched some men to find them. Gama was getting increasingly suspicious, and he was convinced the governor was bluffing. As a precaution he quietly told three men to head along the beach and look out for Nicolau Coelho's boats; if they found him, they were to tell him to make himself scarce. The scouts found nothing, but by the time they came back the rest of the party had disappeared.

As soon as the wali had realized that three sailors were missing, he had escorted the remaining foreigners to the mansion of a Muslim merchant and had left them there, explaining that he and his soldiers were going to search for the stray men. It was late, and Gama had Fernão Martins purchase some food from their hosts. After their exhausting ramble the men were ravenous and, slumping awkwardly on the floor, they started in on dishes of chicken and rice.

The search party did not return until morning, and by then Gama's mood had improved. The Indians seemed well meaning, after all, he brightly said to his men; no doubt they had been right to warn against setting out in the dark. For once the men were less sanguine than their commander, and they looked mistrustfully around.

It was now June 1. The three scouts had not been found, and Gama assumed they had got away with Coelho. Once again he asked for boats, but rather than agree, the wali's men began to whisper among themselves. Eventually they said they would provide them, if the captain-major ordered his fleet to anchor nearer the shore.

This was tricky, since the Zamorin had made the same request, but Gama was determined not to put his ships and crews in harm's way. If he gave any such order, he replied, his brother would assume he was a prisoner and would immediately set sail for home.

Unless he gave exactly that order, the Indians countered, he and his men would not be allowed to leave.

The two sides seemed to have reached an impasse, and Gama reddened with indignation. In that case, he said tersely, the best thing was for him to return to Calicut. If the Zamorin wanted him to stay in his country and refused to let him leave, he added, that was one thing; he would gladly oblige. If not, the Zamorin would doubtless be interested to know that his orders had been blatantly disobeyed.

The Indians seemed to relent, but before anyone could make a move, a large force of armed men appeared in the house and the doors banged shut. No one was allowed out, even to relieve himself, without his own personal detachment of guards.

The officials soon came back with a new demand. If the ships were not going to come in to shore, they said, they would have to give up their sails and rudders.

They would do no such thing, Gama retorted. The Indians could do what they liked with him, but he would give up nothing. His men, though, he added, were starving; if he was going to be detained, surely they could be let go?

The guards refused to be moved. The Portuguese must stay where they were, they answered. If they died of hunger, so be it; it meant nothing to them.

The captain-major and his men were starting to fear the worst, though they did their best to put on a brave face. While they were awaiting their captors' next move, one of the missing sailors showed up. The three scouts, he reported, had indeed found Nicolau Coelho the night before, but rather than keeping out of the way, as Gama had urged, Coelho was still stationed off the beach and was expecting them.

Gama quietly told one of his men to slip away and pass on to

Coelho strict orders to return to the ships and move them to a safer place. The sailor sneaked out, ran down the beach, and jumped in one of the boats, which immediately set off to the fleet. The guards, though, had spotted him, and they raised the cry. Suddenly the missing Indian boats appeared and the guards dragged a sizable flotilla into the water. They rowed furiously after the retreating Portuguese, but they soon realized they could not overtake them. Instead they returned to the shore and directed the captain-major to write to his brother, commanding him to bring the ships into port.

Personally, Gama replied, he was perfectly willing to comply, but as he had already explained, his brother would never go along with it. Even if he did, his sailors were not keen to die and they would not budge.

The Indians refused to believe him. He was the commander, they protested; surely any order he gave would be obeyed?

The Portuguese huddled together and talked things over. Gama was now resolved to keep the ships out of the port at any cost; once inside, he explained, their long-range guns would be useless and they could easily be captured. When the Indians had seized the fleet, he added, they would undoubtedly kill him first and the rest of them after. His men agreed; they had already reached the same conclusion.

The day wore on and the tension rose. That night a hundred guards clustered around the prisoners and took turns to keep watch. They were armed with swords, two-edged battle-axes, and bows and arrows, and they were getting restless. The Portuguese were convinced they would be marched off one by one and roughed up at the very least, though they still managed to make a good supper off more of the local produce.

The next morning, the wali returned and proposed a compromise. Since the captain-major had informed the Zamorin that he intended to land his goods, he should order it done. It was the custom of Calicut for every ship to unload its cargo without delay, and for the crews and merchants to stay on land until their business was over. This time they would make an exception, and he and his men could return to their ships as soon as the merchandise arrived.

Gama had promised no such thing, but since he was in no position to argue he sat down and wrote a letter to his brother. He explained that he was being held, though he was careful to say he was being well treated, and he told Paulo to send over some—not all—of their trade goods. If he failed to return shortly, he added, Paulo should assume that he was still a prisoner and that the Indians were trying to hijack the ships. In that case, Paulo was to sail for Portugal and explain everything to the king. He trusted, he added, that Manuel would dispatch a great war fleet and his liberty would be restored.

Paulo immediately had some merchandise loaded in a boat, though after a heated discussion with the messengers he sent back word that he could not live with the dishonor if he went home without his brother. He trusted, he added, that with God's help their small force would be able to free him.

The boat arrived at the shore, and the goods were transferred to an empty warehouse. The wali held true to his word, and Gama and his men were let go. They returned to the fleet, leaving behind the clerk Diogo Dias and an assistant to look after the merchandise.

"At this we rejoiced greatly," the Chronicler recorded, "and rendered thanks to God for having extricated us from the hands of people who had no more sense than beasts."

This detail from the Catalan Atlas of 1375 shows the Africa of the Western imagination. Bottom left, an Arab trader on a camel approaches Mansa Musa, the emperor of Mali, who holds out a nugget from his rich gold mines. Bottom right is the Red Sea. The claw-like ochre line represents the Atlas Mountains.

On this Catalan world map of around 1450, a great gulf slices into Africa, picturing Europeans' hopes of reaching Ethiopia, the supposed home of the great Christian emperor Prester John. The colored dots to the right represent the Spice Islands.

This plate from Marco Polo's *Livre des Merveilles* shows three of the fantastic races believed to live in Asia: the Blemmya, the Sciapod, and the Cyclops.

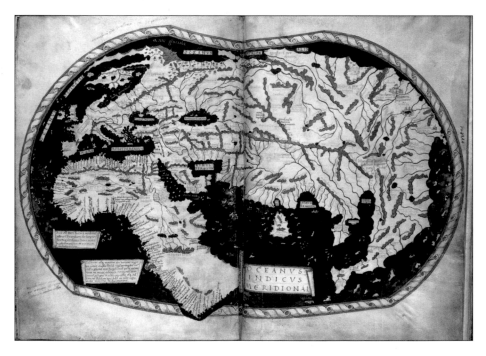

In his world map of 1489, Henricus Martellus responded to Bartolomeu Dias's discovery of the southern tip of Africa by hastily drawing the Cape of Good Hope over the original border. The depiction of Asia has changed little since the first-century maps of Ptolemy.

The final siege of Constantinople, 1453. At the bottom is the Turkish camp; to the left, across the Golden Horn, is Galata, the Genoese quarter. In the distance, across the crowded Bosporus, is the Asian shore.

(Above left) Henry the Navigator, from the fifteenth-century Polytriptych of St. Vincent.

(Above right) King Manuel I "The Fortunate" of Portugal, from a contemporary illuminated manuscript.

Manuel's parents-in-law and rivals, King Ferdinand II of Aragon and Queen Isabella I of Castile, painted for their wedding portrait.

A notably piratical Vasco da Gama, in a portrait by an unknown artist that belonged to Gama's descendants.

·S· graciel

Vasquo da gama,

The *São Gabriel*, Vasco da Gama's flagship on the first voyage, from the *Memórias das Armadas* of 1568.

A sixteenth-century mural in the Veerabhadra Temple at Lepakshi, Andhra Pradesh—originally part of the Vijayanagar Empire—suggests the types of temple paintings that Gama and his men saw at Calicut.

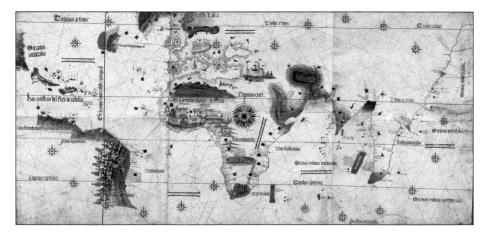

The Cantino planisphere was smuggled out of Lisbon by Alberto Cantino, a secret agent of the Duke of Ferrara, in 1502. The Red Sea is still red and Southeast Asia is still mostly conjecture, but the world is beginning to take on a recognizable shape. The careful charting by Vasco da Gama's crews is evident in the depiction of the east coast of Africa and the west coast of India. Brazil is swimming into view; through it runs the Tordesillas line, the meridian that divided the world between the Spanish and Portuguese.

The *Santa Catarina do Monte Sinai*, Vasco da Gama's flagship on his final voyage to India in 1524.

A portrait of Vasco da Gama painted around 1524 on the eve of his last voyage.

Lisbon in 1572, from the *Civitates Orbis Terrarum* by Braun & Hogenberg. The old Moorish castle is at top right; the new royal castle juts out to the waterfront left of center, well positioned to keep an eye on the loading and unloading of ships. Lisbon, the legend reads, is "the most noted trading center for the entire Orient."

Portuguese roughnecks swaggering like lords in Goa, from the *Itinerario* of Jan Huygen van Linschoten.

CHAPTER 12

DANGERS AND DELIGHTS

T HE SUN SETS on the Malabar Coast in a giant orange fireball that majestically drowns itself in the Indian Ocean. The sky is striated with orange and lemon, cream and blue. Out at sea puffs of cumulus cloud are caught in the glow, lit from beneath like the lumpy underside of heaven. Over land, wispy cirrus clouds turn a delicate but intense violet and seem to brush the tops of the palm forests. The soft waves send bronzed ripples to the shore; the floating clumps of weed, the last few boats out at sea, and the crows flying between the branches of shoreline trees are all silhouetted against the dying fire. Day fades in a riot of turquoise, cerulean, sherbet yellow, salmon pink, umber, and sand, and as the clouds darken, then turn a watercolor smudge of blues, grays, and white, night falls over Calicut.

Not even the toughest sailor was immune to the beauty of India. Yet the old tales that talked of dangers lurking in Paradise had turned out to be true. To the Portuguese, there were, after all, snakes guarding the pepper plantations of the East.

In the days following Gama's return to his ship, the Portuguese warehouse received a steady trickle of visitors but no buyers. The Muslim merchants seemed to come only to scoff, and after a few days Gama sent a messenger to the palace with an official complaint about the way he, his men, and his goods were being treated. He awaited the Zamorin's orders, he pointedly added; he and his ships were at his service when he decided what action to take.

The messenger quickly returned with a Nair noble who was to

guard the warehouse, as well as seven or eight merchants who were to inspect the goods and buy any they thought fit. The Zamorin, he reported, was angry with the men who had detained the captain-major, and he intended to punish them for being bad Christians. As for the Muslims, he authorized the Portuguese to kill any who entered their warehouse without fear of reprisals. Not knowing just how powerful the king of Portugal might be, the ruler had decided to hedge his bets.

The merchants stayed for eight days, but they, too, took a dim view of the European merchandise and bought nothing. The Muslims kept their distance, but the mood had turned ugly. Every time the sailors landed, their rivals spat on the ground. "Portugal, Portugal," they hissed, turning the name of their country into a jeer. Gama ordered his men to laugh it off, but tempers frayed.

It was painfully clear that no one in Pantalayini was going to buy a single bale of cloth, and Gama sent another message to the Zamorin asking his permission to forward the merchandise to Calicut itself. Once again the ruler obliged, and he had the wali assemble a team of porters to carry the whole lot on their backs. This, the Zamorin reassured the captain-major, was to be done at his own expense; nothing belonging to the king of Portugal would be burdened with costs in his country.

It was now June 24. Heavy swells were pitching the ships up and down, and fat raindrops crashed on the decks like marbles. The unsold goods were on their way to Calicut by back and by boat, but few expected much to come of it. Gama concluded that his brother had been right all along, and he vowed never again to set foot on a foreign shore. In the circumstances, he decided it was only fair to let his men try to rescue something from the debacle by bartering their few belongings for spices. The safest course, he told them, was for one man from each ship to go ashore at a time; that way everyone would have his turn without putting a temptingly large body of hostages in harm's way.

Off they went, in twos or threes, past the boats pulled up on the beach and the fishermen's shacks and small temples, past children playing and dancing in the rain, along the long path to Calicut. They caught glimpses of arcaded pavilions painted in fresh greens and blues set amid lush gardens and orchards, and they watched with delight as the ubiquitous gray monkeys stood on their hind legs, ground their teeth, and sneaked inside. Whether grand or simple, each house had a large entrance porch with a gleaming wood floor as clean as a table where strangers were readily given food and drink and a place to rest. After their recent experience, the Portuguese were relieved to find that the locals, at least, were warmly hospitable to their brothers. The sailors, noted the Chronicler, "were made welcome by the Christians along the road, who showed much pleasure when one of them entered a house, to eat or to sleep, and they gave them freely of all they had."

After a year wedged into an all-male tub, the explorers stared unabashedly at the Indian women. They went naked from the waist up, though they wore much jewelry around their necks and on their legs and arms, hands and feet. Gaping holes in their ears were filled with gold and precious stones, and it was clearly the height of fashion to stretch the earlobes to the greatest possible length; the Zamorin's queen, one traveler reported, wore her ears down to her nipples. To their undoubted delight, the sailors soon discovered that marriage was not a sacred union among most of the higher and middle castes. Women could take several "visiting husbands" at once; the most popular had ten or more. The men pooled their resources to keep their wife in her own establishment, and when one husband came for an overnight visit, he left his weapons propped up outside the door as a signal to the others to stay away.

The women stared back at the Portuguese; they were equally mystified by the way they tangled themselves up in cumbersome clothes and sweated like sponges in the heat. Perhaps some took their mutual investigations further; if not, "public women," some of whom were also part-time wives, were everywhere to be had. Between the system of socialized courtesanship, the skilled prostitutes, and the oriental aromas of perfumes and ointments, European men thought they had arrived in a kind of sexual paradise, a discovery that elicited much moral bellyaching and more indulgence. Satisfaction, though, had its price. Niccolò de' Conti had come across many shops run by women who sold strange objects, the size of a small nut and made of gold, silver, or brass, that tinkled like a bell. "The men," he explained, "before they take a wife, go to these women (otherwise the marriage would be broken) who cut the skin of the virile member in many places and put between the skin and the flesh as many as twelve of these 'ringers' (according to their pleasure). After the member is sewn up, it heals in a few days. This they do to satisfy the wantonness of the women: because of these swellings, or tumor, of the member, the women have great pleasure in coitus. The members of some men stretch way down between their legs so that when they walk they ring out and may be heard." Not Conti: the Italian, though "scorned by the women because he had a small member and invited to rectify this," was not willing to give others pleasure through his pain.

The more curious sailors reported even stranger customs. Cows wandered everywhere, including into the royal palace, and were treated with great honor; even the Zamorin ceded place to them. Yet many men and women were shunned as if they were lepers. As the Brahmins and Nairs walked along the streets they cried out *"Po! Po!"*—"Go! Go!"—a warning to the lower castes to get out of the way. If an inferior failed to shrink to the side and bow his head, however rich and influential he might be, his superior could "freely thrust him through, and no man aske him why he did it." Once touched—even by the Portuguese—the highborn had to purify themselves with a ritual bath; if they didn't take precautions, they explained, they would have been bathing all day.

The lowest castes were not allowed anywhere near the city; they lived in the fields and ate dried mice and fish, and if they touched their betters, both they and their relatives were fair game. Unsurprisingly, many converted to Islam. One of the most pol-

luting of all castes, though—the sorcerers and exorcists—came
into their own when the Zamorin was sick. They set up a tent
at his gate, painted their bodies in a rainbow of color, donned
crowns made from grasses and flowers, and lit a bonfire. To a ca-
cophony of trumpets, kettledrums, and cymbals, they leapt out of
the tent yelling and pulling faces, breathing fireballs, and jumping
in naked flames. After two or three days they drew circles on the
ground and spun around inside until the devil entered them and
revealed how to cure the royal ailment. Without fail, the Zamorin
did as he was told.

Stranger still, even to Europeans brought up on stories of saintly
self-abuse, were the Indians' religious rituals. Some ecstatics, they
discovered, presented themselves to priests already prepared for self-
immolation:

> These have on their neck a broad, circular piece of iron, the
> front part of which is round and the back part extremely sharp.
> A chain attached to the front part hangs suspended on the breast.
> Into this the victims insert their feet, sitting down with their
> legs drawn up and their necks bent. Then, when the speaker
> pronounces certain words, they suddenly stretch out their legs
> and at the same time, drawing up their neck, cut off their own
> heads, yielding up their lives as a sacrifice to their idols. These
> men are regarded as saints.

Festivals were a particularly popular time for suicidal acts of devotion. On one day of the year, an idol accompanied by bejew-
eled girls singing hymns was pulled through the street on a wagon
drawn by a file of elephants. A European onlooker reported that
numerous Indians, "carried away by the fervor of their faith, cast
themselves on the ground before the wheels, in order that they
may be crushed to death, a mode of death which they say is very
acceptable to their gods. Others, making an incision in their sides
and inserting a rope through their bodies, hang themselves to the

chariot by way of ornament, and thus suspended and half dead accompany their idol. This kind of sacrifice they consider the best and most acceptable of all."

Yet to foreign eyes—Muslim as much as Christian—the ceremony of suttee was the most alien custom of all. By law, the first wife was compelled to be burned, while further wives, one traveler reported, were married "under the express agreement that they should add to the splendor of the funeral ceremony by their death, and this is considered a great honor for them. . . . When the pile is lighted the wife, richly dressed, walks gaily around it, singing, accompanied by a great concourse of people, amid the sounds of trumpets, flutes and songs . . . and springs in the fire. If some show fear (for it frequently happens that they become stupefied by terror at the sight of the struggles of the others suffering in the fire), they are thrown into the fire by bystanders, whether willing or not." Westerners found the spectacle morbidly fascinating. "'Tis remarkable," another onlooker observed, "that the Body of the Woman hath such an Oyley Property, that one Body will serve like Oil or Greese to consume the Bodies of 5 or 6 men."

After their crash course in Indian culture, the sailors headed to the teeming market squares and bazaars behind the harbor. There they tried to sell their few belongings—a brass or copper bracelet, a new shirt, or even the old linen shirts off their backs. They, too, found they had been wildly optimistic about the value of Portuguese goods in the East: what in Portugal counted as a very fine garment was worth a mere tenth of the price it would fetch at home. Here they sold them for whatever they could—a handful of cloves, a bundle of cinnamon, perhaps one or two garnets, sapphires, or tiny rubies—if only to take back souvenirs. At night the merchants locked up their shops with bars and heavy iron padlocks, the Zamorin's officials lowered barriers around the business area, and the sailors started back to the ships.

While the crews were making themselves at home in the town, the townsfolk rowed out and climbed on board the ships, offering coconuts, chickens, and fish in exchange for bread, biscuits, or coins. Many brought their sons and children to see the outlandish vessels. Some were clearly hungry and Gama ordered his men to feed them, not so much from an outbreak of generosity but "for the sake of establishing relations of peace and amity, and to induce them to speak well of us and not evil." The public relations exercise went so well that it was often late at night before the visitors left, and the captain-major took heart. He decided to leave a factor, a clerk, and a small staff in Calicut to bypass the merchants and sell direct to the people. With the help of the friendly local Christians, he hoped the Portuguese might put down roots in India after all.

By the time every man had taken his turn it was well into August, and Gama was more than ready to head for home. Before giving the order he dispatched his clerk Diogo Dias to inform the Zamorin that the fleet was preparing to depart and to ask for the promised ambassadors. Dias was also to offer one last gift to the ruler—a chest full of amber, corals, scarves, silks, and other pretty things—and in return he was to request large quantities of cinnamon and cloves, together with samples of other spices. If necessary, he was to say, the factor who was staying behind would pay for them when he had the funds. It was a long shot, but Gama was well aware that Christopher Columbus had returned without clear proof that he had reached the Indies, and he was not keen to make the same mistake.

Dias was kept waiting for four days. When he was finally admitted to the audience court, the Zamorin gave him a withering glance and listened impatiently. He brushed away the gifts, and when Dias had finished he warned him that the Portuguese would need to pay the customary departure tax before they could leave.

Dias bowed out, saying he would pass on the message, but he never made it to the fleet. He was tailed from the moment he left the palace, and when he stopped at the Portuguese warehouse a force of armed men burst inside and blocked the door. At the same time a proclamation went out across the city, forbidding any boat from approaching the foreigners' ships on pain of death.

Dias, the factor, the clerk, and their assistants were prisoners in the warehouse. An African boy had come with them as a servant, and they told him to find his way to the fleet and explain their predicament. The boy slipped away to the fishermen's quarter and paid a captain to take him out on his boat. Under cover of darkness the fisherman rowed over to the fleet, saw his passenger aboard, and raced back to the shore.

When they heard what had happened, the Portuguese were more dismayed and puzzled than ever.

"This news made us sad," the Chronicler noted; "not only because we saw some of our men in the hands of our enemies, but also because it interfered with our departure. We also felt grieved that a Christian king, to whom we had given of ours, should do us such an ill turn. At the same time we did not hold him as culpable as he seemed to be, for we were well aware that the Moors of the place, who were merchants from Mecca and elsewhere, and who knew us, could ill digest us." They still could not understand why the Zamorin failed to share their excitement at this historic moment—the moment when his fellow Christians had sailed into the East.

Another caller soon enlightened them. Monçaide, the merchant from Tunis, had often visited the fleet, not least because Gama had paid him to bring intelligence from the shore. With his help, the Portuguese pieced together a plausible version of what had gone wrong.

The foreigners' failure to bring a fitting tribute for the Zamorin, Monçaide explained, had been a gift to the city's Muslims. The Mappilas had begun to worry that the Portuguese might ruin their business, and they had plotted to take Gama prisoner, seize his ships, and kill his men. They had intimated to the Zamorin's advisers that the captain-major was no ambassador but a pirate bent on robbing and plunder, and they had taken their case to the wali. The wali had duly reported to the Zamorin that everyone said the

Portuguese were privateers banished from their own country. The letter purporting to come from the Portuguese king, he had added, was doubtless a fiction; what king in his right mind would send an embassy so far merely in pursuit of friendship? Even if it was real, friendship meant communication and assistance, but Portugal was a world away from India in both geography and culture. Besides, this supposedly mighty king had given poor proof of his power in the gifts he had sent. Far better, he had urged, that the Zamorin safeguard the profits he made from the Muslims than trust the promises of men who came from the extremities of the earth.

According to Monçaide, the Zamorin had been taken aback by the news, and his attitude to the Europeans had hardened. The merchants, meanwhile, had bribed the wali to detain Gama and his men so they could surreptitiously have them killed. The wali had rushed out of town after the departing explorer, and he had only let his captives go when the Zamorin had had second thoughts. Though the plot had failed, the Muslims had carried on with their campaign, and eventually the Zamorin had made up his mind in their favor. Monçaide warned Gama and his men not to set foot in the city if they valued their lives, and two Indian visitors amplified his ominous words. "If the captains went ashore," they declared, "their heads would be cut off, as this was the way the king dealt with those who came to his country without giving him gold."

"Such then was the state of affairs," the Chronicler bleakly recorded.

So the Portuguese believed. There was, though, a simpler explanation for Vasco da Gama's troubles. It was the custom for ambassadors to present the Zamorin with lavish gifts. It was the law for visiting merchants to pay a tithe in return for enjoying his hospitality and protection. Gama had presented himself as both ambassador and merchant, and on both counts he had failed to deliver.

The truth lay somewhere between the two, but in any case little could be done. In the absence of Christian allies or spices that could be scooped up like spring blossom, the Portuguese had only one lever left: brute force.

THE NEXT DAY no one visited the ships, but the day after, four young men approached with jewels for sale. The wary captain-major decided the Muslim merchants had sent them as spies, but he gave them a warm welcome in the hope that more important figures would follow.

After four or five days a party of twenty-five drew alongside, and among them were six Nair nobles. Gama sprang his trap and had the six men seized, together with a dozen more for good measure. The rest were bundled into a boat and were sent to shore with a let-ter, written in Malayalam by two of the Indians, for the Zamorin's factor. Its gist was that the Portuguese proposed a hostage swap.

The news spread fast. The hostages' relatives and friends gath-ered at the Portuguese warehouse, forced the guards to give up their captives, and pointedly delivered them to the factor's house.

It was now August 23, and Gama decided to make a show of leaving. The monsoon was still gusting strongly, and the ships were blown farther out to sea than he intended. The next day they were blown back toward land. Two days later, with still no sign of their men and a steadier wind, they moved away again until the shore was just visible on the horizon.

The day after, a boat approached with a message. Diogo Dias had been moved to the royal palace. If the Portuguese freed their hostages, he would be returned to them.

Gama was sure his men had been killed and his enemies were trying to gain time. He was aware that the Arab fleets were due within weeks, and he was convinced the Muslims of Calicut were arming in preparation for a joint attack on the Christians. He threatened to open fire on the boat, and he warned the messengers not to return without his factor, or at the very least a message from him. They had better act quickly, he barked, or he would chop off his hostages' heads.

A stiff breeze sprang up and the fleet tacked along the coast.

In Calicut, Gama's maneuvers seemed to have worked. The Zamorin sent for Dias, and this time he received him in a markedly friendlier manner. Why, he asked him, was the captain-major sailing off with his subjects on board?

The Zamorin knew perfectly well why, Dias acidly answered, at last venting his spleen. He had imprisoned him and his men, and he was still preventing them from returning to their ships.

The Zamorin feigned astonishment. The captain-major had done the right thing, he declared, and he turned on his factor.

"Are you unaware," he asked in a menacing tone, "that quite recently I killed another factor because he levied tribute upon some merchants who had come to my country?"

He turned back to Dias.

"Go back to the ships," he told him, "you and the others who are with you. Tell the captain to send me the men he took. Tell him that the pillar which I understood him to say he desires to be erected on the shore will be brought back by those who take you and will be put up, and that you may remain here with your merchandise."

Before he left, the Zamorin had Dias write a letter with an iron pen on a palm leaf. It was addressed to the king of Portugal.

"Vasco da Gama," it read, after the usual niceties, "a gentleman of your household, came to my country, at which I was pleased. My country is rich in cinnamon, cloves, ginger, pepper, and precious stones. In exchange I ask you for gold, silver, corals, and scarlet cloth."

The Zamorin instructed the clerk to give the captain-major the letter to forward to his king. In the end, he had decided it was worth seeing whether the foreigners might return with more valuable goods.

On the morning of August 27, seven boats sailed toward the Portuguese fleet with Dias and his men on board. The Indians were reluctant to get too close to Gama's ship, and after some debate they gingerly approached the longboat that was tied to the *São Gabriel's* stern. The freed men climbed inside and the boats backed off a little, waiting for the response.

The Indians had not brought the Portuguese merchandise with them, since they expected the factor and his staff to return to the city. Gama had other ideas. Now that his men were safely on board, he was not going to give them up. He had the pillar transferred to the boats and he sent back several of the hostages, including the six Nairs. But he kept six more, promising to release them if his goods were returned the following day.

The next morning the friendly Tunisian merchant showed up in a great fluster. Monçaide climbed aboard and panted out a plea for asylum. All his possessions had been seized, and he was afraid for his life. The Indians had seen him on easy terms with the Portuguese, and they had accused him of being a covert Christian who had been sent to spy on their city. Given his usual run of luck, he lamented, he would undoubtedly be murdered if he stayed. Monçaide had proved a useful informant, and Gama agreed to take him to Portugal.

At ten o'clock seven more boats approached. Spread along the benches were twelve bales of striped cloth belonging to the Portuguese. That, the Zamorin's men insisted, was all they had found in the warehouse.

Gama unceremoniously told them to get lost. He did not give a fig for the goods, his translator shouted back, and he was going to take his prisoners to Portugal. It was true that plenty of merchandise was still unaccounted for, but more to the point, Gama needed some Indians to stand witness to his discovery and the Zamorin had reneged on his promise to send ambassadors. As a parting shot, he warned the men in the boats to watch out. With luck, he vowed, he would soon be back, and then they would find out whether they should have listened to the Muslims who called him and his crew thieves. On his command the gunners echoed his words with a salvo from the bombards, and the Indians rowed away in a hurry.

It was almost the end of August. Gama conferred with his captains, and they quickly reached a decision. The Chronicler set it down:

"Inasmuch that we had discovered the country we had come in search of, as also spices and precious stones, and it appeared impossible to establish cordial relations with the people, it would be as well to take our departure. And it was resolved that we should take with us the men whom we detained, as, on our return to Calicut, they might be useful to us in establishing friendly relations. We therefore set sail and left for Portugal, greatly rejoicing at our good fortune in having made so great a discovery."

No one could pretend that things had gone smoothly. The young commander had talked a good talk, but he had failed to cut a deal with the Zamorin. The longer he had stayed, the more humiliating the situation had become. After three months, the ships' holds were almost empty. Worst of all, the Portuguese were deeply shaken by the hostility of men they believed were their brothers in Christ.

The explorers' blunderings would soon come back to haunt them, but even so, there was no question that Vasco da Gama had pulled off an astonishing feat. Where he had led, many thousands would follow, and many millions of lives would be changed for good, if not necessarily for the better.

Now all he had to do was to get home. That would turn out to be the hardest part of all.

THE TROUBLE BEGAN a day into the return journey.

The fleet had only moved a league from Calicut when it found itself becalmed. As the crews waited for the wind, they suddenly saw seventy long rowboats swarming toward them from the shore. They were packed with heavily armed Mappilas wearing padded breastplates and backplates covered in red cloth. As Gama had suspected, the Muslim merchants had been busy preparing a war fleet, though they had not been able to detain the interlopers long enough for the large Arab ships to arrive.

The gunners scrambled to their stations and waited for the captain-major's signal. As soon as the enemy moved within range he gave the order to fire. With a flash and a boom, cannonballs whistled through the air and splashed jets of foam around the boats. Still the rowers kept up their rhythm, and as the wind finally picked up and the foreigners' sails filled out, they rowed even harder. For an hour and a half they pursued the fleeing ships, until a providential thunderstorm blew up and swept the Portuguese out to sea.

With the brief panic past, the ships held their course to the north. To reach home, Gama had learned that he needed to follow the coast until he caught the cool northeast winds of the winter monsoon. In time, they would blow him steadily back to Africa. That time, though, was still at least three months off: the monsoon would not start to turn until November.

To complicate the pilots' task still more, the fleet was now sailing into the doldrums. Breezes wafted this way from land, that way from sea, and then petered out. Squalls blew up without warning and sputtered into dead calms. The ships laboriously tacked along the coast; twelve days after leaving Calicut, they had only made twenty leagues.

Gama had been deeply pondering what had happened, and he chose one of the hostages—a man who had lost one of his eyes—to go ashore with a letter for the Zamorin. In the letter, which Monçaide wrote in Arabic, he apologized for taking six of the Zamorin's people hostage and explained that he intended them to bear witness to his discoveries. He would have left his factor behind, he added, if he had not been afraid the Muslims would kill him; he himself had been deterred from landing more often for the same reason. Ultimately, he hoped, the two nations would establish friendly relations to their mutual advantage and profit. Since he could hardly have expected one letter to transform the situation, he must have keenly noted the information given him by the captives that the Kolattiri of Cannanore, the king of this part of the coast, was at war with the Zamorin of Calicut.

By September 15 the ships had made sixty leagues, and they anchored near a small cluster of islands. The largest was a long, narrow sliver, rocky at its southern end, with low hills fringed by a beach to the north and a canopy of palm trees shading the center like tall umbrellas. Two leagues away on the mainland was a broad sandy bay backed by dense woods. Fishing boats set out from the bay offering their catch for sale; the captain-major handed out a few shirts to the fishermen, who beamed with pleasure.

Gama finally began to unwind in the friendlier atmosphere, and he asked the locals if they would like him to erect a pillar on the island. "They said," recorded the Chronicler, "that they would be very glad indeed, for its erection would confirm the fact that we were Christians like themselves." Or so the Portuguese understood.

The pillar was heaved into place, and the Portuguese named the island, after the saint's name given to the pillar, Santa Maria. It was scarcely a strategic prize, but everyone was desperate to go home.

That night the ships caught a land breeze and carried on north. Five days later they sailed past a series of beautiful, verdant hills and saw five more islands ahead, just off the shore. They anchored in the roadstead near the mainland, and Gama sent out a boat to find sufficient fresh water and wood to see them to Africa.

As soon as they landed, the sailors ran into a young man who led them to a cleft between two hills that rose from a riverbank. There they found a wonderfully clear spring bubbling up, and Gama gave the guide a red nightcap in return. As usual, he asked if he was Christian or Muslim. He was a Christian, the man replied; at least, he was not a Muslim, and he chose the only alternative on offer. Gama told him that the Portuguese were Christians, too, and he seemed very happy at the news.

Soon more friendly Indians appeared and offered to lead the visitors to a forest of cinnamon trees. The sailors returned with armfuls of branches that smelled somewhat of cinnamon and twenty locals carrying chickens, pots of milk, and gourds. After their troubles, things finally seemed to be looking up.

Early the next morning, while they were waiting for the tide to turn so they could enter the river and fill their water casks, the watchmen spotted two ships coasting a couple of leagues away. At first Gama made nothing of the news, and the crews busied themselves chopping wood. After a while, though, he began to wonder whether the distance had made the ships look smaller than they really were. As soon as they had eaten, he ordered some of the men into the boats to find out whether they belonged to Muslims or Christians. As an extra precaution he sent a sailor up to the crow's nest, and the lookout cried out that six leagues away, out in the open sea, eight ships were becalmed.

Gama decided to take no risks. The decks were cleared, and he ordered the gunners to sink the vessels as soon as they came within range.

When the wind picked up the Indian ships moved off, and they quickly drew within two leagues of the Portuguese. On Gama's command the fleet sprang forward, guns at the ready.

When the Indians saw the three strange vessels heading straight for them, they bore away for the coast. In their haste one of their ships broke its rudder, and its crew heaved a boat off the stern, jumped in, and rowed to land. Nicolau Coelho's caravel was nearest to the abandoned ship and his men eagerly boarded her, expecting to find rich booty belowdecks. Instead they uncovered a few coconuts, four jars of palm sugar, and a large cache of bows and arrows, shields, swords, and spears; in the hold was nothing but sand.

The rest of the Indian ships had made it to the shore. Rather than move in and lose the advantage of their guns, the Portuguese fired at them from the boats, sending the crews scrambling inland. After a while Gama's men gave up and retreated to a safe distance, with the captured vessel in tow. They were still none the wiser as to where the ships had come from, but the next morning seven locals rowed over. The fleeing men, they revealed, had told them they had been sent by the Zamorin to hunt down the Portuguese. A notorious pirate named Timoja was their leader, and if he could he would undoubtedly have murdered every last one of them.

There was obviously no returning to the mainland. The fleet moved off the next morning and anchored close to one of the islands, which the Portuguese called Anjediva, after its local name. The Indians had told them they would find another freshwater source there, and after they had run the captured ship aground, Nicolau Coelho set out to reconnoiter.

Coelho landed on a pristine beach and delved into a lush forest of coconut palms and tropical evergreens. Suddenly he came upon the ruins of what appeared to be a large stone church on a hill.

A single chapel was still standing, and it had been reroofed with straw. Coelho peered inside.

Three black stones stood in the center, and a number of Indians were praying to them. When the Portuguese quizzed them, they explained that Arab sailors used the island to restock with water and wood and had driven out the inhabitants; they only came back to worship the sacred stones.

Near to the church the search party discovered a large tank built of the same hewn stone. The water was fresh, and they filled some of their casks. When they explored further, they came upon a much bigger tank on the highest point of the island and filled the rest.

By now the three ships were in a dangerously unseaworthy state. The crews began the long repair process by dragging the *Berrio* to the beach in front of the ruined church, emptying it, and careening it.

While they were hard at work, two large boats approached from the mainland. They reminded the Portuguese of the fast galliots— small oared galleys with a shallow draft and a single mast—in which the pirates of the Barbary Coast pounced on passing ships. The rowers dipped their blades to the beat of drums accompanied by what sounded uncannily like bagpipes. Flags and streamers fluttered from the mast. In the distance the Portuguese could see five other ships creeping along the coast, as if lying in wait to see what happened.

The Indians from Calicut excitedly warned their captors not to let the visitors on board. They were pirates, they said, who roamed the seas in those parts. They would pretend they came in friendship, but at the moment of their choosing they would whip out their firearms, rob them of all they had, and take them as slaves.

Gama ordered the *Rafael* and the *Gabriel* to open fire.

The men in the boats ducked and shouted at the foreigners. *"Tambaram! Tambaram!"* they cried; "Lord! Lord!"

The Portuguese had already concluded that this was the Indians' name for God, and they deduced that the men were trying to tell them they were Christians. Even so, they assumed it was another ruse, and they kept on firing. The rowers hastily turned back toward the shore, and Coelho chased them in his boat until Gama, fearful of any more mishaps, raised a signal flag to call him back.

The next day the work on the *Berrio* was still under way when a dozen men appeared in two smaller boats. They were smartly dressed, and they brought a bundle of sugarcane as a gift for the captain-major. They beached their boats, walked up the sand, and asked permission to take a look at the foreigners' ships.

Gama was not in a hospitable mood. By now it seemed as if the whole coast knew about the Portuguese, while the Portuguese knew next to nothing about the coast. Every day a new threat materialized, and he was sure the newcomers had been sent to spy on him. He shouted at them and they backed away, warning twelve more men who were just arriving in two more boats not to land.

The *Berrio* was refloated, and the crews moved onto the *São Gabriel*.

Despite the hostile reception the locals kept on coming, and some managed to sell the Portuguese fish, pumpkins, cucumbers, and boatloads of the green branches that smelled vaguely of cinnamon. Gama was in a less suspicious frame of mind when a striking figure walked up the beach waving a wooden cross.

The newcomer was about forty years old and spoke excellent Venetian as well as Arabic, Hebrew, Syriac, and German. He was dressed in a long linen gown and a dapper Muslim cap, and he had a short, curved sword thrust through his belt. He made straight for the captain-major and threw his arms around him. After embracing the other captains, he explained that he was a Christian from the West who had arrived in this part of the world as a young man and had entered the service of a powerful Muslim lord. He had had to convert to Islam, he confessed, but in his heart he was still Christian to this day. He had been at his lord's house when news came from Calicut, saying that men who spoke a strange language and wore clothes from head to toe had appeared from nowhere. He had immediately realized they must be Europeans, and he had told his master he would die of sorrow if he was not allowed to pay them a visit.

His lord, he added, was generosity itself. He had told him to invite the foreigners to his country, where they could help themselves to anything they needed—spices, provisions, even ships—and he had even given them permission to stay on permanently, if they liked what they saw.

Gama took a shine to the urbane visitor. In his gruffly cordial way he thanked him for his offers and asked him about his master's land, which it turned out was called Goa. In return his garrulous guest merely asked for a cheese, which he explained he would give to a companion whom he had left on the mainland as a token that the meeting had gone well. The cheese was produced, along with two loaves of freshly baked bread, but he was in no hurry to leave. The Chronicler noted that he had so much to say about so many things that he sometimes contradicted himself.

Paulo da Gama was beginning to get suspicious, and he decided to have a word with the sailors who had delivered the visitor. They were Hindus and no particular friends of their Muslim customer. He was a pirate, they quietly explained, and his ships were waiting near the coast for the order to attack.

Paulo spread the news, and the Portuguese seized their caller. The soldiers thrust him against the hull of the beached ship and interrogated him with the aid of a sound thrashing. He still insisted he was an honest Christian, and Gama had him trussed up, hoisted up to the yard, and hauled up and down by his arms and legs. When he was let down, he panted out some home truths. News of the Portuguese had spread far and wide, he told them; the whole country was out to do them harm. All along the shore, large forces of armed men were stationed on boats hidden up creeks; they were only awaiting the arrival of forty ships that were being armed to lead the attack.

Several bouts of torture failed to make him change the rest of his story. As his voice failed, he seemed to be trying to explain that he had come to find out what sort of people the strangers were and what arms they carried, but it was hard to tell. Gama called a halt, ordered him to be confined on one of the ships, and had his wounds dressed; he had decided to take him back to Portugal as another informant for the king.

The *São Rafael* had still not been careened, but there was no time to lose. By now the Arab fleets from Jeddah, Aden, and Hormuz had already arrived in India, and if the new intelligence was to be believed, a mass attack was imminent. The last piece of business was to break up the captured vessel for spares. From the mainland its captain had been watching in the hope of recovering his ship when the foreigners left. As he saw it disappearing piece by piece, he shot over and offered a large sum of money for its return. It was not for sale, Gama peremptorily replied; as it belonged to the enemy he preferred to burn it, and so he did.

The fleet set sail on Friday, October 5. When the ships were far enough out that it was clear they would not return, the prisoner finally came clean. Perhaps he had had enough of being chained up in the forecastle, where a captive's confinement was made triply uncomfortable by the salt water that washed over him, the lowering and raising of the anchors around him, and the men who went there to do their necessities. The time for dissembling was past, he declared. He was, indeed, employed by the ruler of Goa, and he had been at court when news had arrived that the foreigners were lost on the coast and had no idea how to get home. His lord was aware that many boats had been sent to capture them, and he was loath to see the booty end up in his rivals' hands. He had sent his servant to entice the strangers to his country, where they would have been completely in his power. The Christians, he had heard, were brave and belligerent, and he was in need of men like them in the endless wars he waged against his neighboring kings.

GAMA HAD NOT been able to leave India at the moment of his choosing, and his men would pay a terrible price.

The steady breeze of the winter monsoon had not yet arrived at the latitude the explorers had haltingly reached. Again and again the ships were swept up by cyclones, then deposited in dead calms. October turned to November, November to December, and still there was no sign of land. The heat was insufferable, food was running low, and the water turned foul and began to run out, too. Soon the dreaded scurvy returned to ravage the sailors' gaunt frames. A later passenger on a Portuguese ship vividly described the speedy onset of the disease and the panic that ensued. His knees, he recorded, were so shrunken that he was unable to bend them, his legs and thighs were black as gangrene, and he repeatedly had to pierce his skin to draw off his treacly, putrefied blood. Every day he swung on the rigging over the side and, looking in a little mirror, he took a knife to his rotten gums, which had ballooned over his teeth and made it impossible to eat. When he had cut away the flesh he washed his mouth with urine, but the next morning the swelling was just as bad. With dozens similarly afflicted, he found himself adrift on a ship of death:

> Great numbers Died every day thereof, and there was nothing
> to be seen but Bodies a flinging over-board, and the most part
> Died without help, some behind Chests, having their Eyes and
> the Soles of their Feet eaten up with Rats. Others were found

dead in their Beds, after having been let Blood and moving their Arms, the veins opened, and their Blood ran out: Oftentimes after having received their Allowance, which might be about a Pint of Water, and putting it near them to Drink, when a-dry, their Companions rob'd these poor Sick Wretches of this little Water, they being asleep, or turned to the other side. Sometimes being under Deck in a dark place, not seeing one another, they would fight among themselves, and strike one another, if they caught any about to Steal their Water; and thus, oftentimes were they deprived of Water, and for want of a little Draught they miserably died, without any one offering to help them to never so little, no not the Father the Son, nor the Brother the Brother, so much did every Man's particular Thirst compel him to Rob his Companions.

Racked by pain and far from home, dozens of simple, zealous men died fearful, lonely deaths within days of their symptoms appearing. The end came as a release. As Crusaders for Christ, they had been told they would pass away without the stain of sin. Their eyes squeezed shut against the blinding light, the softer life of a place free from suffering beckoned them on. Their comrades threw their bodies into the sea, with less and less ceremony as more and more succumbed.

In the tropical heat, new diseases assaulted the weakened survivors. Fevers left them shivering and delirious. Abscesses and tumors grew on infected skin. A toxic fungus infected the bread and brought on vomiting and diarrhea, followed by painful spasms, hallucinations, and mania, and finally dry gangrene, dropsy, and death. Among the most terrifying afflictions was one that, a sailor reported, "breaks out at the Fundament like an Ulcer, and is presently full of Worms, which Gnaw as far as the Belly, and so they die in great misery and torment: There hath been no better remedy found for this Disease," he added, "than the Juyce of Lymon, in washing therewith the Fundament; for that obstructs the worms breeding there." There was no privacy on board a ship; now there was no dignity, either.

As Christmas approached, only seven or eight sailors were left fit to man each vessel. Few believed they would survive much longer, and the iron discipline that Vasco da Gama had rigorously enforced utterly broke down. The men shouted out to the saints, vowing to reform their ways if they were saved and begging them to spare their lives. They demanded that the captain-major return to Calicut to submit to God's will rather than let them rot away on the open sea. Gama and his fellow captains had lost all track of where they were, and in desperation they finally agreed to turn back, if a favorable wind allowed.

At the last possible moment the weather changed, and with it the mission's fortunes. "It pleased God in his mercy," recorded the Chronicler, "to send us a wind which, in the course of six days, carried us within sight of land, and at this we rejoiced as much as if the land we saw had been Portugal."

The date was January 2, 1499. A few more days, a couple of weeks at most, and three ghost ships would have been cast adrift on the pitiless ocean blue.

BY THE TIME the ragged fleet neared the coast of Africa it was already night. They lay to, and the next morning they reconnoitered the shore, "so as to find out whither the Lord had taken us, for there was not a pilot on board, nor any other man who could tell on the chart in what place we were." As far as they could see, an unvarying thin green ribbon of vegetation stretched between the vastness of the sea and the sky.

A debate ensued. Some of the men were certain they were still three hundred leagues from the mainland, among some islands off Mozambique; one of the prisoners they had taken there had told them the islands were very unhealthy and rife with scurvy, which made all too much sense.

While the argument was still raging, the watchkeepers sighted a city. It turned out to be the ancient Somali port of Mogadishu, which had once been the dominant Muslim entrepôt on the East African coast. Tall houses surrounded a magnificent palace, and four castles defended the perimeter walls. In their perilous state the explorers did not dare try their luck, and after making their feelings known by firing off repeated rounds from the bombards, they continued south along the shore.

Two days later the ships were drifting in a calm when a thunderstorm blew up from nowhere and tore the ties of the *São Rafael*. More trouble was in store: while the few able-bodied men were making repairs, a pirate spotted the stricken fleet and launched a raid from a nearby island. Eight packed boats bore down on the Portuguese, but the gunners leapt to their stations and a barrage sent the pirates flying back to their town. Perhaps to the crews' relief, there was no wind and they were not ordered to give chase.

Finally, on January 7, the lookouts spotted the familiar bay of Malindi. Even—especially—in such dire straits, Gama would not risk mooring in the port, and the ships anchored off the city. The sultan immediately sent out a large welcoming committee with an offering of sheep and a message of peace and friendship. The captain-major had been expected for a long time, the Africans affably said.

Gama sent the ever-reliable Fernão Martins to shore in the sultan's boat with urgent instructions to procure as many oranges as possible. They arrived the next day, along with an assortment of different fruits and plenty of water. The sultan ordered his Muslim merchants to visit the foreigners and offer them chickens and eggs. It was too late for the worst afflicted: many of the sick died off Malindi and were buried there.

The horrors of the journey had softened Gama, and he was struck by the kindness the sultan showed him and his men when they desperately needed help. He sent him a gift and begged him, through his Arabic translators, to give him an ivory tusk to present to the king of Portugal. As a sign of the friendship between the two nations—one that would be clearly visible to their enemies—he also asked permission to place a pillar and cross on the shore. The sultan replied that he would do everything he was asked out of love for King Manuel. He had a prime spot prepared for the pillar, in front of the town and next to his palace, and as well as the requested tusk, he sent over a Muslim boy who dutifully declared that he wanted nothing more in life than to go to Portugal.

The Portuguese stayed at Malindi for five days, enjoying more of the sultan's entertainments as best they could, "and reposing," recorded the Chronicler, "from the hardships endured during a passage in the course of which all of us had been face to face with death." They left on the morning of January 11, and the next day they sailed as quickly as possible past Mombasa.

When they were safely out of sight of the city they anchored in a bay, unloaded the goods from the *São Rafael*, and set fire to it. There were not enough hands left to sail three ships, and in any case the *Rafael*, which had not been repaired for many months, was on its last legs. The whole process took fifteen days, during which numerous Africans came out and bartered chickens for the sailors' last few shirts and bracelets.

Two days after they resumed their journey, the two remaining ships passed a large island, six leagues from the mainland, that they had missed on the outward voyage. This, the boy from Malindi explained, was Zanzibar, one of the most important trading centers of the Swahili Coast. The explorers had never heard of it: there was a great deal more exploring left to do.

On February 1 the ships reached Mozambique during a heavy downpour. They avoided the town and anchored off the island where they had celebrated mass almost a year earlier. They said mass this time, too, and Gama decided to erect another pillar. The rain fell so hard that the landing party could not light a fire to melt the lead that was used to fix the cross on top, and the pillar stayed crossless.

A few days later the survivors left East Africa for the voyage around the Cape. For all the rumors that large communities of Christians lived there, they had stayed frustratingly out of sight. Prester John remained as stubbornly elusive as ever. The Swahili Coast still guarded its secrets; only on another voyage would it yield up its greatest treasures.

A month later the Portuguese reached the bay where the captain-major had been shot in the leg. They stayed for more than a week, catching and salting anchovies, seals, and penguins and replenishing their water for the Atlantic passage. On March 12 they set out for home, but they made it only a dozen leagues before a fierce westerly wind sent them pitching back into the bay. As soon as the wind dropped they started again, and on March 20 they doubled the Cape of Good Hope. By now, the Chronicler recorded, "those who had come so far were in good health and quite robust, although at times nearly dead from the cold winds which we experienced." After the tropical heat, the southern Atlantic felt like the chills that accompany a fever.

For twenty-seven days a following wind drove the two ships to within a hundred leagues of the Cape Verde Islands. They were back in home waters, but after everything they had been through a strange air of unreality clung to the familiar sights.

The easy passage turned out to be too good to be true. There was one final hardship to come.

Before the ships could reach the islands they were becalmed again. The little breeze there was came from ahead, and they plied to windward as best they could. Thunderstorms rolled along the African coast and helped the pilots fix their position, but soon the skies darkened overhead and a violent tornado whipped up the seas. Though lightning crashed around them, the two vessels lost sight of one another.

Nicolau Coelho was still in charge of the *Berrio*. This time there was no assigned meeting place, and he set his course straight for home. On July 10, 1499, his tattered, leaking caravel limped into the fishing port of Cascais, on the cusp of the Atlantic just below

Lisbon. The Portuguese had long ago decided the fleet was lost, and they rushed to welcome the heroes home.

Coelho made his way to the king and reported the discovery of the sea route to India. The momentous mission had lasted 732 days. The ships had covered no less than 24,000 miles. It was by some way the longest voyage known to history, whether measured by time or by distance traveled.

Vasco da Gama's ship arrived a few weeks later, its seams split and its pumps groaning to keep it afloat. Perhaps 170 men had set out; perhaps only 55 had returned alive.

The captain-major was not among those on board. On the return journey his brother had been seized by tuberculosis, and by the time the ships had become separated Paulo's condition had taken a marked turn for the worse. Gama had waited a day for the caravel to reappear before setting a course for Santiago, the port where the fleet had reunited on the outbound voyage. As soon as he arrived he had put João de Sá, the former clerk of the *São Rafael*, in charge of repairing his flagship and sailing it home.

Gama chartered a small, fast caravel to speed his dying brother to Lisbon. Soon after they left, Paulo's condition became desperate, and Vasco changed course for the island of Terceira in the Azores.

Paulo died the day after they reached the island. Vasco da Gama buried his beloved brother in the church of a Franciscan monastery, and the discoverer of the sea route to India slowly, sadly made his way home.

CHAPTER 13

A VENETIAN IN LISBON

O<small>N</small> A<small>UGUST</small> 20, 1501, the newly appointed ambassador extraordinary of the Republic of Venice swept before the royal court of Portugal and launched into a long and extravagant eulogy to King Manuel I.

Until very recently, La Serenissima—the name, meaning "The Most Serene," by which Venetians knew their republic—had barely deigned to notice the existence of Portugal. Yet two years earlier a letter had arrived in Venice that had made its citizens swallow their pride. The Venetian diarist Girolamo Priuli recorded its contents:

> Letters of June arrived from Alexandria, which wrote that through letters from Cairo written by men who had come from India, it was understood that at Calicut and Aden in India, principal cities, there were arrived three caravels of the King of Portugal, which had been sent to enquire after the Spice Islands, and of which the commander was Columbus.

If the details were wide of the mark, the thrust was clear enough. Venice had a new competitor for its Eastern trade.

Priuli, like many of his fellow Venetians, greeted the news with a skeptical shrug. It would be incendiary news if it were true, he admitted, but he did not believe a word of it. Backward little Portugal had always been too busy haring after Prester John and dregs of African gold to think of challenging the greatest trading republic in the West. Soon, though, a flurry of enormously long and frantic

letters began to arrive at Italian merchant houses from their countrymen based in Lisbon. The Portuguese, a merchant named Guido
Detti wrote home to Florence, had "found all the treasure and all
the commerce in spices and precious stones of the whole world."
The news, he predicted—with more than a touch of satisfaction at
a rival's suffering—was "truly bad for the [Egyptian] Sultan, and as
for the Venetians, when they lose the commerce of the East, they
will have to go back to fishing, because by this route the spices
will arrive at a price they won't be able to match." It was a fine
discovery, he added, "and the king of Portugal deserves the hearty
congratulations of all Christians. Certainly, every king and great
lord, especially those whose lands border the sea, must seek after
unknown things and expand our knowledge, because that's how to
win honor and glory, reputation and riches."

The Signoria, the supreme council of Venice, pondered the matter for a while and finally sent its Spanish ambassador to investigate.
He quickly reported back that the Portuguese king had already sent
thirteen more ships to Calicut to buy spices, and another fleet stood
in the port ready to depart within days. Along with his letter another arrived in Venice, this one from a certain "Dom Manuel, by
the Grace of God King of Portugal and of the Algarves on this side
of and beyond the sea in Africa, Lord of Guinea and of the Conquest the Navigation and Commerce of Ethiopia, Arabia, Persia and
India." Despite his grandiloquent new title it was far from obvious
precisely what Manuel had conquered, but it was crystal clear that
his letter was a flagrant attempt to upturn Venice's entire way of life.
Henceforth, the king provocatively proposed, the Venetians should
buy their spices from Portugal, not Egypt. Since Venice's wealth
was based on its near monopoly of trade with the Islamic world, the
offer to split its profits was hardly enticing, but Manuel was determined to make Venice treat Portugal with the respect due an equal.

Three days after the letters arrived, the Venetian senate voted to
appoint its first ambassador to Portugal. It chose Pietro Pasqualigo, a
twenty-nine-year-old product of centuries of breeding. Pasqualigo

held a doctorate from the prestigious University of Paris, and his oration to the Portuguese court—delivered in flawless Latin—was intended to impress.

What was needed was flattery, and he laid it on thick. Every age, he declared, would celebrate Manuel's amazing deeds; for the rest of time Europeans would acknowledge that they owed a greater debt to him than to any king present or past:

> People, islands, and shores unknown until now have either sur-
> rendered to your military might or, overawed by it, have volun-
> tarily begged for your friendship. The greatest kings and uncon-
> quered nations of the past used to boast justifiably that they had
> extended their power to the ocean, but you, invincible King,
> are entitled to take pride in having advanced your power to the
> lower hemisphere and to the Antipodes. What is greatest and
> most memorable of all, you have brought together under your
> command peoples whom nature divides, and with your com-
> merce you have joined two different worlds.

Manuel, he marveled with a straight face, had outdone the Egyptians, the Assyrians, the Carthaginians, the Greeks, the Romans, and even Alexander himself. His high character was known throughout the world, and across Europe people and nations were giving thanks that God had sent them a king "who in his virtue, wisdom and felicity will not only protect the weary and tottering Christian Commonwealth but even extend it far and wide."

The soft-soaping over, Pasqualigo broached the real subject of his mission. Sailing the oceans was a fine thing, he acknowledged, but "a far fairer thing it is, far more splendid and more promising for the immortality of your name, to defend the most noble part of the world from the fury of the infidels." Naturally, he was talking not of Paradise or Jerusalem but of Venice. The republic was imperiled by that "most ferocious monster," the fierce and powerful Turkish sultan, who was doubtless even then constructing diabolical new weapons with which to pound Christendom. "I do not know of anything you could do or conceive that is finer, braver, or more lofty," the ambassador wheedled away, "of anything, in short, more worthy of your godlike character and brilliant abilities."

Venice was indeed in deadly peril. In 1499, while the republic was still recovering from the stinging naval losses it had sustained in seeing off a French invasion of Italy, the Ottomans had launched a ferocious attack with an armada of nearly three hundred ships. In an unprecedented admission of weakness, La Serenissima had conscripted its own cititzens—three of Pietro Pasqualigo's brothers were at sea fighting the Turks—and as the war lurched from disaster to defeat it had petitioned Rome to declare a new Crusade. Venice's novel pose as the champion of Christendom came late in the day— in 1483 the papacy had excommunicated the entire city for refusing to call off a war against an Italian duke, albeit a war that Rome had itself engineered—but the threat to Europe was undeniable and the Crusade was called. Recalling the zeal of Manuel's forebears to fight the Turks, the young envoy framed his request as a holy war on behalf of the Christian faith against the sultan, that "pernicious destroyer of the Christian people . . . that barbarian stained with Christian blood."

Manuel had already sent thirty-five heavily armed warships and a sizable force of men-at-arms to Venice's aid. Like his uncle Afonso, he had even angled for an invitation to lead the new Crusade in person, though in fact the fleet arrived without the king and too late to be of much use. Officially Pasqualigo had come to convey the republic's gratitude and to exhort Manuel to greater sacrifices. Unofficially, he was there to keep a close eye on the king's Indian enterprise, and to assist him, he was accompanied by a squad of seasoned spies masquerading as a diplomatic delegation.

The young ambassador's very first communiqué relayed deeply disquieting news. Two months before he had arrived, the second Portuguese fleet to reach India had returned.

"This is more important to the Venetian State than the Turkish

War or any other war that might take place," the chastened Priuli wrote in his diary:

> Now that this new route has been found by Portugal this King of Portugal will bring all the spices to Lisbon and there is no doubt that the Hungarians, the Germans, the Flemish and the French, and all the people from across the mountains who once came to Venice to buy spices with their money will now turn to Lisbon because it is nearer to their countries and easier to reach; also because they will be able to buy at a cheaper price, which is most important of all. This is because the spices that come to Venice pass through all of Syria and through the entire country of the Sultan and everywhere they pay the most burdensome duties. Likewise, in the State of Venice they pay insupportable duties, customs, and excises. Thus with all the duties, customs, and excises between the country of the Sultan and the city of Venice I might say that a thing that cost one ducat multiplies to sixty and perhaps to a hundred. . . .
>
> Thus I conclude that if this voyage from Lisbon to Calicut continues as it has begun there will be a shortage of spices for the Venetian galleys and their merchants will be like a baby without its milk and nourishment. And in this I clearly see the ruin of the city of Venice, because lacking its traffic it will lack money from which has stemmed Venetian glory and fame.

In Lisbon, the Venetians turned up the heat. A number of Indian envoys had returned with the latest fleet to establish diplomatic relations with Portugal, and Pasqualigo's attachés covertly approached them. The king of Portugal, they explained, was broke, and they had come from Venice to bail him out. Venice was the preeminent power in Christendom, and nothing could be done without its say-so. Besides, while Venice was purely interested in trade, the Portuguese were warmongers, and they were hell-bent on attacking India's Muslims. The Indians began to believe that they had fallen into a terrible trap, and their fears were alleviated only when Vasco da Gama took them on a tour of Portugal's treasury and gave them a good look at its growing stacks of gold.

EVEN BEFORE VASCO da Gama had returned to Portugal, Manuel had ordered celebratory processions to be held throughout the land, "returning many thanks to Our Lord." With equal alacrity, he had dashed off a letter to Ferdinand and Isabella of Castile. As a statement of how inextricably religion and trade were entwined in the discoveries, it could hardly be bettered.

"Most high and excellent Prince and Princess, most potent Lord and Lady!" it began:

> Your Highnesses already know that we had ordered Vasco da Gama, a nobleman of our household, and his brother Paulo da Gama, with four vessels to make discoveries by sea, and that two years have now elapsed since their departure. And as the principal motive of this enterprise has been, with our predecessors, the service of God our Lord . . . it pleased Him in His mercy to speed them on their route. From a message which has now been brought to this city by one of the captains, we learn that they did reach and discover India and other kingdoms and lordships bordering upon it; that they entered and navigated its sea, finding large cities, large edifices and rivers, and great populations, among whom is carried on all the trade in spices and precious stones, which are forwarded in ships (which these same explorers saw and met with in good numbers and of great size) to Mecca, and thence to Cairo, whence they are dispersed throughout the world. Of these they have brought a quantity, including cinnamon, cloves, ginger, nutmeg, and pepper, as well as other kinds, together with the boughs and leaves of the same; also many fine stones of all sorts, such as rubies and others. And they also came to a country in which there are mines of gold, of which, as of the spices and precious stones, they did

not bring as much as they could have done, for they took no merchandise with them.

As we are aware that your Highnesses will hear of these things with much pleasure and satisfaction, we thought well to give this information. And your Highnesses may believe, in accordance with what we have learnt concerning the Christian people whom these explorers reached, that it will be possible, notwithstanding that they are not as yet strong in the faith or possessed of a thorough knowledge of it, to do much in the service of God and the exaltation of the Holy Faith, once they shall have been converted and fully fortified in it. And when they shall have thus been fortified in the faith there will be an opportunity for destroying the Moors of those parts. Moreover, we hope, with the help of God, that the great trade which now enriches the Moors of those parts, through whose hands it passes without the intervention of other persons or peoples, shall, in consequence of our regulations be diverted to the natives and ships of our own kingdom, so that henceforth all Christendom, in this part of Europe, shall be able, in a large measure, to provide itself with these spices and precious stones. This, with the help of God, who in His mercy thus ordained it, will cause our designs and intentions to be pushed with more ardor [especially as respects] the war upon the Moors of the territories conquered by us in these parts, which your Highnesses are so firmly resolved upon, and in which we are equally zealous.

And we pray your Highnesses, in consideration of this great favor, which, with much gratitude, we received from Our Lord, to cause to be addressed to Him those praises which are His due.

Manuel was well aware that Christopher Columbus's star was waning in Spain. The Genoese explorer had still found no spices, no gems, no Christians, and no Chinese Great Khan. In 1498, just as Vasco da Gama was sailing into the Indian Ocean, Columbus had finally reached the mainland he had long sought, but the experience had been distinctly unsettling. As he made his way down the coast his ships had lurched into the vast outflow of the Orinoco River, and the disoriented navigator decided that such a torrent must cascade down a great slope. From that he deduced he was sailing up the foothills of the Holy Mountain of Paradise, a vast protuberance that he pictured thrusting up from the earth's surface like a nipple from a breast. Since he knew no human could enter the Garden of Eden and live, he fled in fear. Columbus, who often wore the simple habit of a Franciscan monk, had always believed he had been chosen to save souls; lately he had begun to hear the voice of God and considered it his destiny to fulfill the old prophecies by discovering a new paradise on earth. His confidence, though, had been badly shaken, and he hanged some of his crew for insubordination. When he returned to Hispaniola his sailors and the settlers he had promised untold riches accused him of torture and gross mismanagement, and the fifty-three-year-old explorer, afflicted with arthritis and a painful inflammation of the eye, was manacled, thrown in jail, and transported back to Spain in chains.

To most observers, Vasco da Gama had clearly trumped his archrival. What Columbus had promised, Gama had delivered. While Columbus had sailed west with a fair wind and reached land in thirty-six days, Gama had swept around the Atlantic, followed the east coast of Africa, crossed to India, and made it home against terrible odds. Where Columbus had parleyed with a few tribesmen, Gama had survived hostile sultans and negotiated with powerful kings, and he had brought home spices, letters, and hostages to prove it. Whatever Columbus had found—and it was by no means yet clear—Gama had opened the sea route to the East and had shown the way to circumvent the Islamic world. The whole of Europe was astonished, and the Portuguese king was only too happy to rub his in-laws' noses in it.

Having performed that pleasant duty, Manuel shored up his position by addressing letters to the pope, the College of Cardinals, and the Cardinal Protector of Portugal in Rome. He instructed them to hold public thanksgivings for God's favoritism toward the Portuguese nation, and he reminded them that by virtue of a papal bull of 1497—the latest attempt to try to adjudicate between the rival powers—he and his heirs enjoyed "very fully the sovereignty and dominion of all we have discovered." Nothing else, he carefully added, was surely needed, but he affectionately begged "for a fresh expression of satisfaction with reference to a matter of such novelty and great and recent merit, so as to obtain His Holiness's renewed approval and declaration."

As the midpoint of the millennium approached, Manuel was determined to push his claim to be the chief monarch of Christendom. His discovery, he declared, was not just for Portugal: it would benefit every Christian nation, "from the damage to the Infidels that is expected." Soon the Muslims would be vanquished, the Holy Land would be repossessed, and Eastern Christians would return to the true Catholic path. Even so, he was not minded to share the glory with rival nations. It was next to impossible to obtain a map of the Portuguese voyages, wrote the secretary to Venice's ambassador in Spain, "for the king has decreed the death penalty for anyone who sends it out of the country."

At home the messiah-king began to level and rebuild Lisbon in a style lavish enough to match his soaring ambitions. Along with majestic new palaces and spacious warehouses to receive the expected flood of goods from India, he ordered a vast church and monastery to be built at Belém, on the site of Henry the Navigator's modest chapel, where prayers were to be said for the souls of Manuel the Conqueror and his great forebear. To honor his immediate predecessor, he decided to rehouse King John II's remains in imperial splendor. Manuel paraded around the country with the coffin, accompanied by a procession of lords, bishops, and chaplains, a choir, torchbearers, and "a barbarous orchestra of trumpets, reed pipes, sackbuts, and drums." When the ceremonies were over, he had it opened at dead of night. "He beheld the body covered with lime dust," it was said, "and ordered the monks to blow it off with tubes of cane, and he himself aided them, and then kissed the dead man's hands and feet again and again. It was a dramatic meeting, this of the dead and the living kings, and a sight for a man to look upon."

A prophecy had long swirled around Europe that a Last Emperor would unite Christendom, subdue the Infidel, and lead the Last Crusade to take back the Holy Land. Then the peoples of the world would be shepherded into the fold, a New Jerusalem would descend from the heavens, and Christ would return to rule over the world. Manuel had begun behaving like an emperor before he had conquered a single patch of land, but the empire he had in mind was not merely territorial. Like Columbus, he was certain that he was nothing less than the Hand of God on Earth; like the Crusaders of old, he was convinced it was God's will for him to destroy Islam and lead his people in glory to Jerusalem.

THE KING'S UNWAVERING conviction owed much to the news that Christians had been found in India. Prester John himself was still conspicuously at large, but Calicut, Nicolau Coelho and his crew had explained on their arrival, was "bigger than Lisbon, and peopled by Christian Indians." It was true that the churches had no regular clergy and the divine offices went unperformed, but they had bells and a type of font. "These Christians," a Florentine merchant named Girolamo Sernigi reported to his compatriots, "believe that Jesus Christ was born of the Virgin Mary, without sin, was crucified and killed by the Jews, and buried at Jerusalem. They also have some knowledge of the Pope of Rome, but know nothing of our faith beyond this."

A few weeks later the *São Gabriel* had docked in Lisbon, and on board was the Venetian-speaking man from Goa.

Sernigi managed to snatch an interview with him, and he immediately wrote to Florence to correct his earlier letter. The new informant told the Florentine that there were many idolaters in India who worshipped cows, and only a few Christians. He added that the supposed churches "are in reality temples of idolaters, and that the pictures within them are those of idols and not of Saints."

"To me," Sernigi wrote home, "this seems more probable than saying that there are Christians but no divine administrations, no priests and no sacrificial mass. I do not understand that there are any Christians there to be taken into account, excepting those of Prester John."

Soon, though, the informant changed his story. He was presented to the king, and he quickly realized that the way to get ahead was to say what was wanted, not to tell an unpalatable truth. His first act—alongside Monçaide, the merchant from Tunis—was to ask to be baptized. He took the name Gaspar, after one of the three Eastern kings who had followed the star to Bethlehem, and da Gama, after his captor, torturer, and now godfather. It turned out that Gaspar had been Jewish before he had become Muslim, but now that he was Christian he began to paint a fantastical picture of India's religions. Christians, he explained, lived in fourteen Indian states, of which twelve were purely or very largely Christian. At least ten had Christian kings, and between them they boasted 223,000 foot soldiers, more than 15,000 cavalry, and 12,400 war elephants that each carried a dozen warriors in a wooden castle and charged forward with five swords protruding from its tusks.

Manuel was ecstatic. The well-traveled Gaspar, he was certain, had been sent by God to advance his great project. Time was of the essence if he was to forge alliances with India's Christian rulers before his rivals stole a march, and he had four ships and two well-armed caravels readied to sail to India in the suggestive month of January 1500. The mission's aims soon expanded from establishing trading bases to drubbing the African and Indian coasts, and the fleet swelled to thirteen ships. In command was Pedro Álvares Cabral, another minor nobleman and a knight of the Order of Christ; under him were more than a thousand men, including five priests. Cabral's orders were to deliver a stark Crusading message to the Muslims and pagans of the Indian Ocean—convert, or die:

Before he attacked the Moors and idolaters of those parts with the material and secular sword, he was to allow the priests and monks to use their spiritual sword, which was to declare to them the Gospel, with admonitions and requisitions on the part of the Roman Church, asking them to abandon their idolatries, diabolical rites and customs, and to convert themselves to the faith of Christ, for all men to be united and joined in charity of religion and love, since we were all the work of one Creator, and redeemed by one Redeemer, who was Christ Jesus, promised by prophets, and hoped for by patriarchs for so many thousand years before he came. For which purpose they brought them all the natural and legal arguments which the Canon Rights disposes of. And should they be so contumacious as not to accept this law of faith, and should reject the law of peace, which ought to be maintained amongst men, for the conservation of the human kind, and should they forbid commerce and exchange, which are the means by which peace and love amongst all men is con- ciliated and obtained . . . in that case they should put them to fire and sword, and carry on fierce war against them.

Manuel had a very different message for the Christians. He gave Cabral a letter for the Zamorin of Calicut, in which he explained that the Portuguese had been led to India by the Hand of God and were about His business:

For one should truly believe that God, Our Lord, has not per- mitted this feat of our navigation solely in order to be served in trade and temporal profits between you and us, but equally in the spiritual profit of souls and their salvation, which we ought to place higher. He considers Himself better served by the fact that the holy Christian faith is communicated and joined be- tween you and us as it was for six hundred years after the com- ing of Jesus Christ, until the time that, for the sins of men, there arose some sects and contrary heresies as predicted . . . and these sects occupy a great part of the Earth between your lands and ours.

Having delivered his public history lesson, Cabral was to convey another message in private. He was to request the Zamorin to banish every last Muslim from his harbors; the Portuguese would henceforth supply the commodities the Arabs had brought, only better and cheaper. Manuel gave his commander a final, top-secret order: if the Zamorin didn't quietly consent to trade solely with the Portuguese, Cabral "should make cruel war upon him for his injurious conduct to Vasco da Gama." The Zamorin might be a fellow Christian, but he was clearly misguided, and Manuel was in a hurry.

Cabral's orders, which were drawn up with Gama's advice, also instructed him to establish relations with the other Christian states of India and to do all he could to interfere with Muslim shipping. Among his captains were Bartolomeu Dias, the discoverer of the Cape of Good Hope, and Gama's close comrade Nicolau Coelho. Pêro Escobar, the pilot of the *Berrio*, again went as a pilot, and João de Sá and other veterans of Gama's mission were among the company. Gaspar da Gama was taken along as an interpreter, and also on board were the five men who had been brought as captives from Calicut and the young envoy of the sultan of Malindi.

Even with their combined experience, the mission lurched from mishap to disaster. Soon after the delayed fleet set out on March 9, 1500, a ship was lost off the Cape Verde Islands. When Cabral tried to replicate Gama's sweep around the Atlantic, he set his course too far to the southwest and hit land. He thought he had discovered a new island, and after holding a mass and erecting a cross he sent one of his captains home with the unexpected news. A terrible tempest struck the remaining eleven ships off the Cape of Good Hope and four were lost with all hands, including the vessel captained by Bartolomeu Dias, who never saw his stormy Cape again. On the crossing to India another ship disappeared in bad weather, and the fleet's strength was reduced to six.

By then it was late summer, and in line with his orders, Cabral stationed himself off the Malabar Coast to attack the Arab shipping that was expected from the north. The crews were confessed and received the sacraments, but the quarry failed to turn up for the hunt. Instead Cabral carried on to Calicut, where he arrived, flags flying and cannon blazing, in mid-September.

The old Zamorin had died shortly after Gama's departure, and his ambitious young successor was much keener to open trade with the Europeans. Several local notables came straight out to the ships, followed by a welcoming committee, an orchestra, and the Zamorin himself. This time the Portuguese had come prepared with a treasure trove of gold and silver basins, ewers, and flagons, together with plenty of gold-colored soft furnishings including cushions, canopies, and carpets. Cabral presented Manuel's remarkable letter, and though the Zamorin's reaction to the Portuguese king's expressions of joy at being united with his fellow Christian is not recorded, the Zamorin gave Cabral a royal grant engraved on a gilded plate that guaranteed the Portuguese security of trade. The meeting fell apart amid a panicky exchange of hostages, but within two months a permanent Portuguese factory was established in a large house behind the seafront, the royal coat of arms fluttering from its roof.

The Portuguese, though, soon discovered that they had arrived when the Arab fleets were already in port. The merchants who had run rings round Vasco da Gama had been unpleasantly surprised to see a much larger Portuguese fleet sail into view, and matters finally came to a head in December. The Portuguese seized a Muslim-owned ship that was leaving for Jeddah, claiming its departure violated their agreement with the Zamorin that they would be given first call in loading spices. In retaliation a large band of Muslim merchants attacked the new Portuguese factory. Seventy men, including the fleet's priests, were trapped in the building. After three hours' fighting they tried to force their way out and head to the boats, and nearly all were killed.

When a day passed with no message from the Zamorin, Cabral decided he had approved the assault and went on the rampage against the Arab ships in the harbor.

It was an uneven contest; the six Portuguese vessels far outgunned the entire Muslim fleet.

For centuries the trade of the Indian Ocean had rarely been ruffled by conflict, and it had no tradition of naval warfare. Its sewn ships were not stout enough to mount heavy guns, and their design made it almost impossible to adapt them to the new threat. In any case, while cannon had originated in China and had long been used by Muslim armies, they had only reached isolated patches of India and the few examples that existed were small and crude. Portugal, like all the maritime nations of Europe, had been waging war at sea for generations, and though its shipborne cannon were far from perfect, there was no denying their capacity to induce terror in a tight corner. Gunpowder might have taken the chivalry out of war, but it was the agent of Portugal's empire in the East.

Cabral seized a dozen large vessels and killed, drowned, and imprisoned hundreds of men. He carted off their cargoes of spices along with three elephants, which were slaughtered and salted for food, and he burned the vessels. At night he ordered his captains to lower their boats and tow their ships as close as was safe to the shore. They lined up in front of the city, and at daybreak they opened fire. Cannonballs plowed into the crowds on the seafront and tore through houses and temples, killing hundreds more. "So great was the consternation," it was reported, "that the zamorin fled from his palace, and one of his chief nayres was killed by a ball close beside him. Part even of the palace was destroyed by the cannonade."

The Zamorin quickly changed his mind about his new allies. As Cabral was preparing to leave, a large war fleet appeared on the horizon. Before the two sides could engage, a sudden storm forced them to anchor for the night. The next morning Cabral thought better of renewing hostilities and broke for the open sea, with the boats from Calicut in hot pursuit until nightfall. The Portuguese commander heeded Vasco da Gama's advice and made the crossing to Africa at the right time of the year, but near Malindi one of his ships was driven onto the shore in a storm. It caught fire and had to be abandoned, and only five of the thirteen vessels made it back to Lisbon.

The voyage had not been a complete loss. Acting on Gama's intelligence, Cabral had discovered two notable African ports that his predecessor had bypassed—Sofala, the conduit for much of West Africa's gold, and Kilwa, the island capital of a dynasty of sultans that had long dominated the Swahili Coast. He had been welcomed with marked friendliness by the chastened ruler of Mozambique, and the sultan of Malindi had been his usual hospitable self. He had made contact with Cannanore and Cochin, two busy Indian ports whose kings were on bad terms with the Zamorin. He had loaded his ships with spices in both cities, and he had left a party of men at Cochin to establish a factory. The vessel that had disappeared in the Indian Ocean finally resurfaced with the news that it had stumbled across Madagascar. Not least, the island Cabral had thought he had discovered on his outward journey turned out to be Brazil, and moreover, the coast was well to the east of the demarcation line established at Tordesillas. By complete accident Cabral had pulled off a historic first: his ships had touched four continents.

Europe's horizons were expanding at a bafflingly fast rate, but Cabral would not reap the glory. He had found no Christian allies, and he had not made a single convert. He had lost hundreds of experienced sailors and half his fleet. He had let the merchants of Calicut destroy the Portuguese factory, and though he had exacted bloody revenge he had failed to stamp out the rebellion. All told, he had not been bold or successful enough for his king's liking. It was a harsh judgment on a man who had been set an impossible task, but Cabral spent the rest of his life in disgrace.

Manuel put the best spin on things he could. A feast was held in the palace to mark the fleet's return, bells pealed across Lisbon, a procession set off around the country, and more crowing letters were dispatched to Spain. But the king's grandiose claims were in danger of looking threadbare, and many of his counselors once again urged him to take the glory and abandon the perilous enterprise. Besides, Manuel had sent many ships to fight the Turks and more to attack the Moroccans—none of which had met with much success—never mind the fleets that were even then headed into the North Atlantic to search for more lands on the Portuguese side of the line. The country was overextended and too many lives had already been lost; goodness knew, they murmured in private, how many more would be sacrificed to Manuel's insane quest for world domination.

The king was not to be brooked. Before Cabral had even returned, Manuel had sent out another four ships under the command of João da Nova, a middling official with strong connections at court. By then, Manuel had assumed, Cabral's intimidating fleet would have either made mass conversions or cowed India into submission, and Nova's orders were merely to follow on where Cabral had left off.

According to one report, the new fleet rounded the Cape of Good Hope and found a message left by Cabral in an old shoe hung from the branch of a tree. Having read of the ruction at Calicut, Nova set off across the Indian Ocean and burned and sank several ships around the Zamorin's harbor. He visited the factory at Cochin and set up another at Cannanore, but as he waited for the monsoon to take him home, dozens of vessels crammed with armed Muslims sprang at him from Calicut. The Portuguese guns pounded at the boats, and as the light faded and the wind dropped, the Muslims hung out a flag of parley. Nova suspected a trick and carried on firing, but eventually, with his guns nearly burnt out, he answered with a flag of his own. The two sides agreed to desist until the next day, and a tense night followed with the enemies anchored at close quarters and the jittery Portuguese firing blindly into the dark. Like Cabral, Nova thought better of fighting another day, and the fleet returned to Lisbon in September 1502 with a large cargo of spices and a fine haul of booty.

It was not enough for the impatient king. To put the flagging Crusade back on track an overwhelming display of force was clearly needed, and it would have to be masterminded by Portugal's most valiant knight.

There was only one man for the job.

VASCO DA GAMA had finally returned to Lisbon in the late summer of 1499. He was still in mourning for his brother, but he was not allowed to grieve for long.

After stopping to give thanks to God for preserving him from peril, he sent notice of his arrival to the king. Manuel dispatched a cortege of nobles to conduct him to court. Huge crowds pressed in, eager to see the new national hero whom they had long thought dead. When he came into the royal presence, the chronicles recorded, "the king honored him as one who by the discovery of the Indies had done so much for the glory of God, for the honor and profit of the king of Portugal, and for the perpetual fame of the Portuguese name in the world."

Gama was asked to name his reward, and he chose the hereditary lordship of Sines, the town where his father had been governor. The title was granted him in December, but the Order of Santiago refused to give up its rights over its fiefdom, even to its own prodigal son. The explorer pressed his case in person, and as the matter dragged on, fights broke out between his servants and the governor's men. Nearly two years later he was still waiting, and a substantial royal pension was cobbled together to make up for the dues he had been denied.

Meanwhile the king ordered his scribes to draft an elaborate grant letter that formally celebrated Gama's great feat. The long letter traced the history of the discoveries from Henry the Navigator to Vasco da Gama himself. It recognized that Gama had triumphed over mortal dangers unlike any faced by his predecessors—dangers that had taken the lives of his brother and many of his men. It commended him for performing a "most excellent service" by discovering "that India, which all those who have given descriptions of the world rank higher in wealth than any other country, which from all time had been coveted by the Emperors and Kings of the world, and for the sake of which such heavy expenses had been incurred in this kingdom, and so many captains and others forfeited their lives." It predicted that great advantages would flow from the discovery, "not only to our kingdoms but to all Christendom: the injury done to the infidels who, up to now, have enjoyed the advantages offered by India: and more especially the hope that all the people of India will rally round Our Lord, seeing that they may easily be led to a knowledge of His holy faith, some of them already being instructed in it."

Princes, Manuel added, should be generous, and the details followed. Gama, his family, and their descendants were permitted to add the prefix *Dom* to their names, an honorific comparable to the English "Sir." The explorer was appointed to the royal council. He was granted another substantial annual pension, to be paid in perpetuity to his heirs, and the right to send money to India every year to buy spices, which he could import free of royal duties. Finally, he was named Admiral of India, "with all the honors, prerogatives, liberties, power, jurisdiction, revenues, quit-rents, and duties that by right should accompany the said Admiralty." Spain had Christopher Columbus, Admiral of the Ocean Sea; now Portugal had Vasco da Gama, Admiral of India. The title outrageously flouted anything the Indians themselves might have to say about the matter, but to its intended audience nearer home the message was unmistakable: while Columbus had been busy sailing around the Atlantic, Gama had won the prize that both had sought.

It was a handsome settlement; Nicolau Coelho, who was also a fidalgo of the court, received about a tenth the amount. Besides, Gama was widely reported to have returned from India with a lucrative cache of pepper, ginger, cinnamon, cloves, nutmeg, lac, and precious stones that he had bartered for his personal silverware.

Like every ambitious man of his age, though, he knew that real power lay with land and titles. He kept pressing for his promised estate, and meanwhile he set about courting the well-connected Dona Catarina de Ataíde. When they married, Gama's pedigree rose another notch. Like most women of her time, Catarina has remained utterly inscrutable to history, though the large brood that gradually surrounded her suggests the match was not purely political.

Gama was a man on the make. When the opportunity to take charge of a great new fleet came his way, he could not resist the chance to redouble his stature.

It was a dangerous move worthy of a gambler who played the odds. If he succeeded in subduing India, he would strengthen his claims on the king's favor. If he failed, he might suffer, like the hapless Cabral, the ignominy of royal neglect. He calculated the risks and took the bet.

On January 30, 1502, Vasco da Gama was formally commissioned as Admiral of India in Lisbon Cathedral. Among the throng of assembled dignitaries was one Alberto Cantino, the envoy of the Duke of Ferrara, and Cantino carefully reported the important occasion to his employer:

> First, every one attended a sumptuous Mass, and when it was over, the above-mentioned Don Vascho, dressed in a crimson satin cape in the French style, lined with ermine, with cap and doublet matching the cape, adorned with a gold chain, approached the King, who was attended by the whole court, and a person came forward and recited an oration, praising the excellence and virtue of the King, and went so far as to make him superior in every way to the glory of Alexander the Great. And then, he turned to the Admiral, with many words in his praise and in praise of his late predecessors, showing how by his indus-

try and vivacity he had discovered all this part of India, [and] when the oration was over, there appeared a herald with a book in his hand, and made the above-mentioned Don Vascho swear perpetual fidelity to the King and his descendants, [and] when this had been done, he knelt before the King, and the King taking a ring from his hand, gave it to him.

The royal standard was carried to the presiding bishop, who solemnly blessed it and returned it to the king. Manuel unsheathed a sword and placed it in his admiral's right hand. He placed the standard in his left, and Gama rose to his feet and kissed the royal fingers. The rest of the knights and lords filed past and followed suit. "And thus it ended, with the most splendid music."

Dom Vasco da Gama, Admiral of India, marched out of the cathedral to a trumpet fanfare, a figure far grander than the young adventurer who had set sail less than five years before.

AMONG THE GRANDEES who lined up that day to pay his homage was the young ambassador from Venice.

Spy or not, Pietro Pasqualigo had struck up a cordial relationship with the Portuguese king. Manuel had knighted him, and he had even asked him to be his son's godfather. The personal warmth between the two men did not disguise the fact that Venice was increasingly horrified by Portugal's obsession with the East. Nor did the shiny black gondola, its cabin festooned with gold cloth, that Venice sent Manuel in the month of Gama's departure. The Most Serene Republic was still trying to convince the king to attack Muslims in the Mediterranean, rather than sail halfway around the world and strike at the trade arteries through which its lifeblood flowed.

Two months later, Venice changed tack and recalled its ambassador. Instead, in December 1502, the Signoria established a special *giunta* of fifteen prominent men to deal with the Portuguese peril.

Since persuasion had failed and cooperation was out of the question, the only remaining option was sabotage.

That same month, the giunta dispatched a confidential agent named Benedetto Sanuto to Cairo. Sanuto's mission was to convince the sultan of Egypt that the Portuguese were as much a menace to Muslims as they were to the Venetians. He was mandated to suggest two strategies to counter the threat. The first was for the sultan to cut his custom duties so that the Venetians could compete with the Portuguese. Even Venice knew that was a long shot. The second was "to find rapid and secret remedies" to deter the Portuguese from sailing to India. The Venetians could not quite bring themselves to ask their Muslim allies to use force against their Christian competitors, but there was little doubt where their sympathies lay. If the Portuguese met with concerted opposition in India, Sanuto predicted, they would soon think again. Perhaps the sultan could have a word with the Zamorin of Calicut and urge him "to do the things that seemed appropriate to his wisdom and power." There was little doubt, either, what he meant by that.

PART III

CRUSADE

CHAPTER 14

THE ADMIRAL OF INDIA

ONCE AGAIN SEA biscuit was baked, barrels of wine rolled along gangplanks, and the banners, standards, and crosses fluttered in the winter breeze. The usual devotions were made, the artillery fired a farewell salvo, and Vasco da Gama sailed out of Lisbon on February 10, 1502.

Altogether the fleet numbered twenty ships, though only fifteen were ready in time. Gama had chosen as his flagship the sturdy *São Jerónimo*. From the *Esmerelda*, his maternal uncle Vicente Sodré, a knight of the Order of Christ, commanded a subfleet of five ships. Also among the captains was Brás Sodré, another of Gama's maternal uncles, and Álvaro de Ataíde, Gama's brother-in-law. Gaspar da Gama, the admiral's unlikely godson, was again prominent among the personnel. The remaining five vessels were due to leave in early April, with Vasco's first cousin Estêvão da Gama in command on the big new warship *Flor de la Mar*. Paulo da Gama's steadfast support and calm voice would be much missed, but the new mission was even more a family business than the first.

It was also a European affair. Lisbon was buzzing with foreign financiers, merchants, and sailors, all talking India and spices. Englishmen, Frenchmen, Germans, Genoese, Spaniards, Flemings, Florentines, and even a few renegade Venetians were arriving daily to try their luck in the East. The new fleet was too big to be crewed or financed by the Portuguese alone, and large numbers of foreigners signed up.

Gama's sailing instructions were astonishingly ambitious, though they were at least more specific than the apocalyptic agenda the king had set Cabral. The combined fleet was to shore up the fragile Portuguese factories, force more African and Indian cities to agree to advantageous trade terms, and deal with the truculent Zamorin of Calicut. When it had imposed its will on the Indian Ocean, it was to split in two. Vasco da Gama was to return to Portugal with the main body of the fleet and its precious cargoes of spices. Vicente Sodré's strongly armed subfleet, meanwhile, was to stay behind and escalate the war against Islam. As well as protecting Portugal's interests, he was to mount a permanent blockade of Arab shipping, stanch the flow of spices into the Red Sea, and strangle Egypt's economy. If all went according to plan, before long the Portuguese would sail up the Red Sea, rendezvous with troops trekking east across Africa from Morocco, and march on Jerusalem.

The first fifteen vessels made the customary first stop at the Cape Verde Islands, where the priests said mass. There were plenty of novices among the crews, and a Flemish sailor aboard the *Leitoa Nova*, one of the ships in Gama's main fleet, ogled the islands' inhabitants. "The people there were stark naked," he blurted out to his diary, "men and women, and they are black. And they have no shame, for they wear no clothes, the women have converse with their men like monkeys, and they know neither good nor evil."

Even more than usual, the Atlantic passage was a test of nerves. On March 6 the fleet left the Cape Verdes with a fair wind, but it was soon becalmed. For days the men had little to do but reel in huge fish, which one sailor noted had a strange and horrible appearance and were as heavy as Frisian cows. Then the wind picked up and brought with it six weeks of changeable weather marked by heavy seas, violent squalls, and hailstorms that swept the ships in every direction. By the end of March the Great Bear and the Pole Star had disappeared from the night sky, and on April 2 the sun burned so high overhead that nothing could be seen in the shadowless light. Even the nights were stifling, and the whole company was sick from the heat.

Soon the ships crossed the equator, the noon sun swung behind them, and the Southern Cross appeared in the night sky, shining clearly through wispy clouds. For company the men watched huge schools of flying fish leap out of the sea in unison and flocks of gray, white-headed frigate birds keep pace with them, every so often dipping on their huge wings to make a catch in their long beaks. When larger predators appeared on their tail, the schools jumped so high that ten or twenty at a time flopped into the boats. For days on end even the fish and the birds disappeared and there was no living thing to be seen. Only the usual minor disasters broke the eerie silence: a mast breaking, or one ship ramming another so hard that it took hours to disentangle them.

By April 23, St. George's Day, the fleet finally had a fair wind and was back on track. Gama consulted with his captains, asking how far they thought they were from the Cape, and set a course to the east-southeast. Then the wind turned against them again, and they were driven west toward Brazil. By late May, having once more regained their course, they were far enough south that the early winter days lasted barely eight hours, and amid a spectacular storm of "rain, hail, snow, thunder and lightning" the westerlies drove them past the Cape of Good Hope.

By now the suffocating heat had given way, a German sailor recorded, to "a chill such as in Germany cannot occur. We were all cold, for the sun lay to the north, and many of our men died of the cold. The sea is of such storminess there as it is wondrous to behold." He pulled his sodden cloak tightly around him, but his shivers sharpened when he was told that four ships—including the vessel captained by Bartolomeu Dias—had been wrecked at this very spot less than two years before. For days the fleet plowed with furled sails through the high seas and driving rain, and nerves were badly frayed by the time the admiral pointed out a flock of birds that fished by day and slept on land at night; a clear sign, he promised, that the coast was near. The captains made what headway they could with shortened sails, and on May 30 they sighted land and dropped anchor. As the relieved sailors celebrated, the pilots peered at the coastline, compared it to their charts, and reckoned they were a hundred leagues past the Cape.

The elements were not ready to let go. "Then we weighed anchor and continued further," the German sailor resumed; "and when we found ourselves at sea, a great storm overtook us, and the sea was more tempestuous than we had ever seen it." Bowsprits and masts snapped like twigs, and three of the ships disappeared from sight. Waves pounded the sides and washed over the decks, and as they battled the swells, currents, and winds for three days and nights, even the seasoned mariners were convinced their time was up. At the worst point a giant dolphin leapt out of the sea and almost overshot the masts, panicking the superstitious sailors. Soon after, a humpback whale with fins as tall as sails swam around for so long and made so much noise that they trembled with foreboding. To their intense relief, the visitors turned out to be good omens: the storm gave way to a fair wind, and the men spread out their drenched clothes to dry in the weak sun.

Soon after the fleet sailed into the Indian Ocean, the admiral called a conference of all fifteen captains. They decided to split up: Vicente Sodré's five ships would head straight for Mozambique, while the rest would stop off at the famed gold-trading town of Sofala. The goods intended for sale at Sofala were transferred to Gama's ships, and a week later the main fleet arrived there, anchoring well away from the low shifting sands of the shore.

In Western lore, Sofala was believed to be the fabulously wealthy biblical port of Ophir, the location of King Solomon's Mines, the capital city of the Queen of Sheba, or all three. "Our Captain told us that the king lived here who came to offer gold to our Lord Jesus Christ at Bethlehem; but the present king is a heathen," the German sailor noted; by heathen he meant, of course, Muslim. The location of the town shifted with the sands; when the Portuguese arrived it was set amid palm groves and plantations on an island at the mouth of a river. The mainland embraced the island to form a broad horseshoe-shaped bay, and boats sailed down the river ferry-ing gold mined in the hinterland.

Gama called another meeting of the captains. The question, he put it to them, was how to be prepared to respond to hostile action, without appearing so aggressive as to invite a preemptive attack. A decision was reached: each captain would fully arm his boats and his men, but the weapons would be concealed.

At daybreak the boats rowed out. The beach was already full of people, and as the Europeans approached, fifteen or twenty men dragged a canoe into the water. Five or six Arabs climbed inside and pushed off to meet the strangers. When the canoe was within hailing distance, Gama's spokesman impressively announced that he bore a message from the admiral of Portugal. The Arabs reported back to the sultan and returned with gifts of bananas, coconuts, and sugarcane. The sultan welcomed them, they said, and he was wait-ing for their message.

Gama was taking no risks, and he asked for hostages before he would let his men land. Two important-looking Arabs soon ar-rived, and two Portuguese set out for the palace. They came back with more welcoming words, together with more bananas and co-conuts and a cow. After a boat had taken soundings of the shallow but navigable harbor, the flagship and three other ships sailed into the bay. Ten or twelve days of trading began, in the course of which the Europeans loaded a hoard of gold in exchange for simple glass beads, copper rings, woolens, and small mirrors. The exchanges stayed friendly, though according to one report, Gama spent his time secretly surveying the surrounding area for the best place to build a fort.

Financially the mission had got off to a flying start, though its fortunes quickly plummeted when one of the gold-laden ships struck a reef on leaving the harbor and was barely evacuated before it sank. The rest of the fleet sailed on to Mozambique, where a week later it reunited with Sodré's squadron.

This time around the sultan of Mozambique was all smiles and cooperation. Two of the three ships that had been lost in the storm were also sheltering in the port, while Sodré's men had been busy constructing an armed caravel, which was to be left to patrol the African coast, from parts that had been brought from Portugal. The fleet loaded fresh water and wood and exchanged more beads for gold, and when all was ready, the admiral dictated a letter outlining the course he intended to follow. He sent it to the town with instructions for it to be delivered to the second wave of ships, and the thirteen vessels sailed on to their next port of call.

Kilwa, the island about which Gama had heard so much on his first voyage, had for centuries been the home of the most powerful sultans in east Africa, the Arab overlords of the entire coast from Sofala and Mozambique in the south to Mombasa and Malindi in the north. The dynasty's star had been waning for some time—the ruins of a monumental palace, with spacious suites of courtyards, bathing pools, and throne rooms, moldered magnificently on a headland overlooking the Indian Ocean—and three years earlier it had been extinguished for good when the last sultan was murdered by his own emir. Yet the island was still seriously rich. Its heavyweight Muslim merchants acted as middlemen for the gold and ivory trade of Sofala and Mozambique, which were too far south for vessels from India and Arabia to arrive and leave with the turning monsoon; they also shipped the gold that was mined inland on the great granite plateau of Zimbabwe, together with silver, amber, musk, and pearls. The city's tall houses were handsomely built of stuccoed stone embellished with ornamental niches and set amid fine gardens and orchards. The Great Mosque, with its egg-box roof of concrete domes and forest of coral columns, looked like a miniature version of the Mezquita in Córdoba. Kilwa's glory days might have gone, but it was still a glittering prize.

Two years earlier, on Gama's advice, Cabral had sailed up to the island to propose a treaty of trade and friendship. At first the usurping Emir Ibrahim had made encouraging noises, but he had soon decided the Portuguese looked too warlike for comfort and had retreated to his palace, where he locked the doors and surrounded himself with armed guards. The Portuguese, as usual, were convinced the Muslims were determined not to trade with Christians, and Gama was under orders to take proud Kilwa down a peg.

The fleet anchored off the island on the afternoon of July 12, and Gama took in the scene. The harbor was thick with masts, and more ships were hauled up on the beach. Men and women waded through the sands and mangrove roots for their daily dip in the sea. The black slaves and the poorer men were all but naked; the Arabs were dressed in long silk and cotton robes. "Their bodies are well shaped," noted one European, "and their beards large and frightening to see."

Gama was expecting a cool reception, and he announced himself with a noisy burst of cannon fire. A boat soon approached, but it turned out to contain only a degredado left behind by Cabral. The convict handed over a letter that João da Nova had given him on his way home; in addition to updating his successors on the fracas at Calicut and the progress at Cannanore, Nova warned that they would not get anywhere by being friendly to the ruler of Kilwa.

Gama sent the man back with a message for the emir. The admiral of Portugal, he was to announce, had been sent by the king his lord to make peace with Kilwa, and he had many goods to trade.

The emir heard the message and immediately fell ill.

Gama summoned all his captains to a council on his ship. Emir Ibrahim was clearly trying to avoid meeting him, and he asked each man to give his advice. They agreed a strategy, and the next morning the captains had their boats fully armed and manned and set out for the shorefront. They drew up in front of the palace, and Gama, who was directing the operation from his own boat, sent a new edict to the emir. If he did not do what he was told and meet the admiral, the envoy declared, the fleet would open fire on his palace.

After much to-ing and fro-ing, the emir's health recovered sufficiently for him to come to the shore, accompanied by a crowd that the German sailor estimated at more than two thousand strong.

Four men took the ashen-faced Ibrahim in their arms and carried
him to the admiral's boat. When he was seated on a carpet, Gama
informed him that he had brought a letter from his king but that,
as time was short, he would tell him its gist. If the emir wanted
the protection of the Portuguese, he would have to fork out a huge
sum in gold and provide all the merchandise they required at the
local price. As a token that he was a loyal vassal, he would have to
send the Portuguese queen an annual tribute of ten pearls and fly
the Portuguese flag from his palace. If he disobeyed, Gama would
throw him in the hold and batten down the hatches.

The shaken emir, who was not used to being addressed in such
terms, asked if the admiral had come to make peace or war. Peace,
if he wanted, or war, if he wanted, Gama replied; it was up to him.
He had no doubt, he added, which he would prefer if he were in
his shoes.

The emir chose peace, but he tried to wriggle. He didn't have
enough money to pay the tribute, he regretted, though he would do
what he could. Gama insisted it was useless to argue, but Ibrahim
drew out the negotiations long enough that he finally agreed to take
a much smaller sum. It was the principle, after all, that mattered.

The emir handed over three dignitaries as hostages and was carried back to the shore. The crowd burst out in applause and cries
of joy that war had been averted, and they rushed to scatter twigs
before the murderous usurper's feet. The Europeans rowed back to
their ships, and soon boats approached containing a whole farmyard
of sacrificial goats, chickens, and oxen.

Within three days the protection money arrived to the ac-
companiment of women chanting "Portugal! Portugal!" in what
seemed intended as a spontaneous demonstration of joy. In return
the emir received his hostages, some scarlet capes, fourteen lengths
of crimson velvet, letters patent in the name of King Manuel that
graciously accepted the emir as a vassal and promised to defend his
realm, and a silk standard embroidered in gold with the royal coat
of arms. The standard was tied to a spear and was sent ashore ac-

companied by an honor guard, a cannon salvo, and a band playing trumpets, castanets, and drums. The pragmatic Ibrahim accepted the precious token with a salute. He had decided to go all out, and the flag was paraded around the city to more shouts of "Portugal! Portugal!" before being hoisted with great ceremony from his topmost tower.

While the Flemish sailor ogled the half-naked local women and marveled at the island's fat-tailed sheep and enormous onions, Gama had his clerk draw up a memorandum for the edification of the following fleet. The emir, he declared, had behaved very discourteously to him, "on account of which I armed myself with all the men I had, determined to destroy him, and I went in my boats before his house, and placed the prow on dry land, and had him sent for much more discourteously than he had behaved with me, and he agreed to do so and came, and I made peace and friendship with him on the condition that he should pay a tribute to the King, my lord." Since the emir was now a vassal of Portugal, Gama ordered his successors to keep the peace as long as the emir kept his word. He added a detailed rundown of his intended itinerary and instructed the latecomers to travel day and night to catch up, and he signed the letter "The admiral Dom Vasco."

The ships had been careened, scoured, and recaulked, and they made ready to leave. It took them two days to reach the open sea; the tides, as Gama had warned in his letter, made the harbor tricky to exit. Irritation turned to joy when, while they were still trying to extricate themselves, Estêvão da Gama sailed into view on the *Flor de la Mar*. He had left Lisbon in May; two of his ships, though, had been lost amid more tempests at the Cape, and Gama left his message in the hope that they would pick it up.

The combined armada of sixteen ships sailed north to Malindi. If the men were looking forward to the sultan's famous hospitality, they were to be disappointed. The monsoon winds had begun to howl, the rain pelted down, and the ships were driven five leagues past the city. They anchored in a cove, and men set out to look for water. Meanwhile Gama ordered his captains to make a list of the spices they hoped to load and the money and merchandise they had brought. While crossing the ocean, he explained, he wanted to work out exactly what business he needed to conduct in India. He had a hidden agenda: private merchants had funded several of the ships, and he was determined not to let them compete with each other—or with the king's factors—for the precious spices. "We all thought it was advisable to notify him of our merchandise and funds, as well as what we would buy, keeping to us the possibility to take more or less spices depending on the quality and prices we found," noted Matteo da Bergamo, the factor of an Italian merchant.

The sultan of Malindi had seen the ships passing by, and he sent a letter to the admiral. The messengers waded waist-deep through the sea to reach him, avoiding the wild beasts that roamed the shore at night, and Gama sent back friendly greetings and more instructions to the remaining ships not to tarry. The African part of his mission had gone more or less according to plan, and Gama had decided to head straight for India. After stopping for just two days, the fleet set sail on Friday, July 29.

The monsoon did not oblige. A storm drove the armada nearly to Arabia, and when it finally arrived in India, it found itself far to the north of Calicut in Muslim-controlled territory. The ships sailed south along the coast and passed a city whose sultan, the Flemish sailor recorded, owned at least eight thousand horses and seven hundred war elephants. The Europeans, he added, captured four hundred ships, "and we killed the people and burned the ships."

Whether or not such horrifying slaughter took place—if anything did, it was almost certainly on a far smaller scale—the Admiral of India was determined to rid the Arabian Sea of Arabs once and for all. The king had ordered it. The massacre at Calicut and the attacks on the Portuguese fleets had made it more urgent. Gama was ready to do his Christian duty, and no doubt the prospect of exacting personal revenge for his earlier treatment steeled his soul.

After a few days the fleet arrived at Anjediva Island, where Gaspar da Gama had been taken captive on the first voyage. By now hundreds of sailors were stricken with scurvy, and they were carried ashore and housed in makeshift shelters. The mysterious disease terrified the new hands, though the Flemish sailor distracted himself by hunting and killing a five-foot-long lizard. The friendly locals brought plenty of food—fresh and cooked fish, cucumbers, and the bananas that the Portuguese, who were obsessed with them, called "Indian figs"—but sixty or seventy died.

One morning a sail appeared on the horizon, and the admiral sent out three ships and two caravels to head off the vessel. As they drew near, it put out its flags and standards and wild cheering broke out. The ship was one of the two that had sailed in May and had been delayed at the Cape. It was owned by a wealthy "New Christian" named Rui Mendes de Brito and was captained by a Florentine named Giovanni Buonagrazia; also on board was a scribe named Tomé Lopes, who had taken it upon himself to make a full record of the voyage. As it joined the rest of the fleet, sailors swarmed aboard to hear the news from Portugal and ask if they had any letters. The new arrivals had called at Malindi, and they gave the recuperating patients chickens and oranges from the sultan.

The second ship missing from the May fleet showed up soon after, and the huge armada sailed off toward Cannanore, the northernmost of the three great ports of the Malabar Coast. Along the way the Europeans captured several boats and looted their cargoes of rice, honey, and butter. The men belonging to friendly rulers were set free; the rest were taken as slaves, and their vessels were burned.

RATHER THAN ENTER the port of Cannanore and start trading, the admiral ordered his captains to wait out at sea. They stopped opposite Mount Eli, the landmark to which Arab pilots steered and the point where Gama himself had first arrived in India.

By now the entire company was in on the plan. The Flemish sailor put it as simply as possible. They were to lie in wait for the merchant convoys heading from Arabia to Calicut, "the ships which carry the spices that come to our country, and we wished to destroy them so that the King of Portugal alone should get spices from there."

Every few hours one of the ships set out to scan the sea-lanes, and when its turn was up another took its place. The relay kept going for days without achieving much. A captain named Fernão Lourenço tried to board an enormous four-masted dhow carrying a large crew, but after shooting off six or seven bombards, the gunners ran out of ammunition, and as night fell they lost their quarry. The ship belonging to Rui Mendes de Brito managed to capture a sambuk, a small, double-ended dhow, but it was carrying little more than oakum threads and yams and it turned out to be headed to friendly Cannanore. Gama kept its twenty-four Muslim sailors under close watch for a few days while he decided what to do; in the end the need for allies prevailed over the urgings of faith, and he put them under the care of an ambassador from Cannanore who had returned to India with the fleet.

The twenty-four men soon found out what a narrow escape they had had.

The armada stayed at the ready, its guns loaded, the officers plated up for action and spurring on their crews, who were growing increasingly restless as the supplies ran down. Finally, two days before the end of September, the traffic from Jeddah and Aden began to arrive on the late monsoon winds and a suitable target sailed into view.

Tomé Lopes, the clerk on Rui Mendes de Brito's ship, later set down a full account of the horrors that unfolded over the following days.

The *São Gabriel* was on reconnaissance duty when the huge Arab vessel appeared on the horizon. As the watchkeepers shouted out, the gunners sprang into action and fired warning shots across its bow.

Strangely, since the Europeans could see it was armed, it came to a halt and lowered its flag. The *São Gabriel* closed in, and its soldiers boarded the vessel without meeting any opposition.

The Arab ship was called the *Mîrî*. To the deep satisfaction of the Portuguese, it was headed for Calicut. It was crammed with 240 men and more than 50 women and children. Most were pilgrims coming home from the hajj to Mecca, but a dozen of the wealthiest merchants of Calicut were also on board. They were used to running the gauntlet of pirates along the Malabar Coast, and rather than put up a fight they had decided to buy their freedom with a portion of the riches they were carrying.

The foremost merchant was named Jauhar al-Faqih, and he was, the Europeans learned, none other than the factor in Calicut of the sultan of Mecca. The *Mîrî* was part of his personal fleet, and he took charge of the negotiations.

At al-Faqih's request, the Admiral of India met him in person. The Muslim grandee opened with a high bid, and in the usual Arab manner, to save face he presented a blatant bribe as a regular business transaction. His mast was broken, he explained, and he could offer a handsome sum in gold for a new one; moreover, he would personally ensure that every ship in the Portuguese fleet would fill its hold with spices.

Gama refused. Five years earlier he had made a great play of being outraged when the Muslims of Calicut called him a pirate. With good reason, he was now being treated like one. Yet much had changed in the meantime. Gama's first expedition was a voyage of exploration conducted on three small ships. His second was a voyage of conquest backed up by a bristling armada. Then he was a pathfinder. Now he was a Crusader, and he had designs far darker than simple extortion.

Al-Faqih upped his offer. If he, his nephew, and one of his wives were set free, he guaranteed to load four of the biggest ships with a full cargo of spices at his own charge. He himself would remain on the flagship as a hostage; the admiral merely had to allow his nephew ashore to make the arrangements. If, say, within fifteen or twenty days, the shipment did not arrive, his life would be theirs to do with as they wished, and so would the valuable cargo of the *Mîrî*. On top of that, he would mediate with the Zamorin to ensure the return of the goods in the Portuguese warehouse and to restore friendly relations in place of the unfortunate hostilities that had broken out.

The admiral brusquely ordered the merchant to return to his ship and tell his fellow Muslims to hand over everything of value on board.

There was clearly no negotiating with the uncouth European, and al-Faqih's pride had taken enough knocks.

"When I commanded this ship," he answered, "they did as I said; now that you command it, you tell them!"

Nonetheless he went back to the *Mîrî*, and after a heated debate, the merchants sent a modest amount of gold to the Portuguese fleet. Gama took it, then dispatched his boats to rake the Arab ship for more booty. One of his own crewmen was transferring the seized goods when he lost his footing and slipped over the side. The current forced the two vessels against each other with the sailor in between, and his body was shattered. The admiral became even more implacable.

Waylaying ships at sea was a military affair. The representatives of the European merchants looked on, unsure what was happening, while Gama held closed councils with his captains. Matteo da Bergamo heard that the soldiers had seized a great deal of gold and silver coin as well as Turkish velvets, quicksilver, copper, and opium from the *Mîrî*. "We couldn't even speak about this capture," he noted, "all the more so because we had no part in it. We were told that it was none of our business."

The standoff had already lasted five days. "It was a Monday, the 3rd of October 1502," wrote Tomé Lopes: "a date that I will remember every day of my life."

By now Gama's soldiers had removed all the weapons they could find from the Arab ship. It was a sitting duck, and the admiral ordered his men into their boats. Their task was simple. They were to tow the *Mírí* out to sea until it was safely away from the Portuguese fleet. Then they were to set it alight and burn it with everyone on board.

The soldiers marched onto the *Mírí*, set fires across the decks, and jumped back into the boats as the flames licked and the smoke billowed. Some of the Muslims rushed to smother the fires, and one by one they stamped them out. Others dragged out several small bombards they had managed to hide from the search party, and they hurriedly set them up. The pilgrims and merchants ran to grab anything that could serve as ammunition, including fist-sized stones from the piles of ballast in the hold. There was clearly no chance of surrender, and they were determined to die fighting rather than burn to death.

When the soldiers in the boats saw the fires go out they rowed back to light them again. As they approached, women and men alike fired the bombards and hurled the stones. The Europeans cowered under the hail of missiles and beat a fast retreat. From a distance they tried to sink the *Mírí* with their bombards, but the guns carried on the boats were too small to inflict real damage.

The Muslim women tore off their jewelry, clutched the gold, silver, and precious stones in their fists, and shook them at the boats, screaming at their attackers to take everything they had. They held up their babies and little children and desperately pleaded with the Christians to take pity on the innocents. One last time, the merchants shouted and gestured that they would pay a great ransom if their lives were spared.

Gama watched, hidden from sight, through a loophole in the side of his ship. Tomé Lopes was stunned: shocked by the admiral's refusal to relent, and amazed that he was willing to turn down such wealth. There was no doubt in his mind that the ransom would have been enough to buy the freedom of every Christian prisoner in Morocco and still leave great treasure for the king. Bergamo and his fellow factors were no doubt wondering just how much of their profit would go up in smoke. Yet there were plenty of zealous

Christians among the crews who had no more qualms than their Crusader forebears about killing peaceful merchants and pilgrims. The dehumanizing notion that their enemies in faith were somehow not real people was too deeply ingrained to be shaken. Like holy warriors before and after, they avoided looking into the whites of their victims' eyes and got on with their godly business.

The *Mîrî* was still afloat. The desperate Muslims had dragged their mattresses and the mats that covered the cargo into the center of the deck, and they kept up their barrage from behind their makeshift shelters. Tomé Lopes's ship was nearest, and he and his crew could see their comrades in the boats waving flags and calling them to come to the rescue. They sailed over and took the soldiers on board, half on the ship itself and half on the sambuk they had seized earlier, which they were still towing along. The gunners trained a large bombard on the *Mîrî* and the cannonball crashed into the base of its mast, splintering the wood. Thinking they had the situation under control, they sailed right up to the enemy ship.

The *Mîrî* was much the bigger and taller of the two, and the Christians turned their ship astern so that the top of its castle came up against the waist of the Arab vessel. The Muslims sprang into action. They threw ropes onto Lopes's ship, and so quickly that the sailors had no time to act, they leapt across the gap. They clung to the netting that was meant to ward off boarders, climbed up the rigging, and threw the ropes back. The men on the *Mîrî* grabbed the ends and pulled the two vessels tight against one another.

Suddenly the Christians were in deep trouble. At such close quarters their guns were useless. The forty or so sailors were heavily outnumbered, and every time they poked their heads out into the open, a hail of stones thudded around them. A few soldiers scrambled up to the crow's nest and returned fire with their meager supply of lances and arrows, but the Muslims picked them up and sent them thwacking back into the decks. Lopes and his comrades were forced to cower out of sight: only one soldier armed with a crossbow stopped the men on the *Mîrî* from swarming aboard.

It was the longest day of the year, Lopes later noted—it certainly felt like it—and yet as the light finally began to fade the battle showed no sign of letting up. The Muslims were still fighting "with such vehemence that it was marvelous to see, and even though we wounded and killed many, it seemed as if no one was dying and no one felt their wounds." They tore arrows from their skin, flung them back at their attackers, and threw themselves back into the action without a second's pause. Fourteen or fifteen Muslims jumped on the Portuguese ship and hurled themselves at the sterncastle with the superhuman force of men who knew they were wronged. The victims were now the avengers, and they pushed at the door, brushing away the lances that pierced their chests. The officers and soldiers who had barricaded themselves inside beat a bruised and bloody retreat down the ladder to the main deck. Only Tomé Lopes and Giovanni Buonagrazia, the ship's captain, stayed to fight on. The cuirass the captain had strapped around his torso was already dented and broken from the barrage of stones, and as he stood there the straps gave way and his breastplate fell to the ground. He turned to the faithful friend at his side.

"O Tomé Lopes, scribe of this ship," he said, "what are we doing here, while everybody has left?"

They quit the castle, too, both heavily wounded. The Muslims charged in and raised a triumphant cry. The men on the *Mîrî* took heart and rushed the decks of the Portuguese ship. By now most of the Europeans were wounded and several were dead. The rest cowered behind the sails, the only cover they had left.

With the wind against them the rest of the armada had been unable to act, but eventually a few ships closed in on the action. They were powerless to fire lest they hit their own men, and as they looked on, several of their comrades abandoned all hope and threw themselves in the sea. Some of the wounded and exhausted men of the *Mîrî* lost their footing as they tried to drag themselves back to their ship and fell into the sea, too, but still new waves of attackers took their place.

Finally one of the larger Portuguese ships caught a breeze and headed straight for the *Mîrî*. The Muslims scrambled back to their decks, cut the ropes, and pushed off. The *Julioa* was bigger than its stricken sister ship, but the men on board took one look at the fired-up enemy and decided to leave them alone. The *Mîrî* was getting away.

It was only then that Vasco da Gama managed to arrive on the scene on the *Lionarda*. The principal warships were close behind, and they set off in pursuit of their fleeing quarry. The wind was now gusting and the sea was swelling in great waves, and as they pitched up and down they were driven far ahead of the *Mîrî* and then blown far back behind. As they swayed within range they let loose a few off-target cannonballs and veered off again. The ghastly chase continued for four days and nights, the wounded men and women on the *Mîrî* lying prone on the deck, calling to the Prophet to deliver them from the hands of the Christians.

The end was as sordid as the whole engagement. A young Muslim jumped off the side of the *Mîrî* and swam through the rough sea to the nearest Portuguese ship. He would give them the secret of how to sink the Arab vessel, he blurted to the captain, if they promised to save his life. He would tie a rope to her rudder, and with the *Mîrî* crippled they would no longer have to follow her all over the sea.

The traitor carried out his task and the cannons fired. "And so," recorded Tomé Lopes, "after all those battles, the Admiral ordered the ship burnt with the men who were on it, very cruelly and without the slightest pity." Screams rent the air. Some of the Muslims leapt in the sea with hatchets in their hands and swam to the boats, but they were killed in the water as they tried to hack at the bottoms or clamber on board. Almost all the rest—nearly three hundred men and women—were drowned.

The young traitor was sufficiently chastened by the ghastly sight to relish a small moment of revenge. There had been great treasures on the *Mîrî*, he told the Christians, that they had never found.

Gold, silver, and jewels had been hidden in casks of oil and honey, and when the merchants had realized their lives were lost, they had thrown them all in the sea.

The Portuguese had shown one small sign of mercy, and one of pragmatism. Before they sank the *Mîrî*, they had taken off seventeen children. They believed they were saving their souls when they baptized them by force. They had also seized the ship's pilot, a hunchback with useful experience of sailing the Indian Ocean, and they found an immediate job for him.

With grim satisfaction, Gama dictated a letter to the Zamorin of Calicut and handed it to the pilot to deliver. The letter explained that of all the souls on board the *Mîrî*, the admiral had spared the lives of only some children and the man who was now his messenger. The rest, Gama declared, had been killed in revenge for the Portuguese who had been murdered in Calicut, and the children had been baptized as reckoning for a Portuguese boy whom the Moors had taken to Mecca to make a Muslim. This, he added, "was a demonstration of the manner that the Portuguese had in amending the damage that they had received, and the rest would be in the city of Calecut itself, where he hoped to be very soon."

Vasco da Gama had returned to India in the service of a king who dreamed of ushering in a universal Christian age. A visionary's sense of proportion lessens as his vision grows in grandeur, and world domination and fair play have no common border. If the admiral had any notion of natural justice, it, too, was sacrificed to the call of holy war.

CHAPTER 15

SHOCK AND AWE

THE CRUSADER FLAGS snapped boldly from the masts and the crow's nests of the European fleet. On the unfurled sails the crimson Crusader crosses could be seen from far away. They were not there for decoration, or simply as signs of piety and pleas for protection. Not everyone had enlisted for the voyage knowing of Manuel's mad ambition to crush Islam and anoint himself Universal Emperor, but few if any had believed they were going on a peaceful trading trip.

The vast majority of Vasco da Gama's men knew exactly where their sympathies lay. To the sailors and soldiers, the admiral was a proven leader who had earned their unblinking loyalty. To the captains, he was an astute commander who consulted them regularly and passed no bucks. To the priests, he was a Crusader engaged in God's work. Civilians had always been swept up in war, enemy peoples had always been caricatured as scarcely human, and war's inhumanity had often escalated when men believed they were fighting for their faith. In an age when it was commonplace for conquerors to slaughter entire cities, Gama's followers and foes alike did not see his attack on the *Mîrî* as an unconscionable act. Only a few contemplative men, like the clerk Tomé Lopes, were struck by the human tragedy of holy war.

The merchants' representatives had different reasons to prefer caution. Their employers had funded a large part of the fleet, and yet Matteo da Bergamo privately noted that the admiral appeared determined to put Crusade before trade. Dom Vasco had made it clear that he would only allow a few of them to leave the ships, and he had suggested in no uncertain terms that they buy their spices in the places he arranged and at the prices he fixed. They had little choice; as Bergamo put it, "we knew his will and didn't want to oppose him. So we were all agreed, with lively voice." If there were more episodes like the brutal attack on the *Mîrî*, though, they wondered if they would have anything at all to take home.

Crusading might be bad for business, but Gama had a longer prospect in view. The hard-nosed captain had become an iron-fisted admiral. He had no qualms about being more feared than loved, and he had no intention of slackening his attacks on anyone who hindered the Portuguese cause. He was, though, quickly reminded that nature had no truck with the aspirations of admirals and kings.

Within days four more big dhows appeared on the horizon, and the *São Paulo* set off in pursuit. The Arab ships fled toward land, and three disappeared down a river. In its haste the fourth hit a shoal, and the *São Paulo* came alongside and grappled it, lowering its anchors to keep clear of the shoal. A boarding party swung onto the deck, and many of the Muslims jumped in the sea. Yet no sooner were the Christians on board than the captive ship creaked alarmingly and rolled over onto its side. The *São Paulo* tipped with it, and the crew was forced to uncouple the two vessels. The stricken ship lurched into the waves, and the marooned men hung on to anything they could and waited to be rescued. The Europeans put out their boats, but in the heavy swells their oars were useless. The waves began to break up the lightly built dhow, and with the boarding party still beyond rescue, it filled with water and sank. Its cargo, including a large cache of shields and swords, washed toward the shore, where a crowd of locals emerged to scavenge the wreckage.

On October 13 the last of the three ships that Gama had lost at the Cape of Good Hope sailed into view. It had been missing so long that everyone had assumed it had foundered, and as so often happens at sea the mood instantly switched from dismay to celebration.

The fleet had been hunting Arab ships for a month, and no more had fallen into its net. The whole time the admiral had been receiving letters from the Kolattiri of Cannanore, who repeatedly assured him that he was at his service and would give him all the spices in his land at the price he named. The time for loading the ships was running out, and Gama reluctantly gave the order to set sail. On October 18 the nineteen vessels rounded a rocky headland, passed a jutting promontory, and moored within sight of the secluded harbor of Cannanore.

The Kolattiri had been markedly friendly to the Portuguese on their last two sorties. He became even better disposed when the ambassador he had sent to Portugal sailed up with the twenty-four men who had been seized in the sambuk. They had heard the battle with the *Mîrî* at close quarters—they had been battened under the hatches of their boat, which had been tied to Tomé Lopes's ship— and as they arrived home their trumpets pealed their relief.

Soon envoys bearing gifts approached the Christian fleet. They were at the service of the king of Portugal, they bowed, and they added that the Kolattiri was most eager to meet the admiral. Gama was equally keen to meet the Indian king, but he refused to step onshore. He was determined to trust no one; possibly he realized that his recent behavior might not incline them to trust him, either.

If Gama was not going to leave his floating realm, the Kolattiri was not going to set foot outside his kingdom. To solve the dilemma an elaborate compromise was drawn up. Elephants appeared on the shore dragging dozens of tree trunks, and a team of carpenters set to work constructing a sturdy wooden pier. In no time it reached well out to sea.

The next day the admiral took charge of one of the caravels. He seated himself on the poop deck, on a fine cushion set on a richly carved chair under a crimson and green velvet awning. He was wearing a silk robe and two heavy gold chains, one around his neck and the other slung across his chest. Twenty-six boats accompanied him, each decked out with the flags of the Order of Christ and the full panoply of arms. The pages struck up a dignified tune on their trumpets, drums, and castanets, the sailors danced a jig, and the flotilla set off toward the pier.

On land the Kolattiri appeared accompanied by four hundred Nair soldiers—most likely not, as a Portuguese chronicler claimed, ten thousand—and a menagerie of exotic animals that the wide-eyed Flemish sailor found it impossible to name. The newcomers to India were equally surprised to see that all the dignitaries, including the king, were naked from the waist up.

At each end of the pier the workmen had erected a pavilion draped with painted cloths. The soldiers halted in front of the shoreside pavilion, and the Kolattiri and thirty of his attendants disappeared inside. It took them a while to emerge: the sun was scorching, the Kolattiri was seventy years old, and the party had run out of puff.

When the admiral's caravel drew alongside the seaside pavilion, the Kolattiri moved off down the pier. Two men went in front of him swinging heavy sticks decorated with bull's heads, and two more men danced around with sticks painted with white sparrow hawks; Tomé Lopes mockingly noted that they looked like a couple of Portuguese girls.

The Kolattiri dismounted from his palanquin and arrayed himself on a sumptuously draped daybed. Still Gama refused to disembark, and the perplexed king was forced to bend down and shake his hand across the water. The audience went ahead with the interpreters shouting diplomatic niceties back and forth between the pier and the poop deck.

Since the Kolattiri had been so accommodating, Gama passed him with his own hands—a diplomatic breach that set tongues wagging—a lavish set of gilded silver tableware filled with saffron and rosewater. The Kolattiri gave the admiral, through the more humble hands of his servants, a collection of enormous gems. Smaller precious stones—mere trifles, he let it be known—were handed out to the captains and officers.

Gama moved swiftly on to business, but his attempts to fix a tariff for the spices he wanted to buy were royally rebuffed. The visitors had come too early in the year, the king replied, and the spices hadn't yet arrived. In any case, he did not concern himself with such matters. He would command merchants to call on them, and then they could discuss trade.

After two hours the Kolattiri left, saying he was tired. The Portuguese fired a ceremonial salute as he retreated down his pier, and when Gama returned to the fleet he informed the merchants' representatives that complete accord had broken out. The Kolattiri, recorded Matteo da Bergamo, would do everything the king of Portugal and his admiral asked, including making war on the Zamorin of Calicut and compelling his merchants to sell spices at the price the admiral had set. Gama was determined to call the shots and get the best deal for his king, but in reality the Kolattiri had agreed to nothing of the sort.

The merchants arrived the next day, and to Gama's dismay they all turned out to be Muslims. As usual they turned up their noses at the European goods—a bargaining strategy, the Portuguese were convinced—but worse, the prices they asked were a great deal higher than before. After much haggling the negotiations fell apart, and Gama began to detect a fiendish conspiracy at work.

The admiral was in severe danger of losing face, and he worked himself into a professional rage against foreigners who refused to play by his rules. He dismissed the merchants and immediately dispatched a warning message to the Kolattiri. Clearly, he railed, the king was not a true friend of the Portuguese. There was no other explanation for his sending Muslim merchants to them, "who as he well knew had an ancient hatred for the Christians and were our greatest enemies." He would return the small quantities of spices that had already been loaded, he darkly added, with a great fanfare of bugles and plenty of salutes from his guns.

As the tension mounted, the Portuguese factor who had been left behind by the last fleet showed up in a fluster. Paio Rodrigues and his men had been in Cannanore for nearly a year and, he assured the admiral, they had found its king and people extremely obliging. Gama told him to stay on the ship; he was done with the Kolattiri, he fumed. Paio, who was not under Gama's command, point-blank refused: he was going back, he insisted, whether the admiral liked it or not.

Gama bristled, then stepped back an inch. Instead he gave Rodrigues a new message for the Kolattiri. The fleet, he announced, would sail off and buy spices at a friendlier port, but the Muslims of his land had better not think they were safe any longer. Moreover, if the Christians who were staying on were hurt or dishonored in any way, his people would pay the price.

The ships weighed anchor before dawn on October 22, just four days after they had arrived. They sailed along the coast, stopping to intercept a small sambuk and seize twenty men with a cargo of coconut fiber. Soon they saw a small port where three large ships were pulled up on the shore, and Gama himself set out toward them with two caravels and eight boats packed with troops. As the bombards fired and the Europeans closed in, a number of figures jumped overboard and fled to land. A man raced down the beach and set out in a boat, rowing furiously to dodge the cannonballs. He was a vassal of the Kolattiri, he shouted at the admiral; all the land around here was subject to Cannanore. He was therefore at peace with the Portuguese—to his cost. He had refused to rent the very ships they had just attacked to the Zamorin of Calicut for his war against the Christians, and for that reason he himself was at war with Calicut. If the admiral doubted his word, he added, he would leave his men as hostages and prove everything he said.

Gama reluctantly desisted.

Late at night one of Paio Rodrigues's men rowed up in haste with a letter from the Kolattiri. He was replying to the messages he had received, the king said with some forbearance and dignity. If the admiral wanted to kill or kidnap his people he could do so, because he would not mount a guard against his Portuguese allies.

Even then, he would keep the peace he had made with the king of Portugal, which he cared about deeply. He would, though, be sure to inform King Manuel of everything that had happened. As for the Christians in his city, the admiral could attack him to his heart's content and it would bring them no harm or shame.

A covering letter from Rodrigues contained a similar message.

Gama glowered. Clearly the Portuguese factor had tutored the Kolattiri to treat the admiral as a renegade and threaten to appeal over his head.

The scale of Portugal's ambitions had always required India's rulers to switch their entire trade to the West and oust every last Muslim from their lands. The hope that they would do so voluntarily was receding daily, and Gama was more sure than ever that they would have to be shocked into compliance. With his mind set on vengeance, he sailed on to Calicut.

As the fleet passed Pantalayini, the town where Gama had first landed in India, it overtook another small sambuk. As usual the sailors were taken captive, and two of them attracted the attention of the children who had been taken from the *Mîrî*. The children were frightened and eager to oblige their new masters, and they accused the prisoners of having taken part in the attack on the Calicut factory. One boy said that one of the men had boasted of killing two Christians while he was staying at his home, and another said the second man had cut off a Christian's arm. Gama had it proclaimed that the sailors were dying for the cause of justice and hanged them from the mast. They were not the first casualties of the children's terror: a few days before, Gama had ordered another Muslim lanced to death when they accused him of stealing goods from the Portuguese warehouse.

THE ZAMORIN HAD heard that a powerful European fleet was on its way almost as soon as it had reached India.

Rather than wait to be attacked, he had decided to make the first move. While the fleet was still at Cannanore, word had reached

Gama that the Zamorin had written to the king of Cochin, the southernmost of the three richest ports on the Malabar Coast. The Portuguese, the Zamorin had predicted, would do great damage to the whole of India, and the only way to deal with them was for the rulers to close ranks and refuse to sell the foreigners the spices they coveted. If they combined their efforts, he argued, the Christians would give up and go home; if not, they would all end up as subjects of the Portuguese king.

The king of Cochin had refused. He was no more a friend of the high and mighty Zamorin than was the Kolattiri of Cannanore, and he wrote back that he had already signed a highly satisfactory treaty with the Portuguese. He showed the Zamorin's letter and his reply to the Portuguese factor, who copied them and forwarded them to the admiral.

His plan thwarted, the Zamorin had instead sent an ambassador to Gama himself. His king wanted nothing but peace and friendship, the emissary declared, and though the trouble had all been the fault of the Portuguese factors, who had brought about their own deaths, naturally he would restore the goods the Christians had left in his city. Some, it was true, should have been handed over in lieu of the tax they owed, and some he had given to the master of the ship that Cabral had burned; but judges could be appointed to decide who owed what to whom. As for the dead, he added, they could never be brought back, even though, when everything was accounted for, the Christians were more than revenged for their losses.

As the fleet neared Calicut, an extraordinary exchange of messages began to fly back and forth between the admiral and the Zamorin.

Gama made no reply until he reached Pantalayini. If the Zamorin wanted to have good relations with him, he finally responded via a Nair soldier who had come along from Cannanore, he must first return all the stolen merchandise; he had one day to comply.

The deadline passed without an answer.

The fleet passed in front of Calicut on October 29 and lined up ominously on the horizon. Soon a new envoy arrived in a boat flying a flag of truce. He was dressed in the habit of a Franciscan friar, and he climbed on board exclaiming *"Deo gratias!"*—"Thanks to God!" He was quickly unmasked as a Muslim, and he apologized for disguising himself to secure permission to come aboard. He saluted the admiral and made appropriate noises about how welcome he was, then repeated the terms set out in the Zamorin's first message. Not only had the Portuguese sunk the *Mîrî* and drowned hundreds of men and women, he added; even now they were hanging the Zamorin's subjects. Surely their injuries had been more than redressed?

By any reckoning they had been, but Gama was no longer interested in reparations. He was bent on severing the ties that for centuries had bound together peoples and nations. He would not make any treaty, he replied, until every last Arab, visiting or resident, had been expelled from Calicut, "because since the beginning of the world the Moors have been the enemies of the Christians, and the Christians of the Moors, and they had always been at war with each other, and because of that no agreement that we made would stick." If he wanted peace, he concluded, the Zamorin must never again let an Arab ship into his port.

The Zamorin heard Gama's outrageous demands and sent back a measured reply. There were more than four thousand Arab households in his lands, he pointed out; among them were many rich and powerful merchants who ennobled his kingdom. For generations his ancestors had welcomed them, and they had always found them to be honest men. Like his forebears, he had received many services from them; to name just one, they had often loaned him money to defend his borders. It would seem to the whole world an ugly and improper act to reward them by forcing them into exile. He would never do such a perfidious thing, and the admiral should not tempt him. He was, though, ready to oblige the Portuguese in any honorable way, and he had sent his ambassadors to express his great desire for peace.

Gama threw down the letter. "An insult!" he growled, and he had the messengers seized.

While the diplomatic wrangling was going on, the Portuguese had been busy capturing fishermen and raiding boats in the backwaters. The illustrious Zamorin had had enough of foreigners treating him as an inferior while they behaved like bloodthirsty pirates, and he sent another envoy with a much less diplomatic message. If the Portuguese wanted peace, he declared, there could be no conditions attached, and if they wanted their goods back, he required compensation for the loss and damage they had inflicted on his city. To begin with, they must return everything they had taken from the *Mîrî*, which belonged to his people. Calicut, he reminded them, was a free port; he could not prevent anyone from coming there to trade, nor could he send away a single Muslim. If the admiral agreed they would come to terms, but he would give no surety. His word as king was enough, and if the strangers doubted it, they should leave his port immediately and never show their faces in India again.

Gama abandoned all restraint and sent the messenger back with a declaration of war. If he did not receive complete satisfaction, he threatened, he would open fire on the city at noon the next day. The Zamorin need not bother sending any more messages unless they named the sum of money he was ready to pay up. He, a mere knight of the mighty king of Portugal, was a better man than the Indian ruler. "A palm tree," he exploded, "would make a king as good as him," and for good measure he threw in some derisory comments about the royal habit of chewing paan.

THAT EVENING, A SUNDAY, the Europeans set their foresails and lined up fifteen ships with their prows jutting at the shore; only the four largest stayed a little back. The Zamorin, they could see, had been expecting them. He had improvised a stockade, by transplanting rows of palm trees near the water's edge, to obstruct their landings and deflect their fire.

As the gunners shifted the large pieces of artillery to the fore-decks, they saw hundreds of lanterns flicker to life like fallen stars on the shore. By their light, men began to crawl around, digging hollows in the beach. Then they hauled over iron cannon and installed them in the sandy emplacements, with the barrels poking out over the top.

When morning came, Gama ordered the front line of ships to anchor as close as possible to the waterfront. As the men took to their battle stations, ranks of defenders emerged from the cover of the palms. There were far more of them than anyone had imagined at night.

Noon on November 1, the appointed day, passed with no reply.

The admiral made his move. On his command, boats went around the fleet distributing the Muslim captives who had been seized over the previous days. Two or three were dropped off at each ship, along with a message to look out for a signal flag on the topmast of the *Leitoa*.

One hour after midday the flag was run up. On each ship the prisoners' necks were placed in nooses and the ends of the ropes were thrown over the yards. The struggling men were hoisted to the top and were hung in full sight of the city. Tomé Lopes saw thirty-four bodies jerking amid the rigging; Matteo da Bergamo counted thirty-eight.

On the shore the swelling crowd watched in horror. Gama's flagship and a caravel each fired a cannonball into their midst, sending them diving for the ground. The rest of the ships opened fire and the Indians fled, throwing themselves into hollows as the stone balls thudded around them and crawling off the beach on their stomachs. The Europeans shouted mocking taunts as they ran away. The men in the sand bunkers fired back, but they only had a few old bombards, their aim was wide of the mark, and they took precious minutes to reload. The ships turned their fire on them, and one by one they surfaced and ran to the town. Replacements inched forward on all fours, but within an hour the beach was deserted.

The bombardment of the city started in earnest. Cannonballs thundered overhead and smashed into the earth walls and thatch roofs of the houses near the shore. Decapitated palm trees splintered, groaned, and toppled. Many men, women, and children were killed, and thousands fled.

With dusk gathering, Gama ratcheted up the terror. As his orders were shouted from ship to ship, the corpses were cut down from the rigging. Their heads, hands, and feet were hacked off, and the body parts were sent to the flagship. Gama had them piled in one of the captured boats. The boat was tied to a ship's skiff, and a solitary sailor towed it out and left it to float on the tide to the shore.

An arrow stuck out from the bloody heap, and tied to its shaft was a letter from the admiral. In Malayalam, Gama advised the Zamorin to take a good look at the punishment he had meted out to men who had not even been party to the attack on the Portuguese factory—men who were not even residents of the city but merely their cousins. A far more cruel death, he avowed, awaited the murderers. The price of the Christians' friendship, he added, had risen: now the Zamorin would have to reimburse them not only for the goods he had plundered, but also for the powder and ammunition they had expended in bombarding him to his senses.

The Portuguese tossed the dismembered trunks of the hung men overboard to wash up on the shore with the incoming tide.

As the boat touched the seafront, a few townspeople approached and gaped at its ghastly cargo. The Europeans could clearly see the scene in the bright moonlight, and Gama ordered his men not to shoot. It was late at night, but soon large crowds came down to the shore. They turned away in disgust, bewildered and frightened, and trudged back to their homes, some with their relatives' heads cradled in their arms. The bereaved held a vigil, with no candles or lanterns to light their grief in case the Portuguese tried to set their houses on fire. Until the early hours the dirges and lamentations carried on the breeze to the Portuguese fleet, waking the sailors and plaguing their dreams.

Having given the Zamorin the night to ponder, Vasco da Gama woke early to deliver the coup de grâce. As the new day dawned, he ordered the gunners to prime the biggest artillery. The simple houses near the shore had already been pulverized, and now the cannonballs smashed into the grand mansions on the higher ground behind. Then, no doubt with particular relish, Gama told his men to aim for the Zamorin's palace. As the hours passed, Tomé Lopes counted more than four hundred cannonballs exploding from the bombards on eighteen ships.

At noon Gama ordered a cease-fire and waited for the Zamorin to surrender. The front line of ships pulled back, but there was no answer from the shore.

The admiral emptied a captured sambuk of its barrels of honey and nuts and distributed the delicacies among the ships. Then he had it anchored near the shore and set on fire. As the Europeans began eating dinner and the warning beacon blazed away, a dozen boats put out from the beach to cut the sambuk's cable and tow it off. Gama's men pushed aside their trenchers, climbed into their boats, and rowed over at high speed, chasing the Indians as they headed back to the shore. As they drew near a menacing crowd gathered at the water's edge. They thought better of getting any closer and retreated to the fleet.

By now darkness had fallen. The sambuk was still smoldering away, and Gama decided he had done enough. Realistically, there was little else he could do. As long as he kept to the water, he had the advantage of massively superior firepower and unseasoned enemies. The famously fierce Nair soldiers were forbidden on religious grounds from eating at sea, and they rarely set foot on board a ship. Their Muslim counterparts labored under no such proscription, but they were traders and sailors, not warriors. In hand-to-hand combat on land, though, the Nairs would have vastly outmatched Gama's men. The Admiral of India had escalated the standoff with the Zamorin of Calicut into a full-blown war, but like any attacking force that balks at putting boots on the ground, he could only hope that he had applied enough pressure to make the enemy collapse from within.

On November 3, Gama gave the order to depart the half-ruined city. He left Vicente Sodré in command of six ships and a caravel to blockade the harbor and sailed on down the coast to Cochin.

COCHIN WAS AN upstart among the port cities of the Malabar Coast. It was only a century and a half old, and it had been created not by man but by monsoon. Locals still talked of the violent monsoon season of 1341, when the backwaters near the ancient port of Muchiri—a prosperous place well known to the Romans, and to Jews fleeing the Roman destruction of Jerusalem—radically shifted and re-formed into a watery new riddle of islands and lakes. The old harbor had silted up, and a nearby prince had taken advantage of the new landscape to redirect its traffic to his capital.

The city of Cochin was built on a thumb of land at the end of a straggling seaboard peninsula. The thumb was opposed to the north by three heavily wooded fingers; a fourth curled toward the mainland. Vypeen Island, the westernmost finger, nearly brushed the tip of the city, leaving a narrow opening into a skein of calm lagoons and waterways fed by seven major rivers. The harbor was by far the finest on the Malabar Coast, and it had quickly begun to thrive. Cochin's signature sight—great spidery fishing nets, raised and lowered from the shore on huge wooden pivots—was a legacy of decades of Chinese visitors, and a large community of Jewish merchants had their own quarter and their own prince.

The royal family nursed grand ambitions to outdo its richer and older neighbors, and it was particularly keen on trumping the supercilious Zamorin of Calicut. As the paramount rulers on the coast, the Zamorins had long reserved the right to turn up in Cochin and imperiously pass judgment on whether its kings were fit to serve. The sudden arrival of the Portuguese was too good an opportunity to miss, and Unni Goda Varma, the Cochin raja, had greeted the strangers with open arms. If the Admiral of India was welcome anywhere, it should have been in Cochin.

The fleet sailed into sight on November 7 and a welcoming committee, including the two factors whom Cabral had left behind, immediately hailed the admiral. The city's Muslim merchants had also been expecting the Europeans. Letters had already reached them from their cousins in Calicut, detailing the death and destruction inflicted on them and appealing for help to lift the blockade. The Christians, they bitterly complained, had even stopped them from fishing and they were on the verge of starvation. The factors told Gama to count on a hostile reception.

There was more news, both good and bad. The factors had also caught wind of a massive armada that had been gathering to make war on the Christians. The Zamorin had reportedly rented and requisitioned more than two hundred ships, and they had sailed out in search of the Portuguese. One of the biggest vessels had crashed into the coast at Cochin, and its crew had revealed that the rest of the vast fleet had been lost in a terrible storm. The king, the factors reported with satisfaction, had seized all the men and had not returned a bean to the Zamorin. As always when the weather was on their side and against their enemies, the Portuguese deduced that the hand of God had worked another miracle and gave thanks for their deliverance.

The same day one of the king's sons arrived and saluted the admiral. He had come, he explained, especially to thank him for leaving ships belonging to Cochin unharmed as he burned and pillaged his way along the coast. He passed on his royal father's appreciation for the favor that had been shown to his people out of respect for him; in return, he promised, his father would personally make the most advantageous arrangements to load their ships with spices.

Gama slowly began to unbend. His men set about repairing the ships and clearing space for the bumper cargo they expected. Three days after their arrival the king sent word that it was an auspicious day to start loading, and hillocks of pepper began to pile up on the docks. The prices, though, had yet to be fixed, and the merchants soon went on strike. After four days Gama was forced to ask the king for a meeting. His holds were still empty, and he was running out of places to do business.

The meeting was arranged for the fourteenth, a week after the fleet's arrival. The admiral set out in a caravel with the usual trumpets, bombards, and standards, and he and his captains sailed into the mouth of the harbor. The king came down to the shore in his palanquin, accompanied by six war elephants and—so claimed a Portuguese sailor—ten thousand men. With his servants fanning him and his ushers holding back the crowds with maces, he drew to a halt. The royal trumpeters lifted their instruments and tooted a tune, and a few cannon fired a salute. The Portuguese responded with their own fanfare and a great blast of their guns. Envoys shuttled back and forth to finalize the diplomatic niceties, but just as the meeting was about to go ahead, the wind whipped up, rumbles of thunder burst the air, and the inky heavens opened. The king sent word that it was a bad omen, and the meeting was rescheduled for two days later.

When Gama returned, the raja was already out in the harbor, seated on a large raft made from four sambuks lashed together and covered with planks. Tomé Lopes noted that the crowds had lost interest, or had not been summoned, and there were only four or five guards with him.

As soon as the admiral's caravel drew alongside, the king came beamingly on board. In a replay of the scene at Cannanore, Gama gave him—again, with his own hands—more silver basins, jugs, and saltcellars gilded to look like solid gold, together with a throne embellished with silver, a hundred cruzados, a piece of velvet, and two rich brocade cushions. The raja presented the admiral and his officers with more jewels. After a long, cheerful conversation, he agreed to Gama's conditions and signed off on his schedule of prices, and the admiral accompanied his floating platform back to the palace jetty.

The merchants grumbled about the prices, but sellers clustered on the shore. The Portuguese began to fill their holds day and night with the exotica of the East: pepper, ginger, cardamom, myrobalans, canafistula, zerumba, zedoary, wild cinnamon, cloves, benzoin, and alum.

Soon Vicente Sodré sailed into view with three of the ships that had stayed at Calicut. It turned out they had had a narrow escape. The Zamorin had secretly prepared another armed fleet of twenty large sambuks to attack them. When it was ready, a flotilla of fishing boats had lured the Christians into the mouth of the river that Gama had crossed in great state on his first visit. The fleet was lying in wait among the palm trees, and the Indians quickly surrounded the European boats on every side, unloosing volleys of arrows. The trapped and wounded men panicked, and they were saved only when a gunner tried to shoot one of the fishing boats, aimed too high, and sent a cannonball smashing down onto the sambuk carrying the captain of the fleet. As it capsized, the Indians went to the rescue, and the Portuguese had enough time to extricate themselves.

With Sodré was an envoy from Cannanore who had arrived in Calicut and had asked to be taken to the admiral. His king, he told Gama, had sent him to say that he would match the prices the Europeans had been given anywhere else, if necessary by making up the difference out of his own pocket; moreover, he would buy any goods they had for sale at the price they set.

Gama dispatched Sodré to check out the story and load the king's ships. His high-stakes gamble had paid off in the nick of time: instead of letting the European merchants compete to buy spices, he had made the Malabar kings compete for their business. Still, Matteo da Bergamo and his fellow traders continued to grumble about conditions in Cochin. The consignments of pepper had begun to run out, and the European merchandise was as impossible as ever to shift. The city's merchants were always asking for more money or finding another reason to stop loading, and more than once they rebelled against the king's orders and refused to trade at all. Several times Gama was forced to pull out his factors and rant to the raja about the dastardly behavior of the Muslims: one day he crept up to his palace and fired off his bombards, in the guise of a fete, while the king pretended to be entertained on his terrace. Nothing was enough for Matteo da Bergamo and his profit-hungry colleagues. "We kept asking ourselves," the Italian noted, "whether we would be able to load our ships even half full on this voyage." They were no more enthused by the offer from Cannanore. "The admiral sent three royal ships," he added, "because no one among us wanted to go there, since from what we had learned they had too little pepper and the cinnamon was of bad quality."

With the king firmly on the side of the Portuguese, the Muslim merchants hatched a plot. Three farmers approached the *Julioa*, which was in the harbor to load spices, and sold the sailors a cow. The Hindu king, naturally, got wind of the matter and made a forceful complaint to the admiral; like the Zamorin, on taking the throne he had sworn to protect cows first and Brahmins second. Gama promptly had it proclaimed that his men, on pain of being beaten, were forbidden to buy cows and were immediately to arrest and bring to him anyone who tried to sell anything remotely bovine. The three men came back with another cow and were dragged before the admiral, who sent both cow and captives to the king. They were instantly impaled without trial, reported Tomé Lopes, "in this way, that each one had a stake thrust up through the kidneys and chest that propped up the face, and they were set in the ground, as high as a lance, with the arms and legs splayed and tied to four poles, and they could not pull down the post, because there was a piece of wood across it that held them in place. And so they carried out justice on them, because they sold the said cows."

It was at that satisfying moment of cross-cultural cooperation that a large party of Indians turned up and announced they were Christians.

THE NEW ARRIVALS told Dom Vasco that they had come on behalf of thirty thousand Christians who lived farther down the coast. They were the descendants, they explained, of the followers of the Apostle Thomas, who was buried in their city. They were, reported Tomé Lopes, "most honorable in appearance," and they brought offerings of sheep, chickens, and fruit.

Gama's voyages had revolutionized Europe's maps, but much of the West's world picture was still colored by the surmises of scriptural geographers. There was thus nothing in the least surprising about the notion that one of Jesus's disciples had traveled to India. Farther south, the newcomers explained, was a great trading city called Quilon, and nearby, where the land projected into the sea, the apostle had miraculously built a great church just before he died. St. Thomas, the story went, had arrived dressed in rags on a mission to convert the lowest castes of Indians to the new religion. One day a gigantic log had floated into the harbor and had lodged on the strand. The king had sent many men and elephants to drag it inland, but it refused to budge. The ragged apostle swore he could move it, if the king would give him a piece of land on which to build a church in honor of his Lord. He summoned every carpenter he could find, and they sawed away at the log until they had fashioned the frame and the cladding for the church. At midday Thomas took a scoop and filled it with sand; the sand turned into rice, and the workers were fed. When their work was done, he transformed a wood chip into money to pay them. Soon afterward the apostle assumed the form of a peacock and was shot by a hunter. Having risen into the air as a bird, he had fallen back to earth as a man. He was buried, but his right arm refused to stay in the ground. Every time someone pushed it back under the soil it popped up again the next day. Eventually the grave diggers gave in and left it poking out, and pilgrims flocked to see the miracle from many lands. Some Chinese visitors tried to cut off the arm and take it home, but when they struck it with a sword it finally drew back into the grave.

A touch more prosaically, the visitors explained that the saint's followers had sent five men out into the world to make contact with their fellow Christians. They had eventually arrived in Persia, where a community of Christians who spoke Syriac, a language similar to Jesus's Aramaic tongue, had flourished independently of the rest of Christendom for centuries. Ever since, the Persian Church had sent bishops to tend to its Indian flock.

After the long, fruitless search for Prester John, after the initial euphoria at finding countless Christians in India and the dawning realization that they belonged to an entirely different religion, here, at last, were real Indian Christians. True, like their Persian mentors they were Nestorians who believed that Jesus had two natures, one human and one divine, and so, strictly speaking, they were heretics. True, their priests wore turbans, went barefoot, and, the German sailor noted, were as black as the other Indians. But they had six bishops, they said mass at an altar before a cross, and they took communion, albeit with soaked raisins instead of wine. It was a start.

Gama welcomed the visitors with great joy and gave them gifts of silk cloth. They asked about Europe's churches and priests and about the sailors' homes and habits, and they were astonished to hear how far they had come. They offered to become vassals of the Portuguese king, and as a symbol of their allegiance they brought the admiral a scarlet crook tipped with silver and adorned with little bells, together with a letter from their leaders. Though they were hardly huge in number, they were clearly ready to support their fellow Christians against their Hindu rulers and the Muslims who dominated their cities. If the Portuguese king built a fortress in their neighborhood, they bravely suggested, he could dominate the whole of India.

As the news traveled back to the Christian communities, a second delegation arrived from Quilon in mid-December. They told the admiral that there were plenty of spices in their city, and Gama dispatched three ships down the coast. The Flemish sailor was on board, and he reported that there were "nearly 25,000 Christians" in Quilon who worshipped at "nearly 300 Christian churches, and they bear the names of the apostles and other saints." When he visited the church of St. Thomas he found it cut off by the sea, and the nearby town, which the Christians inhabited on condition of paying a tribute, was mostly ruined. Still, the Europeans loaded large quantities of pepper and some cinnamon and cloves, which they paid for with cash, copper, and the opium seized from the *Mîrî*.

Back in Cochin the new pepper harvest had at last arrived. Matteo da Bergamo was still complaining that he had to sell his wares at a loss, that Cochin was badly supplied with drugs and precious stones, and that he was being given short measure by the merchants, but the holds were filling up fast. Meanwhile, a caravel returned from Cannanore with the news that Vicente Sodré had not only loaded a bumper haul of spices but had also captured and looted three large vessels at sea. One had had more than a hundred men on board, and most had been captured or killed. If honest trade failed, piracy was always another way to make ends meet.

CHAPTER 16

STANDOFF AT SEA

CHRISTMAS PASSED IN high spirits for the Europeans in Cochin and Quilon. The festive mood was only slightly spoiled on December 29, when the soundly sleeping sailors on the *Santo António* woke up with a jolt to find their anchor rope had snapped, they had hit the coast, and they were letting in water at an alarming rate. They fired off two shots and the boats raced to their aid, but the ship stayed beached all night until it could be towed off for emergency repairs in the morning.

As the year 1503 began, even the excruciating display of barbarity that Gama had inflicted on Calicut seemed to be paying off. The Zamorin had already sent two sambuks to spy on the fleet; the Portuguese had captured them and had summarily executed their crews. Now, though, an embassy arrived with a new letter from the Zamorin and renewed assurances of friendship. If the admiral would come back, the Zamorin promised to make restitution for the seized goods; for his security, he would give him anyone he named to keep as a hostage until he was completely satisfied.

A Brahmin delivered the letter, and his son and two Nairs accompanied him. "This Brahmin," noted Lopes, "is like a bishop and a monk, and is a man of great estate." Like the rest of his caste, he added, the Brahmin was able to travel in perfect safety even if the country was at war, because anyone who harmed him would immediately be excommunicated with no possibility of absolution. The Portuguese were flattered all the more when the Brahmin announced that he wanted to go to Portugal with them. He had brought enough jewels, he explained, to pay his way, and if they would allow him, he would buy some cinnamon to do a little trading. He even asked if his sons and nephews could come with him to learn Latin and be instructed in the Christian faith.

This was music to Gama's ears, and he was coaxed out of his professional distrust. Clearly, he thought, he had bombarded some sense into the Zamorin, and he decided to return with the ambassador in person. When his captains protested, he bluntly replied that if the Zamorin broke his word he would hang the Brahmin and his fellow messengers. The risk was worth taking: if he humbled Calicut and turned it over to Portuguese control, he would go home in triumph.

The admiral had the distinguished visitor's jewels and spices secured on the flagship. He boarded the *Flor de la Mar*, his cousin Estêvão's ship, and accompanied by a solitary caravel he set sail for Calicut.

The merchants of Cochin watched the admiral leave and immediately put down their scales. All their king's blandishments had failed, they complained: the fickle Christian was headed back to Calicut to buy spices. Gama had given command of the Cochin fleet to Dom Luís Coutinho, a wealthy nobleman who was captain of the *Lionarda*, and Coutinho went to reason with the merchants. By two o'clock in the morning he had still failed to hammer out an agreement, and he sent Giovanni Buonagrazia after the admiral with letters asking for his orders. On board was Buonagrazia's brother in arms Tomé Lopes, and once again Lopes recounted the story.

The winds were feeble, and it took the Italian captain three days to reach Calicut. When he arrived he edged within half a league of the shore, but the *Flor de la Mar* was nowhere to be seen. He sailed straight on to Cannanore, thinking the admiral had already made peace and had left to join his uncle, but since a strong northeast wind made it impossible to approach the harbor he returned to Calicut, still convinced that all was well. Luckily the wind again refused to cooperate, and he headed back to Cannanore, where he finally found the missing vessels in full battle rig, "as if they were ready to fight with a thousand ships." The captains sent up the flags and banners, and the crews exchanged stories.

As soon as Gama had arrived outside Calicut, Lopes heard, he had dispatched the caravel to Cannanore to fetch his uncle. With only a few dozen sailors left to protect him, he had made a warm speech to the Brahmin and had asked him to repeat it to the Zamorin. It often happened, he said, that two enemies became great friends, and so the Christians would become to the Zamorin. From this moment on, they would do business as if they were brothers.

The Brahmin promised to return by nightfall, but in his stead a different messenger arrived. The money and spices were ready for the admiral, he announced, if he would send a man of quality to the city to settle their accounts.

Gama began to suspect that he had been taken for a fool. He wouldn't even send the smallest ship's boy, he furiously replied. For the umpteenth time, he told the Zamorin to send what he owed or forget the whole thing.

The messenger advised him to stay at least another day; he knew the will of the Zamorin and his people, he added, and it would soon become clear. He, too, promised to return with an answer.

That night, during the last quarter before dawn, the watchkeepers sighted a sambuk setting out from the shore. When they took a second look, they saw that what looked like one boat was really two tied together, and they were now heading straight for their ship.

The officers woke up the admiral. He threw on some clothes and came on deck, confident that the Zamorin was at last sending the long-awaited goods. Instead he made out seventy or eighty more sambuks rowing silently from the shore. He decided it must be the fishing fleet heading out for its morning catch.

Without warning the two leading boats opened fire. Iron cannonballs skipped across the sea and smashed into the *Flor de la Mar*. The rest of the war fleet came up behind and fired at will. As soon as one of the Christians showed himself, arrows thudded from the moonlit sky like black rain. The enemy was already too close for the bombards to be of any use, and the Europeans could only climb up the masts and throw back stones.

Along the way Gama had seized a sambuk, and it was tied to the stern of the *Flor de la Mar.* The Indians filled it with wood and gunpowder and set it on fire. The flames leapt up the sternpost, and the sailors scrambled to cut the rope. The current took the blazing boat away just in time.

As dawn glowed on the horizon, more boats were still starting out from the shore. Soon there were two hundred swarming around the lone Portuguese vessel, all shooting as soon as they were in range. Their guns were small, but the vengeful Zamorin had clearly gone all out to procure every weapon he could find.

The *Flor de la Mar* was in desperate straits. The slow business of hauling in the anchors would have exposed the sailors to lethal fire, and instead they dashed to hack at the cables.

The sails were set, but the ship did not budge. The night before, Gama had secretly ordered a special anchor to be dropped in case the Zamorin's men tried to cut the others loose. It was attached with several iron chains. Cowering beneath the relentless barrage of arrows, the men had no choice but to take a hatchet to each in turn.

The day was already well advanced when the ship finally moved off, with the enemy fleet in full pursuit. Almost immediately the wind dropped, the sails sagged, and the rowing boats swarmed around again.

Just in time Vicente Sodré's ship and two caravels drifted into view. As they took in the sight, they put out their oars and laboriously rowed toward the Indian fleet. When they were near enough they opened fire with their big guns, and the Indians scattered and retreated to the town.

The Admiral of India was fast losing face. He had fallen for the Brahmin's blandishments and had sailed straight into a trap. He had been wounded—eleven times, according to a Portuguese sailor. He had misjudged his opponent's mettle, and he had nearly paid for his mistake with his life.

Gama had the remaining envoys—including the Brahmin's son—hung from the masts of the caravels, and he ordered the ships to parade up and down as near as possible to the city. A crowd came out to watch and shout insults, and the Portuguese shot at them. When the Indians had had plenty of time to see the grisly show, the admiral had the bodies taken down and thrown into a captured boat. He sent it to the shore with one last letter for the Zamorin.

"You vile man!" it read: "you had me called for, and I came in answer to your call. You did as much as you could, and if you could have, you would have done more. The punishment will be as you deserve: when I come back here, I will make you pay what you owe, and not in cash."

The threats were wearing thin, and Gama did not have the forces to back up his words. He beat a retreat to Cannanore, where he met up with Tomé Lopes's ship. They stopped for several days to load spices, then sailed back to Cochin, giving Calicut a wide berth.

THE RUNNING BATTLE with Calicut was threatening to capsize the entire mission, but once again Vasco da Gama found a safe haven in Cochin. The fleet regrouped, the sailors swapped stories, and the admiral met twice more with the king. Their final agreement established a permanent Portuguese factory in the city with a staff of thirty, but it went much further. The chief factor henceforth had jurisdiction over all the Portuguese in Cochin—and over all the Christians in India. As a mark of how strongly the king had sided with the Europeans—if not of Gama's confidence in the attractions of his faith—the factor was explicitly given the authority to deal as he saw fit with any Christian who defected to Islam. This was no mere trade treaty: it established Europe's first Indian colony, and in theory at least it made India's Christians subjects of the Portuguese crown. For the raja, at the ostensibly low cost of a few words it gave the Europeans a vested interest in aggrandizing his power. The cost would soon turn out to be a great deal higher: the agreement dangerously trespassed on the rights of his neighboring rulers.

By February 10, with letters and envoys to King Manuel safely on board, Gama's business in Cochin was done. His plan was to return one last time to Cannanore and then sail for home; if he made a similar pact with the Kolattiri, he reasoned, he could box in the headstrong Zamorin—and if necessary play off his new allies against one another. Before he could depart, though, more unnerving news traveled down the coast. The Zamorin had managed to regroup and amass a fearsome new war fleet, and this time he was determined to rid himself once and for all of the truculent Portuguese.

Gama, in a cold fury, steeled himself for one final battle. His plan was to draw out the enemy and provoke them into attacking before they were fully prepared. The admiral and his uncle Vicente set all their sails and moved off at full speed, while Don Luís Coutinho toured the rest of the fleet in a boat, telling the captains to hold back and follow at a distance.

Two days later, as Coutinho's convoy edged within four or five leagues of Calicut, the lookouts saw a great armada of Arab dhows heading toward them from the north. Lopes counted thirty-two vessels—the Flemish sailor thirty-five—a Portuguese sailor thirty-six—Matteo da Bergamo thirty-eight. With as many as five hundred troops on each, they were far bigger than the boats that had attacked the Europeans before—and far bigger than the largest Portuguese ships. Gama had drawn them out, but there was no sign that they had been caught off guard.

The Christians were sailing close-hauled against the wind and were making slow progress. The Muslims had the wind with them and their sails were fully set. They were bearing down fast, and as the Europeans ran to their battle stations, the ominous rhythm of a war tattoo beaten on big Arab castanets came to them on the breeze.

A new cry went up on the Portuguese ships. A swarm of sambuks and long rowing boats was heading toward them from the city, all armed and with their guns already firing. Gama's men scrambled to return fire, but the boats kept on coming. The Indians had learned to push on until they were past the range of the European guns; that way, they could put their numerical advantage to use in hand-to-hand fighting. In no time the light, fast boats reached the fleet and darted in and out, letting loose flocks of arrows.

The Portuguese ships were heavily laden and in poor condition. They responded sluggishly as the helmsmen heaved on the tillers, and they drifted apart toward land and sea. To complicate matters more, two trading vessels from Cochin were following them. They were even slower sailers, and the Zamorin's boats targeted them, trying to pick them off first. Both the ships' owners were Muslims, but Gama thought better of sacrificing them and endangering the treaty he had just signed with their king. On his urgent signal the fleet slowly re-formed around them.

The situation was dire, but the Europeans had one signal advantage: their big cannon were still much more powerful than anything the enemy possessed. By now the Arab fleet had come within range, and a Portuguese ship that was farther out to sea than the rest opened fire. The gunners scored several direct hits and the dhows fell back toward Calicut. Almost immediately the wind died down, and the Europeans were left powerless to give chase.

Gama barked out new orders. With the Indians still firing at them, the crews put out the boats, tied them to the ships' bows, and strained at the oars to tow the entire fleet along the coast. After a backbreakingly long time they drew level with the seafront of Calicut and closed in on the enemy. A great fusillade of cannonballs ripped holes in the sides of the Arab ships, which scattered toward the city.

The two caravels put out their long oars and set off in pursuit of the Arab flagship. A sudden gust of wind blew the light, freshly tarred dhows to the shore, and the heavily laden caravels creaked after them, their guns blazing away. The flagship refused to surrender, and the caravels were forced to keep their distance. There were only a few dozen men between them, and they were heavily outnumbered.

Eventually a big Portuguese ship lumbered into the harbor. As it grappled one of the Arab vessels, another crashed into its side. The Muslim sailors threw themselves overboard and swam to the shore. The Christians went after them in the boats, throwing lances at them and skewering them in the sea; according to Tomé Lopes, only one of the hundreds of men slipped away and escaped with his life.

The Europeans boarded the two dhows and found a young boy cowering in a corner. Gama immediately sent him to be hanged, then changed his mind and instead had him interrogated. The Zamorin, the boy told his captors, had suffered such losses that he had demanded that his Muslim merchants fight their own battles; otherwise, he had threatened, he would "cut off their heads and those of their women, too." Every piece of artillery he could buy, beg, or borrow had been loaded onto their vessels, and every day he had raged at them, saying he was at war with the Christians on their account. Seven thousand had joined the armada and had sworn to defeat the Portuguese or die trying, but in the end the Zamorin had had to have them beaten with sticks to make them go on board. Their unpreparedness had proved their undoing: when the battle was barely under way a few bombards had been fired from the shore, and the jittery captains had decided it was a signal to retreat.

There was little booty in the captured ships: some nuts and rice and water, seven or eight stubby bombards in poor condition, some shields and swords, and plenty of bows and arrows. During the search the Portuguese found two more Muslims hiding and killed them before they could pray. When they were done, they set the vessels ablaze.

The Europeans' blood was up. The rest of the fleet bore down until their prows were leaping at the seafront, but the crews of the other Arab ships had already escaped to land. Even Tomé Lopes wondered why the admiral did not give the order to burn the city.

The only thing in the Zamorin's favor, he acerbically noted, was that "for the whole night the wind blew from the sea with great fury, sending all the dead to the shore, where they could be counted at leisure."

With the ships full of spices and time running out to return home, the guns stayed silent. Hoping—if not quite believing— that he had finally done enough to quell the maddening Zamorin, Gama set a course for Cannanore.

The nineteen ships arrived at midday on February 15, and boat-loads of Muslim merchants immediately came to meet them. The merchants had already heard the news from Calicut, and they had some startling information. There had been sixteen thousand men on board the war fleet, they said, and the Portuguese had killed as many as a thousand. Nearly seven hundred had died on the two captured vessels alone. Out of five hundred men on the flagship, half had died in the bombardment, and the other half had had their arms or legs blown off. The ship itself had been smashed so badly that it had nearly sunk before it made it to land.

To Gama's violent satisfaction, the merchants added that the Zamorin had seen the whole engagement from the turret of a house on a hill. Even better, among the informants were several who had given up on the Zamorin and his wars and had brought their wives and children to Cannanore. They had been starving to death in Ca-licut, they said; food had reached twice its usual price, and the city could only hold out on its own resources for a few more months. Many of the most powerful merchants, they added, had also aban-doned the city, since nothing was arriving by sea. The Zamorin was beside himself with fury, and he had vowed to take the first Chris-tians who fell into his hands and roast them alive.

Rather than blame the foreigners, these men seemed on the whole to be content at their victory. The Kolattiri was delighted. He had welcomed the refugees from Calicut and had given them money to hire crews, and he had been on the point of send-ing ships to go to the Europeans' aid. Vasco da Gama's merciless attacks on his old rival had finally convinced him to side with the Christians.

Gama decided he could trust the ruler of Cannanore after all. He made arrangements to set up a permanent factory in a spacious house with a staff of twenty, and he promised that his countrymen would return every year. The Kolattiri swore to protect them and supply them with spices, and the admiral engaged to defend his kingdom from attack. Before he left, Gama presented the king with some splendid gold and scarlet robes—the very Turkish velvets he had stolen from the *Mîrî* more than four months before.

The holds were now stacked high with spices, and the stores were freshly stocked with water, fish, and rice. On February 22, with the last preparations complete, Vasco da Gama left India for the second time. Vicente and Brás Sodré, his two uncles, stayed on with their three ships and two caravels to police the Indian Ocean—the first permanent European naval presence in Eastern waters.

THE ADMIRAL HAD decided to try a new tack across the Indian Ocean, and he set his course directly for Mozambique Island. The route bypassed Malindi and its loyal sultan, without whose help Gama might never have made it to India, but it promised to shave valuable days off the return journey.

Vast stretches of the ocean were still uncharted water to the Europeans. During the crossing they passed chains of unknown islands, and they skirted the shallows to take a look. The inhabitants of one island lit a large bonfire to attract them, but mindful of his precious cargo, Gama decided to press on.

For seven weeks the ships plowed close-hauled into storms and drifted under full sail in calms. They were sluggish in the water and leaking badly, and the sailors began praying that they would reach land before they sank. Two of the smaller ships went on ahead, and finally, before dawn on April 10, they sounded the seafloor and fired their bombards. The next morning the sailors made out the familiar green ribbon of the African coast, and on the evening of April 12 they anchored off Mozambique.

The long journey, the heavy loads, and the repeated battles had tested Europe's maritime technology to the limits. Many of the fourteen ships were now in an utterly unseaworthy state, and once more they were unloaded and tipped on their sides. The hulls were so perforated with wormholes that they looked as if they were made of pegboard, and there was nothing to do but pore over the wood and plug the holes with little wooden sticks—five or six thousand of them, estimated Lopes. Then the ships had to be recaulked, refloated, restocked, and loaded with water and wood.

Gama chose the *São Gabriel* and the *Santo António*, which were in better condition than the rest, to sail ahead and deliver the news to King Manuel. Each ship also carried a copy of Matteo da Bergamo's report to his employer. For several days the opinionated Italian had been busy putting the finishing touches to his letters, and he must have hoped that no one would decide to take a peek. The Indians and Arabs, he wrote, were more formidable foes than the Portuguese had reckoned them:

> It seems to me that the argument made at Lisbon, that our ships are better than theirs, is wrong; we've seen from experience that the opposite is true. It seems to me that as long as we don't make peace with Calicut they will always arm themselves, and in consequence, if we are to defend ourselves and not run away, we need big, well-armed vessels. Because if they hadn't suffered great losses this year, during the storm that destroyed more than a hundred and sixty of their ships between Calicut, Cannanore, and Cochin without a single person saved, none of ours, I fear, or rather I'm certain, would have stayed there, or perhaps wouldn't have been able to load their cargo. But if at least twelve or fifteen ships with a tonnage of 200 tons and more came to this region well armed and equipped, they could load quite safely and would find a cargo. That's what I think.

Vasco da Gama himself, he added, had several times insisted that the king would never let any merchants arm themselves, but he advised his employer to defend his interests against the Portuguese as well as against the Indians. Gama, he complained, had refused to let him and his colleagues negotiate their own terms, he had ordered them to leave their unsold goods with the king's factors against payment in Lisbon or else throw them in the sea, and he had kept the spoils from every captured vessel for the crown. The merchants, the Italian urged, should examine their articles of agreement and claim compensation for the admiral's injurious actions.

The two ships left Mozambique on April 19. The admiral himself set out ten days later with eight ships, and the last five followed after another two days.

The final convoy had barely left the harbor when the lookouts saw Gama's fleet heading back toward them. Two of his ships, the *Flor de la Mar* and the *Lionarda*, were taking on so much water that it was almost impossible to bail them out. The admiral ordered all thirteen vessels back to Mozambique for more repairs.

On May 4 Gama chose two more ships to go on ahead in case the first pair had encountered any trouble. It was just as well. On May 20, with the hulls patched as best they could be, the eleven remaining vessels once again set out to sea. Within days, they were back again.

Tomé Lopes's ship was among them, and he reported what had happened.

All had gone well until they were eight days out. Then, without warning, a tempest had whipped up the sea like a bubbling cauldron. Night had fallen and ardent prayers had been said when the *Lionarda* crashed straight into Lopes's ship. The collision sheared away part of its forecastle and splintered the topsides. The shrouds became entangled, and the waves were so high that the men swung wildly in the rigging as they tried to disengage them. When Lopes's ship finally broke free, the *Lionarda* came straight at it again and smashed into the side near the bow. A huge gash opened up, and shrouds, planks, chains, and sails went crashing around. The sailors were convinced they were doomed, and every new crack and bang made their hearts jump. Most gave up, kneeled down, and prayed.

Eventually a few stouter men managed to cut the rigging, and the two ships sheered apart. Relays of sailors bailed out the rising water, some with the pumps and others with any container to hand. Another party waded into the hold carrying lanterns and found the bottom of the hull still watertight. Even so, many were convinced the vessel was about to founder, and thirteen deserters jumped ship to the *Lionarda.*

Lopes and the rest who stayed on board were sure their lives had been spared by an act of God. It was impossible to be saved from such calamity by natural forces, the clerk recorded, and they all vowed to go on a pilgrimage when they reached home. Miracle or not, they were not safe yet. As soon as they tried to come around to the heading set by the admiral, the water rushed in again and the ship listed dangerously toward the holed side. With the waves still rearing high, the officers decided to risk lighting bonfires on the decks as a signal to the rest of the fleet.

Gama's vessel was the first to arrive on the scene, and he shouted to the men to ask if they wanted to abandon ship. With God's help, they cried back, they could last until morning. The *Flor de la Mar* appeared next and offered to send out its boat. Its crew tried to persuade their comrades that they were bound to sink in such furious seas, but Lopes and his men were convinced they were under supernatural protection.

On May 31 the fleet once again turned back toward land, and the pilots found they had made only ten leagues from Mozambique. It took them three attempts to enter the harbor, and the next day Lopes's ship limped in after them. The *Lionarda*, too, was leaking and badly in need of repair, and the process of careening started all over again.

So much time had passed that the supplies of food had run dangerously low. Already the men were on reduced rations of bread

350 ~ Holy War

and wine. Four days after they arrived in Mozambique for the third time, the rice they had bought ran out. They moved on to African millet, and that ran out, too. Eventually they were reduced to cooking up the biscuit crumbs from the bottom of the barrels—at least, the ones the mice had missed. Since there was no oil or honey left, the crumbs were boiled in water. The result, Tomé Lopes mordantly noted, "needed no condiments since it smelled like a dead dog, but we ate it because we were starving."

By June 15 conditions had become so bad that Gama ordered three of the ships to leave immediately for home. They set out early the next morning, and after surviving a blizzard that separated and nearly sank them, they finally came within sight of the Cape of Good Hope. There, as if to show just how much had changed in the five years since Vasco da Gama had first sailed into the Indian Ocean, they ran into two Portuguese ships newly bound for India. The bombards fired and the boats went out. News of a prince born to the king passed one way, and sacks of bread passed the other. The homeward-bound crews went on their way, watching pods of whales swimming around the Cape, shooting large, sleek tuna with their artillery, and stopping on an island to trap and roast flocks of birds that had never learned to beware of humans. According to the Flemish sailor, birds were not the only victims. By mid-July the provisions were again running out, and on the thirtieth, he matter-of-factly reported, "we found an island, where we killed at least 300 men, and we caught many of them, and we took there water." No doubt he was exaggerating as usual, though Tomé Lopes, whose ship was waiting offshore, was unusually reticent about what went on.

The flotilla sailed on toward the Cape Verdes. The islands were still some way off when it ran into a raging storm and was forced to anchor in the pitching sea. All the men fell ill, and for twenty days they had no bread to eat. The German sailor was among them. In the nick of time, he reported, another Portuguese ship sailed past, "from which we took flour and baked cakes and made porridge, and helped ourselves as best we could. Every second or third day a man died, and the rest were ever sicker and more despondent from the change of air." Eventually the three vessels reached the Azores, took on plenty of fresh food, and scudded on the westerlies to Lisbon.

Back in Mozambique, the remaining ships set out in twos and threes as soon as they could be provisioned. The Admiral of India waited for the very last departure and left on June 22. Two of the ships lost the rest on a dark, stormy night and limped home taking in water, accompanied by nothing, recorded a Portuguese sailor, but their fears. As they headed to the Azores, the entire company sickened and no one was left to sail the ships. There was nothing to eat but moldy biscuits crawling with maggots, and the ailing men devoured two dogs and two cats that had been taken on board to eat rats.

THE SCENT OF spices reached land before the ships. Seventeen hundred tons of pepper, cinnamon, cloves, ginger, nutmeg, cardamom, brazilwood, aloeswood, myrobalans, canafistula, zerumba, zedoary, benzoin, camphor, tamarind, musk, and alum perfumed the holds and masked the odors of men who had been nearly two years at sea.

The first vessels reached Lisbon in late August, and the news they brought set the seal on Vasco da Gama's fame. "In every place that he has been," Matteo da Bergamo's boss Gianfranco Affaitati reported to Pietro Pasqualigo, who was then in Spain, "either through love or through force, he has managed to do everything that he wanted."

On October 10, the Admiral of India sailed triumphantly into Lisbon. By the end of the month at least thirteen ships had returned. One vessel had come aground off Sofala early in the voyage; another, the oldest and smallest of the fleet, arrived home during a fierce storm and had to anchor five miles off Lisbon. "Such a strong wind blew," a witness reported, "that all the anchor lines broke and the waves dashed the ship to pieces, and the men saved themselves on these pieces, so that not more than four were drowned." Otherwise, Gama had not lost a single vessel.

His success stood in stark contrast to the disasters that had befallen his great rival. Three months after the Admiral of India had embarked on his second voyage, the Admiral of the Ocean Sea had set out from Spain for the fourth and final time. When Christopher Columbus arrived at Hispaniola, the governor ignored his warning that a hurricane was brewing and refused him entry to the port. Two days later the first Spanish treasure fleet left the colony and sailed straight into the tropical storm. Twenty of the thirty ships foundered, taking a vast haul of gold and five hundred men, including the governor himself, to the bottom of the sea. Columbus's four venerable vessels had taken refuge in an estuary, and when the storm passed he set off to explore the mainland he had struck on his previous voyage. In Panama he learned that a whole new ocean lay a few days' march away, and he was convinced he was close to finding a strait through which he could sail directly to India.

He was never able to search for it. Having evaded the hurricane, his fleet was pummeled by an even fiercer storm. One of the damaged ships was trapped in a river, and under attack from a nearby tribe, he was forced to abandon it. The three remaining vessels were riddled with wormholes and were leaking fast, and they had barely set sail for home when another had to be abandoned. As the last two ships headed for Cuba they were lashed by another tempest, and Columbus was forced to beach them in Jamaica before they sank. There were no Spaniards on Jamaica, and the men were marooned. One of the captains bought a canoe from a local chief and paddled to Hispaniola, where the new governor promptly threw him in prison for seven months. Columbus was still stuck on Jamaica, trying to put down a mutiny among half his crew and startling the islanders into feeding the castaways by predicting a lunar eclipse, when Vasco da Gama arrived home.

The court came down to the sea to welcome Dom Vasco and accompany him to the palace. He paraded through the streets to drumrolls and fanfares, preceded by a page boy carrying a huge silver basin filled with the golden offering from Kilwa. When he arrived at the palace, he presented the heap of gold to Manuel.

For the first time, a valuable tribute had been brought back from a celebrated Eastern city. For the first time, a Muslim ruler had made himself a vassal of the Portuguese king. For the first time, Manuel had thousands of Christian subjects in India. The doubts sown by Cabral's troubled mission were silenced.

Manuel praised his admiral in unstinting words that redounded to his own credit. Vasco da Gama had outmatched the ancients, he rhapsodized. He had attacked "the Moors from Mequa, enemies of our Holy Catholic Faith," he had made solemn treaties with two Indian kings, and he had brought his fleet safely home, "well-laden and with great riches." As for the gold from Kilwa, Manuel had it melted down and made into a glittering monstrance for the vast monastery church that was rising at Belém, its lavish detailing a candy store of African carvings and Eastern marvels, proof in soaring stone of Portugal's new power and the profit from spices.

CHAPTER 17

EMPIRE OF THE WAVES

J UST A FEW years earlier Lisbon had been a city on the edge of the world. Now it was transformed into a commercial hub that rivaled the richest entrepôts of the East. Ships from three continents crowded its harbor. Bulging sacks of pepper filled its warehouses. Carts heaped with muslins and brocades, musk and ambergris, frankincense and myrrh, cloves and nutmeg rumbled through its alleys. Persian carpets covered its floors and oriental tapestries lined its walls. Men from across Europe flocked to look, to buy, and to taste the thrill of the new.

To the footloose, the newly expanded world brought a heady surge of freedom. The chance to see new lands, meet new peoples, and bring home eyewitness accounts, striking souvenirs, and even exotic pets was irresistible to Europe's adventurers, and a steady stream of latter-day Marco Polos abandoned their homes and set out on lengthy journeys to the East. These were men like Lodovico de Varthema, who quit Bologna in 1502 with a raging thirst for adventure, fame, and exotic sexual encounters. According to his riveting *Travels*, Varthema disguised himself as a Mamluk soldier in Syria, fought fifty thousand Arabs at a time while guarding a camel caravan, slipped into the precinct of the Kaaba in Mecca and the tomb of Muhammad in Medina, conducted an impassioned affair with a wife of the sultan of Aden, and achieved a reputation as a Muslim saint before returning to Europe on a Portuguese ship.

The doughty Portuguese had not opened a path to the East for the titillation of a few daredevils. The little nation had set itself a task of monumental proportions, and the work had just begun.

Vasco da Gama had sailed east, declared an Italian banker in Lisbon, with the express object of "subjugating all of India" to his master's will. His own iron will had set the course for decades of ruthless battles for domination. Yet India was no longer an idea, a glorious figment of the European imagination. It was a vast subcontinent, beset by its own internal strife, vibrant with its own intricate complexities, and disconcertingly oblivious to the foreigners scratching at its shores. The Portuguese had only begun to chart the coastline, while the interior was still an impenetrable mystery: that was the limitation of conducting warfare by sea.

To be fair, the banker had jumped ahead of the game. For Vasco da Gama and his men, India was a means to an end. That end was Manuel's vaulting ambition to install himself as king of Jerusalem, and the first step in that Crusade was not the conquest of India but the expulsion of its Muslim merchants. Gama had thrown everything at the task, yet his royal nemesis was still ensconced in his Calicut palace and the merchants were still plying their trade. As for the path ahead, the Portuguese had found no Prester John waiting to put his cohorts at their command, and the few Christians they had met were powerless to rally to their cause. They had yet to stanch the flow of spices to Egypt, and they had come nowhere near the Red Sea, the channel they believed would deliver them to the Holy Land. To all but the most credulous in faith, it was clear that Manuel's master plan would require a vast commitment of time, manpower, and wealth that would draw Portugal ever deeper into the East.

The king was undeterred. Faith, and artillery, would conquer all. Yet India was halfway around the world, and without the right man in charge the crown was impotent to control the actions carried out in its name.

The rot set in with Gama's own relatives.

Vicente Sodré and his brother Brás had stayed on in India with a broad remit to protect the Portuguese factories and despoil Muslim shipping. As soon as their stern nephew left they decided the second of those tasks was more profitable than the first, and they sailed off to loot ships carrying spices and silks to the Red Sea. Their crews were furious, not from moral outrage but because the brothers refused to share out the spoils. One irate captain denounced the brothers to King Manuel himself; Brás, he wrote, had made off with all manner of goods "without entering them in the books of Your Lordship, besides many others that he took when he wanted, for no one dared to go against him, since his brother permitted him to do whatever he wanted." The cocky siblings got their comeuppance when they laughed off the advice of some Bedouin herders to move their ships out of the path of an oncoming gale, and the captain self-righteously reported the consequences to the king:

"So that, my lord, the next day, the wind rose so high and the sea became so rough that the ship of Vicente was dashed against the shore, and after it that of Brás Sodré with its mast broken, each of them having six cables for the prow." Vicente was immediately killed; the thuggish Brás scrambled ashore and thrust his sword first into a pilot he had seized from one of the vessels he had looted, and then into the hunchback pilot who had been taken from the *Mîrî*. The admiral himself had instructed his uncles to make use of the hunchback's expertise; he was, Manuel's informant added, the best pilot in the whole of India, and "most necessary for Your Lordship."

With the fleet absent, the Zamorin seized his chance. He turned his wrath on the rebellious king of Cochin, who was still stubbornly refusing to break his treaty with the Christians, and marched across the border with a large army. The raja and the Portuguese factors, clerks, and guards were forced to flee the ruined city and hide out on a nearby island. They were still there when the next Portuguese fleet arrived, and when they reinstalled the raja on his throne, the first European fort in India, a hastily constructed wooden structure named Fort Manuel, went up at Cochin.

It was fast becoming clear that only a permanent armed oc-

cupation could hope to achieve Manuel's aim of clearing the seas
of Muslim trade. That called for a commander who could make
decisions on the ground, and in 1505 Manuel appointed the first
Viceroy of India. Like the titles the king had concocted for himself
and his admiral, it was a signal of intent rather than an expression
of reality, but it marked the beginning of a mission drift that saw
the Portuguese move inexorably from sea to land. Manuel chose
Dom Francisco de Almeida, a tried and trusted old soldier who had
fought at the siege of Granada in 1492, and besides giving him full
powers to make treaties, wage war, and dispense justice, Manuel
ordered him to construct a chain of forts around the Indian Ocean.

Almeida began at Kilwa. His soldiers landed and made straight
for the palace of the usurping emir, benevolently "sparing the lives
of the Moors along the way who did not show fight." A courtier
furiously waved the flag left by Gama from a window and shouted
"Portugal! Portugal!" The Portuguese ignored him, broke down
the palace doors, and hacked and looted away while a priest and
a party of Franciscan friars held crosses aloft and chanted the Te
Deum. The emir fled, and Almeida appointed a puppet in his place.
He commandeered the strongest seafront house, razed the buildings around it to the ground, and turned it into a heavily armed fort
manned by a captain and eighty soldiers.

The Europeans moved on to Mombasa. The sultan had been
expecting them, and cannonballs whistled toward them from the
bastion at the harbor entrance. They shot back until the fort's gunpowder store ignited and the building went up in flames, then sailed
into the harbor with all guns blazing. The soldiers landed in force,
advanced through a hail of stones and arrows, and torched the
city's wooden houses. The walls and thatched roofs went up like
kindling, taking nearby masonry buildings with them; Mombasa,
reported a German sailor named Hans Mayr, who was with the
expedition, "burned like one huge fire that lasted nearly all night."
The surviving inhabitants fled to the palm groves outside the city,
and after breakfast the next day the invaders ransacked the smolder-

ing ruins, breaking down doors with axes and battering rams and stopping to pick off the last defenders on the rooftops with their crossbows. When they reached the palace they smashed through its sumptuous rooms, while a Portuguese captain climbed to the roof and ran up the royal standard. Great heaps of treasure were carted away, including a magnificent carpet that was sent to King Manuel. According to the German sailor, when it was all over fifteen hundred Muslim men, women, and children lay dead but only five Christians had been killed, a disparity he put down more to divine grace than human skill.

The fleet headed for India, and after putting up a fort at Cannanore the Portuguese set off for their annual confrontation with the Zamorin.

In March 1506, fully 209 vessels from Calicut—84 of them big ships—attacked the 11-strong Portuguese fleet. The Bolognese adventurer Lodovico de Varthema happened to be passing by at the time, and he threw himself into the fray.

The Zamorin had finally managed to arm himself with efficient artillery—ironically for Varthema, the cannon were of Italian manufacture—and the odds were stacked against the Europeans. Almeida's son Lourenço, who was in command, called together his men and steeled them to their sacrifice in the words of a true Crusader:

"O sirs, o brothers, now is the day that we must remember the Passion of Christ, and how much pain He endured to redeem us sinners. Now is that day when all our sins will be blotted out. For this I beseech you that we determine to go vigorously against these dogs; for I hope that God will give us the victory, and will not choose that His faith should fail." Then a priest, crucifix in hand, gave a rousing sermon and granted a plenary indulgence. "And he knew so well how to speak," Varthema later recalled, "that the greater part of us wept, and prayed God that He would cause us to die in that battle."

The drums rolled, the guns boomed, and, wrote Varthema, "a

most cruel battle was fought with immense effusion of blood." The fighting raged on into a second day. "It was a beautiful sight," the Italian remembered, "to see the gallant deeds of a very valiant captain who, with a galley, made such a slaughter of the Moors as it is impossible to describe." Another captain leapt on board an enemy boat. "Jesus Christ, give us the victory! Help thy faith," he cried, and he hacked off some more heads. The Indians fled before the relentless assault, and the Europeans mercilessly hunted them down. When they returned to the scene, the young commander sent his men to count the corpses. Varthema recorded the outcome: "They found that those who were killed on the shore and at sea, and those of the ships taken, were counted at three thousand six hundred dead bodies. You must know that many others were killed when they took to flight, who threw themselves in the sea." The would-be martyrs had to make do with victory, because according to Varthema, the Italian guns notwithstanding, not a single Christian died.

While the victor was still celebrating his triumph, a Portuguese captain who was barely younger than Lourenço's father was busy stealing his thunder.

Afonso de Albuquerque was already fifty when he first arrived in the Indian Ocean. He was of middling height, with a ruddy complexion, a large nose, and "a venerable beard reaching below his girdle to which he wore it knotted." As a nobleman who was distantly related to the royal family he had been well educated, and he was noted for his elegant turn of phrase. He was also a confirmed Crusader who as a young man had served for ten years in the Moroccan wars. He was a commander of the Order of Santiago, the same Moor-slaying society into which Vasco da Gama had been inducted as a boy, and he had decided the future lay in the East. There was more than a touch of Gama in the determined set of his eyes, but if he was a match for his predecessor in personal courage and sheer force of personality, the older man outstripped the younger in his capacity for unflinching cruelty—and left him behind in his willingness to turn his temper on his own people.

In 1506 Albuquerque set out with a squadron of six ships to cut off the supply chains to Egypt, Arabia, and Iran. He quickly captured a rocky island near the mouth of the Red Sea and built a fortress on it. From his new base he dispatched raiders to sweep the Gate of Tears for ships heading to Aden and Jeddah. The next year he set off for the other side of Arabia to blockade the Persian Gulf. His attack fleet anchored in the horseshoe-shaped harbor of Muscat, an ancient port at the entrance to the Gulf, and let loose an opening salvo. The soldiers scaled the high earth walls of the venerable city and stormed the streets. They sliced their way to victory and cut off the ears and noses of the men and women who were left alive. Then they took an ax to the main mosque, "a very large and beautiful edifice, the greater part of timber, finely carved, and the upper part of stucco," and set it on fire. Albuquerque went on to terrorize a string of nearby ports and towns before continuing to his main target, Hormuz. When he arrived he threatened to build a fort out of its inhabitants' bones and nail their ears to the door, and, having terrorized them, he wiped out their entire fleet with a virtuoso display of seamanship and superior firepower. The boy king of Hormuz became a vassal of King Manuel, and a Portuguese fort named Our Lady of Victory—built of stone, not bones—rose over the fabled city.

Albuquerque was systematically shutting down the ocean termini of Islam's Eastern trade. As more and more spices ended up in the holds of Portuguese ships, the markets of Alexandria emptied. The Egyptians were no longer willing to stand by and watch their monopoly vanish, and nor were their allies, the Venetians.

IN THE YEAR 1500 a garden of balsam trees on the outskirts of Cairo had suddenly wilted away.

The news would have been unremarkable were it not for the fact that the Coptic monks who tended the grove claimed that the infant Jesus had planted the first sapling; the precious spice, it was said, was the essence of his sweat, which Mary had wrung out of his shirt after washing it in a spring he had made gush forth. For centuries, under the watchful eye of the sultan's men, the monks had extracted a resinous gum from the trees. The gum was infused in oil, and the decoction was prized as a miracle cure for all manner of ailments. Its sale was carefully controlled—the Venetians, naturally, were among the favored clients—and Europeans paid exorbitant prices for tiny vials of the holy oil. Yet all of a sudden the ancient trees were gone, as if they had never been, and Egyptians of every faith mourned their passing.

It was a curious emblem of the devastation Vasco da Gama had wrought on the spice routes. For nearly a thousand years, trade in the Indian Ocean had been conducted on Muslim terms. Suddenly, the Portuguese had torn up the old order. Swaths of the Islamic world were faced with economic decline, and a hard, swift blow had been delivered to their pride. Like the balsam grove, an ancient, settled way of life had suddenly caught a chill wind and shriveled up.

In the summer of 1504, a Franciscan friar arrived at the papal court with an ultimatum from the sultan of Egypt. The friar was custodian of the monastery of Mount Zion in Jerusalem, which was still in Egyptian hands. The sultan, he warned, had threatened to demolish the Christian pilgrimage sites in the Holy Land if the Portuguese did not immediately leave the Indian Ocean. The pope washed his hands of the affair and sent the friar to King Manuel with a letter asking him how he should respond. If the holy places were touched, Manuel replied, he would launch a massive new Crusade in their defense. He reminded the pope of his family's victories over Islam and vowed to stay the course until the Infidel was crushed. He had already overcome such formidable obstacles, he added, that his quest was undoubtedly blessed by God.

On his way to see the pope the friar had stopped off in Venice. The Signoria officially requested the Egyptians not to act on their threat, then immediately dispatched a new secret agent to Cairo. The envoy, Francesco Teldi, disguised himself as a jewel merchant and revealed his identity only when he secured a private audience with the sultan. The European powers, he assured the Egyptian ruler, were far too disunited to march on the Holy Land. The Portuguese were threatening the livelihood of Venice and Egypt alike, and the sultan had to break them before it was too late.

Venice was Cairo's partner in gloom. In 1498, as Vasco da Gama was crossing the Indian Ocean for the first time, such a bumper haul of spices had arrived in Alexandria that even the Venetians ran out of funds to buy them. In 1502, the year Gama returned on his second voyage, their ships went away half-empty. Three-quarters of Venice's merchant galleys were mothballed, and the remaining ships sat out three of every four of their usual trips.

The Venetians abandoned all pretense of friendship with Portugal and threw in their lot with Egypt. The Signoria sent more spies to Lisbon—one was unmasked and was slung in Manuel's dungeons—and for a while it even revived an ancient scheme to dig a canal from the Red Sea to the Mediterranean, beginning at Suez. In the end the idea was shelved before the sultan had been approached, and instead Venice set about building him a navy.

In an extraordinary inversion of Portugal's long-nursed plans, Venice was about to launch Muslim ships into the Red Sea to destroy Christian trade.

In Istanbul the Ottomans had also been watching with alarm as their Eastern commerce slipped away. The Turkish sultan was on even worse terms with his Egyptian counterpart than he was with Venice, but the three threatened powers forged an unlikely alliance. Istanbul provided Egypt with the materials to build a war fleet, together with officers and gunners to man it, and Venice's skilled shipbuilders arrived to supervise its construction. The Venetians watched as the parts arrived at Alexandria, saw them loaded on camels and transported across the desert, and assembled them on the shores of the Red Sea.

Twelve splendid oak-and-pine Venetian-style galleys rose on the scaffolds at Suez. Turkish cannon forged from solid bronze were mounted fore and aft—though not along the sides, where oars and oarsmen took up too much space—and the armada set out for India.

After a long delay it arrived in early 1508 and anchored in the harbor of Diu, a Gujarati port strategically located at the mouth of the Indus delta in northwest India. The plan was to rendezvous with a fleet being sent by the Zamorin of Calicut, who had once again rebuilt his navy after his recent defeat, then sail south and destroy every Portuguese fort and factory along the coast. The Egyptians, though, were late, and the Zamorin's ships had been and gone. Instead they joined forces with a squadron provided by the Muslim ruler of Diu and severely mauled a small Portuguese fleet at nearby Chaul. Among the Portuguese dead was Almeida's son Lourenço, the hero of the battle of Calicut.

It was Portugal's first naval defeat in the Indian Ocean, and the victory drums rolled in Cairo for three days. Yet the Egyptians failed to follow it up. The fleet returned to Diu and stayed put through the winter monsoon, the hulls fouling up and the crews drifting away. The next year eighteen Portuguese warships bore down on the port, with Almeida leading the charge on the old *Flor de la Mar.* The battle-hardened Europeans won a bloody victory within hours, and the avenging viceroy sailed along the coast, shooting his prisoners point-blank with his cannon and firing their heads and limbs at passing towns. The Zamorin finally sued for peace, and the Portuguese built a fortress at Calicut.

The Venetians mounted a new diplomatic offensive with the aim of persuading Istanbul to sponsor another Egyptian fleet, but the appeal fell on deaf ears. Seven years after the Battle of Diu, Turkish cannon cut down the cream of Egypt's sword-wielding cavalry and brought 267 turbulent years of Mamluk rule to a swift end. The Ottomans turned their attention back to Europe, and they would not send another major fleet against the Portuguese for thirty years. The papacy, meanwhile, leagued with the French and the Spanish to cut Venice down to size. La Serenissima was stripped of a century of territorial gains, and though it recovered, it was never again quite the major power it had been.

Like the first Crusaders, the Portuguese were providentially lucky with their timing. With Venice humbled and its Egyptian ally crushed, Portugal's naval supremacy in the Indian Ocean was assured. The seaways to the rest of Asia lay open for the taking.

Viceroy Almeida, for all the fury with which he avenged his son's death, had turned out to be a less than fully paid-up subscriber to Manuel's messianic agenda. Under the influence of the merchant lobby and groups of nobles who were making a fortune from plundering Arab ships, he had become convinced that fighting on land was a sure way to fritter away the wealth Portugal was amassing by sea. Far better, he advised the king, to use naval power to intimidate India's rulers and step up the profitable business of organized piracy. His case was strengthened when the Kolattiri of Cannanore enlisted the help of his erstwhile enemy, the Zamorin of Calicut, to attack the Portuguese fortress in his city. The Kolattiri who had negotiated with Gama had died, and the new ruler had vowed to exact blood for a gruesome episode in which the Portuguese had sunk an Indian ship, stitched its crew into lengths of sail, and thrown them alive in the sea. A huge army besieged the fort for four months, and the Portuguese were only saved from starvation when a tidal wave of lobsters washed to their door, closely followed by a relief fleet.

Just as Almeida was urging Manuel to scale down his ambitions, the fires of religious intolerance had begun to rage in Portugal. In 1506 a man suspected of being a *marrano*—a "New Christian," or baptized Jew, who secretly practiced his former faith—had caused outrage in Lisbon by venturing to suggest that an ethereal glow that seemed to emanate from a crucifix might have had a less than miraculous explanation. A crowd of women dragged the doubter from the church and beat him to death, and a priest preached a fiery sermon urging his flock to root out the enemy within. Two more priests marched through the streets brandishing crucifixes, and a mob of local men and sailors from ships in the harbor went on the rampage. In two bloody days, two thousand men and women—including some Catholics who looked vaguely Jewish—were massacred. Crusading fever, once unleashed, was hard to control.

Manuel executed the ringleaders, including the priests. Yet he was more convinced than ever that it was his historic mission to usher the East into the Christian fold, and he replaced the reluctant Almeida with Afonso de Albuquerque.

The Crusade leapt forward. Like his king, Albuquerque envisioned a colossal Asian empire united by a universal Christianity in which a subsumed Islam would dwindle away. To pay for the astronomic cost of it all, Portugal's grip on the spice trade would have to become a stranglehold—and a crown monopoly, despite the squeals of aggrieved merchants. No longer would royal factors haggle for sacks of pepper on the quay fronts of India. The ultimate origin of the most valuable spices would have to be discovered, more fortresses would have to be built to funnel the fragrant treasure into Portuguese hands, and a fleet of floating warehouses, escorted by squadrons of fighting ships, would have to be built to ferry them home.

Albuquerque's enthusiasm sometimes got the better of him. On one occasion he contemplated diverting the Nile to dry up Egypt; another time he hatched a plot to steal the body of the Prophet Muhammad and hold it for ransom in exchange for the Holy Sepulcher in Jerusalem. He never hesitated to hang his men from the yardarm or hack off their noses, ears, and hands at the slightest sign that insubordination threatened his grand schemes. Yet the fanatic was also a startlingly gifted naval strategist. He quickly realized that an empire founded on ships alone—especially badly maintained ships crewed by badly trained men—would soon founder. Raw recruits were now flooding in from Portugal, but many of them were simple farmhands and they had to be trained from scratch. A reserve force had to be built up to fill the boots of the sick. The vessels needed to be repaired, refitted, and reliably provisioned. What Albuquerque needed was a secure naval base, and he soon found the ideal spot.

The island of Goa was separated from the mainland by tidal creeks that made it easy to defend and formed a fine protected harbor. After Calicut it was the busiest port in India, and it boasted plenty of skilled shipbuilders. It did a roaring trade in Arabian horses from Hormuz, which were much in demand among Indian potentates and were impossible to breed in the subcontinent's sultry air. The city was old, large, and rich—Lodovico de Varthema colorfully claimed that the king's servants sported rubies and diamonds on the insteps of their shoes—and like the rest of north India it was in Muslim hands. With the help of an ambitious Hindu privateer named Timoja—the same man whom the Zamorin had once sent to hunt down Vasco da Gama—Albuquerque took Goa from its illustrious sultan. Within weeks he was forced to retreat before a huge Muslim army, but three months later he returned with a new war fleet. His men slaughtered the defenders on the shore, pursued them into the city, and ran amok through the streets. In the bloody sack many Goans drowned or ended their lives in the jaws of alligators while trying to swim across the river to freedom. Six thousand men, women, and children had been massacred, Albuquerque contentedly wrote home to the king, while just fifty Portuguese had lost their lives.

Goa was now the headquarters of an expansionist colonial power with bases around the western Indian Ocean, and ambassadors from neighboring states called to congratulate the warlike new ruler. To entrench the colony, Albuquerque bribed his men with land, houses, and jobs to marry local Hindu women. The mixed marriages were not without problems from the start, a chronicler reported:

> On one night that some of these marriages were celebrated, the brides became so mixed and confounded together, that some of the bridegrooms went to bed with those who belonged to others; and when the mistake was discovered next morning, each took back his own wife, all being equal in regard to the point of honor. This gave occasion to some of the gentlemen to throw

ridicule on the measures pursued by Albuquerque; but he persisted with firmness in his plans, and succeeded in establishing Goa as the metropolis or centre of the Portuguese power in India.

From Goa, Portuguese fleets set out to explore Southeast Asia. They had already reached Ceylon, the source of the world's finest cinnamon, and in 1511 Albuquerque sailed on east to the Malay Peninsula. His destination was an international port city that controlled the narrow chokepoint of the Strait of Malacca, the busy shipping lane between the Indian and Pacific oceans. The city was also named Malacca, and its influence was felt far away. "Whoever is lord of Malacca has his hand on the throat of Venice," a Portuguese factor dramatically declared. That was not mere hyperbole: Malacca was the western terminus for Chinese sailors, thousands of whom lived in their own quarter called Chinese Hill, and merchants from India, Persia, and Arabia sailed there to buy silks and porcelains. A powerful Muslim sultan ruled the city and the lands far around, but to the Christians that made it an irresistible target.

Albuquerque sailed into the harbor, flags flying and cannon blazing, and burned dozens of ships. His troops marched ashore, and after fierce hand-to-hand fighting—and a few well-aimed spears that made the enemy's war elephants rear up and throw its army to the ground—the last sultan fled. Another fortress went up, and from Malacca the Portuguese set out for points north and south.

To the north, the king of Siam—Thailand—had long had his eye on wealthy Malacca. Albuquerque sent an ambassador to negotiate an alliance, and after finding passage on a Chinese junk he became the first European to visit Thailand. In 1513 an expedition sailed east from Malacca and reached the Chinese city of Guangzhou, which the Portuguese christened Canton. The first contacts were a disaster; the Chinese sank two Portuguese ships, and the envoys were sentenced to death for the misbehavior of their compatriots, who the Chinese were convinced were cannibals. One of the condemned men, a former apothecary from Lisbon named Tomé Pires, set pen to paper and reassured himself that it was worth paying the ultimate price to further the Crusade of the Holy Catholic Faith against the false and diabolical religion of the abominable and phony Muhammad. Eventually the Portuguese established a permanent base on nearby Macau and began to carry China's overseas trade, while three merchants who were blown off course stumbled across Japan and founded another lucrative trading post at Nagasaki.

To the south and east, the Portuguese sailed on to Indonesia and the Spice Islands themselves. With Malay pilots as guides, squadrons weaved their way around Sumatra and Java, among the Lesser Sunda Islands, and on to the Moluccas. Here, at last, on a handful of cone-shaped volcanic islets, they found the source of the world's cloves, nutmeg, and mace. Islam had taken root even here as Hinduism and Buddhism had waned, but the Christians found enough allies to establish a beachhead; among them was the sultan of Ternate, who together with his bitter enemy, the sultan of neighboring Tidore, was the world's major producer of cloves.

Portugal's possessions were only tiny pinpricks on the map, but joined together they formed the outline of a vast maritime empire. Settlements, strongholds, and dependencies stretched around the west and east coasts of Africa, across to the Persian Gulf, down the western shores of India, and deep into Southeast Asia. Astonishingly, a mere fourteen years had passed since Vasco da Gama had first sailed into the East. "It appears to me," concluded Lodovico de Varthema after a lengthy tour of Southeast Asia, "that, if it please God and if the King of Portugal is as victorious as he has been hitherto, he will be the richest king in the world. And truly he deserves every good, for in India, and especially in Cochin, every feast day ten and even twelve pagans are baptized in the Christian faith, which is daily extending by means of this King; and for this reason it may be believed that God has given him victory, and will ever prosper him in the future."

Manuel had not been bashful about showing off his newfound

magnificence to an astonished Europe, and in 1514 he sent a spectacular embassy to the pope in Rome. The centerpiece was an elephant accompanied by 140 attendants in Indian costume and a menagerie of exotic beasts, including a cheetah from Hormuz. Embarrassingly, Manuel had skimped on his ambassador's expenses, and the envoy had to borrow a large sum to keep the show on the road. The pope, who was a Medici and not easily impressed, nevertheless signed another bull and sent back generous gifts of his own. Determined to outdo him, Manuel returned the favor the next year by dispatching a fully laden spice ship and a rhinoceros to Rome, though the vessel carrying the horned beast sank off Genoa before it arrived.

As he basked in oriental splendor, the Portuguese king began his final push toward Jerusalem and eternal glory.

Steeled with Crusading fervor and spurred on by the lust for spices, the Portuguese had broken the Muslim monopoly of the world's richest trading routes with astonishing speed. Yet Manuel's megalomaniacal ambition to sweep from east and west into the Holy Land had never been matched by a realistic strategy or the means adequate to achieve it. God, he had always believed, would step in on behalf of His people and help them to carry out His supreme plan.

That plan soon began to unravel with bewildering speed.

IN 1515, TEN thousand Portuguese soldiers landed in Morocco and marched into the maws of banked Muslim cannon. The wooden fort they had come to build was blasted to splinters along with most of their ships, and the panicked Crusaders fled for home. Manuel had sent four thousand men to their deaths, and his plan to march east across Africa blew up in a cloud of sulfurous smoke.

That same year, Afonso de Albuquerque's many enemies finally conspired to relieve him of his command, a task made much easier by Albuquerque's rash request that the king ennoble him as Duke of Goa. The sixty-three-year-old empire builder heard the news while returning to his capital city after reconquering Hormuz, and

he straightaway fell into a deep despond. He wrote a dignified letter to the king accounting for his actions, his clerk taking over as
his hand shook, and died as his ship crossed the bar. He was buried in full Crusader armor, as was fitting for a man who had done
more than anyone except Vasco da Gama to unfurl bloodred crosses
across the East.

With the warrior gone, weaker, greedier figures came out to
play.

In 1517, a massed Portuguese fleet carrying more than three
thousand soldiers and sailors set out from India to seize control of
the Red Sea. The invasion had been years in the making, but the
timing could hardly have been more propitious. The Ottoman sultan Selim the Grim had just conquered Egypt and its dependencies, Syria and Arabia, but the former Mamluk lands were still in
turmoil. For a brief moment Manuel's ultimate goal seemed easily
within reach: from Suez, it was only a few days' march to Jerusalem
itself.

The fleet arrived in Aden, where the Crusaders were unexpectedly welcomed with open arms. Aden was in the grip of a mass
panic about the encroaching Ottomans, who had long been notorious for their atrocious treatment of Arabs. The Portuguese only had
to say they wanted the city, reported a German merchant named
Lazarus Nürnberger, and it would have been handed to them on the
spot. Yet instead of accepting the key to the Red Sea, the vacillat-
ing commanders continued to Jeddah. They dropped anchor, held
a conference, and decided the gateway to Mecca was too strongly
defended to risk an attack. Instead they headed back to Aden, but by
then its governor had lost faith in the irresolute Christians and the
fleet meandered back to India. By the time it arrived, most of the
men who had not already deserted had been lost in violent storms.

As corruption and profiteering became rife and the fledgling
empire lost its bearings, Portugal's old rivalry with Spain again
reared its head. In 1516 King Ferdinand of Castile and Aragon
had died, twelve years after his beloved Isabella had gone to her

grave. The throne passed to their daughter Joanna the Mad—who earned her sobriquet from her violent jealousy of her philandering husband, Philip the Handsome—and Joanna's son Charles. With Aragon came the thrones of Sicily, Sardinia, and Naples. From his Hapsburg father Charles had acquired the extensive family lands in Burgundy and the Netherlands. In 1519, on the death of his grandfather, he inherited the Archduchy of Austria and was elected Holy Roman Emperor. A more powerful threat to Portugal's interests could scarcely have been conjured.

Charles I of Spain—now also Charles V of the Holy Roman Empire—had barely arrived in Seville when a Portuguese sailor approached him with a startling proposal.

Ferdinand Magellan had spent eight years exploring and fighting for his nation in the Indian Ocean. He had taken part in Albuquerque's conquests of Goa and Malacca, and when he returned home he had gone Crusading in Morocco. He was sure he deserved advancement, and yet his petitions for the captaincy of a ship had fallen on deaf ears at the Portuguese court. In frustration, like Columbus before him, he had taken himself and his accumulated knowledge to Spain.

Magellan put an astonishing case to his prospective patron. Say, he suggested, you were to extend the demarcation line drawn at Tordesillas around the eastern half of the globe. According to his calculations, you would discover that the Spice Islands were on the Spanish side of the line. Of course the line did not exist—just twenty-three years earlier no one had dreamed that Europeans would be contesting ownership of the farthest reaches of the planet—but if the Spanish were to show up in Southeast Asia, their very presence would surely force the issue.

There was only one problem: the Portuguese had a monopoly on the Cape route to the East. It was not just a question of practicality. Since Europe's overseas expansion largely depended on the skills of navigators, it was widely accepted that the sea routes they discovered were a kind of intellectual property owned by the sponsor nation. The Spanish would have to find another way—a way that went west.

In 1506 Christopher Columbus had died, less than two years after he had finally made it home from Jamaica and still convinced he had reached Asia. By then Amerigo Vespucci, another Italian in Portugal's service, had explored the coast of Brazil and had concluded that the landmass stretched much farther south than Columbus had envisaged. The following year, a new continent had appeared on a world map for the first time, called America, after Vespucci's first name.

America was still seen as a barrier to reaching the East more than a destination in its own right, and it was still no clearer that it could be rounded than had been the case with Africa. Yet Magellan boldly promised to succeed where Columbus had failed—to sail west to the East. He renounced his Portuguese citizenship and signed a contract with Charles, who invested him as a commander of the Order of Santiago. In September 1519 he set out with a fleet of five ships to find a southern route around America, with a squadron sent by an irate King Manuel in hot pursuit.

Three years later a single ship limped back to Spain. More than two hundred sailors had been lost to storms, shipwrecks, mutinies, and battles, including Magellan himself, who was stabbed to death in the Philippines when he waded into a squabble between local chiefs. There were just eighteen survivors, but they were the first men to circumnavigate the globe. Portugal's obsession with reaching the East had driven its old rival around America and across the vast expanse of the Pacific Ocean—a continent and an ocean whose existence had not even been suspected just three decades earlier. Soon Spanish galleons would be shipping Chinese silks and porcelains across the Pacific to Mexico and Peru and returning with small mountains of freshly mined silver.

By now Charles, too, had decided he was divinely mandated to destroy Islam and beget a new Christian world. The emperor dispatched a war fleet to follow Magellan's course, occupy the Spice

Islands, and claim them for himself. Once again Portuguese and Spanish negotiators locked themselves away to divide up the world, this time at the Spanish border town of Badajoz. Portugal's astronomers worked around the clock to fix the Spice Islands' position, and just to be on the safe side their cartographers hurriedly doctored their charts. The Spanish had a high-placed informant among the Portuguese delegation, but still the bad-tempered discussions broke up without an agreement. For years the Iberian neighbors skirmished halfway around the globe, and the dispute was only settled when Portugal paid Spain an astronomical sum in gold to acknowledge its rights. It was much longer before Magellan was proved wrong: the Moluccas had been on Portugal's side of the imaginary line after all.

By then Manuel the Fortunate was long dead. The visionary king had never stopped believing in his God-sent mission, and a few months before he died, from an epidemic that struck Lisbon in December 1521, his prayers finally seemed to have been answered. That spring, reports arrived that a Portuguese expeditionary force had landed in Ethiopia and had reached the imperial court. A "Letter with the News that came to the King Our Lord, of the discovery of Prester John" was rushed into print, and Manuel dreamed his vainglorious dreams one last time. An alliance was even then being struck with Prester John, he informed the pope in a letter; soon Mecca, the tomb of the Prophet, and "the evil sect of Mafamede" would all be destroyed. The flurry of excitement turned to quiet despond when the Ethiopian monarch turned out to be far from the answer to centuries of Christian prayers.

Manuel's ships had set out from little Portugal and had forged the first European empire. They had explored the seas from Brazil to China. They had transformed Europe's picture of the world, and they had exploded the limits of its power. Yet set against his vast ambitions, he had failed. His plan to march across Africa, sail up the Red Sea, vanquish Turks and Egyptians, and retake Jerusalem had turned out to be nothing more than a mirage. For all his grandiose talk about leading the Last Crusade, Manuel had never left home.

King John III, Manuel's estranged nineteen-year-old son and successor, was crowned with imperial pomp but inherited an empire as directionless as a rudderless ship. What he desperately needed was a larger-than-life figure who could stamp his authority on his far-flung lands.

For one last time, Vasco da Gama was pressed into service.

CHAPTER 18

THE KING'S DEPUTY

F OR TWENTY-ONE YEARS, Dom Vasco da Gama had been busy hoarding the fruits of his fame.

The admiral had returned from India a rich man. He had brought back chests stuffed with luxury goods, including, it was rumored, a trove of magnificent pearls. The king had given him more lavish grants, he had allowed Gama to send his own men east to look after his interests, and he had exempted his whole household from paying taxes. Dom Vasco was even permitted to hunt in the royal forests and to collect fines from poachers.

He was not satisfied. Rank meant everything, and he was still a mere fidalgo, a gentleman of the court. The honor he desired most—the overlordship of his father's town of Sines—continued to elude him. Typically, he moved his growing family there anyway and began building himself a lordly new home. The Grand Master of the Order of Santiago reported his presumptuous knight to the king, who had no choice but to order Dom Vasco, his wife, and his children to leave Sines within thirty days and never show their faces there again, under penalty of such punishment as was "meted out to those who do not obey the command of their king and lord." Gama never returned to the town he had hoped to pass on to his descendants, and he switched his allegiance from the Order of Santiago to the Order of Christ.

Plenty of patricians thought the explorer's pushiness was beyond the pale. For refusing to be satisfied with how far he had already risen above his origins, he was scolded as intemperate, ungrateful, and unreasonable. Gama pushed on regardless. In 1518—the year after Magellan had defected to Spain—he brought matters to a head by threatening to quit Portugal himself and offer his services abroad. To lose a couple of navigators to one's rival was one thing; to lose one's admiral was quite another. The king refused to let him go until he had cooled off for several months, "by which time we hope you will have seen the error you are committing and will decide to serve us again rather than take the extreme step you propose." Dom Vasco stayed put, and the following year, twelve years after his brusque dismissal from Sines and sixteen after his return from India, he was invested as Count of Vidigueira. His elevation, the royal letter that delivered the news proclaimed, was a reward for his services, "especially in the discovery of the Indies, and the settling of them, from which there resulted, and results great profit not only to us and the Crown of our kingdoms and lordships, but generally universal profit to their residents and to all of Christianity, on account of the exaltation of Our Holy Catholic Faith." Gama had always been politically active as an adviser on imperial affairs; now he was one of only nineteen high noblemen in the nation and a resplendent presence at ceremonial events.

When the young new king wooed the grand old man of fifty-five to return to the scene of his triumph, he decided to risk it all. The empire was his legacy, and the opportunity to remake it in his image was too important to refuse.

On April 9, 1524, Vasco da Gama set sail for India for the third and last time. With him came two of his sons: Estêvão, who at the tender age of nineteen was to assume the title Captain-Major of the Indian Seas, and Paulo, who was even younger. Before leaving, Gama had extracted from the king a guarantee that in the event of his death his titles and estates would pass directly to his eldest son, Francisco, who stayed safely at home.

Vasco da Gama had been a mere captain-major himself on his first voyage east. This time out, titles hung around him like impenetrable suits of armor. The Admiral of India and Count of Vidigueira was now Viceroy of India to boot. The new viceroy—only the second man, after Almeida, to bear that title—had received the commission shortly before he left, and he had sworn the solemn oath of fealty three times before the king.

It was in every way a major mission. State-of-the-art ordnance had been procured in Flanders and several large ships had been built to order; Gama's flagship, the *Santa Catarina do Monte Sinai*, had as its figurehead the Alexandrian martyr who was condemned to die on a Roman torture wheel and was reportedly disinterred half a millennium later, her luxurious locks still growing. Altogether there were fourteen ships and caravels carrying three thousand men—and a few women. Many of the men were old India hands, and an unusual number were knights, gentlemen, and nobles who had been attracted or persuaded into serving with the great Gama. The women had sneaked on board at the last minute. Taking wives, lovers, or "comfort women" on the harrowing voyage was strictly forbidden, more for the morale-sapping quarrels their presence provoked than for the sake of their souls. The prohibition was regularly flouted; on one voyage, a passenger noted, the sailor who hoisted the mainsail was taken prisoner because he "kept a Concubine, which he had brought from Portugal, and she being with Child when she Embark'd, was brought to Bed in our Ship." Gama, ever the disciplinarian, had vowed to put a stop to the onboard orgies; before leaving Lisbon he had had it proclaimed on ship and shore that any woman found at sea "should be publicly scourged, even though she were a married woman, and her husband should be sent back to Portugal loaded with fetters; and should she be a slave and a captive she should be confiscated for the ransom of captives: and the captain who should find a woman in his ship and not give her up should for that lose his commission." The warning was also written on signs and nailed to the masts; no one could have missed it, or doubted that the count would carry out his word.

After the familiar trials of the voyage past the Cape, the fleet arrived in Mozambique on August 14. As soon as it anchored, three

women were dragged over to the flagship. A vessel at sea was the
least private place in the world, and it had been impossible to keep
them hidden for long. Grim-faced at the insubordination that had
broken out among the India crews, Gama took the women into
custody to be dealt with later.

There was much worse in store. As he prepared to leave Africa,
Gama sent a caravel to make his apologies and deliver letters and
gifts to the ever-patient sultan of Malindi. The caravel's crew, master, and pilot had already taken a violent dislike to their Majorcan
captain. Once they were on their own they murdered him, then
absconded toward the Red Sea to cruise for plunder.

Nature, too, seemed to be conspiring against the returning admiral. One ship ran into a reef off the African coast and had to be
abandoned, though the crew was saved. As the southwest monsoon
battered the fleet on the crossing to India, a ship and a caravel disappeared in mid-ocean and were never seen again. When the ten
remaining ships neared the coast, the fierce wind gave way to a
dead calm. Suddenly, during the daybreak watch, the water began
to tremble violently, as if the whole sea were boiling. A tidal wave
smacked into the hulls with such force that the sailors thought they
had hit a huge shoal, and one man threw himself overboard. The
rest struck the sails and lowered the boats, shouting out warnings as
the vessels pitched and rolled. When they realized the entire fleet
was firing off distress signals from its cannon, they cried to God to
have mercy on them, certain they had been gripped by a diabolical
force. They lowered the leads to sound the depth, and when the
lines paid out without reaching the seafloor they crossed themselves
even harder.

The tremors died down, then came back as strong as before.
Again the ships lurched so violently that men toppled up and down
the decks and chests skidded and banged from one end to the other.
For an hour the convulsions came and went, "each time during the
space of a Credo."

The admiral stood planted on his deck like an oak. A doctor

who dabbled in astrology had explained to him that the fleet had sailed into the epicenter of a submarine earthquake.

"Courage, my friends!" he shouted to his men. "The sea trembles for fear of you."

Gama was back.

THREE DAYS AFTER the seaquake subsided, one of the ships captured a dhow on its way home from Aden. On board were sixty thousand gold coins and goods worth more than three times that amount. With no Zamorin to teach a lesson, Gama took the valuables and let the crew go. This time he was determined above all to set an example to his own people, and to avoid any semblance of impropriety, he ordered his clerks to itemize every last cruzado.

The Muslims inadvertently had their revenge. The coast, they had told their captors, was just three days' sailing away. Six days later there was still no sight of land, and the more credulous crewmen began to whisper that it had been swallowed up in the quake. Panic gripped them when they recalled the forecast by several of Europe's leading astrologers that a conjunction of all the planets in the house of Pisces was about to unleash a second Great Flood. A number of Portuguese nobles had prepared themselves by building mountaintop shelters stocked with enough barrels of crackers to last until the waters receded, though in the end the year turned out to be drier than usual.

It soon transpired that the ships had taken the wrong heading. Two days later they arrived in Chaul, the port where Lourenço Almeida had met his end. Another Portuguese fort had gone up there three years earlier, and a settlement had already grown around it.

Gama published the king's commission that installed him as viceroy and set about business.

Vasco da Gama had never been a great dreamer. He was a loyal servant of his lord who unflinchingly carried out his commands, a born leader who set his course and unswervingly stuck to it, and from afar he had watched in disgust as his ocean turned into a free-for-all at a heavy cost to the crown. If he could, he dutifully declared, he "would make the King rich, as the greatest benefit the people could obtain was to have their King well supplied." He was determined to clear away the scroungers and deadweights accumulated after a decade of bribery and patronage, and he had brought his own handpicked men to fill many posts. Chaul's officers were summarily dismissed, and it was announced in the streets that anyone not there on official business was to embark immediately or lose his pay. Before leaving, Gama gave the new captain of the fort his first command: If Dom Duarte de Meneses, the governor whom Gama was replacing, showed up as expected, the captain was to refuse Meneses permission to disembark, disregard his orders, and only supply him with enough food to last four days.

Ignoring the appeals of his cabin-fevered and scurvy-ridden sailors to allow them ashore, Gama moved on to Goa. He was received with a public oration and lavish festivities and was carried in procession to the cathedral and the fort. The next day he relieved its captain, Francisco Pereira, of his command and opened an inquiry into a long list of accusations leveled against him by the townspeople. The charges included the imprisonment of his adversaries—among them the city's lawyers and judges—without charge or trial, the seizure of their property, and the expulsion of their wives and children from their homes. Crowds arrived to denounce Pereira for more "great evil doings," and Gama peremptorily sentenced the apoplectic former captain to pay reparations to them all.

Pereira had at least put the property he seized toward a good cause: a palatial hospital for the hundreds of Europeans who fell ill each year in the East. Yet so much money had been lavished on the hospital and the equally grandiose monastery of St. Francis that nothing had been left over for essentials, such as artillery. Gama took one look at the infirmary and its patients, some of whom appeared to be using it as a hotel, and ordered the doctor in charge not to admit anyone unless they could show their sores. Even the wounded were to be banned if they had been involved in a brawl;

trouble with women, the viceroy stiffly pointed out, was invariably the cause, and there was no medicine for that. Meanwhile, the many sick men on board the ships had begun to complain bitterly at their treatment. Gama retorted that he knew exactly how to make them feel better, and he announced that their shares of the booty from the vessel he had seized were ready to be disbursed. The attraction also drew forth large numbers of inmates from the hospital; when they tried to return, they found they had been locked out.

There was still the case of the three women stowaways to be dealt with. The town crier proclaimed the sentence:

"The justice of the King our sovereign! It orders these women to be flogged, because they had no fear of his justice, and crossed over to India in spite of his prohibition." It was, of course, Gama's justice that was sovereign in the East, and it was his punishment that had to be meted out.

Portuguese women were a rarity in Goa, whatever the state of their souls, and their plight immediately became a cause célèbre. Franciscan friars, Brothers of Mercy, and even the bishop of Goa protested to the viceroy's officials, and the gentlemen of the town offered a ransom for their release.

Gama paid no heed, and the flogging was fixed for the following day. Shortly before the appointed hour, the Franciscans and the Brothers of Mercy paraded to the viceroy's residence waving a crucifix and announced that they had come to make a last plea for a pardon. Gama ordered them to return the crucifix to its altar, and when they came back he launched into a long harangue. Marching on his house under the sign of the cross, he said in icy tones, "was a kind of conspiracy, and done to show the people that he was cruel and pitiless," and it must never happen again. When the brothers tried to explain the value of mercy, he brusquely retorted that mercy was for God, not men, and he vowed that if a single man dared commit a crime during his tenure, he would have him cut down inside the city gates.

The women were duly flogged, and the example had the

intended effect. "The people were much scandalized at what happened to these women," reported Gaspar Correia, a self-appointed chronicler who was in India at the time, "and judged the Viceroy to be a cruel man; but seeing such great firmness in carrying out his will, they felt great fear, and were wary, and reformed many evils which existed in India, especially among the gentlemen who were very dissolute and evil-doers."

For all his dictatorial ways, the new viceroy was undoubtedly a man of much greater probity than his immediate predecessors. The members of Goa's Municipal Council wrote a long report to King John III extolling Gama's determination to serve the crown, to rectify abuses, and to redress injuries. They were particularly astonished that he refused to accept the gifts—a polite word for bribes—that were offered as a matter of course to new governors. Gama, though, was in a hurry to continue his work, and to the council's dismay he moved on from Goa while petitioners were still lining up at his door. Leaving instructions that Dom Duarte de Meneses was not to be welcomed or obeyed there, either, he boarded a galliot and sailed down the coast, closely followed by his fleet.

In the long interval since Gama's last visit, the river mouths and harbors on the way to Cochin had become infested with nests of militant Muslim pirates. Many were merchants who had been driven out of business and who nursed a deep hatred of the Portuguese. Every summer they fortified themselves with paan and opium and sailed out to make war on the occupiers; the threat of being put to forced labor for life in the king's galleys made them more reckless, not less, and any Portuguese they captured who were not quickly ransomed were summarily killed. Gama had heard a great deal about the menace, and he insisted on nosing into the rivers to take a look for himself. The pirates spotted the intruders from their lookout towers, and to the viceroy's indignation the extravagantly mustachioed men in their light, fast boats darted brazenly around the lumbering Portuguese ships, even when the eight-strong squadron that was intended to police the coast sailed into view. Gama immediately dispatched his son Estêvão with a flotilla of armed boats to teach them a lesson, and he stationed six ships in the bars of the rivers. When he had put his own house in order, he vowed, he would return to deal with the scourge.

The former governor was still at large, but Gama finally ran into his brother off the coast. Dom Luís de Meneses was sailing north from Cochin to meet Dom Duarte, who was due to return south from Hormuz. The flags went up and the drums and trumpets sounded, but Gama insisted that Luís turn back and accompany him to Cochin.

The fleet briefly stopped at Cannanore, where Gama replaced another captain and threatened to punish the new Kolattiri for allowing Muslims to do business in his city and for failing to root out the pirate lairs. The alarmed king handed over a leading Muslim, and the sacrificial victim was imprisoned and later hanged.

Steering clear of Calicut, which was still a thorn in Portugal's side after twenty-six years, Gama arrived in Cochin in early November.

THE FLEET ANCHORED after dark, its guns firing a salute and inadvertently killing two men on a caravel. The flashes from the bombards also lit up a ship that had gone missing the night before and was sneaking into the harbor. It belonged to a merchant who had slipped away to steal a march on his competitors, and Gama clapped him in irons.

The next day Dom Luís sailed up on a richly decorated galley rowed by slaves, with the gentlemen of Cochin lining the poop deck and a lavish breakfast laid on a table, and offered to conduct Gama to land. He refused and set out for the city in his own boat.

Twenty-one years had passed since he had last been in Cochin, and much had changed. A new Portuguese town had grown up along the shore, and its leaders welcomed the new viceroy with an effusive oration. Clergymen with crucifixes conducted him to the main Portuguese church, and after the service the king stopped by on his elephant. Gama installed himself in the fortress, dismissed its captain, and set about refashioning the corrupt, bloated empire into a well-oiled machine run with martial efficiency from his office. Nominees for even the lowliest positions were ordered to report to the viceroy for a personal grilling. The clerks, some of whom were barely literate, were summoned to produce a writing sample in his presence. He insisted on personally licensing every captain, on pain of death if they tried to avoid his audit. He threatened to seize merchants' vessels and property and banish them from the East if they carried on embezzling from the royal weighing houses. He revoked the pay and rations of married men, unless they were called up to fight or to serve on the ships. He investigated allegations that officials had been pocketing tax revenues, and he had several arrested. He forbade his captains to load barrels of wine without his express permission, and he banned men from fighting if they had not proved themselves in war. He would give the honors of the battle, he pointedly declared, to soldiers who won them with their sword arm, whether or not they were gentlemen.

The old explorer had always ruled his ships with steely discipline, and now he was adopting a zero-tolerance approach to running his empire. "He had it proclaimed," reported Gaspar Correia, "that no seafaring man should wear a cloak except on a Sunday or Saint's day on going to church, and if they did, that it should be taken away by the constables, and they should be put at the pump-break for a day in disgrace; and that every man who drew pay as a matchlock man should wear his match fastened to his arm. He upbraided the men-at-arms very much for wearing cloaks, because with them they did not look like soldiers. He ordered that the slaves they might have should be men who could assist in any labor, for they were not going to be allowed to embark pages dressed out like dolls on board the King's ships." Anyone who disliked the new austerity, the viceroy announced, was free to go back to Portugal, as long as he had no debts and was not under investigation. So as not entirely to depopulate the empire, he declared a three-month amnesty during which crimes that predated his arrival would be pardoned. The period was reduced to one month for those who had purloined artillery; some of the captains and officers, it turned out, had been selling their guns to merchants, who had sold them to Portugal's enemies, and they responded to requests for their record books by burning them.

Gama had set himself a punishing program, and he refused to slow down even as the heat mounted. Mornings and evenings he visited the beach and the warehouses to hurry up the unloading of the fleet. He dispatched two ships to Ceylon to buy cinnamon, and four to the Maldives to attack a nest of Muslim pirates who preyed on supply convoys crossing the Indian Ocean. He readied a squadron to head to the Red Sea under the command of his son Estêvão, and he summoned a Genoese master builder to design a fleet of new vessels that could outpace the pirate craft of the Malabar Coast. "Sir, I will build you brigantines which would catch a mosquito," the shipwright answered.

There were more threats on the horizon. The Spanish had to be confronted; treaties or no treaties, Gama vowed, if he had his way Spain's ships would mysteriously vanish, along with their crews. The Ottomans were massing to the north, and with every passing year it seemed increasingly likely that they would go all out to challenge Portugal's control of the oceans. Meanwhile, a bishop had written to the Portuguese king to complain that the Zamorin and his Muslim subjects had been persecuting India's Christians; many, he said, had been robbed and killed, and their houses and churches had been burned down. Once again, Gama planned to launch a massive attack against his old foe, and the old hatred came flooding back. As soon as the merchant fleet had left, he declared, "he would go and destroy Calicut and all the coast of India, so that there should not remain one Moor on land nor at sea." Even in an empire troubled with internal strife and threatened by its Iberian neighbor, the fires of holy war still burned bright and true.

Many of the five thousand Portuguese in Cochin had had a

much easier life before the Count of Vidigueira had shown up, and
his iron-jawed rigor earned him plenty of enemies. Public meetings
took on a menacing edge, and Christians as well as Muslims began
to quit Cochin to conduct their business away from the viceregal
gaze. The sidelined Dom Luís de Meneses was behind much of the
dissent; half of Cochin, noted Gaspar Correia, seemed to eat at his
table, and over dinner, plots began to be hatched. Matters came to a
head when Luís's brother Duarte finally reached Cochin after being
cold-shouldered in Chaul and Goa. Gama had brought to India a
long list of complaints against his predecessor, and he had begun, in
secret, to call witnesses. Meneses, it was variously alleged, had used
the king's money for his own trade and had broken the royal spice
monopoly. He had stolen the estates of Europeans who had died in
India, and he had handed out slaves to soldiers and sailors in lieu
of salaries. He had slept with the wives of European settlers, not to
mention Hindu and Muslim women, and he had even taken bribes
from Muslim rulers to go easy on them. As soon as the former governor sailed into the port, Gama sent a delegation to ban him from
coming ashore and arranged to transfer him to a ship that would
take him home as a prisoner.

Meneses was the son of a count, a powerful nobleman in his
own right, a major figure in the Order of Santiago, and a renowned
war leader. He had nothing but contempt for the new Count of
Vidigueira, and he had taken his time in coming. Along the way he
had stopped off to stock up his chests for the voyage home, and he
had also brought with him a vast haul of booty, tributes, and bribes
from Hormuz. He refused to hand it over, and he treated the viceroy's emissaries with lordly disdain. Meneses had, though, reckoned
without the loyalty that Gama inspired in men who admired his
determination to serve his lord. When he reminded one member
of the delegation that his father had personally made him a knight,
the messenger retorted that he would cut off his own father's head
if the king commanded it.

The ousted governor had still not officially handed over power, and he waited in the harbor, hoping that events would somehow conspire to rid him of the self-righteous viceroy. His supporters kept him well informed about events on land, and they soon gave him startling grounds for hope.

Vasco da Gama had been suffering for days from severe and inexplicable pains. Hard boils had broken out at the base of his neck, and it became sheer agony to turn his head. He took to his room in the fortress and issued orders from his bed. His forced confinement, Gaspar Correia reported, brought on "great fits of irritation, with the heavy cares which he felt on account of the many things which he had to do, so that his illness was doubled." Soon the pain became so excruciating that he was only able to croak out commands in a hoarse whisper.

Secretly, at night, Gama called his confessor to his side. He was moved to the house of a Portuguese grandee, and he summoned his officials to join him. He made each man sign an oath to press on with his plans until another governor replaced him. Then he confessed and took the sacraments.

As he drew sharp breaths and murmured his last wishes, his clerk wrote down his will. He told his sons to go back to Portugal with the spice fleet and take with them any of his servants who so desired. He directed them to give his clothes and best furniture to the churches and hospital; the rest of his belongings they were to take home, not selling anything. He asked for his bones to be returned to Portugal, and he charged one of the witnesses to write to the king, begging him to look after his wife and sons and to take on his attendants. Finally, or so it was later rumored, he ordered a large sum of money to be sent to each of the three women he had flogged at Goa, so they could find good husbands and marry.

He died at three o'clock in the morning. It was Christmas Eve, 1524.

NO ONE CRIED, no one wept. The house was silent. The doors stayed shut all day. After dark his sons and his servants announced his death, and many of his friends and relatives came to mourn. Soon the entire city had gathered in the nearby courtyard of the Portuguese church.

The mood was solemn, but for some relief outweighed their grief. "The captains, factors, scriveners and other officials would be very satisfied at the death of the viceroy," one of Gama's admirers wrote to the king four days after his death, "for they do not wish to have the justice in their own house that he brought."

The great explorer's body was dressed in silks. His gilded belt was buckled around his waist, and his sword was placed in its scabbard. His spurs were fastened on his buskins, and his square cap was placed on his head. Finally, the mantle of the Order of Christ was draped over the old Crusader's back.

The uncovered bier was moved into the hall of the house. The coffin bearers, each wearing the cloak of a military brotherhood, raised it on their shoulders. Gama's loyal men walked alongside holding lit tapers, and the townspeople followed. For good or ill, none of them would have been in India were it not for Vasco da Gama.

The Count of Vidigueira, Admiral and Viceroy of India, was buried in the simple Franciscan church of St. Anthony. The next day the friars said a dignified funeral mass, with Gama's sons sitting in their midst. At night the two young men came back to the church to grieve in private, "as was reasonable," said Gaspar Correia, "on losing so honored a father, and of such great deserts in the kingdom of Portugal.

"For it pleased the Lord," he continued, "to give this man so strong a spirit, that without any human fear he passed through so many perils of death during the discovery of India . . . all for the love of the Lord, for the great increase of his Catholic faith, and for the great honor and glory and ennobling of Portugal, which God increased by His holy mercy to the state in which it now is."

GAMA HAD BROUGHT to India a letter of succession sealed with the king's insignia. It was ripped open in church and was read aloud.

To his indignation, Duarte de Meneses discovered that he and his brother were out of a job.

The spice fleet sailed for home with Gama's sons and the Meneses brothers on board. The disgruntled brothers made life as difficult as possible for the two young mourners, but in the end they got more than they gave. Luís de Meneses's ship was lost in a storm after rounding the Cape; a French pirate later revealed that his brother had seized it and had killed Luís and his crew before setting it on fire. Dom Duarte was nearly shipwrecked, too, but he finally made it to Portugal. It was rumored that he stopped off on the coast to bury his treasure while his ship sailed on to Lisbon. The ship sank before it reached the port; some said it was sabotage to cover up the theft of riches that should have been the crown's. Whether for that reason or for his other nefarious activities, the king slung Dom Duarte in prison for seven years. The buried treasure, of course, was never found.

❧

CHAPTER 19

THE CRAZY SEA

THE YOUNG KING who had sent Vasco da Gama to fix his Indian problem soon succumbed to his dynasty's delusions of grandeur. Like his father he, too, began to fantasize about wringing the Indian Ocean drop by drop until it was purified into a Christian lake. More brutal campaigns were waged against Muslims, more forts went up, and Gama's drive to rein in the unwieldy empire was quickly forgotten. As its outposts were flung still farther across the map and the annual spice shipments that reached Lisbon barely covered the cost of maintaining the garrisons, Portugal steadily evolved into a territorial power, its income dependent on taxing peasants.

With spices still a royal monopoly, Portuguese ships backed by European merchants began to crisscross the Indian Ocean carrying Persian horses to India, Indian textiles to Indonesia and East Africa, and Chinese silks and porcelains to Japan. The so-called country trade proved more profitable than the long Cape route, and the Portuguese soon outstripped Muslim merchants in Asia; by the mid-sixteenth century pidgin Portuguese had replaced Arabic as the language of commerce in ports across the East. Yet as regular links with Portugal were increasingly severed, large swaths of the empire became all but impossible to control.

Only the hardiest and most desperate men were eager to serve in the remotest corners of the earth, and like their Crusader forebears, many who went east had small horizons at home. They were determined to live like lords, and they were not overly fussy about how they made their fortunes. As dropouts, jailbirds, criminal gangs, kidnapped youths, and penniless younger sons poured out of Portugal, shocking tales of depravity began to filter back to Europe.

The French traveler Jean Mocquet penned the most devastating of many exposés. As apothecary royal to the king of France, Mocquet was responsible for concocting the king's drugs from a global range of resins, minerals, and aromatics. Perhaps because of his daily exposure to the exotica of the East, he developed a bad case of wanderlust. The king granted him permission to roam the globe on condition that he brought back weird and wonderful souvenirs for the royal cabinet of curiosities, and Mocquet set out on a ten-year odyssey. After he had visited Africa, South America, and Morocco, his fourth voyage took him to Goa. Like many of the era's adventurers, he kept an exhaustive account of his travels, and he sat down and dashed off page after page devoted to trashing the Portuguese.

By the mid-sixteenth century Goa had grown into a colonial city grand enough to earn the sobriquet "Rome of the East." Its streets and squares were lined with fifty churches and numerous convents, hospices, and colleges staffed by thousands of ecclesiastics. Its lofty white cathedral was the seat of an archbishop whose dominion stretched from the Cape of Good Hope to China. The governor's palace, public buildings, and potentates' mansions were magnificent examples of Renaissance and early Baroque architecture sprouting among the lush Indian foliage, and pomp and pageantry filled the streets to celebrate festivals and victories. Barely hidden behind the stately facade, though, was a frontier town of bars, brothels, and brawls where gangs of soldiers roamed the streets and a self-appointed Portuguese aristocracy wielded power at the point of a sword.

The social pressure on new arrivals was intense. As soon as they stumbled half dead off the ships in their home-style clothes, they were jeered at with such venom—"licehead" was a favorite insult—that they hid in their lodgings, under a boat, or at the back of a church until they worked out how to pawn their cloak or sword and dress like old hands. Within weeks, Jean Mocquet acerbically noted, they began calling themselves gentlemen, "tho they be but Peasants and Tradesmen." One gallant named Fernando, he reported, had caught the eye of a rich woman and was parading around decked out in gold chains and attended by a retinue of slaves when he was recognized by the son of his old employer in Portugal. Fernando pretended not to know him and asked who he was, "to which the other made answer, Was he not the same who formerly kept Hogs for my Father; This Gallant hearing this, drawing him aside, told him, he was, and was here called *Don*, and was looked upon as a great Gentleman, praying him to hold his peace, and gave him Money; yet this hindered not his being known by several, who made their own profit thereof." Other newcomers were less fortunate: if they breathed the truth, they were quickly roughed up. Even lowly soldiers equipped themselves with a boy to carry their parasol or cloak and assumed an air of majestic gravity, and if they quarreled—as they often did—any of their gang who refused to back them to the hilt was cast out and was fair game, too.

At its high point Goa was home to more than two hundred thousand inhabitants—as many as lived in Paris, more than in London or Lisbon itself. Only a few thousand, though, were Portuguese, and most of those were *mestiços*, or the mixed-race offspring of colonists and indigenous women. The rest were Hindus, Indian Christians, and slaves, who were kept in large numbers by every Portuguese household and by every seminary, monastery, and nunnery. None were well treated. Indians who failed to bow down to the new rulers or doff their caps were slashed with swords, cudgeled with bamboo poles, or beaten with long sandbags. One cabal of captains set out at night to steal a golden idol from a Hindu temple, pausing to torch the nearby houses to cause a diversion. Inside they found five hundred temple women dancing an all-night vigil. At the sight of the intruders the dancers linked their arms and legs together, and before the Portuguese could prize them apart the fires they had lit began licking at the walls. They snatched the jewelry from the women's ears, hacked off their fingers to get their rings, and beat a hasty retreat without the idol. The women, it was reported, "made such a lamentable noise, that 'twas a great pity to hear them: The Portugals flying away from the Fire, let all these Religious young Women to be Burnt, none being able to succor them; and thus cruelly do the Portugals treat their best Friends and Confederates."

No doubt the dancers had feared for their honor, because women were rarely safe in Portuguese India. Especially vulnerable were mestiços who retained their ties to the Indian community and unmarried daughters with any portable property. The latter's slaves were bribed to gain access to them, they were swept off on a whirlwind elopement, and when their lovers had gambled their way through their jewelry they were regularly strangled and buried, in at least one case under the floorboards of their own lodgings. Portuguese husbands, meanwhile, were paranoid that their mestiço wives were drugging them while they cavorted with lovers before their insensate eyes; they were so suspicious, warned Mocquet, that it was courting disaster to look their womenfolk in the face, while if they saw them speaking to another man,

> they presently Strangle or Poison them; and when they have Strangled them, they call their Neighbours to their Succour, saying, that a Swooning Fit has taken their Wife upon the Chair; But they never come again to themselves: Sometimes they send for a Barber to Blood them, saying, that they are not well; When the Barber is gone away, they undo the Fillet, and let the Blood run out until the poor miserable Creature dies; and then also they call in the Neighbours, to see as they say, what a sad Disaster has happened to their Wife in Sleeping.

Others took their wives for a dip in a brook or pond, "and there make them Drink their Belly full; and a little while after, send their Slaves to look for their Mistress, whom they find Drown'd, which the husband knowing before, seems to be mightily astonished and grieved at." He knew of some, the Frenchman added, who had

done away with three or four wives, though women, too, reportedly rid themselves of adulterous husbands, usually with the help of
poison. Many blamed it on the climate: it was, said Mocquet, "so
hot, that where any Man can only have the means to speak with a
Woman or Maid, he is sure to obtain of them what he desires."

Most egregious of all was the colonists' treatment of slaves. Hundreds at a time, seized across Asia and Africa, were stripped and dis-
played on the auction block in Goa, where they went for less than a
tenth the cost of an Arabian horse. Girls sold as virgins were examined
to make sure their hymens were intact; some were kept as concubines,
others were doused in perfumes and sent out to prostitute themselves.
Whatever their task, Mocquet claimed, slaves who dissatisfied their
master or mistress were beaten to the point of death. "For they run
them through with double Irons, then give them with a Cudgel, 500
blows at a time, and make them lie along the ground on their Belly, and
then come two, who by turns strike the poor Body as a Log of Wood."
If an owner was particularly religious, Mocquet sharply noted, he kept
a count of the blows on his rosary. "And if by chance they who thus
strike are not strong enough to his mind, or have an inclination to spare
their Companion, he causes them to be put in the place of the Patient,
and to be soundly banged without any Mercy."

Of Mocquet's long litany of accusations, it was this vicious mistreatment that shocked even a violent age. The Frenchman piled example
on example to make his point. At night at his lodgings, he wrote, he
was kept awake by the noise of blows "and some weak Voice, which
Breathed a little, for they stop their Mouth with a Linnen Cloth, to
hinder them from crying out. After they have been well beaten, they
cause their Bodies to be sliced with a Razor, then rub it with Salt
and Vinegar for fear it should Fester." Sometimes, he claimed, owners
made their slaves lie on their bellies, heated a shovel until it was red hot,
and dripped lard from it on their naked flesh. One Indian girl came
running to his lodgings, "crying out for help, and praying me to be a
means to obtain Mercy; but I could not save her, to my great Sorrow;
For she was taken and laid all along on the Ground and Bastinadoed

without pity." A mestiço woman had killed five or six slaves and had buried them in her garden; while she was punishing her latest victim, the slave administering the blows left off and told his mistress she was dead. "'No, no,' she answered, 'she counterfeits . . . *Lay on, lay on, 'tis an old Fox.'*" One slave who was slow to answer her owner's summons had a horseshoe nailed on her back and died soon after of gangrene; another had her eyelids sewn to her eyebrows. A male slave was hung up by his hands for two or three days for spilling some milk, and afterward he was "well Bang'd." When Mocquet heard a young woman being beaten in his own lodgings, his host's brother explained that it was nothing to what others had endured:

> He told me also, how his Brother, who was Master of the Lodging, having one day bought a Japan Slave, a beautiful Girl, and how in Dineing with his Wife, he happened to say in Jesting, that this Slave had exceeding White Teeth, his Wife said nothing at present, but having watched her opportunity when her Husband was abroad, she caused this poor Slave to be taken and bound, and pluck'd all her Teeth out without Compassion; And another's Privy-Parts, whom she conceited her husband entertained, she ordered a red-hot Iron to be run up, of which the miserable Creature Died.

"Such," Mocquet concluded, "is the cruel and Barbarous treatment, which the Portugals and others use to their slaves of Goa, whose condition is worse than that of Beasts." Years later, the experience still made him shudder with horror.

Justice was rarely done. Posses of Portuguese pulled on masks, barged into houses at dinnertime, and swept the plate off the tables into their swag bags; then they demanded a bribe to return it, and another not to kill the master of the house. In case they were caught they had bags of gunpowder at the ready, with matches tied around them, and they threatened to blow up anyone who approached. Murderers ran away to the mainland and waited for an amnesty to be declared: with desertions rife, soldiers were always in demand. Successive governors, meanwhile, lined their pockets and tyrannized the poor. Vast quantities of spices, gold, and ivory vanished without ever showing up in the royal ledgers. Captains pocketed half the money they were allowed for provisions and left their men on half rations, adding starvation to the toll from scurvy, cholera, dysentery, and malaria. In desperation the crown cut back the royal cargo fleets and sold the captaincies of the forts to the highest bidders for three-year terms. That only encouraged the debt-laden officials to pump the system all the harder before their time was up. One captain of Sofala murdered one Muslim merchant to whom he was deeply in debt, went on a killing spree to shore up the position of another Muslim merchant with whom he was in cahoots, and tried to stab to death the king's factor when he complained. The Portuguese East had become a forerunner of the Wild West, with soldiers paid in gold dust by the carat and captains shooting up each other's ships.

The forces of lawlessness that had been the camp followers of every previous Crusade had been exported east. Violence bred violence. When the king of Siam captured some miscreant Westerners, reported Mocquet, he showed little self-restraint:

> For some of them he causes to be put stark-naked in Frying Pans of Copper, upon the Fire and thus to be roasted by little and little: Others he causes to be put betwixt two great Fires and set down, and thus to Die in Torments; others, he exposes in the Park of his Elephants to be crushed and knocked down by them, and a thousand sorts of barbarous Cruelties, which he exercises upon these poor Portugals.

Southeast Asia had hardly been an enlightened place before the Portuguese had appeared. The same Siamese ruler, when he heard that his commanders had failed to turn up for battle because their wives could not bear their absence, "sent for these Women, and having caused their Privy Parts to be cut off, and to be fastened upon their Husbands Foreheads, he caused them thus to walk about all the City, and then to have their Heads choped of." Sorcerers reportedly so inflamed one Burmese king against his people that he resolved to exterminate them all: for three years he forbade anyone, on pain of death, to plow or sow the land, and the country resorted to cannibalism. Yet the Portuguese were foreign devils, and as their aggressions mounted, their former friends turned on them one by one. "The Portuguese are much detested in almost all the parts of the Indies," a Venetian ambassador to Spain reported with no little satisfaction, "as the countrymen have seen that they go about fortifying themselves little by little, and making themselves the lords of those lands. . . . I think that the difficulties will increase every day."

Amid all the troubles the original purpose of the Portuguese explorations was virtually forgotten. Portugal's Crusading kings had planned to siphon vast wealth out of the Islamic East and into Christian Europe, then conquer and convert the Infidels and heathens of the world. The first part of the plan had met with some success, even though much of the money ended up in pockets other than their own. Yet if faith had led the charge to the East, to the majority of the empire builders who followed it came a distant second to the scramble for filthy lucre.

The Portuguese were fond of claiming that their arrival in the East had stopped all of India from succumbing to Islam. They had certainly pummeled the Muslims of the Malabar Coast, who responded to their loss of power by seeking martyrdom in a jihad that intermittently lasted into the twentieth century. Even so, their policies were hardly designed to win converts to the Christian way of life, let alone to usher in the universal Christendom of which their kings had dreamed. Eventually they resorted to the old stratagem of forced conversions, and the dark figures of the Inquisition arrived to stalk the streets of Goa.

As EARLY As 1515, Manuel I had petitioned the pope to establish the Inquisition in Portugal.

Manuel's request was yet another consequence of his marriage to the daughter of the Catholic Monarchs. Early in their reign Ferdinand and Isabella had pressured Rome into authorizing the revival of religious tribunals to torture, try, and execute heretics, a practice that had been dormant since the early thirteenth century. By the time Manuel made his request, the Inquisition had already wreaked such havoc that the papacy delayed its debut in Portugal by twenty-one years. Four years later, in 1540, the first batch of marranos was publicly sentenced at the first Portuguese auto da fé, and the burnings began.

By then John III had become as evangelical as his father, and he was increasingly embarrassed by his colonists' unchristian lifestyle. Violence, naturally, was not the problem; what was really worrying was that so many settlers had succumbed to the earthy pleasures of India and had gone native. The king turned to the newly formed Society of Jesus, all but one of whose founders, including Ignatius Loyola himself, were Spanish or Portuguese. In 1541, a year after John had ordered the destruction of every Hindu temple in Goa, the Jesuits sent Francis Xavier, a Basque from Navarre, to the East.

Xavier's labors to improve the colonists' morals evaporated in a sultry haze of indifference. After four years he gave up the struggle and wrote to King John, recommending that the Inquisition be installed at Goa as the only way to cleanse his colony. Xavier left for Indonesia, where his evangelism found a much more receptive audience, and died while trying to reach China several years before the Inquisition finally arrived.

By then Portugal had had more than half a century to shepherd Africa and India into the Catholic fold. Rome had begun to take a dim view of what it saw as Portuguese apathy, and it reminded the king that it had only given him authority over the lands he discovered on condition that he spread the faith. Since the quid pro quo seemed to have been forgotten, the Church threatened to throw open Asia to all comers. The threat worked, after a fashion. The colonial government offered rice to poor Hindus and jobs to the higher castes if they submitted to baptism. Many of the "Rice Christians" were dunked under water, took their reward, and carried on with life as normal.

In theory the Inquisition only had jurisdiction over Christians, but its first act was to outlaw the open practice of Hindu rites on pain of death. Having only recently been mistaken by Vasco da Gama and his contemporaries for Christians, Hindus found themselves herded into churches to hear their religion ridiculed and were subjected to a regime of discrimination that ranged from the petty   prohibitions against riding on horseback or being carried in palanquins—to the ruinous. At the latter end of the scale were bans on Christians employing Hindus and on Hindus employing Christians. More Indians lined up for baptism, failed to shake off their old habits of keeping small idols or chanting under their breath, and like the Rice Christians, found themselves caught under the Inquisition's burning lens of religious purification.

Many "New Christians" who had fled the Inquisition in Portugal also became its victims in India. Hundreds were burned at the stake in the cathedral square, and thousands sought refuge in Muslim territory. Finally, the inquisitors turned on the St. Thomas Christians who had been so eager to give their allegiance to Vasco da Gama and his nation. In 1599, on the grounds that they practiced a heretical form of Eastern Christianity, they were converted en masse to Catholicism. Their books were burned, their ancient liturgical language was banned, and their priests were imprisoned and targeted by assassins. As the dungeons and torture chambers filled up, the inquisitors awarded themselves their victims' property and connived with the colonial government to terrorize them into submitting to Portuguese control.

The Goan Inquisition was one of the most brutal and iniquitous of all those scandalous tribunals of the soul. It was also spectacularly unsuccessful. Obsessing over doctrinal purity was no way to convert people who came from radically different religious traditions. Missionaries who tried to understand those traditions and graft native churches onto them were much more effective, though some were persecuted by the Inquisition for their very success. The educated Jesuits, who on the whole were mercifully free of the inquisitors' superiority complex, arrived in China, learned the language, and dressed their hair and beards in the local style; even though preaching in public meant instant death, they made large numbers of converts, among them influential mandarins and even a few regional governors. Yet they, too, were hampered by the rebarbative behavior of their Portuguese hosts, while Jean Mocquet had a typically caustic explanation for the missionaries' grueling experiences in Japan. The Japanese, he reported,

> who are a subtile and wary People, seeing that the design of the Portugals, after having made them Christians, was to dispossess them of their Lands and Goods by all inventions; therefore they did not care for their Amity, much less did they desire 'em to Govern, and this perhaps was one of the causes that they have Martyred so many Jesuits who were utterly innocent of all this: For these Japans are mightily Jealous of their Wives, and the Portugals had no other aim but to gain them, especially those of the greatest, with whom afterwards they do what they please.

"I have found out in the Indies," Mocquet blisteringly added, "that the Whoredoms, Ambition, Avarice, and Greediness of the Portugals, has been one of the chiefest causes why the Indians become not Christians so easily." For all the Frenchman's anti-Portuguese prejudice, the missionaries had no hope of making major inroads without the sheltering umbrella of an effective empire, and many met with a martyr's death.

Strangely, while Hindus and Christians were persecuted with increasing enthusiasm, the animus against Muslims that had driven Vasco da Gama to India was muted for a long while.

It was not for want of Muslim threats. In 1524 an Uzbeki warlord named Babur, who was terrifyingly descended from Tamerlane on his father's side and Genghis Khan on his mother's, rode into India through the mountain passes of Afghanistan. Babur had decided to retake his rightful inheritance, and he founded the Delhi Empire of the House of Timur, called by Europeans the Mughal Empire. The Mughals swept across northern India, but they had no navy to challenge Portugal's supremacy at sea and the Portuguese pragmatically refused to fight them. More alarmingly for the Westerners, the increasingly almighty Ottoman Empire finally refocused its attention on the seaways of the East. Muslims and Christians fought sea battles from India to Indonesia, but the Ottomans never managed to project their naval power convincingly beyond the Red Sea. In 1538, a massed fleet of eighty warships set out from Egypt to wage "holy war . . . and to avenge the evil deeds of the Portuguese infidels" once and for all, but a second Battle of Diu ended in a comprehensive Portuguese victory and by 1557 the Turkish threat had lifted for good.

Closer to the hub of Portugal's activities, the once-formidable Vijayanagar Empire finally fell in 1565 to the Muslim sultans across its borders. The sultans' armies marched to the coasts to oust the Portuguese, and the colonists only held on to Goa after a brutal ten-month siege. Yet long before then, most of the empire's freewheeling monopoly holders had decided it was more profitable to ally with Muslim merchants than to try to uproot them. So had the increasing numbers of wanted men and deserters from the fleets who wandered around Asia and Africa, married into local trading networks, and adopted the local lifestyle and beliefs. Many eked out a living as middlemen to the empire, which gradually became barely recognizable as a Portuguese empire at all. In East Africa a sort of mercenary convivencia was established, and it endured until the 1570s, when a young Portuguese king caught Crusading fever and sent new armies to massacre Muslims around the Indian Ocean.

As the sixteenth century drew to a close, the Crusader fleets petered out for good. The reason was simple. There were no longer enough Portuguese who were willing and available to sail to the East.

DEATH HAD ALWAYS stalked the explorers, but in an age that held life cheap the risk had been worth the reward. Men who lived in hope of heaven and fear of hell had been eager to serve as Crusaders; men born into poverty had hungered to touch the wealth of the East. Yet the wealth had stuck to the fingers of the elite, and faith had proved a poor defense against disease, famine, and storms. Even the devout had begun to wonder whether God had really chosen them to carry out His plan. Christians or not, Portugal's greatest chronicler lamented in the mid-sixteenth century, "It seems that— on account of our sins or as a result of some judgment of God hidden from us—at the entrance to this great land of Ethiopia where our ships go, he placed a menacing angel with a sword of fire in the form of mortal fevers which prevent us from penetrating into the interior to find the springs which water this earthly garden and from which flow down into the sea, in so many of the regions we have conquered there, rivers of gold."

In the three decades following Vasco da Gama's first voyage, perhaps eighty thousand Portuguese men—and a few women—had set out for the colonies. Perhaps eight thousand had returned. For a nation of a million men, women, and children it was an insupportable loss. As the dreaded plague once again struck Portugal and cut down countless more lives, towns and villages across the kingdom emptied and sleepily decayed.

Complete collapse was only averted when the attractions of the East began to wear off.

The voyage around Africa had always been a deadly obstacle course. Now it had become tediously familiar, too. There were no new coastlines to explore, people to encounter, or stars to chart, and there was little hope of finding fabulous wealth at the end. The Portuguese still clung to the old system that separated sailors from soldiers and put both under the command of men qualified by birth

rather than ability, and shipboard brawls became a depressingly regular feature of life at sea. They broke out all the more as merchants
commissioned towering two-thousand-ton vessels that were built
for their carrying capacity, not for seaworthiness or comfort. With
their rearing castles and bulbous hulls the ships' design had changed
little since Vasco da Gama's time, and the bigger they got, the more
top-heavy and unstable they became. They were overloaded with
goods and passengers, they were badly maintained and crewed by
inexperienced hands and slaves, and out of every four, one met with
disaster.

Of all the Portuguese vessels lost to shipwreck, piracy, and war,
the fate of one reverberated on every subsequent voyage.

In February 1552 the *São João* left Cochin, its holds crammed
with one of the greatest hauls of all time. It was late in the season,
and it sailed into a storm near the Cape of Good Hope. The mainmast and rudder sheared off, and the ship crashed into the coast of
Natal. A hundred and twenty survivors—among them the captain,
a nobleman named Manuel de Sousa de Sepúlveda, and his wife,
Dona Leonor—dragged themselves ashore with as many valuables
as they could stuff under their clothes. They had no provisions,
they were soon parched and starving, and when they encountered a
group of Africans, they asked to be taken to their king.

The king sent word that strangers were not allowed to enter his
village, but if they camped under a clump of trees he would give
them food. Since they had no idea where they were, they did as
they were told, ate the food they were given, and decided to wait
until another ship passed by. To defend themselves they had just five
muskets they had rescued from the wreck.

Manuel de Sousa sent one of his men to ask for a house for
himself, his wife, and his two small sons. The king replied that he
would lend him one, but only if his people split up among the local villages, since he could not feed them all. His chiefs, he added,
would lead them to their new homes and would take care of them,
but first they had to lay down their weapons. Ignoring the advice

of a chief who warned the castaways to stick together—and the protests of his wife, who was made of stronger stuff than her husband—Sousa ordered his men to hand over their muskets.

"You lay down your arms," Dona Leonor said sadly, "and now I give myself up for lost with all these people."

The captain abandoned all pretense of leadership and told his people to make their own way home. He would stay where he was, he said, and die with his family if it pleased God. The Africans led the sailors in groups through the bush to their villages, where they stripped them, robbed them, and beat them. Back in the king's village Manuel de Sousa, his family, five women slaves, and a dozen or so men who had stayed with him were relieved of their jewels and coins and were told to go and find the others.

Many of the scattered party had managed to regroup, but no one took charge. Without arms, clothes, or money they trekked across the arduous terrain, some taking to the woods, some to the mountains. The humiliated and half-delirious captain set off on their track with the rest of his weakening party, but they had barely started out when more Africans fell upon them, stripping them of their clothes and wounding Sousa in the leg. Dona Leonor tried to fend off her assailants with her fists, but her husband begged her to let herself be stripped, "reminding her that all are born naked and that, since this was the will of God, she should submit." With her sons crying and begging for food she threw herself on the ground and covered her modesty with her long hair, scrabbling in the sand to bury herself to the waist. She refused to move, even when her old nurse gave her the torn mantle with which she was protecting her own dignity, and she never moved again.

The other men stood off in embarrassment. "You see how we are and that we can go no further, but must perish here for our sins," Leonor said to one, the pilot of the wrecked ship. "Go on your way and try to save yourselves, and commend us to God. If you should reach India or Portugal at any time, say how you left Manuel de Sousa and me with my children."

Most of the men shambled into the bush, while Sousa, his wound suppurating and his mind wandering, dragged himself off to look for fruit. When he came back, Dona Leonor was half faint from weeping and hunger, and one of his sons was dead. He buried the little body in the sand. The next day he returned to find the slaves crying over the corpses of his wife and his other son. He sent the women away and sat motionless, his chin resting on his hand, staring fixedly at his wife's body. After half an hour he got to his feet, made a hollow in the sand, and buried the rest of his family. When he was finished, he disappeared into the bush and was never seen again.

Three of the women slaves managed to escape to Goa, where they told the sorry tale. Thirty-seven years later another Portuguese ship was wrecked not far away, and a local chief who came to see the castaways cautioned them not to travel overland, as thieves would rob and kill them. "He added that his father had warned Manuel de Sousa de Sepúlveda of this when he had passed that way," a chronicler recorded, "and he was lost through not following his advice." Instead the sailors waded out to an islet and camped in a deserted Portuguese settlement that had been built by ivory traders. As the sailors and soldiers began to bicker and fight, the captain—another Portuguese nobleman—shut himself up in a half-derelict hut and begged his men to leave him alone, "since he was old and weary, and finding himself with his wife in these straits, he determined to lead a hermit's life there, passing the remainder of his days in penance for his sins." Four years after that, another shipwrecked party behaved with much better discipline and marched overland for more than three months to meet up with the rest of their fleet. Along the way, they encountered an African who bowed and doffed his cap to their leader. "I kiss your worship's hands," he said, in the Portuguese manner; it turned out he had been brought up among the Portuguese survivors of the *São João*.

To superstitious sailors, the horror story of the *São João*, the half-witted Manuel de Sousa, and the tragic Dona Leonor kept resurfacing like a ghostly reminder of everything that had gone wrong. The hulking, unwieldy treasure ships disappeared at sea with terrifying regularity. Their captains, however noble, often proved desperately poor leaders. The indigenous peoples were inhospitable at best, and at worst they were seized with a violent loathing of the intruders. The climate wreaked havoc with European constitutions, and tropical diseases finished them off. The casualty figures were terrifying: twenty-five thousand patients died in the course of the seventeenth century at the Goa hospital alone. Around the Indian Ocean gravestones marked the deaths of countless young men taken before their prime. Countless more were buried or lost at sea, and the scars of absence were the only marks they left.

A Jesuit priest named Father António Gomes summed up the feelings of the unfortunate many. In the 1640s Gomes was himself shipwrecked on the Swahili Coast. He made his way to the nearest village and asked for the local chief. An old man with leathery skin and a gray beard appeared; Gomes cheekily suggested that he must have been around in Vasco da Gama's days.

"I started to complain about the sea that had done us so much wrong," the priest reported, "and he gave me an answer which I considered very wise.

"'Master, if you know the sea is crazy and has no brain, why do you venture upon it?'"

I N 1516, AT the grand old age of sixty-four, Leonardo da Vinci moved to France. With him he brought three samples of his wares: two religious paintings and one enigmatic portrait that would become known as the *Mona Lisa*.

A tunnel linked Leonardo's turreted manor house to the Château d'Amboise, the favored residence of the French king. Francis I was only twenty-two, but the two men saw each other nearly every day and became fast friends. When Leonardo died three years after his arrival, Francis cradled his head in his arms. "There had never been another man born in the world," the king lamented, "who knew as much as Leonardo."

The Renaissance had reached France. Born in the competing city-states of Italy, nourished by the splendors that flooded there from the East, and carried north on the winds of war, the intellectual transformation brought a new taste for learning and art to a nation obsessed by battle. Francis dispatched his agents to Italy to buy up paintings, sculptures, and manuscripts; they even tried to transport Leonardo's *Last Supper* to France, wall and all. Magnificent palaces and castles shot up across his kingdom, including the Château de Chambord, the most astonishing hunting lodge in the world, which Leonardo himself may have had a hand in designing and where, in 1539, Francis hosted his bitter enemy Charles I of Spain.

The two men had a long history. Twenty years earlier the nineteen-year-old Charles had beaten the twenty-four-year-old

Francis to the crown of the Holy Roman Empire. They had been sworn adversaries ever since, so much so that Charles several times challenged the French king to single combat. Most woundingly to French pride, in 1525 Charles's troops had captured Francis while both were vying for control of the Duchy of Milan, and the French king was carted off to Madrid and thrown in prison.

Francis had left his mother, Louise of Savoy, in charge as regent during his campaign. When she heard of her son's captivity Louise decided bold action was needed, and she sent an embassy to Istanbul.

The first envoy disappeared in Bosnia, but the second reached the Ottoman capital. Concealed in his shoes were letters to the sultan Suleiman the Magnificent asking him to form an alliance with France. Leonardo da Vinci might well have disapproved. More than a decade before he moved to the Loire, he had designed a soaring single-span bridge to adorn Istanbul. Suleiman's grandfather had rejected the bravura proposal as absurdly impractical, and instead he had turned to Leonardo's fellow Tuscan, Michelangelo.

The alliance was eventually struck, and Suleiman, who detested his rival claimant to the title of Caesar, sent Charles an ultimatum to release the French king and pay an annual tribute or face the consequences. Charles refused, and in the spring of 1529 the Ottomans marched on his city of Vienna. Suleiman's 120,000 troops far outnumbered the defending force of Hapsburg soldiers and Viennese militiamen, but the Turks were in a poor state of health after trudging through the winter mud, their supplies were running short, and as a heavy snowfall set in they beat a dismal retreat.

The failed siege marked the high-water mark of Turkish power, but the Ottoman Empire was still the sole superpower of the Renaissance world. Tracing the path taken by the early Arab conquerors, the Turks had marched west from Egypt and had stormed across North Africa. Sixty thousand Ottoman soldiers and mariners had ousted the last five hundred Knights Hospitaller from their stronghold at Rhodes and had pushed them back to Malta. A Barbary pirate named Khayr ad-Din—better known as Barbarossa—had been co-opted as the Ottoman fleet admiral, and he had imposed his will across the Mediterranean. The French alliance with the Turks scandalized their fellow Christians, but it reflected reality.

In 1535 France established a permanent embassy at the Sublime Porte, the gate in Istanbul's Topkapi Palace where ambassadors were received and, by extension, the diplomatic byname for the Ottoman Empire. Ottoman warships wintered in Marseilles and launched joint attacks with the French on Italy and Spain. The French fleet then wintered in Istanbul, and the allies carried on their campaign until Francis and Charles finally called a truce. It was soon after that that the French king invited his imperial foe to Chambord and showed off his magnificent new pile.

The thaw soon frosted over. Charles's men assassinated Francis's Ottoman ambassador, and once again Christians teamed up with Muslims to fight Christians. Barbarossa's ships joined forces with France's navy and laid waste to Nice, which belonged to an ally of Charles, though the former pirate was famously unimpressed by his confederates. "Are you seamen to fill your casks with wine rather than powder?" he asked the bibulous French. When the Ottoman fleet and its thirty thousand sailors and soldiers wintered in Toulon, Francis displaced the town's entire population and turned the cathedral into a mosque. The alliance between Turks and French endured through the overwhelming defeat of the Ottoman navy by the Christian Holy League at Lepanto in 1571, through another Ottoman siege of Vienna in 1683, and all the way into the nineteenth century.

France was not the only European power to turn to Istanbul. In 1578, an English businessman named William Harborne arrived at the Sublime Porte and paid his respects to Sultan Murad III. The next year, Murad instigated a long correspondence with Queen Elizabeth I. The queen responded by sending the sultan a fancy carriage clock and, more controversially, a large quantity of lead for making munitions, much of it stripped from the roofs of Catholic monasteries. It was not the first time Elizabeth had compacted with a Muslim nation: she had already authorized the sale of armor and ammunition to Morocco and had dispatched warm letters and ambassadors to its ruler.

By then the Protestant Reformation had cleaved Europe into two warring theological camps. In 1570 the pope had excommunicated "Elizabeth, the pretended Queen of England and the servant of crime," and Elizabeth had turned to the Islamic world for potential allies against Spain, the foremost Catholic power. Like the ruler of Morocco, the Ottoman sultan was receptive to the overtures. In stark contrast to the pope's invective, he addressed his letters to "the pride of the women who follow Jesus, the most excellent of the ladies honored among the Messiah's people, the arbitress of the affairs of the Christian community, who trails the skirts of majesty and gravity, the queen of the realm of Inglitere, Queen Elizaide." Islam and Protestantism, he suggested, were kindred faiths; unlike Catholics, both abhorred the worship of idols and believed in the power of the book. Elizabeth wrote back in wholehearted agreement and enclosed some fragments of broken icons, while William Harborne, who by 1583 had become England's first ambassador to the Sublime Porte, returned the compliment by addressing Murad, in terms that would have pleased Mehmet the Conqueror, as "the most august and benign Caesar." With Harborne murmuring sage advice in the ears of the sultan's counselors, the two sovereigns discussed mounting a joint campaign against Spain.

By Spain, Elizabeth also meant Portugal. The same year that William Harborne arrived in Istanbul, the twenty-four–year–old King Sebastian I of Portugal had disappeared during a disastrous Crusade in Morocco. He was last seen charging at full tilt into the Moorish host and was presumed dead, though many Portuguese took to espousing Sebastianism, the belief that the young king would suddenly show up and rescue Portugal in its darkest hour, and a number of impostors capitalized on their hopes. The popularity of Sebastianism had much to do with the succession crisis triggered by the royal vanishing act. Three of Manuel I's grandchildren laid claim to the throne, and in 1580 one of the three marched into Portugal and defeated the people's favorite. The new king was the son of France's old adversary Charles, and on his father's death he had become King Philip II of Spain. He was also king of Naples and Sicily, archduke of Austria, duke of Burgundy and Milan, lord of the Low Countries, and for four years of marriage to Henry VIII's Catholic daughter Mary, king of England and Ireland as well. To the dismay of many of his new subjects, proudly independent Portugal had been subsumed into a mighty empire, and a Spanish-led empire to boot.

For sixty years the two nations that had spearheaded the Age of Discovery were yoked in an uncomfortable union. By association, Portugal now found itself on the wrong side of its old allies, the English and the Dutch. The Dutch, who for decades had resold Portugal's Eastern goods in northern Europe, had revolted against Philip II's rule in 1568, thus launching the Eighty Years' War; in retaliation, Philip had banned them from visiting Lisbon. In 1585 Queen Elizabeth, Philip's half sister-in-law, sent an army to the aid of the Dutch Protestants and inaugurated nineteen years of the Anglo-Spanish War. Sir Francis Drake began privateering against Spanish ports and treasure fleets and in the process circumnavigated the globe, and the Spanish Armada disastrously set sail for the English Channel.

For years English and Dutch explorers had been braving the icy wastes of Russia and Canada in search of a northern passage to the warm seas of the East. Now Portugal was the enemy, and any scruples about hijacking its ocean route to Asia went up in a blaze of nationalism.

In 1592, four years after the remnants of the Spanish Armada had limped home, an English naval squadron captured an enormous Portuguese ship off the Azores. One hundred and sixty-five feet in length, with thirty-two huge brass cannon mounted between seven decks and more than six hundred passengers and crew, the *Madre de*

Deus was three times bigger than any English vessel afloat, and she was returning from India laden with treasure. Her captors sailed her back to England, where she towered over the houses of the Dartmouth dockyard. An inventory was taken, and the entire nation was dumbfounded. Five years later Richard Hakluyt summarized the findings in his great compendium of English travels, under the exceedingly misleading heading "The Madre de Dios taken. Exceeding humanity shewed to the enemy." As well as a great haul of jewels that had mysteriously disappeared before the list was made,

> it was found, that the principall wares . . . consisted of spices, drugges, silks, calicos, quilts, carpets and colours, &c. The spices were pepper, cloves, maces, nutmegs, cinamom, greene ginger: the drugs were benjamim, frankincense, galingale, mirabolans, aloes zocotrina, camphire: the silks, damasks, taffatas, sarcenets, altobassos, that is, counterfeit cloth of gold, unwrought China silke, sleaved silke, white twisted silke, curled cypresse. The calicos were book-calicos, calico-launes, broad white calicos, fine starched calicos, course white calicos, browne broad calicos, browne course calicos. There were also canopies, and course diaper-towels, quilts of course sarcenet and of calico, carpets like those of Turky; wherunto are to be added the pearle, muske, civet, and amber-griece. The rest of the wares were many in number, but lesse in value; as elephants teeth, porcellan vessels of China, coco-nuts, hides, eben-wood as blacke as jet, bedsteds of the same, cloth of the rindes of trees very strange for the matter, and artificiall in workemanship.

All hell broke loose on the docks, and an irate Queen Elizabeth dispatched Sir Walter Raleigh to save what was left of her share of the loot. The total value of the cargo was calculated at the astronomical sum of half a million pounds sterling, or almost half the wealth of the English treasury. Even after every sailor, fisherman, and thief from miles around had stuffed his shirt, the remainder amounted to 150,000 pounds sterling, "which being divided among the adventurers (whereof her Majesty was the chiefe) was sufficient to yeeld contentment to all parties."

To his ravishing catalog Hakluyt added a thought that would have had a familiar ring to Vasco da Gama and his fellow pioneers:

> And here I cannot but enter into the consideration and acknowledgement of Gods great favor towards our nation, who by putting this purchase into our hands hath manifestly discovered those secret trades & Indian riches, which hitherto lay strangely hidden, and cunningly concealed from us; whereof there was among some few of us some small and unperfect glimpse onely, which now is turned into the broad light of full and perfect knowledge. Whereby it should seeme that the will of God for our good is (if our weaknesse could apprehend it) to have us communicate with them in those East Indian treasures, & by the erection of a lawfull traffike to better our meanes to advance true religion and his holy service.

Helpfully, the Portuguese ship also yielded a document, "inclosed in a case of sweete Cedar wood, and lapped up almost an hundred fold in fine calicut-cloth, as though it had beene some incomparable jewell," that described in great detail the system of trade in the Far East.

It was not the only commercial secret that had leaked out of the East. Hakluyt also included the report of Ralph Fitch, an Englishman who had set out in 1583 with letters from Queen Elizabeth to the emperor of China. The Portuguese captured Fitch at Hormuz and imprisoned him in Goa, but he broke out and embarked on a tour of India, Burma, and Malacca. At almost the same time Jan Huygen van Linschoten, a staunchly Calvinist Dutchman who nevertheless spent six years in India as secretary to the archbishop of Goa, published an account of Portuguese navigation in Asia that became an instant bestseller in three languages. Both travelers painted a brilliant picture of the exotic East and an excoriating portrait of the lawless Portuguese Empire, but Linschoten, as well as providing detailed sailing directions for the routes between Europe, India, China, and Japan, also included a sheaf of nautical maps that he had covertly copied in Goa.

The secrets that Portugal had fiercely guarded for a century were suddenly thrown open to the world. A new race was on to break Portugal's century-old monopoly of the Eastern trade, and this time the two rivals were the East India Companies that were formed by the English and the Dutch.

Two years after the *Madre de Deus* made England goggle, the first English fleet returned home from India. The next year the first Dutch fleet left Amsterdam. Both voyages were deadly for their crews, but they proved that Portuguese vessels were not the only ones that could survive the journey.

The Dutch sent ships east as fast as they could be built, and they quickly overtook the English. In 1603 a Dutch fleet seized a Portuguese vessel off Singapore that was carrying twelve hundred bales of Chinese silk and an extraordinary quantity of musk, and in the furor that followed, the Dutch jurist Hugo Grotius formulated the radical notion of the *Mare Liberum*—the sea as an international realm that was open to all. Covered by that judicial fig leaf, the Dutch began to pick off the scattered strongholds of the Portuguese Empire. In 1604 the Zamorin of Calicut eagerly sided with the Dutch against the Portuguese, having just sided with the Portuguese to put down a Muslim rebellion. From their new Indonesian capital at Batavia—modern Jakarta—the Dutch sailed out each winter to blockade Goa. In 1641 they took the great fortress and emporium at Malacca, and in 1656 they conquered Cochin. Ceylon fell in 1658, and Cannanore in 1663. As the world's spices flowed due west from Batavia to the Dutch colony at the Cape of Good Hope and onward to the Netherlands, the monsoon winds of the Arabian Sea no longer ruled the world's trade. The ancient ports of the Red Sea and the Persian Gulf were stilled, their markets emptied of everything but slaves and dates. The resourceful merchants of Cairo and Alexandria survived and even flourished, but only by switching their business to the latest craze: coffee.

The Dutch and the English had followed where the Portuguese had led, and they had the advantage of learning from the pioneers' mistakes. Both nations began to build sleek galleons that were more maneuverable and had greater firepower than the ponderous Portuguese ships, and they turned their crews into unified fighting units of sailor-soldiers led by professional naval commanders. Portugal had driven its rivals to create the first modern navies, and its failed attempt to enforce a crown monopoly on the spice trade had encouraged the new players to put their faith in free enterprise. Free enterprise did not mean a free-for-all: the bitter clashes that had wreaked havoc with Portuguese commerce showed the vital importance of keeping a ruthless grip on the chain of supply. The Dutch drove native traders out of business, took direct control of many of the Spice Islands, and killed or enslaved large numbers of their inhabitants.

With the Dutch ensconced in Southeast Asia, the English learned a different lesson from Portugal's difficulties. By now the Mughals, who spoke Persian and were no more native to India than were the Europeans, had conquered all but a southern sliver of the Indian subcontinent. In 1615 an English ambassador named Sir Thomas Roe arrived at the Mughal court, made himself the emperor's drinking companion, and struck a treaty that gave the East India Company exclusive trading rights across the empire. At the same time the English joined forces with Persia, which was now ruled by Shia shahs who were bent on challenging the Ottoman dominance of Islam, and in 1622 the allies ejected the Portuguese from Hormuz after a century of troubled occupation. Though the company's traders eventually took to arms, its readiness to cooperate across the religious divide allowed it to insinuate itself into local power structures in a way the Portuguese had never managed—or wanted—to do. The consequences were even more catastrophic for the ancient cultures of the East. When the spice mania finally faded and tea became the latest exorbitantly expensive European craze, Britain exchanged opium grown in India for tea grown in China and turned an entire nation into addicts.

As the English, the Dutch, and the Portuguese fought bitter wars for land and trade, the seas of the East became infested with the warships and pirate craft of rival European nations, each trying to outmaneuver and outgun the other. The seaway that Vasco da Gama had opened up had become the conduit for a vicious colonial scramble that seemed to have no end.

TODAY THE OLD Portuguese capital of Goa is a ghost town. Not a trace is left of its warehouses, hospitals, mansions, and palaces. The sprawling city had always been a fever-ridden place, and in the nineteenth century it was abandoned and mostly leveled. Only half a dozen spectacular churches remain, dramatically dotted around landscaped lawns like the attractions in a religious theme park. Busloads of tourists arrive to puzzle at their purpose and to visit the monumental tomb of St. Francis Xavier, the inadvertent scourge of India's Christians, Hindus, and Jews. As the sun sets and the tour parties leave, these outsize reminders of outstripped dreams brood like great jilted brides in the care of a few patient priests and nuns.

Across the Indian Ocean lie the ruins of the capital of Portuguese Africa. Mozambique Island lost its purpose a few decades after Goa's demise, when the opening of the Suez Canal finally cashiered the Cape route to the East. Trees sprout from the debris of colonial houses. Rusting cannon litter the ground in the old naval yard. A vast neoclassical hospital molders magnificently over a grand square, complete with a bandstand, which serves as a playground for the local children who live, as they always have, in a tight-packed village of thatched huts. In front of the handsome redbrick Jesuit College stands the statue of a strong, stern figure in Crusader garb, his fist clenched against his chest, his sword ready to be drawn from its scabbard, his unbrookable eyes gazing out to sea.

The statue was toppled in a recent cyclone, and though it was put back on its plinth, the letters that once spelled the name VASCO DA GAMA were torn off and were never replaced. Larger than life but stripped of its meaning, it seems a fitting comment on its subject's latter-day reputation.

In Ceuta, where it all started, the sanctuary of Santa Maria de Africa still gives pride of place to an image of Our Lady donated by Henry the Navigator in 1421. The Portuguese prince sent the icon to the knights of the Order of Christ who were defending the city and it is said to have wrought many miracles, though it failed to stop Ceuta from siding with the Spanish in 1640, when Portugal fought its neighbor to regain its independence. Spanish it remains, but its ownership is as vigorously contested by Morocco, to whose coast it clings, as that of Gibraltar, its opposite Pillar of Hercules, is by Spain. Here the paths tramped by centuries of holy warriors have not yet faded away.

In recent years, in fact, Ceuta has received more attention than it has seen for centuries. In 2006 Ayman al-Zawahiri, the former leader of Egyptian Islamic Jihad who has been dubbed the brains of al-Qaeda, called for Ceuta's "liberation" from Christian occupation; two years later, he labeled the United Nations an enemy of Islam because it considered Ceuta an inseparable part of Crusader Spain. Ceuta is no longer the strategic prize it once was, but thirteen hundred years after an Islamic army departed there for Europe, and nearly six centuries after a Portuguese army arrived there at the beginning of its odyssey around Africa, for some it still symbolizes a hoped-for Muslim countermove into the West.

A similar message was behind Zawahiri's 2001 declaration that the fall of al-Andalus was a "tragedy." To many Muslims al-Andalus was an ideal society, a paradise of learning and culture, and its loss marked the beginning of Islam's long retreat. Extremists do not mourn the tolerance that made al-Andalus thrive; in their view Spain and Portugal occupy Islamic territory that needs to be reclaimed. Three years after Zawahiri's paean to the past, a jihadist group claimed responsibility for the Madrid bombings that ripped apart four commuter trains. "We have succeeded in infiltrating the heart of crusader Europe and struck one of the bases of the crusader alliance," it boasted, adding that it was intent on settling ancient scores. "Crusade" is another word that has been heard a lot recently, both in the invective of terrorists and, in the wake of the September 11 attacks, from the lips of President George W. Bush. In one statement, Islamist leaders proclaimed that it was the duty of every Muslim to kill the Americans and their allies in the "Crusader-Zionist alliance" in order to liberate Jerusalem's al-Aqsa Mosque.

It hardly needs saying—and yet it needs saying—that the actions of terrorists are an affront to mainstream Islam. What is painfully clear is that many of these proclamations are essentially a mirror image of Christian polemic in the decades leading up to the Age of Discovery. Even more striking is al-Qaeda's preferred means of hitting back at the West: to disrupt its commerce by blowing up planes and causing "a haemmorhage in the aviation industry, an industry that is so vital for trade and transportation between the U.S. and Europe." Substitute ships for planes and the Indian Ocean for the Atlantic, and we are back five hundred years. The terrorists' trap, tragically, has been sprung. As we commit vast resources to the so-called war on terror and our armies are yet again bogged down in the Middle East, the Islamist case that a new Crusade is under way wins a wider hearing, especially when linked to the West's support of Israel. Many Westerners, meanwhile, begin to fear their Muslim neighbors as the enemy within, and all sides flirt with the old, raw language that caricatures the others as medieval fanatics or degenerate devils.

From what until recently was our securely modern viewpoint, and after all the obituaries historians have written of history, it can be hard to understand why an age-old conflict has come back to haunt us. The explanation lies in our mutual past, if we take the longer perspective needed to see it.

Nearly fourteen hundred years ago, two great religions crashed into each other and competed for the wealth and the soul of the world. Both grew from the same roots, and both were nourished by the same soil. They were neighbors with a common heritage, and they were rivals for the same lands. They each claimed to possess the ultimate truth, and they each aimed to deliver God's final revelation to all mankind. Both celebrated victory and removed the sting from death, and for all the glories they unfolded and all the succor they gave, militarism became their shared dark side. Faith, to Muslims and Christians alike, was not merely a personal matter, an inner striving toward an impossible ideal. It was a public trust, given by God to His people, to forge His society on earth, and few saw anything strange about doing God's work with swords and guns.

More than eight centuries later, Christians were still fighting a seemingly losing battle with Muslims over the same old ground when a handful of men sheared free and opened up a new front. They were headed for Islam's heartlands, with the aid of the allies and wealth they believed they would find in the East. Driven by an ironclad certainty that they were destined to spread the true faith, the Portuguese changed the course of history. In 1552 the Spanish chronicler Francisco López de Gómara declared the discovery of the sea routes to the East and West Indies "the greatest event since the creation of the world, apart from the incarnation and death of Him who created it." Two centuries later, humanists were still putting the same case in a more secular way. "The discovery of America, and that of a passage to the East Indies by the Cape of Good Hope, are the two greatest and most important events recorded in the history of mankind," wrote Adam Smith in 1776. Both events sprang from Portugal's quest, and to most minds both had equal weight. Even when the magnitude of Christopher Columbus's discovery became clear, it was long apparent that for the West to be won, the East first had to be overcome.

The moment when Vasco da Gama arrived in the Indian Ocean was the moment when Europe could begin to believe that the global balance of power had shifted its way. As centuries of cribbed fantasies gave way to clearly charted facts, new mental as well as geographical horizons opened up. Colonies were founded, churches sprang up in unheard-of places, and Islam's supremacy no longer seemed unassailable. Vast wealth in natural resources—bullion, manpower, and of course spices—fell under Christian control, and at long last the West had the means to hold off and eventually repel the Ottoman challenge at its gates. But for that, the fate of much of Europe, the settlement of America, and the discovery of new worlds then unknown might have taken a very different path.

It was Vasco da Gama who fired the starting gun on the long, fraught centuries of Western imperialism in Asia, and it was the success of the global Crusade known as the Age of Discovery that allowed the Christian West to dismiss its old rivalry with Islam as a relic of darker times. Yet that rivalry remained a powerful undercurrent of history even as Christians fought Christians, Muslims fought Muslims, and—occasionally—both joined forces to fight a common enemy. To Islamists who dream of a reborn caliphate ruling a restored empire it is unfinished business, and the world order founded in the wake of colonialism—including the United Nations and the very concept of democracy—is an ongoing Western plot to impose an alien way of life, the Crusades in a subtler guise. Meanwhile a new era begins in which China and India retake their traditional places as the engines of the world's economy—and yet just when we should be competing for global markets and minds, we find ourselves drawn back into the old religious conflict.

It is easy to be fatalistic. Christians and Muslims, it can seem, barricaded themselves into hostile camps so long ago that nothing can be done. No one has a monopoly on right and everyone has an interest in understanding, yet our mutual distrust is too deep-seated to dislodge. Cooperation sometimes thrives, but holy wars never end.

There is another way—a way shown by the many men and women who instinctively rejected the division of the globe into rival religious blocs. There were the Muslims of Córdoba and Baghdad, the alchemists of wild explosions of cultural interaction. There were the Christians of Toledo and Sicily, who carried on that progressive tradition. There was Frederick II, who sat down with a sultan and negotiated a lease on Jerusalem. There was Mehmet the Conqueror, the cultivated tyrant who turned Istanbul into an international melting pot. There was Leonardo da Vinci, who sought enlightened patrons wherever his mind took him. There were even the kings and queens of France and England and their allies, the Ottoman sultans. Like the early Crusaders, there were also countless Europeans who were captivated by the ancient cultures of Asia and went native, to the horror of their compatriots back home.

The clash between East and West has consistently been as creative as it has been destructive. The one thing it has never been is stilled, and dogmatists and diehards of all stripes have soon enough found themselves left behind. Among those were the pathfinders, the Portuguese themselves. In the end, the religious certainty that drove Vasco da Gama and his fellow explorers halfway around the world was also their undoing. For all their astonishing achievements, the idea of a Last Crusade—a holy war to end all holy wars—was always a crazy dream.

ACKNOWLEDGMENTS

WRITING THIS BOOK has been an education and an adventure. During my research, I delved into the past in Lisbon and Rome, sailed the Swahili Coast in search of ruined cities, and was buffeted by the monsoon in Kerala and Goa. As I journeyed from Portugal, Spain, Italy, and Morocco to Mozambique, Tanzania, Kenya, and India, I was privileged to enjoy the unstinting advice, help, and friendship of numerous people. Most were previously strangers, like Karisa Keah, who went especially out of his way to steer me through the remote backwaters of East African history. My obligations to all are too many to mention, but their conversation and companionship are unfading memories.

A book of this scope would have been impossible to conceive without the scholarly work of generations of historians. In particular, the translators and editors of the Hakluyt Society's editions of rare travel accounts have made an invaluable trove of primary sources available in English. My great debts to other scholars past and present are recorded in the notes. The congenial atmosphere and ever-helpful staff of the London Library made the process of tracking down elusive material a pleasure. My thanks, too, to the librarians and curators of the British Library and National Maritime Museum in London, the Museu Nacional de Arte Antiga, Arquivo Nacional da Torre do Tombo, and Sociedade de Geografia in Lisbon, the Biblioteca Estense in Modena, the Heidelberg University Library, the library of the Universidad Complutense de Madrid, and the Bibliothèque nationale de France.

Massimiliano Durante and Francisco Vilhena patiently helped me to unravel the knottier clauses of medieval Italian and Portuguese. Angelica von Hase read the manuscript and made many cogent suggestions. Julia Kaltschmidt was always ready with advice during the long and sometimes winding journey that brought me to this subject.

In the United States, my agent, Henry Dunow, has been the best possible friend to a writer feeling his way into his second book, and a guru when sage advice was needed. My sincere thanks to Terry Karten, my editor at Harper, for her ready support and advocacy. Thanks, too, to Harper's David Koral, Sarah Odell, Bill Ruoto, and copy editor Tom Pitoniak, and also to Nancy Miller.

While working on this book I met and married my wife. Wedding planning wreaks havoc with deadlines, and splendors of the heart sit strangely with often dark and invariably male material. I could wish the subject at hand was more romantic, but the dedication is for life, not for now.

Prologue

1   **The light was fading:** For my sources for Vasco da Gama's first voyage, see the notes to chapter 7.

4   **Spanish and Italian:** Specifically, the Tunisian merchants spoke Castilian and Genoese; the former evolved into modern Spanish, while the latter is still spoken in the Genoa region today.

6   **the medieval and the modern ages:** Historians have offered a variety of dates for the end of the Middle Ages; two leading contenders are 1453, the year of the fall of Constantinople, and 1492, the year of Columbus's first voyage. If the overriding theme of the medieval age is Europe's decline and the rise of Islam, the dominant theme of the modern age is the Christian West's global surge to power. From that perspective, it makes little sense to start the latter with the fall of the final bastion of the classical world to the Ottomans. Columbus did not reach the mainland of the Americas until August 1498, and it was decades before the impact of his discoveries became clear. Vasco da Gama arrived in India in May 1498, and it was his achievement, I argue, that allowed Europe to believe the historical tide had finally turned.

Chapter 1: East and West

12   **god of the Jews:** Jews traced their ancestry to Isaac, Abraham's son by his wife Sarah; Muslims to Ishmael, Abraham's son by Sarah's Egyptian slave girl Hagar. Arab tradition holds that Abraham re-

stored the Kaaba, which was founded by Adam and rebuilt by Noah, while he was visiting Hagar and Ishmael, whom his jealous wife had forced him to send into exile.

13   **"dark-eyed houris":** N. J. Dawood, trans., *The Koran: With a Parallel Arabic Text* (London: Penguin, 2000), 497.

14   **Church of the Holy Sepulcher:** The site was uncovered by Constantine's mother Helena, who set out in 325 on a relic-hunting trip to the Holy Land and miraculously unearthed parts of the True Cross on which Jesus was believed to have died, the nails that pierced his hands and feet, and, according to some accounts, the Holy Tunic and the rope with which he was tied to the cross. Some of the finds accompanied her home, including two of the nails, one of which ended up in Constantine's helmet and the other on his bridle; others stayed to be housed in the new church. Since tradition held that Jesus was crucified over the exact spot where Adam's skull was buried, the church was also believed to enclose the tomb of the first man. See Colin Morris, *The Sepulchre of Christ and the Medieval West* (Oxford: Oxford University Press, 2005).

14   **a blackened sky:** The Persians sacked Jerusalem in 614 CE. In 70 CE the Romans had put down a mass Jewish uprising by burning down the Second Temple, razing the city, and massacring or carting away the entire population; never since had Jews been permitted to live in the city of David. The Jews allied with the Persians to wreak 544 years of revenge, only to be massacred again when the Romans marched back in; they would soon ally more successfully with the Arabs.

15   **churning Christian controversy:** The main bone of contention was the precise degree of Christ's divinity. The orthodox position, hammered out at a series of great councils, was that Jesus was both fully divine and fully human, two distinct states united in one perfect being. Many of the empire's subjects begged to differ. Arians denied Jesus's divinity, Monophysites denied his humanity, Nestorians declared he was two beings, one divine and one human, and other groups fixed on a variety of intermediate states. Successive emperors decreed that a united empire required a unified faith and charged the dissenters with heresy. Heraclius, the victor over Persia, had reopened the fraught question in search of a compromise, but the resulting creed of Monothelitism, which declared that Jesus had

two natures but only one will, satisfied no one and was rejected as heretical within five decades.

15 **a new regime:** Centuries later, leaders of the independent Eastern churches that survived under Islam still saw the Arabs as saviors. "The God of vengeance," wrote a twelfth-century patriarch of the Syriac Orthodox Church, "having observed the malice of the Greeks, who cruelly pillaged our churches and monasteries wherever they had dominion and condemned us mercilessly, brought the sons of Ishmael from the south to deliver us." Michael the Syrian, quoted in Stephen O'Shea, *Sea of Faith: Islam and Christianity in the Medieval Mediterranean World* (London: Profile, 2006), 52.

15 **"Damn this world":** The quotation is from the great epic poem *Shahnameh*, or *Book of Kings*, by Ferdowsi, which was written at the turn of the first millennium CE. The best translation is by Dick Davis (New York: Viking, 2006). The Persian aristocracy, though it quickly adopted Islam, long nursed an animosity to Arab culture and an attachment to the splendors of pre-Islamic Persia.

15 **Jerusalem was starved into submission:** The city fell in April 637. According to tradition, Muhammad's successor Umar arrived dressed in rags and rode through the Gate of Repentance astride a white ass (or camel). He asked the patriarch where King David had prayed and was led to the Temple Mount, which he found had long been used as a rubbish dump. Umar rounded up some Christians and put them to work clearing the refuse, then erected a simple wooden house of worship that would later be replaced by the al-Aqsa Mosque (see chapter 2).

16 **Saracens:** The term *sarakenoi* or *saraceni* originally referred to the non-Arab peoples of northern Arabia, but it was subsequently applied to Arabs and then to all Muslims. Its etymology is unclear, but by the fourth century the historian Ammianus Marcellinus noted that it was used to refer to the region's desert nomads.

16 **commanded from on high:** So feared the Armenian bishop Sebeos; see Alfred J. Butler, *The Arab Conquest of Egypt—and the Last Thirty Years of the Roman Dominion* (Oxford: Clarendon, 1902), 152. Of the five great patriarchates of the Church, three—Antioch, Jerusalem, and Alexandria—now operated under the sufferance of Islamic rulers.

16   **stabbed with a poisoned sword:** Ali's assassin was fanatically certain that piety, not genealogy, should be the sole qualification for Islam's leader. His simple, puritanical version of Islam would become known as Kharijism and would take root most firmly in North Africa. Pockets survive today in Arabia and Africa.

16   **the Umayyads:** Muawiya, the founder of the dynasty, was the son of Abu Sufyan Ibn Harb, a prominent Meccan who led the attack on Medina that nearly annihilated Islam. At the end of the same battle Muawiya's mother, Hind, ripped out and dined on the liver of Muhammad's uncle Hamza. The civil war also left Muhammad's grandson murdered and the Kaaba itself in flames; pragmatic power politics had dramatically won out over pious purity.

17   **blue-eyed Berbers:** The Berbers, whose lands stretched from the Nile to the Atlantic, called themselves *Imazighen*, or "Free Men." They were masters of survival, and their tribes were an eclectic mix of pagans, Jews, and Christians. The legend of the Prophetess has been the focus of much arcane dispute; see Abdelmajid Hannoum, *Post-Colonial Memories: The Legend of the Kahina, a North African Heroine* (Westport, CT: Heinemann, 2001).

17   **smashed a mountain in two:** Geryon was said to live on the island of Erytheia, near modern Cadíz. In Apollodorus's version, Hercules threw up the two mountains to commemorate his journey; Diodorus Siculus says he narrowed the existing strait to keep out the monsters of the Ocean Sea. Pliny the Elder, in the "Introduction" to Book 3 of his *Natural History*, records that the first-century inhabitants of the coasts believed the mountain was "dug through by [Hercules]; upon which the sea, which was before excluded, gained admission, and so changed the face of nature." The Pillars of Hercules still stand proud on Spain's coat of arms; the motto *Plus ultra*— "further beyond"—wreathes around them, suggesting they mark an entrance, not a closure.

18   **Old Man of the Sea:** The mythical character, also identified as the sea god Nereus, appears in Hercules's eleventh labor. In it, Hercules is sent to fetch the golden apples of immortality from the garden of the Hesperides, the daughters of the Titan named Atlas who holds the heavens on his shoulders. Hercules seizes the shape-changing Nereus and extracts from him the location of the garden, then frees

Prometheus from his fiery torment and in return learns that only Atlas can fetch the apples. Hercules offers to bear Atlas's burden while he goes off to the garden; on his return Atlas tries to trick the hero into taking the weight off his shoulders for good. Hercules asks Atlas to hold the skies while he rearranges his cloak, and runs away. In one variant, Hercules builds his pillars to liberate Atlas.

18   **a millennium of mariners:** One or two earlier navigators were bolder. Around 500 BCE, the Carthaginian explorer Hanno the Navigator sailed through the Pillars of Hercules and likely reached the Senegal River; his journey is recorded in his *Periplus*, a Greek translation of the text on a tablet that Hanno deposited in a temple. Herodotus briefly mentions the earlier circumnavigation of Africa, in a clockwise direction, by a Phoenician-crewed fleet sent by the Egyptian pharaoh Necho II; his skeptical report that the Phoenicians found the sun on their right as they sailed west around the southern tip of Africa lends the only credence to a story for which there is no other evidence and which is mainly remembered by those who posit a link between the pyramids of Egypt and Mexico.

18   **the Seven Peaks:** The mountain range culminates in the near three thousand feet height of Jebel Musa, the Mountain of Moses, which is the alternative candidate for the southern Pillar of Hercules.

19   **sinful wickedness of their rulers:** While divine punishment for the Goths' constant civil wars was seen behind the defeat, divine providence was detected when the exiled nobles managed to put aside their differences, elect a ruler, and found Asturia, the kernel of the Christian kingdoms that would eventually push back against Islam. In 722 Pelayo, the first king of Asturia, won a minor victory against the Berbers that was later identified as the start of the Christian comeback. "I will not associate with the Arabs in friendship," a chronicler had him grandly proclaim, "nor will I submit to their authority . . . for we confide in the mercy of the Lord that from this little hill that you see, the salvation of Spain and of the army of the Gothic people will be restored." Repeated claims of continuity between Gothic Spain and the new Christian kingdoms helped justify the wars against Islam as the reconquest of Iberia by its rightful rulers. Joseph F. O'Callaghan, *Reconquest and*

Crusade in Medieval Spain (Philadelphia: University of Pennsylvania Press, 2003), 5–6.

19   **Arab armies had besieged Constantinople:** The sieges took place in 674–78 and 717–18. Between 80,000 and 120,000 troops marched on Constantinople in 717; eighteen hundred war galleys attacked by sea. Starvation, freezing temperatures, and disease decimated the land army; Greek fire destroyed much of the fleet, and its remnants were wiped out in a freak storm.

20   **that day in 732:** Western tradition has accorded the Battle of Poitiers a significance that was lost on Arab writers and is lost, too, on revisionist historians. In Europe's foundation stories, though, Poitiers became paramount. In chapter 52 of *The Decline and Fall of the Roman Empire*, Edward Gibbon famously supposed that if the battle had gone the other way, "perhaps the interpretation of the Koran would now be taught in the schools of Oxford, and her pulpits might demonstrate to a circumcised people the sanctity and truth of the revelation of Mohammed." See Maurice Mercier and André Seguin, *Charles Martel et la Bataille de Poitiers* (Paris: Librarie orientaliste Paul Geuthner, 1944); Jean-Henri Roy and Jean Deviosse, *La Bataille de Poitiers* (Paris: Gallimard, 1966).

20   **the Hammer:** Charles Martel was the greatest in a long line of seventh- and eighth-century palace mayors who were the powers behind the throne of the Frankish Merovingian kings. Martel, the bastard son of the palace mayor Pepin of Herstal, scythed through the customary mayhem that followed Pepin's death and united much of present-day France, western Germany, and the Low Countries under his rule. In 751 his son, also called Pepin, finally seized the throne with the backing of the pope.

20   **tactics that had reaped such spectacular rewards:** The Arab maneuver known as *karr wa farr*—"attack and withdrawal"—was impracticable for Europe's soldiers, who were weighed down by heavy helmets, coats of armor, and shields. See Hugh Kennedy, *The Armies of the Caliphs: Military and Society in the Early Islamic State* (London: Routledge, 2001); David Nicolle, *Armies of the Muslim Conquest* (London: Osprey, 1993).

20   **rancorous power struggles:** As late as 807, the governor of Toledo invited hundreds of prominent rebels to a feast in his palace,

decapitated them, and threw their bodies into a prepared pit; the grisly event became known as "La Jornada del Foso," or the Day of the Pit.

21   **a king's ransom:** Mayeul, the abbot of Cluny, was kidnapped in 972.

21   **"a plank on the water":** Ibn Khordabeh, *Book of Routes*, quoted in Jack Turner, *Spice: The History of a Temptation* (New York: Random House, 2004), 96.

21   **"Europeans":** In the *Chronicle of 754.* The reliability of the text has been disputed, and some medievalists date the term to the late Middle Ages.

22   **Augustus, Emperor of the Romans:** The papacy derived its sovereignty over the secular rulers of the former western lands of the Roman Empire from a document called the Donation of Constantine, which was purportedly written in the fourth century, was first seen in the eighth century, and was proved to be a forgery in the fifteenth century.

22   **schism with the Orthodox Church:** Even in Western Europe, dissenters repudiated St. Peter's successors long before the Protestant Reformation split its society in two. Among the most determined and most unfortunate were the puritanical Cathars of southern France, who held that the material world was evil and broke off with opulent, corrupt Rome; the heresy was eventually wiped out, at the cost of as many as a million dead.

23   **Peoples of the Book:** The Quran names the Sabians as a third People of the Book; Islamic scholars later added Zoroastrians and Hindus.

23   **"with wooden saddles":** Philip Khuri Hitti, *History of Syria, Including Lebanon and Palestine* (London: Macmillan, 1951), 543. The caliph was Mutawwakil. Even under less petty regimes, the dhimmi were forbidden to build new places of worship and sometimes to repair old ones, church bells had to be muffled, and proselytizing was a capital crime.

23   **all-powerful foreign minister:** Hasdai ibn Shaprut started out as Abd al-Rahman III's personal physician; from medic to minister was a classic career path for ambitious medieval men.

23   **Sephardi Jews:** Many of Iberia's Jews had migrated there following

the Roman sack of Jerusalem in 70 CE. The Goths had energetically persecuted them; at the end of the seventh century, paranoid that Jews were conspiring to overthrow them, they seized their property and distributed it to their slaves, then enslaved them and forbade them to practice their religion.

24   **Christians took just as happily to Arab culture:** Paul Alvarus, a Jewish convert to Christianity, famously let out a great wail of complaint that the supple, sophisticated Arabic tongue had seduced his coreligionists: "The Christians love to read the poems and romances of the Arabs; they study the Arab theologians and philosophers, not to refute them but to form a correct and elegant Arabic. Where is the layman who now reads the Latin commentaries on the Holy Scriptures, or who studies the Gospels, prophets or Apostles? Alas! All talented young Christians read and study with enthusiasm the Arab books; they gather immense libraries at great expense; they despise the Christian literature as unworthy of attention. They have forgotten their language. For every one who can write a letter in Latin to a friend, there are a thousand who can express themselves in Arabic with elegance, and write better poems in this language than the Arabs themselves." Quoted in John Tolan, *Saracens: Islam in the Medieval European Imagination* (New York: Columbia University Press, 2002), 86.

24   **deflower the Virgin Mary:** Eulogius was eventually arrested for harboring a Muslim girl who had converted to Christianity. At his trial he offered to induct the judge into the Christian religion, then launched into a lecture about the manifold errors of Islam. The judge threw up his hands and sent the prisoner before the ruling council, which was treated to a sermon on the glories of the Gospels. The stubborn monk's Muslim peers admired him as a scholar and a man and begged him to stop his insane mission of self-destruction, but he started up again and was beheaded. See Tolan, *Saracens*, 93; Olivia Remie Constable, ed., *Medieval Iberia: Readings from Christian, Muslim, and Jewish Sources* (Philadelphia: University of Pennsylvania Press, 1997), 51–55.

24   **individuals with their own perceptions and desires:** The awakening is preserved in the era's poetry and song. See Peter Cole, trans. and ed., *The Dream of the Poem: Hebrew Poetry from Muslim*

and Christian Spain, 950–1492 (Princeton, NJ: Princeton University Press, 2007); Salma Khadra Jayyusi, "Andalusi Poetry: The Golden Period," in Jayyusi, ed., *The Legacy of Muslim Spain* (Leiden: Brill, 1992), 317–66.

24 **exotic new crops:** Among them were lemons, limes, grapefruit, figs, pomegranates, watermelons, apricots, almonds, saffron, spinach, artichokes, eggplants, cotton, rice, sugarcane, mulberry trees, henna plants, and palm trees. See Olivia Remie Constable, "Muslim Merchants in Andalusi International Trade," in Jayyusi, *Legacy of Muslim Spain*, 759–73; Richard A. Fletcher, *Moorish Spain* (London: Weidenfeld & Nicolson, 1992), 62–64.

25 **"ornament of the world":** María Rosa Menocal adopts the famous saying as the title of her book about the culture of convivencia. The nun was Hroswitha of Gandersheim.

25 **fifty-two battles:** Or thereabouts; fifty-two is the number given by the pioneering North African historian Ibn Khaldun in the fourteenth century. Al-Mansur owed his initial advancement to a commission by the then chancellor to murder the uncle of the heir to the throne, thus ensuring the delicate boy's accession and the chancellor's influence.

26 **orgies of fratricide:** One king, Sancho of Leon, was pushed off a cliff by his sister to make way for their brother (and possibly her lover) Alfonso the Brave, the future conqueror of Toledo.

27 **a war of religious liberation:** In the late eleventh century, the 27 of Aragon and Navarre declared that his conquests were intended "for the recovery and extension of the Church of Christ, for the destruction of the pagans, the enemies of Christ . . . so that the kingdom . . . might be liberated to the honour and service of Christ; and that once all the people of that unbelieving rite were expelled and the filthiness of their wicked error was eliminated therefrom, the venerable Church of Jesus Christ our Lord may be fostered there forever." O'Callaghan, *Reconquest and Crusade*, 8. It hardly needs saying that the kings of the Reconquest were hungry for land and booty, but in an age when faith defined life it is too easy to read such statements as mere posturing, as opportunism cloaked in a holy habit.

27 **a Spanish field:** The field, the *Campus stellae* or "Field of the star,"

was later held to have lent its name to Santiago de Compostela, the city that grew up around the purported tomb. In 997, Almanzor attacked and burned Santiago and carted away its church bells to be melted down into lamps for Córdoba's Mezquita; more than anything else, his actions made St. James the rallying cry of the Reconquest and Santiago a magnet for international pilgrims. When the Reconquest reached Córdoba, the lamps went back home.

27 **El Cid:** The champion's real name was Rodrigo Diaz; El Cid was the Spanish version of the Arabic honorific *al-sayyid*, or "the lord," which was given him by his Muslim troops.

27 **a synagogue designed by Muslim architects:** The synagogue was eventually stormed by a Christian mob and was turned into the church of Santa Maria la Blanca. The eddy of competing city-states and commingling cultures unleashed by the breakup of al-Andalus has been likened to the Italian Renaissance; see María Rosa Menocal, *The Ornament of the World: How Muslims, Jews, and Christians Created a Culture of Tolerance in Medieval Spain* (Boston: Little, Brown, 2002), 40–41, 144.

27 **fashions, and songs:** Among the most culturally influential figures of al-Andalus was a singer from Baghdad named Ziryab, who became Islamic Spain's arbiter of fashion and manners and brought his repertoire of ten thousand songs of love, loss, and longing to the West. When the Arabic songs crossed the Pyrenees, not least in the mouths of captured *qiyan* or singing girls, they came to the ears of French troubadours, heavily influenced European music and literature, and may have inspired the concept of courtly love. Fletcher, *Moorish Spain*, 43–45; Menocal, *Ornament of the World*, 123.

28 **help from abroad:** The invitation to the Almoravids was extended by Muhammad ibn Abbad al-Mutamid, the emir of Seville, who famously remarked after Toledo fell to Alfonso the Brave that he "would rather be a camel-driver in Africa than a swineherd in Castile." Fletcher, *Moorish Spain*, 111.

28 **The Almohads:** The new rulers did not entirely eradicate al-Andalus's ingrained habits of learning. Ibn Rushd, known in the West as Averroës, was the chief judge of Seville before the Almohads sent him to their Moroccan capital Marrakech as a royal physician. His commentaries on Aristotle, which insisted that science was superior

to religion since God had created a logical universe that could be divined by the application of reason, were translated in Toledo and spurred the development of Scholasticism, the dominant philosophical and theological movement of medieval Europe. Averroës's rationalist beliefs found an unlikely supporter in the Almohad caliph Abu Yaqub Yusuf and were enshrined in the Almohad Creed of 1183, but as religious intolerance mounted, the philosopher was sent into exile and his books were burned. Averroës's contemporary Musa ibn Maymun, known in the West as Maimonides, represents the end of convivencia. The scion of a long line of Arabized Córdoban Jews, he escaped the Almohads' persecutions by moving to Egypt, where he became another royal physician, only to fall foul of more pogroms against Jews. He turned his back on his past, repudiated (in Arabic) Jews' cooperation with Muslims as a disaster, and predicted the eclipse of Islam. Yet his schooling in al-Andalus prepared him to write the most influential of all the Arabic works that tried to reconcile Aristotelian logic with religion, the *Guide for the Perplexed*, as well as medical textbooks that were still heavily used in the Renaissance. The intellectual impact of Muslim Iberia was felt in Europe long after its eclipse.

29 **mysteries of Islam:** The first Latin translation of the Quran was made in 1143.

30 **marched south across Spain:** The pivotal Battle of Las Navas de Tolosa was fought in 1212 across a plain in the eastern foothills of the Sierra Morena, the mountain range that separates Andalusia from La Mancha. According to several contemporary reports, the entire Spanish army became trapped on a plateau and was only saved from catastrophe when a shepherd showed them a sheep run that led down to the Muslim camp. In the usual manner, the shepherd was later revealed to have been none other than a long-dead saint in disguise.

Chapter 2: The Holy Land

31 **Pope Urban II:** Ironically, the pope who inspired vast armies to march east was barely able to enter Rome; a rival pope installed by the Holy Roman Emperor Henry IV, who had been embroiled

in an infamous struggle with Urban's predecessor, Gregory VII, over which of the two wielded supreme power, was nestled there. For years Urban wandered Italy as an exile, dependent on charity and deeply in debt; on the few occasions he made it to Rome, he was forced to barricade himself on an island in the Tiber, hole up in a loyalist's fortress, or helplessly anathematize his rival from outside the walls, while his supporters fought running battles with the so-called antipope's troops. Urban's position was still precarious in 1095, and the backbone of the Crusading army came from his homeland in northern France.

32   **excommunicated the patriarch:** The patriarch returned the favor and excommunicated the legates. Despite doubts about the legality of the decrees, the long-strained ties between the Eastern Orthodox Church and the Roman Catholic Church had finally snapped and would never be restored.

32   **ousted the Umayyad caliphs:** The Abbasids defeated the Umayyads in 750 and moved their capital to Baghdad in 762. Among the few survivors of the bloody banquet was a young prince named Abd al-Rahman, who evaded the bounty hunters all the way to Spain, where he reestablished the Umayyads as the ruling dynasty of al-Andalus.

33   **an embassy from Constantinople:** The extravaganza is recounted by the eleventh-century historian al-Khatib al-Baghdadi; see Hugh Kennedy, *The Court of the Caliphs: The Rise and Fall of Islam's Greatest Dynasty* (London: Weidenfeld & Nicolson, 2004), 153.

34   **a Shia sect:** The sect is the Ismailis, who trace the legitimate line of successors to Muhammad through an imam named Ismail ibn Jafar. A Baghdadi missionary carried their teachings to Tunisia and in 909 roused the local population to overthrow their ruler in favor of a self-proclaimed descendant of the Prophet via Fatima, Ali, and Ismail. In 969 the Fatimids conquered Egypt, which had been ruled for twenty-two years by a eunuch and former slave named Abu al-Misk Kafur (Musky Camphor). One story holds that the new ruler, the caliph al-Muizz, answered religious scholars who doubted his lineage by drawing his sword and showering the floor with gold coins: "There is my lineage," he retorted.

34 **Persian power revived for a time:** The Samanid Empire lasted through most of the ninth and tenth centuries; Bukhara, its capital, rivaled Baghdad as a cultural center. Foremost among its luminaries was the philosopher and physician Ibn Sina, who was long revered in the West as Avicenna; his *al-Qanun* ("The Canon"), a vast encyclopedia of Greek and Arab medical knowledge, was a primary text in European and Asian medical schools well into the modern era.

34 **smashed its armies:** At the Battle of Manzikert in 1071. To complete the humiliation the victorious sultan Alp Aslan killed the vanquished emperor Romanos IV Diogenes with kindness; he lavished gifts on him and sent him home, where his domestic enemies gouged out his eyes. As Constantinople distracted itself with new civil wars the Turks walked virtually unopposed into the vast Anatolian peninsula—Rome's great province of Asia Minor, today the Asian lands of Turkey. In a trice, the empire was reduced to its capital and a vulnerable straggle of hinterland.

34 **Scandalous rumors:** One especially incendiary letter was purportedly addressed to Count Robert of Flanders by the Byzantine emperor Alexius I Comnenus. As well as detailing the wholesale defilement of churches, it alleged that the Turks lined up to violate virgins while making their watching mothers sing obscene songs, and sodomized men of all ages, including clergymen, monks, and even bishops. The letter, which is written in a lurid tabloid style, may be apocryphal, or it may be a later forgery based on real material; either way, the accusations give a startling insight into the pitch to which enmity between Christians and Muslims had risen. Andrew Holt and James Muldoon, eds., *Competing Voices from the Crusades* (Oxford: Greenwood, 2008), 9.

34 **"have completely destroyed":** Robert the Monk, quoted in Thomas F. Madden, *The New Concise History of the Crusades* (Lanham, MD: Rowman & Littlefield, 2005), 8–9. A verbatim report of Urban II's speech has not survived; Robert's version was written twenty years after the event, and its catalog of Muslim depravities may have been intended to validate the First Crusade after the fact.

35 **toward Jerusalem:** Robert the Monk reports Urban II's focus on Jerusalem. In the account of Fulcher of Chartres, who was present at Clermont, the pope instead stresses the need to defend Constanti-

nople against the fast-advancing Turks. In his own letter to the Crusaders, written shortly after the council, Urban II talks about the outrages of the Muslims who had seized "the Holy City of Christ" but does not overtly call for its liberation. In all probability, though, that was his hope. Edward Peters, *The First Crusade: The Chronicle of Fulcher of Chartres and Other Source Materials* (Philadelphia: University of Pennsylvania Press, 1971), 30–31, 16.

35   **one Egyptian ruler:** The Fatimid caliph Al-Hakim, who then controlled Jerusalem, launched a widespread program to destroy Christian churches in Egypt and Palestine. His more tolerant son and heir allowed Constantinople to bribe him into agreeing to the shrine's reconstruction. The Fatimids lost Jerusalem to the Turks in 1073 but recaptured the city in 1098, the year before the Crusaders arrived.

35   **"and does not cease":** Robert the Monk, quoted in Peters, *First Crusade*, 4.

36   **"Hence it is":** Ibid., 3–4.

37   **"marvelous works":** Raymond of Aguilers, quoted in Thomas Asbridge, *The First Crusade: A New History* (London: Free Press, 2004), 316. The estimate of 100,000 dead was considerably in excess of Jerusalem's population at the time, which likely numbered around 30,000.

37   **"seizing infants":** Albert of Aachen, in ibid., 317.

37   **"gulped down":** Fulcher of Chartres, in ibid., 318.

37   **the al-Aqsa Mosque:** The name means "the farthest mosque." A lofty stone building at the southern end of the Temple Mount, it was built well after Muhammad's time but had become popularly identified as the earthly destination of the Prophet's Night Journey. Since there were soon no Muslims left in Jerusalem to explain this, the Crusaders decided it must be the Jewish First Temple built by King Solomon. There were no Jews left, either, to point out that the Babylonian king Nebuchadnezzar had destroyed Solomon's Temple some sixteen centuries before the Crusaders showed up. The first Crusader kings unsuspectingly used the mosque as their palace and then gave it to a new knightly fraternity known as the Poor Fellow-Soldiers of Christ. After the Hebrew history they imagined lay buried beneath the Islamic floor at their Christian feet, the Poor Fellow-Soldiers became known as the Knights Templar.

37   **a nearby rock:** The rock is located under the Dome of the Rock, the Muslim shrine built at the end of the seventh century in a wholly successful attempt to outdo the city's rival religious structures. In Jewish belief, it is the Foundation Stone from which the earth was formed, the altar where Abraham offered to sacrifice his son, and the resting place of the Ark of the Covenant, though all three locations are heavily disputed. In 2000, Israel's then opposition leader Ariel Sharon took a walk on the Temple Mount that provoked a six-year intifada; so the religious layers of Jerusalem continue to pile up.

37   **up to their ankles, their knees, or their bridle reins in blood:** While Muslim writers exaggerated the number of the dead to outrage their coreligionists' feelings, Christian writers exaggerated the number out of pride at performing God's work. Fulcher of Chartres, who was in Jerusalem five months after the conquest, says that nearly 10,000 were killed in the "Temple of Solomon" alone; the Muslim historian Ali ibn al-Athir puts the figure at 70,000. None are to be taken literally; Raymond of Aguilers's line about the blood rising to the horses' bridles is straight out of the book of Revelation.

37   **"in mounds as big as houses":** The anonymous *Gesta Francorum* ("Deeds of the Franks"), quoted in Asbridge, *First Crusade*, 320.

37   **one rapturous monk:** Robert the Monk. Some Christian fundamentalists now believe that Israel is that precursor state.

38   **galloped in silent, tight formation:** For the impression the Templars made on the battlefield, see the anonymous pilgrim's account known as the *Tractatus de locis et statu sanctae terrae* ("Tract on the places and state of the Holy Land"), quoted in Helen Nicholson, *The Knights Templar: A New History* (Stroud, UK: Sutton, 2001), 67–68.

38   **The Templars and Hospitallers lived like monks:** The Templars were allowed no possessions and were sworn to chastity. A dauntingly detailed rulebook laid out their every move; even minor transgressions meant a year of whippings and eating off the ground. The rule eventually ran to 686 clauses. See Malcolm Barber, *The New Knighthood: A History of the Order of the Temple* (Cambridge: Cambridge University Press, 1994), 182, 219–21.

38   **a renegade sect of Shia fanatics:** The Assassins were a radical

band of Ismailis who were frustrated by the failure of the Egyptian Fatimids to impose Shiism on the ummah. The result of their campaign of terror was the discrediting of the whole Shia movement. "To shed the blood of a [Muslim] heretic," wrote one Assassin acolyte, "is more meritorious than to kill seventy Greek infidels." Quoted in Bernard Lewis, *The Assassins: A Radical Sect in Islam* (London: Weidenfeld & Nicolson, 1967), 48.

39 **another devastating defeat on Constantinople:** At the Battle of Myriocephalum. The Christians' cause was not helped when, six years later, the emperor stood by while Orthodox mobs massacred thousands of Catholics who lived in Constantinople and dragged the severed head of the pope's representative through the streets tied to the tail of a dog, an event that in part motivated the mayhem of the Fourth Crusade.

40 **"so as to free the earth of anyone who does not believe in God":** Saladin's words were recorded by his retainer and biographer Baha ad-Din; quoted in Francesco Gabrieli, *Arab Historians of the Crusades* (Berkeley: University of California Press, 1984), 101.

40 **the fresh Muslim troops crushed them in hours:** By the ferocious standards of his age, Saladin was magnanimity itself. The foot soldiers were sold into slavery, and the nobles were held for ransom. The feared warrior-monks of the Hospital and the Temple were not so fortunate. Among their Muslim enemies they were reputed to be more devils than men; clerics lined up to behead them one by one while Saladin, his secretary Imad ad-Din recorded, looked on with a face full of joy. See Barber, *New Knighthood*, 64.

41 **cosmopolitan Sicily:** In the eleventh century two Norman brothers named Roger and Robert Guiscard had wrested Sicily from its Muslim rulers, who had wrested it from Constantinople. The Normans were the descendants of Vikings, or Norsemen, and long after they converted to Christianity, wherever there was a war there were sure to be Normans. Yet the peripatetic warriors quickly adapted to their new homes, and they were especially seduced by sophisticated Sicily. Its governance was put in the capable hands of a meritocracy of Jews, Muslims, and Christians, and religious freedom flourished. Muslim travelers were taken aback at their enthusiastic reception in Christian Palermo, where women went to mass in an Eastern cloud

of silk robes, colored veils, gilt slippers, and henna tattoos, and they were even more surprised to discover that some Normans spoke decent Arabic.

42   **"Rage and sorrow are seated in my heart":** Quoted in Stephen Howarth, *The Knights Templar* (New York: Atheneum, 1982), 223.

43   **the death of their Great Khan:** The Khan then was Ogedei, Genghis Khan's third son and first successor.

44   **"Their situation approached the point of annihilation":** Quoted in Michael W. Dols, *The Black Death in the Middle East* (Princeton, NJ: Princeton University Press, 1977), 67. While Christians saw the plague as God's punishment for mankind's sins, Muslims dealt with the disaster by interpreting it as God's offer of martyrdom for the faithful. That belief was shaken, though not destroyed, when the plague hit Mecca despite Muhammad's prediction that no disease would touch either it or Medina.

45   **the Council of Constance:** The numbers and professions of the attendees are given in Jerry Brotton, *The Renaissance Bazaar: From the Silk Road to Michelangelo* (Oxford: Oxford University Press, 2002), 96. The council, which met from 1414 to 1418, ruled that all men, including the pope himself, were duty-bound to obey its decisions, and it appointed Martin V as the first uncontested pope in nearly a century.

45   **an eternal building site:** "Houses have fallen into ruins, churches have collapsed, whole quarters are abandoned; and the town is neglected and oppressed by famine and poverty," lamented the new pope. Rome's inhabitants, he added, "have been throwing and illicitly hiding entrails, viscera, heads, feet, bones, blood, and skins, besides rotten meat and fish, refuse, excrement, and other fetid and rotting cadavers into the streets . . . and have dared boldly and sacrilegiously to usurp, ruin, and reduce to their own use streets, alleys, piazzas, public and private places both ecclesiastical and profane." From the start the new Rome was planned on a scale to represent and reinforce the glory of the revived church; the people's faith, said Pope Nicholas V, would be "continually confirmed and daily corroborated by great buildings" that were "seemingly made by the hand of God." Eamon Duffy, *Saints and Sinners: A History of the*

Popes, 3rd ed. (New Haven, CT: Yale University Press, 2006), 193; Brotton, *Renaissance Bazaar*, 106.

48   **"We lost the day":** Barbara Tuchman, *A Distant Mirror: The Calamitous Fourteenth Century* (New York: Knopf, 1978), 561.

Chapter 3: A Family War

50   **Crusaders from northern Europe:** In 1147, several boatloads of English, Scottish, Flemish, German, and Norman knights en route to the Second Crusade stopped off for provisions in the port town of Porto. Porto had grown around an old Roman outpost called Portus Cale, which had been retaken from the Berbers in the ninth century; as the scrappy statelet expanded, the name Portus Cale evolved into Portugal. The Crusaders were enticed with tall tales of magnificent treasure to reinforce the army that was besieging Lisbon, and for four burningly hot months they bombarded the citadel. Finally the English built a series of siege towers, breached the walls, and set about pillaging with intent. In the spring of 1189 more Crusaders piled into the Algarve, where they massacred six thousand Muslims and brutally besieged the city of Siles. With the final conquest of the Algarve in 1249, Portugal became the first European nation-state to fix its borders.

50   **a royal chronicler:** Duarte Galvão, *Crónica de D. Afonso Henriques*, quoted in Sanjay Subrahmanyam, *The Career and Legend of Vasco da Gama* (Cambridge: Cambridge University Press, 1997), 162.

51   **routed the attackers:** At the Battle of Aljubarrota. The victory came at the cost of the death or dispersal of most of the old nobility who had sided with Castile; John I confiscated their lands and created a new nobility from among his supporters.

51   **The English and Portuguese had been allies:** After the siege of Lisbon a number of English knights had stayed on; one, Gilbert of Hastings, was installed as Lisbon's first bishop. English soldiers fought on John's side at Aljubarrota, and the year after the battle John I signed the Treaty of Windsor, enshrining between the Portuguese and English kings, "their heirs and successors, and between the subjects of both kingdoms an inviolable, eternal, solid, perpetual and true league of friendship, alliance and union." The treaty is the

oldest extant alliance between European nations. H. V. Livermore, *A New History of Portugal*, 2nd ed. (Cambridge: Cambridge University Press, 1976), 67.

52 **Philippa arrived in Portugal:** Philippa's captivating story is told in T. W. E. Roche, *Philippa: Dona Filipa of Portugal* (London: Phillimore, 1971).

52 **"little blue Englishwoman's eyes":** Ibid., 57.

52 **The prospect of such a pampered entrée:** The primary authority for the planning and execution of the Crusade against Ceuta is the Portuguese chronicler Gomes Eanes de Zurara. His account originally formed a supplement to the Chronicle of King John I by Fernão Lopes, Zurara's predecessor as court chronicler. A recent Portuguese edition is Gomes Eanes de Zurara, *Crónica da tomada de Ceuta* (Mem Martins: Publicações Europa-América, 1992). An abridged translation is given in *Conquests and Discoveries of Henry the Navigator*, ed. Virginia de Castro e Almeida and trans. Bernard Miall (London: Allen & Unwin, 1936).

53 **"great exploits":** Zurara, *Conquests and Discoveries*, 33.

54 **"excellent exercise of arms":** Letter of Duarte I, quoted in Peter Russell, *Prince Henry 'the Navigator': A Life* (New Haven, CT: Yale University Press, 2000), 40.

55 **several times it had granted bulls of Crusade:** The bulls were issued by the Roman popes, whom the Portuguese, along with the English, had supported against the French claimants. The first bull was dated 1341; it was renewed in 1345, 1355, 1375, and 1377.

56 **"I am going to make a request":** Zurara, *Conquests and Discoveries*, 52–53.

57 **"On with you, greybeards!":** Ibid., 57. Behind the scenes, the council was far from unanimous in its support for the plan; many young nobles still hankered after renewing the war with Castile. Zurara's claim that men of ninety were lining up to take part is best read as a poetic assurance that the nation's wisest voices were behind the Crusade.

57 **Italian merchants and sailors:** The Genoese, who were driven to seek out new commercial opportunities when Venice cornered the trade in Asian luxury goods, were the dominant group. In 1317 one Genoese was appointed Portugal's first admiral.

58 **a ruinous piece of chivalric nonsense:** Decades later, creditors were still trying to recover the large sums they had loaned the crown. See Russell, *Prince Henry*, 44.

59 **"I do not know":** Zurara, *Conquests and Discoveries*, 66–67.

60 **the assembled army numbered more than 19,000:** The figures were given by a spy in the service of Ferdinand I of Aragon; Russell, *Prince Henry*, 31. Other estimates ranged as high as 50,000 men.

62 **The king's confessor:** As Peter Russell notes, the priest made much of John I's guilt at having spilled a great deal of Christian blood during the wars against Castile; to salve his conscience, he explained, the king was determined to spill a matching amount of infidel blood. "Presumably," Russell comments, "no one in the royal entourage thought it odd that John's moral discomfort was to be assuaged at huge expense to his people and by yet more spillage of their blood." Ibid., 46.

62 **a new papal bull:** The pope from whom John I secured the bull was John XXIII, the second of the Pisan line of pontiffs elected in opposition to the French and Roman popes. Having been ritually accused of piracy, murder, rape, simony, and incest, John XXIII was deposed at the Council of Constance in May 1415 and was declared an antipope, two months before the Crusade he had endorsed set sail.

63 **The elderly governor:** Salah ben Salah, the governor of Ceuta, was the lord of a string of nearby cities and came from a prominent African seafaring family.

64 **the town would be at their feet:** At this point, Zurara has a throng of young Moroccans seek out the governor of Ceuta and suggest how to seize the enemy fleet, win a great victory, and reap a rich bounty. The Christians were weighed down with heavy armor, they supposedly explained; all that was needed was to meet them on the beaches and knock them to their feet, and they would be unable to get up. Whether or not the governor was given such sage advice—it is hard to conceive how Zurara might have got wind of it—he was mindful of his depleted forces and decided his best hope was to prevent the Portuguese from entering the city. Many of his troops left their defensive positions and swarmed onto the beaches, with disastrous results.

65   **"And to you, Lord":** Zurara, *Conquests and Discoveries*, 98.

65   **"black as a crow":** Ibid., 99.

66   **"Our poor houses look like pigsties":** Quoted in C. R. Boxer, *The Portuguese Seaborne Empire 1415–1825* (London: Hutchinson, 1969), 13.

67   **"did not trouble themselves about such things":** Ibid.

68   **They destroyed the cistern with the townspeople inside:** Valentim Fernandes, *Description de la Côte d'Afrique de Ceuta au Sénégal*, ed. and trans. P. de Cenival and T. Monod (Paris: Larose, 1938), 18–19. The huge cistern was filled from the city's springs; ships that wanted to replenish their water supply from it paid handsomely for the privilege.

68   **long-awaited invasion of France:** Malyn Newitt notes the coincidence in *A History of Portuguese Overseas Expansion, 1400–1668* (London: Routledge, 2005), 19.

Chapter 4: The Ocean Sea

70   **the carefully cultivated legend:** The image of Henry as a lonely man of science who founded a groundbreaking school of navigation dates back to the sixteenth-century Portuguese chronicles; written at the height of empire, they inevitably romanticized its founding father. The legend was enshrined in R. H. Major's nineteenth-century biography of "Prince Henry of Portugal, Surnamed the Navigator," and it has proved hard to dislodge. See Peter Russell, *Prince Henry 'the Navigator': A Life* (New Haven, CT: Yale University Press, 2000), 6–7.

71   **"one large garden":** G. R. Crone, trans. and ed., *The Voyages of Cadamosto, and Other Documents on Western Africa in the Second Half of the Fifteenth Century* (London: Hakluyt Society, 1937), 10.

71   **The Temple in London:** The Temples were not always as secure as their reputation held. In 1263 the future Edward I of England, who was broke along with his father Henry III and the rest of the royal family, was admitted to the London Temple on the pretext of taking a look at the crown jewels; instead he took a hammer to a series of chests and carried off a great haul of other people's money. See Helen Nicholson, *The Knights Templar: A New History* (Stroud, UK: Sutton, 2001), 163.

71   **Philip the Fair:** The French arrest warrants were issued on Fri-

day, October 13, 1307; a papal bull dated that November ordered every Christian ruler in Europe to follow suit. The pope had second thoughts and convened a court that acquitted the Templars on every count, but under renewed French pressure and on the basis that the order was tainted by the scandal that Philip had single-handedly whipped up, it was disbanded by a bull of 1312.

72 **had settled huge tracts of newly seized lands:** In 1131 King Alfonso I of Aragon tried to leave his entire kingdom to the Templars, the Hospitallers, and the monks of the Holy Sepulcher. His brother Ramiro hastily came out of his monastery, fathered a daughter, and married her to the count of Barcelona, who took over as ruler of Aragon. Ramiro retreated to his monk's cell; the Templars were compensated with vast lands and revenues.

72 **the Order of Christ:** In Henry's time the renamed Templar chapter controlled twenty-one towns and extensive lands in central Portugal. By then, though, it had long run out of Muslims to attack, and the knights had enraged the king by refusing to take part in the Crusade against Ceuta on the grounds that they were only obliged to fight at home. John's appointment of Henry as the order's governor amounted to a royal takeover.

73 **push ahead with the Reconquest:** Henry was not alone in refusing to see the Strait of Gibraltar as an obstacle to the Reconquest. As early as 1291, Castile and Aragon agreed a boundary between their prospective fiefdoms in Morocco; in 1400 Castile destroyed the Moroccan town of Tétouan, which was located some twenty-five miles south of Ceuta and was a notorious pirate base. In Roman times northern Morocco had been part of the diocese of Spain, though Castile's claim rested more on its spurious self-identification as the heir to the old Gothic kingdom that it imagined had ruled Morocco as well as Spain.

74 **He never intended to honor the accord:** Henry's reputation rested on his heroics at Ceuta, and his father had put him in charge of the city's defense; to hand it back so soon would have been a desperate personal humiliation, as well as making a mockery of Portugal's newly burnished Crusading credentials.

74 **the Catalan Atlas:** The atlas was made in Majorca by the leading Jewish cartographer Abraham Cresques for Charles V of France.

74   **"So abundant is the gold":** Quoted in Jerry Brotton, *The Re-naissance Bazaar: From the Silk Road to Michelangelo* (Oxford: Oxford University Press, 2002), 55. For once the stories contained a kernel of truth; gold mined in the western Sudan was indeed transported to trading towns like Timbuktu on the edge of the Sahara, where it was forged into ingots and was sent by caravan to North Africa. Mansa Musa, a king of the powerful state of Mali, gained his reputa-tion from the spectacular display of opulence, including 100 camels loaded with gold and 500 slaves bearing heavy gold staffs, which accompanied his hajj to Mecca in 1324.

76   **crept up to the fearsome headland:** Europe's mapmakers, and Henry's sailors, may have mistaken the more dangerous Cape Juby, 140 miles north of Cape Bojador, for the famous landmark; Cape Bojador itself was likely rounded almost unnoticed a decade later. See Russell, *Prince Henry*, 111–13.

76   **Sagres Point:** It was here that Henry's academy was later said to have been located. According to the chronicler João de Barros, Henry had begun to restore an existing village that was subse-quently renamed Vila do Infante, or the Prince's Town; it was likely intended as a service station for passing ships. In the mid-fifteenth century, when Zurara was writing, it was still going up and con-sisted of a perimeter wall, a fortress, a few houses, and no school of navigation. Henry's own fleets left from Lagos, along the Algarve coast to the east.

77   **"ten blacks, male and female":** Gomes Eanes de Zurara, *The Chronicle of the Discovery and Conquest of Guinea*, trans. C. R. Beazley and Edgar Prestage (London: Hakluyt Society, 1896–98), 1:57. The bumper haul was exacted as a ransom for three Muslim prisoners.

77   **"They related so much in this strain":** Crone, *Voyages of Cada-mosto*, 5. Alvise Cadamosto was the Portuguese version of the Vene-tian's real name, Alvide da Ca' da Mosto.

77   **borrowed via the Arabs from the Indian Ocean:** The process of diffusion has been a matter of long debate. See I. C. Campbell, "The Lateen Sail in World History," in *Journal of World History* 6, no. 1 (Spring 1995): 1–23.

79   **built entirely of blocks of salt:** Taghaza, now in the desert of northern Mali, was the site of immensely valuable salt mines, con-

trolled by the Moroccans, that were long a commercial and political hub of North Africa. The rock salt was taken south by throngs of merchants and was exchanged for gold in the Sudan, where it was so prized that it was cut into pieces and used as a currency. The exchange took the form of a silent auction that had been famous since the time of Herodotus. The salt was piled in rows and the merchants retired; the miners approached, placed a quantity of gold by each row, and disappeared. The salt sellers came back and calculated whether to take the gold or hold out for more, the gold sellers returned to take their salt or raise their offer, and the process continued until all deals were done.

79   **Senegal River:** For some time the Portuguese believed the Senegal was a branch of the Nile; the error found its way into the papal bull *Romanus Pontifex* of 1455. The Gambia, Niger, and Congo rivers were also successively mistaken for branches of the Nile.

79   **"It appears to me a very marvelous thing":** Crone, *Voyages of Cadamosto*, 28. To the south were the Wolof and Serer tribes. To the north were the Azanaghi (the modern-day Sanhaja or Zenaga), one of the major groups of the Tuareg peoples, nomadic Berbers who were (and are) the principal inhabitants of the Sahara.

80   **a nearby royal capital:** The capital belonged to one of two Wolof kingdoms with which the Portuguese established trading relations.

81   **"he showed good powers of reasoning":** Crone, *Voyages of Cadamosto*, 41.

81   **"a handsome young negress":** Ibid., 36.

81   **"exceedingly black":** Ibid., 58.

81   **"did not want our friendship":** Ibid., 60.

82   **a German bishop:** Otto of Freising, a half brother of the Holy Roman Emperor. In his *Chronica de duabus civitatibus*, a dual history of Jerusalem and Babel, Otto reports that Bishop Hugh of Jabala in Syria had told him of a Nestorian king in the east named Prester John.

83   **"seven kings":** Quoted in Robert Silverberg, *The Realm of Prester John* (Garden City, NY: Doubleday, 1972), 2. The letter was still in wide circulation in Vasco da Gama's time.

83   **"horned men, one-eyed ones":** Quoted in L. N. Gumilev, *Searches for an Imaginary Kingdom: The Legend of the Kingdom of Prester*

John, trans. R. E. F. Smith (Cambridge: Cambridge University Press, 1987), 6.

84   **Genghis Khan's estranged foster father:** Europeans identified him as Toghrul, king of the Kerait tribes of central Mongolia. Toghrul was the blood brother of Genghis Khan's father and may have been a Nestorian Christian. The story was lent further credence when Toghrul tried to assassinate his former protégé, who had grown too powerful for his liking. The older man was killed when fleeing the battle, and Genghis Khan married his son to Toghrul's niece.

84   **He was briefly killed off when reports arrived:** The reports came from none other than Marco Polo. The Crusader and historian Jean de Joinville has the same story. In the chronicle of William of Rubruck, the king of the Keraits is Prester John's brother; the Mongols defeat both, and Genghis Khan's son marries the Prester's daughter.

84   **The Prester's population:** Much of the gilding on the Prester John legend derives from the inscriptions on world maps; see Russell, *Prince Henry*, 122.

84   **Middle India:** So called to differentiate it from Greater India and Lesser India, or roughly the Indian subcontinent and Indochina. The names are Marco Polo's; Ethiopia was also termed *India Tertia*, or the Third India. The divisions were for the experts; to most people, any mysterious place east of the River Nile was generally believed to be one part or another of the Indies.

84   **Some said it was separated from Egypt:** See *Travelers in Disguise: Narratives of Eastern Travel by Poggio Bracciolini and Ludovico de Varthema*, trans. John Winter Jones, rev. Lincoln Davis Hammond (Cambridge, MA: Harvard University Press, 1963), 42.

85   **"as far as the Indians":** Russell, *Prince Henry*, 121.

86   **the goods the explorers brought home:** Ibid., 202, 211.

86   **another way of advancing the struggle against Islam:** The claim was not as hypocritical as it now sounds. At a time when church and state were inextricably linked, the religious health and the secular wealth of nations were impossible to disentangle. The old Crusaders had never seen anything odd about yoking together religion, war, power, and profit, and neither did the new. Wealth

was God's blessing; one medieval Italian merchant headed every page of his ledgers with the invocation "In the name of God and of Profit." C. R. Boxer, *The Portuguese Seaborne Empire 1415–1825* (London: Hutchinson, 1969), 18.

86 **"There you might see mothers abandoning their children":** Gomes Eanes de Zurara, *Conquests and Discoveries of Henry the Navigator*, ed. Virginia de Castro e Almeida and trans. Bernard Miall (London: Allen & Unwin, 1936), 160–61.

87 **"for these could not run so fast":** Ibid., 164–66.

88 **"For some kept their heads low":** Zurara, *Discovery and Conquest of Guinea*, 1:81–82.

89 **"Now," recorded Zurara:** Russell, *Prince Henry*, 246.

90 **pirates of the Barbary Coast:** The slaves were mainly seized from coastal villages in Spain, Portugal, and Italy, but the Barbary slavers also raided France, England, Ireland, and the Netherlands, and even Iceland and North America. Europe was forced to fork out tributes in an attempt to keep them off, while the United States' first overseas military action was conducted against the pirates, in the First and Second Barbary Wars of 1801–1805 and 1815. See Joshua E. London, *Victory in Tripoli: How America's War with the Barbary Pirates Established the U.S. Navy and Shaped a Nation* (Hoboken, NJ: Wiley, 2005).

90 **"wonderful new things that await them":** Russell, *Prince Henry*, 244. For Zurara's Noah and Cain theory, see *Discovery and Conquest of Guinea*, 2:147. Within forty years the Portuguese were acting as middlemen between African chiefs and Muslim slavers, and any pretense that they were in the business of saving souls was dropped. The practice was eventually stopped when King John III (1521–1557) realized he was consigning the captives to eternal damnation, something that had apparently escaped his predecessors.

90 **20,000 Africans:** The estimate is given in Russell, *Prince Henry*, 258. The figure of 150,000 is in Boxer, *Portuguese Seaborne Empire*, 31.

91 **the pope issued a bull:** *Dum Diversas*, dated June 18, 1452, issued by Pope Nicholas V. Not every pope countenanced slavery; in the bull *Sicut dudum* of 1435, Eugene IV threatened slavers with excommunication.

Chapter 5: The End of the World

92   **a besieged Constantinople:** Eyewitness accounts of the siege include the detailed diary of Nicolò Barbaro, an aristocratic Venetian surgeon fond of talking up his fellow citizens' role in the defense; the chronicle of George Phrantzes, the city's chancellor; and the letter to the pope written by Leonard of Chios, the bishop of Lesbos, who was in Constantinople to negotiate the union of the Churches. These narratives are collected in J. R. Melville Jones, ed., *The Siege of Constantinople: Seven Contemporary Accounts* (Amsterdam: Hakkert, 1972). For histories of Byzantium and the siege, see Steven Runciman, *The Fall of Constantinople: 1453* (Cambridge: Cambridge University Press, 1965); John Julius Norwich, *Byzantium: The Decline and Fall* (London: Viking, 1995); and Roger Crowley, *Constantinople: The Last Great Siege, 1453* (London: Faber & Faber, 2005).

93   **a keen student of history:** During the siege, Mehmet employed a small staff of Italian humanists to read him edifying excerpts from the classical historians. See Franz Babinger, *Mehmed the Conqueror and His Time* (Princeton, NJ: Princeton University Press, 1978).

93   **visited the pope:** In 1438 Emperor John VIII Paleologus journeyed to Florence and proposed the union as the only way to prevent the fall of Constantinople. Delegations arrived from across the lands of the Eastern Church, bringing with them a treasure trove of classical and early Christian manuscripts, and the Decree of Union was signed on July 6, 1439. It was never put into effect; the people of Constantinople refused to accept the merger, and the Italians refused to provide them with military aid. In 1452, with the Ottomans at the gates, the last emperor Constantine XI wrote to Rome promising to enact the agreement, but the pope failed to convince the European powers to act in time.

93   **a charnel house of holy relics:** The relics played an important part in the imperial mythos. The passion relics represented the emperor's divinely ordained authority; Moses's rod and the trumpets from the fall of Jericho, which held pride of place in the old palace, conferred the legitimacy of deep history. The perhaps spurious letter addressed by the emperor Alexius to Count Robert of Flanders

on the eve of the First Crusade took care to list the city's full panoply of covetable relics.

94 **a mark of his extreme holiness:** Andrew lived rough on the
streets of Constantinople and only revealed his holy wisdom to his
disciple Epiphanios. The popular phenomenon of Fools-for-Christ
found corroboration in Paul's first letter to the Corinthians: "Let
no man deceive himself. If any man among you seemeth to be wise
in this world, let him become a fool, that he may be wise. For the
wisdom of this world is foolishness with God." They were believed
to be engaged in a battle with self-pride by deliberately inviting
ridicule, insults, and beatings, or to be feigning madness so they
could provide spiritual guidance without earning praise, and their
pronouncements were combed for prophetic wisdom unavailable to
saner sermonizers.

94 **"No nation whatever":** Nikephoros, *The Life of St. Andrew the
Fool*, ed. and trans. Lennart Rydén (Stockholm: Uppsala University,
1995), 2:261.

95 **"But what is that terrible news":** Quoted in Jerry Brotton, *The
Renaissance Bazaar: From the Silk Road to Michelangelo* (Oxford: Oxford University Press, 2002), 49.

96 **spurred on the gathering Renaissance:** A direct bridge was thus
built between the classical age and the Renaissance that allowed Europe to forget the vital contribution of the Islamic world to its rebirth
of learning. While the rediscovery of Latin and subsequently Greek
literature was largely a Western undertaking, the work of Muslim
philosophers, astronomers, and physicians continued to inspire Europe's scientists and thinkers well into the modern era.

96 **George of Trebizond:** See John Monfasani, *George of Trebizond: A
Biography and a Study of His Rhetoric and Logic* (Leiden: Brill, 1976),
131–36. George's zeal to serve the Conqueror landed him in jail and
nearly cost him his life.

97 **set sail for Italy:** Mehmet's fleet captured the Italian port city of
Otranto in 1480, but the invasions stopped with his death the next
year and the consequent tussle among his sons over the Ottoman
throne. If they had continued, Europe might have had a very different future; a few years later, the French conquered much of Italy
with little trouble.

97   **the Feast of the Pheasant:** See Marie-Thérèse Caron and Denis Clauzel, eds., *Le Banquet du Faisan* (Arras: Artois Presses Université, 1997). Phillip had founded an order of chivalry named the Knights of the Golden Fleece to celebrate his marriage to Isabel of Portugal.

98   **"the sublimity of spirit":** Peter Russell, *Prince Henry 'the Navigator': A Life* (New Haven, CT: Yale University Press, 2000), 320.

99   **the long papal bull:** *Romanus Pontifex*, issued by Nicholas V on January 8, 1455. The original text and English translation are in Frances Gardiner Davenport, ed., *European Treaties Bearing on the History of the United States and Its Dependencies to 1648* (Washington, DC: Carnegie Institution of Washington, 1917), 13–26. In 1456, the new pope Callistus III confirmed the terms of the previous bulls and, at Henry's request, conceded to his Order of Christ spiritual jurisdiction over all regions conquered then or in the future from Cape Bojador, through Guinea, and beyond to the Indies.

100   **his contract was terminated:** Gomes was so successful that he was ennobled by the king and was given a new coat of arms—"a shield with crest and three heads of negroes on a field of silver, each with golden rings in ears and nose, and a collar of gold around the neck, and 'da Mina' as a surname, in memory of its discovery." G. R. Crone, trans. and ed., *The Voyages of Cadamosto, and Other Documents on Western Africa in the Second Half of the Fifteenth Century* (London: Hakluyt Society, 1937), 109–10.

100   **Europe was born of an abduction from the East:** Mark P. O. Morford and Robert J. Lenardon, *Classical Mythology*, 6th ed. (Oxford: Oxford University Press, 1999), 291–93. According to Herodotus, the pattern of revenge kidnappings continued until the Trojan prince Paris abducted Helen of Sparta and provoked the Trojan War.

101   **"Thus saith the Lord God":** Ezekiel 5:5.

101   **the spring of humanity itself:** The Bible revealed that the world was a little over six thousand years old, and civilizations were known to have flourished long ago in the East. Asia was thus the natural location for the birthplace of mankind, a belief that was still taken for granted in the early seventeenth century by the French traveler Jean Mocquet. Asia, he wrote, "is of very great Extent, Riches, and Fertility, and ever very renowned for having born the greatest Mon-

archies, and first Empires, as of the Assyrians, Babylonians, Persians, Greeks, Parthians, Arabians, Tartars, Mongols, Chineses, and other Indians. But above all, this Part is the most esteemed, for the Creation of the first Man, planted in the Terrestrial Paradise, Colonies and Peoples coming from thence, and dispersed through the rest of the World, and moreover, for the Redemption of Mankind, and the Operation of our Salvation acted therein; besides, for having given Religion, Science, Arts, Laws, Policy, Arms, and Artifices, to all the other Parts." "Preface," *Travels and Voyages into Africa, Asia, and America, the East and West Indies; Syria, Jerusalem, and the Holy Land,* trans. Nathaniel Pullen (London, 1696).

101   **The vast encyclopedia compiled by St. Isidore:** St. Isidore was a seventh-century archbishop of Seville who was instrumental in converting the Goths to Catholicism. His *Etymologiae,* the first medieval encyclopedia, was a *summa* of universal knowledge that ran to 448 chapters in twenty volumes.

101   **"makes up a sizeable part of the earth's mass":** Quoted in Jean Delumeau, *History of Paradise: The Garden of Eden in Myth and Tradition,* trans. Matthew O'Connell (New York: Continuum, 1995), 53. The *Polychronicon* was written by an English Benedictine monk named Ranulf Higden.

102   **an actual encounter with Paradise:** The story was told in *Alexandri Magni iter ad paradisum* ("The Journey of Alexander the Great to Paradise"); written by a Jewish author between 1100 and 1175, it was subsequently translated into French and was incorporated, with variations, into the *Roman d'Alexandre* and other Alexandrian tales. See Delumeau, *History of Paradise,* 46.

102   **"monstrous races":** Pliny the Elder categorized the races in the first century CE. For a wide-ranging account of the monstrous, particularly the canine, in folklore and myth, see David Gordon White, *Myths of the Dog-man* (Chicago: University of Chicago Press, 1991).

102   **Adam and Eve fleeing the garden:** See Scott D. Westrem, "Against Gog and Magog," in Sylvia Tomasch and Sealy Gilles, eds., *Text and Territory: Geographical Imagination in the European Middle Ages* (Philadelphia: University of Pennsylvania Press, 1998), 54–75, 60.

103   **the End Times of the earth:** At first many Europeans believed the Mongols were the biblical scourge; see Kurt Villads Jensen, "Dev-

ils, Noble Savages, and the Iron Gate: Thirteenth-Century European Concepts of the Mongols," in *Bulletin of International Medieval Research* 6 (2000): 1–20. Andrew the Fool painted a vivid picture of what would happen when God opened the gates. Seventy-two kings would pour out, he prophesied, "with their people, the so-called filthy nations, who are more disgusting than any conceivable defilement and stench. They will spread over the whole earth under heaven, eating the flesh of living men and drinking their blood, devouring dogs, rats, frogs and every kind of filth on earth with pleasure. . . . The sun will turn into blood, seeing the abominations vying with each other on earth." Nikephoros, *Life of St. Andrew*, 2:277–83.

104 **a king's ransom of Eastern delights:** Paul Freedman, *Out of the East: Spices and the Medieval Imagination* (New Haven, CT: Yale University Press, 2008), 6.

104 **Spices did not just tickle the palate:** The persistent notion that the purpose of spices was to mask the taste of rancid meat has long been disproved. Since nearly all food was produced locally, it was usually fresh; in any case, spices were considerably more expensive than meat. Spices were used to liven up meat and fish that were salted to last through the winter and to make rough wines palatable, but mostly their taste was enjoyed for its own sake.

105 **"a small member":** Sheikh Mohammed al-Nefzaoui, *The Perfumed Garden*, trans. Sir Richard Burton, quoted in Jack Turner, *Spice: The History of a Temptation* (New York: Random House, 2004), 222. Among a great deal else, the sheikh also advised applying chewed cubeb pepper or cardamom grains to the head of the member to "procure for you, as well as for the woman, a matchless enjoyment."

105 **"so imperfectly that the bottom layer is left undisturbed":** Desiderius Erasmus, letter to Francis, physician to the Cardinal of York, n.d. [Basel, December 27, 1524?], quoted in E. P. Cheyney, *Readings in English History Drawn from the Original Sources* (Boston: Ginn, 1922), 317. The full letter is in *The Correspondence of Erasmus: Letters 1356 to 1534, 1523–1524*, trans. R. A. B. Mynors and Alexander Dalzell (Toronto: University of Toronto Press, 1992), 470–72.

106 **the Black Death:** The bubonic plague was of course spread by the bite of an infected flea found on rodents.

106 **ambergris:** Arab tradition generally held that ambergris floated upward from a fountain on the ocean floor, though in *The Arabian Nights*, Sinbad places the spring on an island and says that monsters gobble up the precious substance before regurgitating it in the sea. It was also believed to ease childbirth, to prevent epilepsy, and to relieve suffocation of the womb, a peculiarly medieval disease in which the uterus was said to move around the belly and up to the throat and induce hysteria. Copious sex, according to one authority, was the best remedy, but anointing the vagina with aromatic oils or inserting burnt herbs in a penis-shaped metal fumigator helped lure the womb back down. Freedman, *Out of the East*, 15; Helen Rodnite Lemay, *Women's Secrets: A Translation of Pseudo-Albertus Magnus's De Secretis Mulierum with Commentaries* (Albany: State University of New York Press, 1992), 131–32.

106 **the apothecaries' under-the-counter goods:** *Circa Instans* (1166), quoted in Freedman, *Out of the East*, 14. Freedman notes that fine linens, cottons, and silks, rare dyes, animal pelts, ivory, and even parrots were sometimes classed alongside spices.

108 **"that damned pepper":** Ulrich von Hutten, quoted in Freedman, *Out of the East*, 147.

108 **clung to visiting angels:** Angels, revealed St. Andrew the Fool, smelled of a marvelously sweet perfume "which emanates from the terrible and unapproachable Godhead. For as they stand before the terrible throne of the Almighty they receive the fragrance of the lightning which it emits, after which they cense with the ineffable fragrance of the Godhead incessantly. Now when they have decided to give somebody a share of this sweetness they place themselves in front of him and tap his face with the divine fragrance to the degree they find appropriate, so that this person in his rejoicing is at a loss to explain whence comes this most pleasant odour." Nikephoros, *Life of St. Andrew*, 2:287.

108 **had established a regular trade:** The voyage to India is described in the *Periplus of the Erythraean Sea*, a detailed set of sailing instructions written by a Greek-speaking sailor in the first century CE.

109 **"The greedy merchants":** Quoted in Turner, *Spice*, 81; John Dryden's translation. Like their medieval successors, Roman moralists complained that spices were at best superfluous, at worst harm-

ful, and in any case a huge waste of money. Hunger, Cicero declared in the plain old Roman style, was the best spice.

109 **the earthly Paradise:** Adam, explained the fourth-century theologian St. Ephrem the Syrian, fed on nothing but the perfumed unguents that dripped from the garden's trees. Freedman, *Out of the East*, 90.

110 **"When morning comes":** Jean de Joinville, *History of Saint Louis*, in *Chronicles of the Crusades*, trans. M. R. B. Shaw (Harmondsworth, UK: Penguin, 1963), 212. Joinville was a participant in the Seventh Crusade; less alluringly, he also saw the bloated, plague-ridden bodies of his companions float down the Nile after the disastrous Battle of al-Mansurah.

110 **"The pepper forests are guarded by serpents":** Quoted in Freedman, *Out of the East*, 133–34.

110 **"The Arabians say that the dry sticks":** So Herodotus had reported long ago, and no Westerner had the wherewithal to doubt him. Quoted in Andrew Dalby, *Dangerous Tastes: The Story of Spices* (London: British Museum Press, 2000), 37.

111 **Missionaries led the way:** In 1253 a Franciscan friar named William of Rubruck set out from Constantinople, trekked four thousand miles across the steppes and deserts of Central Asia, and reached the court of the Great Khan at Karakorum, where he took part in a remarkable debate with representatives of Islam, Buddhism, Manicheanism, and rival Christian denominations. Though William failed to win any converts, he enjoyed plenty of the Mongols' potent national beverage of fermented mare's milk and took care to record their customs and culture. Notable among his successors was the Franciscan missionary John of Montecorvino, who arrived in Beijing in 1294, built two churches, trained Chinese altar boys and choirboys, translated the New Testament into the Mongol language, made several thousand converts, and was consecrated archbishop of Beijing. In 1361 Catholicism disappeared from China along with the Mongols. See Peter Jackson, trans., *The Mission of Friar William of Rubruck: His Journey to the Court of the Great Khan Möngke 1253–1255*, ed. David Morgan (London: Hakluyt Society, 1990).

111 **merchants soon followed:** By 1340 the nine-month journey from

the Crimea to Beijing was common enough to merit its own guide-book. Its author, a Florentine merchant named Francesco Pego-lotti, assured his readers that the road was "perfectly safe whether by day or by night," though he advised growing a long beard as a precaution. Italian merchants settled along the route, and a few other Europeans eventually followed. One papal envoy arrived at the Mongol court only to find several Russians, an Englishman, a Parisian goldsmith, and a Frenchwoman who had been abducted in Hungary already there. See Pegolotti, *Pratica della Mercatura*, in Henry Yule and Henri Cordier, trans. and eds., *Cathay and the Way Thither, Being a Collection of Medieval Notices of China* (London: Hakluyt Society, 1913–1916), 3:143–71.

112   **two missionary friars:** The two were John of Montecorvino, the future archbishop of Beijing, and the Dominican Nicholas of Pistoia. John spent more than a year preaching on India's Coromandel Coast; Nicholas died there.

112   **Odoric of Pordenone:** The friar was among the best traveled of all medieval Europeans. Setting out from Constantinople, he headed for Tabriz, Baghdad, and Hormuz, took ship to India and Ceylon (Sri Lanka), and struck out for Sumatra and Java before arriving in China.

112   **the Malabar Coast:** The narrow coastal plain of southwest India between the Arabian Sea and the Western Ghats, now in the states of Kerala and Karnataka.

114   **"Who could count the many shops":** Canon Pietro Casola, quoted in Brotton, *Renaissance Bazaar*, 38. The Milanese priest visited Venice in 1494.

115   **One deputation arrived in Florence:** Ibid., 2.

115   **"Everything that is sold in Egypt":** Quoted in C. F. Beckingham, "The Quest for Prester John," in C. F. Beckingham and Bernard Hamilton, eds., *Prester John: The Mongols and the Ten Lost Tribes* (Aldershot, UK: Variorum, 1966), 276. In 1322 Adam became archbishop of Sultaniyah and thus head of the Catholic Church in Persia.

116   **"If our lord the Pope":** Quoted in Harry W. Hazard, ed., *A History of the Crusades*, 2nd ed. (Madison: University of Wisconsin Press, 1975), 3:543. Sévérac was made bishop of Quilon, now Kollam.

116   **an elaborate manual for reviving the Crusades:** Sanudo's work,

Liber secretorum fidelum crucis, was first submitted to Pope Clement V in 1309 and then, with revisions, to King Charles IV of France in 1323. As well as maps, Sanudo supplied ready-made battle plans and a wealth of logistical information.

117 **the mapmakers did not think the earth was flat:** The notion that everyone before Columbus believed the earth was flat is a nineteenth-century fable, largely propagated by Washington Irving's 1828 fantasy *The Life and Voyages of Christopher Columbus*. See Jeffrey Burton Russell, *Inventing the Flat Earth: Columbus and Modern Historians* (New York: Praeger, 1991).

117 **they would have been unreachable by the Gospel:** Romans 10:18.

118 **Niccolò de' Conti:** Conti's story amply repays further study. The Venetian learned Arabic in Syria and Persian in Iran, then traveled with Muslim merchants to India. There he married, and he dragged his growing brood around Indonesia and Indochina, Arabia and East Africa. In Cairo he converted to Islam to protect them, but almost immediately the plague carried off his wife and two of his four children. He set out for home and sought a papal audience to ask forgiveness for renouncing his faith; as penance, the pope ordered him to dictate an account of his travels to Poggio Bracciolini, an apostolic secretary and leading humanist. Despite its occasional fantasies—including two neighboring islands, one inhabited solely by men and the other by women, whose amorous exchanges were curtailed by the fact that anyone who stayed off their own island for six months dropped dead on the spot—his report corroborated many of Marco Polo's claims, clarified others, and was a major step forward in Europe's knowledge of the Indian Ocean. An English translation by John Winter Jones was published in 1857 by the Hakluyt Society and is reprinted, revised by Lincoln Davis Hammond, in *Travelers in Disguise: Narratives of Eastern Travel by Poggio Bracciolini and Ludovico de Varthema* (Cambridge, MA: Harvard University Press, 1963).

118 **Fra Mauro's map:** The cartographer monk also displaced Jerusalem from its customary bull's-eye position, a move so radical that he felt it necessary to mount an ingenious self-defense. "Jerusalem is indeed the center of the inhabited world latitudinally, though longitudinally it is somewhat to the west," he carefully inscribed on

his map, "but since the western portion is more thickly populated by reason of Europe, therefore Jerusalem is also the center longitudinally if we regard not empty space but the density of population." See Piero Falchetta, *Fra Mauro's World Map* (Turnhout, Belgium: Brepols, 2006).

119   **a junk had rounded Africa:** The caption actually reads "an Indian ship or junk," which suggests that it may not have been Chinese at all. Despite the ambiguities, Fra Mauro's comment has been taken as a major plank of evidence that the Chinese explored the Atlantic Ocean and may have reached the Americas before the Spanish or Portuguese.

120   **much farther to the north:** Given the topographical details Fra Mauro draws in the hinterland, the region he puts at the continent's southern extremity may be the Horn of Africa; or perhaps, given the large island he places off Africa's southern tip, the channel he shows flowing around Africa is the Mozambique Channel and the island is Madagascar.

Chapter 6: The Rivals

121   **La Beltraneja:** Joan's cause was not helped by the fact that her mother subsequently had two children with the nephew of a bishop, a flagrant demonstration of fecundity that finally drove Henry to divorce her.

121   **War broke out:** The War of the Castilian Succession was fought from 1475 to 1479, when the two nations concluded the Treaty of Alcáçovas. As well as settling the succession on Isabella, the treaty also tidied up, for a while, the competing Portuguese and Spanish claims in the Atlantic. Portugal was finally forced to accept Castilian control of the Canaries; Spain confirmed Portugal's possession of the Azores, Madeira, and Cape Verde islands and its sole rights to "lands discovered or to be discovered . . . from the Canary Islands down toward Guinea." Frances Gardiner Davenport, ed., *European Treaties Bearing on the History of the United States and Its Dependencies to 1648* (Washington, DC: Carnegie Institution of Washington, 1917), 44.

122   **Abraham Zacuto:** Zacuto was a famous teacher of astronomy in

Spain until 1492, when he joined the exodus of Jews to Portugal and became John II's astronomer royal. Five years after arriving, he escaped Manuel I's forced conversions and moved to Tunis and Jerusalem. As well as drawing up astronomical tables that were developed by his pupil Joseph Vizinho for practical use at sea, he designed the first metal astrolabe and was an influential proponent of Vasco da Gama's expedition. Joseph Vizinho arrived in Portugal shortly after John II's accession in 1481; in 1485 he went to sea to conduct experiments in calculating a ship's latitude. According to the chronicler João de Barros, also on the junta were Rodrigo, the king's physician, and the German cartographer and astronomer Martin Behaim, who was in Lisbon from 1480.

123   **"In the year 6681":** Quoted in Edgar Prestage, *The Portuguese Pioneers* (London: A. & C. Black, 1933), 208.

123   **Whale Bay:** Or Walvis Bay, as it was renamed by the Dutch and, along with the Namibian port it shelters, is still known.

123   **he died on his way home:** Years later, a carved stone inscribed with Cão's name was found on the banks of the Congo (which the Portuguese named the Zaire). Barros, though, says Cão returned to Portugal, while other sources say he died at Cape Cross. See Prestage, *Portuguese Pioneers*, 210.

124   **proselytization was painfully slow:** The rate increased with the baptism of the king of Kongo, the dominant ruler of western Central Africa, in 1491; named Nzinga Nkuwu, he took the Christian name John. Though he and many of his court soon returned to their traditional beliefs, his son and heir Afonso defeated his lapsed brother with the aid of Portuguese weapons and, he claimed, a timely apparition of St. James. Afonso's descendants entrenched the Catholic Church at the cost of a fraught relationship with the Portuguese and much damage to Kongo's traditional culture.

124   **a more promising pair:** The fullest account of Covilhã and Paiva's mission is still that of the Conde de Ficalho, *Viagens de Pedro da Covilhan* (Lisbon: A. M. Pereira, 1898). The report of the priest who discovered Covilhã in Ethiopia is in Francisco Alvares, *Narrative of the Portuguese Embassy to Abyssinia During the Years 1520–1527*, trans. and ed. Lord Stanley of Alderley (London: Hakluyt Society, 1881); a revised edition edited by C. F. Beckingham and G. W. B. Hunting-

ford was published in 1961. The Portuguese chronicles supply more details, and I have used the accounts of near-contemporary travelers to fill in the background of the journey.

124 **Pêro da Covilhã:** His first name is also given as Pedro (of which Pêro is an archaic form), João, João Pêro, or Juan Pedro; his last name as da Covilhã, da Covilhã, de Covilhã, de Covilham, or Covilhão. In an entertaining coincidence, the Indian Embassy in Lisbon is today located on Rua Pêro da Covilhã.

125 **Afonso de Paiva:** His birthplace was Castelo Branco, a little to the south of the town of Covilhã. On its conquest from the Moors it had been given to the Templars, who defended the town against the frequent attacks from across the nearby Spanish border.

125 **Joseph Vizinho:** The third expert is named Master Moyses (or Moses) in some sources. Ficalho concludes that Moyses was christened Joseph Vizinho when he was baptized; see *Viagens de Pedro da Covilhã*, 55.

125 **whether it was really possible to sail around Africa:** According to Giovanni Battista Ramusio, in his *Navigazioni e Viaggi*, a famous compendium of travel writing published in Venice between 1550 and 1559. This last instruction is not mentioned in the Portuguese sources; see Ficalho, *Viagens de Pedro da Covilhã*, 56–63.

126 **"his capacity was not greater":** Alvares, *Portuguese Embassy*, 267.

126 **"which were so long":** Damião de Góis, quoted in Henry H. Hart, *Sea Road to the Indies* (London: William Hodge, 1952), 239. Góis also says that Manuel was of good stature, held his head erect, and had a pleasant expression, but his description is unusually free of the usual airbrushing.

126 **a powerful Florentine banker:** The banker was named Bartolomeo Marchionni; he was reputedly the richest man in Lisbon. By now there was a sizable Florentine community in Portugal involved in banking and shipping; Marchionni was its most prominent member and did a good deal of business with the crown.

126 **cashed in their check:** The bank they visited was run by the sons of Cosimo de' Medici; the hugely wealthy Florentine family had offices throughout Italy.

127 **"At this time [Alexandria] looks very glorious without":** Ibid., 392.

127   **"sav'd a great part":** "The Travels of Martin Baumgarten . . . through Egypt, Arabia, Palestine and Syria," in Awnsham Churchill, ed., *A Collection of Voyages and Travels* (London: A. and J. Churchill, 1704), 1:391.

129   **"one little hand":** Wilfred Blunt, *Pietro's Pilgrimage: A Journey to India and Back at the Beginning of the Seventeenth Century* (London: James Barrie, 1953), 58.

129   **"in sport":** Ibid., 55.

129   **dated back to classical times:** "On the pyramid," wrote Herodotus, "there is an inscription in Egyptian characters which records the quantity of radishes, onions, and garlic consumed by the laborers who constructed it." Ibid., 57.

129   **"They do positively aver":** "Travels of Martin Baumgarten," 397. For more on medieval Cairo and other Islamic cities, see Joseph W. Meri, ed., *Medieval Islamic Civilization: An Encyclopedia* (New York: Routledge, 2006); Michael Dumper and Bruce E. Stanley, eds., *Cities of the Middle East and North Africa: A Historical Encyclopedia* (Oxford: ABC-Clio, 2007).

130   **"metropolis of the world":** Quoted in Albert Habib Hourani, *A History of the Arab Peoples* (Cambridge, MA: Harvard University Press, 2002), 3.

130   **"surpasses reality":** Ibn Khaldun, *An Arab Philosophy of History: Selections from the Prolegomena of Ibn Khaldun of Tunis (1332–1406)*, trans. and ed. Charles Issawi (Princeton, NJ: Darwin, 1987), 4.

132   **"and tho' one should deface them":** "Travels of Martin Baumgarten," 401.

134   **the same sewn planks:** Nails were unknown in Indian Ocean ships; superstitious sailors were said to believe that great undersea magnets would pull them out, while the more practical prized the dhow's flexibility, which made it easier to beach and more resilient if it struck a shoal.

135   **"very strangely attyred":** The sixteenth-century English traveler Ralph Fitch, quoted in Hart, *Sea Road to the Indies*, 71.

135   **"the dirtiest, most disagreeable, and most stinking town":** Quoted in Ross E. Dunn, *The Adventures of Ibn Battuta* (Berkeley: University of California Press, 1989), 122. The Somali town is mostly known today as Seylac.

137   **He wrote a long dispatch to the king:** The question of whether Covilhã's letter ever reached Lisbon has long fascinated historians. The sixteenth-century chronicler Fernão Lopes de Castanheda first said it did and then, in a later edition, suggested it didn't. His contemporaries Gaspar Correia and Garcia de Resende say it did, but only after John II's death; Resende adds that it arrived after Vasco da Gama had left. Ramusio says it did, and it contained the news that Portugal's ships could easily reach the Indian Ocean. James Bruce, an eighteenth-century Scottish explorer of Ethiopia, was adamant that it did and added an imaginative account of its contents, including detailed maps, to boot. Vasco da Gama certainly knew where to head for when he reached India, though he was undoubtedly ignorant of what he would find when he got there. It seems most likely that at least one of the two Jewish travelers made it home with news, if not written proof, of Covilhã's discoveries, but the truth, alas, will almost certainly never be known.

138   **Muhammad's burial place:** According to tradition, Muhammad was buried in the apartment of his favorite wife, Aisha, the site of which was later covered by repeated rebuildings of the adjoining mosque, including a total reconstruction after a fire in 1481. Medieval Christians spread the rumor that the iron tomb was suspended in the air and then ridiculed the supposed miracle by explaining that it was held up by magnets.

138   **the court of Alexander:** The name Alexander is the Westernized version of Eskender. At its height around the third century CE, Ethiopia was an important power whose lands stretched south to Sudan and east to Arabia. The Solomonid Dynasty, of which Alexander was a member, survived from 1270 to 1974.

139   **he was Christian:** Ethiopia officially adopted Christianity in the early fourth century, after its ruler was converted by a Greek courtier who as a boy had been kidnapped by pirates from a passing ship. Isolated from much of Christendom by the Islamic conquests, it had preserved its own traditions, including polygamy.

139   **"with much pleasure and joy":** Alvares, *Portuguese Embassy*, 270.

139   **"he was not in a position to grant it":** Ramusio, quoted in Hart, *Sea Road to the Indies*, 76. To his surprise, Covilhã discovered he was not the only European in Ethiopia. An Italian friar turned

artist claimed to have lived there for forty years; Alvares noted that
"he was a very honorable person, and a great gentleman, although a
painter." Another European, a throwback to the ascetic masochism
of the desert fathers, lived in a cavern in a ravine; after twenty years
he bricked up the entrance from the inside and presumably died
soon after. Other Europeans intermittently showed up; some came
voluntarily, some were cast ashore by pirates, and almost none were
permitted to leave.

139   **fat, rich, happy:** The Portuguese embassy arrived around May
1520, and Covilhã, now seventy-three or seventy-four, regaled
Francisco Alvares with his adventures. He was, the friar wrote with
nice understatement, a man "who did everything he was ordered to
do, and gave an account of it all."

140   **August 1487:** The record is unusually silent on Dias's voyage. No
official report, log, journal, or chart survives; not all the chroniclers
mention it even in passing. Barros, who gives a brief summary, says
Dias left in August 1486 and returned in December 1487. The few
contemporary witnesses—including Duarte Pacheco Pereira, whose
fever-stricken and shipwrecked crew was rescued by Dias on his
way home—say he discovered the Cape of Good Hope in early 1488
and returned that December, and a departure date of August 1487
has become accepted.

140   **herders were tending their cattle:** Dias seems to have named the
bay the Bahia dos Vaqueiros, or Bay of Cowherds, and the protected
cove where he landed the Aguada de São Bras, or Watering-Place
of St. Blaise, after a spring he found there on the saint's feast day.
The Portuguese later named the bay after St. Blaise, and it was subsequently renamed Mossel Bay by the Dutch.

141   **The storeship had been left far behind:** When the rest of the
company returned to it, they discovered that six of the nine men who
had been left on board had been killed. A seventh, a clerk, was so overjoyed at seeing his companions that he reportedly expired on the spot.

141   **Cape of Storms:** According to Barros; Duarte Pacheco says Dias
himself named it the Cape of Good Hope.

141   **Europe's maps were hastily redrawn:** In 1489 Henry Martellus
published a world map that was originally intended to show Africa
extending to the bottom of the page. He had already engraved it

when news of Dias's discovery reached him, and rather than start over he added the Cape of Good Hope on top of the border.

142   **married a nobleman's daughter:** For Columbus, Filipa was connected in all the right ways. She was the daughter of Bartolomeu Perestrello, who was of Genoese origins and was one of the captains sent by Henry the Navigator to claim Madeira for Portugal; her maternal grandfather had fought at Ceuta.

142   **"a shorter way":** *The Journal of Christopher Columbus (During His 1st Voyage, 1492–93), and Documents Relating to the Voyages of John Cabot and Gaspar Corte Real,* trans. Clements R. Markham (London: Hakluyt Society, 1893), 4–5. Toscanelli's letter to Columbus is reproduced in the same volume: "I perceive your magnificent and grand desire to navigate from the parts of the east to the west," he wrote, and added: "The said voyage is not only possible, but it is true, and certain to be very honorable and to yield incalculable profit, and very great fame among all Christians." The kings and princes of the East, he confidently declared, were even keener to meet Europeans than Europeans were to meet them, "because a great part of them are Christians. . . . On account of all these things, and of many others that might be mentioned, I do not wonder that you, who have great courage, and all the Portuguese people who have always been men eager for all great undertakings, should be with a burning heart and feel a great desire to undertake the said voyage" (10–11).

143   **Columbus stretched Asia:** The Catalan Atlas of 1375 represented Eurasia as measuring 116 degrees from east to west; on his 1492 globe Martin Behaim famously stretched its breadth to 234 degrees, an increase even on Marinus of Tyre. The correct figure is 131 degrees. All things taken together, Columbus underestimated the distance from the Canaries to Japan by a factor of more than four.

144   **against the consensus of his age:** Columbus's ideas evolved over time, and his first recorded references to some of his sources and calculations postdate his first voyage. Even so, the doggedness with which he presented his case suggests that he had early on found sufficient grounds to support his grand scheme.

144   **"promises and offers were impossible":** Quoted in Samuel Eliot Morison, *Admiral of the Ocean Sea: A Life of Christopher Columbus* (Boston: Little, Brown, 1942), 97.

145 **"It pleased our Lord":** Quoted in Joseph F. Callaghan, *Reconquest and Crusade in Medieval Spain* (Philadelphia: University of Pennsylvania Press, 2003), 214.

146 **"You call Ferdinand a wise ruler":** Quoted in David F. Altabé, *Spanish and Portuguese Jewry Before and After 1492* (Brooklyn, NY: Sepher-Hermon, 1983), 45.

146 **Columbus's wealthy rescuer:** The minister, Luis de Santangel, did fund much of the voyage himself, and he raised additional funds to keep Isabella from having to pawn her jewels. It was to Santangel that Columbus sent his letter describing the first voyage.

147 **"IN THE NAME OF OUR LORD":** The excerpts are quoted in Morison, *Admiral of the Ocean Sea*, 152–55. Clearly Columbus did not have time to construct an elaborate address at the start of his voyage; the Prologue was written piecemeal and was appended later.

150 **Rodrigo Borgia:** In one of the brighter spots of his papacy, Alexander VI refused to condone Ferdinand and Isabella's edict of expulsion against the Jews. He received some of the refugees from Spain—and later from Portugal—in Rome, an act that earned him many Spanish enemies but was hardly, as his bitter rival Giuliano della Rovere alleged, proof that he was a secret Jew himself.

150 **a hundred leagues:** A league was originally the distance the average ship could sail in average conditions in an hour, or around three modern nautical miles.

150 **"discover islands or mainlands":** *Dudum Siquidem*, dated September 26, 1493. The original text and English translation are in Davenport, *European Treaties*, 79–83. The earlier bull was *Inter Caetera*, dated May 4, 1493, which is reproduced at pp. 71–78; it was itself the third of three bulls, issued in quick succession, which progressively ratcheted up the pope's favoritism toward Spain.

151 **The Spanish set about pillaging and slaughtering:** Bartolemé de las Casas, an early settler who later took his vows and became a bishop, reported that the colonists, many of whom were convicted felons, "made bets as to who would slit a man in two, or cut off his head at one blow; or they opened up his bowels. They tore the babes from their mother's breast by their feet, and dashed their heads against the rocks. . . . They spitted the bodies of other babies, to-

gether with their mothers and all who were before them, on their swords." Prisoners were hung on the gallows "just high enough for their feet to nearly touch the ground, and by thirteens, in honour and reverence for our Redeemer and the twelve Apostles, they put wood underneath and, with fire, they burned the Indians alive." Quoted in Kirkpatrick Sale, *The Conquest of Paradise: Christopher Columbus and the Columbian Legacy* (London: Hodder & Stoughton, 1991), 157. The quarterly tribute system was soon replaced by institutionalized slavery; disease, of course, annihilated far more of the indigenous population than even the most wanton cruelty could accomplish.

Chapter 7: The Commander

155 **A high forecastle and an even taller sterncastle:** The castles were the legacy of the cogs of northwest Europe, merchant and fighting ships that carried battlemented towers fore and aft from which archers could fire at enemies. By the fifteenth century the sterncastle had morphed into cabin accommodation topped by a poop deck and the forecastle into a high triangular platform that projected forward, resting on the knee of the stem.

157 **he would not even see them leave Lisbon:** There is no clear answer to the question of why the discoveries paused for nearly a decade between the voyages of Bartolomeu Dias and Vasco da Gama. Probably John II was waiting for news from his spies and for the treaty with Spain to be settled; no doubt he was mourning his dead son, and there was the flood of Jewish refugees from across the border to deal with. Manuel I, who was reported by the Venetian spy Leonardo da Ca' Masser to be spineless, capricious, and hopelessly indecisive, was preoccupied for the first two years of his reign with negotiations for his marriage and was faced with concerted domestic opposition to the explorations. The theory beloved of some Portuguese historians that numerous fleets set out to reach India between 1488 and 1497—and even discovered the Americas before Columbus—has never been proven. It rests on the apparent confidence with which Gama pursued a new route to the Cape of Good Hope; John II's determination to move the demarcation line

with Spain 270 leagues farther west, which put Brazil on the Portuguese side; an apparent reference by the celebrated Arab navigator Ahmad ibn Majid to "Frankish" vessels that visited Mozambique in 1495; and the order book of a Lisbon bakery, which did a roaring trade in sea biscuit between 1490 and 1497. There are reasonable explanations for all these particulars that do not assume the remarkable discretion of hundreds of hypothetical sailors, never mind the unlikely reluctance of the Portuguese king to trumpet his besting of Columbus.

157 **"for I am only a sack of earth and worms":** Quoted in Edgar Prestage, *The Portuguese Pioneers* (London: A. & C. Black, 1933), 246.

158 **heir to Castile:** Isabella's brother John had married six months before he died on his way to the wedding; his widow was pregnant but their daughter was stillborn, leaving Isabella as heiress of Castile. Manuel's hopes of ruling both kingdoms were dashed when Isabella died in childbirth in 1498; their son, who was also briefly heir to both thrones, died aged two.

158 **every Jew in Portugal was ordered to leave:** In a ceremony held in 2008, Portugal's Justice Minister José Vera Jardim called the expulsion of Portugal's Jews a black piece of the nation's history; the state, he declared, owed Jews moral reparation for centuries of brutal persecution.

159 **A maze of streets:** The Lisbon district is known as the Alfama, from the Arabic *al-Hamma*, "the fountain" or "the bath." In the fifteenth century only one mosque remained, though so long as they kept their heads down, its worshippers were permitted to meet there to regulate the affairs of the neighborhood.

161 **sea biscuit:** Also known as ship's biscuit or hardtack. *Biscuit* comes from the Medieval Latin *bis coctus*, or "twice baked," though the ship's version, a kind of dense wholemeal bread, was baked up to four times to give it a longer shelf life. It was the inescapable sailor's staple, and during John I's reign a Royal Biscuit Office had been established to ensure a sufficient supply.

161 **"coarse, poor, lacking in good manners and ignorant":** Nicholas of Popelau, quoted in Henry H. Hart, *Sea Road to the Indies* (London: William Hodge, 1952), 44. Nicholas's opinion of Por-

tugal's women was based on keen observation. "They allow one to look upon their faces without hindrance," he noted, "and also upon much of their bosoms, for which purpose their shifts and outer dresses are cut generously low. Below their waist they wear many skirts so that their posteriors are broad and beautiful, so full that I say it in all truth in the whole world nothing finer is to be seen." They were, though, he warned prospective suitors, lewd, greedy, fickle, mean, and dissolute.

162   **a gentleman of the king's household:** *Fidalgo* literally meant "the son of somebody." It was originally applied to anyone of noble lineage, then to the new nobility created by John I. By Vasco da Gama's time it distinguished those families from the new wave of parvenus, knights appointed from among the bourgeoisie.

162   **the best man Manuel could find:** Gama's most recent (and best) scholarly biographer closely argues the case that Gama was not the king's choice but that of a group of nobles opposed to the king; Manuel accepted him, he ingeniously suggests, so that if the under-powered fleet met with disaster, he could pin the failure on the opposition. A fleet of four ships, though, was not unusually small for a voyage of exploration; Dias and Columbus had only three. It would have been small for a voyage of trade or colonization, a fact that belies the notion that Portugal was already on the brink of reaching India. See Sanjay Subrahmanyam, *The Career and Legend of Vasco da Gama* (Cambridge: Cambridge University Press, 1997), 67.

162   **He was most likely born in 1469:** Fourteen sixty is the alternative year sometimes given for Gama's birth. The primary piece of evidence is a pass issued in 1478, in the name of Isabella of Castile, to a Vasco da Gama who must have been older than nine; Gama's name, though, was not uncommon. Other sources, scant as they are, speak for 1469, which is now the consensus.

163   **the Order of Santiago:** The Portuguese chapter split from those in the rest of Iberia when Portugal became independent. Its power base was in southwest Portugal, where Gama was born; the extent of its lands made it virtually a state within a state.

163   **the novice Crusader:** Sanjay Subrahmanyam gives a comprehensive survey of the handful of documents bearing on Gama's family and early life: see *Career and Legend*, 58–68.

165   **the full company:** Of the chroniclers, Castanheda and Goís say
        148; Barros says 170. There are other, unlikelier, estimates, rang-
        ing from the Florentine merchant Girolamo Sernigi's 118 to the
        Portuguese historian Gaspar Correia's 260. Correia and the later
        Portuguese historian Manuel de Faria e Sousa each have a (different)
        priest aboard, though Correia's was likely a clerk and no contempo-
        rary mention is made of either.

166   **the Chronicler:** A remarkable quantity of ink has been spilled
        since the journal was discovered in 1834 on theories about the au-
        thor's identity. By a process of elimination, two candidates emerged
        as front-runners: João de Sá, the clerk of the *São Rafael* and later
        treasurer of the Casa da Índia, and Alvaro Velho, a soldier. A minor
        conflict between the author's credulity that India was full of Chris-
        tians and the more skeptical viewpoint later ascribed to Sá has gone
        against the clerk, and most Portuguese historians have definitively
        named Velho as the diarist. The evidence is circumstantial at best,
        and the attribution remains speculative. A standard Portuguese edi-
        tion is *Diário da viagem de Vasco da Gama*, ed. António Baião, A. de
        Magalhães Basto, and Damião Peres (Porto: Livraria Civilização,
        1945); an English translation by E. G. Ravenstein was published as
        A Journal of the First Voyage of Vasco da Gama, 1497–1499 (London:
        Hakluyt Society, 1898) and is hereafter cited as *Journal*. Any other
        diaries, logbooks, or reports that once existed were lost, perhaps,
        along with countless other documents, in the devastating Lisbon
        earthquake of 1755, and the *Journal* remains the only eyewitness
        source for the voyage. To complete the picture I have drawn selec-
        tively on the early Portuguese chronicles, especially those of João
        de Barros and Fernão Lopes de Castanheda, and on the accounts
        of near-contemporary travelers. As usual the literature disagrees on
        virtually everything, including the types and names of the ships;
        the dates of the mission's preparation, departure, and return; the
        numbers, names, and survival statistics of the crews; and the route
        the fleet followed. I have only noted discrepancies from my account
        where they add interest to the story.

166   **"Praised be God":** Barros gives the fullest report of the royal au-
        dience; see *Ásia de João de Barros, Dos feitos que os Portuguezes fizeram
        no descobrimento e conquista dos mares e terras do Oriente*, ed. Hernani

Cidade and Manuel Múrias, 6th ed. (Lisbon: Divisão de publicações e biblioteca, Agência geral das colónias, 1945–1946), 1:131.

167   **the Order of Christ:** Manuel had been grand master of the order since 1484, and though John II's will stipulated that on his coronation he should hand over to John's illegitimate son Jorge, he refused to let go.

167   **Belém:** The village was formerly known as Restello; it was renamed Belém by Manuel I, who commissioned the great monastery that was built there to commemorate Vasco da Gama's voyage.

169   **The seamen wore loose shirts:** For the sailors' garb, see A. H. de Oliveira Marques, "Travelling with the Fifteenth-Century Discoverers: Their Daily Life," in Anthony Disney and Emily Booth, eds., *Vasco da Gama and the Linking of Europe and Asia* (Delhi: Oxford University Press, 2000), 34.

169   **"weeping and deploring":** Fernão Lopes de Castanheda, in Robert Kerr, *A General History and Collection of Voyages and Travels* (Edinburgh: William Blackwood, 1811–1824), 2:303. Castanheda's account of Gama's first voyage is based on a version of the *Journal* but adds much valuable detail. His *História do descobrimento e conquista da Índia pelos Portugueses* was translated into English by Nicholas Lichfield and was published in 1582 as *The First Booke of the Historie of the Discoverie and Conquest of the East Indias, Enterprised by the Portingales, in their Daungerous Navigations, in the Time of King Dom John, the Second of that Name: Which Historie Conteineth Much Varietie of Matter, Very Profitable for all Navigators, and Not Unpleasaunt to the Readers*. A revised version of this text was reprinted in Kerr's collection.

170   **the fleet edged forward:** A fifth ship left Lisbon with Gama's fleet; commanded by Bartolomeu Dias, it was headed to the Gold Coast, where Dias was to take up an appointment as captain of the fort of São Jorge da Mina.

170   **"May God our Lord":** *Journal*, 1.

Chapter 8: Learning the Ropes

171   **the first of the islands:** The Ilha do Sal, or Salt Island, named by the Portuguese after the mines they had dug there.

172   **off the known face of the earth:** Gama's bold move is a main

plank in the argument advanced by the Portuguese historian Armando Cortesão and others that a series of exploratory fleets set out in the years following Bartolomeu Dias's voyage. The author of the *Journal* tacitly adds to the speculation by showing scant interest in the course Gama followed. The complete silence of the record has been ingeniously adduced as evidence that something important enough to demand strict secrecy was afoot, but a sudden obsession with investigating the sailing conditions of the southern Atlantic does not fit in with the pattern of the discoveries. It seems likeliest that Gama's course was determined by the lessons learned from Dias's voyage, the limitations of his ships, and the vagaries of the weather. Whatever the level of premeditation, the execution by a fleet equipped with rudimentary navigational devices of a three-month sweep around the Atlantic that ended a mere hundred miles north of the Cape of Good Hope was a historic feat of navigation by any yardstick.

173   **on another voyage:** *The Voyage of François Pyrard of Laval to the East Indies, the Maldives, the Moluccas and Brazil,* trans. and ed. Albert Gray and H. C. P. Bell (London: Hakluyt Society, 1887–1890), 1:325.

173   **"The watch is changed":** Quoted in John Villiers, "Ships, Seafaring and the Iconography of Voyages," in Anthony Disney and Emily Booth, eds., *Vasco da Gama and the Linking of Europe and Asia* (Delhi: Oxford University Press, 2000), 76.

173   **"And while this Prince":** Quoted in Peter Padfield, *Tide of Empires: Decisive Naval Campaigns in the Rise of the West,* vol. 1, *1481–1654* (London: Routledge & Kegan Paul, 1979), 33. Padfield gives a useful summary of the few known facts about the munitions carried by the fleet.

174   **the same basic daily rations:** The quantities varied between voyages; the biscuit ration ranged from less than a pound to nearly two pounds. See Oliveira Marques, "Travelling with the Fifteenth-Century Discoverers," 32. Also among the foodstuffs commonly carried were salted or smoked fish, flour, lentils, onions, garlic, salt, mustard, sugar, almonds, and honey.

177   **"Amongst us was the greatest Disorder and Confusion":** Jean Mocquet, *Travels and Voyages into Africa, Asia, and America, the East and West Indies; Syria, Jerusalem, and the Holy Land,* trans. Nathaniel Pullen (London, 1696), 203–4.

178   **thirty leagues north of the Cape of Good Hope:** St. Helena Bay is thirty-three leagues north of the Cape, or about one hundred miles: Pêro de Alenquer, who made the estimate, was less than ten miles out.

178   **ninety-three restless days:** The time Gama and his crews went without seeing land was unprecedented as far as we know; it was certainly much longer than the five weeks endured by Columbus's mutinous crews.

179   **a group of locals:** The Bushmen or San people, hunter-gatherers and pastoralists who had lived in southern Africa since the late Stone Age.

179   **"The inhabitants of this country":** *Journal*, 6.

180   **"one of the sheaths":** Ibid., 7.

182   **a paste of urine:** A common remedy; the Portuguese had dealt with poisons made from snake venom or deadly sap from their first encounters with hostile forces in sub-Saharan Africa.

182   **"All this happened":** *Journal*, 8.

183   **ninety or so men emerged from the hills:** The people were the Khoikhoi, pastoralists who had migrated to southern Africa by the fifth century CE and had intermixed with the San; the name for both is the Khoisan. Hottentot, the old name for the Khoikhoi, is now considered pejorative.

184   **"We found him very fat":** *Journal*, 11.

184   **"but to prove that we were able":** Ibid., 12.

185   **"as big as ducks":** Ibid., 13. After several months of punishing conditions at sea, sailors invariably took out their pent-up aggression on defenseless animals.

186   **a terrifying storm:** At this point the sixteenth-century chronicler Gaspar Correia confronts Gama with a full-scale mutiny that dramatically ends when he summons the ringleaders to the flagship on pretense of charting the course home, claps them in irons, and flings their navigational equipment overboard. God will be their master and pilot, he vows; as for himself, he will never give up until he finds what he has come to seek. Correia's account of Gama's first two voyages is peppered with flights of fancy and no other source has the story, though Osorius briefly mentions a mutiny near the Cape of Good Hope. See Henry E. J. Stanley, trans. and ed., *The*

Three Voyages of Vasco da Gama, and His Viceroyalty (London: Hak-luyt Society, 1869), 56–64.

187   **the last pillar:** Gama had bypassed a bay that Dias christened Bahia da Roca (Bay of Rocks; later renamed Algoa Bay) and the largest of those rocks, where Dias celebrated mass and which he named Cross Island. The low islands—Dias's Flat Islands—were five leagues past Cross Island and 125 leagues from the Cape. The headland where Dias erected his pillar was formerly known as False Inlet and is now called Kwaiihoek; the river that marked the point where Dias turned home is either the Great Fish River or the Keiskamma River.

187   **"Henceforth," noted the Chronicler:** *Journal*, 16.

Chapter 9: The Swahili Coast

188   **All were remarkably tall:** The Bantu, a large family of African peoples who moved into southern Africa from around the fourth century CE and displaced many of the indigenous population; they were farmers, herders, and metalworkers. The river was probably the Inharrime, in southern Mozambique; Gama named it the Rio do Cobre, or Copper River.

189   **"Look what I have been given!":** *Journal*, 17.

189   **a much larger river:** The Qua Qua River, in Mozambique. About ten miles upstream was the Muslim trading settlement of Quelimane, which was doubtless where the two distinguished visitors came from. The rest of the people, as before, were Bantu.

190   **"These tokens":** *Journal*, 20.

191   **"a man of such unprepossessing appearance":** Wilfrid Blunt, *Pietro's Pilgrimage: A Journey to India and Back at the Beginning of the Seventeenth Century* (London: James Barrie, 1953), 10.

192   **the local sultan:** The sultans of the Swahili Coast were sole governors of their lands; they controlled trade, exacted a levy on imports and exports, and provided warehouses, pilots, and facilities for repairing ships. With extensive links to inland trading networks, often forged through polygamous marriages, they were also the coast's dominant merchants in their own right. They were powerful men, and they were not used to being ordered around by foreigners. See Malyn Newitt, *A History of Mozambique* (London: Hurst, 1995), 4.

193 **"a jar of bruised dates":** *Journal*, 28. The details of the street life are from Jean Mocquet, *Travels and Voyages into Africa, Asia, and America, the East and West Indies; Syria, Jerusalem, and the Holy Land*, trans. Nathaniel Pullen (London, 1696), 215.

194 **"gold, silver, cloves, pepper":** *Journal*, 23.

194 **"great merchants and owned big ships":** Ibid., 24.

195 **"This information":** Ibid., 25.

196 **"But when they learned":** Ibid., 28.

198 **warring tribes of naked tattooed men:** The Dutch traveler Jan Huygen van Linschoten was unusually perceptive about the cultural norms that made white people caricature black people as figures out of hell—and vice versa. Some of the Bantu, he noted, seared their faces and bodies with irons until their skin looked like raised satin or damask, "wherein they take great pride, thinking there are no fairer people than them in all the world, so that when they see any white people, that wear apparell on their bodies, they laugh and mocke at them, thinking us to be monsters and ugly people: and when they will make any devilish forme and picture, then they invent one after the forme of a white man in his apparel, so that to conclude, they thinke and verily perswade themselves, that they are the right colour of men, and that we have a false and counterfeit colour." *The Voyage of J. H. van Linschoten to the East Indies*, ed. Arthur Coke Burnell and P. A. Tiele (London: Hakluyt Society, 1885), 1:271.

198 **The pilot whom Gama had hired from the sultan:** Most likely the pilot who was so keen to get away was the local man, not the Meccan pilot who had asked for passage, though the sources do not specify one or the other.

199 **"When we were weary with this work":** *Journal*, 30. Estimates of the islanders' strength range from a hundred to Barros's two thousand; the lower estimate, as usual, is probably nearer the mark.

200 **"*Pisce Mulier,* which is to say Women Fish":** Mocquet, *Travels and Voyages*, 233–35. The fishermen, Mocquet reports, were also said to cut the throats of humans and drink their blood while it was still hot. The king was the ruler of Matapa, a state of the Karanga (now Shona) people that stretched between the Limpopo and Zambezi rivers and flourished from around 1200 to 1500 CE on the back of its trade in gold and ivory. Great Zimbabwe, a monumental stone

city on the Zimbabwe plateau, was the royal palace and trading center. The Portuguese called the kingdom Monomotapa, which they derived from the Karanga royal title *Mwene Matapa*, or "Ravager of the Lands," and which they initially thought was the personal name of the ruler. Though Matapa had declined by the time the Portuguese arrived, the latter long believed it was a great power and went to great lengths to infiltrate it.

201   **"Chaine of mens members":** Linschoten, *Voyage*, 1:275.

201   **a large archipelago of tropical islands:** The Quirimbas Archipelago, which stretches for sixty miles along the northern coast of Mozambique. The low-lying mainland is virtually hidden from view when coasting outside the reefs.

202   **a large island ahead:** Probably Mafia Island, which was likewise perfectly free of Christians. By standing out to sea Gama missed Zanzibar, a hundred miles to the north.

204   **the Holy Ghost painted as a white dove:** Castanheda says the merchants were Indian; Sir Richard Burton suggested the drawing was of a Hindu pigeon-god. *Journal*, 36.

205   **"These and other wicked tricks":** Ibid., 37–38. According to Castanheda, the Mombasans tried further attempts at sabotage during the two following nights.

208   **huge horns:** The Siwa, or Royal Trumpet, was imported to East Africa by Persians from Shiraz, who settled along the coast in the eleventh and twelfth centuries. Siwas were made of copper and wood as well as ivory.

211   **"Our Lady at the foot of the cross":** *Journal*, 44.

212   **the pilot appeared to be another Christian from India:** The pilot has often been romantically misidentified as the great Arab navigator Ahmad ibn Majid. The only plausible evidence is a short passage in a mid-sixteenth-century Arabic chronicle that calls the arrival in India of the "accursed Portuguese" one of the "astounding and extraordinary occurrences of the age" and in passing claims that the Portuguese—"may they be cursed!"—only made it across the Indian Ocean by getting Ibn Majid drunk. Castanheda, Barros, and Goís all say the pilot was from Gujarat. Barros and Goís say he was a Muslim, but given the explorers' ongoing confusion about India's religions, the *Journal's* line—"We were much pleased

with the Christian pilot whom the king had sent us" (46)—can be taken to imply that he was a Hindu. For the Arabic chronicle, see Sanjay Subrahmanyam, *The Career and Legend of Vasco da Gama* (Cambridge: Cambridge University Press, 1997), 124.

212 **Indians preferred another device:** The kamal, an Arab invention that the Portuguese developed in the early sixteenth century into the cross-staff.

212 **"would never leave his heart":** Gaspar Correia, in Henry E. J. Stanley, trans. and ed., *The Three Voyages of Vasco da Gama, and His Viceroyalty* (London: Hakluyt Society, 1869), 143. Colorful as always, Correia paints a picture of "true friendship and sincere love" developing between Gama and the sultan of Malindi, so much that on their departure he "could not endure it, and embarked in his boat and went with them, saying very affectionate things" (141, 144).

Chapter 10: Riding the Monsoon

213 **scorching temperatures:** The Great Indian Desert, or Thar Desert, reaches 50 degrees Celsius during summer; the sea temperature remains in the low 20s Celsius. The dates and intensity of the monsoon vary widely from year to year, but the Malabar Coast is always the first area to receive heavy rain. The rest of the air mass flows over the Bay of Bengal, where it picks up more moisture and roars into the eastern Himalayas at speeds of up to twenty-five miles an hour before turning west and drenching the Indo-Gangetic Plain.

214 **"As soon as I caught the smell of the vessel":** "Narrative of the Journey of Abd-er-Razzak," in R. H. Major, ed., *India in the Fifteenth Century: Being a Collection of Narratives of Voyages to India in the Century Preceding the Portuguese Discovery of the Cape of Good Hope* (London: Hakluyt Society, 1857), 7–8.

215 **Mount Eli:** Also known as Mount Dely and now as Ezhimala; the hill, which stands out prominently into the ocean, is now the construction site of a naval academy and is inaccessible to the public.

215 **"saying the *salve*":** Castanheda, in Robert Kerr, *A General History and Collection of Voyages and Travels* (Edinburgh: William Blackwood, 1811–1824), 2:344.

215 **the Promised Land:** On a recent visit, paradise was tainted with a

liberal scattering of discarded sandals, ointment tubes, and medicine bottles. The surf rolls heavily on the sand, whipped up by treacherous-looking rocks in the shallows. Just behind the coast is an unprepossessing concrete post bearing the inscription:

Vasco-da-Gama

landed

Here

Kappkadavu

in the year

1498

Kappad, which the Portuguese called Capua or Capocate, is ten miles north-northwest of Calicut, which is now known as Kozhikode. Strictly speaking, Gama did not land there; he first set foot on Indian soil at Pantalayini Kollam, the Portuguese Pandarani, four miles farther up the coast. Pantalayini Kollam was later supplanted by the nearby town of Quilandy, now known as Koyilandy.

216 **"Why," he and his colleague had asked:** *Journal*, 48–49.

216 **"They all then joined in humble and hearty thanks":** Castanheda, in Kerr, *General History*, 2:357.

217 **"all the spices, drugs, nutmegs":** Ibid., 346–47. In the 1330s, when Ibn Battuta arrived in Calicut, it was already a busy port thronged with international merchants. In 1421 and 1431 the Chinese traveler Ma Huan visited Calicut and Cochin with Zheng He's fleets and described the hubbub of trade in his widely read *Ying-yai Sheng-lan* ("The Overall Survey of the Ocean's Shores"); an English translation by J. V. G. Mills was published by the Hakluyt Society in 1970.

218 **"The officers of the custom-house":** "Narrative of the Journey of Abd-er-Razzak," 14.

218 **"You mistook one thing for another":** K. V. Krishna Ayyar, *The Zamorins of Calicut* (Calicut: University of Calicut, 1999), 86.

219 **"The city of Calicut is inhabited by Christians":** *Journal*, 49–50.

219 **elegant, pagoda-like mosques:** The striking mosques still stand around the Kuttichira pool in central Kozhikode, although the Mishkal mosque, which was built by a Yemeni trader and ship

owner in the fourteenth century, was reconstructed after the Portuguese torched it in 1510. With louvers painted in fresh turquoises and blues, carved floral designs, and multitiered tiled roofs, they bear more than a passing resemblance to the city's ancient Hindu temples.

219   **"commonly very hayrie":** *The Voyage of J. H. van Linschoten to the East Indies*, ed. Arthur Coke Burnell and P. A. Tiele (London: Hakluyt Society, 1885), 1:278. The Indians, Linschoten pruriently added, were "the most leacherous and unchast nation in all the Orient, so that there are verie few women children among them of seven or eight yeares old, that have their maiden-heades."

220   **"We did not":** *Journal*, 510.

222   **"This reception was friendly":** Ibid., 51.

222   **"They can keep nothing free":** Jean Mocquet, *Travels and Voyages into Africa, Asia, and America, the East and West Indies; Syria, Jerusalem, and the Holy Land*, trans. Nathaniel Pullen (London, 1696), 241–41v.

224   **"the Christians of this country":** *Journal*, 54.

224   **"teeth protruding an inch from the mouth":** Ibid., 55.

224   **another ancient church:** Though it would have meant taking a circular route to the palace, this may have been the Tali Temple, the most important Hindu shrine in Calicut and the focal point from which the city grid was laid out in the fourteenth century. A large porch opens into a courtyard that leads to a hall lined with burnished copper; in the inner shrine is a two-foot-high *shivalinga*, the phallic symbol of Shiva, made of gold and encrusted with gems.

224   **five thousand people:** See the letter of the Florentine merchant Girolamo Sernigi, quoted in *Journal*, 126. Sernigi also passed on the news, brought home by Gama's sailors, that eighty years earlier huge fleets of four-masted vessels crewed by "white Christians, who wore their hair long like Germans, and had no beards except around the mouth," had regularly visited Calicut. "If they were Germans," he reasoned, "it seems to me that we should have had some notice about them" (131). They were, in fact, Chinese. Memories of Zheng He's treasure fleets, which had paid their last visit sixty-seven years before Gama arrived, were clearly still alive in Calicut; the Indians who gave the Portuguese such a rapturous welcome may at first have thought the Chinese had returned.

225   **"more than is shown in Spain to a king":** *Journal*, 55.

225   **"They little think in Portugal":** Castanheda, in Kerr, *General History*, 2:364.

225   **Inside was a vast, leafy courtyard:** As well as the *Journal* and the chronicles, my description of the palace and of Calicut in general draws on the accounts of earlier and later travelers including Abd al-Razzaq, Duarte Barbosa, François Pyrard, Ludovico de Varthema, and Pietro della Valle; the last gives a particularly full picture of the palace, complete with diagrams. The site of the palace is now a public park called Mananchira Square; the Zamorins' vast bathing tanks can still be seen.

225   **"giving many blows to the people":** *Journal*, 56.

225   **King of the Hills and the Waves:** The Portuguese *Zamorin* was a corruption of *Samuri*, the common abbreviation of the fuller title *Samutiri Tirumulpad*. Beyond that, the derivation is unclear. *Samutiri* may be a corruption of *Svami* (Sanskrit for "master") and the honorific *Sri*, or *tiri* may itself be a contraction of the honorific *Tirumulpad*. Alternatively, *Samutiri* may be a condensed form of *Samudratiri*, which without the honorific *tiri* means "he who has the sea for his border," though another of the Zamorin's titles, *Kunnalakonatiri*, means (again without the honorific) "king of the hills and the waves." K. V Krishna Ayyar delves into the matter in *Zamorins of Calicut*, 24–26.

226   **"very white, delicate and sumptuous":** Letter of Girolamo Sernigi, quoted in *Journal*, 126.

226   **expensive simplicity:** So say most of the sources, though a few indulge in lavish Orientalist fantasies. "He wore so many ornaments," wrote the Portuguese chronicler Diogo do Couto, "and on his arm such a quantity of jeweled bracelets, that they extended from the bend of his elbows down to his thumbs, wherewith he was so weighted that he was obliged to have two pages each sustaining one arm. From his neck hung a collar of inestimable value. In his ears, earrings of the same assay, set with beautiful rubies and diamonds, whose weight extended the ears down to the shoulders, so that the value of what he carried upon him was indeed great. He was naked from the waist to the head, while round the waist was bound a cloth of gold and silk in many folds, the ends reaching half-way down the

leg, and round the head a jeweled coronet of four fingers' width, very richly set and of great value." Quoted in *The Voyage of François Pyrard of Laval to the East Indies, the Maldives, the Moluccas and Brazil*, trans. and ed. Albert Gray and H. C. P. Bell (London: Hakluyt Society, 1887–1890), 1:415.

226 **bitter betel leaves:** The Persian ambassador Abd al-Razzaq was an enthusiastic convert to the ancient habit of chewing betel. "This substance," he wrote, "gives a colour to and brightens the countenance, causes an intoxication similar to that produced by wine, appeases hunger, and excites appetite in those who are satiated; it removes the disagreeable smell from the mouth, and strengthens the teeth. It is impossible to express how strengthening it is, and how much it excites to pleasure." Major, *India in the Fifteenth Century*, 32.

Chapter 11: Kidnap

232 **Vijayanagar:** The name derives from the Sanskrit for "City of Victory." The village of Hampi in northern Karnataka now sits within its spectacular ruins; Muslim armies sacked it after they defeated the empire in 1565, and it was never repopulated. Robert Sewell, *A Forgotten Empire: Vijayanagar* (London: Sonnenschein, 1900), includes vivid accounts of the city by two sixteenth-century Portuguese travelers.

232 **"is by far more distinguished":** Quoted in *Travelers in Disguise: Narratives of Eastern Travel by Poggio Bracciolini and Ludovico de Varthema*, trans. John Winter Jones, rev. Lincoln Davis Hammond (Cambridge, MA: Harvard University Press, 1963), 9–10. Suttee, Conti explained, was performed "in order to add to the pomp of the funeral." Outside the prostitutes' bazaars and the royal household, Vijayanagar's women were also civil servants, merchants, poets, and artists.

233 **Islamic empires:** One, the Delhi Sultanate, founded in 1206 and ruled by Turkish and Afghan dynasties, became a new Indian powerhouse and shielded India from the Mongol apocalypse. After surviving endless bloody intrigues that saw nineteen of its thirty-five sultans assassinated, its nemesis appeared in 1398 in the unstoppable form of Tamerlane. On his whirlwind campaign to restore the

Mongol Empire—or, as he proclaimed in words that would have had a familiar ring to the Portuguese, to plunder the wealth of the infidel Hindus, convert them to the true faith, and strengthen Islam—he swept through the Khyber Pass and sacked Delhi, killing a hundred thousand prisoners in one day and leaving the city in ruins. He stormed on to China, where he died during a deadly cold winter, but the sultanate was fatally weakened and much of India fell back into the hands of independent rajas.

235   **"And when the king":** *The Book of Duarte Barbosa*, trans. Mansel Longworth Dames (London: Hakluyt Society, 1921), 2:26.

236   **"It is strictly forbidden":** *The Voyage of François Pyrard of Laval to the East Indies, the Maldives, the Moluccas and Brazil*, trans. and ed. Albert Gray and H. C. P. Bell (London: Hakluyt Society, 1887–1890), 1:404–5. According to the Dutch traveler Jan Huygen van Linschoten, India's Muslims were equally convinced that there was little difference between Hindus and Christians.

237   **"As to us others":** *Journal*, 19.

238   **"I expected you yesterday":** Ibid., 62–63.

239   **unable to read it:** One wonders why Gama could not have had Martins translate the Portuguese letter aloud into Arabic; presumably his Arabic was not up to the task. In any case, the Arabic letter had to be left and needed checking.

241   **"When they saw the dark looks of the captain":** *Journal*, 64.

244   **"At this we rejoiced greatly":** Ibid., 67.

Chapter 12: Dangers and Delights

247   **"were made welcome by the Christians":** *Journal*, 69.

248   **"The men," Conti explained:** *Travelers in Disguise: Narratives of Eastern Travel by Poggio Bracciolini and Ludovico de Varthema*, trans. John Winter Jones, rev. Lincoln Davis Hammond (Cambridge, MA: Harvard University Press, 1963), 13–14.

248   **"freely thrust him through":** *The Voyage of J. H. van Linschoten to the East Indies*, ed. Arthur Coke Burnell and P. A. Tiele (London: Hakluyt Society, 1885), 1:281. The rules of pollution were utterly perplexing to Europeans. If a non-Hindu touched a high-caste Hindu's servant while he was bringing them food or drink, the food

was thrown on the ground. If he entered his house and touched anything, no one would eat there again until it was ritually cleansed. If a Christian came to sit next to a Brahmin or Nair, he would immediately get up; if the Christian sat down unnoticed, the Hindu would wash his whole body. Fear of pollution also accounted for the practice of tossing items to those of other religions rather than passing them by hand and pouring liquids into their mouths rather than letting them drink directly from vessels.

249 **"These have on their neck"**: *Travelers in Disguise*, 32–33. The witness was Niccolò de' Conti; he also reported the deadly festival, which he saw at Vijayanagar. Linschoten mentions a similar temple festival during which the faithful hacked out lumps of their flesh and threw them before the wagon; Pietro della Valle has the martyrs insert hooks in their backs and suspend themselves from a beam that whirls them around when a lever is pulled. Less violent acts of devotion also spooked Europeans: Jean Mocquet reported seeing a naked Hindu "squat up on his Tail before a Fire of Cow Dung, and with Ashes thereof all bepowdered his Body, having long Hair like a Woman, which he held on the top of his Shoulders: This was the most hideous and monstrous Spectacle that ever was seen: For he remained still looking on the Fire, without so much as turning his Head." *Travels and Voyages into Africa, Asia, and America, the East and West Indies; Syria, Jerusalem, and the Holy Land*, trans. Nathaniel Pullen (London, 1696), 244.

250 **"under the express agreement"**: Niccolò de' Conti, in *Travelers in Disguise*, 28. Conti was one of the first Europeans to describe suttee, which was banned in Muslim areas of India.

250 **"'Tis remarkable"**: Mocquet, *Travels and Voyages*, 242. Mocquet goes on to tell the tale of a prostitute whose client "heated himself so with her, that he Died upon the spot, at which she was so afflicted, that when they Burnt his Body, she Burnt her self with him, seeing he had Died for Love of her, tho' she was no other than a good Friend."

251 **"for the sake of establishing relations of peace and amity"**: *Journal*, 69.

252 **"This news made us sad"**: Ibid., 71.

253 **"If the captains went ashore"**: Ibid., 72.

255   **"Are you unaware":** Ibid., 74–5.

257   **"Inasmuch that we had discovered":** Ibid., 76.

259   **"They said," recorded the Chronicler:** Ibid., 80.

259   **five more islands ahead:** The *Journal* incorrectly says there were six. The Panchdiva Islands are forty miles south of Goa; the largest, off which the Portuguese anchored, was named Anjediva by the Portuguese and is now known as Anjadip. In Canto Nine of the *Lusiads*, the Portuguese epic of the discoveries, Luís Vas de Camões calls it the Isle of Love and describes it in lush detail as a miniature paradise; Venus, he says, put it in the voyagers' path as a sanctuary from their weary toils.

259   **smelled somewhat of cinnamon:** The branches were from cassia trees; the dried bark produces a spice similar but inferior to cinnamon.

260   **A notorious pirate named Timoja:** The Hindu privateer Thimayya, known to the Portuguese as Timoja, would later serve them as an informant and supplier; he was instrumental in the capture of Goa and was briefly installed as the governor of its Indian population.

265   **"Great numbers Died every day":** Mocquet, *Travels and Voyages*, 205–6.

266   **A toxic fungus infected the bread:** The disease was known as St. Anthony's fire after the monks of the Order of St. Anthony, who were renowned for their prowess in curing it; the modern term is ergotism. It results from eating the *Claviceps purpurea* fungus, which grows on cereals, particularly rye. Episodes of mass convulsions blamed on witchcraft have been controversially ascribed to the disease; the psychotic effects are similar to those of LSD.

266   **"breaks out at the Fundament like an Ulcer":** Mocquet, *Travels and Voyages*, 231–32.

267   **"It pleased God in his mercy":** *Journal*, 87.

267   **"so as to find out whither the Lord had taken us":** Ibid., 88.

267   **some islands off Mozambique:** The Seychelles are some 300 leagues or 900 miles from Mozambique; Madagascar is more plausibly "off" the coast, but by only 60 leagues or 180 miles.

268   **a nearby island:** The town was Pate; the island of the same name is the largest of the Lamu Archipelago and is located off the north Kenyan coast.

269   **a pillar and cross:** A pillar surmounted by a cross still stands on a small rocky promontory almost eaten away by the tide, a little south of the town of Malindi in the middle of the bay. It is not the original, which offended the local population and was soon removed—owing to "odium," says the sign—though the sultan carefully stored it in his palace and the cross may have survived.

269   **"and reposing":** *Journal*, 91.

269   **six leagues from the mainland:** The *Journal* incorrectly gives the distance as "quite ten leagues."

270   **"those who had come so far":** Ibid., 92–93.

Chapter 13: A Venetian in Lisbon

272   **ambassador extraordinary of the Republic of Venice:** For the story of the Venetian envoy I am indebted to Donald Weinstein's *Ambassador from Venice: Pietro Pasqualigo in Lisbon, 1501* (Minneapolis: University of Minnesota Press, 1960). See also George Modelski, "Enduring Rivalry in the Democratic Lineage: The Venice-Portugal Case," in *Great Power Rivalries*, ed. William R. Thompson (Columbia: University of South Carolina Press, 1999).

272   **"Letters of June":** Quoted in Sanjay Subrahmanyam, *The Career and Legend of Vasco da Gama* (Cambridge: Cambridge University Press, 1997), 20.

273   **"found all the treasure":** See Paul Teyssier and Paul Valentin, trans. and eds., *Voyages de Vasco de Gama: Relations des expeditions de 1497–1499 et 1502–3*, 2nd ed. (Paris: Chandeigne, 1998), 186–88.

274   **"People, islands, and shores unknown":** Quoted in Weinstein, *Ambassador from Venice*, 45–46.

274   **the fierce and powerful Turkish sultan:** For some decades, while Europe remained under dire threat of an Ottoman conquest, there were plenty who agreed with Pasqualigo that the new obsession with discovering distant lands had left the homeland dangerously unguarded. Many Christians, wrote Ogier Ghiselin de Busbecq, Austria's ambassador to the Ottoman Empire in the mid-sixteenth century, had abandoned the medieval valor that sought honor in defending the faith on the battlefield in favor of a predilection for "seeking the Indies and the Antipodes across vast fields of ocean, in

search of gold." Only with time would the impact of the voyages on the global balance of power become clear. Bernard Lewis, *Islam and the West* (New York: Oxford University Press, 1993), 15.

275   **"This is more important to the Venetian State":** Quoted in Weinstein, *Ambassador from Venice*, 29–30.

277   **"returning many thanks to Our Lord":** Letter of Manuel I to the Cardinal Protector, dated August 28, 1499, quoted in *Journal*, 115.

277   **"Most high and excellent Prince and Princess":** Ibid., 113–114.

279   **the old prophecies:** Columbus staked his place in the eschatological scheme that would lead to the end of the world in his *Book of Prophecies*; he started work on it in 1501 and was still revising it in the year before his death.

279   **the settlers he had promised untold riches:** Columbus turned their argument back on them: the colonists, he complained, had come "in the belief that the gold and spices could be gathered in by the shovelful, and they did not reflect that, though there was gold, it would be buried in mines, and the spices would be on the treetops, and that the gold would have to be mined and the spices harvested and cured." Quoted in Felipe Fernández-Armesto, *Columbus* (Oxford: Oxford University Press, 1991), 134.

279   **rub his in-laws' noses in it:** At the time Manuel was in fact briefly unmarried to one of the Catholic Monarchs' daughters. Isabella had died in 1498; in 1501 Manuel married her younger sister Maria, who bore him his son and heir, John III.

280   **"very fully the sovereignty and dominion":** Quoted in *Journal*, 115–16. Manuel also wrote to the Holy Roman Emperor Maximilian I.

280   **"from the damage to the Infidels that is expected":** Grant letter of January 1500 (?), quoted in Subrahmanyam, *Career and Legend*, 171.

280   **"for the king has decreed the death penalty":** Angelo Trevisan, secretary to Domenico Pisani, to the chronicler Domenico Malipiero; quoted in Henry H. Hart, *Sea Road to the Indies* (London: William Hodge, 1952), 28. Guido Detti made a similar point: Manuel, he said, had ordered Gama and his men to hand over their navigational charts on pain of death and the confiscation of their goods, from fear that their route and intelligence would be leaked to

foreign powers. "But I believe that, whatever they do, everyone will know, and other ships will start to go there," he added. See Teyssier and Valentin, *Voyages de Vasco de Gama*, 188.

280 **"a barbarous orchestra of trumpets":** Quoted in Hart, *Sea Road to the Indies*, 203.

281 **"bigger than Lisbon":** Letter of Girolamo Sernigi, n.d. [July 1499], quoted in *Journal*, 125, 134–35. Guido Detti echoed the news; the people of Calicut, he explained, "are not strictly speaking Christians, because they baptize themselves once every three years as a means of confession and purifying their sins. But they recognize the existence of Christ and Our Lady. They have churches equipped with bells, where there are only two basins, one for holy water and the other for balm, without any other sacrament, without priests or monks of any kind." The notion that Hinduism was a variant of Christianity, or at least had some kinship with it, proved hard to shake. "The whole of Malabar believes, as we do, in the Trinity of Father, Son and Holy Ghost, three in one, the only true God. From Cambay to Bengal all the people hold this," wrote Tomé Pires, an apothecary to the Portuguese royal family who was posted to India as "factor of drugs" and wrote a comprensive survey of Asia between 1512 and 1515. By 1552, João de Barros was still referring to the Hindu threefold god of Brahma with Vishnu and Siva as a Brahman trinity, though he noted that it was quite different from the Christian trinity. See Teyssier and Valentin, *Voyages de Vasco de Gama*, 183; *The Suma Oriental of Tomé Pires*, trans. and ed. Armando Cortesão (London: Hakluyt Society, 1944), 1:66.

282 **"are in reality temples of idolaters":** Second letter of Sernigi, n.d. [1499], quoted in *Journal*, 138.

282 **Gaspar had been Jewish:** Ibid., 137. Sernigi says Gaspar was born in Alexandria, as does Manuel in his letter to the Cardinal Protector. Barros adds that his parents had fled from Poznan in Poland when the Jews were banished in 1450. Castanheda says he had a Jewish wife; he also had a son, who was later christened Balthasar.

282 **a fantastical picture of India's religions:** Separate statistics for each region of India and other "kingdoms on the coast to the south of Calecut," some of which are in fact in Southeast Asia, are appended to the *Journal*, 96–102.

283   **"Before he attacked the Moors":** Barros's summary is cited in Henry E. J. Stanley, trans. and ed., *The Three Voyages of Vasco da Gama, and His Viceroyalty* (London: Hakluyt Society, 1869), 186–87.

283   **"For one should truly believe that God":** Castanheda, quoted in Subrahmanyam, *Career and Legend*, 162.

286   **"So great was the consternation":** Castanheda, in Robert Kerr, *A General History and Collection of Voyages and Travels* (Edinburgh: William Blackwood, 1811–1824), 2:418.

288   **headed into the North Atlantic:** The commander was Gaspar Corte-Real. In 1500 he reportedly reached Greenland and Newfoundland, where John Cabot, an Italian sailing under an English flag, may have already landed in 1497. The next year Corte-Real set out again and may have seen Chesapeake Bay and Nova Scotia, but he and his ship were lost; so, when he sailed to find him the following year, was his brother Miguel.

289   **There was only one man for the job:** In fact, the command was first offered to Cabral, who still had his supporters at court. Cabral's detractors, notably Gama's maternal uncle Vicente Sodré, denounced Cabral as incompetent and successfully maneuvered against him. The problem was solved when Gama was given the right for life to assume command of any India-bound fleet.

289   **the late summer of 1499:** The sources disagree over the date of Gama's return. Barros, Góis, and Resende give the date as August 29, Castanheda as September 8, and other sources as September 18. Possibly, as Barros suggests, Gama spent his first days on home soil in seclusion before he publicly entered the city.

289   **"the king honored him":** Castanheda, in Kerr, *General History*, 2:394.

289   **an elaborate grant letter:** Quoted in *Journal*, 230–32. The letter has traditionally been dated to January 10, 1502, but was likely issued in January 1500; see Subrahmanyam, *Career and Legend*, 169–70.

290   **"with all the honors, prerogatives, liberties":** Subrahmanyam, *Career and Legend*, 172.

291   **"First, every one attended a sumptuous Mass":** Ibid., 194–95.

292   **the shiny black gondola:** The impressively gaudy vessel can still be seen in Lisbon's Museu da Marinha.

293　**"to find rapid and secret remedies":** Quoted in Weinstein, *Ambassador from Venice*, 77–78.

Chapter 14: The Admiral of India

297　**Vasco da Gama sailed out of Lisbon:** Several eyewitness accounts of Gama's second voyage have survived. Much the fullest is by Tomé Lopes, a Portuguese clerk who sailed on a ship, financed by Rui Mendes de Brito and captained by Giovanni Buonagrazia, which left Lisbon in April 1502 as part of the fleet under the command of Estêvão da Gama. Lopes's narrative is known only in an Italian translation that was sent to Florence and was published in the 1550s by Giovanni Battista Ramusio; see "Navigazione verso le Indie orientali scritta per Tomé Lopez," in Ramusio, *Navigazioni e viaggi*, ed. Marica Milanesi (Turin: Einaudi, 1978–1988), 1:687–738. A second account was written in Portuguese by a sailor with Gama's main fleet; it is particularly informative on the first leg of that fleet's voyage, but then becomes more piecemeal. The manuscript is in the Österreichische Nationalbibliothek in Vienna and is reprinted in Leonor Freire Costa, ed., "Relação anónima da segunda viagem de Vasco da Gama à Índia," in *Cidadania e história: Em homenagem a Jaime Cortesão* (Lisbon: Livraria Sá da Costa Editora, 1985), 141–99. A third source is a pair of letters written by an Italian factor named Matteo da Bergamo, whose ship was part of Estevão da Gama's fleet; though they vary in length and detail, both are dated Mozambique, April 18, 1503, and were sent, by different ships for safety, to his employer, a Cremonese named Gianfranco Affaitadi, who ran a merchant business in Lisbon. Two copies are in the Biblioteca Marciana in Venice; both versions, in French translation, are in Paul Teyssier and Paul Valentin, trans. and eds., *Voyages de Vasco de Gama: Relations des expeditions de 1497–1499 et 1502–3*, 2nd ed. (Paris: Chandeigne, 1998), 319–40. The other surviving accounts are shorter but are valuable for recounting the experiences of ordinary seamen, especially those who were wide-eyed newcomers to the ways of Africa and India. The first, which was already known by 1504, is by a Fleming who sailed with the main fleet on the *Leitoa Nova*. A facsimile of the original with English translation was published as

Calcoen: A Dutch Narrative of the Second Voyage of Vasco da Gama to Calicut, trans. J. P. Berjeau (London: B. M. Pickering, 1874). The second, which follows the Portuguese account in the Vienna manuscript, is in German; the writer was also with Gama's fleet, but the surviving text is incomplete and often confused and is likely a copy of a report put together from notes or a diary on the fleet's return. It was first published along with the Portuguese manuscript in Christine von Rohr, ed., *Neue quellen zur zweiten Indienfahrt Vasco da Gamas* (Leipzig: K. F. Koehler, 1939). A variant, generally abridged version of this account, which probably belonged to a commercial agent named Lazarus Nuremberger, who was active in Lisbon and Seville, was found in the 1960s in the Lyceum Library, Bratislava (now in the Central Library of the Slovak Academy of Sciences), and is published, with English translation, together with other manuscript fragments on the early voyages of discovery, in Miloslav Krása, Josef Polišenskyâ, and Peter Ratkoš, eds., *European Expansion (1494–1519): The Voyages of Discovery in the Bratislava Manuscript Lyc. 515/8 (Codex Bratislavensis)* (Prague: Charles University, 1986). The different accounts are inconsistent or contradictory in many details, but as before I have steered clear of long-winded explanations of my deductions. Except where English versions are noted above, translations are my own.

298 **"The people there were stark naked":** *Calcoen*, 22.

299 **"rain, hail, snow, thunder and lightning":** Ibid., 23.

299 **"a chill such as in Germany cannot occur":** Krása, Polišenskyâ, and Ratkoš, *European Expansion*, 78.

300 **the famed gold-trading town of Sofala:** Though the Christian beliefs about Sofala were mere fantasies, Muslim writers described it as an important source of gold as early as the tenth century. The sands have shifted dramatically since Gama's arrival, and the once-thriving port is long lost to the sea. The author of *Calcoen* dramatically claims that its inhabitants refused to trade with the Portuguese out of fear that they might sail up the river and find their way into the realm of Prester John, which was located inland and was otherwise entirely enclosed by walls. The sultan of Sofala, he adds, was at war with Prester John's people; from some who had been taken as slaves, the Portuguese learned that their land was awash with silver,

gold, and precious stones. Shipboard gossip was no doubt behind the rumors.

302 **the most powerful sultans in East Africa:** Kilwa's ruins are still impressive, though the island can now only be reached by wading through the shallows. For its fascinating history, see H. Neville Chittick, *Kilwa: An Islamic Trading City on the East African Coast* (Nairobi: British Institute in Eastern Africa, 1974). For a near-contemporary view, see Hans Mayr, "Account of the Voyage of D. Francisco de Almeida, Viceroy of India, along the East Coast of Africa," in Malyn Newitt, ed., *East Africa* (Aldershot, UK: Ashgate, 2002).

303 **"Their bodies are well shaped":** Hans Mayr, in Newitt, *East Africa*, 14.

304 **The emir handed over three dignitaries:** According to Castanheda and Correia, who for once more or less agree, the emir handed over his archenemy as a hostage and refused to pay the tribute, in the hope that Gama would kill him; in the end the hostage came up with the money himself. When the deal was done, Gama graciously asked his new vassal if he had any enemies he could help him with; the emir, trying to salvage something from the situation, told him they greatly feared Christians in Mombasa—his main rival—and would no doubt shell out a handsome tribute if asked.

305 **"on account of which I armed myself":** Letter dated Quiloa [Kilwa], July 20, 1502, Biblioteca Nacional de Lisboa, Reservados, Mss. 244, No. 2, quoted in Sanjay Subrahmanyam, *The Career and Legend of Vasco da Gama* (Cambridge: Cambridge University Press, 1997), 202.

305 **Gama had warned in his letter:** "If before you enter this port, this letter is handed to you outside, do not enter it, because this port is difficult to exit from, but instead go on ahead, and follow everything that has been said above," he wrote.

306 **"We all thought it was advisable":** See Teyssier and Valentin, *Voyages de Vasco de Gama*, 328. Of the chroniclers, Barros says the fleet put in at a bay eight leagues south of Malindi; Castanheda says Gama briefly visited the city; Correia offers an elaborate description of Gama's meeting with the sultan, who once more embraces him as a brother. All are contradicted by the eyewitness accounts.

306 **"and we killed the people and burned the ships":** *Calcoen*, 26.

The Flemish sailor says the fleet headed northeast on the monsoon winds and arrived on August 21 off "a great city called Combaen." The city was Cambay, an important Gujarati port for six hundred years; now known as Khambhat, its harbor has long ago silted up. Sailing down the coast, he says the fleet reached a city named Oan (likely Goa); it was there, he claims, that they captured and burned 400 ships. The attack is not corroborated in the other accounts. Matteo da Bergamo says the storm blew them to Dhabul (Mumbai); Lopes describes a similar place but calls it Calinul.

307 **Rui Mendes de Brito:** The shipowner was likely a member of a family of "New Christians" who were prominent Portuguese gem dealers and merchant bankers. Rui Mendes is mentioned as a financier of armadas at Antwerp between 1504 and 1508, when the city was already becoming the main European entrepôt for Portugal's spices. In 1512 a Diogo Mendes, possibly of the same family, moved permanently to Antwerp and became a fabulously rich spice baron; by the mid-sixteenth century the dynasty handled the lion's share of the spice trade and controlled several stock markets. See Marianna D. Birnbaum, *The Long Journey of Gracia Mendes* (Budapest: Central European University Press, 2003), 15–22.

308 **"the ships which carry the spices":** *Calcoen*, 27.

308 **sambuk:** Different types of dhows were distinguished by their keel design rather than their purpose or their size, which could vary widely. Even the keel design evolved over time: sambuks, which were among the most successful of all dhows, later developed a square stern under Portuguese influence.

308 **a full account of the horrors:** My account of the battle is based on Tomé Lopes's blow-by-blow report, with additional details from the other eyewitnesses and the chronicles.

309 **240 men:** The figure is given by the dependable Lopes, but estimates vary widely. Matteo da Bergamo and the anonymous Portuguese writer put the number at about 200; the Flemish sailor says 380 and the German sailor 600. Barros says 260, plus more than fifty women and children; Correia, exaggerating as usual, says 700.

309 **Jauhar al-Faqih:** Lopes's "Ioar Afanquy."

310 **"When I commanded this ship":** See Lopes, "Navigazione verso le Indie orientali," 701.

310   **"We couldn't even speak about this capture"**: See Teyssier and Valentin, *Voyages de Vasco de Gama*, 330. "On this subject there are moreover certain stories that it's neither the time nor the place to reveal," Bergamo darkly added.

310   **"It was a Monday"**: See Lopes, "Navigazione verso le Indie orientali," 703.

313   **"with such vehemence"**: Ibid., 704.

314   **"And so"**: Ibid., 705.

314   **Almost all the rest**: On the return of the first ships to Lisbon, the Florentine merchant Francesco Corbinelli was told that Gama burned the *Mîrî* with all its gold but saved all the Muslim merchants. Unless he made a glaring mistake, at least one person was ashamed of Gama's actions. Letter dated Lisbon, August 22, 1503; see Teyssier and Valentin, *Voyages de Vasco de Gama*, 354.

315   **seventeen children**: The figure given by the anonymous Portuguese writer; Matteo da Bergamo says twenty. At least some were later given to the monastery at Belém as apprentice friars.

315   **"was a demonstration of the manner"**: João de Barros, quoted in Subrahmanyam, *Career and Legend*, 208.

Chapter 15: Shock and Awe

317   **"we knew his will"**: See Paul Teyssier and Paul Valentin, trans. and eds., *Voyages de Vasco de Gama: Relations des expeditions de 1497–1499 et 1502–3*, 2nd ed. (Paris: Chandeigne, 1998), 329.

320   **a fiendish conspiracy**: The Portuguese factors regularly complained that they were being charged inflated prices; in reality, they were often short on hard currency, their trade goods were seldom in demand, and they invariably refused to pay market rates.

320   **"who as he well knew"**: See "Navigazione verso le Indie orientali scritta per Tomé Lopez," in Giovanni Battista Ramusio, *Navigazioni e Viaggi*, ed. Marica Milanesi (Turin: Einaudi, 1978–1988), 707.

324   **"because since the beginning of the world"**: Ibid., 712.

325   **"A palm tree"**: Ibid., 714.

326   **distributing the Muslim captives**: According to the German sailor, Gama asked the captives, through a Dutch Jew who

had been baptized in Portugal, whether they wanted to die as Christians or keep their own faith. Most, he insists, asked to be baptized, not because they thought it would save their necks but so they could breathe their last believing in the all-powerful God. The anonymous Portuguese account says thirty-two were hanged.

327   **a letter from the admiral:** Barros reports the first part, Lopes the second. Gaspar Correia, typically, manages to make the episode even more ghastly. The fake friar, he says, was put in a boat with his ears, nose, and hands strung around his neck and a message to the Zamorin suggesting he make a curry out of them. The rest of the surviving prisoners were similarly mutilated and their body parts were thrown in the boat; then Gama "ordered their feet to be tied together, as they had no hands with which to untie them: and in order that they should not untie them with their teeth, he ordered them to strike upon their teeth with staves, and they knocked them down their throats; and they were thus put on board, heaped up upon the top of each other, mixed up with the blood which streamed from them; and he ordered mats and dry leaves to be spread over them, and the sails to be set for the shore, and the vessel set on fire." More than eight hundred Muslims, Correia declares, were so murdered; more were strung up by their feet and were used by the Portuguese for target practice. Three of those begged to be baptized, and after they had prayed with a priest, Gama charitably strangled them so "that they might not feel the arrows. The cross-bow men shot arrows and transfixed the others; but the arrows which struck these did not go into them nor make any mark upon them, but fell down." Correia's story is uncorroborated and is almost certainly invented; even so, Gama's gruesome actions have to be seen in the context of an age in which such claims were made not to indict the admiral but to glorify him and his Crusade. Henry E. J. Stanley, trans. and ed., *The Three Voyages of Vasco da Gama, and His Viceroyalty* (London: Hakluyt Society, 1869), 331–34.

333   **"We kept asking ourselves":** See Teyssier and Valentin, *Voyages de Vasco de Gama*, 332–33.

333   **"in this way":** See Lopes, "Navigazione verso le Indie orientali," 720.

334   **Quilon:** Now known as Kollam; the burial place of St. Thomas, though, is traditionally held to be Mylapore, in southern Chennai.

334   **the story went:** The legends are recounted in *The Book of Duarte Barbosa*, trans. Mansel Longworth Dames (London: Hakluyt Society, 1921), 2:97–99, 127–29. There are numerous variant versions; the episode of the martyrdom of the peacock likely derives from a Hindu or Buddhist story.

335   **They had eventually arrived in Persia:** Most likely it was the Persians who first arrived in India. Missionaries belonging to the Persian Church or Church of the East, one of several denominations of Syriac Christianity that emerged from the fifth-century Christological controversies, reached the Malabar Coast and China in the sixth century; in the ninth century many Syriac Christians migrated to southern India. Tamerlane virtually wiped out Persian Christianity at the end of the fourteenth century; the Indian community was one of the few survivors, though it had split into two groups that followed different Syriac rites. In the seventeenth century it fell into further schisms as some St. Thomas Christians entered communion with Rome under Portuguese pressure and others rebelled against the Portuguese and broke with Rome, creating a patchwork of West Syriac St. Thomas Christians, East Syriac St. Thomas Christians, West Syriac Roman Catholics, East Syriac Roman Catholics, non-Syriac Roman Catholics, two Orthodox Syriac denominations, and others that still persists today.

336   **"nearly 25,000 Christians":** *Calcoen: A Dutch Narrative of the Second Voyage of Vasco da Gama to Calicut,* trans. J. P. Berjeau (London: B. M. Pickering, 1874), 29.

Chapter 16: Standoff at Sea

337   **"This Brahmin":** See "Navigazione verso le Indie orientali scritta per Tomé Lopez," in Giovanni Battista Ramusio, *Navigazioni e Viaggi,* ed. Marica Milanesi (Turin: Einaudi, 1978–1988), 724. Correia luridly and no doubt spuriously claims that Gama tortured the Brahmin with burning embers before cutting off his lips and ears and sewing dog's ears in their place. The sources differ on the number and estate of the messengers, their mission, and their fates.

339   **"as if they were ready to fight"**: Ibid., 726.

340   **Soon there were two hundred:** Matteo da Bergamo gives the figure. By the time the fleet was home the count of the enemy boats, according to the Florentine merchant Francesco Corbinelli, had grown to four hundred or even five hundred.

341   **"You vile man!"**: See Lopes, "Navigazione verso le Indie orientali," 728.

344   **"otherwise he would cut off their heads"**: Ibid., 730.

344   **little booty:** According to Castanheda there was plenty, including much porcelain and silver and a golden idol with emerald eyes and a huge ruby on its chest. Correia adds that the sailors found many women belowdecks, including some pretty girls whom Gama kept for the queen. Neither claim is credible.

345   **"for the whole night the wind blew from the sea"**: See Lopes, "Navigazione verso le Indie orientali," 730.

346   **chains of unknown islands:** The Laccadives and Maldives. Nearer Africa the fleet sailed through the Seychelles, Comoros, and Amirante islands; the last were named after Vasco da Gama, Admiral of India.

347   **"It seems to me"**: See Paul Teyssier and Paul Valentin, trans. and eds., *Voyages de Vasco de Gama: Relations des expeditions de 1497–1499 et 1502–3*, 2nd ed. (Paris: Chandeigne, 1998), 338. For unknown reasons, here and throughout his letter the Italian merchant substitutes "Constantinople" for "Lisbon."

348   **The two ships left Mozambique:** Lopes says fifteen ships left Mozambique; if his figure is correct, the caravel that had been built there may have replaced the ship that had been lost off Sofala. The accounts disagree about some of the dates of departure and other details of the return journey; Lopes is my primary guide, but eyewitnesses on different ships fill out the story. Lopes and the German sailor left on June 16; though he later muddles his dates, the Flemish sailor almost certainly left with the same group. The Portuguese sailor left with Gama and the final convoy on June 22. Matteo da Bergamo put the finishing touches to his letters on April 18; with his usual confidence, he assured his employer that he expected to leave within six days and to outrun the other, less seaworthy ships on the way home. He dispatched his reports the next day and his

testimony ends there, but his patience was doubtless sorely tested one last time.

350   **"needed no condiments"**: See Lopes, "Navigazione verso le Indie orientali," 736.

350   **"we found an island"**: *Calcoen: A Dutch Narrative of the Second Voyage of Vasco da Gama to Calicut*, trans. J. P. Berjeau (London: B. M. Pickering, 1874), 32.

350   **"from which we took flour and baked cakes"**: Miloslav Krása, Josef Polišenskyâ, and Peter Ratkoš, eds., *European Expansion (1494–1519): The Voyages of Discovery in the Bratislava Manuscript Lyc. 515/8 (Codex Bratislavensis)* (Prague: Charles University, 1986), 80–81.

351   **"In every place that he has been"**: Letter dated Lisbon, August 20, 1503, quoted in Sanjay Subrahmanyam, *The Career and Legend of Vasco da Gama* (Cambridge: Cambridge University Press, 1997), 225.

351   **"Such a strong wind blew"**: Krása, Polišenskyâ, and Ratkoš, *European Expansion*, 81. The German sailor says one ship returned on August 19, one on August 27, one on October 7, nine on October 10, and one on October 14. The old ship was wrecked off Lisbon on the 24th. "One small ship is still out," the German adds, "and there are fears that it too was wrecked." According to other sources, though, ships were still arriving as late as November.

353   **"the Moors from Mequa"**: Grant letter of February 1504, quoted in Subrahmanyam, *Career and Legend*, 227.

Chapter 17: Empire of the Waves

354   **the precinct of the Kaaba in Mecca:** While disguised as a pilgrim, Varthema teased a Meccan merchant about the effects of the Portuguese voyages: "I began to say to him, if this was the city of Mecca which was so renowned through all the world, where were the jewels and spices, and where were all the various kinds of merchandise which it was reported were brought there. . . . When he told me that the King of Portugal was the cause, I pretended to be much grieved and spoke great ill of the King, merely that he might not think that I was pleased that the Christians should make such a journey." *Travelers in Disguise: Narratives of Eastern Travel by Poggio*

Bracciolini and Ludovico de Varthema, trans. John Winter Jones, rev. Lincoln Davis Hammond (Cambridge, MA: Harvard University Press, 1963), 82.

355   **"subjugating all of India":** Quoted in Sanjay Subrahmanyam, *The Career and Legend of Vasco da Gama* (Cambridge: Cambridge University Press, 1997), 227. The banker was Bartolomeo Marchionni, the same plutocrat who had issued a letter of credit to Pêro da Covilhã.

356   **"without entering them in the books":** Letter from Pêro de Ataíde to Manuel I, dated Mozambique, February 20, 1504, quoted in ibid., 230. Soon afterward, Brás Sodré died in mysterious circumstances; Castanheda and Goís insist that the brothers were condemned by God for the sin of abandoning the king of Cochin. Ataíde took the remaining ships to India and wrote to Manuel asking for a reward, but he died the next year at Mozambique before his letter could do him any good.

357   **"sparing the lives of the Moors":** Hans Mayr, in Malyn Newitt, ed., *East Africa* (Aldershot, UK: Ashgate, 2002), 12.

357   **"burned like one huge fire":** Ibid., 15.

358   **"O sirs, o brothers":** *Travelers in Disguise*, 214–19.

359   **"a venerable beard":** Manuel de Faria e Sousa, *The Portuguese Asia*, trans. Captain John Stevens (London: C. Brome, 1694–1695), 1:207–8.

360   **the Persian Gulf:** Or the Arabian Gulf; the nomenclature is a point of controversy between Iran and the Arab states.

360   **"a very large and beautiful edifice":** Walter de Gray Birch, ed., *The Commentaries of the Great A. Dalboquerque, Second Viceroy of India* (London: Hakluyt Society, 1875–1894), 1:81.

360   **the fabled city:** Hormuz was quickly lost when several of Albuquerque's captains rebelled against the heavy work of building the fortress in the parching heat and absconded to India. It was not properly retaken until 1515, again by Albuquerque but with a much larger force. Hormuz gave Portugal overlordship of the ports of the Persian Gulf and eastern Arabia; the island remained under Portuguese rule until it was taken in the seventeenth century by a combined Persian-English force.

360   **a garden of balsam trees:** See Stefan Halikowski Smith, "Mean-

ings Behind Myths: The Multiple Manifestations of the Tree of the Virgin at Matarea," in *Mediterranean Historical Review* 23, no. 2 (December 2008): 101–28; Marcus Milwright, "The Balsam of Matariyya: An Exploration of a Medieval Panacea," in *Bulletin of the School of Oriental and African Studies* 66, no. 2 (2003): 193–209.

360   **the infant Jesus:** For the story of Mary washing Jesus's shirt, see William Schneemelcher, ed., *New Testament Apocrypha*, vol. 1, *Gospels and Related Writings* (Louisville, KY: Westminster John Knox Press, 2003), 460. In another version, Jesus breaks up Joseph's staff, plants the pieces, and waters them from a well he digs with his own hands; they immediately grow into balsam saplings. See Otto F. A. Meinardus, *Two Thousand Years of Coptic Christianity* (Cairo: American University in Cairo Press, 1999), 21.

361   **a Franciscan friar:** The friar was named Fra Mauro; the sultan was Qansuh al-Ghuri, who took power in 1501 after a succession struggle unleashed by the death of the long-reigning Qaitbay saw four sultans dispatched in quick succession. See Donald Weinstein, *Ambassador from Venice: Pietro Pasqualigo in Lisbon, 1501* (Minneapolis: University of Minnesota Press, 1960), 78–79.

362   **one was unmasked:** The spy was named Ca' Masser; he posed as a merchant and sent his coded reports care of Venice's ambassador in Spain. The nephew of the Florentine banker Bartolomeo Marchionni exposed him before he even arrived in Lisbon, but Manuel eventually freed him. In his report he correctly predicted that the Portuguese would be able to dominate the waters around India but would not be able to conquer Mecca, blockade all Arab shipping, or permanently monopolize the spice trade. His intelligence encouraged the Venetians to throw in their lot with their Muslim partners and plot reprisals against Portugal. See Robert Finlay, "Crisis and Crusade in the Mediterranean: Venice, Portugal and the Cape Route to India, 1498–1509," in *Studi Veneziani* n.s. 28 (1994): 45–90.

363   *Flor de la Mar:* The big carrack was one of the most famous ships of the Age of Discovery. After returning to Lisbon with Gama, she went back east with Almeida in 1505; besides winning the day at Diu, she took part in the conquest of Hormuz, Goa, and Malacca. The aging ship sank in a storm while carrying a vast haul of treasure

back from Malacca; many of the crew died, and Albuquerque, who was on board, had to paddle to safety on a makeshift raft. Despite the best efforts of treasure hunters the wreck has never been found.

363   **The papacy, meanwhile:** The three powers formed the League of Cambrai; the decisive encounter was the Battle of Agnadello in 1509. The league soon disintegrated and Venice recovered many of its losses, if not all of its pride. In the end, it was the revolution in global trade instigated by the Portuguese that condemned Venice—like its Ottoman ally—to a slow decline.

364   **a man suspected of being a** *marrano*: Many of the New Christians, or *conversos*, were suspected of being secret Jews and were labeled *marranos*, from the Spanish for "pig." Some did indeed continue to observe Jewish precepts in private, though many became fully signed-up Catholics. Paranoia mounted during periods of social upheaval; shortly before the Lisbon Massacre the plague hit the city, and suspected marranos were the scapegoat. As well as executing the ringleaders, Manuel extended the moratorium on investigations into the conversos' religion by twenty years. Estimates of the dead range as high as four thousand.

365   **he replaced the reluctant Almeida:** Albuquerque was appointed in 1508, but the outgoing viceroy refused to accept the appointment and slung his successor in jail. The canny Albuquerque bided his time and finally took office in November 1509. Almeida was killed on his way home when his men engaged in some unwise cattle rustling near the Cape of Good Hope.

365   **he hatched a plot to steal the body of the Prophet Muhammad:** For Albuquerque's schemes, see Birch, *Commentaries of the Great A. Dalboquerque*, 4:36–37. Albuquerque was not the first Crusader to contemplate the theft of Muhammad's remains. Back in the time of the Second Crusade, a particularly unhinged Frenchman named Reynaud de Châtillon had launched an outrageous plot to invade the Red Sea. Reynaud had married into the lordship of Transjordan, a barren corner of the Kingdom of Jerusalem that stretched south toward the Gulf of Aqaba and straddled the trade and pilgrimage routes from Syria to Arabia and Egypt. In an uncanny anticipation of Venice's later activities at Suez, he had a fleet of galleys constructed in prefabricated sections and transported on

camels to the gulf port of Eilat, where they were assembled and launched on the Red Sea. Along with intercepting merchant shipping from India and Africa, Reynaud planned to track down Muhammad's tomb, dig up his body, and bring it back to be reburied in his backyard. That way, he predicted, the hajj would be diverted to Transjordan and he would become fantastically rich. A detachment of Crusaders landed in Arabia and began plundering and raping pilgrims; by the time they were finally cornered they were within a few miles of Medina. An outraged Saladin sent orders to kill every last man, not least to stop them spilling the secrets of the Red Sea trade; four years later, at the Horns of Hattin, he fulfilled his pledge to behead the truculent Frenchmen. By drawing Saladin out, Reynaud had sabotaged the entire Crusading movement.

366   **"On one night":** Manuel de Faria e Sousa, in Robert Kerr, *A General History and Collection of Voyages and Travels* (Edinburgh: William Blackwood, 1811–1824), 6:137.

367   **"Whoever is lord of Malacca":** *The Suma Oriental of Tomé Pires*, trans. and ed. Armando Cortesão (London: Hakluyt Society, 1944), 2:287. Malacca owed its wealth to Tamerlane, who wreaked such destruction on the cities of the Silk Road that, in 1402, China rerouted its exports by sea.

368   **the false and diabolical religion:** Ibid., 1:2.

368   **Eventually the Portuguese:** The merchants reached Japan in 1542; the Portuguese were permitted to establish a permanent settlement at Macao in 1557. The shipping lane between the two was the key to a hugely lucrative trading loop. From Goa, merchants shipped ivory and ebony to Macao, where they bought silks and porcelain. Since China had banned direct trade with Japan they headed to Nagasaki, where they exchanged the prized goods for a small fortune in silver. Since silver was worth much more in China than in Japan, on their way home they returned to Macao and purchased vast quantities of Chinese luxuries for onward shipment to Europe.

368   **"It appears to me":** *Travelers in Disguise*, 230.

369   **ten thousand Portuguese soldiers landed in Morocco:** Their objective was to establish a fortress at Mamora (now Mehdia), which commanded the route up the Sebou River to Fez. Despite

his setbacks in Africa, Manuel was still hoping to march through southern Morocco and onward to Egypt and Palestine.

370   **The fleet arrived in Aden:** In 1513, in the only signal failure of his governorship, Albuquerque's forces were beaten back from the high walls of Aden; the defenders were steeled by the knowledge that their defeat would threaten the holy cities of Mecca and Medina themselves. That failure only made the lapse of judgment four years later even more galling, and in 1538 Aden fell to the Ottomans. Without complete control of the Aden–Hormuz–Calicut trade triangle, Portugal was never fully able to stop spices reaching the Muslim world.

372   **America was still seen as a barrier to reaching the East:** It was during Charles I's reign that Cortés and Pizarro destroyed the Aztec and Inca empires and began to export Christianity to South America. Even so, they were still hankering after the East. In 1526 Cortés felt it necessary to apologize to the Spanish monarch for not finding a western route to the Spice Islands, and in 1541 Pizarro's brother Gonzalo mounted a disastrous expedition across Ecuador in search of the fabled Country of Cinnamon. Cortés likened the Aztec cities to Muslim Granada and called their temples mosques; in the conquistadores' onslaught, the holy vengeance against Muslims fanned by the Iberian Reconquest was visited on a new world where Islam had never existed.

373   **the dispute was only settled:** As well as ceding the Moluccas to Portugal, the Treaty of Zaragoza (1529) confirmed Spain's rights over the Philippines. They, too, would turn out to be in the Portuguese hemisphere.

373   **"the evil sect of Mafamede":** Quoted in Subrahmanyam, *Career and Legend*, 283. Manuel was still under the common misapprehension that Muhammad was buried at Mecca.

Chapter 18: The King's Deputy

375   **"meted out":** Royal order dated Tomar, March 21, 1507; see A. C. Teixeira de Aragão, *Vasco da Gama e a Vidigueira: Estudo Histórico*, 2nd ed. (Lisbon: Imprensa Nacional, 1898), 250–52.

376   **"by which time":** Letter of Manuel I to Gama dated August 1518; see ibid., 257–58.

376 **"especially in the discovery of the Indies":** Letter of Manuel I dated December 17, 1519, quoted in Sanjay Subrahmanyam, *The Career and Legend of Vasco da Gama* (Cambridge: Cambridge University Press, 1997), 281. Subrahmanyam notes that Portugal could then only muster "two Dukes, two Marquises, a Count-Bishop, and twelve other Counts."

376 **Vasco da Gama set sail for India:** Gaspar Correia, a fanciful chronicler of Gama's first two voyages, is more reliable on the third. By 1524 he had been in India for more than a decade; he first arrived, aged sixteen, as a soldier, but to his relief he was instead appointed secretary to Afonso de Albuquerque. As usual, the official chronicles and contemporary documents fill out the story.

376 **two of his sons:** Paulo da Gama died in a naval battle off Malacca in 1534. Estêvão da Gama became governor of India in 1540; in 1541 he led a naval expedition into the Red Sea to attack the Ottoman fleet, but when he reached Suez he found he had been expected and was forced to retreat. His younger brother Cristóvão disembarked to lead a Crusade in Ethiopia, which had been invaded by a Muslim army that had declared holy war and was equipped with Ottoman cannon. Cristóvão was captured and executed the next year, but his intervention was instrumental in Ethiopia's successful defense. Estêvão died in Venice, where he had absconded to avoid marrying the wife chosen for him by the king. Of the other brothers, the eldest, Francisco, succeeded as Count of Vidigueira, while the two youngest, Pedro and Álvaro, served in turn as captains of Malacca.

377 **"kept a Concubine":** Jean Mocquet, *Travels and Voyages into Africa, Asia, and America, the East and West Indies; Syria, Jerusalem, and the Holy Land*, trans. Nathaniel Pullen (London, 1696), 207.

377 **"should be publicly scourged":** Henry E. J. Stanley, trans. and ed., *The Three Voyages of Vasco da Gama, and His Viceroyalty* (London: Hakluyt Society, 1869), 394.

378 **they murdered him:** The captain was known as Mossem Gaspar Malhorquim; the caravel was captured the following year and was taken to India, where many of the crew were hanged.

378 **"each time during the space of a Credo":** Stanley, *Three Voyages*, 383.

379 **"Courage, my friends!":** Various versions of the quotation are attributed to Gama; this is from Manuel de Faria e Sousa, *The Portuguese Asia*, trans. Captain John Stevens (London: C. Brome, 1694–1695), 1:280.

379 **a second Great Flood:** The belief was widespread across Europe. Fifty-six authors rushed 133 books into print, thousands of Londoners fled to higher ground, and numerous arks were constructed. See Lynn Thorndike, *History of Magic and Experimental Science*, vols. 5 and 6, *The Sixteenth Century* (New York: Columbia University Press, 1941), 5:178–233.

380 **"would make the King rich":** Stanley, *Three Voyages*, 396.

380 **"great evil doings":** Ibid., 390.

380 **a palatial hospital:** Grand though it was, the hospital's effectiveness was limited by the fact that its chief doctors were subject to the same three-year term limit as other Portuguese officials. Just as they got the hang of the unfamiliar tropical diseases, they went home.

381 **"The justice of the King":** Stanley, *Three Voyages*, 394–96.

382 **The members of Goa's Municipal Council wrote:** See ibid., Appendix, pp. x–xvi, for the original text and pp. 385–90 for Stanley's translation. The new captain of Goa had a different take on the colony's troubles: he thought Goa was too full of priests and men too comfortably married with local women to mount a proper defense. See Subrahmanyam, *Career and Legend*, 316.

384 **"He had it proclaimed":** Stanley, *Three Voyages*, 397–98.

385 **"Sir, I will build you brigantines":** Ibid., 405.

385 **The Spanish had to be confronted:** Juan de Zúñiga, the Spanish ambassador in Portugal, reported to Charles I that Spain could expect no quarter from Gama. According to Zúñiga, in addition to threatening to sink Spain's ships, the viceroy had vowed to disregard any agreement that gave Spain rights over the Moluccas and to do whatever it took to keep the islands in Portuguese hands. Letter dated Tomar, July 21, 1523, quoted in Subrahmanyam, *Career and Legend*, 299–300.

385 **a bishop had written to the Portuguese king:** Ibid., 325. The main church at Cranganore had been attacked and burned down in 1523.

385 **"he would go and destroy Calicut":** Stanley, *Three Voyages*, 412.

386 **Gama sent a delegation:** Even with the powers vested in him as viceroy, Gama overstepped his authority. According to Castanheda,

a royal letter was handed to Dom Duarte that exempted him and his men from Gama's jurisdiction and gave him permission to stay in India until the homebound fleet was ready; if necessary he was to bide his time at the Cannanore fortress, which would become his personal fiefdom for the duration. Correia says that Duarte refused to board the ship Gama specified and Gama threatened to sink the ship he was on; after a raging argument with the viceroy and a tearful farewell to his dining companions, Luís joined his brother and persuaded him to disembark. Ibid., 417–20.

387 **"great fits of irritation":** Ibid., 422. One theory is that Gama was suffering from oropharyngeal anthrax.

387 **He asked for his bones to be returned to Portugal:** Gama's remains were not repatriated until 1538. In the nineteenth century they were moved with great ceremony to Lisbon and were reburied in the monastery at Belém that had been built to commemorate his first voyage. Some years later it was discovered that the wrong set of bones had been disturbed, and a more discreet ceremony was held to rehouse the correct remains.

388 **"The captains":** Letter of Pêro de Faria, dated Cochin, December 28, 1524, quoted in Subrahmanyam, *Career and Legend*, 343.

388 **"as was reasonable":** Stanley, *Three Voyages*, 427.

389 **a French pirate:** In retribution for his brother's behavior the pirate and his crew had their hands cut off and their ship burned, an act that set off years of cruel reprisals by French pirates against the Portuguese.

Chapter 19: The Crazy Sea

391 **the most devastating of many exposés:** The following quotations are from Jean Mocquet, *Travels and Voyages into Africa, Asia, and America, the East and West Indies; Syria, Jerusalem, and the Holy Land*, trans. Nathaniel Pullen (London, 1696), 246–46v, 267–68, 249–52v, 259–60, 262–63. Jan Huygen van Linschoten and François Pyrard paint only slightly less lurid portraits of Goa.

391 **Goa had grown into a colonial city:** For Old Goa, see José Nicolau da Fonseca, *An Historical and Archaeological Sketch of the City of Goa* (Bombay: Thacker, 1878); Anthony Disney, *The Portuguese in India and Other Studies, 1500–1700* (Farnham, UK: Ashgate, 2009).

392   **a Hindu temple:** The temple was near Cochin; the Portuguese attacked it even though it was sacred to their allies.

396   **One captain of Sofala:** The captain was Dom Jorge Teles de Meneses; the factor was João Velho, who in 1547 dispatched a long and vehement letter about his mistreatment to the king. See M. D. D. Newitt, *A History of Mozambique* (London: Hurst, 1995), 1–3.

397   **"The Portuguese are much detested":** Gasparo Contarini, address to the Venetian Senate on November 16, 1525, quoted in Sanjay Subrahmanyam, *The Career and Legend of Vasco da Gama* (Cambridge: Cambridge University Press, 1997), 350.

397   **seeking martyrdom:** A Mappila epic titled *The Gift to the Holy Warriors in Respect to Some Deeds of the Portuguese* chronicles and glorifies the campaign of defiance. As many as 10,000 may have died in a Mappila uprising of 1921–1922. See Stephen Frederic Dale, "Religious Suicide in Islamic Asia," in *Journal of Conflict Resolution* 32, no. 1 (March 1988): 37–59.

398   **died while trying to reach China:** The pioneering missionary died of fever in 1552 and was buried on a beach; the next year his body was taken to Goa. It still rests in a magnificent tomb in the Basilica of Bom Jesus in Old Goa, except for two arm bones, one of which was taken to the Gesù in Rome and the other of which was intended for Japan, where Xavier had worked for two years, but only made it as far as Macau.

399   **The Goan Inquisition:** The tribunal was not abolished until 1812. Most of its records were destroyed; the number of its victims is unknown, though at least sixteen thousand cases are believed to have been brought to trial. See A. K. Priolkar, *The Goa Inquisition* (Bombay: Bombay University Press, 1961). *L'inquisition de Goa: La relation de Charles Dellon (1687)*, ed. Charles Amiel and Anne Lima (Paris: Chandeigne, 1997), is a modern edition of the famously chilling account of a French eyewitness.

401   **"holy war":** Quoted in K. M. Mathew, *History of the Portuguese Navigation in India, 1497–1600* (New Delhi: K. M. Mittal, 1988), 214.

401   **a young Portuguese king:** King Sebastian, who succeeded to the throne at three years of age in 1557, was heavily influenced by his Jesuit tutors and was determined to stiffen efforts to spread the faith.

In 1569 he took up a plan that had been heavily touted by Portugal's merchants to seize the legendary African gold mines of Monomotapa, but before proceeding he put the question of the morality of the enterprise to a committee of lawyers and theologians. The answer came back that the proposed war was just on the grounds that a Jesuit priest had been murdered in the region and that the local king harbored Muslims, providing that spreading the gospel and saving souls was its primary objective. Sebastian dispatched Francisco Barreto, a former governor of Portuguese India, at the head of a large army; with him went a Jesuit priest whose advice Barreto was under royal orders to heed. Instead of heading for the mines, they spent a year and a half massacring Muslims on the coast and then set off on the trail of the priest's murderers. Before they reached their goal Barreto and most of his men died of fever, but the expedition marked the beginning of a concerted campaign of colonization and evangelism in the African interior.

402   **"it seems that—on account of our sins"**: João de Barros, quoted in Peter Russell, *Prince Henry 'the Navigator': A Life* (New Haven, CT: Yale University Press, 2000), 343.

403   **the *São João* left Cochin:** For its story, see M. D. D. Newitt, ed., *East Africa* (Aldershot, UK: Ashgate, 2002), 99–103. The account first appeared in Bernardo Gomes de Brito's *História Trágico-Marítima*, a two-volume collection of marine disasters published in Lisbon between 1729 and 1736. For a partial English translation, see C. R. Boxer, ed. and trans., *The Tragic History of the Sea, 1589–1622* (London: Hakluyt Society, 1959) and *Further Selections from 'The Tragic History of the Sea,' 1559–1565* (Cambridge: Hakluyt Society, 1968).

405   **another Portuguese ship was wrecked:** Newitt, *East Africa*, 105–6.

406   **"I started to complain":** Ibid., 65. Gomes was shipwrecked shortly before 1645.

Epilogue

407   **"There had never been another man":** As reported by the sculptor Benvenuto Cellini; cited in A. Richard Turner, *Inventing Leonardo* (Berkeley: University of California Press, 1994), 52.

409   **Christians teamed up with Muslims to fight Christians:** "I
cannot deny," Francis told the Venetian ambassador Giorgio Gritti
in 1531, "that I wish to see the Turk all-powerful and ready for war,
not for himself—for he is an infidel and we are all Christians—but
to weaken the power of the emperor, to compel him to make major
expenses, and to reassure all the other governments who are opposed to such a formidable enemy." Quoted in André Clot, *Suleiman
the Magnificent*, trans. Matthew J. Reisz (London: Saqi, 1992), 137.

409   **"Are you seamen to fill your casks":** Harold Lamb, *Suleiman the
Magnificent: Sultan of the East* (Garden City, NY: Doubleday, 1951),
229.

410   **the Protestant Reformation:** Martin Luther rejected the whole
notion of holy war as contrary to the teachings of Christ, though he
did revise his early view that the Turks were the scourge that would
destroy the Antichrist—the pope—and so should not be resisted.

410   **"Elizabeth, the pretended Queen":** Quoted in Kate Aughterson, ed., *The English Renaissance: An Anthology of Sources and Documents* (London: Routledge, 1998), 36.

410   **"the pride of the women":** Quoted in Susan A. Skilliter, *William
Harborne and the Trade with Turkey, 1578–1582: A Documentary Study
of the First Anglo-Ottoman Relations* (Oxford: Oxford University
Press, 1977), 123. Both English and Turks wrote in Latin. For the
Anglo-Ottoman entente, see Albert Lindsay Rowland, *England and
Turkey: The Rise of Diplomatic and Commercial Relations* (New York:
Burt Franklin, 1968); for a broader view, see Nabil Matar, *Islam
in Britain, 1558–1685* (Cambridge: Cambridge University Press,
1998).

410   **"the most august and benign Caesar":** Susan A. Skilliter,
"William Harborne, the First English Ambassador, 1583–1588," in
Four Centuries of Turco-British Relations, ed. William Hale and Ali
Ihsan Bagis (Beverley, UK: Eothen, 1984), 22.

412   **"The Madre de Dios taken":** Richard Hakluyt, *The Principal
Navigations, Voyages, Traffiques and Discoveries of the English Nation*
(Glasgow: MacLehose, 1903–1905), 7:116–17. The discovery of the
document is revealed in "The Epistle Dedicatorie in the Second
Volume of the Second Edition, 1599" (1:lxxii).

413   **an instant bestseller in three languages:** In 1595 Linschoten

published a description of Portuguese navigation in the East; the following year he capitalized on his instant fame by rushing into print a full account of his travels. An English translation of the latter, titled *Iohn Huighen van Linschoten his Discours of Voyages into ye Easte & West Indies*, was published in 1598; a German edition appeared the same year. A Spanish sailor and priest named Bernardino de Escalante beat both Fitch and Linschoten into print; his revelations about Portugal's route to China were published in an English translation in 1579.

414   **the first English fleet returned home from India:** Sir James Lancaster, an Englishman who had sailed with and fought for the Portuguese, set out in 1591 with three ships and reached Zanzibar, Malacca, and Ceylon; a single ship limped home in 1594 with twenty-five survivors on board. In 1600 Lancaster took command of the East India Company's first fleet and reached Indonesia, where he established the first English factory, at Bantam in west Java. The Dutch expedition of 1595 was led by Cornelius de Houtman, who had earlier been sent to Lisbon to dig up information on the Spice Islands. The voyage was beset by scurvy, murderous brawls, pirate attacks, and battles that Houtman largely incited. Two-thirds of the crew died, and Houtman returned home only to find he had been preceded and trounced by Linschoten. In 1599 he was reportedly killed by the female admiral of Aceh and her all-woman navy.

415   **Sir Thomas Roe:** For the accomplished ambassador's life, see Michael J. Brown, *Itinerant Ambassador: The Life of Sir Thomas Roe* (Lexington: University Press of Kentucky, 1970). The journals and letters pertaining to his Indian journey are in *The Embassy of Sir Thomas Roe to the Court of the Great Mogul, 1615–1619*, ed. William Foster (London: Hakluyt Society, 1899).

416   **the handsome redbrick Jesuit College:** The building, which dominates the old administrative heart of the town, was commandeered for the governor's palace when Portugal outlawed the Society of Jesus. It is now a sleepy museum.

417   **Ceuta's "liberation":** *Time*, June 26, 2007.

418   **"We have succeeded":** *The Times* (London), March 13, 2004.

418   **President George W. Bush:** At a press conference on September 16, 2001, George W. Bush referred to the newly declared war on

terror as a "crusade." His spokesman later expressed regret for his terminology, but the next year the president again called the ongoing war a crusade. Ron Suskind, "Faith, Certainty and the Presidency of George W. Bush," *New York Times Magazine,* October 17, 2004.

418 **"Crusader-Zionist alliance":** The statement, released in February 1998, was titled "Jihad Against Jews and Crusaders." The Arabian Peninsula, it also declared, "has never—since Allah made it flat, created its desert, and encircled it with seas—been stormed by any forces like the Crusader armies spreading in it like locusts, eating its riches and wiping out its plantations." Peter L. Bergen, *The Osama Bin Laden I Know: An Oral History of Al Qaeda's Leader* (New York: Free Press, 2006), 195.

418 **"a haemmorhage":** *Sunday Times* (London), November 28, 2010.

419 **"the greatest event since the creation of the world":** Francisco López de Gómara, "Dedication" to *Historia general de las Indias* (Saragossa, 1552).

419 **"The discovery of America":** Adam Smith, *An Inquiry into the Nature and Causes of the Wealth of Nations,* ed. Edwin Cannan (London: University Paperbacks, 1961), 2:141.

420 **hold off and eventually repel the Ottoman challenge:** Other factors, of course, were at play, not least the Ottomans' unshakable belief, even as their empire was hamstrung by harem intrigues and endemic patronage while the West emerged into the Enlightenment, that their way was best. In the long run, though, the global pressure exerted by the voyages of discovery crucially tipped the balance. The point is well made by Bernard Lewis, a leading scholar of Islam and the Middle East. "The final defeat and withdrawal of the armies of Islam was no doubt due in the first instance to the valiant defenders of Vienna," writes Lewis, "but in the larger perspective, it was due to those self-same adventurers whose voyages across the ocean and greed for gold aroused [the ire of their European rivals]. Whatever their motives, their voyages brought vast new lands under European rule or influence, placed great wealth in bullion and resources at European disposal, and thus gave Europe new strength with which to resist and ultimately throw back the Muslim invader." *Islam and the West* (New York: Oxford University Press, 1993), 16.

420 **Western imperialism in Asia:** In India, the entire colonial era from Gama's arrival to independence has been labeled the Vasco da Gama epoch of history; see K. M. Panikkar, *Asia and Western Dominance: A Survey of the Vasco da Gama Epoch of Asian History, 1498–1945* (London: Allen & Unwin, 1959). It has conversely been argued that the Portuguese had little direct impact on the great empires of South and East Asia. Narrowly speaking, yes; but then the balance of trade with India, never mind with China, was never a factor in Portugal's calculations. India was the destination, but to weaken Islam was the aim. On a broader view, the impact of the discoveries was profound; when Vasco da Gama sailed east, India and China between them accounted for half the world economy.

420 **joined forces to fight a common enemy:** In the Crimean War of 1853–1856, Anglican Britain and Catholic France joined forces with the Muslim Ottomans to fight the Orthodox Russians. The British and French were not just keen to halt Russia's expansion; they deliberately set out to support Islam's fight with Eastern Christianity, which Western clerics readily denounced as a semi-pagan heresy. Ever since 1453, the Russians had claimed they were the rightful heirs of the Byzantine Empire; *tsar* is Russian for "Caesar," and Moscow was declared the third Rome. The Western allies were particularly aghast at the prospect of the Russians reversing the Muslim conquest of Constantinople and installing themselves—and the Orthodox Church—in the second Rome.

SELECT BIBLIOGRAPHY

Alam, Muzaffar, and Sanjay Subrahmanyam, eds. *Indo-Persian Travels in the Age of Discoveries, 1400–1800.* Cambridge: Cambridge University Press, 2007.

Altabé, David F. *Spanish and Portuguese Jewry Before and After 1492.* Brooklyn, NY: Sepher-Hermon, 1983.

Alvares, Francisco. *Narrative of the Portuguese Embassy to Abyssinia During the Years 1520–1527.* Translated and edited by Lord Stanley of Alderley. London: Hakluyt Society, 1881.

————. *The Prester John of the Indies: A True Relation of the Lands of the Prester John, Being the Narrative of the Portuguese Embassy to Ethiopia in 1520.* Revised and edited by C. F. Beckingham and G. W. B. Huntingford. 2 vols. Cambridge: Hakluyt Society, 1961.

Ames, Glenn J., trans. and ed. *En Nome De Deus: The Journal of the First Voyage of Vasco da Gama to India, 1497–1499.* Leiden: Brill, 2009.

Armstrong, Karen. *The Battle for God: Fundamentalism in Judaism, Christianity and Islam.* London: HarperCollins, 2000.

————. *Islam: A Short History.* London: Weidenfeld & Nicolson, 2000.

————. *Muhammad: A Biography of the Prophet.* London: Gollancz, 1991.

Asbridge, Thomas. *The First Crusade: A New History.* London: Free Press, 2004.

Aslan, Reza. *No God but God: The Origins, Evolution, and Future of Islam.* London: William Heinemann, 2005.

Aughterson, Kate, ed., *The English Renaissance: An Anthology of Sources and Documents.* London: Routledge, 1998.

Ayyar, K. V. Krishna. *The Zamorins of Calicut.* Calicut: University of Calicut, 1999.

Babinger, Franz. *Mehmed the Conqueror and His Time.* Princeton, NJ: Princeton University Press, 1978.

Baião, António, A. de Magalhães Basto, and Damião Peres, eds. *Diário da viagem de Vasco da Gama*. Porto: Livraria Civilização, 1945.

Barber, Malcolm. *The New Knighthood: A History of the Order of the Temple*. Cambridge: Cambridge University Press, 1994.

Barbosa, Duarte. *The Book of Duarte Barbosa*. Translated by Mansel Longworth Dames. 2 vols. London: Hakluyt Society, 1921.

Barros, João de. *Ásia de João de Barros: Dos feitos que os Portugueses fizeram no descobrimento e conquista dos mares e terras do Oriente*. Edited by Hernani Cidade and Manuel Múrias. 6th ed. 4 vols. Lisbon: Divisão de publicações e biblioteca, Agência geral das colónias, 1945–1946.

Baumgarten, Martin von. "The Travels of Martin Baumgarten . . . through Egypt, Arabia, Palestine and Syria." In *A Collection of Voyages and Travels*, edited by Awnsham Churchill, 1:385–452. London: A. & J. Churchill, 1704.

Beckingham, C. F. *Between Islam and Christendom: Travellers, Facts and Legends in the Middle Ages and the Renaissance*. London: Variorum Reprints, 1983.

Bergen, Peter L. *The Osama Bin Laden I Know: An Oral History of Al Qaeda's Leader*. New York: Free Press, 2006.

Bergreen, Laurence. *Marco Polo: From Venice to Xanadu*. London: Quercus, 2008.

———. *Over the Edge of the World: Magellan's Terrifying Circumnavigation of the Globe*. London: HarperCollins, 2003.

Berjeau, J. P., trans. *Calcoen: A Dutch Narrative of the Second Voyage of Vasco da Gama*. London: B. M. Pickering, 1874.

Bernstein, William. *A Splendid Exchange: How Trade Shaped the World*. London: Atlantic, 2008.

Birch, Walter de Gray, ed. *The Commentaries of the Great A. Dalboquerque, Second Viceroy of India*. 4 vols. London: Hakluyt Society, 1875–1894.

Blake, J. W., trans. and ed. *Europeans in West Africa, 1450–1560*. London: Hakluyt Society, 1942.

Blunt, Wilfred. *Pietro's Pilgrimage: A Journey to India and Back at the Beginning of the Seventeenth Century*. London: James Barrie, 1953.

Boas, Adrian J. *Jerusalem in the Time of the Crusades: Society, Landscape, and Art in the Holy City Under Frankish Rule*. London: Routledge, 2001.

Bonner, Michael. *Jihad in Islamic History: Doctrines and Practice*. Princeton, NJ: Princeton University Press, 2006.

Boorstin, Daniel J. *The Discoverers*. New York: Random House, 1983.

Bovill, Edward William. *The Golden Trade of the Moors*. 2nd ed. Revised by Robin Hallet. London: Oxford University Press, 1970.

Boxer, C. R. *The Portuguese Seaborne Empire 1415–1825*. London: Hutchinson, 1969.

Bracciolini, Poggio, and Ludovico de Varthema. *Travelers in Disguise: Narratives of Eastern Travel by Poggio Bracciolini and Ludovico de Varthema*. Translated by John Winter Jones and revised by Lincoln Davis Hammond. Cambridge, MA: Harvard University Press, 1963.

Brett, Michael, and Elizabeth Fentress. *The Berbers*. Oxford: Blackwell, 1996.

Brotton, Jerry. *The Renaissance Bazaar: From the Silk Road to Michelangelo*. Oxford: Oxford University Press, 2002.

Butler, Alfred J. *The Arab Conquest of Egypt—And the Last Thirty Years of the Roman Dominion*. Oxford: Clarendon Press, 1902.

Camões, Luiz Vaz de. *The Lusíads*. Oxford: Oxford University Press, 1997.

Campbell, I. C. "The Lateen Sail in World History." *Journal of World History* 6, no. 1 (Spring 1995): 1–23.

Carboni, Stefano, ed. *Venice and the Islamic World, 827–1797*. New Haven, CT: Yale University Press, 2007.

Caron, Marie-Thérèse, and Denis Clauzel, eds. *Le Banquet du Faisan*. Arras: Artois Presses Université, 1997.

Castanheda, Femão Lopes de. *The First Booke of the Historie of the Discoverie and Conquest of the East Indias, Enterprised by the Portingales, in their Daungerous Navigations, in the Time of King Don John, the Second of that Name*. . . . Translated by Nicholas Lichefild. London: Thomas East, 1582.

———. *História do descobrimento e conquista da Índia pelos Portugueses*. Edited by Manuel Lopes de Almeida. 2 vols. Porto: Lelloe Irmão, 1979.

Chaudhuri, K. N. *Trade and Civilization in the Indian Ocean: An Economic History from the Rise of Islam to 1850*. Cambridge: Cambridge University Press, 1985.

Cheyney, E. P. *Readings in English History Drawn from the Original Sources*. Boston: Ginn, 1922.

Chittick, H. Neville. *Kilwa: An Islamic Trading City on the East African Coast*. 2 vols. Nairobi: British Institute in Eastern Africa, 1974.

Clot, André. *Suleiman the Magnificent*. Translated by Matthew J. Reisz. London: Saqi, 1992.

Cohen, J. M. *The Four Voyages of Christopher Columbus*. Harmondsworth, UK: Penguin, 1969.

Cole, Peter, trans. and ed. *The Dream of the Poem: Hebrew Poetry from Muslim and Christian Spain, 950–1492*. Princeton, NJ: Princeton University Press, 2007.

Constable, Olivia Remie, ed. *Medieval Iberia: Readings from Christian, Muslim, and Jewish Sources*. Philadelphia: University of Pennsylvania Press, 1997.

———. "Muslim Merchants in Andalusi International Trade." In *The Legacy of Muslim Spain*, edited by Salma Khadra Jayyusi, 759–773. Leiden: Brill, 1992.

Correia, Gaspar. *Lendas da Índia*. Edited by M. Lopes de Almeida. 4 vols. Porto: Lello e Irmão, 1975.

Cortesão, Armando. *The Mystery of Vasco da Gama*. Coimbra. Universidade de Coimbra, 1973.

Costa, Leonor Freire, ed. "Relação Anónima da Segunda Viagem de Vasco da Gama à Índia." In *Cidadania e história: Em homenagem a Jaime Cortesão*, 141–99. Lisbon: Livraria Sá da Costa Editora, 1985.

Crone, G. R., trans. and ed. *The Voyages of Cadamosto, and Other Documents on Western Africa in the Second Half of the Fifteenth Century*. London: Hakluyt Society, 1937.

Dalby, Andrew. *Dangerous Tastes: The Story of Spices*. London: British Museum Press, 2000.

Dale, Stephen Frederic. *The Mappilas of Malabar, 1498–1922*. Clarendon: Oxford, 1980.

———. "Religious Suicide in Islamic Asia." *Journal of Conflict Resolution 32*, no. 1 (March 1988): 37–59.

Das Gupta, Ashin. *The World of the Indian Ocean Merchant 1500–1800*. Oxford: Oxford University Press, 2001.

Davenport, Frances Gardiner, ed. *European Treaties Bearing on the History of the United States and Its Dependencies to 1648*. Washington, DC: Carnegie Institution of Washington, 1917.

Dawood, N. J., trans. *The Koran: With a Parallel Arabic Text*. Penguin: London, 2000.

Delumeau, Jean. *History of Paradise: The Garden of Eden in Myth and Tradition*. Translated by Matthew O'Connell. New York: Continuum, 1995.

Diffie, Bailey W., and George D. Winius. *Foundations of the Portuguese Empire, 1415–1580*. St. Paul: University of Minnesota Press, 1977.

Disney, Anthony. *A History of Portugal and the Portuguese Empire: From Beginnings to 1807*. 2 vols. Cambridge: Cambridge University Press, 2009.

————. *The Portuguese in India and Other Studies, 1500–1700*. Farnham, UK: Ashgate, 2009.

Disney, Anthony, and Emily Booth, eds. *Vasco da Gama and the Linking of Europe and Asia*. Delhi: Oxford University Press, 2000.

Dols, Michael W. *The Black Death in the Middle East*. Princeton, NJ: Princeton University Press, 1977.

Donner, Fred McGraw. *The Early Islamic Conquests*. Princeton, NJ: Princeton University Press, 1981.

Duffy, Eamon. *Saints and Sinners: A History of the Popes*. 3rd ed. New Haven, CT: Yale University Press, 2006.

Dumper, Michael, and Bruce E. Stanley, eds. *Cities of the Middle East and North Africa: A Historical Encyclopedia*. Oxford: ABC-Clio, 2007.

Dunn, Ross E. *The Adventures of Ibn Battuta*. Berkeley: University of California Press, 1989.

Edson, Evelyn. "Reviving the Crusade: Sanudo's Schemes and Vesconte's Maps." In *Eastward Bound: Travel and Travellers, 1050–1550*, edited by Rosamund Allen, 131–55. Manchester: Manchester University Press, 2004.

————. *The World Map, 1300–1492: The Persistence of Tradition and Transformation*. Baltimore: Johns Hopkins University Press, 2007.

Falchetta, Piero. *Fra Mauro's World Map*. Turnhout, Belgium: Brepols, 2006.

Faria e Sousa, Manuel de. *The Portuguese Asia*. Translated by Capt. John Stevens. 3 vols. London: C. Brome, 1694–1695.

Fernandes, Valentim. *Description de la côte d'Afrique de Ceuta au Sénégal*. Paris: Larose, 1938.

Fernández-Armesto, Felipe. *Columbus*. Oxford: Oxford University Press, 1991.

————. *Pathfinders: A Global History of Exploration*. New York: Norton, 2006.

Finnlay, Robert. "Crisis and Crusade in the Mediterranean: Venice, Portugal and the Cape Route to India, 1498–1509." *Studi Veneziani* n.s. 28 (1994): 45–90.

Firdowsi. *Shahnameh: The Persian Book of Kings*. Translated by Dick Davis. New York: Viking, 2006.

Fletcher, Richard A. *The Cross and the Crescent: Christianity and Islam from the Prophet Muhammad to the Reformation*. London: Penguin, 2005.

————. *Moorish Spain*. London: Weidenfeld & Nicolson, 1992.

Flint, Valerie. *The Imaginative Landscape of Christopher Columbus*. Princeton, NJ: Princeton University Press, 1992.

Fonseca, José Nicolau da. *An Historical and Archaeological Sketch of the City of Goa*. Bombay: Thacker, 1878.

Freedman, Paul. *Out of the East: Spices and the Medieval Imagination*. New Haven, CT: Yale University Press, 2008.

Freeman-Grenville, Greville Stewart Parker. *The Medieval History of the Coast of Tanganyika: With Special Reference to Recent Archaeological Discoveries*. London: Oxford University Press, 1962.

Gabrieli, Francesco. *Arab Historians of the Crusades*. Berkeley: University of California Press, 1984.

Gibbs, James, trans. *The History of the Portuguese, During the Reign of Emmanuel written originally in Latin by Jerome Osorio, Bishop of Sylves. . . .* 2 vols. London: A. Millar, 1752.

Góis, Damião de. *Crónica do felicíssimo rei Manuel. . . .* Edited by J. M. Teixeira de Carvalho and David Lopes. 4 vols. Coimbra: Imprensa da Universidade, 1926.

Gordon, Stewart. *When Asia Was the World: Traveling Merchants, Scholars, Warriors, and Monks Who Created the "Riches of the East."* New Haven, CT: Yale University Press, 2008.

Greenlee, William Brooks, trans. and ed. *The Voyage of Pedro Álvares Cabral to Brazil and India, from Contemporary Documents and Narratives*. London: Hakluyt Society, 1938.

Gumilev, L. N. *Searches for an Imaginary Kingdom: The Legend of the Kingdom of Prester John*. Translated by R. E. F. Smith. Cambridge: Cambridge University Press, 1987.

Hakluyt, Richard. *The Principal Navigations, Voyages, Traffiques and Discoveries of the English Nation*. 12 vols. Glasgow: MacLehose, 1903–1905.

Hannoum, Abdelmajid. *Post-Colonial Memories: The Legend of the Kahina, a North African Heroine*. Westport, CT: Heinemann, 2001.

Harris, Jonathan. *Constantinople: Capital of Byzantium*. London: Hambledon Continuum, 2007.

Hart, Henry H. *Sea Road to the Indies*. London: William Hodge, 1952.

Hazard, Harry W., ed. *A History of the Crusades*. 2nd ed. Vol. 3, *The Fourteenth and Fifteenth Centuries*. Madison: University of Wisconsin Press, 1975.

Hillenbrand, Carole. *The Crusades: Islamic Perspectives*. New York: Routledge, 2000.

Hitti, Philip Khuri. *History of Syria, Including Lebanon and Palestine*. London: Macmillan, 1951.

Hobson, John M. *The Eastern Origins of Western Civilization*. Cambridge: Cambridge University Press, 2004.

Holt, Andrew, and James Muldoon, eds. *Competing Voices from the Crusades*. Oxford: Greenwood Press, 2008.

Hourani, Albert Habib. *A History of the Arab Peoples*. Cambridge, MA: Harvard University Press, 2002.

Hourani, George F. *Arab Seafaring in the Indian Ocean in Ancient and Early Medieval Times*. Princeton, NJ: Princeton University Press, 1951.

Howarth, Stephen. *The Knights Templar*. New York: Atheneum, 1982.

Ibn Battuta. *The Travels of Ibn Battuta, A.D. 1325–1354*. Translated and edited by H. A. R. Gibb and C. F. Beckingham. 5 vols. London: Hakluyt Society, 1958–2000.

Ibn Khaldun. *An Arab Philosophy of History: Selections from the Prolegomena of Ibn Khaldun of Tunis (1332–1406)*. Translated and edited by Charles Issawi. Princeton, NJ: Darwin, 1987.

Ibn Majid, Ahmad. *Arab Navigation in the Indian Ocean Before the Coming of the Portuguese. . . .* Translated and edited by G. R. Tibbetts. London: Royal Asiatic Society of Great Britain and Ireland, 1971.

Jack, Malcolm. *Lisbon: City of the Sea, A History*. London: I. B. Tauris, 2007.

Jackson, Peter, trans. *The Mission of Friar William of Rubruck: His Journey to the Court of the Great Khan Möngke 1253–1255*. Edited by David Morgan. London: Hakluyt Society, 1990.

Jayne, K. G. *Vasco da Gama and His Successors, 1460–1580*. London: Methuen, 1910.

Jayyusi, Salma Khadra. "Andalusi Poetry: The Golden Period." In *The Legacy of Muslim Spain*, edited by Salma Khadra Jayyusi, 317–66. Leiden: Brill, 1992.

Jensen, Kurt Villads. "Devils, Noble Savages, and the Iron Gate: Thirteenth-Century European Concepts of the Mongols." *Bulletin of International Medieval Research* 6 (2000): 1–20.

Joinville, Jean de. *Vie de Saint Louis*. Edited by Jacques Monfrin. Paris: Garnier, 1995.

Jones, J. R. Melville, ed. *The Siege of Constantinople: Seven Contemporary Accounts*. Amsterdam: Hakkert, 1972.

Karabell, Zachary. *People of the Book: The Forgotten History of Islam and the West*. London: John Murray, 2007.

Keen, Maurice. *Chivalry*. New Haven, CT: Yale University Press, 1984.

Kelly, Jack. *Gunpowder: Alchemy, Bombards, and Pyrotechnics: The History of the Explosive That Changed the World.* New York: Basic Books, 2004.

Kennedy, Hugh. *The Armies of the Caliphs: Military and Society in the Early Islamic State.* London: Routledge, 2001.

———. *The Court of the Caliphs: The Rise and Fall of Islam's Greatest Dynasty.* London: Weidenfeld & Nicolson, 2004.

———. *Muslim Spain and Portugal: A Political History of al-Andalus.* London: Longman, 1996.

Kerr, Robert, ed. *A General History and Collection of Voyages and Travels.* 18 vols. Edinburgh: William Blackwood, 1811–1824.

Krása, Miloslav, Josef Polišenskyâ, and Peter Ratkoš, eds. *European Expansion (1494–1519): The Voyages of Discovery in the Bratislava Manuscript Lyc. 515/8 (Codex Bratislavensis).* Prague: Charles University, 1986.

Lach, Donald F. *Asia in the Making of Europe.* 3 vols. in 9 books. Chicago: University of Chicago Press, 1965–1993.

Lamb, Harold. *Suleiman the Magnificent: Sultan of the East.* Garden City, NY: Doubleday, 1951.

Latino Coelho, J. M. *Vasco da Gama.* Lisbon: Bertrand Editora, 2007.

Levenson, Jay A., ed. *Encompassing the Globe: Portugal and the World in the 16th and 17th Centuries.* Washington, DC: Arthur M. Sackler Gallery, Smithsonian Institution, 2007.

Lewis, Bernard. *The Assassins: A Radical Sect in Islam.* London: Weidenfeld & Nicolson, 1967.

———. *Cultures in Conflict: Christians, Muslims, and Jews in the Age of Discovery.* New York: Oxford University Press, 1995.

———. *Islam and the West.* New York: Oxford University Press, 1993.

———. *The Muslim Discovery of Europe.* London: Norton, 2001.

Lewis, David Levering. *God's Crucible: Islam and the Making of Europe, 570 to 1215.* New York: Norton, 2008.

Linschoten, Jan Huygen van. *The Voyage of J. H. van Linschoten to the East Indies.* Edited by Arthur Coke Burnell and P. A. Tiele. 2 vols. London: Hakluyt Society, 1885.

Livermore, H. V. *A New History of Portugal.* 2nd ed. Cambridge: Cambridge University Press, 1976.

Logan, William. *Malabar.* 3 vols. Madras: Government Press, 1887–1891.

Lomax, Derek W. *The Reconquest of Spain.* London: Longman, 1978.

Lopes, Tomé. "Navigazione verso le Indie orientali scritta per Tomé Lopez."

In Giovanni Battista Ramusio, *Navigationi e Viaggi*, edited by Marica Milanesi, 1:687–738. Turin: Einaudi, 1978.

Ma, Huan. *Ying-yai Sheng-lan: The Overall Survey of the Ocean's Shores*. Translated and edited by J. V. G. Mills. Cambridge: Cambridge University Press, 1970.

Madden, Thomas F. *The New Concise History of the Crusades*. Lanham, MD: Rowman & Littlefield, 2006.

Major, R. H. *India in the Fifteenth Century: Being a Collection of Narratives of Voyages to India.* . . . London: Hakluyt Society, 1857.

Mandeville, John [pseud.]. *Mandeville's Travels*. Edited by M. C. Seymour. Oxford: Clarendon Press, 1967.

Maqqari, Ahmad Ibn Mohammed. *The History of the Mohammedan Dynasties in Spain*. Translated by Pascual de Gayangos. 2 vols. London: Oriental Translation Fund, 1840–1843.

Margariti, Roxani Eleni. *Aden and the Indian Ocean Trade: 150 Years in the Life of a Medieval Arabian Port*. Chapel Hill: University of North Carolina Press, 2007.

Markham, Clements R., trans. *The Journal of Christopher Columbus (During His First Voyage, 1492–93), and Documents Relating to the Voyages of John Cabot and Gaspar Corte Real*. London: Hakluyt Society, 1893.

Mathew, K. M. *History of the Portuguese Navigation in India, 1497–1600*. New Delhi: K. M. Mittal, 1988.

Meinardus, Otto F. A. *Two Thousand Years of Coptic Christianity*. Cairo: American University in Cairo Press, 1999.

Mello, Francisco de, Conde de Ficalho. *Viagens de Pedro da Covilhã*. Lisbon: Imprensa Nacional, 1898.

Menocal, María Rosa. *The Ornament of the World: How Muslims, Jews, and Christians Created a Culture of Tolerance in Medieval Spain*. Boston: Little, Brown, 2002.

Mercier, Maurice, and André Seguin. *Charles Martel et la Bataille de Poitiers*. Paris: Librairie orientaliste Paul Geuthner, 1944.

Meri, Joseph W., ed. *Medieval Islamic Civilization: An Encyclopedia*. 2 vols. New York: Routledge, 2006.

Milwright, Marcus. "The Balsam of Matariyya: An Exploration of a Medieval Panacea." *Bulletin of the School of Oriental and African Studies* 66, no. 2 (2003): 193–209.

Mocquet, Jean. *Travels and Voyages into Africa, Asia, and America, the East and*

West Indies; Syria, Jerusalem, and the Holy Land. Translated by Nathaniel Pullen. London, 1696.

Modelski, George. "Enduring Rivalry in the Democratic Lineage: The Venice-Portugal Case." In *Great Power Rivalries*, edited by William R. Thompson. Columbia: University of South Carolina Press, 1999.

Monfasani, John. *George of Trebizond: A Biography and a Study of His Rhetoric and Logic.* Leiden: Brill, 1976.

Moraes, G. M. *A History of Christianity in India, From Early Times to St. Francis Xavier: A.D. 52–1542.* Bombay: Manaktalas, 1964.

Morford, Mark P. O., and Robert J. Lenardon. *Classical Mythology.* 6th ed. Oxford: Oxford University Press, 1999.

Morison, Samuel Eliot. *Admiral of the Ocean Sea: A Life of Christopher Columbus.* Boston: Little, Brown, 1942.

Morris, Colin. *The Sepulchre of Christ and the Medieval West.* Oxford: Oxford University Press, 2005.

Neill, Stephen. *A History of Christianity in India: The Beginnings to AD 1707.* Cambridge: Cambridge University Press, 1984.

Newitt, M. D. D., ed. *East Africa.* Aldershot, UK: Ashgate, 2002.

———. *A History of Mozambique.* London: Hurst, 1995.

———. *A History of Portuguese Overseas Expansion, 1400–1668.* London: Routledge, 2005.

———. "Mozambique Island: The Rise and Decline of an East African Coastal City, 1500–1700." *Portuguese Studies* 20, no. 1 (September 2004): 21–37.

Nicholson, Helen. *The Knights Templar: A New History.* Stroud, UK: Sutton, 2001.

Nicolle, David. *Armies of the Muslim Conquest.* London: Osprey, 1993.

———. *Constantinople 1453: The End of Byzantium.* Oxford: Osprey, 2000.

Nikephoros. *The Life of St. Andrew the Fool.* Edited and translated by Lennart Rydén. 2 vols. Stockholm: Uppsala University, 1995.

Norwich, John Julius. *Byzantium: The Decline and Fall.* London: Viking, 1995.

O'Callaghan, Joseph F. *Reconquest and Crusade in Medieval Spain.* Philadelphia: University of Pennsylvania Press, 2003.

Of the newe lādes and of ye people founde by the messengers of the kynge of portỹgale named Emanuel. Of the X dyuers nacyons crystened. Of pope Johñ and his landes, and of the costely keyes and wonders molodyes that in that lande is. Antwerp, 1520?

Oliveira Marques, A. H. de. *Daily Life in Portugal in the Late Middle Ages.* Madison: University of Wisconsin Press, 1971.

————. *History of Portugal.* 2nd ed. 2 vols. New York: Columbia University Press, 1976.

————. "Travelling with the Fifteenth-Century Discoverers: Their Daily Life." In Disney and Booth, *Vasco da Gama and the Linking of Europe and Asia*, 30–47. Delhi: Oxford University Press, 2000.

Oliver, Roland, and Anthony Atmore. *Medieval Africa, 1250–1800.* Cambridge: Cambridge University Press, 2001.

O'Shea, Stephen. *Sea of Faith: Islam and Christianity in the Medieval Mediterranean World.* London: Profile, 2006.

Osorius, Jerome [Jerónimo Osório]. *The History of the Portuguese During the Reign of Emmanuel: Containing all their Discoveries, from the Coast of Africa to the Farthest Parts of China. . . .* Translated by J. Gibbs. 2 vols. London, 1752.

Padfield, Peter. *Tide of Empires: Decisive Naval Campaigns in the Rise of the West.* Vol. 1, *1481–1654.* London: Routledge & Kegan Paul, 1979.

Pagden, Anthony. *Worlds at War: The 2,500-Year Struggle Between East and West.* Oxford: Oxford University Press, 2008.

Panikkar, K. M. *Asia and Western Dominance: A Survey of the Vasco da Gama Epoch of Asian History, 1498–1945.* London: Allen & Unwin, 1959.

Parry, J. H. *The Age of Reconnaissance.* London: Weidenfeld & Nicolson, 1963.

————, ed. *The European Reconnaissance: Selected Documents.* New York: Harper & Row, 1968.

Partington, J. R. *A History of Greek Fire and Gunpowder.* Baltimore: Johns Hopkins University Press, 1999.

Partner, Peter. *God of Battles: Holy Wars of Christianity and Islam.* London: HarperCollins, 1997.

Pearson, M. N. *The Indian Ocean.* London: Routledge, 2003.

————. *The New Cambridge History of India.* Vol. 1, pt. 1, *The Portuguese in India.* Cambridge: Cambridge University Press, 1987.

————. *The World of the Indian Ocean, 1500–1800: Studies in Economic, Social and Cultural History.* Aldershot, UK: Ashgate, 2005.

Pegolotti, Francesco. *Pratica della Mercatura.* In *Cathay and the Way Thither, Being a Collection of Medieval Notices of China*, translated and edited by Henry Yule and revised by Henri Cordier, 3:143–171. London: Hakluyt Society, 1916.

Peters, Edward. *The First Crusade: The Chronicle of Fulcher of Chartres and Other Source Materials.* Philadelphia: University of Pennsylvania Press, 1971.

Peters, F. E. *The Children of Abraham: Judaism, Christianity, Islam.* Princeton, NJ: Princeton University Press, 2004.

Phillips, J. R. S. *The Medieval Expansion of Europe.* 2nd ed. Oxford: Oxford University Press, 1988.

Phillips, Jonathan. *The Fourth Crusade and the Sack of Constantinople.* London: Jonathan Cape, 2004.

Pires, Tomé. *The Suma Oriental of Tomé Pires.* Translated and edited by Armando Cortesão. 2 vols. London: Hakluyt Society, 1944.

Polo, Marco. *The Travels.* Translated and edited by R. E. Latham. Harmondsworth, UK: Penguin, 1958.

Prestage, Edgar. *Afonso de Albuquerque, Governor of India: His Life, Conquests and Administration.* Watford, UK: Voss & Michael, 1929.

———. *The Portuguese Pioneers.* London: A. & C. Black, 1933.

Priolkar, Anant Kakba. *The Goa Inquisition.* Bombay: A. K. Priolkar, 1961.

Pyrard, François. *The Voyage of François Pyrard of Laval to the East Indies, the Maldives, the Moluccas and Brazil.* Translated and edited by Albert Gray and H. C. P. Bell. 2 vols. London: Hakluyt Society, 1887–1890.

Ravenstein, E. G., trans. and ed. *A Journal of the First Voyage of Vasco da Gama, 1497–1499.* London: Hakluyt Society, 1898.

Raymond, André. *Cairo.* Translated by Willard Wood. Cambridge, MA: Harvard University Press, 2000.

Resende, Garcia de. *Crónica de Dom João II e miscellanea.* Lisbon: Imprensa Nacional, 1973.

Riley-Smith, Jonathan. *The Crusades: A Short History.* London: Athlone, 1987.

———. *The Crusades, Christianity and Islam.* New York: Columbia University Press, 2008.

———. *The First Crusade and the Idea of Crusading.* London: Athlone, 1986.

Roche, T. W. E. *Philippa: Dona Filipa of Portugal.* London: Phillimore, 1971.

Roe, Sir Thomas. *The Embassy of Sir Thomas Roe to the Court of the Great Mogul, 1615–1619.* Edited by William Foster. 2 vols. London: Hakluyt Society, 1899.

Rohr, Christine von, ed. *Neue quellen zur zweiten Indienfahrt Vasco da Gamas.* Leipzig, 1939.

Rowland, Albert Lindsay. *England and Turkey: The Rise of Diplomatic and Commercial Relations.* New York: Burt Franklin, 1968.

Roy, Jean-Henri, and Jean Deviosse. *La Bataille de Poitiers.* Paris: Gallimard, 1966.

Runciman, Steven. *The Fall of Constantinople: 1453.* Cambridge: Cambridge University Press, 1965.

Russell, Peter, *Prince Henry 'the Navigator': A Life*. New Haven, CT: Yale University Press, 2000.

Russell-Wood, A. J. R. *A World on the Move: The Portuguese in Africa, Asia, and America, 1415–1808*. Manchester: Carcanet, 1992.

Sale, Kirkpatrick. *The Conquest of Paradise: Christopher Columbus and the Columbian Legacy*. London: Hodder & Stoughton, 1991.

Sanceau, Elaine. *The Perfect Prince: A Biography of the King Dom João II*. . . . Porto: Livraria Civilização, 1959.

———. *Portugal in Quest of Prester John*. London: Hutchinson, 1943.

Scafi, Alessandro. *Mapping Paradise: A History of Heaven on Earth*. London: British Library, 2006.

Schneemelcher, William, ed. *New Testament Apocrypha*. Vol. 1, *Gospels and Related Writings*. Louisville, KY: Westminster John Knox Press, 2003.

Schulze, Franz. *Balthasar Springers Indienfahrt, 1505/06*. Strasbourg, 1902.

Schwartz, Stuart B., ed. *Implicit Understandings: Observing, Reporting, and Reflecting on the Encounters Between Europeans and Other Peoples in the Early Modern Era*. Cambridge: Cambridge University Press, 1994.

Sewell, Robert. *A Forgotten Empire: Vijayanagar*. London: Sonnenschein, 1900.

Shaw, M. R. B., trans. *Chronicles of the Crusades*. Harmondsworth, UK: Penguin, 1963.

Silverberg, Robert. *The Realm of Prester John*. Garden City, NY: Doubleday, 1972.

Skilliter, Susan A. *William Harborne and the Trade with Turkey 1578–1582: A Documentary Study of the First Anglo-Ottoman Relations*. Oxford: Oxford University Press, 1977.

———. "William Harborne, the First English Ambassador, 1583–1588." In *Four Centuries of Turco-British Relations*, edited by William Hale and Ali Ihsan Bagis. Beverley, UK: Eothen, 1984.

Smith, Adam. *An Inquiry Into the Nature and Causes of the Wealth of Nations*. Edited by Edwin Cannan. 2 vols. London: University Paperbacks, 1961.

Smith, Stefan Halikowski. "Meanings Behind Myths: The Multiple Manifestations of the Tree of the Virgin at Matarea." *Mediterranean Historical Review* 23, no. 2 (December 2008): 101–28.

Southern, R. W. *Western Views of Islam in the Middle Ages*. Cambridge, MA: Harvard University Press, 1962.

Soyer, François. *The Persecution of the Jews and Muslims of Portugal: King Manuel I and the End of Religious Tolerance (1496–7)*. Leiden: Brill, 2007.

Stanley, Henry E. J., trans. and ed. *The Three Voyages of Vasco da Gama and His Viceroyalty.* London: Hakluyt Society, 1869.

Stein, Burton. *Vijayanagara.* Cambridge: Cambridge University Press, 1989.

Subrahmanyam, Sanjay. *The Career and Legend of Vasco da Gama.* Cambridge: Cambridge University Press, 1997.

————. *The Portuguese Empire in Asia, 1500–1700.* London: Longman, 1992.

Teixeira de Aragão, A. C. *Vasco da Gama e a Vidigueira: Estudo Hisórico.* 2nd ed. Lisbon: Imprensa Nacional, 1898.

Teyssier, Paul, and Paul Valentin, trans. and eds. *Voyages de Vasco de Gama: Relations des expeditions de 1497–1499 et 1502–3.* 2nd ed. Paris: Chandeigne, 1998.

Thomas, Hugh. *The Slave Trade: The History of the Atlantic Slave Trade, 1440–1870.* London: Picador, 1997.

Tolan, John. *Saracens: Islam in the Medieval European Imagination.* New York: Columbia University Press, 2002.

Tuchman, Barbara. *A Distant Mirror: The Calamitous Fourteenth Century.* New York: Knopf, 1978.

Turner, A. Richard. *Inventing Leonardo.* Berkeley: University of California Press, 1994.

Turner, Jack. *Spice: The History of a Temptation.* New York: Random House, 2004.

Vallé, Pietro della. *The Travels of P. della Valle in India.* Edited by E. Grey. 2 vols. London: Hakluyt Society, 1892.

————. *The Travels of Sig. Pietro della Valle, a Noble Roman, Into East-India and Arabia Deserta.* Translated by G. Havers. London: J. Macock, 1665.

Varthema, Ludovico de. *The Travels of L. di Varthema in Egypt, Syria, Arabia Deserta, Arabia Felix, in Persia, India, and Ethiopia, A.D. 1503–1508.* Translated by John Winter Jones and edited by G. P. Badger. London: Hakluyt Society, 1863.

Villiers, John, "Ships, Seafaring and the Iconography of Voyages." In Disney and Booth, *Vasco da Gama and the Linking of Europe and Asia,* 72–82. Delhi: Oxford University Press, 2000.

Watt, W. Montgomery. *Muslim-Christian Encounters: Perceptions and Misperceptions.* London: Routledge, 1991.

Weinstein, Donald. *Ambassador from Venice: Pietro Pasqualigo in Lisbon, 1501.* Minneapolis: University of Minnesota Press, 1960.

Westrem, Scott D. "Against Gog and Magog." In *Text and Territory: Geograph-*

ical Imagination in the European Middle Ages, edited by Sylvia Tomasch and Sealy Gilles, 54–75. Philadelphia: University of Pennsylvania Press, 1998.

Wheatcroft, Andrew. *The Infidels: The Conflict Between Christendom and Islam, 638–2002*. London: Viking, 2003.

White, David Gordon. *Myths of the Dog-Man*. Chicago: University of Chicago Press, 1991.

Whitfield, Peter. *New Found Lands: Maps in the History of Exploration*. London: British Library, 1998.

Wolpert, Stanley. *A New History of India*. 8th ed. New York: Oxford University Press, 2009.

Zurara, Gomes Eanes de. *The Chronicle of the Discovery and Conquest of Guinea*. Translated by C. R. Beazley and Edgar Prestage. 2 vols. London: Hakluyt Society, 1896–1898.

———. *Conquests and Discoveries of Henry the Navigator, Being the Chronicles of Azurara*. Edited by Virginia de Castro e Almeida and translated by Bernard Miall. London: Allen & Unwin, 1936.

———. *Crónica da tomada de Ceuta*. Mem Martins: Publicações Europa-América, 1992.

INDEX

NIGEL CLIFF IS a historian, biographer, and critic. He was educated at Oxford University, where he was awarded the Beddington Prize for English Literature. He is a former theater and film critic for the London *Times* and a contributor to the *Economist* and other publications. His first book, *The Shakespeare Riots*, was a finalist for the National Award for Arts Writing and was selected as one of the best nonfiction books of 2007 by the *Washington Post*. He lives in London with his wife, the ballerina Viviana Durante.

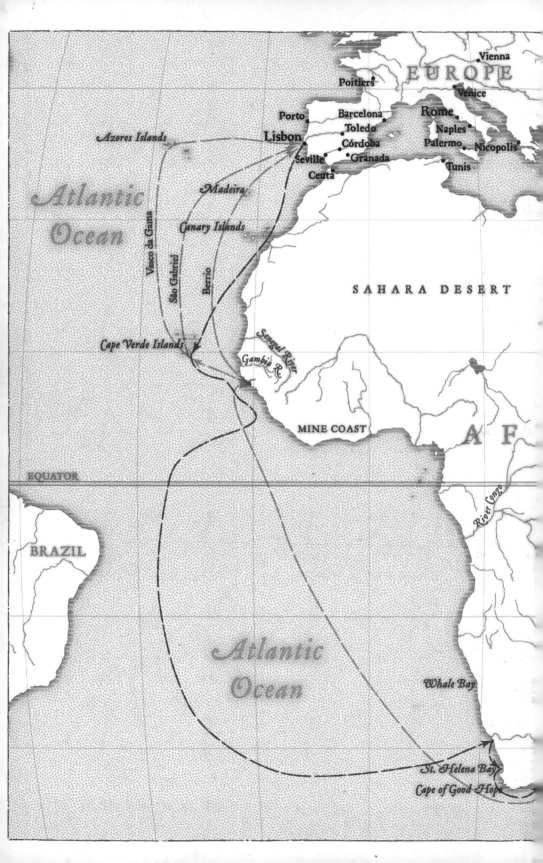